WHEN CHINA RULES THE WORLD

THE END OF THE WESTERN WORLD
AND THE BIRTH OF A NEW GLOBAL ORDER

MARTIN JACQUES

PENGUIN BOOKS

WHEN CHINA RULES THE WORLD

MARTIN JACQUES is a senior visiting fellow at IDEAS, a centre for diplomacy and grand strategy at the London School of Economics and a visiting professor at Tsinghua University, Beijing. He is also a Bosch Public Policy Fellow at the Transatlantic Academy, Washington, DC. He has previously been a visiting professor at Renmin University, Beijing, the International Centre for Chinese Studies, Aichi University, Nagoya, and Ritsumeikan University, Kyoto, and a senior visiting research fellow at the Asia Research Institute, National University of Singapore. He co-founded the think-tank DEMOS, and until its closure in 1991 was editor of the renowned London-based monthly *Marxism Today*. He has been a columnist for several newspapers (and is a former deputy editor of the *Independent*), and has made many television programmes. He took his doctorate while at King's College, Cambridge. He lives in London with his son, Ravi. *When China Rules the World* was first published in 2009 and has since been translated into eleven languages, and sold approaching a quarter of a million copies worldwide. The book has been shortlisted for two major literary awards.

* * *

Praise for Martin Jacques
and *When China Rules the World*

'This important book, deeply considered, full of historical understanding and realism, is about more than China. It is about a twenty-first-century world no longer modelled on and shaped by North Atlantic power, ideas and assumptions. I suspect it will be highly influential.'
—Eric Hobsbawm

'Interesting . . . and disturbing.'
—Larry Summers, former chief economic adviser to President Obama

'Martin Jacques's scholarship, perspective and experience in observing Asia are all manifested brilliantly in this book, which performs a very valuable service to all who really want to understand China and anticipate world politics in the coming decades. It will be difficult to argue against his innovative central thesis that a modernizing and modernized China will keep her essential Chineseness in a new era of "contested modernity."'
—Shi Yinhong, professor of international relations, Renmin University, Beijing

MARTIN JACQUES

When China Rules the World

The End of the Western World and the
Birth of a New Global Order

Second Edition

PENGUIN BOOKS

PENGUIN BOOKS

Published by the Penguin Group
Penguin Group (USA) Inc., 375 Hudson Street, New York, New York 10014, U.S.A.
Penguin Group (Canada), 90 Eglinton Avenue East, Suite 700, Toronto,
Ontario, Canada M4P 2Y3 (a division of Pearson Penguin Canada Inc.)
Penguin Books Ltd, 80 Strand, London WC2R 0RL, England
Penguin Ireland, 25 St Stephen's Green, Dublin 2, Ireland (a division of Penguin Books Ltd)
Penguin Group (Australia), 250 Camberwell Road, Camberwell,
Victoria 3124, Australia (a division of Pearson Australia Group Pty Ltd)
Penguin Books India Pvt Ltd, 11 Community Centre, Panchsheel Park, New Delhi – 110 017, India
Penguin Group (NZ), 67 Apollo Drive, Rosedale, Auckland 0632,
New Zealand (a division of Pearson New Zealand Ltd)
Penguin Books (South Africa) (Pty) Ltd, 24 Sturdee Avenue,
Rosebank, Johannesburg 2196, South Africa

Penguin Books Ltd, Registered Offices:
80 Strand, London WC2R 0RL, England

First published in Great Britain by Allen Lane, an imprint of Penguin Books Ltd 2009
First published in the United States of America by The Penguin Press,
a member of Penguin Group (USA) Inc. 2009
Second edition published in Penguin Books (UK) 2012
Published in Penguin Books (USA) 2012

1   3   5   7   9   10   8   6   4   2

Copyright © Martin Jacques, 2009, 2012
All rights reserved

ISBN 978-0-14-311800-8
CIP data available

Printed in the United States of America

For Hari

My love for you knew no limits, nor has it dimmed with time.
I miss you more than words can ever say.

For Ravi
Hari's greatest gift. And my reason

Contents

CONTENTS

List of Figures

List of Maps

List of Tables

List of Illustrations

Acknowledgements

My interest in East Asia dates back to a visit to the region in 1993 when I also happened to meet my wife-to-be, Harinder Veriah, on Tioman Island, Malaysia. The idea for this book dates back to 1996. In 1997–8 contracts were signed and plans drawn up for us to be based in Hong Kong for three years. At the beginning of November 1998 we arrived in Hong Kong with our nine-week-old son, Ravi. Just fourteen months later, Hari died in the most tragic circumstances. It was five years before I could resume work on the book. I would like to thank everyone who, in their different ways, gave support and helped me survive the darkest days anyone could possibly imagine, especially Marlene Hobsbawm, Karena Ghaus, Ian Selvan, Rabindra Singh, Jasvinder Kaur, Graham Huntley, Joe Collier, Stuart Hall, Antonio Borraccino, Selvi Sandrasegaram, Paul Webster, Dhiren Norendra, Bob Tyrrell, Frances Swaine, Douglas Hague and Shariza Noordin.

I am very grateful to Eric Hobsbawm (a very close friend for over thirty years), Niall Ferguson (who first planted the idea in my mind that I should write this book), Christopher Hughes and Arne Westad for reading the manuscript and making many valuable suggestions as to how it might be improved and hopefully at least saving me from the worst of my mistakes and indiscretions. Chen Kuan-Hsing read Chapter 8 and has discussed many of the ideas in it with me over the last few years. I, of course, remain solely responsible for the book as it now appears, warts and all.

I would like to express my gratitude to Tony Giddens, former director of the London School of Economics, and Meghnad Desai, then chairman of the Asia Research Centre, who arranged for me to become a visiting research fellow at the Centre in 2004, a connection which has continued to this day. I am also now a senior visiting fellow at the LSE's IDEAS, an association for which I would like to thank Michael Cox and Odd Arne Westad. I was a visiting professor at the International Centre for Chinese Studies, Aichi University, Nagoya, for four months in early 2005, where I received splendid hospitality from Professor Mitsuyuki Kagami and Professor Kazumi Yamamoto, who I would like to thank most warmly. For three separate periods in 2005–6 I was a visiting professor at Renmin University, which I enjoyed immensely; in particular I would like to thank my generous host, Professor Song Xinning. In autumn 2005 I was invited by Professor Nishi to be a visiting professor at Ritsumeikan University, Kyoto, which proved rewarding. I spent four months at the beginning of 2006 as a senior research fellow at the Asia Research Institute, National University of Singapore, for which I would like to thank the then Director Professor Anthony Reid. These visits assisted me enormously in both my research and writing.

The Barry Amiel and Norman Melburn Trust gave me generous financial assistance to enable me to carry out my research. Having had the privilege of knowing both while they were still alive, I hope they would think their money has been put to good purpose. I am grateful to the trustees for their support.

During the course of 1999, before my wife died, I spent almost a month in each of Shanghai, Tokyo and Taipei. I am very grateful to the following for sparing me the time to share their ideas with me: Dai Badi, Tong Shijun, Gu Xiao-ming, Xie Xia-ling, Melvin Chu, Jiao Chun-xue, Ma Lian-yuan, Wang Xiaoming, Wu Jiang, Yang Qingqing, Christopher Tibbs, Lu Hao, Ge Jianxiong, Zhou Jun, Shen Kai, Graham Earnshaw, Sun Xiaolong, Cao Jingyuan, Chen Xiaoming, Teng Xuekun, Yu Zhiyuan, Yu Ming, Qiao Yiyi, Zhang Xiaoming, Wang Jianxiong, Huang Yongyi, James Harding, Ma Chengyuan, Shen Guanbao, Gao Rui-qian, Frank Gao, Hsu Feng,

Qui Genxiang, Kevin Tan, Ji Guoxing, Xu Jilin, Bao Mingxin, Qiao Yiyi, Lu Yongyi (Shanghai); Chen Kuan-Hsing, Sechin Yung-xiang Chien, Chu-Joe Hsia, Liang Lu, Ling Mei, Hsu Hsin-liang, Hung Tze Jan, Stan Lai, Johnny Tuan, Bing C. P. Chu, Sen Hong Yang, Sheena Hsu, Wei-Chung Wang, Ti-Nan Chi, Ku Chung-Hwa, Yun-Peng Chu, Wan-Wen Chu, Chihyu Shih, Andrew Nien-Dzu Yang, Ping Lu, Jian-San Feng, Edward Wong, Szu-Yin Ho, Chen-Kuo Hsu, Chunto Tso, Chieh-Fu Chen, Chiang Sung, Hsiung-Ping Chiao, Christopher R. Fay, Benny T. Hu, Allen Chun, Antonio Chang, W. S. Lin, Darlene Lee (Taipei); Chie Nakane, Kiyoshi Kojima, Kosaku Yoshino, Kiyohiko Fukushima, Tatsuro Hanada, Shunya Yoshimi, Noriko Hamo, Yukiko Kuroda, Mitsutoshi Kato, Odaka Naoko, Tadashi Nakamae, Peter Tasker, Martin Reeves, Takashi Kiuchi, Yoichi Funabashi, Kiichi Fujiwara, Shinji Fukukawa, Toshiya Uedo, Sahoko Kaji, Takashi Yamashita, Kang Sangjung, Yoshiji Fujita, Masamoto Yashiro, Sadaaki Numata, Richard Jerram, Valerie Koehn, Mark Dytham, Astrid Klein, Tetsuo Kanno, Tadashi Yamamoto (Tokyo).

I am grateful to Kenneth Yeang, Zeti Akhtar Aziz, Mohamed Arif Nun, Jomo Kwame Sundaran, Shad Saleem Faruqi, Francis Yeoh Sock Ping and many others for interviews in Kuala Lumpur. In particular, I owe a large debt of gratitude to the late Noordin Sopiee, who always found time to chew the fat during my frequent visits. Although Hong Kong was more a base than a place for field research, I would like to mention Frank Ching, John Gittings, Oscar Ho, Andy Xie, Christine Loh, Lian Yi-Zheng and K. Y. Tang, again amongst many others, who gave of their time. During a visit to San Francisco I gained a better insight into the Chinese community there, especially through my conversations with L. Ling-Chi Wang and Albert Cheng. I interviewed Xin Hu, Miles Lee, Zhang Jiansen and Charlie Zheng in Shenzhen. I would particularly like to thank Wang Gungwu, Geoff Wade, Kishore Mahbubani, Chua Beng Huat and Anthony Reid for their stimulation and assistance during my stay in Singapore.

Professor Mitsuyuki Kagami and Professor Kazumi Yamamoto

never failed to find time for our many conversations during my stay at Aichi University, while Chunli Lee shared with me the fruits of his studies on the Chinese automobile industry and Uradyn E. Bulag discussed China's relationship with Mongolia. I also learnt a great deal from my Chinese doctoral students whom I had the privilege of teaching whilst I was there. I would like to thank my friend Chen Kuan-Hsing for providing me with constant advice and assistance during my various stays in East Asia, especially Taiwan, Japan and Singapore.

My stay in Beijing in 2005–6 was the source of much enlightenment. I whiled away the time in many fascinating conversations. I would particularly like to thank Song Xinning, Jin Canrong, Zhu Feng, Fang Ning, Zhang Yunling, Wang Yizhou, Zhu Wenhui, Wang Yuqing, Feng Zhongping, Wang Zhengyi, Pan Wei, Wang Hui, Wang Xiaodong, He Zengke, Kang Xiaoguang, He Guangbei, Ye Zicheng, Yu Zengke, Zha Daojiong, Cheng Lu, Liu Xiu and Liu Hua. My greatest debt of all is to Yu Yongding, Huang Ping and especially Shi Yinhong, who have been unfailingly helpful and hugely stimulating in the many conversations I have enjoyed with them.

Zhang Feng has assisted me with great thoroughness and efficiency on the footnotes and bibliography, as well as doing some background research for Chapter 11. Sherlyn Wong and Chris Thwaite have conscientiously sought to obtain the necessary permissions.

I must admit that I had not expected the hardback edition – and the numerous translations that have followed – to have sold so extraordinarily well, to the extent that the book has become a global bestseller. As a result of its success, I have found myself on what seemed at times like a perpetual world tour. I am grateful to all those who have acted as my host and organized the many events to which I have been invited. It all began in Kuala Lumpur with a splendid occasion organized by Munir Majid. These many events have been the source of great stimulation and enlightenment, especially those in China. As a result, together with the inevitable passage of time, the paperback is not simply the hardback in soft cover but, on the contrary, a fully fledged second edition which is almost halfway to being a new book. I would particularly like to mention my stay in Washington DC as a Bosch Public Policy Fellow at the Transatlantic Academy from November 2010 to February 2011, where I was afforded ample time to work on the paperback text. I am grateful to Stephen Szabo for this opportunity. I would also like to thank Joseph Quinlan, a Wall Street analyst. We both happened to be Bosch fellows during the same period and we found, to our pleasure, that we had a great deal in common. Joe, together with Alexis Cedeno, has provided me with numerous charts and tables for this edition for which I am very grateful. During my stay in DC, I met David Shambaugh for the first time and he was, as I expected, full of interesting thoughts and views. Chen Xingdong, chief China economist, and Richard Iley, chief Asia economist, at BNP Paribas have also furnished me with very useful charts and data. Finally, I spent an immensely stimulating five weeks in October to November 2011 as a visiting professor at Tsinghua University, Beijing, in the Institute of Modern International Relations. I am very grateful to Professor Yan Xuetong for this opportunity. My stay gave me much food for thought and even the genesis, perhaps, of a new book.

I am very fortunate in having a fine agent in Andrew Wylie, to whom I owe a debt of gratitude. I would also like to thank Scott Moyers, James Pullen and Jordyn Ostroff at Wylie for all the help they have given. I am also appreciative of the efforts of my previous agent Georgina Capel, who helped to initiate the project.

I have been blessed with an excellent editor in Stuart Proffitt. He has been enormously conscientious and painstaking in his editing, for which I am extremely grateful. Perhaps most of all, I am indebted to Stuart for his sensitivity towards me after my wife's death, when he realized that it was impossible for me to work on the book; his timing was perfect two years later when he gently broached the question again with me. I would also like to thank my former US editor, Laura Stickney, for her perceptive comments on the Afterword and her general support. I am grateful to Penguin for their patience and forbearance with an author who took far longer to complete his book than was originally intended. I would like to thank Peter Carson for originally commissioning the book, Phillip Birch for his assistance on numerous occasions, Jane Birdsell for her conscientiousness, patience and good humour during the copy-editing of the hardback edition, Samantha Borland for taking admirable care of the maps, tables and figures, and Richard Duguid for overseeing the production of the hardback and making sure that it somehow managed to meet the prescribed publication date. Rebecca Lee has overseen the production of the paperback, notwithstanding its voluminous changes, with great efficiency and unfailing bonhomie, while Richard Duguid took responsibility for the final stages in his typically calm and hugely competent way. Jane Robertson has copy-edited the paperback with a light touch, singular efficiency and agreeable good nature.

It would be remiss of me not to mention the efforts of all those at Penguin around the world who have assisted in the promotion of the book: in particular I would like to thank Mari Yamazaki in London, Abigail Cleaves in New York, Debbie Gaudet in Toronto, Jo Lusby and Joy Ma in Beijing, Emily Wang in Shanghai, Vijaya Mohan and Daina Neoh in Kuala Lumpur, and Eddy Teo and Loi Zhi Wei in Singapore.

Finally, I would like to thank Cristina Pilien, who helped to look after our son Ravi when we were in Hong Kong and has continued to do so in London ever since, for her extraordinary kindness, loyalty and devotion. Ravi and I are very proud that she now has a degree in Chinese and spent a very successful year studying the language at Beijing University.

My greatest debt of all is to Ravi, our son, who has just turned thirteen and was sixteen months when Hari died. It has been an unspeakably painful, sad and cruel decade, but together we have found a way to play, live and grow. Ravi, you have been my reason, the source of such pride and pleasure. Thank you for putting up with all those endless days and months when Daddy has been, in your words, in 'his prison', otherwise known as my study. What has kept me going are all the times in between that I have spent with you, messing about, enjoying your company, listening to you play

ACKNOWLEDGEMENTS

the violin and taking delight in your ever-expanding range of interests, gifts and accomplishments: Mummy would have been thrilled. This book is for you and, of course, for Mummy, who I loved beyond all reason or belief. I miss her desperately. She would have been so proud of us for having found the will and fortitude to complete the book despite the cruel hand of Fate. She cannot share this moment of pleasure with us. The aching emptiness of her absence will forever still any sense of elation.

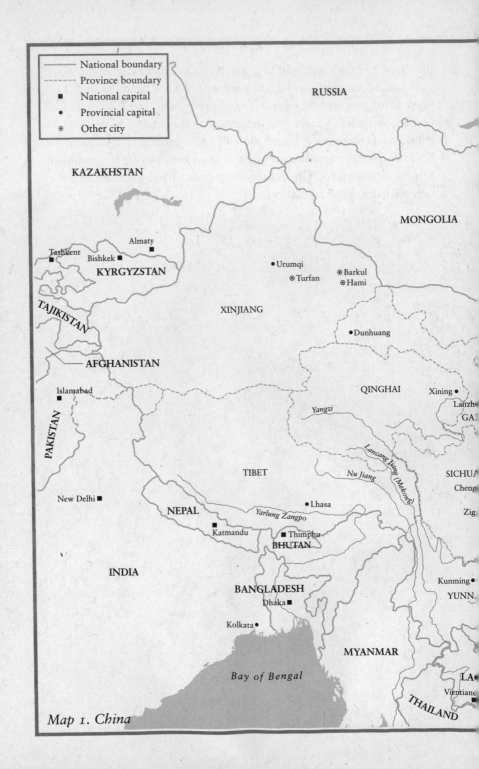

Map 1. China

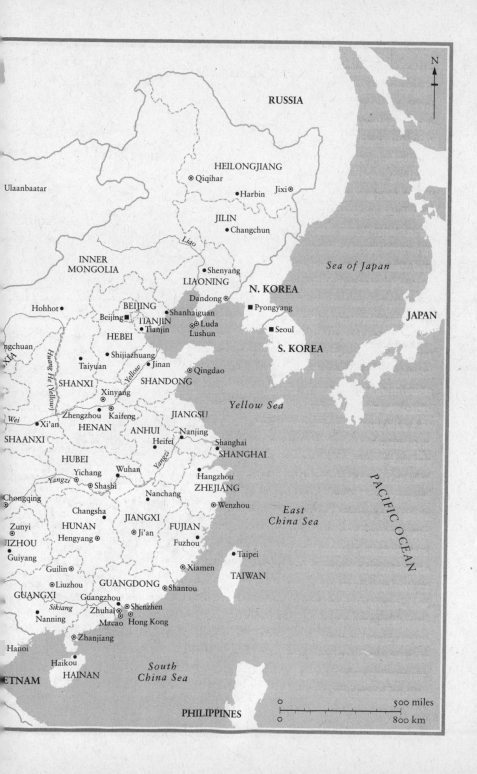

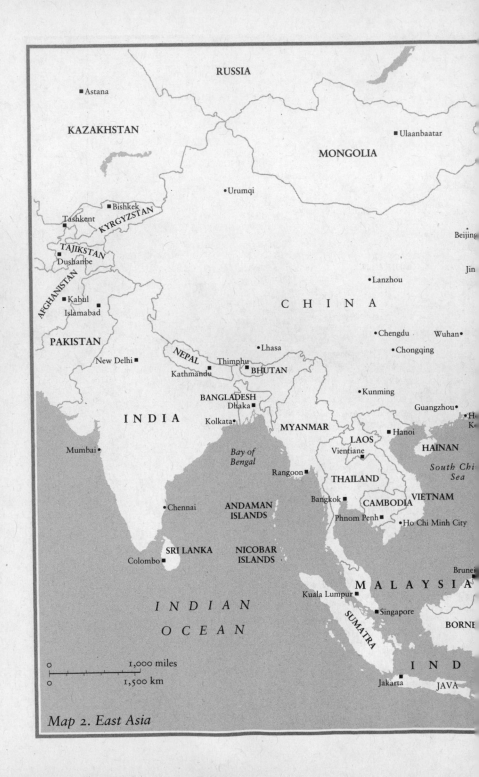

Map 2. East Asia

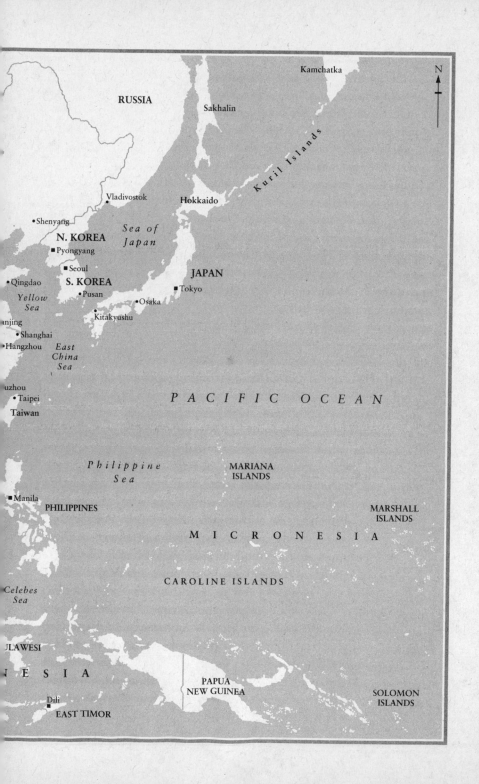

Note on Transliteration, Names and Currency

The Pinyin system of transliteration, adopted in the People's Republic of China in the 1950s and now generally used worldwide, has been employed in this book, with the exception of some names which are most familiar in the older Wade-Giles system (for example, Sun Yat-sen and Chiang Kai-shek).

Chinese names are generally written in English style, with the family name first, except in those few cases where they are usually written in Western form with the family name second. Japanese names vary, with the family name sometimes written first (as in Japan), but where they are usually written in English with the family name second, as is often the practice, the same approach has been followed.

The Chinese currency, often known as the yuan, is referred to in this book as the renminbi.

Major Periods in Imperial China

Eastern Zhou	771–256 BC
Warring States	403–221 BC
Qin	221–206 BC
Han	206 BC–AD 220
Tang	618–907
Northern Song	960–1126
Southern Song	1127–1271
Yuan (Mongols)	1271–1368
Ming	1368–1644
Qing (Manchus)	1644–1912

I

The Changing of the Guard

Since 1945 the United States has been the world's dominant power. Even during the Cold War its economy was far more advanced than, and more than twice as large as, that of the Soviet Union, while its military capability and technological sophistication were much superior.[1] Following the Second World War, the US was the prime mover in the creation of a range of multinational and global institutions, such as the United Nations, the International Monetary Fund and NATO, that were testament to its new-found global power and authority. The collapse of the Soviet Union in 1991 greatly enhanced America's pre-eminent position, eliminating its main adversary and resulting in the countries of the former Soviet bloc opening their markets and turning in many cases to the US for aid and support. Never before, not even in the heyday of the British Empire, had a nation's power enjoyed such a wide reach. The dollar became the world's preferred currency, with most trade being conducted in it and most reserves held in it. The US dominated all the key global institutions bar the UN, and enjoyed a military presence in every part of the world. Its global position seemed unassailable, and at the turn of the millennium terms like 'hyperpower' and 'unipolarity' were coined to describe what appeared to be a new and unique form of power.

The baton of pre-eminence, before being passed to the United States, had been held by Europe, especially the major European nations like Britain, France and Germany, and previously, to a much lesser extent, Spain, Portugal and the Netherlands. From the beginning of Britain's Industrial Revolution in the late eighteenth century until the mid twentieth century, Europe was to shape global history in a most profound manner. The engine of Europe's dynamism was industrialization and its mode of expansion colonial conquest. Even as Europe's position began to decline after the First World War, and precipitously after 1945, the fact that America, the new rising power, was a product of European civilization served as a source of empathy and affinity between the Old World and the New World, giving rise to ties which found expression in the idea of the West[2] and which served to mitigate the effects of the latent imperial rivalry between Britain and the United States. For over two centuries the West, first in the form of Europe and subsequently the United States, has dominated the world.

We are now witnessing an historic change which, though still in its relative infancy, is destined to transform the world. The developed world – which for over a century has meant the West (a shifting idea over time, but basically the United States, Canada, Western Europe, Australia and New Zealand) plus Japan – is rapidly being overhauled in terms of economic size by the developing world.[3] In 2001 the developed countries accounted for just over half the world's GDP, compared with around 60 per cent in 1973, and by 2025 that figure is likely to be just above one third. It will be a long time, of course, before most of the developing countries acquire the economic and technological sophistication of the developed, but because they collectively account for the overwhelming majority of the world's population, and their economic growth rate in recent times, and especially since the Western financial crisis, has been rather greater than that of the developed world, their rise has already resulted in a major shift in the balance of global economic power. There is a battery of indices that illustrate this. After declining for over two decades, commodity prices began to increase around the turn of the century, driven by buoyant economic growth in the developing world, above all from China, until the onset of the global recession reversed this trend, which was resumed again a couple of years after the financial crisis.[4] Whereas the developed world was responsible for 65 per cent of global manufacturing in 1970, compared with 35 per cent in the developing world, by 2010 the share of developed countries had fallen to 53 per cent, while that of the developing countries had risen to 47 per cent. In 1999 developing countries' share of total foreign currency reserves was 38 per cent,

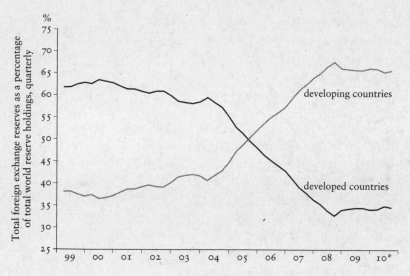

Source: International Monetary Fund, *preliminary data through the third quarter of 2010

Figure 1. Savings in the East, debt in the West.

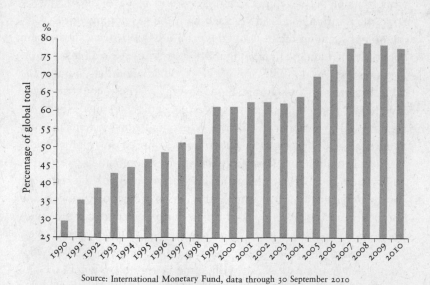

Source: International Monetary Fund, data through 30 September 2010

*Figure 2. Developing countries' share of world
international reserves.*

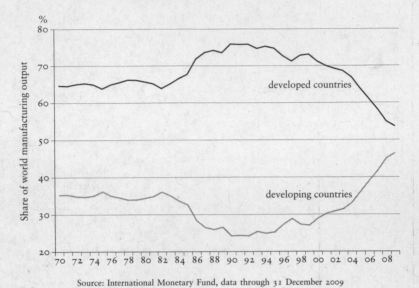

Source: International Monetary Fund, data through 31 December 2009

Figure 3. The global shift in world manufacturing.

while that of the developed countries stood at 62 per cent, but by 2010 the position had been reversed with the developing world holding 66 per cent and the developed world only 34 per cent. East Asian countries, including China, Singapore and South Korea, enjoy enormous reserves, as do some commodity-producing nations, notably the oil-rich states in the Middle East. Several of these countries have invested a portion of their reserves in state-controlled sovereign wealth funds whose purpose is to seek profitable investments in other countries, including the West. These funds acquired powerful new leverage as a result of the Western financial crisis, commanding resources which the major Western financial institutions palpably lacked.[5] The sovereign wealth funds of Qatar, Abu Dhabi, Singapore, Kuwait and South Korea pumped billions of dollars into US banks between mid-2007 and mid-2008. The meltdown of some of Wall Street's largest financial institutions in September 2008 underlined the shift in economic power from the West, with some of the fallen giants seeking further support from sovereign wealth funds and the US government stepping in to save the mortgage titans Freddie Mac and Fannie Mae, partly in order to reassure countries like China, which had invested huge sums of money in them: if China had started to withdraw these sums, it would have precipitated a collapse in the value of the dollar.

The financial crisis graphically illustrated the disparity between an East Asia cash-rich from decades of surpluses and a United States cash-poor following many years of deficits. It has typically been described as a global financial crisis but this is a misnomer because it was over-whelmingly a Western financial crisis. While the United States, Japan, France, the UK and Italy (Germany being the nearest to an exception) have been hobbled by the financial crisis, with their banks remaining in an extremely fragile state, their economies mired in debt, GDP (in autumn 2010) still below pre-crisis levels, and their economies operating at up to 10 per cent below their past trends, China continued to grow very strongly, with its banks enjoying very healthy balance sheets. East Asia, apart from Japan, recovered very rapidly from the contraction in Western export markets, while India and Latin America also soon resumed their economic growth. If the developed economies told one story, the developing economies told a very different one.

According to projections by Goldman Sachs in 2007, as shown in Figure 4, the Chinese economy will be almost the same size as the US economy by 2025, with the Indian economy the fourth largest after Japan. By 2050, they project that the largest economy in the world will be China, which will be almost twice the size of the US economy, with the Indian economy following a close third, almost on a par with the US. These three will be followed by Brazil, Mexico, Russia and Indonesia.[6] Only two European countries feature in the top ten, namely the UK and Germany in ninth and tenth place respectively. Of the present G7, only four appear in the top ten. In similar forecasts, Pricewaterhouse-Coopers suggest that the Brazilian economy could be larger than Japan's, and that the Russian, Mexican and Indonesian economies could each be bigger than the German, French and UK economies by 2050.[7] If these projections, or something similar, are realized in practice, then during the next four decades the world will come to look like a very different place indeed. Of course, these are projections based on past trends, though they include the assumption, for example, that over time the Chinese growth rate will decline as its economy matures.

It goes without saying that the future can never be a simple extrapolation of the past. But it should be borne in mind that this does not necessarily mean that these projections inevitably exaggerate the rise of the developing countries while overstating the decline of developed countries. On the contrary, the opposite could be the case: these projections predate the Western financial crisis and therefore, at the time of writing, understate the underlying shift in economic power from the developed to the developing world, a process which has been accelerated by the crisis.

Such a transformed world was far from people's minds in 2001. Following 9/11, the United States not only saw itself as the sole superpower but attempted to establish a new global role which reflected that pre-eminence. The neo-Conservative think-tank Project for the New American Century, established in 1997 by, amongst others, Dick Cheney, Donald Rumsfeld and Paul Wolfowitz, adopted a statement

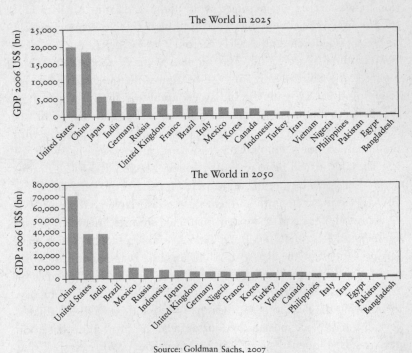

Source: Goldman Sachs, 2007

Figure 4. Projected size of national economies.

of principles which articulated the new doctrine and helped prepare the ground for the Bush administration:

> As the twentieth century draws to a close, the United States stands as the world's pre-eminent power. Having led the West to victory in the Cold War, America faces an opportunity and a challenge: Does the United States have the vision to build upon the achievements of past decades? Does the United States have the resolve to shape a new century favourable to American principles and interests?[8]

In 2004 the influential neo-Conservative Charles Krauthammer wrote:

> On December 26, 1991, the Soviet Union died and something new was born, something utterly new – a unipolar world dominated by a single superpower unchecked by any rival and with decisive reach in every corner of the globe. This is a staggering development in history, not seen since the fall of Rome.[9]

The new century dawned a little more than a decade ago with the global community deeply aware of and preoccupied by the prospect of what appeared to be overwhelming American power. The neo-Conservatives chose to interpret the world through the prism of the defeat of the Soviet Union and the overwhelming military superiority enjoyed by the United States, rather than in terms of the underlying trend towards economic multipolarity that we have just discussed, the significance of which was downplayed and largely ignored. The new doctrine placed a premium on the importance of the United States maintaining a huge military lead over other countries in order to deter potential rivals, and on the US pursuing its own interests rather than being constrained either by its allies or international agreements.[10] In the post-Cold War era, US military expenditure was almost as great as that of all the other nations of the world combined: never in the history of the human race has the military inequality between one nation and all others been so great.[11] The Bush presidency's foreign policy marked an important shift compared with that of previous administrations: the war on terror became the new imperative; America's alliance with Western Europe was accorded reduced significance; and the principle of national sovereignty was denigrated and that of regime-change affirmed,[12] culminating in the invasion of Iraq. Far from the United States presiding over a reshaping of global affairs, however, it rapidly found itself beleaguered in Iraq and enjoying less global support than at any time since 1945.[13] The exercise of overwhelming military power proved ineffectual in Iraq, while eroding the reserves of soft power – in Joseph S. Nye's words, 'the attractiveness of a country's culture, political ideals and policies'[14] – that the United States had accumulated since 1945.[15] Failing to comprehend the significance of deeper economic trends, as well as misreading the situation in Iraq, the Bush administration overestimated American power and thereby overplayed its hand, with the consequence that its policies had exactly the opposite effect to that which had been intended: instead of enhancing the US's position in the world, Bush's foreign policy seriously weakened it. The neo-conservative position represented a catastrophic misreading of history.

Military and political power rest on economic strength. As Paul Kennedy argued in *The Rise and Fall of the Great Powers*, the ability of modern nations to exercise and sustain global hegemony has ultimately depended on their productive capacity.[16] America's present superpower status is a product of its rapid economic growth between 1870 and 1950

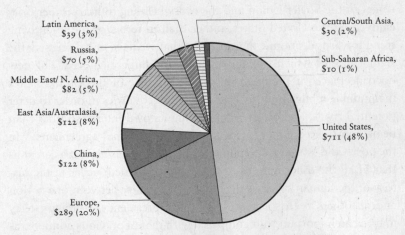

Source: The Center for Arms Control and Non-Proliferation

Figure 5. Global distribution of military expenditure in 2008 (billions of US dollars).

and the fact that during the second half of the twentieth century it was the world's largest and often most dynamic economy. This economic strength underpinned and made possible its astonishing political, cultural and military power from 1945 onwards. According to the economic historian Angus Maddison, the US economy accounted for 8.8 per cent of global GDP in 1870. There then followed a spectacular period of growth during which the proportion rose to 18.9 per cent in 1913 and 27.3 per cent in 1950. This was followed by a slow and steady decline to 22.1 per cent in 1973, with the figure now hovering around 20 per cent.[17] This still represents a formidable proportion, given that the US accounts for only 4.6 per cent of the world's population, but the long-run trend is unmistakable.[18] One could make a similar point in relation to Victorian Britain's imperial reach between 1850 and 1914. This was made possible because Britain accomplished the world's first industrial revolution and, as a consequence, came to enjoy a big economic lead over all other countries. Compared with the United States, however, whose share of global GDP peaked at 35 per cent in 1944 (albeit in a war-ravaged world), the highest figure for the UK was a much smaller 9 per cent in 1899. The precipitous decline of Britain as a global power after 1945 has been the predictable result of its deteriorating relative economic position, its share of global GDP having sunk to a mere 3.3 per cent by 1998.[19] If Britain took its place alongside the United States in Iraq, its military contribution was largely cosmetic. A precondition for being a hegemonic power, including the ability or otherwise to preside over a formal or informal empire, is economic strength. In the long run at least, it is a merciless measure. Notwithstanding this, imperial powers in decline are almost invariably in denial of the fact. That was the case with Britain from 1918 onwards and, to judge by the behaviour of the Bush administration – which singularly failed to read the runes, preferring to believe that the US was about to rule the world in a new American century when the country was actually in decline and on the eve of a world in which it would find its authority considerably diminished – the US may well make the same mistake, perhaps on a much grander scale. Belatedly, the financial meltdown finally persuaded a growing number of the American elite, albeit still a somewhat small minority, that the United States might after all be in decline: in a poll of leading Washington Democrats and Republicans conducted in January 2010, 24 per cent of the former and 28 per cent of the latter agreed that 'the financial crisis of 2008 marked the end of American international dominance'.[20] This represents a significant shift of opinion amongst Washington's political elite, though still a far cry from a more general recognition on the part of Americans of the extent and irreversibility of decline and how it might diminish US power and influence in the future.

It has been estimated that the total budgetary and economic cost to the United States of the Iraq war will turn out to be around $3 trillion.[21] Even with this level of expenditure, the armed forces came under huge strain as a result of the war. Deployments got steadily longer and redeployments more frequent, retention rates and recruitment standards fell, while the army lost many of its brightest and best, with a remorseless rise in the number of officers choosing to leave at the earliest opportunity.[22] Such was the inordinate cost of the Iraqi occupation that, regardless of political considerations, the financial burden of any similar proposed invasion of Iran – in practice likely to be much higher – would probably have been too great: for military and financial as well as political reasons then, the Bush administration was unable to seriously contemplate similar military action against Iran and North Korea, the other two members of its 'axis of evil', especially given its already very considerable military commitment in Afghanistan.[23] The United States, in other words, was confronted with the classic problem of imperial overreach. The burden of maintaining a huge global military presence, with roughly 800 American bases dotted around the world, has been one of the causes of the US's enormous current account deficit, which in 2006 accounted for 6.5 per cent of US GDP.[24] In future the American economy will find it increasingly difficult to support such a military commitment.[25] The United States has lost considerable ground as a major manufacturer and as a large-scale exporter of manufactured goods, having steadily ceded that position to East Asia and especially China.[26] In recent times it has persistently been living beyond its means: the government has been spending more than it saves, households have been doing likewise, and since 1982, apart from one year, the country has been buying more from foreigners than it sells to them, with a consequent huge current account deficit and a growing volume of IOUs. Current account deficits can of course be rectified, but only by reducing growth and accepting a lower level of economic activity. Growing concern on the part of foreign institutions about these deficits led to a steady fall in the value of the dollar until 2008, and this could well be resumed at some point, further threatening the dollar's role as the world's reserve currency and American financial power.[27] The credit rating agency Moody's already warned in 2008 that the US faced the prospect of losing its top-notch triple-A credit rating, first granted to US government debt when it was assessed in 1917, unless it took radical action to curb government expenditure.[28] This was before the financial meltdown in 2008, which, with the huge taxpayer-funded government bail-out of the financial sector, greatly increased the size of the US national debt. And in August 2011 the credit rating agency Standard & Poor's downgraded US government debt from AAA to AA+. This is not to suggest that, in the short run, the US will be required to drastically reduce its military expenditure for reasons of financial restraint: indeed, given the position that the US military occupies in the national psyche, and the primary emphasis that US foreign policy has traditionally placed on military power, this seems most unlikely.[29] Being an imperial power, however, is a hugely expensive business and, peering into the future, as its relative economic power declines, the United States will no longer be able to sustain the military commitments and military superiority that it presently enjoys.[30] Meanwhile, there is abundant evidence that American global hegemony is steadily eroding: in Latin America its authority is at its lowest point for over a century; in East Asia the US is increasingly being overshadowed by China; in Africa Chinese influence is in the process of overtaking that of the US; while the power and reach of American-dominated institutions like the IMF and World Bank has declined significantly. The American-made world that has held sway since 1945 is on the wane.

A NEW KIND OF WORLD

We stand on the eve of a different kind of world, but comprehending it is difficult: we are so accustomed to dealing with the paradigms and parameters of the contemporary world that we inevitably take them for granted, believing that they are set in concrete rather than themselves being the subject of longer-run cycles of historical change. Given that American global hegemony has held sway for almost a lifetime, and that Western supremacy transcends many lifetimes, this is not surprising. We are so used to the world being Western, even American, that we have little idea what it would be like if it was not. The West, moreover, has a strong vested interest in the world being cast in its image, because this brings multifarious benefits. As a matter of course, hegemonic powers seek to project their values and institutions on to subordinate nations and the latter, in response, will, depending on circumstances, adapt or genuflect towards their ways; if they don't, hegemonic powers generally seek to impose those values and arrangements on them, even *in extremis* by force. For reasons of both mindset and interest, therefore, the United States, and the West more generally, finds it difficult to visualize, or accept, a world that involves a major and continuing diminution in its influence.

Take globalization as an example. The dominant Western view has been that globalization is a process by which the rest of the world becomes – and should become – increasingly Westernized, with the adoption of free markets, the import of Western capital, privatization, the rule of law, human rights regimes and democratic norms.[31] Much political effort, indeed, has been expended by the West towards this end. Competition, the market and technology, meanwhile, have been powerful and parallel pressures fostering the kind of convergence and homogeneity which is visible in many developing cities around the world in the form of high-rise buildings, expressways, mobile phones, and much else. There are, however, also strong countervailing forces, rooted in the specific history and culture of each society, that serve to shape indigenous institutions like the family, the government and the company and thereby pull in exactly the opposite direction.[32] Furthermore, as countries grow more prosperous they become increasingly self-confident about their own culture and history, and thereby less inclined to ape the West.[33] Far from being a one-way process, therefore, globalization is rather more complex: the United States may have been the single most influential player, exerting enormous power in successive rounds of global trade talks, for example, but the biggest winner has been East Asia and the greatest single beneficiary China. The process of globalization involves an unending tension between on the one hand the forces of convergence, including Western political pressure, and on the other hand the counter-trend towards divergence and indigenization.

Prior to 1960, the West and Japan enjoyed a huge economic advantage over the rest of the world, which still remained largely agrarian in character, but since then a gamut of developing countries have closed the gap with the West, especially those in East Asia. As a consequence, it is becoming increasingly difficult to distinguish between the developed world and the more advanced parts of the developing world: South Korea and Taiwan, for example, should now be counted as developed. This brings us to a critical question. As countries reach Western levels of development, do they become more like the West, or less like the West, or perhaps paradoxically a combination of the two? Clearly the pressures for convergence indicate the former but the forces of divergence and indigenization suggest the contrary. Previously, the overarching difference between the developed and the developing world was the huge disparity in their levels of economic development. It is only with the arrival of these countries at the lower reaches of Western levels of development that the question of convergence or divergence becomes pertinent. There has been an assumption by the Western mainstream that there is only one way of being modern, namely by adopting Western-style institutions, values, customs and beliefs, such as the rule of law, the free market and democratic norms.[34] This, one might add, is an attitude typically held by peoples and cultures who regard themselves as more developed and more 'civilized' than others: that progress for those who are lower down on the developmental scale involves them becoming more like those who are higher up.

The significance of this debate for a world in which the developing nations are increasingly influential is far-reaching: if their end-point is similar to the West, or, to put it another way, Western-style modernity, then the new world is unlikely to be so different from the one we inhabit now, because China, India, Indonesia and Brazil, to take four examples, will differ little in their fundamental characteristics from the West. This was the future envisaged by Francis Fukuyama, who predicted that the post-Cold War world would be based on a new universalism embodying the Western principles of the free market and democracy.[35] If, on the other hand, their ways of being modern diverge significantly, even sharply, from the Western model, then a world in which they predominate is likely to look very different from the present Western-made one in which we still largely live. As I discuss in the prologue to Part I, modernity is made possible by industrialization, and until the middle of the last century this was a condition which was exclusive to a small part of the world. As a result, before the second half of the twentieth century the West enjoyed a de facto monopoly of modernity, with Japan the only exception, because these were the only countries that had experienced economic take-off. It might be argued that the Soviet Union also constituted a form of modernity, but it remained, contrary to its claims, far more backward than Western nations in terms of GDP per head, the proportion of the population living in the countryside, and its technological level. Moreover, although it was Eurasian, the USSR was always dominated by its European parts and therefore shared much of the Western tradition. Japan is a fascinating example which I will consider at length in Chapter 3. Until the Second World War it remained a relative outsider, having commenced its industrialization in the last quarter of the nineteenth century. After 1945 Japan became a powerful economic competitor to the West, and by the 1980s it had established itself as the second largest economy behind the United States. Japan in this period, however, always sought to assert its Western credentials and play down its political and cultural distinctiveness. Defeated in the Second World War, occupied by the United States until 1951, endowed with a constitution written by the Americans, disqualified from maintaining a significant military force (and thereby dependent on the US–Japan security pact first signed in 1951 for its defence), Japan, if not a vassal state of the Americans, certainly enjoyed an attenuated sovereignty.[36] It is this which largely explains why, although it is a highly distinctive country which culturally shares little with the West, it has nonetheless persistently sought to emphasize its Western characteristics.

With the exception of Japan, the modern world has thus until recently been exclusively Western, comprising Western Europe, the United States, Canada, Australia and New Zealand; in other words, Europe plus those countries to which European settlers migrated and which they subsequently conquered, or, as the economic historian Angus Maddison described them, the 'European offshoots'. Western modernity – or modernity as we have hitherto known it – rests, therefore, on a relatively small fragment of human experience. In every instance, that experience is either European or comes from Europe, sharing wholly or largely the cultural, political, intellectual, racial and ethnic characteristics of that continent. The narrowness, and consequent unrepresentativeness, of the Western experience is often overlooked, such has been the dominance that the West has enjoyed over the last two centuries. But as other countries, with very different cultures and histories, and contrasting civilizational inheritances, embark on the process of modernization, the particularism and exceptionalism of the Western experience will become increasingly apparent. In historical terms, we are still at the very beginning of this process. It was only in the late 1950s that the first Asian tigers – South Korea, Taiwan, Hong Kong and Singapore – began their economic take-offs, to be joined in the 1970s by Malaysia, Thailand, Indonesia and others, followed by China.[37] And what was once more or less confined to East Asia – by which I mean Japan, China, Taiwan, Hong Kong and South Korea in North-East Asia, and countries like the Philippines, Malaysia, Indonesia, Thailand and Vietnam in South-East Asia – has rapidly spread to other regions and continents, including Latin America and the Indian subcontinent. In 1950 the US GDP was almost three times that of East Asia and almost twice that of Asia. By 2001, US GDP was only two-thirds that of Asia, and rather less than that of East Asia.[38] In Part I, I will discuss more fully the nature of modernity, arguing that rather than there being a single way of being modern, we are witnessing the birth of a world of multiple and competing modernities. This will be a quite new and novel feature of the twenty-first century, ushering in an era of what I characterize as contested modernity.[39]

Although we are witnessing the rise of a growing number of developing countries, China is by far the most important economically. It is the bearer and driver of the new world, with which it will enjoy an increasingly hegemonic relationship, its tentacles having stretched across East Asia, Central Asia, South Asia, Latin America and Africa in little more than a decade. China is very different from earlier Asian tigers like South Korea and Taiwan. Unlike the latter, it has never been a vassal state of the United States;[40] furthermore, it enjoys a huge population, with all that this implies. The challenge represented by China's rise is, as a consequence, on a different scale to that of the other Asian tigers. Nonetheless, the consensus in the West, at least up until very recently, has been that China will eventually end up – as a result of its modernization, or as a precondition for it, or a combination of the two – as a Western-style country. American policy towards China over the last three decades has been informed by this belief. It has underpinned America's willingness to co-operate with China, open its markets to Chinese exports, agree to its admission to the World Trade Organization (WTO) and allow it to become an increasingly fully-fledged member of the international community.[41]

The mainstream Western attitude has held that, in its fundamentals, the world will be relatively little changed by China's rise. This is based on three key assumptions: that China's challenge will be primarily economic in nature; that China will in due course become a typical Western nation; and that the international system will remain broadly as it now is, with China acquiescing in the status quo and becoming a compliant member of the international community. Each of these assumptions is misconceived. The rise of China will change the world in the most profound ways.

The effects of China's economic rise are being felt around the world, most notably in the falling price of many consumer products and the rise in commodity prices. Goldman Sachs has projected that in 2027, with a population four times the size of that of the United States and a double-digit growth rate, China will overtake the United States as the world's largest economy,[42] although even then China will still only be in the mid-stage of its transformation into a modern economy. Breathtaking as these economic forecasts are, however, why should we assume that the effects of China's rise will be primarily or exclusively economic in nature? Rising powers in time invariably use their new-found economic strength for wider political, cultural and military ends. This is one of the great advantages of being a hegemonic power, and China will surely become one. The West, however, finds it difficult to imagine such a scenario. Having been hegemonic for so long, the West has, for the most part, become imprisoned within its own assumptions, unable to see the world other than in terms of itself. Progress is invariably defined in terms of degrees of Westernization, with the consequence that the West must always occupy the summit of human development since by definition it is the most Western, while the progress of others is measured by the extent of their Westernization. Political and cultural differences are seen as symptoms of backwardness which will steadily disappear with economic modernization. It is inconceivable, however, that China will become a Western-style nation in the manner to which we are accustomed. China is the product of a history and culture which has little or nothing in common with that of the West. It is only by discounting the effects of history and culture and reducing the world to a matter of economics and technology that it is possible to conclude that China will become Western.

As Chapter 5 will show, it is striking how limited in many respects East Asia's Westernization has been, notwithstanding the effects of a century or more of European colonization followed by a half-century of American ascendancy in the region. If that is true of East Asia as a whole, it is even truer of China. There are four key themes, each rooted in Chinese history, which mark China as distinct from the West and which, far from being of diminishing significance, are likely to exercise an increasing influence over how China both sees itself and also conceives of its place and role in the world. These constitute much of the subject matter of the second part of the book, but as a taster I can outline them in brief as follows.

In the first place, China should not be seen primarily as a nation-state, even though that is how it presently describes itself and how it is seen by others. China has existed within roughly its present borders for two thousand years and only over the last century has it come to regard itself as a nation-state. The identity of the Chinese was overwhelmingly formed before China assumed the status of a nation-state, unlike in the West, where the identity of people, in both Europe and the United States, is largely expressed in terms of the nation-state. The Chinese, in constantly making reference to what they describe as their 5,000-year history, are aware that what defines them is not a sense of nationhood but of civilization. In this context, China should not primarily be seen as a nation-state but rather as a civilization-state. The implications of this are far-reaching: it is simply not possible to regard China as like, or equivalent to, any other state. I will explore this question more fully during the course of the book, especially in Chapter 7.

Likewise, China has a different conception of race to that held by the other most populous nations, notably India, Indonesia, Brazil and the United States, which acknowledge, in varying degrees, that they are intrinsically multiracial in character. It is self-evident that a country as vast as China, comprising a fifth of the world's population, was originally composed of a huge diversity of races. Yet the Han Chinese, who account for around 92 per cent of the population, believe that they comprise one race. The explanation for this lies in the unique longevity of Chinese civilization, which has engendered a strong sense of unity and common identity, with, over a period of thousands of years, a process that has included mixing, melding, absorption, assimilation and effective elimination of a multitude of diverse races. There is also an ideological component to the Chinese attitude towards race: at the end of the nineteenth century, as the dynastic state found itself increasingly beleaguered in the face of the European, American and Japanese occupying powers, the term 'Han Chinese' acquired widespread popularity as part of a nationalist reaction against both the invaders and also the Manchu character of the Qing dynasty. But in practice this is a far less influential factor than the effects of China's long history. Race is rarely paid the attention it deserves in political and cultural writing, but attitudes towards race and ethnicity are integral to understanding all societies. As I demonstrate in Chapter 8, they shape and define how the Chinese see the non-Chinese, whether within China or the rest of the world. The Chinese attitude towards difference will be a powerful factor in determining how China behaves as a global power.

Until little more than a century ago, China's hinterland – what we know today as East Asia – was, for thousands of years, organized on the basis of tributary relationships which involved neighbouring states acknowledging China's cultural superiority and its overwhelming power by rendering tribute to the Middle Kingdom (which is the Mandarin Chinese name for China, namely *Zhǒngguó*) in return for benevolence and protection. The tributary system, as it is known, fell victim to the colonization of East Asia by the European powers and Japan, and was replaced by the Westphalian nation-state system in its colonial form. Is it possible that the tributary system could return to the region? China, as before, is set to economically dwarf the rest of the region. The Europeans have long since departed East Asia, while the American position is progressively weakening. It should not be taken for granted that the interstate system that prevails in the region will continue to be a version of the Westphalian. If, with the rise of China, we are entering a different world, then that is even truer of East Asia, which is already in the process of being reconfigured in terms of a renascent China. I consider the nature of the tributary state system, past and possible future, in Chapter 9.

Finally, the most single important characteristic of China concerns its unity. In the aftermath of the Tiananmen Square repression it was widely believed in the West that China would fracture in a manner similar to the Soviet Union. This was based on a fundamental misreading of China. The latter has occupied roughly similar territory – certainly in terms of where the great majority of the population live – for almost two millennia. When the Roman Empire was in the process of fragmenting into many smaller states, China was moving in the opposite direction, acquiring a unity which has, despite long periods of Balkanization, lasted until the present. The result is a single country that is home to a huge slice of humanity. This profoundly affects how it sees the rest of the world as well as providing it with – potentially at least – exceptional power. The sheer size of China defines it as different from all other countries, bar India. The nature and ramifications of China's unity are considered at various stages in the book, notably in Chapters 4, 7, 8 and 11.

It is obvious from the profundity of these four points – civilization-state, race, tributary state, and unity – let alone many others that I will consider during the course of the book – that China has enjoyed a quite different history to that of the West. Countries invariably see the world in terms of their own experience. As they become hegemonic powers – as China will – they seek to shape the world in the light of their own values and priorities. It is banal, therefore, to believe that China's influence on the world will be mainly and overwhelmingly economic: on the contrary, its political and cultural effects are likely to be at least as far-reaching. The underlying argument of the book is that China's impact on the world will be as great as that of the United States over the last century, probably far greater, and certainly very different.

This brings us to the question of whether, in the long run, China will accept the international system as presently constituted or seek a fundamental change in that system. It is an impossible question to answer with any certainty because we are still at such an early stage of China's rise. Since 1978 China has progressively sought to become a fully-fledged member of the international community and has gone to considerable lengths to reassure the West that it is a 'responsible power', as it likes to describe itself. John Ikenberry, an influential American writer on international relations, has argued that:

> The postwar Western order is historically unique. Any international order dominated by a powerful state is based on a mix of coercion and consent, but the US-led order is distinctive in that it has been more liberal than imperial – and so unusually accessible, legitimate, and durable. Its rules and institutions are rooted in, and thus reinforced by, the evolving global forces of democracy and capitalism. It is expansive, with a wide and widening array of participants and stakeholders. It is capable of generating tremendous economic growth and power while also signalling restraint – all of which make it hard to overturn and easy to join.[43]

Ikenberry argues that the present American-created international order has the potential to integrate and absorb China rather than instead being replaced in the long run by a Chinese-led order. This is a crucial barometer of what the rise of China might mean. Hitherto, the arrival of a new global hegemon has ushered in a major change in the international order, as was the case with both Britain and then the United States. Given that China promises to be so inordinately powerful and different, it is difficult to resist the idea that in time its rise will herald the birth of a new international order. It is a question I will return to towards the end of the book.

I
The End of the Western World

Until the second half of the eighteenth century, life was conceived of largely in terms of the past. The present was seen as no more than the latest version of what had gone before. Similarly, the future, rather than being a separate and distinct idea, was regarded as a repetition or re-creation of the past. In a world in which the overwhelming majority worked on the land and where change was glacial, this is understandable. Material circumstance and daily experience complemented a philosophy and religious belief that reproduced and venerated the past. The values that counted – in everyday life, art, literature – were those of experience, age, wisdom, hierarchy and tradition. Change was acceptable and legitimate as long as it did not threaten the cherished ideas of the past. Even the Renaissance and the Reformation, two great efflorescences of European life, were, as their names suggest, couched in terms of the past, despite the fact that they contained much that was forward-looking and novel.[1] Scholars of Renaissance Europe believed that the learning of classical antiquity was being restored even while they were busy transforming the very manner in which people understood history.[2] From the sixteenth century, this retrospective way of thinking gradually began to be eroded, not just in Europe but also in China, India, Japan and the Islamic world, though the process has been best chronicled in Europe. The growth of scientific knowledge, the expanding influence of the scientific method, the spread of secularism, and the burgeoning importance of the market and commerce slowly undermined the idea that the present and the future were little more than replays of the past.

From the late eighteenth century, a fundamentally different outlook began to take root with the arrival of modernity. Instead of the present being lived as the past, it became increasingly orientated towards the future. From change being seen as so many variants of the past, it acquired a quite new power and promise as a way of making a different future. A new set of words and concepts became the bearers of the values that were intrinsic to modernity: progress, change, modernization, reason, enlightenment, development and emancipation. There was growing conflict between these attitudes and those – such as tradition, custom, heritage, experience and conservative – associated with the old modes of thinking. The modernity–tradition divide became a new central organizing principle of social life.

The coming of modernity cannot be considered in neat chronological terms like the reign of a king, or the period of a dynasty, or the duration of a war, or (though with less precision) the boundaries of an industrial revolution. Its inception cannot be given a date, only a period; so far, moreover, there appears, as yet at least, to be no obvious end but rather a process akin to perpetual motion. It was the onset of industrialization that marked the arrival and diffusion of modernity and, rather like the ever-expanding universe, modernity has relentlessly kept on moving ever since. According to Göran Therborn, modernity marked the emergence of 'an epoch turned to the future'.[3] Christopher Bayly argues that modernity should be seen as an open-ended process, 'which began at the end of the eighteenth century and has continued up to the present day'.[4] If modernity was a novelty at the time of the British Industrial Revolution, it has since become a compelling and seemingly omnipotent narrative, sweeping all before it, with the 'new' exercising a magnetic attraction on the popular imagination from North America to Europe, from China to Japan. The extent to which so many contemporary conflicts are fought out between 'progressive' on the one hand and 'conservative' or 'traditionalist' on the other underlines the degree to which the language of modernity has insinuated itself into the bloodstream of societies.

The decisive moment for modernity was, and remains, economic take-off and the coming of industrialization. It is with the arrival of industrial capitalism that the new mentality – the orientation towards change and uncertainty, the belief that the future will be different from the past – slowly moves from being the preserve of a few elites to eventually infecting the psyche of the entire population. The locus of economic activity shifts from the field to the factory, and that of residence from the countryside to the cities. Every aspect of human life is progressively transformed: living standards, family structure, working conditions, skills and knowledge, self-organization, political representation, the relationship with the natural environment, the idea of time, and the perception of human existence. Like modernity itself, and as its key driver, the Industrial Revolution unleashed a process of economic transformation which continues unabated to this day.[5]

Even though one can trace some of the origins of the modern in Europe back to the sixteenth century, the decisive period of change was the nineteenth century, when industrialization swept across north-west Europe, the economic power of European nations was transformed, the modern nation-state was born, and virtually the entire world was brought into a global system dominated by Europe. The merging of all these trends marked a qualitative shift in human organization. This was the period when modernity began to acquire a global reach, and people aspired to be modern and to think of themselves as modern – from dress and ways of being named to the possession of objects like fob watches and umbrellas – not only in Europe and North America, but also even amongst elite groups, though not amongst the masses (with the exception of Japan), in Asia and Africa.[6]

This process has been gathering speed ever since. By previous standards, Britain's Industrial Revolution between 1780 and 1840 was breathtakingly rapid, but, when judged by later examples, especially those of the Asian tigers, it was, paradoxically, extremely slow. Each successive economic take-off has got faster and faster, the process of modernization, with its attendant urbanization and rapid decline in agrarian employment, steadily accelerating. Although Europe has, in the debates about post-modernity, recently expressed qualms about modernity, seen from a global perspective, it is abundantly clear – as it sweeps across the Asian continent, home to 60 per cent of the world's population – that the insatiable desire for modernity is still the dominant force of our time; far more, in fact, than ever before. Europe's confidence and belief in the future may have dimmed compared with that of Victorian Britain, but the United States is still restlessly committed to notions of progress and the future. And if one wants to understand what 'the embrace of the future' means in practice, then China is now the best vantage point of all.

Europe was the birthplace of modernity. As its tentacles stretched around the globe during the course of the two centuries after 1750, so its ideas, institutions, values, religion, languages, ideologies, customs and armies left a huge and indelible imprint on the rest of the world. Modernity and Europe became inseparable, seemingly fused, the one inconceivable without the other: they appeared synonymous. But though modernity was conceived in Europe, there is nothing intrinsically European about it: apart from an accident of birth it had, and has, no special connection to that continent and its civilization. Over the last half-century, as modernity has taken root in East Asia, it has drawn on the experience of European – or, more precisely, Western – modernity. However, rather than simply being clones of it, East Asian modernities are highly distinctive, spawning institutions, customs, values and ideologies shaped by their own histories and cultures. In Part I, I will explore how modernity came to be indelibly associated with Europe, and more broadly the West, and how East Asia is now in the process of prising that relationship apart.

2

The Rise of the West

By the mid-nineteenth century, European supremacy over East Asia had been clearly established, most graphically in Britain's defeat of China in the First Opium War in 1839–42. But when did it start? There has been a tendency to date it from considerably earlier. Part of the reason for this, perhaps, is that China's history after the Ming dynasty (1368–1644), and especially after the genius of the Song dynasty (960–1279), was to blaze an altogether less innovative trail. Writing of the Qing dynasty (1644–1912), for example, the historian David Landes suggests that: 'China had long slipped into technological and scientific torpor, coasting along on previous gains and losing speed as talent yielded to gentility.' As a result, he argues: 'So the years passed and the decades and the centuries. Europe left China far behind.'[1]

As China disappointed compared with its previous record, Europe, on the other hand, grew steadily more dynamic. From around 1400, parts of it began to display steady economic growth, while the intellectual ferment of the Renaissance provided some of the foundations for its later scientific and industrial revolutions. The emphasis on the long-run nature of Europe's transformation, however, has probably been exaggerated by what might be described as hindsight thinking: the belief that because of the dazzling success and extraordinary domination of Europe from the beginning of the nineteenth century, the roots of that success must date back rather longer than they actually did. The result has been a view – by no means universal – that Europe's lead over China, and China's own relative decline, commenced rather earlier than was in fact the case.[2]

The idea that Europe enjoyed a comfortable lead over China and Japan in 1800 has been subject to growing challenge by historians. Kaoru Sugihara has argued that, far from going into decline after 1600, over the course of the next three centuries there was an 'East Asian miracle' based on the intensive use of labour and market-based growth – which he describes as an 'industrious revolution' – that was comparable as an economic achievement to the subsequent 'European miracle' of industrialization. He shows that Japanese agriculture displayed a strong capacity for innovation long before the Meiji Restoration in 1868, with major improvements in crops and productivity helping to support a growing population.[3] It is clear, as Adam Smith pointed out, that in the late eighteenth century China enjoyed a rather more developed and sophisticated market than Europe.[4] The share of the Chinese harvest that was marketed over long distances, for example, was considerably higher than in Europe. A key reason for the early development of the market in China was the absence of feudalism. In medieval Europe the serf was bound to the land and could neither leave it nor dispose of it, whereas the Chinese peasant, both legally and in reality, was free, provided he had the wherewithal, to buy and sell land and the produce of that land.[5]

In 1800 China was at least as urbanized as Western Europe, while it has been estimated that 22 per cent of Japan's eighteenth-century population lived in cities compared with 10–15 per cent in Western Europe. Nor did Western Europe enjoy a decisive advantage over China and Japan before 1800 in terms of capital stock or economic institutions, with plenty of Chinese companies being organized along joint-stock lines. Even in technology, there appears to have been little to choose between Europe and China, and in some fields, like irrigation, textile weaving and dyeing, medicine and porcelain manufacture, the Europeans were behind. China had long used textile machines that differed in only one key detail from the spinning jenny and the flying shuttle which were to power Britain's textile-led Industrial Revolution that started around 1780. China had long been familiar with the steam engine and had developed various versions of it; compared with James Watt's subsequent invention, the piston needed to turn the wheel rather than the other way round.[6] What is certainly true, however, is that once Britain embarked on its Industrial Revolution, investment in capital- and energy-intensive processes rapidly raised productivity levels and created a virtuous circle of technology, innovation and growth that was able to draw on an ever-growing body of science in which Britain enjoyed a significant lead over China.[7] For China, in contrast, its 'industrious revolution' did not prove the prelude to an industrial revolution.

Living standards in the most advanced regions of China and Western Europe appear to have been roughly comparable in 1800, with Japan perhaps slightly ahead, while the figures for life expectancy and calorie-intake were broadly similar.[8] European life expectancy – an important measure of prosperity – did not surpass that of China until the end of the nineteenth century, except in its most affluent regions.[9] Paul Bairoch has calculated figures for per capita income which put China ahead of Western Europe in 1800, with Asia as a whole behind Western Europe but in advance of Europe.[10] In referring to China and Europe, of course, we need to bear in mind that we are dealing with huge land masses populated by very large numbers of people: in 1820, China's population was 381 million while that of Western Europe was 133 million, and that of Europe as a whole 169 million. Levels of economic development and standards of living inevitably varied considerably from region to region, making comparisons between the two problematic. The key point is that the most advanced regions of China, notably the Yangzi Delta, seem to have been more or less on a par with the most prosperous parts of north-west Europe, in particular Britain, at the end of the eighteenth century.[11] Given the crucial role played by the most advanced regions in pioneering industrial take-off, the decisive comparison must be that between Britain and the Yangzi Delta.

The general picture that emerges is that, far from Western Europe having established a decisive economic lead over China and Japan by 1800, there was, in fact, not that much to choose between them.[12] In this light, the argument that industrialization was the product of a very long historical process that took place over several centuries, rather than a few decades, is dubious: instead, it would appear more likely that industrialization was, in large measure, a consequence of relatively contingent factors.[13] This still begs the question, however, as to why Western Europe, rather than Japan or China, was able to turn its fortunes around so rapidly from around 1800 and then outdistance Japan, and especially China, by such a massive margin during the nineteenth century.

Here the fortuitous or chance factor, while by no means the sole reason, played a critical role. Around 1800 the most heavily populated regions of the Old World, including China and Europe, were finding it increasingly difficult to sustain rising populations. The basic problem was that food, fibre, fuel and building supplies were all competing for what was becoming increasingly scarce land and forest. This was particularly serious in China because its heartland, which lay between the Yellow and Yangzi rivers, had always supported a very large and relatively dense population as a result of its fertility; now, however, it became increasingly exhausted through overuse.[14] This, combined with the fact that new land brought under cultivation was not of a high quality, posed an increasingly acute problem.[15] For two crucial reasons, Europe – or rather specifically Britain – was able to break this crucial land constraint in a way that was to elude China. First, Britain discovered large quantities of coal that were accessibly located for the new industries, thereby helping to ease the growing shortage of wood, and able to play a vital role in fuelling the Industrial Revolution. In contrast, although China also had very considerable deposits of coal, they lay a long way from its main centres of population, the largest being in the north-west, far from the textile industries and canals of the lower Yangzi Valley.[16] Second, and much more importantly, the colonization of the New World, namely the Caribbean and North America, was to provide huge tracts of land, a massive and very cheap source of labour in the form of slaves, and an abundant flow of food and raw materials: the early growth of Manchester, for example, would have been impossible without cheap and plentiful supplies of cotton from the slave plantations. Raising enough sheep to replace the yarn made with Britain's New World cotton imports would have required huge quantities of land (almost 9 million acres in 1815 and over 23 million acres by 1830). Overall, it is estimated that the land required in order to grow the cotton, sugar and timber imported by Britain from the New World in 1830 would have been between 25 and 30 million acres – or more than Britain's total arable and pasture land combined.[17] The role played by colonization, in this context, is a reminder that European industrialization was far from an endogenous process.[18] The New World – together with the discovery of large quantities of coal in Britain – removed the growing pressure on land that was endangering Britain's economic development. China was to enjoy no such good fortune. The consequences were to be far-reaching: 'England avoided becoming the Yangzi Delta,' argues the historian Kenneth Pomeranz, 'and the two came to look so different that it became hard to see how recently they had been quite similar.'[19]

The fact that the New World colonies proved a vital source of raw materials for Britain at such a critical time was a matter of chance, but there was nothing fortuitous about the way that Britain had colonized the New World over most of the two previous centuries. Colonization also provided Europe with other long-term advantages. Rivalry over colonies, as well as the many intra-European wars – combined with their obvious economic prowess – helped to hone European nation-states into veritable fighting machines, as a result of which, during the course of the nineteenth century, they were able to establish a huge military advantage over every other region in the world, which thereby became vulnerable to European imperial expansion. The scale of this military expenditure should not be underestimated. HMS *Victory*, commanded by Admiral Nelson during the Battle of Trafalgar in 1805, cost five times as much as Abraham Crowley's steelworks, one of the flagship investments of Britain's Industrial Revolution.[20] Colonial trade also provided fertile ground for innovations in both company organization and systems of financing, with the Dutch, for example, inventing the joint-stock company for this purpose. Without the slave trade and colonization, Europe could never have made the kind of breakthrough it did. It is true that China also had what might be termed colonies – newly acquired territories achieved by a process of westward imperial expansion from 1644 until the late eighteenth century – but these were in the interior of the Eurasian continent, bereft of either large arable lands or dense populations, and were unable to provide raw materials on anything like the scale of the New World.[21] South-East Asia, which was abundant in resources, would have been a more likely candidate to play the role of China's New World. Admiral Zheng's exploits in the early fifteenth century, with ships far larger than anything that Europe could build at the time, show that China was not lacking the technical ability or financial means, but the attitude of the Chinese state towards overseas interests and possessions was quite different from that of Europe. Although large numbers of Chinese migrated to South-East Asia, the Chinese state, unlike the European nations, showed no interest in providing military or political backing for its subjects' overseas endeavours: in contrast, the Qing dynasty displayed great concern for its continental lands in the north and west, reflecting the fact that China saw itself as a continental rather than maritime civilization. Ironically, it was the European powers that were to begin the colonization of South-East Asia, especially from the mid nineteenth century.

This raises the wider question of the extent to which the contrasting attitudes of the European and Chinese states, and their respective elites, were a factor in China's failure to make the breakthrough that Europe achieved. The capacity of the Chinese state was certainly not in question: as we shall see in Chapter 4, it was able to achieve quite extraordinary feats when it came to the mobilization of economic and natural resources.[22] The highly developed granary system, the government-built 1,400-mile-long Grand Canal and the land settlement policies on the frontiers all demonstrated a strong interventionist spirit. The imperial Chinese state also had the experience and ability to transport bulk commodities over long distances, though its priority here was not coal but grain, salt and copper, since these were crucial for maintaining the stability, cohesion and subsistence of the population, always an overriding concern of the Chinese state.[23] Herein, in fact, lay a significant difference: the priorities of the imperial state tended to be focused on the maintenance of order and balanced development rather than narrow profit-making and industrialization. The state was resistant to excessive income differentiation and marked displays of extravagance, which were seen as inimical to Confucian values of harmony.[24] The state did not block market activities and commerce – on the contrary, it strongly supported the development of an agrarian market economy – but it did not, for the most part, promote commercial capitalism, except for those merchants engaged in the monopolies for salt and foreign trade. In contrast, the European state, especially the British, tended to be more responsive to the new industrial possibilities.[25] Nor did the imperial state believe in pitting one province against another, which would clearly have made for instability, whereas in Europe such competition took the form of nation-state rivalry. The main reason for the different mentalities of the Chinese and Western European states was that while the rising merchant classes were eventually incorporated, in one form or another, into European governance, in China they remained firmly outside, as they have to this day.[26] Rather than enjoying an independent power base, the merchants depended on official patronage and support to promote and protect large-scale commercial undertakings. Western European states, and in the first instance the British, were more favourably orientated towards industrial development than China, where the administrative class and landed interest still predominated.[27]

In 1800, therefore, Britain enjoyed two long-term – as opposed to contingent – advantages over China. The British state (and, in varying degrees, other Western European states) was more favourably disposed towards industrial capitalism (and therefore industrialization) than the Chinese state, while colonization and persistent intra-European wars had furnished Western Europe with various strategic assets, notably raw materials and military capacity. The fact that colonization was to provide Britain with the means by which to side-step its growing land and resource problem towards the end of the eighteenth century, however, was, in the event, entirely fortuitous. The point remains, therefore, that in 1800 China (and, indeed, Japan) found itself in a rather similar economic position to Western Europe and possessed a not dissimilar potential for economic take-off. What made the key difference were those contingent factors – New World resources and, to a lesser extent, accessible supplies of coal – that enabled Britain to deal with its resource constraints; though the supportive attitude of the British state towards industrialization was also of considerable importance. China enjoyed no such contingent salvation and, as a result, found itself in a hole from which it was unable to extricate itself, a situation that was to be exacerbated within less than half a century by the growing incursions of the European powers, especially Britain, beginning with the Opium Wars. The historical consequences were to be enormous: China was at least as agrarian in 1850 as it was in 1750 and not much less so even in 1950. According to the economic historian Angus Maddison, China's GDP in 1820 was $228.6 billion – almost four times greater than in 1600 – but had barely increased at all by 1913, by which time it had nudged up to $241.3 billion, and actually fell to $239.9 billion in 1950.[28]

If the root cause of China's catastrophic performance between 1800 and 1950 lay not circa 1600 but circa 1800, then the antecedents of China's present economic dynamism, rather than being lost in the mists of time, are, on the contrary, relatively recent.[29] This makes China's remarkable economic transformation since 1978 rather more explicable.[30] Far from being a basket-case, the Chinese economy in 1800 remained, in many respects, very dynamic; society continued to be highly competitive, the peasantry displayed a powerful capacity to adapt and innovate, and merchants possessed considerable commercial acumen. While these characteristics may have remained relatively dormant in the inclement intervening period, after 1978 they have once again come to the fore.[31] To this we might add a further contemporary point. In 1800, rather than being Eurocentric, the global economy was, in fact, polycentric, economic power being shared between Asia, Europe and the Americas, with China and India the world's two largest economies. The global economy is now once more becoming increasingly multipolar. Rather than regarding this as unusual, perhaps instead we should see the last two centuries, in which economic power became concentrated in the hands of a relatively small part of the world's population, namely Europe, North America and later Japan, as something of an historical aberration. Colonization, furthermore, was to play a crucial role in this outcome, by providing some of the preconditions for Europe to break into Promethean growth while at the same time also bestowing on it the power and opportunity to stifle and distort the economic development of much of the rest of the world for a century or more.

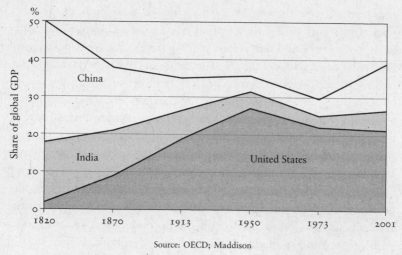

Source: OECD; Maddison

*Figure 6. The fall and rise of China and India:
changing shares of global GDP, 1820–2001.*

PRECONDITIONS OR
CHARACTERISTICS?

If, towards the end of the eighteenth century, Western Europe was in
a rather similar position to China, the implications for our understanding of history and subsequent events are far-reaching. It suggests
that the explanation for the rise of Europe was in large part to do
with relatively short-term factors rather than preordained by its slow
but steady transformation over previous centuries; in other words, we
need to rethink the idea that the ensemble of characteristics which
Europe had been acquiring over centuries, and enjoyed on the eve of
economic take-off, were, as has often been assumed, also *preconditions* for that take-off. They might have been desirable, they could
have been advantageous, but were they also conditions without which
the process would never have happened at all? Japan, China and India
were not too far away from achieving a similar economic breakthrough but their political and cultural histories contrasted sharply
with that of Europe. If they had succeeded and Europe failed, then the

characteristics of their subsequent paths of development, and the institutions and values they would have spawned, would certainly have looked very different from those we have come to associate with Europe. Indeed, as we shall see later, as these countries have modernized they have diverged markedly from the European template.

It is clear from the experience of the last half-century, during which a growing number of countries have achieved rapid industrialization, that the processes and conditions that characterized European take-off, and particularly that of Britain, were in many respects peculiar to Western Europe and that there are, in fact, many ways of achieving take-off. As the historian Peter Perdue writes: 'Industrial growth does not have to be an outcome of a centuries-long accumulation of the particular skills found in north-west Europe; there are numerous paths to economic modernity, and England followed only one of them.'[32] As a small example, the nature of class differentiation in the English countryside, including the rapid decline of the peasantry, has not been repeated in the case of China's industrialization nor, indeed, have countless other characteristics either.[33]

This brings us to the broader political, cultural and intellectual framework of Europe's passage to modernity. The roots of European civilization are usually traced back to Greek democracy, Roman law and Judaeo-Christian religion. It has been commonplace to regard these as preconditions for, as well as characteristics of, European modernity. Although the impact of democracy in ancient Greece has been exaggerated, with the West not adopting it, except for small minorities, until the late nineteenth century at the earliest, there is no mistaking the broad influence that Greek civilization has exercised on European history down the ages, including the way we think about right and wrong, the tradition of debate and oratory, the notion of independent citizenship, and the idea of democracy. A more prosaic example is the constant recycling of mainly Doric but also Ionic and, via the Roman Empire, Corinthian columns as the preferred architectural style for buildings that seek to convey a sense of eternal authority, from the Bank of England to the French National Assembly; the same, of course, is true in the United States, with the Supreme Court, the White House and Capitol Hill.[34] Similarly, the development of Roman-inspired law – essentially through Christianity in the eleventh and twelfth centuries – helped to establish the concept and reality of an independent legal system, which played a significant role in the subsequent entrenchment of property rights.[35] Finally, Christianity was to imbue Europe with a powerful sense of universalism, which was to shape the continent's attitudes towards not only itself but also other cultures and races, playing an important role in moulding the colonial mentality and the notion of a civilizing mission.[36]

It is not difficult, then, to see the lines of continuity. It is rather more difficult, however, to argue that they were necessary conditions for take-off. These cultural characteristics certainly helped to shape European modernity, but that is not the same as them being preconditions. Something similar can be said of Western individualism and the Western family. It would appear, with the benefit of hindsight, for example, that many different types of family are compatible with the process of industrialization. A significant area of European advantage was in the field of science, based on the growing autonomy of intellectual inquiry, spreading networks of scientific activity, and the routinization of research and its diffusion.[37] But other intellectual traditions, notably the Chinese during the Qing dynasty and the Islamic, also gave rise to forms of debate, argument and empirical observation that stand comparison with the emerging scientific rationalism of Western Europe. The rider – and a very important one – is that in these other traditions there was still a strong tendency to seek to reconcile new arguments with those of older authorities, instead of rejecting them.[38]

By 1800 Europe had accumulated an array of such cultural assets, but these were not the key to its economic breakthrough. They should be seen as characteristics of European modernity rather than as preconditions for it.[39] There is no reason to believe that other cultures – with their own diverse characteristics – were incapable of achieving the breakthrough into modernity: this, after all, is precisely what has been happening since 1960. Central to an understanding of why Europe succeeded and China failed at the end of the eighteenth century are conjunctural factors rather than long-run cultural characteristics. Christopher Bayly draws the following conclusion: 'If, in terms of economic growth, what distinguished Europe from China before 1800 was only its intensive use of coal and the existence of a vast American hinterland to Europe, then a lot of cultural baggage about inherent European political superiorities looks ready to be jettisoned.'[40]

EUROPEAN EXCEPTIONALISM

Far from Europe being the template of modernity which every subsequent transformation should conform to and be measured by, the European experience must be regarded – notwithstanding the fact that it was the first – as highly specific and particular.[41] In practice, however, it has seen itself, and often been seen as, the defining model. This is not surprising. The extraordinary global hegemony enjoyed by Europe for almost two centuries has made the particular seem universal. What, then, have been the peculiar characteristics of Europe's passage to, and through, modernity?

Although European nations spent an extraordinary amount of time and energy fighting each other, the European passage to modernity from the mid sixteenth century onwards was achieved without, for the most part, a persistent threat from outside, with the exception of the Ottoman Empire in the south-east. By the seventeenth century, however, the latter was progressively being rolled back, though it was not until the nineteenth century that it was finally excluded from the Balkans.[42] Europe was the only continent to enjoy this privilege. Every subsequent aspirant for modernity – Asia, Africa, Latin America, the Middle East – had to confront and deal with an outside predator in the form of the modern European nations. Even the European settlers in North America had to fight the British in the American War of Independence to establish their sovereignty and thereby enable the conditions for economic take-off. A consequence of this is that Europe has been little concerned in recent centuries with dealing with the Other, or seeking to understand the Other, except on very much its own, frequently colonial, terms. Only relatively recently did this begin to change.

Europe's colonial history, in fact, is a further distinguishing characteristic. From the sixteenth century to the 1930s European nations, in a remarkable display of expansion and conquest, almost uniquely (the nearest similar example being Japan) built seaborne empires that stretched around the world. The colonies, especially those in the New World and, in the case of Britain, India and the Malay Peninsula,[43] were to be the source of huge resources and riches for the imperial powers. Without them, as we have seen, Europe could not have achieved its economic take-off in the way that it did. No non-European country, bar Japan after 1868, was to achieve take-off in the nineteenth century: as a result, a majority found themselves colonized by the European powers.

Although the passage through modernity universally involves the transition from an agrarian to a service-based society via an industrial one, here we find another instance of European exceptionalism. European countries (sixteen in all) – with Britain, Belgium and Germany (in that order) at the head – are the *only* ones in the world that have been through a phase in which the relative size of industrial employment was *larger* than either agrarian or service employment.[44] In Britain, industrial employment reached its peak in 1911, when it accounted for 52.2 per cent of the total labour force: by way of contrast, the peak figure for the United States was 35.8 per cent in 1967 and for Japan 37.1 per cent in 1973. It was the sheer weight of industrial society that was to lend modern Europe many of its most distinctive characteristics, notably the centrality of class conflict and importance of trade unions. From a global perspective, a different and far more common path has been to move directly, in terms of employment, from a largely agrarian to a mainly service society, without a predominantly industrial phase, a route that has been followed by the United States, Canada, Japan and South Korea.[45]

Although the pace of European industrialization was extremely rapid by the standards of previous economic change, it was slow compared with subsequent take-offs, the United States included, but especially East Asia.[46] The transformation of Western Europe was a long and protracted affair: it took Britain, after all, over two centuries to get where it is now. One consequence has been that the conflict between modernity and tradition has been relatively muted. The European city neatly illustrates this point: it is like a geological formation, one era of architecture existing cheek by jowl with another, a living museum embracing centuries of history, in contrast to North America, where cities were newly created, and East Asia, where little survives from the past in places like Tokyo, Seoul, Singapore, Shanghai, Kuala Lumpur and Hong Kong.

Another peculiar characteristic of Europe has been a succession of intra-continental conflicts or what might be described as internal wars.[47] Perhaps this was in part due to the relative lack of an external threat, which meant that the dominant fault lines were national or intra-European rather than to do with the outside, as was to be the case, in varying degrees, with colonized societies. The initial cause of these internal wars was religious conflict, starting in 1054 with the struggle between eastern and western Christianity followed, after 1517, by the division between Catholicism and Protestantism, which was to split the continent largely on a north–south axis. The persistence of these religious conflicts was to lend Europe a strongly doctrinal way of thinking which was initially expressed in theological and then later ideological forms. This was to be a far more pronounced characteristic than in any other continent: most of the major non-religious 'isms' – for example, liberalism, anarchism, socialism, communism, republicanism, monarchism, Protestantism and fascism – were European in origin.[48] From the 1540s to the 1690s, Europe's internal wars were largely concerned with the consolidation of the early modern states. After the French Revolution, class assumed growing importance, and from the early nineteenth century until the late twentieth century it formed the overarching language of European politics and society in a way that was never to be the case anywhere else in the world. From 1792 through to around 1870 the establishment of nation-states was to play a fundamental role in Europe's internal wars. By the late nineteenth century these national rivalries were increasingly transposed on to the global stage, with the struggle over colonies, notably in Africa, contributing to the First World War. The Second World War started as a further instalment of Europe's internal wars but rapidly spread to engulf most of the world, although its heartland remained in Europe. This penchant for internal war found global projection in the very European phenomenon of the

Cold War, in which the fundamental divide was ideological, with the two great 'isms' of the time – capitalism and communism – ranged against each other. Ultimately, this appetite for internal war was to prove near-fatal for Europe: it fought itself to a standstill in the two world wars of the twentieth century and thereby rendered itself both exhausted and, in terms of global power, largely a spent force.[49]

Finally, the transformation of Europe has also been distinguished by individualism. The historian and anthropologist Alan Macfarlane has described individualism as 'the view that society is constituted of autonomous, equal units, namely separate individuals, and that such individuals are more important, ultimately, than any larger constituent group'.[50] This is very different from East and South Asian cultures, where group rather than individual identity is central. Take the family, for example. The English family system had its origins in the thirteenth century and, courtesy of the Pilgrims, it also became the basis of the family system in North America. This individualistic system, with its emphasis on the nuclear family, stands in stark contrast to the traditional extended-household, arranged-marriage, kinship-based systems to be found in societies like China and India, whose values and distinctive characteristics persist to this day, notwithstanding urbanization and a dramatic fall in the size of the nuclear family.[51] Thus, while marriage in the West is essentially a union of two individuals, in Chinese and Indian culture it involves the conjoining of two families.

Europe's journey to and through modernity took highly specific and unique forms – the relative absence of an external threat, colonialism, the preponderance of industry, relatively slow growth, a pattern of intra-European conflict (or what I have termed 'internal wars'), and individualism. We should not therefore be surprised that the characteristics of its modernity are also more distinctive than is often admitted. Since Europe has enjoyed such a huge influence on the rest of the world, however, differentiating between the specific and the universal is often difficult and elusive. Europeans, unsurprisingly, have long believed that what they have achieved must be of universal application, by force if necessary. It is only with the rise of a range of new modernities that it is becoming possible to distinguish between what is universal and what is specific about the European experience.

THE DOMINANCE OF EUROPE

At the beginning of the nineteenth century, GDP per head in Western Europe and on the North American seaboard was perhaps twice that of South Asia and roughly on a par with Japan and the southern and eastern seaboard of China. By 1900, income per head in Western Europe and the North American seaboard dwarfed that of China by a margin of at least ten times. China was to pay dearly for its inability to overcome the economic constraints that began to bear down on it during the late eighteenth century; in contrast, Europe luxuriated in its good fortune. The key to Europe's transformation was the Industrial Revolution. Britain's was well under way before 1800; by the second half of the nineteenth century, it had been joined by much of Western Europe. Previously economic growth was of a glacial speed; now compound rates of growth ensured that Western Europe far outdistanced every other part of the world, the United States being the most important exception. Apart from North America, the old white settler colonies[52] and Japan after 1868, Europe enjoyed a more or less total monopoly of industrialization during the nineteenth century, a scenario with profound consequences for everyone else.

The economic chasm that opened up between Europe and nearly everywhere else greatly enhanced its ability to dominate the world.[53] The colonial era had started in the seventeenth century, but from the middle of the eighteenth century onwards, with the progressive acquisition of India, it rapidly expanded. In the name of Christianity, civilization and racial superiority, and possessed of armies and navies without peer, the European nations, led by Britain and France, subjugated large swathes of the world, culminating in the scramble for Africa in the decades immediately prior to 1914.[54] Savage wars took place between whites and non-whites as Chinese, Indians and native peoples in North America, Australasia and southern Africa made their last stand against European assaults on their religions, rulers, land and resources.[55] Niall Ferguson writes:

Western hegemony was one of the great asymmetries of world history. Taken together, the metropoles of all the Western empires – the American, Belgian, British, Dutch, French, German, Italian, Portuguese, and Spanish – accounted for 7% of the world's land surface and just 18% of its population. Their possessions, however, amounted to 37% of global territory and 28% of mankind. And if we regard the Russian empire as effectively another European empire extending into Asia, the total share of these Western empires rises to more than half the world's area and population.[56]

As the world's leading power, Britain sought to shape the new global trading system according to its interests. Its national wealth depended on exporting its manufacturing products to as many markets as possible while importing food and raw materials at the lowest possible prices. Laissez-faire was not simply an abstract principle or a disinterested policy. It was the means by which Britain tried to take advantage of its overwhelming advantage in manufacturing and prevent others from seeking to erect tariffs to protect their nascent industries. The international free trade regime championed by Britain had a stifling effect on much of the rest of the world outside north-west Europe and North America. Industrial development in the colonial world was for the most part to prove desperately slow, or non-existent, as the European powers tried to prevent or forestall direct competition for their domestic producers. 'Whatever the official rhetoric,' writes Eric Hobsbawm, 'the function of colonies and informal dependencies was to complement metropolitan economies and not to compete with them.'[57] The urban population – a key measure of industrialization – in the British and French empires in Asia and North Africa remained stuck at around 10 per cent of the total in 1900, which was barely different from the pre-colonial period, while standards of living may even have fallen over the course of the nineteenth century.[58] India – by far Britain's most important colony (it was colonized by the East India Company from the mid eighteenth century, and formally annexed by Britain in 1857)[59] – had a per capita GDP of $550 in 1700, $533 in 1820, and $533 in 1870. In other words, it was lower in 1870 than it had been in 1700, or even 1600 (when it was also

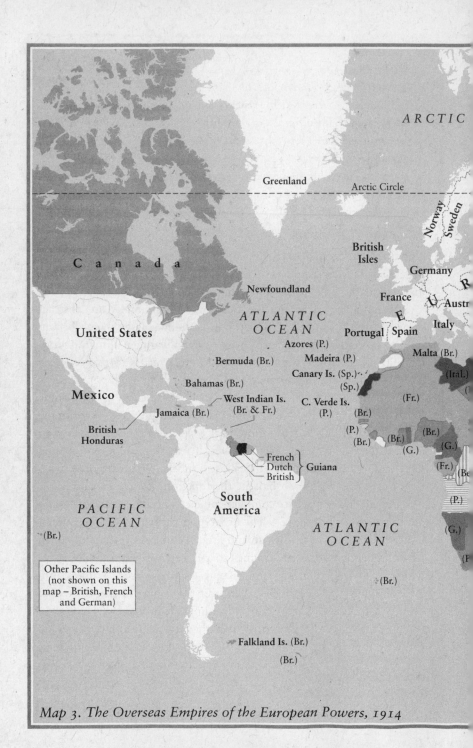

Map 3. *The Overseas Empires of the European Powers, 1914*

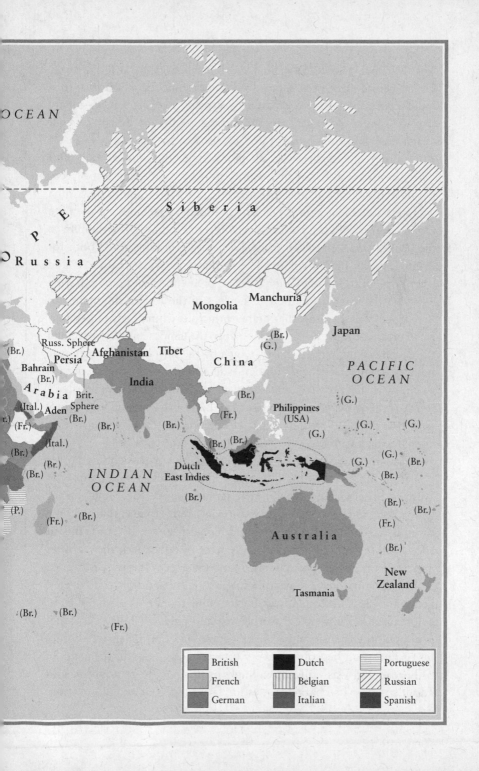

OCEAN

Russia

P
E

Siberia

Mongolia   Manchuria

Japan

(Br.)
(G.)

Russ. Sphere
(Br.)
Afghanistan   Tibet   China
Bahrain
(Br.)
Arabia   Brit.
(Ital.) Aden   Sphere
r.)   -(Br.)
(Fr.)   (Br.)
(Ital.)

India

(Br.)

PACIFIC
OCEAN

(Br.)

(Fr.)   Philippines
(USA)

(G.)

(Br.)   (Br.)   (Br.)

(G.)   (G.)

(Br.)
(Br.)
(P.)

(Br.)
(Br.)   (Br.)

INDIAN
OCEAN

Dutch
East Indies

(G.)

(Br.)   (Br.)

(Br.)

(G.)   (G.)
(G.)   (G.)   (Br.)
(G.)   (Br.)

(Br.)

(Fr.)   (Br.)

(Br.)

(Fr.)

(Br.)

Australia

(Br.)

New
Zealand

(Br.)   (Br.)

(Fr.)

Tasmania

	British		Dutch		Portuguese
	French		Belgian		Russian
	German		Italian		Spanish

$550). It then rose to $673 in 1914 but fell back to $619 in 1950. Over a period of 250 years, most of it under some form of British rule, India's per capita GDP increased by a mere 5.5 per cent. Compare that with India's fortunes after independence: already by 1973 its per capita GDP had risen to $853 and by 2001 to $1,957.[60]

Not only did Europe take off in a manner that eluded Asia after 1800, but it forcibly sought to prevent – by a combination of economic and military means – Asia from taking the same route. China was a classic case in point. The British fought the Chinese in the First Opium War of 1839–42 over the right to sell Indian-grown opium to the Chinese market, which proved a highly profitable trade both for Britain and its Indian colony. The increasingly widespread sale and use of opium following China's defeat predictably had a debilitating effect on the population, but in the eyes of the British the matter of 'free trade' was an altogether higher principle. China's ensuing inability to prevent the West from prising open the Chinese market hastened the decline of the Qing dynasty, which by the turn of the century was hopelessly enfeebled, with foreign rule entrenched in the numerous so-called treaty ports. When European and American expeditionary forces invaded China in 1900 to crush the Boxer Uprising, it was evident that little, other than imperial differences, stood in the way of China being partitioned in a similar manner to Africa.[61]

Paradoxically, nothing serves to illustrate the overwhelming power of Europe more vividly than the rise of Japan. Stalked by the threat of Western invasion and fearful that it might meet the same fate as China, following the Meiji Restoration in 1868, Japan embarked on a carefully calculated process of rapid modernization. It sent teams of specialists to study the European systems of education, their armies and navies, railways, postal systems and much else. It rejected the idea that it was any longer a meaningful part of Asia and instead coveted acceptance as a Western power. It even emulated the Western model of colonialism, occupying Taiwan, Korea and part of China. The Meiji project of modernization was testament to the comprehensive character of European hegemony. Every other country lived in the shadow of Europe and was obliged, willingly or unwillingly, to adapt to and adopt some of its characteristics, or face the threat of colonization.

The rise of Europe changed the rules of the game for everyone else. The consequences were by no means exclusively negative: above all, Europe demonstrated what was possible through industrialization and thereby confronted the world with the ineluctable choice of modernization. Although imperial powers saw their colonies as the servant of their needs, and prohibited them from competing with their masters, some, nonetheless, acquired from their colonizers a few of the building blocks of their subsequent development. India obtained a widely shared language in English, Taiwan inherited the Japanese education system, and the Chinese in the treaty ports, especially Shanghai, learnt about Western commerce.[62] But the balance of outcome was largely negative, as reflected in the economic evidence presented earlier as well as the profound popular hostility towards what was perceived by the great majority in the colonial world, then and now, as alien rule; in some cases, notably Africa, moreover, it was almost entirely negative. The one great exception was the white settler colonies of Australia, Canada and New Zealand: these were always treated entirely differently – for straightforward racial and ethnic reasons – and prospered greatly as a consequence.[63]

The high-point of European power was probably just before the First World War, although as late as the 1930s Italy still managed to annex Abyssinia. By then, however, the United States had begun to emerge as the successor power, enjoying not only great economic strength but also growing cultural and intellectual influence. The full impact of its rise, though, continued to be obscured by a combination of its isolationism and its obvious affinity with Europe. This latter perception was reinforced by the huge numbers of migrants from Europe to the United States between 1850 and 1930, equivalent to 12 per cent of the former's entire population in 1900.[64] The decline of Europe became manifest after 1945 with the rapid and dramatic collapse of its empires, with the Indian subcontinent, Indonesia, much of Africa, Indo-China and Malaysia, for example, all gaining independence. In the process, the number of nation-states grew by three times.[65] The global map was once again redrawn, as it had been in the nineteenth century – but this time far more rapidly and in the opposite direction. Independence opened up new possibilities, although these proved to be extremely diverse and uneven. India's performance was transformed, as the figures cited earlier for its economic growth illustrate, but Africa was left debilitated by the experience of the slave trade and then colonialism. It has been estimated that the slave trade may have reduced Africa's population by up to a half as a result of the forcible export of people combined with deaths on the continent itself.[66] In contrast East Asia, which was far less affected by colonialism and did not suffer slavery (though it did experience indentured labour), was much less disadvantaged. In the light of the economic transformation of so many former colonies after 1950, it is clear that the significance of decolonization and national liberation in the first two decades after the Second World War has been greatly underestimated in the West, especially Europe. Arguably it was, bar none, the most important event of the twentieth century, creating the conditions for the majority of the world's population to become the dominant players of the twenty-first century. As Adam Smith wrote presciently of the European discovery of the Americas and the so-called East Indies:

> To the natives, however, both of the East and West Indies, all the commercial benefits which can have resulted from these events have been sunk and lost in the dreadful misfortunes which they have occasioned . . . At the particular time when these discoveries were made, the superiority of force happened to be so great on the side of the Europeans, that they were enabled to commit with impunity every sort of injustice in those remote countries. Hereafter, perhaps, the natives of those countries may grow stronger, or those of Europe may grow weaker, and the inhabitants of all the different quarters of the world may arrive at that equality of courage and force which, by inspiring mutual fear, can alone overawe the injustice of independent nations into some sort of respect for the rights of one another.[67]

THE RISE OF THE UNITED STATES

Although American and European modernity are often conflated into a single Western modernity, they are in fact rather different.[68] The point of commonality was that the settlers, who first arrived in 1607, were Europeans. By 1790 the total population of the United States was 3,929,000, of whom 698,000 were slaves and thereby not regarded as part of American society: of the white population, 80 per cent were British (the rest being largely German and Dutch).[69] Successive waves of European settlers brought with them the values, beliefs, customs, knowledge and culture with which they had grown up. Their intention was to re-create the Old World in the New World.[70] In contrast to Europe, however, where capitalism was shaped by its feudal antecedents, the settlers were not constrained by pre-existing social structures or customs. In effect, they could start afresh, unencumbered by the past. This, of course, entailed the destruction of the native population of Amerindians in what we would now describe as a most brutal act of ethnic cleansing.[71] While Europe was mired in time-worn patterns of land tenure, the American settlers faced no such constraints and, with the decimation of the native population, enjoyed constantly expanding territory as the mythical frontier moved ever westwards. Where Europeans possessed a strong sense of place and territory, the Americans, in contrast, formed no such attachment because they had no need or experience of it. The fact that the United States started as a blank piece of paper enabled it to write its own rules and design its own institutions: from the outset, steeped in Protestant doctrine, Americans were attracted to the idea of abstract principles, which was to find expression in the Constitution and, subsequently, in a strong sense of a universalizing and ultimately global mission.

The fact that the European settlers brought with them a powerful body of values and religious beliefs, but were largely devoid of the class attitudes of their ancestral homes, lent the white American population a sense of homogeneity. The exclusion of African slaves from American society together with the destruction of the Amerindians imbued their identity with a strongly racial dimension. The boundless opportunities presented by a huge and well-endowed territory and a constantly moving frontier instilled the nation with a powerful sense of optimism and a restless commitment to change. The domestic market was unconstrained by the local and regional preferences and the class and status distinctions that prevailed in Europe and, being relatively homogeneous, was much more receptive to standardized products.[72] The relative scarcity of labour stimulated a constant desire to introduce labour-saving machinery and improve productivity. Unlike in Europe, there was little resistance to the process of deskilling and the routinization of tasks. The result was an economy which showed a far greater proclivity for technological innovation, mechanization, the standardization of products, constant improvement in the labour process, economies of scale and mass production than was the case in Europe. The American model was distinguished by a new kind of mass market and mass consumer, with all the attendant innovations in areas such as advertising. As a result, from the late nineteenth century American capitalism was to prove far more dynamic and innovative than its European counterparts.

In 1820, the US economy accounted for a mere 1.8% of world GDP compared with 5.2% and 3.9% for the UK and Germany respectively. By 1870, the US share of world GDP had risen to 8.8% while the equivalent figures for the UK and Germany were 9.0% and 6.5% respectively. By 1914, the US had pulled well ahead with a share of 18.9% compared with 8.2% for the UK and 8.7% for Germany. In 1950, America's economic high noon, its share of world GDP was 27.3%, compared with 6.5% for the UK, 5.0% for Germany and 26.2% for the whole of Western Europe.[73] The damage wrought by two world wars notwithstanding, the American economy hugely outperformed the European economies in the period 1870–1950 and this underpinned the emergence of the United States as the premier global power after 1945. Largely eschewing the formal colonies which had been the characteristic form of European global influence,[74] the United States became the first truly global power: the dollar was enshrined as the world's currency, a new constellation of global institutions, like the IMF, the World Bank and GATT, gave expression to the US's economic hegemony, while its military superiority, based on airpower, far exceeded anything that had previously been seen. The United States succeeded in creating a world system of which it was the undisputed hegemon but which was also open and inclusive, finally reaching fruition after the collapse of the Soviet bloc and with the progressive inclusion of China.[75] By 1960, if not earlier, the United States had supplanted Europe as the global exemplar to which other societies and peoples aspired. It demonstrated a new kind of cultural power and influence, through Hollywood and television soaps, and also through such icons of its consumer industry as Coca-Cola and Levi jeans. Its universities increasingly became magnets for the best scholars and students from all over the world. It dominated the list of Nobel Prize winners. And it was the power and appeal of the United States that lay behind the rise of English as the world's first true lingua franca.

The United States became the new metaphor for modernity: untrammelled by the baggage of the past, gravity-free, in perpetual motion, and possessed of the spirit of the new frontier. It was born in the present and has never grown old, its lodestar an abstract set of principles enshrined in a constitution, the whole society committed to a non-stop process of reinvention, a flow of immigration constantly shifting the composition and identity of the population. The rise of Silicon Valley, the penchant for cosmetic surgery and the growing importance of the Hispanic minority are all, in their different ways, but the latest expressions of the American psyche. This is so different from Europe as to be quite alien; and yet the fact that modern America literally comes from Europe has meant that the bond between the two, that sense of affinity, particularly in the global context, has always been very powerful and is likely to remain so. Ancestry, race, history, culture, religion, beliefs and a sense of shared interest have prevailed over profound differences, as evinced by the pervasiveness of the term 'West', whose meaning is not simply geopolitical but more importantly cultural, racial and ethnic, as personified in the word 'Westerner'.[76] Whatever the differences between Europe and the United States, the West is likely to retain a powerful sense of meaning and identity: indeed, it may be that the rise of non-Western countries and cultures will serve to reinforce that sense of affinity.[77] It is true, of course, that the growth of new ethnic minorities in Europe and the increasing importance of non-white minorities in the United States, epitomized by Barack Obama's election, is steadily changing these societies, but the extent of this process should not be exaggerated. It will be a very long time, if ever, before the still overwhelming white majorities on either side of the Atlantic cease to dominate their societies.

The West has shaped the world we live in. Even now, with signs of

a growing challenge from China, the West remains the dominant geopolitical and cultural force. Such has been the extent of Western
influence that it is impossible to think of the world without it, or
imagine what the world would have been like if it had never happened. We have come to take Western hegemony for granted. It is so
deeply rooted, so ubiquitous, that we think of it as somehow natural.
The historian J. M. Roberts wrote, in a somewhat triumphalist vein:
'What seems to be clear is that the story of western civilisation is now
the story of mankind, its influence so diffused that old oppositions
and antitheses are now meaningless.'[78] Not quite. Western hegemony
is neither a product of nature nor is it eternal. On the contrary, at
some point it will come to an end.

3

Japan – Modern But Hardly Western

Crossing a road in Tokyo is a special experience. Virtually every junction, seemingly even the smallest, has its traffic lights, including one for pedestrians. Even if there is no sign of a car, people wait patiently for the lights to change before crossing, rarely if ever breaking rank, young and old alike. The pressure to conform is immense. As an inveterate jogger, I found Tokyo posed problems I had never before encountered: the sheer number of lights proved a serious obstacle to that all-important rhythm of running, and yet at every red light I found myself overcome by guilt at the thought of making a bolt for it, even though there was not a vehicle in sight, perhaps not even a person. This is a society that likes moving and acting together and it is infectious.

Swimming hats appear on a certain day in all the supermarkets, just like suntan lotion and mosquito repellent, and then duly disappear when their allocated time is up. All schoolchildren wear the same uniforms, irrespective of their school or city, the only variation being according to whether the pupil is at junior high or senior high. Once a product gains acceptance among a critical 5 or 10 per cent of the population, it spreads like wildfire. Whereas it took well over twenty years for 90 per cent of Americans to acquire a colour TV, in Japan the process was compressed into less than a decade, the curve climbing almost vertically around 1970. According to Yoshiyuki, a former editor of the teen magazine *Cawaii!*, once 5 per cent of teenage girls take a liking to something, 60 per cent will jump on the bandwagon within a month. Although young Japanese are very style-conscious, fashion is marked by a powerful conformity and a lack of individualism, with the same basic look, whatever that might be, acquiring near universality.

Sahoko Kaiji, an economist at Keio University, explains: 'Here you can leave your car outside in the street, even forget to lock it, and it will still be there in the morning. You can leave your stereo on the dashboard and a smart bag on the seat, and nothing will happen.' Women happily travel on the metro with their wallets clearly visible at the top of an open handbag; men will stick their mobile phone in the back pocket of their jeans in a crowded carriage entirely confident that no one will steal it. Kaiji continues: 'People are always nice and friendly and they keep their promises. If you order something in a store and they say it will take two weeks to deliver, they will always phone you if it arrives early, and nine times out of ten it does arrive early.' You never see any litter anywhere, not even at Tokyo's Shinjuku Station, which handles two million commuters a day. The only exception I can recall is when I was at Toyahashi Station near Nagoya, where I saw a small piece of paper on the ground. When I expressed surprise to my Japanese friend, he said, 'Don't worry, someone will pick it up in a minute.'

The Japanese are exquisitely polite. People invariably greet you with a pleasant acknowledgement and a gentle bow. When you arrive in a supermarket or department store, there will be someone at the entrance to welcome you. There is no surly behaviour or rudeness. Your space is respected, whether you are queuing or leaving a lift. You are made to feel that you matter. This idea of inclusivity extends to social attitudes more widely. Chie Nakane, a famous Japanese sociologist, remarked to me: 'Unemployment is not a problem for the unemployed, it is a problem for the whole of society.' Japan believes in taking care of the individual. At Tokyo's Narita Airport, a uniformed attendant will politely beckon you to the appropriate queue, and on the ground you will find painted footprints, just in case you are in any doubt as to where you should stand. You can never get lost in a station or airport, however large, because the Japanese are punctilious in providing directions. This sense of consideration includes an exceptional commitment to punctuality. At a metro station, the train indicator includes not only when the next train is due but when it will arrive at every single station until it reaches the terminus. And it is invariably on time, to the nearest minute, if not second. One could safely set one's watch by a Japanese train.

On the surface, Japan might look similar to any Western country. But inside it is very different. Or, as Chie Nakane told me: 'Japan is outwardly Western but inwardly Japanese.'[1]

Japan was the only Asian country to begin industrialization in the nineteenth century, the only intruder in an otherwise exclusively Western club. By any standards, it was phenomenally successful in its attempt to emulate the West, industrializing rapidly prior to 1914, and then again before 1939; it had colonized a large part of East Asia by 1945, and then overtook much of the West in GDP per head by the 1980s. Not surprisingly, Japan served as an influential economic model when the East Asian tigers began their economic take-off from the late 1950s. If we want to understand the nature of Asian modernity, Japan is the best place to start because it was first and because it remains easily the most developed example. Just because Japan is part of East Asia, however, does not mean that it is representative of the region: on the contrary, Japan is, as we shall see, in many respects unique.

WHERE DOES JAPAN COME FROM?

Japan has been shaped by two momentous engagements with the most advanced civilizations of their time: China in the fifth and sixth centuries and the West in the nineteenth and twentieth centuries. Japan's early history was influenced by its proximity to China, which was a far more advanced and sophisticated country. Prior to its engagement with China, Japan had no writing system of its own, but subsequently adopted and Japanized many Chinese characters and blended them with its own invented writing system. This was an extremely difficult process because the two languages were completely different and unrelated. In the process, the Chinese literary tradition became one of the foundation stones of Japanese culture. Taoism,

Buddhism and Confucianism were to enter Japan from China via Korea more or less simultaneously around the sixth century.[2] Taoism melded with Japanese animist traditions and mutated into Shintoism, while Confucianism became, as in China, the dominant intellectual influence, especially amongst the elite, and even today, in its Japanese form, still dominates the ideology of governance.[3] Confucianism was one of the most sophisticated philosophies of its time, a complex system of moral, social, political and quasi-religious thought, its greatest achievement perhaps being to widen access to education and culture, which previously had been confined to the aristocracy. The Chinese influence was to continue for many centuries, only finally being displaced by that of the West with the Meiji Restoration in 1868. Japan, thus, lived in the shadow of China for some fourteen centuries, for most of that time as one of its tributary states, paying tribute to the Chinese emperor and acknowledging the superiority of Chinese civilization. This left a deep imprint on the Japanese psyche and nurtured an underlying sense of inferiority together with a defensive, and incipiently militant, nationalism.[4]

Though Chinese influence was profound, it was refracted through and shaped by Japan's own experience and traditions. Japanese Confucianism differed markedly in various respects from Chinese Confucianism. While the latter explicitly included benevolence amongst its core values, the Japanese instead laid much greater emphasis on loyalty, a difference that was to become more pronounced with the passage of time. Loyalty, together with filial piety and a duty to one's seniors – based on authority, blood and age – were amongst the key defining characteristics of the hierarchical relationships that informed Japanese culture.[5] China and Japan were both ruled by an imperial family; there were, however, two crucial differences between them. First, in China a dynasty could be removed and the mandate of Heaven withdrawn: there have been thirty-six dynasties in Chinese history. In contrast, the Japanese imperial family was regarded as sacred: the same family has occupied the imperial seat throughout its 1,700-year recorded history. Second, while a Chinese dynasty enjoyed absolute power, the Japanese imperial family did not. For only a third of its history has the Japanese imperial family ruled in both name and reality. For much of Japan's history, there has been dual or even triple government, with the emperor, in practice at least, obliged to share power.[6] The most typical form was dual government, with political power effectively controlled either by shoguns (the military chiefs), or by prime ministers or chief advisers backed by military power. The price of eternity, in other words, has been a greatly diminished political role. During the Tokugawa era (1603–1867), real political power was exercised by the military in the person of the shogun. The emperor enjoyed little more than symbolic and ceremonial significance, although formally the shogun remained answerable to him. Ruth Benedict, in her classic study of Japan, *The Chrysanthemum and the Sword*, makes the interesting observation that: 'Japan's conception of her Emperor is one that is found over and over among the islands of the Pacific. He is the Sacred Chief who may or may not take part in administration. In some Pacific Islands he did and in some he delegated his authority. But always his person was sacred.'[7] To understand Japan we need to see it in its Pacific as well as East Asian context.

The Tokugawa era, the 250-year period prior to the Meiji Restoration, saw the creation of a highly centralized and formalized feudal system.[8] Beneath the imperial family and the lords (*daimyo*), society was organized into four levels in such strict hierarchy that it possessed a caste-like quality: these were the warriors (*samurai*), the farmers, the artisans and the merchants respectively. One should also, strictly speaking, include the *burakumin*, Japan's outcasts or untouchables – descended from those who worked in occupations associated with death, such as undertakers, buriers of the executed, skinners of dead animals – who were regarded and treated as invisible, just as they still are today, the exception (along with those of Chinese and Korean ancestry) to the social inclusivity described earlier.[9] One's rank was determined by inheritance and set in stone. The head of every family was required to post on his doorway his class position and the details of his hereditary status. His birthright determined the clothes he could wear, the foods he could buy and the type of house he could live in. The *daimyo* took a portion of his farmers' rice every year and out of that, apart from catering for his own needs, he paid his *samurai*. The *samurai* possessed no land: their formal function was to defend the *daimyo*, his land and property. They were the only members of society allowed to carry a sword and enjoyed wide and arbitrary power over the lower classes. During the Tokugawa era the *daimyo* were answerable to the shogun, who, in turn, was, at least formally, accountable to the emperor in his seclusion in Kyoto. Unlike Chinese Confucianism, which valued educational excellence above all (the mandarins being products of a highly competitive examination system), the Japanese, in giving pre-eminence to the *samurai*, and indeed the shogunate, extolled martial qualities.[10] During the Tokugawa period, China was, in effect, a civilian Confucian country and Japan a military Confucian country.

Not long after the Tokugawa family began their shogunate at the beginning of the seventeenth century, they closed Japan off to the outside world and suppressed Christianity, rejecting foreign influences in favour of Japanese customs and religious traditions. No European ships were allowed to use Japanese ports, with the exception of the Dutch, who were permitted to use the small island of Deshima in Nagasaki. The Japanese were forbidden from sailing in larger boats – it became an offence to build or operate a boat over a certain size – thereby bringing to an end extensive trading activity along the Japanese coast. The reasons appear to have been a desire to limit the activities of merchants together with a fear of outside influences, and especially the import of European firearms, which it was believed might serve to destabilize the delicate balance of power between the various provinces and the shogun.[11] Notwithstanding this retreat into autarchy, the Tokugawa era saw many dynamic changes. Japan became an increasingly unified community, standardizing its language, engendering similar ways of thinking and behaving between different provinces, and evolving a common set of rules and customs. As a result, the conditions for the emergence of a modern nation-state began to take shape. Castle towns were built along a newly constructed road network which served to further unify the country, with these towns at the centre of what became a vibrant trade. By the end of the Tokugawa period, Edo, as Tokyo was then known, was as big as London, with a population of more than a million, while Osaka,

Kyoto, Nagoya and Kanazawa also had sizeable populations. As we saw in the last chapter, Japan's economy in 1800 compared favourably with that of north-west Europe although it suffered from the same intensifying resource constraints as Europe and China. Japan, like China, moreover, could not look to any colonies as a source of relief, though food and fertilizer from long-distance fishing expeditions, and the import of commodity-intensive products from its more sparsely populated regions, provided Japan with rather greater amelioration than was the case with China. On the eve of the Meiji Restoration in 1868, Japan was to possess many of the preconditions for economic take-off apart, that is, from a government committed to that goal.

One final point should detain us: the changing nature and role of the *samurai*. Although their original purpose had been to defend the interests of the *daimyo*, their role steadily broadened as they assumed growing responsibility for the administration and stewardship of their *daimyo*'s estates, as well as for protocol and negotiations with other *daimyo* and the shogun. On the eve of the Meiji Restoration they had, in effect, been transformed from a military caste into a key administrative class within Japanese society. Although steeped in the Confucian tradition of efficient administration, their knowledge and predisposition were essentially military, scientific and technological rather than literary and scholastic, as was the case with their Chinese counterparts: this orientation and inclination was to have a profound impact on the nature and character of the post-1868 era.

THE MEIJI RESTORATION

In 1853 the relative peace and stability of the Tokugawa era was rudely interrupted by the appearance in Tokyo Bay of Commodore Perry, an American naval officer, at the head of a fleet of black ships, demanding on behalf of the United States – along with various European powers, notably Britain – that Japan should open itself to trade.[12] Japan's long period of isolation could no longer be sustained: like so much of the rest of the world in the nineteenth century, Japan could not ignore the West and its metamorphosis into such an expansive and predatory player. In 1858, faced with the continuing threat of invasion, Japan signed the unequal treaties which opened up the country to trade on extremely unfavourable terms, including the imposition of extra-territoriality on its main ports, which excluded Western nationals from the requirements of Japanese law. The unequal treaties represented a major restriction of Japan's sovereignty. In 1859 Japan was obliged to lift the ban on Christianity imposed over 300 years earlier.

The intervention of the Western nations, with the British, American, French and Dutch fleets actively involved, was bitterly resented and led to a huge wave of anti-foreigner (or anti-barbarian, as Westerners were known) sentiment.[13] In the face of growing tumult and unrest, the Tokugawa regime was beleaguered and paralysed. During a process lasting two years, culminating in 1868, the shogunate was overthrown by the combined forces of the Satsuma and Choshu clans, and a new government, dominated by former *samurai*, installed. The *samurai* were the prime movers in the fall of the shogunate and the chief instigators of the new Meiji regime (named after the emperor who reigned between 1868 and 1912). Part of the price the *samurai* paid for their new-found power and prominence in a government committed to the building of a modern state was the forfeiture of their old feudal-style privileges, namely their monopoly of the right to bear arms and their previous payments in kind – with the payments being commuted to cash and rapidly diminishing in value.[14]

This dramatic political change – bringing to an end two and a half centuries of shogunate rule – was driven by no political blueprint, goal or vision. In the early stages, the popular mood had been dominated by anti-Western sentiment. However, it became increasingly clear to a growing section of the ruling elite that isolation was no longer a serious option: if Japan was to be saved from the barbarians, it would have to respond to the challenge posed by the West rather than ignore it. The emergent ruling elite, which had previously shared these xenophobic and isolationist sentiments, underwent a remarkable political transformation, rapidly acquiring a very powerful sense of what needed to be done and implementing it with extraordinary speed. A modern imperial state was instituted, with a chief minister 'advising' the emperor, but with effective power concentrated in the former's hands. By 1869 universal freedom of choice was introduced in marriage and occupation. By 1871 the feudal order had effectively been disbanded. In 1873 universal conscription was decreed, rendering the old *samurai* privilege to bear arms redundant. Almost immediately the government started to establish factories run mainly by former *samurai*, thereby ushering in a new and very different economic era.[15]

If Japan had previously been shaped and influenced by its exposure to Chinese civilization, the threat from the West persuaded the new ruling elite that it had to learn from the West as quickly as possible if it was to preserve the country's independence and forestall the fate that had befallen China after the Opium Wars, with its progressive loss of sovereignty. The speed, single-mindedness and comprehensiveness with which the new government went about this task, particularly in the absence of any prior commitment or programme, is a remarkable historical phenomenon. During a breathtaking period of two decades, it drew hugely on Western experience in the construction of a range of new institutions. It sent envoys and missions to Europe and also to the United States in order to study what might be learnt, borrowed and assimilated.[16] This was done in a highly systematic way, with the object of establishing which country had most to offer in which particular area. The results were almost immediate. The education system introduced in 1873 was modelled on the French system of school districts. The navy was based on Britain's, the army on France's, and later also on Germany's. The railways followed the British example but the universities the American. Between 1871 and 1876 around 300 European experts were brought to Japan by interested institutions and government departments to assist in the process of design and construction.[17] The result was a patchwork of foreign influences that – in what became a typically Japanese manner – were somehow articulated into a distinctively Japanese whole.

From the late 1870s the government began to sell off its newly created factories. By so doing, it created a capitalist class. Many were former *samurai* who used the bonds that they had been given by the government – which had replaced the monetary stipends that they

had previously received, which in turn had replaced their former feudal payments in kind – to buy the new companies. From the outset,
then, the new capitalist owners had two distinguishing characteristics
which have remained a hallmark of post-Meiji Japan to this day: first,
they owed their existence and position to the largesse and patronage
of the government, thereby creating a powerful bond of obligation;
and second, the new owners were by background, training and tem-
perament administrators rather than entrepreneurs.

The Meiji Restoration bore some of the characteristics of a revolution. The purpose was to build a modern state and shed the country's
feudal legacy. The new ruling elite was drawn not from the *daimyo*
but primarily from the *samurai*, including those sections of farmers
that had been latterly incorporated into the *samurai* class, together
with some of the merchant class. There was clearly a shift in class
power. And yet, unlike in Europe, the new rising class, the merchants,
neither instigated the change nor drove it: in fact, for the most part,
they had not come into conflict with the old regime.[18] The leaders of
the Restoration, instead, were part of the existing ruling elite, namely
the warrior class, whose role had steadily been transformed into one
of more generalized administrative leadership.[19] To emphasize this
sense of continuity and in order to consolidate popular support and
provide legitimacy for the new regime, the *samurai* restored the
emperor to a more central role in Japanese life, an act symbolized by
his transfer from Kyoto to Edo, now renamed Tokyo. It was a coup by
the elite rather than a popular uprising from below.[20] Thus, although
it had some of the attributes of a revolution, it is best described as a
restoration, an act that sought to preserve the power of the existing
elite in the name of saving Japan from the barbarian threat. It was
designed to preserve and maintain as much as transform, its instincts
conservative as much as radical. Japan is a deeply conservative country in which the lines of continuity are far stronger than the lines of
discontinuity. Even when discontinuity was needed, as in 1868, it was
instituted, unlike in France and China – both notable exponents of
revolution – by the elite, who, mindful of the need for radical change,
nonetheless sought to preserve as much as possible of the old order. It
is not surprising, therefore, that the Restoration, certainly in contrast

to most revolutions, was relatively bloodless. Furthermore, the ruling elite was to succeed in maintaining the way of life, traditions, customs, family structure, relationships and hierarchies of Japan to a remarkable extent. The Meiji Restoration is testimony to the resilience, inner strength and adaptability of the Japanese ruling elite and its ability to change course when the situation urgently demanded it.[21]

There is one other fundamental difference between the major revolutions in Europe and the Meiji Restoration. The French Revolution was, amongst other things, a response to an internal development – the rise of the bourgeoisie – whereas the Meiji Restoration was a response to an external threat, that of an expansionist West. This was the fundamental geopolitical difference between Europe and the rest of the world: Europe was the leader and, therefore, the predator, while the rest of the world was, in response, obliged to find a way of dealing with Europe's power and expansionist intent. This difference also helps to explain why the Restoration was instigated by a section of the elite rather than a rising antagonistic group: what obliged Japan to change course was not the rise of the merchant class but the external threat from the West.

THE LINES OF CONTINUITY

Japan was the world's first example of reactive modernization: a modernity necessitated by Western power and pre-eminence. As a result, the process of Japanese modernization deliberately and self-consciously walked the tightrope between Westernization and Japanization. Nonetheless, compared with later examples of Asian modernization, Japan was in a relatively privileged position: it could make choices – in particular, how and in what ways to modernize – that were not open in the same way to later-comers. As a result, it is a fascinating case-study: a country whose existing elite made a voluntary and calculated decision to Westernize in order to preserve what it perceived to be the nation's essence.

At critical junctures, notwithstanding the long period of isolation under the Tokugawa, Japan has displayed an openness to foreign

influences which goes back to its relationship with Chinese civilization in the fifth and sixth centuries. This willingness to absorb foreign
approaches, as and when it has been deemed necessary, has been an
underlying strength of Japanese society. Instead of an outright rejection of foreign ideas, the desire to preserve the Japanese 'essence' has
instead been expressed by attempting to delineate what the Japanese
writer Kosaku Yoshino has described as 'our own realm', namely
those customs, institutions and values which are regarded as indigenous. As Yoshino argues:

> In order for 'our realm' to be marked, significant differences have been
> selected and organised not merely to differentiate between 'us' (the
> Japanese) and 'them' (the other countries from which cultural elements
> are borrowed), but, more importantly, to emphasise the existence of
> 'our own realm' and therefore to demonstrate the uninterrupted con-
> tinuation of 'our' nation as a cultural entity. In this way, the sense of
> historical continuity can also be maintained. It is this cultural realm of
> 'ours' to which the Japanese claim exclusive ownership.[22]

The distinctiveness of Japan is thus defined and maintained in two
ways: firstly in the notion of the Japanese realm as described, consisting of those elements regarded as exclusively and authentically
Japanese; and secondly in the unique amalgam of the various foreign
influences combined with those elements regarded as distinctively
Japanese. As one would expect, the notion of a Japanese realm takes
precedence over hybridity in the Japanese sense of self. Although the
former includes material objects as diverse as tatami mats, sake and
sumo wrestling, Japanese uniqueness centres around how the Japanese behave differently from non-Japanese, or where the symbolic
boundary between the Japanese and foreigners should be drawn.[23]
The duality or hybridity embraced in the juxtaposition of the indigenous and the foreign can be found in many aspects of Japanese life.
Somehow the two coexist, often with little leakage between them,
with the foreign influences absorbed and reformatted, blended and
incorporated.[24] Japanese modernity, as a consequence, is a highly
complex, incongruous and at times bizarre phenomenon. This hybridity dates back to the era of Chinese influence but has been most

marked, and traumatic, during the era of Westernization. It is so deeply entrenched that it is now taken for granted as something thoroughly natural and intrinsic to Japan. Western-style clothes may be the norm, but kimonos are a common sight on Sundays, and Japanese clothes are frequently worn at home. Japanese food contains Japanese, Chinese and Western elements, with both chopsticks and cutlery commonly used. Reaching further back into history, as noted earlier, the Japanese language consists of a combination of both Chinese-derived and Japanese characters.

After periods of heightened Westernization, the relationship between Japanese and Western elements in the country has been the subject of intense reflection and debate. Japan's post-1868 history, indeed, has seen alternating phases of Westernization and Japanization. The first twenty years after the Meiji Restoration saw a furious process of Westernization on many fronts, but by 1900 this had given way to a period of introspection and an attempt to specify the nature of the Japanese essence. In this debate three characteristics were used to define Japaneseness: the emperor system, the *samurai* spirit, and the idea of a family society (with the emperor as father). After the defeat in the Second World War and the American occupation, there was again a frantic period of economic catch-up and Westernization followed, in the 1970s and early 1980s, by a further phase of seeking to define the nature of the Japanese realm,[25] though the conception of 'Japaneseness' deployed at this juncture was distinctively different from that of the early 1900s. The *nihonjinron* (meaning 'discussions on the nature of the Japanese') in the 1970s focused on Japan as a homogeneous and group-orientated society, and the Japanese as a non-verbal, non-logical people.[26] Not surprisingly, given the context of the times, these latter characteristics were essentially designed to define Japaneseness in contradistinction to the American influence that had loomed so large in Japanese life during the post-war decades.

In reality, of course, the nature of Japaneseness cannot be expressed in such reductionist terms. The *nihonjinron* were politically inspired cultural responses to Western influence. They tell us much about the Japanese psyche, about the desire to be different and distinct, but they only partially reveal what is continuingly and persistently different about Japan. In *The Chrysanthemum and the Sword*, Ruth Benedict argues:

> In studies of Western nations one who is untrained in studies of comparative cultures overlooks whole areas of behaviour. He takes so much for granted that he does not explore the range of trivial habits in daily living and all those accepted verdicts on homely matters, which, thrown large on the national screen, have more to do with that nation's future than treaties signed by diplomats.[27]

The distinctiveness of Japan – as with other countries, indeed – lies precisely in the stuff of the everyday and the easily overlooked, from the nature of relationships to the values that inform people's behaviour.

Japanese relationships operate according to a strict hierarchy based on class, gender and age. Each relationship is finely graded accordingly, depending on the degree of previous contact and familiarity. The importance of hierarchy is initially learnt in the family, with the father cast as the undisputed head of the household and each member of the family occupying a pre-ordained position. The family is regarded as a microcosm of society, with the firm, like the nation, conceived in its image. The gradations of relationships are reflected in the use of language, with different words for 'you', for example, depending on the status of the other person. The language is also gendered, with men and women required to use different words and modes of address. Japanese is a 'respect language' and its nuances are accompanied by a system of bowing, the degree of bow depending on the status of the other person.[28] Firms often advise their employees on the required extent of the bow based on the importance of the other person.[29]

Japanese conventions require not only a respect for hierarchy but also an onerous and complex system of obligations. There are two kinds of obligation, or *on*: the *gimu*, which is limitless and lifelong, and which one owes to one's parents, for example; and the *giri*, which is finite. These obligations lie at the heart of Japanese society: virtuousness is defined in terms of meeting one's obligations rather than money, which has become the typical measure of virtue in Western society.[30] If one fails to meet one's *giri*, one feels a sense of shame. Broadly speaking,

68

cultures can be divided into those that are based on guilt, like the Christian-derived West, and those that are based on shame. The sense of guilt in the former stems from the idea of original sin and the belief that left to their own devices – and inevitable base instincts – people are inherently sinful. Shame, on the other hand, is the product of monitoring one's actions by viewing one's self from the standpoint of others. Japanese society is rooted in shame: it is how one is regarded by others, rather than one's own individual conscience, which is critical. A sense of guilt can be salved by an act of apology; shame, in contrast, is not nearly as easily assuaged. The consequence is very different patterns of behaviour. While in the West, for example, suicide is frowned upon as a selfish act, in Japan it is seen as the ultimate way of settling one's *giri* and, therefore, as a noble act. As a result, it is far more common:[31] there are 35.6 male suicides per 100,000 population in Japan, in contrast to 17.9 for the US, 10.8 for the UK and 19.7 for Germany.[32]

The latticework of personal relationships, based on hierarchy and obligations, informs the way all Japanese institutions work, from the extended family and the firm to school and government. Take the firm: the relationship between the large corporations and the small- and medium-sized companies that depend upon them is of a distinctly hierarchical character. Lifetime employment, which still predominates in the large corporations, embodies a conception of obligation on the part of both the company and the employee that is quite different from the narrowly contractual – and often short-term – nature of employment in the Anglo-American tradition. The firm is seen as akin to a family, with the company having multifarious obligations to the employee while the employee – mainly male (women still play a relatively peripheral role in the labour force compared with the West) – in return is expected to give most of his life, in terms of both career and the hours of the day, to the company. The seniority system, widely practised in Japanese companies, where one steadily climbs the company ladder as one gets older and enjoys a rising income and growing authority, rather than being dispensed with in the manner of the Western firm, reflects the age-hierarchy of Japanese society.[33]

There are many other ways in which the distinctively Japanese culture of relationships shapes the attitude towards and conduct of institutions. The Japanese, for example, are profoundly averse to the use of the law, primarily because of a desire to avoid the kind of confrontation that characterizes the process of litigation. As a consequence, Japan does not have enough lawyers to support even a fraction of the litigation that takes place in Europe, let alone the United States. Virtually all cases of civil conflict are settled by conciliation, either out of court or before any legal judgment is made.[34]

This picture of Japanese distinctiveness should not come as any great surprise. Even a relatively casual acquaintance with Japanese society conveys this impression.[35] As the accompanying tables and charts illustrate, Japanese attitudes and values remain strikingly different from those of Western societies, notwithstanding the fact that they share roughly the same level of development.[36] The first reason for this hardly needs restating: cultural differences have an extraordinary endurance, with Japan's rooted in a very different kind of civilization.[37] The second is historical: because the Meiji Restoration was a relatively recent event, Japan is still strongly marked by the

	Men should work outside and women should maintain the household (%)	Gender roles should be determined freely (%)
Japan (Tokyo)	16.2	46.4
USA (N.Y. & L.A.)	10.5	81.2
England (London)	10.5	81.8
France (Paris)	3.2	91.3
Germany (Berlin)	2.6	92.1
Sweden (Stockholm)	3.2	80.4

Source: Dentsu Institute for Human Studies

Table 1. Japanese attitudes towards gender.

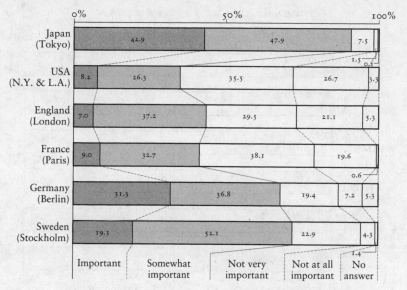

Source: Dentsu Institute for Human Studies

Figure 7. The Japanese commitment to work.

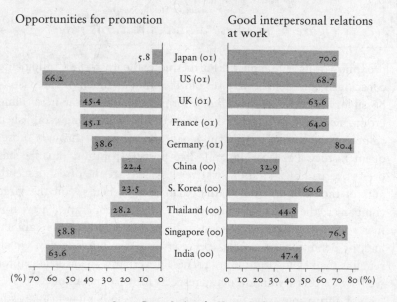

Source: Dentsu Institute for Human Studies

Figure 8. Japanese expectations of the workplace.

71

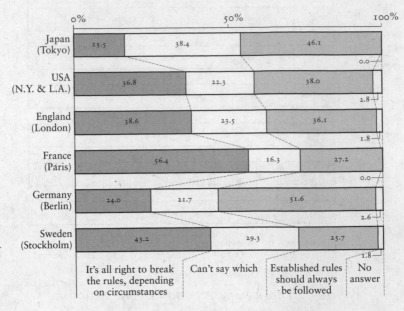

Source: Dentsu Institute for Human Studies

Figure 9. Japanese attitudes towards rules.

proximity of its feudal past.[38] Furthermore, the post-1868 ruling elite consciously and deliberately set out to retain as much of the past as possible. The fact that the *samurai* formed the core of the new ruling group, moreover, meant that they carried some of the long-established values of their class into Meiji Japan and onwards through subsequent history. Post-war Japan – like post-Restoration Japan – has been governed by an administrative class who are the direct descendants of the *samurai*: they, rather than entrepreneurs, run the large companies; they have dominated the Liberal Democratic Party; former administrators have tended to be preponderant in the cabinet; and, by definition, of course, they constitute the bureaucracy, which remains the key institution in Japanese governance, as it has been for well over a century and in many respects for very much longer.[39]

Not surprisingly, the nature of governance in similar fashion still strongly bears the imprint of the past. Throughout most of Japan's recorded history, power has been divided between two or more centres, and that remains true today. The emperor is now of ceremonial and symbolic significance. The Diet – the Japanese parliament – enjoys little real authority. The prime minister is far weaker, relatively speaking, than any other prime minister of a major developed nation and normally enjoys only a relatively brief tenure in office before being replaced; between 2007 and 2011 Japan had no less than six prime ministers. Cabinet meetings are largely ceremonial, lasting less than a quarter of an hour. Although formally Japan has a multi-party system, the Liberal Democrats, until their defeat by the Democratic Party in 2009, were in office almost continuously from the mid 1950s; and during this period its factions were in practice of much greater importance than the various other parties. Power is therefore dispersed across a range of different institutions, although the bureaucracy, in traditional Confucian style, is by far the single most important.[40] Since the end of the American occupation, Japan has been regarded by the West as a democracy in its own image, but in reality it works so differently from any Western democracy that it cannot be meaningfully described as such. Indeed, unlike Western democracies, it is extremely doubtful whether in practice Japan gives primacy to the idea of popular sovereignty, a subject that we will return to in Chapter 7:[41] on the contrary, as in China, another Confucian society, state sovereignty rather than popular sovereignty is predominant. Japan may have changed hugely since 1868, but the influence of the past is remarkably persistent.

THE TURN TO THE WEST

Following the Meiji Restoration, Japan's mission was to close the gap with the West, to behave like the West, to achieve the respect of the West and ultimately to become, at least in terms of the level of development, like the West. Benchmarking and catch-up were the new lodestars.[42] Before 1939, this primarily meant Europe, but after 1945, Europe was replaced in the Japanese mind by an overwhelming preoccupation with the United States. The key objective was economic growth, but Japan's colonial expansion, which started within six years of the Meiji Restoration, also owed much to a desire to emulate

Europe: to be a modern power, Japan believed that it needed to have its own complement of colonies. These territorial ambitions eventually brought Japan to its knees in the Second World War, culminating in its defeat and surrender. It was a humiliating moment: the very purpose of the Meiji Restoration – to prevent the domination of the country by the West – had been undermined. The post-1868 trajectory had resulted in the country's occupation, its desire to emulate the West in disaster.

Nevertheless, the war was to prove the prelude to the most spectacular period of economic growth in Japan's history. In 1952, Japan's GDP was smaller than colonial Malaya's. Within a generation the country had moved from a primarily agrarian to a fully-fledged industrial nation, achieving an annual per capita growth rate of 8.4 per cent between 1950 and 1970, far greater than achieved elsewhere and historically unprecedented up to that time. By the 1980s, Japan had overtaken both the United States and Europe in terms of GDP per head and had emerged as an industrial and financial powerhouse.[43] This represented an extraordinary transformation, but it was not to be sustained. At the end of the 1980s, Japan's bubble economy burst and for the following fifteen years it barely grew at all. Meanwhile, the United States found a new lease of economic life, displaying considerable dynamism across a range of new industries and technologies, most notably in computing and the internet. Japan's response to this sharp downturn in its fortunes was highly instructive – both in terms of what it said about Japan and about the inherent difficulties entailed in the process of catch-up for all non-Western societies.

The apogee of Japan's post-1868 achievement – the moment that it finally drew level with and overtook the West during the 1980s[44] – carried within it the seeds of crisis. Ever since 1868, Japan's priority had been to catch up with the West: after 1945 this ambition had become overwhelmingly and narrowly economic. But what would happen when that aim had finally been achieved, when the benchmarking was more or less complete, when Japan had matched the most advanced countries of the West in key respects, and in others had even opened up a considerable lead? When the Meiji purpose had been accomplished, what was next? Japan had no answer: the country was plunged into an existential crisis. It has been customary to explain Japan's post-bubble crisis in purely economic terms, but there is also a deeper cultural and psychological explanation: the country and its institutions, including its companies, quite simply lost their sense of direction.[45]

Nor was the country endowed by its history with the ability or facility to change direction. Ever since 1868, through every historical twist and turn, it had displayed an extraordinary ability to retain its focus and maintain a tenacious commitment to its long-term objective. Japan might be described as single-path dependent, its institutions able to display a remarkable capacity to keep to their self-assigned trajectory. This has generated a powerful degree of internal cohesion and enabled the country to be very effective at achieving long-term goals. By the same token, however, it has also made changing paths, of which Japan has little experience, very difficult. The only major examples were its response to its defeat in 1945 and the subsequent American occupation, and the 1868 Meiji Restoration, both of which involved a huge and compelling external threat.[46] The difficulty which Japan finds in changing direction has been graphically illustrated over the course of the last two decades.

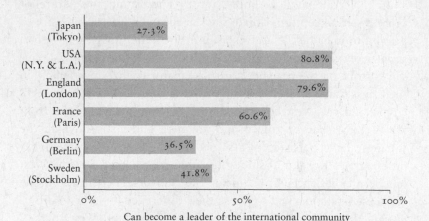

Can become a leader of the international community

Source: Dentsu Institute for Human Studies

Figure 10. Japanese pessimism about their international role and influence.

The post-bubble crisis, which was followed by a long period of very low economic growth, led to much heart-searching and a deep sense of gloom. Some even went so far as to suggest that Japan had suffered two defeats: one in 1945 and another in the 1990s.[47] The pessimism that engulfed the country revealed the underlying fragility of the contemporary Japanese psyche. Having finally achieved their goal, they were filled with doubt as to what to do next. As the United States regained its dynamism and Japan was becalmed, there was a widespread sense that its achievement was little more than a chimera, that it was always destined to live in the shadow of the West.[48] Japan's psychological fragility in the face of the post-bubble crisis is a stark reminder of how difficult the process of catch-up – in all its many aspects – is for non-Western countries. Here was a country whose historical achievement was remarkable by any standards; which had equalled or pulled ahead of the West by most measures and comfortably outstripped the great majority of European countries that it had originally sought to emulate; which had built world-class institutions, most obviously its major corporations, and become the second wealthiest country in the world – and yet, in its moment of glory, was consumed by self-doubt.

In this context, it is important to understand the nature of Japan's self-perception. Unlike the European or American desire to be, and to imagine themselves as, universal, the Japanese have had a particularistic view of their country's role, long defining themselves to be on the periphery of those major civilizations which, in their eyes, have established the universal norm. As we have seen, China and the West constituted the two significant others from which Japan has borrowed and adapted, and against which the Japanese have persistently affirmed their identity. 'For the Japanese,' argues Kosaku Yoshino, 'learning from China and the West has been experienced as acquiring the "universal" civilization. The Japanese have thus had to stress their difference in order to differentiate themselves from the universal Chinese and Westerners.'[49] This characteristic not only distinguishes Japan from the West, which has been *the* universalizing civilization of the last two centuries, but also from the Chinese, who have seen their own civilization, as we shall explore later, in universalistic terms for the best part of two millennia.

In order to understand Japan's present dilemma, we need to take into account the broader coordinates of its post-1868 reorientation: for while Japan sought to embrace the West, it turned against Asia and came to regard its neighbours as its inferiors. The turn to the West saw the rise of many new popular writers, the most famous of whom was Fukuzawa Yukichi, who argued, in an essay entitled 'On Leaving Asia', published in 1885:

> We do not have time to wait for the enlightenment of our neighbours so that we can work together towards the development of Asia. It is better for us to leave the ranks of Asian nations and cast our lot with civilized nations of the West. As for the way of dealing with China and Korea, no special treatment is necessary just because they happen to be our neighbours. We simply follow the manner of the Westerners in knowing how to treat them. Any person who cherishes a bad friend cannot escape his notoriety. We simply erase from our mind our bad friends in Asia.[50]

The Japanese did not wait long to put this new attitude into practice. In 1894–5 they defeated China, gaining control of Taiwan and effectively also Korea. In 1910 they annexed Korea. In 1931 they annexed north-east China, from 1936 occupied central parts of China, and between 1941 and 1945 took much of South-East Asia. Between 1868 and 1945, a period of seventy-seven years, Japan engaged in ten major wars, lasting thirty years in total, the great majority at the expense of its Asian neighbours.[51] In contrast, Japan had not engaged in a single foreign war throughout the entire 250-year Tokugawa era.[52] Meiji Japan was thus intent not only on economic modernization and the emulation of the West, but also on territorial expansion, as the national slogan 'rich country, strong army' (*fukoku kyôhei*), which was adopted at the beginning of the Meiji period, implied.[53] Although Japan presented its proposal for the Greater East Asian Co-Prosperity Sphere during the 1930s as a way of promoting Asian interests at the expense of the West, in reality it was an attempt to subjugate Asia in the interests of an imperial Japan.[54]

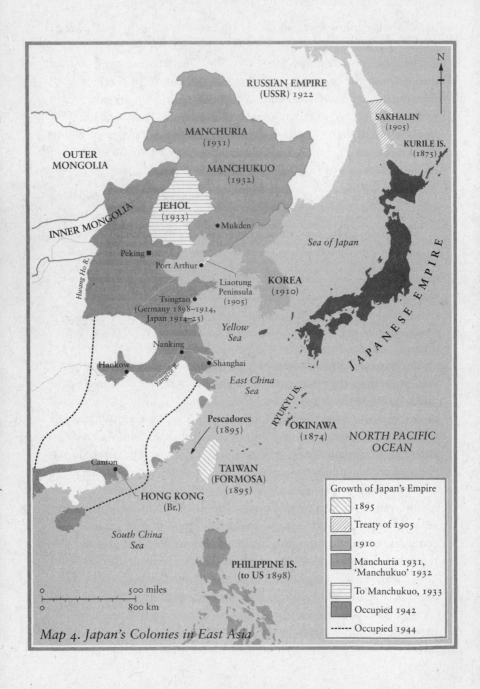

Map 4. Japan's Colonies in East Asia

Japan, unsurprisingly, saw the world in essentially similar terms to the deeply hierarchical nature of its own society.[55] While looking up to the West, it looked down on Asia as backward and inferior, seeking to subjugate its own continent for the purpose of its enrichment and aggrandizement. Where once it had seen Chinese civilization as its superior, it now regarded the Chinese as an inferior race.[56] The idea of a racial hierarchy has long been intrinsic to the Japanese view of the world. Even today it continues to persist, as its relations with its East Asian neighbours demonstrate. Whites are still held in the highest esteem while fellow Asians are regarded as of lesser stock.[57] Racialized ways of thinking are endemic to mainstream Japanese culture,[58] in particular the insistence on the 'homogeneity of the Japanese people' (even though there are significant ethnic minorities), the idea of a 'Japanese race' (even though the Japanese were the product of diverse migratory movements), and the widely held belief that the

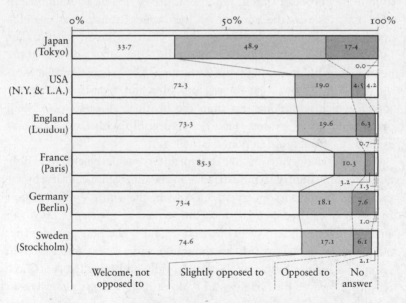

Source: Dentsu Institute for Human Studies

Figure 11. Japanese responses to the question, 'How do you feel about you or a member of your family marrying a foreigner?'

Japanese 'blood type' is associated with specific patterns of cultural behaviour.[59] Racial, ethnic and national categories overlap in Japanese conceptions of both themselves and, by implication, others also.[60] This is illustrated by former prime minister Nakasone's infamous remark in 1986 that the mental level in the United States was lower than in Japan because of the presence of racial minorities – specifically, 'blacks, Puerto Ricans, and Mexicans'.[61] Even today there is no law against racial discrimination.[62]

Over the course of the last half-century, however, East Asia has been transformed from a state of backwardness into the most dynamic region in the world: Japan is no longer alone.[63] And yet its attitudes towards East Asia remain, in large part, fixed in a Meiji time-warp. Japan would still prefer to see itself as Western rather than Asian: I vividly recall a conference on Europe and Japan in Tokyo in 1999 at which it was seriously suggested that Japan might consider applying to join the European Union. Japan's failure to rethink its relationship with East Asia in the context of the latter's transformation adds another important dimension to the crisis that Japan faces today. Indeed, it is this – more than any other question – that now lies at the heart of Japan's deepening sense of trauma. The Japanese find it inordinately difficult to accept the rise of China and what that means for Japan, which is nothing less than the death knell of its post-Meiji orientation. I will explore Japan's relationship with East Asia, and especially China, more fully in Chapter 9.

Japanese modernity is an extraordinary achievement: the only non-Western country to industrialize in the nineteenth century, by far the most advanced country in East Asia, the world's third largest economy (measured by GDP according to market exchange rates), an enviably high standard of living, and arguably the best public transport system in the world; at the same time it has succeeded in remaining highly distinctive, both culturally and socially.[64] For three reasons, however, the novelty and scale of its post-1945 achievement have never received the recognition either in the West or in Asia that they deserve. First, ever since 1945 Japan has been at pains to stress its similarity with the West rather than its difference from it. Following its defeat, Japan entered the American sphere of influence, lost any independent foreign-policy voice, and became to all intents and purposes an American protectorate: under such circumstances, its approach was *sotto voce*, having no reason or desire to emphasize its distinctiveness. Second, its deeply troubled relationship with East Asia has meant that Japan has never enjoyed anything like the political and cultural influence in the region its economic strength would suggest. In varying degrees, Japan remains problematic and tainted. Third, as Japan has always seen itself in particularistic rather than universal terms, it has not regarded itself as a model for others.

The fact remains that Japan was the first East Asian country to modernize, and much of the region has now followed in its wake. Without Japan, it is doubtful whether the Asian tigers would have begun to roar; and without the Asian tigers, China's modernization would certainly have been even further delayed. Japan might have been, in a host of ways, an exception, but it has been the exception that has eventually proved the rule: it is now surrounded by countries that are, in various different ways, following its example, at times to its acute discomfort. If Britain was Europe's pioneer in modernity, so Japan has been Asia's.

4

China's Ignominy

On the orders of King George III, the first British trade delegation to China left London in September 1792, bearing numerous gifts including telescopes, clocks, barometers, a spring-suspension coach and airguns. They sailed in a man-of-war equipped with sixty-six guns, accompanied by two support vessels, on a mission whose purpose was to impress and seduce the Chinese Emperor Qianlong with Britain's growing industrial and technological prowess. The 700-strong party, comprising diplomats, businessmen, soldiers, scientists, painters, gardeners and others, was led by Lord George Macartney, an experienced diplomat with an eye for the main chance, whether personal or national. The British government, represented by the East India Company, which organized the mission (and which acted as Britain's de facto corporate overseas persona, having, for example, ruled India until 1858), was anxious to open up the Chinese market to trade, its previous efforts having been rebuffed. The preparation was meticulous and protracted. The British mission arrived at Macao, the Portuguese enclave on the south coast of China, and then took four months to crawl northwards, as negotiations with the Emperor's representatives dragged on, eventually reaching Beijing for the long-awaited and much-postponed audience with the Emperor.

When the meeting was finally held in September 1793, Macartney asked the Emperor for British diplomatic representation in Beijing, the ending of the system whereby foreigners were only allowed to use Canton (Guangzhou) as their point of entry and for trade, the opening up of new ports for trade, and the provision of fair and equitable tariffs. The Emperor was unmoved, his mind made up long before the mission ever arrived. Instead of informing Macartney, he sent an edict to George III, explaining that China would not increase its foreign trade because it required nothing from other countries. As Qianlong wrote:

> We have never valued ingenious articles, nor do we have the slightest need of your country's manufactures. Therefore, O King, as regards your request to send someone to remain at the capital, while it is not in harmony with the regulations of the Celestial Empire we also feel very much that it is of no advantage to your country.

To the British, possessed of the hubris of a rising power and flush with the early fruits of the Industrial Revolution – by then well under way, though unbeknown to the 81-year-old Emperor, it would appear – the Chinese reaction was incomprehensible. Duly spurned, Macartney was obliged to leave China empty-handed by the only route available to him: over land to Canton. During the course of his journey he kept a copious journal. One entry reads, 'The Empire of China is an old, crazy, first rate man-of-war, which a fortunate succession of able and vigilant officers has contrived to keep afloat for these one hundred and fifty years past, and to overawe their neighbours merely by bulk and appearance.' He was thoroughly bleak about the prospects for the Celestial Empire, which he saw as destined to be 'dashed to pieces on the shore'. In Macartney's opinion, it was futile for China to resist the British demands because it was 'in vain to attempt arresting the progress of human knowledge'. The sense of one era closing and another beginning was apparent not only in Macartney's over-weaning self-confidence but also in the Emperor's blinkered failure to recognize the potential represented by Britain's new manufactures. Meanwhile the clash of civilizations was graphically illustrated by the lengthy and tortuous argument over diplomatic protocol for the audience with the Emperor. From a full six weeks before, the Chinese had pressured Macartney with growing intensity that he should perform the kowtow, the required gesture of deference to the Emperor: a set of three genuflections, each containing three full prostrations with the head touching the ground. Macartney offered to doff his hat, go down on one knee and even kiss the Emperor's hand, but he declined to kowtow unless a Chinese official of similar position kneeled before a portrait of George III. For the Chinese, this was out of the question: the Emperor was the ruler of 'all under Heaven' and therefore could not possibly be regarded as of equal status to a mere king. Even the status of the goods that the British had brought was the subject of dispute: as required by more than a millennium and a half of Chinese convention, foreigners could only visit China as inferior vassals bearing tribute. In the eyes of the Chinese, Macartney was simply a subordinate 'conveyor of tribute': Macartney, for his part, insisted that they were presents from the ambassador of a diplomatic equal. No compromise was reached. Two eras and two civilizations collided without a hint of mutual understanding.

The mission ended in dismal failure. Macartney's prediction of the fate that awaited China was to be borne out more fully than the Chinese could ever have imagined, though the British – filled with the testosterone of growing power and well versed in aggressive intent – clearly had some inkling. Already at the time of Macartney's embassy to Beijing, the East India Company had started to export opium from India to China and this was rapidly to prove a highly profitable trade. In 1829 the Chinese government banned the import of opium, much to the fury of the British. As relations deteriorated, the British launched the First Opium War (1839–42) and bombarded south China into submission. In the Treaty of Nanjing, the Chinese were forced to hand over Hong Kong, open the first five treaty ports and pay reparations. China's 'century of humiliation had begun'.[1]

If Japan was the great exception, the only non-Western country to begin its industrialization in the nineteenth century, China was an example of the opposite: a country which failed to industrialize, even though it enjoyed a similar level of development to Japan in 1800. As a result, China found itself hugely outdistanced by Europe and the United States over the course of the nineteenth century, and also by Japan towards the end of it. After 1800, and especially from the middle of the century, China suffered from growing economic weakness, near implosion, debilitating division, defeat, humiliation and occupation at the hands of foreign powers, and a progressive loss of sovereignty. Disastrous though its fortunes were in the period between 1850 and 1950, however, their consequences should not be overstated. China's progress after 1949, and especially since 1978, suggests that the roots of its contemporary dynamism lie in its own history: even if it did not appear so at the time, all was far from lost in the century of humiliation.[2] Nonetheless, this period was to leave deep psychological scars. As we shall see, China's modernization, like Japan's, was to take a very different path from that of the West.[3]

A PLACE IN THE SUN

China had already begun to acquire its modern shape in the centuries leading up to the birth of Christ.[4] The victory of the so-called First Emperor (Qin Shihuangdi, the Western name for China being derived from his family name, Qin) marked the end of the Warring States period (403–221 BC) – an endless series of conflicts between the numerous Chinese states of the time which resembled a much later phase of European history – and the beginning of the Qin dynasty (221–206 BC). By 206 BC the boundaries of the Qin Empire contained much of what we now regard as the heartland of modern China, stretching towards Vietnam in the south and as far as the Great Wall in the north, including the densely populated region between the Yangzi and the Yellow rivers (see Map 5). Following the fall of the Qin dynasty, the country continued to expand rapidly during the Han dynasty (206 BC–AD 220) (see Map 6), achieving its furthest extent in the period 141–87 BC, when the Chinese armies penetrated into southern Manchuria and the Korean Peninsula in the north-east, and south and south-west as far as northern Vietnam.[5] Over the next millennium or so, China continued to expand to the north, north-east, north-west, south and south-east.[6] The huge size that China ultimately acquired was related to the natural borders of its continental land mass, bounded by the steppe in the north, the coastline to the south and east, and the mountainous regions to its south-east.[7]

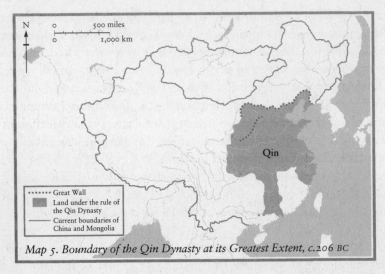

Map 5. *Boundary of the Qin Dynasty at its Greatest Extent, c.206 BC*

Source: Wikimedia Commons

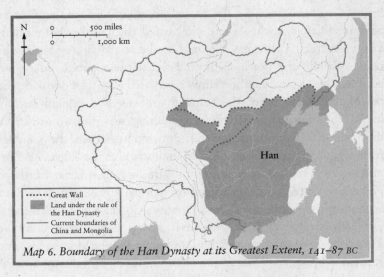

Map 6. *Boundary of the Han Dynasty at its Greatest Extent, 141–87 BC*

Source: Wikimedia Commons

Extensive internal migration, improving communications and many centuries of unity or near unity helped to foster a relatively homogeneous culture across what was, for its time, a massive population. The Qin dynasty, short though its life may have been, constructed over 4,000 miles of imperial highways, as many as the Roman Empire.[8] A centralized state, and a sophisticated statecraft, took root based on the teachings of Confucius (551–479 BC), who was to exercise a huge influence over the Chinese political and moral universe for more than two millennia. Weights, measures and currency were standardized. The distinctive customs that we associate with China – including the Mandate of Heaven, a family structure resting on filial piety, a language that used common signs and symbols, and a religion based on ancestral worship – were already well established by the time of the Qin dynasty. On the basis of these foundations, during the first millennium AD, China was to acquire – given the fact that in practice it embraced many different peoples – an unusually strong sense of cultural identity.[9] One of the most striking features of Chinese history has been that, although it has been invaded from the north many times – notably by the Mongols in the thirteenth century and the Manchu in the seventeenth – all invaders, bar the Mongols (whose rule lasted less than a century) sought to acquire, once secure in power, the customs and values of the Chinese and to rule according to their principles and their institutions: a testament to the prestige enjoyed by the Chinese and the respect accorded to their civilization by their northern adversaries.[10] The persistence and steady spread of the Chinese language is a further indication of the strength of the culture: the constant invasions from the north, by obliging the population to stay mobile, kept the language from becoming atomized into different dialects, at the same time making the Chinese themselves more aware of, and therefore also protective of, both their language and culture.[11] The early emergence of a Chinese identity is, perhaps more than anything else, the key to China as we know it today, for without that, China could not have remained a relatively unified country for over two millennia and would have been shorn of its most striking characteristic: its size.

Relatively advanced forms of agriculture have historically enabled societies to sustain large populations and provided propitious conditions for the development of organized states; China was a classic example of this phenomenon. It is now believed that millet and rice first appeared in northern and southern China respectively 12,000 years ago, earlier even than in Mesopotamia, where sedentary agriculture began about 8,000 years ago. Although North China has long sustained 'dry' agriculture by way of cereals, barley and various kinds of millet, it was the wet cultivation of rice, which developed slowly from the beginning of the first millennium and which was in full swing by its end, that was later to give a major boost to Chinese agriculture, resulting in a shift in the economic centre of gravity from the central plain to the lower Yangzi basin. New methods of wet rice cultivation were introduced, including the planting of seedlings, early ripening varieties of rice, the systematic selection of species, new tools such as a chain with paddles which made it possible to lift water from one level to another, and sophisticated forms of irrigation. These made Chinese wet rice farming one of the most advanced agricultural techniques in the world, generating extremely high yields.[12] During the Song dynasty (AD 960–1279), these advanced techniques were generalized across large tracts of the country, pushing south as the frontier was steadily extended.[13] Sustained by agrarian prosperity, the population expanded rapidly, almost doubling between 1000 and 1300.[14] Between AD 500 and 900 bricked roads were built across the middle of the Chinese empire such that the capital (known then as Chang'an, now as Xian) was only eight to fourteen days' travel from any reasonably sized city. Even more significant was the spread of water transport in the form of rivers, canals and coastal shipping. These various waterway systems became part of an integral network that was to form the basis of a nationwide market that steadily took shape by 1200. As Marco Polo, a resident of Venice, Europe's greatest seaport, observed of the Yangzi in the late thirteenth century:

> I assure you that this river runs for such a distance and through so many regions and there are so many cities on its banks that truth to tell, in the amount of shipping it carries and the total volume and value of its traffic, it exceeds all the rivers of the Christians put together and their seas into the bargain.[15]

The Chinese economy became increasingly commercialized, with paper money firmly established in both north and south China by the twelfth century. A large inter-regional trade developed in both luxuries and staples like rice. During the Song dynasty, coastal trade flourished and extended to Japan and South-East Asia. Urbanization proceeded apace, such that by the late thirteenth century Hangzhou, China's largest city, had a population of almost 7 million, making China by far the most urbanized society in the world, its cities accounting for around 10 per cent of the population.[16] The cities were not, however, to play the same role as centres of political and personal freedom as those in Europe: autonomous urban development was constrained by China's centralized imperial structure, a pattern that only began to change in the twentieth century. Encouraged by the government, there was a flowering of learning and a wave of remarkable inventions during the Song dynasty, especially in the century and a half of the Northern Song (960–1126).[17] What is sometimes described as China's Renaissance witnessed the development of a classical examination system, the birth of neo-Confucianism, the invention of gunpowder, mortars and woodblock printing, the spread of books, and major advances in mathematics, natural sciences, astronomy and geography.[18] A large spinning machine was invented that was to fall only slightly short of what might – at least theoretically – have ushered in an industrial revolution along the lines that Britain was to experience centuries later.[19] In contrast, Europe's Renaissance only began two centuries after the end of the Northern Song. The diffusion of books enabled by woodblock printing, the publication of large encyclopaedias, the growing number of candidates who entered the examination system for the civil service, the great progress made in mathematics (particularly the development of algebra) and the emergence of a gentry-scholar class marked China out as the most literate and numerate society in the world; only the Islamic world could compare, with Europe lagging well behind.[20] During the medieval period Europe was to borrow extensively from China's innovations, including paper, the compass, the wheelbarrow, the sternpost rudder, the spinning wheel and woodblock printing.[21] China was by far the most advanced civilization in East Asia, exercising a huge influence on its neighbours, many of which had long been tributary states of China, paying tribute to the emperor, acknowledging the superiority of Chinese culture while borrowing from it extensively.

After 1300 this efflorescence began to subside and China's medieval economic revolution gave way to a period of stagnation that only came to an end in 1500. The Mongol invasion marked the closure of the Song period, in many respects China's finest age, and led to the establishment of the Yuan dynasty (1279–1368) and the incorporation of China into the Mongol Empire. This was to prove a very traumatic period, with the Chinese finding themselves under alien rule and reduced to lowly status. There were several reasons for the economic slowdown. The dynamic by which China had expanded from its heartlands southwards had involved the addition of rich new farmlands, but this area began to fill up with migrants from the north; as a consequence there was growing pressure on resources, most notably food.[22] The spectacular advances in science, meanwhile, started to dry up. The Song dynasty had placed considerable emphasis on the importance of trade and contact with foreigners, notably Japan and South-East Asia, but also beyond to Central Asia, the Indian subcontinent and even the east coast of Africa. This process slowly went into reverse during the Ming dynasty (1368–1644).[23] In 1371 the Ming dynasty forbade coastal people from sailing overseas because of the threat posed to Chinese shipping by large-scale Japanese piracy. An edict in 1390 declared: 'At present the ignorant people of the Liang-Kuang, Chekiang and Fukien are frequently in communication with the outer barbarians, with whom they carry on a smuggling trade. This is therefore strictly prohibited.'[24] There followed over the next three centuries a succession of restrictions banning first private and then government trade. By 1757 Canton was the only port from which legal trade could be conducted, as Lord Macartney was to complain.

The successful reconstruction in 1411 of the Grand Canal, which had originally been built between the fifth century BC and the seventh century AD, linking Beijing and Tianjin with Hangzhou in the south and the rich rice fields of the Yangzi, was a crucial moment, signalling a greatly reduced need for coastal shipping and, therefore, also for a

A model of one of Zheng He's ships, shown in comparison to one of Christopher Columbus's

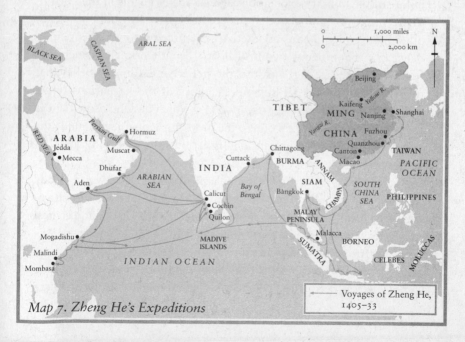

Map 7. Zheng He's Expeditions

navy. For almost four and a half centuries, from the consolidation of the Song Empire until the remarkable seafaring expeditions of the early Ming (1405–33), China was the greatest maritime nation in the world – using big compartmented ships (with up to four decks, four or five masts and a dozen sails), steered by a sternpost rudder, guided by charts and compass, and able to carry 500 men.[25] The ships used by Zheng He for his great voyages to South-East Asia, the Indian Ocean and the east coast of Africa in the early fifteenth century were by far the most advanced in the world. From the moment the voyages were completed, however, China's maritime prowess fell into steep decline. In 1436 the construction of seagoing ships was banned and the number of smaller vessels built was reduced. The reason for this growing isolation and introspection is not entirely clear. It would appear that the failure to continue with Zheng He's great voyages was the result of several factors: a political shift in the attitude of the Ming dynasty; the moving of the imperial capital from Nanjing to Beijing in 1421, which led to heightened sensitivities about the northern border and reduced interest in oceanic and coastal priorities; and growing concern about both the cost of the maritime voyages and the relative failure of the military expeditions against the Mongols in the north.[26] There was also an anxiety that the coastal centres, with their links to other lands, might act as an alternative source of power, the maintenance of social order and control always being a prime consideration for Chinese rulers. Perhaps also the underlying Chinese belief that their civilization was far superior to those of the barbarians (especially the nomadic cultures to its north),[27] which had intensified under the Ming in an ethnic reaction to the previous Mongol rule, made the turn towards a more autarchic and isolationist view seem natural.

Between 1500 and 1800, however, stagnation gave way to vigorous economic growth and reasonable prosperity. There was a steady increase in the food supply, due to an increase in land under cultivation – the result of migration and settlement in the western and central provinces, greater productivity (including the use of new crops like corn and peanuts) and better irrigation.[28] These developments sustained a fivefold increase in China's population between 1400 and 1800, whereas between 1300 and 1400 it had fallen sharply.[29] China's performance during this period has tended to be overshadowed by the dynamism of the earlier medieval economic revolution; unlike during the Song dynasty, this later growth was achieved with relatively little new invention. In the eighteenth century China remained the world's largest economy, followed by India, with Europe as a secondary player. Adam Smith, who saw China as an exemplar of market-based development, observed in 1776 that 'China is a much richer country than any part of Europe.'[30] It was not until 1850, indeed, that London was to displace Beijing as the world's largest city.[31]

As we saw in Chapter 2, Britain was able to escape the growing resource constraints at the end of the eighteenth century by deploying the resources of its colonies, together with an abundant supply of accessible domestic coal. But what exactly happened to China, which enjoyed neither? There was almost certainly enough capital available, especially given the relatively small amounts involved in the take-off of the cotton industry in Britain. Although Chinese merchants did not enjoy the same kind of independent and privileged status that they did in Britain, always being subordinate to the bureaucracy and the land-owning gentry, they were widely respected and enjoyed growing wealth and considerable power.[32] There may have been rather less protection for investment in comparison with Europe, but nonetheless there were plenty of very large Chinese enterprises. China's markets were no less sophisticated than those of Europe and were much longer established. Mark Elvin argues that the reason for China's failure was what he describes as a 'high-level equilibrium trap'.[33] China's shortage of resources in its densely populated heartlands became increasingly acute: there was a growing lack of wood, fuel, clothing fibres, draught animals and metals, and there was an increasing shortage of good farmland. Hectic deforestation continued throughout the nineteenth century and in some places the scarcity of wood was so serious that families burned little but dung, roots and the husks of corn. In provinces such as Henan and Shandong, where population levels were at their most dense, forest cover fell to between 2 per cent and 6 per cent of the total land area, which was between one-twelfth and one-quarter of the levels in European countries like France at the time.[34] The pressure on land and other resources was driven by the continuing growth of population in a situation of relative technological stasis. Lacking a richly endowed overseas empire, China had no exogenous means by which it could bypass the growing constraints.

With the price of labour falling, profit margins declining and static markets, there was no incentive to invest in labour-saving machinery; instead there was a premium on conserving resources and fixed capital. In such a situation there was little reason to engage in the kind of technological leap into the factory system that marked Britain's Industrial Revolution. In other words, it was rational for the Chinese not to invest in labour-saving machinery. As Elvin argues:

> In the context of a civilization with a strong sense of economic rationality, with an appreciation of invention such that shrines were erected to historic inventors . . . and with notable mechanical gifts, it is probably a sufficient explanation of the retardation of technological advance.[35]

With growing markets and a rising cost of labour, on the other hand, investment in labour-saving machinery was entirely rational in the British context and was to unleash a virtuous circle of invention, application, increased labour productivity and economic growth; in contrast, China remained trapped within its old parameters. In Britain the domestic system, based on small-scale family units of production, proved to be the precursor of the factory system. In China, where such rural industrialization was at least as developed as it was in Britain, it did not. While Britain suggested a causal link between the domestic and the factory systems, this was not true in China: widespread rural industrialization did not lead to a Chinese industrial revolution.[36]

THE CHINESE STATE

The most striking difference between Europe and China was not in the timing of their respective industrializations, which in broad historical terms was similar, separated by less than two centuries at the most, but in the disparity between the sizes of their polities, which has persisted for at least two millennia and whose effects have been enormous. For roughly two thousand years, China has been united and Europe has been divided. It is this, above all, which explains why Europe is such a poor template for understanding China. After the collapse of the Roman Empire, Europe was never again to be ruled, notwithstanding the ambitions of Napoleon and Hitler, by an imperial regime with the capacity to exercise centralized control over more or less the entire continent. Political authority, instead, was devolved to many small units. With the creation of the modern nation-state system, and the unification of Germany and Italy, Europe remained characterized by its division into a multi-state system. In contrast, China retained the imperial state system that emerged after the intense interstate competition – the Warring States period – that ended in the third century BC, though this was to assume over time a range of different forms, including, as in the case of the Mongol Yuan and the Manchu Qing dynasties, various phases of foreign rule.[37] Apart from Outer Mongolia, China's borders today remain roughly coterminous with those the country acquired during the period of its greatest geographical reach under the Qing dynasty (1644–1912). China's equilibrium state has been that of a unified agrarian empire in contrast to Europe, which for two millennia has been an agglomeration of states.[38]

From this follows a fundamental difference in contemporary Chinese and European attitudes: while the Chinese attach greater importance to unity than literally anything else, the Europeans overwhelmingly believe in the nation-state rather than European-wide sovereignty, the European Union notwithstanding. The underlying strength of the Chinese desire for unity is illustrated by the fact that, while the rise of nationalism in Europe in the nineteenth century resulted in the break-up of old empires and the creation of many new states, this has never happened, and shows no sign of happening, in China. The Chinese commitment to unity has three dimensions: the fundamental priority attached to unity by both the state and the people; the central role expected of the state in ensuring that this unity is maintained; and a powerful sense of a common Chinese identity that underpins this overarching popular commitment to unity. This unity could never be taken for granted: China has spent around half its history in varying degrees of division, which, in the light of the country's size and diversity (far greater than that of Europe), is not surprising. As a result of its attachment to unity, China has largely escaped the intra-state wars that have scarred Europe's history over many centuries, though its periods of disunity and fragmentation have often carried a very heavy cost in terms of war and famine, notably from the mid nineteenth to the mid twentieth century, when it was chronically divided.[39] Indeed, China's frequent experience of disunity and its baleful consequences have served to reinforce its commitment to unity, a tradition that began with Confucius – who, living on the eve of the Warring States period, was witness to the huge cost of instability and conflict, and preached the importance of harmony.

A further difference between the Chinese state and the various European states was that for over a millennium the former has not faced competition from rival elites seeking to limit its power. By the mid tenth century, the Chinese aristocratic elites had been destroyed, with the consequence that no elite enjoyed authority independent of the state. The opposite, in fact, was the case: the bureaucratic elite enjoyed unrivalled authority and numerous privileges, with all other elites dependent for their position on the patronage of the state.[40] The key mechanism for the selection of the bureaucratic elite was the imperial examination system, which had been more or less perfected by the time of the Tang dynasty (AD 618–907).[41] Although the nobility enjoyed an advantage in these exams, they were open to a wide cross-section of society and were the means by which recruitment to the imperial elite was greatly broadened. Knowledge of the Confucian classics formed the core of the exams and served, for successful and unsuccessful candidates alike, to articulate and reinforce a common set of values.[42] Whereas in Europe the elites remained relatively autonomous, except at extreme moments like war, the Chinese elites were absorbed by and became effectively part of the state, often being called upon to act on its behalf. The imperial bureaucracy, under the aegis of the emperor, faced no challenge from a Church (after the seizure of Buddhist properties in the ninth century), a judiciary, a landed aristocracy, the military or an urban bourgeoisie.[43] The most important exception was the tradition of the literati, like

Confucius himself, who were given licence to write critical things provided that they, in effect, removed themselves from everyday society.

The Chinese state was thus not constrained by independent power elites in the manner of Europe: it enjoyed universal and unchallenged authority. While the boundaries between the state and society in Europe were clearly delineated and constantly contested, this was not the case in China, where the frontiers remained blurred and fuzzy, as they still are today: there has been no need to define them because there were no competing social groups. Given the non-conflictual nature of state–elite relations, the boundaries between state and society were instead determined by practical issues of organization and resource constraints. In Europe, by contrast, autonomous, competing elites – nobles, clerics and burghers – fought to constrain the power of the state. Whereas the contest between state and elites in Europe was intimately bound up with both Church and class, in China the functional differentiation into scholars, peasants, merchants and tradesmen did not translate into independent bases of power or institutionalized voices.

With such a vast territory to govern, the Chinese state could not, and did not, depend solely or even mainly on physical coercion for the exercise of its rule.[44] It would have been neither feasible nor viable, the resources required being too enormous. In comparison with Japan, indeed, the military remained strikingly absent from Chinese life – at least until the early twentieth century. Instead, the power of the state has rested primarily on consent reinforced by forms of coercion. The Chinese state went to great lengths, in both the Ming and Qing periods, to inculcate in the population a sense of shared values and culture based on Confucian principles. Here was another contrast with Europe, where such matters were not considered to be the responsibility of the state and, until the late nineteenth century, were left in the hands of the Church.[45] The Chinese state saw moral instruction, amongst both the common people and the elites, as both desirable in itself and also as a means of exercising social control. For the elites, the state required that the Confucian classics be taught in schools as well as in preparation for the imperial exams. It promoted lectures for the common people on the virtues of Confucian behaviour, and imperial edicts frequently adopted a moral tone on issues such as social hierarchy and the payment of taxes. The state also sought to promote the worship of particular deities, while at the same time discouraging those which it saw as potential sources of social unrest.[46] On these matters, it was, with the exception of religious control, many centuries in advance of European states, which only began to concern themselves with such questions after the emergence of the modern nation-state and concomitant nationalism in the late nineteenth century. As the historian Bin Wong suggests: 'From a Chinese perspective, the lack of concern for education and moral indoctrination in Europe constitutes a basic limitation on European rule, no less important than the absence of representative political institutions in China.'[47] The same can be said of the manner in which the Chinese state, as a matter of course, engaged in surveillance of the population – by registration and other means – in order to be better able to anticipate sources of dissatisfaction and potential unrest.[48] A crucial mechanism in the exercise of social control was the clans or lineages, which were – and remain, even – far more important in China than they generally were in Europe. These were huge extended kinship groups, which traced their origins back to a common male ancestor (at the time of the 1949 Revolution there were still fewer than 500 surnames in China),[49] and were based on formal membership. They enjoyed huge authority, with the power of expulsion and the consequent threat of social ostracism.[50]

The imperial state was mindful of the importance of good governance and the need for restraint. This notion of good governance was intimately linked to the Confucian tradition, with its stress on the moral responsibility of the rulers: a continuing feature of imperial rule, for example, was a recognition that taxes needed to be kept low so that peasants would prosper, harmony would be promoted, resistance and rebellion avoided.[51] Nor was there a complete absence of accountability: imperial rule was always haunted by the possibility that the mandate of Heaven, and therefore its right to rule, might be withdrawn. During the Zhou dynasty (1046–256 BC) emperors claimed for the first time that their sanction to govern came from a broader, impersonal deity, Heaven (*tian*), whose mandate (*tianming*) might be conferred on any family that was morally worthy of the responsibility. This doctrine proclaimed the ruler's accountability to a supreme moral force that guides the human community. The Chinese concept of Heaven differed from the Western concept of a universe created and controlled by a divine power. For the Chinese, Heaven was seen as superior to anything on earth but it was not regarded as the creator of the universe, nor was it visualized in concrete terms. Unlike a Western ruler's accession through the doctrine of the divine right of kings, which rested solely on birth, the Chinese mandate of Heaven established moral criteria for holding power, which enabled the Chinese to distance themselves from their rulers and to speculate on their virtue and suitability.[52] A succession of bad harvests, or growing poverty, or a series of natural disasters such as floods and earthquakes, might bring into question in the minds of the people the right of a particular emperor to continue his rule: such a growing crisis of legitimacy could lead to and sustain huge popular uprisings, the last great example being the Taiping Uprising against the Qing dynasty in the mid nineteenth century, when tens of millions came to believe that the mandate of Heaven had been withdrawn.

The moral role that the Chinese state assumed was only one aspect of a very broad conception of how it conceived of its responsibilities. The mandate of Heaven meant that the state felt obliged to intervene in ecological and economic questions and also in ensuring the livelihood of the people. A striking example was the way the Qing during the eighteenth century managed granary reserves in order to ensure that the local laws of supply and demand worked in a reasonably acceptable fashion and produced relative price stability, a practice which dated back much earlier to the Yuan dynasty (1271–1368) and even before.[53] The state also took on responsibility for what were, by the standards of the time, huge infrastructural projects, such as the maintenance of the Yellow River in order to prevent flooding, and the construction of the Grand Canal, which was completed at the beginning of the seventh century and then added to subsequently.[54] In each of these respects, the Chinese state was very different from European states in that it assumed functions that the latter were only to regard as legitimate areas of concern many centuries later. In these instances too, then, developments in China prefigured those in Europe, and confound the idea of a single Eurocentric path of development that other states are destined to follow. If anything, indeed, quite the reverse: the Chinese state acquired many of the characteristics of a modern state, not least a large-scale bureaucracy, long before, on a European time-map, it should have done. Moreover, those forces that later drove the expansion of the nation-state in Europe from the seventeenth century onwards – the exigencies of warfare, the need for revenue and the demand for political representation – were very different from the factors that shaped China's imperial state. In contrast to Europe, where no nation dominated, China enjoyed overwhelming power over its neighbours for more than a millennium,[55] while political representation was to remain an alien concept, even after the 1911 Revolution and the fall of the Qing dynasty. The dynamics of state-creation in China and Europe were profoundly different in almost every major respect.[56] It is hardly surprising, therefore, that the modern Chinese state should differ so markedly from the European state and enjoy such a different relationship with society, as we shall see in Chapter 7.

IMPLOSION AND INVASION

The problems faced by the Qing dynasty (1644–1912) began to mount in the early decades of the nineteenth century. Its first taste of what lay in wait was its defeat by Britain in the First Opium War (1839–42). Then, around the middle of the century, as economic difficulties began to grow, the Qing were shaken by a series of local revolts together with four major rebellions: a Muslim rebellion in Yunnan in the south-west (1855–73), another Muslim rebellion by those of Turkic descent in the north-west (1862–73), the Nien Rebellion in the north (1853–68), and the Taiping Uprising (1850–64).[57] Of these, the Taiping was by far the most serious. With trust in the imperial regime shaken by its defeat at the hands of the British in the Opium War, together with serious floods and famine in 1848–50, the conditions were ripe for rebellion. The Taiping Uprising started in southern China and laid waste to much of the rich lower Yangzi region before moving north and west, and threatening Beijing: it is estimated that the uprising resulted in the deaths of 20–40 million people. The historian Paul Cohen describes the Taiping's ideology as 'a bizarre alchemy of evangelical Christianity, primitive communism, sexual Puritanism, and Confucian utopianism'.[58] Initially it drew considerable support from various ethnic minorities in the south which had migrated from the north, especially the Hakka, and contained a strongly anti-Manchu element (the Qing dynasty being from Manchuria).[59] The outcome remained uncertain for several years, with the rebellion only finally being crushed by the raising of new armies by the Qing and the support of British and French troops. Although the ultimate ability of the Qing to prevail indicated that it was still a robust and powerful force, its moral authority had been seriously undermined and was never to be restored.[60]

Following the defeat of the Taiping Uprising, the problems posed by growing Western ambition and aggression began to move centre-stage in the 1870s and 1880s.[61] The First Opium War, in which the Qing unsuccessfully sought to resist British demands to allow the import of Indian-grown opium, led to the Treaty of Nanjing.[62] This was the first of the so-called unequal treaties and resulted in the imposition of reparations, the loss of Hong Kong, and the creation of four treaty ports in which the British enjoyed special concessions. The impact of the defeat, however, was limited. The Qing dynasty was not forced to rethink its attitudes in the light of its defeat: the imperial state, indeed, continued to perceive the British in rather similar terms to the way it regarded other foreigners, whether they were the peoples of the northern steppes and Central Asia, or its many tributary states in East Asia, like Korea and Vietnam.[63] The sense of Chinese superiority and self-confidence remained obdurate.[64] This state of affairs began to change with the Second Opium War (1857–60), which culminated in the ransacking and burning of the Summer Palace in Beijing by British and French troops and the resulting Treaty of Tianjin and the Beijing Conventions. These established a whole string of new treaty ports in which Western citizens were granted extra-territoriality; the right to foreign military bases was conceded; missionaries were given freedom to travel in the interior; and further reparations were imposed. As a result, China began to lose control over important aspects of its territory.[65] In 1884 the French succeeded in crushing the Chinese navy in a struggle for influence over Vietnam, which had long been part of the Chinese tributary system but was in the course of being colonized by France. The naval battle revealed the alarming disparity between the power of an advanced European industrial nation, even so far from its home base, and that of an overwhelmingly agrarian China. The Chinese flagship was sunk by torpedoes within the first minute of battle; in less than an hour all the Chinese ships had been destroyed and the way was clear for France to take control of Indochina.[66]

The decisive turning point was the Sino-Japanese War in 1894, which, like the war with the French, concerned China's influence over its tributary states, in this case Korea, which had for many centuries been one of those closest to China. The Chinese suffered a humiliating defeat at the hands of its rapidly industrializing and increasingly aggressive neighbour and in the Treaty of Shimonoseki was forced to pay huge reparations, amounting to three times the government's annual income. Korea effectively became a Japanese protectorate, though not formally until 1905. China lost Taiwan and part of southern Manchuria, four further treaty ports were created, and Japan won the right to build factories and other enterprises in one of the now numerous treaty ports. Japan's victory also proved the occasion for further demands from the Western powers and a series of new concessions from a China impotent to resist.[67] By the turn of the century, China's sovereignty had been severely curtailed by the growing presence of Britain, France, Japan, Germany, the United States, Belgium and Russia on Chinese territory.

The Boxer Uprising of 1898–1901, which received the tacit support of the Empress Dowager Cixi, who held de facto power over the Qing government between 1861 and 1908, was occasioned by growing anti-Western sentiment and resulted in widespread attacks on foreign missionaries and other Westerners. Eventually a joint foreign army drawn from British, Japanese, French and American troops marched on Beijing, suppressed the uprising and then proceeded to base itself in the Forbidden City for over a year. Further concessions were extracted from the Chinese authorities, including another round of reparations. Although China was not colonized, in effect it became a semi-colony, with foreign troops free to roam its territory, the treaty ports resembling micro-colonies, missionaries enjoying licence to proselytize Western values wherever they went,[68] and foreign companies able to establish subsidiaries with barely any taxation or duties. China was humiliated and impoverished.[69] The fact, however, that it never formally became a colony, even though the Japanese were later to occupy Manchuria and then conquer lands much further to the south, was of great importance for China's ability to revive after 1949.

Major Unequal Treaties Imposed on China

Treaty of Nanjing (1842) with the United Kingdom
Treaty of the Bogue (1843) with the United Kingdom
Treaty of Wanghia (1844) with the United States
Treaty of Whampoa (1844) with France
Treaty of Aigun (1858) with Russia
Treaty of Tianjin (1858) with France, the United Kingdom, Russia and the United States
Convention of Peking (1860) with the United Kingdom, France and Russia
Treaty of Tientsin (1861) with Prussia and the German Customs Union
Chefoo Convention (1876) with the United Kingdom
Sino-Portuguese Treaty of Peking (1887) with Portugal
Treaty of Shimonoseki (1895) with Japan
Li-Lobanov Treaty (1896) with Russia
Convention for the Extension of Hong Kong Territory (1898) with the United Kingdom
Boxer Protocol (1901) with the United Kingdom, the United States, Japan, Russia, France, Germany, Italy, Austro-Hungary, Belgium, Spain and the Netherlands
Twenty-One Demands (1915) with Japan

China's impotence in the face of growing foreign intervention stimulated a movement for reform aimed at modernizing the country. Unlike in Japan, however, it failed to command anything like a consensus, its base never extending beyond a small elite, with the consequence that reform was always a hesitant and piecemeal process. It was driven by a small coterie of imperial civil servants, together with various writers and scholars, such as Kang Youwei, a well-connected man adept at showing how new ways of thinking were compatible with traditional Confucian texts.[70] The imperial government for the most part, however, neither understood nor accepted the necessity, let alone the urgency, of modernization, remaining passive or actively opposed – unlike in post-1868 Japan, where the state was the key agent of modernization. Nonetheless, there was some reform of the armed forces and various ministries, including the establishment for the first time of a diplomatic presence in major capitals like London and Paris, while the educational curriculum was revised after the turn of the century to include Western disciplines. In 1898 the reform movement reached its apogee when it finally received the formal blessing of the imperial hierarchy, but the imprimatur only lasted for a few months.[71]

One of the major problems facing the reformers was that modernization became intimately associated with the West at a time when the latter was colonizing and humiliating the country: far from being seen as patriots, they were regarded as tainted by the West or, worse, as traitors. As a result, the growing hostility amongst the Chinese towards the West was to work against the process of reform. The fact that China enjoyed such a unitary and centralized system of government also conspired to inhibit and stifle the development of alternative reforming impulses, in contrast to Japan, where authority was more dispersed. This problem was compounded by the hegemony enjoyed by Confucian thought, which made it very difficult for other ways of thinking to gain ground and influence. Until around 1900 the idea of reform was virtually always articulated within a Confucian framework – with an insistence on the distinction between Chinese 'essence' and Western 'method' (or, in the famous phrase of Zhang Zhidong (1837–1909), 'Chinese learning for the essential principles, Western learning for the practical applications').[72] After the turn of the century, other modes of thought began to acquire some traction, including socialist and Marxist ideas amongst sections of the intelligentsia,[73] a process that culminated in the 1911 Revolution largely being inspired by Western thinking.[74] Although Confucianism certainly declined during this period, it did not die. Nor should it be regarded as having been, or being, inherently incompatible with, or fundamentally antithetical to, change and reform.[75] However, it was in urgent need of revitalization through a process of cross-fertilization with other ways of thinking, as happened to it in earlier periods of history with Buddhism and Taoism.

By the early years of the twentieth century, the Qing dynasty faced an intensifying crisis of authority. Constantly required to seek the approval of the occupying powers, it enjoyed only very limited sovereignty over its territory. Its economic situation, exacerbated by the enormous reparations that it was forced to pay, which required the government to depend on loans from foreign banks in order to meet its obligations, meant that it was permanently in dire financial straits. The armies that it had depended upon to crush the various rebellions, notably the Taiping Uprising, behaved in an increasingly independent manner, and the regime faced gathering disaffection and disillusionment amongst growing sections of the population, with a rising tide of anti-Manchu sentiment directed against the Qing. The Qing finally fell following the 1911 Revolution, after 268 years in power, bringing down the curtain on over two millennia of dynastic government – the most enduring political system in world history. It was replaced by the republican government of Sun Yat-sen, but, far from ushering in a new and more hopeful era, Sun's regime proved the prelude to a further Balkanization of China, in which limited sovereignty gave way to something much worse: a chronic multiple and divided sovereignty. Sun Yat-sen's Kuomintang (or Nationalist) Party was in a very weak situation, with no troops at its command or effective state apparatus at its disposal. He sought to strike a deal with the country's most powerful military overlord, Yuan Shih-kai, but the result was to render Yuan the real power in the land and to sideline Sun. After Yuan's death in 1916, the military governors that he had installed in the provinces quarrelled and shared out China between them, with the support of various foreign powers. The years 1916–28 were the period of warlordism. Not only was the country now – de facto if not de jure – divided, but also, for the first time for many centuries, military power, together with the continuing foreign presence, became the arbiter of China's future.[76]

Only between 1928 and 1937, when Chiang Kai-shek, the heir to the warlords and leader of the Nationalist Party, a position he inherited from Sun Yat-sen, became China's leader and effective dictator, was China relatively united. But even Chiang Kai-shek's power was circumscribed by a combination of the Japanese occupation of the north-east, the presence of other foreign powers and his lack of support in rural areas, together with the opposition of the Communist armies in the south (until he drove them out in the early 1930s), followed by their Long March around China in 1934–5 when they tried to evade the Nationalist offensive against them.[77] The country was to face a further trauma in 1937 with the Japanese drive southwards from their stronghold in the north-east and their seizure of the fertile eastern provinces of China, where most industry was also located. The brutality of Japan's colonization, symbolized by the Nanjing Massacre in December 1937, when Japanese troops killed many tens of thousands of Chinese civilians and soldiers (and possibly as many as 300,000), was to leave a lasting impression on the Chinese and has continued to haunt Sino-Japanese relations to this day.[78] Chiang displayed a persistent ambiguity about who he regarded as the main enemy, the Japanese or the Communists, suggesting that 'the Japanese were the disease of the skin and the Communists were the threat to the heart'.[79] In so doing, he underestimated the impact of Japanese aggression on Chinese national consciousness and popular perceptions. After 1936 he was forced to stop the civil war against the Communists and co-operate with them in a united front against the Japanese, with the former fighting a guerrilla war behind Japanese lines which was to earn them considerable prestige.[80] After the Japanese surrender in 1945, the Nationalists used puppet Chinese forces and Japanese troops against the Communists. Not surprisingly, despite their many losses in the fighting against the Japanese, such episodes served to tarnish

Chiang's nationalist credentials. The Communist victory in the subsequent civil war was a result of manifold factors, including rampant corruption under the Nationalists, their long-running failure to unite and modernize the country, and the inadequacy of the struggle against the Japanese.[81] In the 1949 Revolution, the Communist Party led by Mao Zedong finally took power. Unlike the 1911 Revolution – which, in practice, turned out to be one of history's commas, the prelude to almost four decades of divided authority and foreign occupation – 1949 proved to be the decisive turning point.

From this most bitter period, one is left with two crucial questions: why did China, though chronically divided, never break up; and why – despite everything – did the impact of Western and Japanese occupation prove relatively limited, at least in the long run?

In the period 1911–49, the possibility of China dividing was very real: on three occasions between 1911 and 1916 provinces actually declared independence from the central government. This was done, however, in response to particular actions by central government rather than as a matter of principle. In practice there proved to be no alternative identities strong enough to provide a viable basis for the formation of breakaway states. There were two exceptions to this: the ultimately successful pressure for an independent Outer Mongolia between 1933 and 1941, and the de facto independence enjoyed by parts of Tibet between 1913 and 1933. But in the vast heartlands of China no such movement for separatism or independence ever acquired any serious strength. The Han Chinese identity, bolstered by new forms of anti-Manchu expression from the late nineteenth century, was simply too strong and too exclusive, while provincial identities remained ill-formed and never acquired any nationalist aspirations. Moreover, forced to enter the Western-dominated modern nation-state system in the most adverse of circumstances, China was also to experience the binding effects of modern nationalism: the centuries-old sense of cultural identity and cohesion, born of a unique kind of agrarian civilization, was reinforced by a profound feeling of grievance engendered by foreign occupation.[82]

Finally, why were the effects of foreign occupation relatively limited when elsewhere – Africa and the Middle East most obviously – they were to prove so enduring? China's vastness made colonizing the whole of it, or even the majority of it, a huge task which Britain and the United States saw no advantage in, although Japan and some of the other European nations favoured such an approach;[83] as a consequence, most of the country remained under Chinese sovereignty. Apart from Manchuria, it was largely the many treaty ports that experienced sustained foreign occupation and these were, in effect, small enclaves (albeit, by far the most advanced parts of the country) surrounded by China's huge rural hinterland. This is not to detract from or underestimate the extent to which the country was undermined and dismembered by foreign occupation, but it fell far short of the kind of colonization experienced in Africa, for example. The fact, moreover, that prior to 1800 China was an advanced agrarian economy, with widespread rural industrialization, considerable commercialization and sophisticated markets, meant that once foreign occupation came to an end, China could draw on this culture, knowledge and tradition for its industrialization. Furthermore, China enjoyed the world's oldest and most sophisticated state and statecraft, a huge resource that post-1949 China was able to utilize with great effect. This was in striking contrast to post-colonial Africa and the Middle East, where modern states had to be created more or less from scratch, with their borders drawn by their colonial conquerors. Finally, the powerful sense of Chinese identity helped China resist many of the most negative cultural and psychological effects of Western and Japanese colonialism.[84] The Chinese remained bitterly hostile towards the presence of the Western powers and the Japanese, and felt deeply humiliated by the concessions they were forced to make; this was quite different from India, for example, which learnt to accommodate the presence of the British.[85] Despite everything, the Chinese never lost their inner sense of self-confidence – or feeling of superiority – about their own history and civilization.[86] This notwithstanding, the scale of China's suffering and dislocation in the century of humiliation has had a profound and long-term effect on Chinese consciousness, which remains to this day.

AFTER 1949

By 1949 China had suffered from an increasingly attenuated sovereignty for over a century. After 1911 it had experienced not only limited sovereignty but also, in effect, multiple sovereignty,[87] with the central government being obliged to share authority with both the occupying powers (i.e., multiple colonialism)[88] and various domestic rivals. Most countries would have found such a situation unacceptable, but for China, with its imposingly long history of independence, and with a tradition of a unitary state system dating back over two millennia, this state of affairs was intolerable, gnawing away at the country's sense of pride. The Communists were confronted with three interrelated tasks: the return of the country's sovereignty; the reunification of China; and the reconstruction of the state and the restoration of unitary government. Although the Communists had played a key role in the resistance against the Japanese, it was the Japanese surrender at the end of the Second World War that forced their departure from China.[89] In 1949, with the defeat of the Nationalists by the Communists in the Civil War, the country was finally reunified (with the exception of the 'lost territories', namely, Taiwan, Hong Kong and Macao). The key to the support enjoyed by the Communist regime after 1949 – and, indeed, even until this day – lies, above all else, in the fact that it restored the independence and unity of China.[90] It was Mao's greatest single achievement.

After the ravages of the previous forty years, the disintegration of the imperial state and the failure of the Nationalists, the Communists had to deal with the daunting task of establishing a new ruling system. China, ever since the rise of the West, had been faced with a range of strategic choices concerning its modernization: it could reform the traditional imperial institutions, which was attempted unsuccessfully prior to 1911; it could imitate the Western model, an experiment which failed badly between 1911 and 1949; or it could develop new institutions, drawing on foreign examples where appropriate as well as on the past.[91] The last, in effect, became the Communist project, with inspiration being sought in part from the Soviet Union, although

Maoism was overwhelmingly a home-grown product rather than a foreign import.[92] The Communists had already acquired some initial experience of governance in the areas over which they had enjoyed limited authority during the late twenties and early thirties,[93] subsequently in the expanding territory they controlled during the resistance against the Japanese occupation after 1937, especially North China, and finally in the regions they governed during the Civil War between 1945 and 1949. One of the key problems that faced both the late imperial state and the Nationalists, under Sun Yat-sen and then Chiang Kai-shek, was a loss of control over government revenues. The People's Republic of China (PRC) – as the new regime was known – quickly reasserted central control over revenues and disbursements. Although the actual expenditure of revenues was to remain in local hands, as it had been since the eighteenth century, central government once again determined how they should be used; there was, in this respect, a strong continuity with the late imperial state.[94]

The backbone of the new ruling system was the Communist Party. In many respects, it proved a highly effective mechanism for governing, certainly in comparison with the late imperial state and the Nationalists. The key figure was Mao Zedong. Notwithstanding his colossal abuses of power, which resulted in the deaths of millions, as the architect of the revolution and the founder of an independent and unified China, he played the central role in sustaining the popularity and legitimacy of the new regime, and he remains, even today, a venerated figure in the eyes of many Chinese, even more than Deng Xiaoping, who presided over the reform period from 1978. Prior to 1949, the Communist Party's main base of support lay amongst the peasantry, who constituted the overwhelming majority of the population, rather than in the cities, where the Nationalists were strong.[95] This was very different from the Bolsheviks in the USSR, whose support was concentrated in the cities, where only a very small minority of the population lived, and was very weak in the countryside.[96] As a consequence, the Chinese Communist Party always enjoyed far greater popular support and much deeper roots than did the Soviet Communist Party. The underlying strength and resilience of the new regime was demonstrated by the ability of the Communist Party to reinvent itself after the death of Mao.[97] This was the nadir of the regime. Mao's actions had brought into question its legitimacy and competence. It is estimated that 25 million died as a result of the famine and malnutrition consequent upon the Great Leap Forward in 1958–60. The Cultural Revolution between 1966 and 1969 – although its effects lasted into the mid seventies – led to the death of around 400,000 people as a result of maltreatment and was to deprive a whole generation of their education. Yet after Mao's death in 1976, the Communist Party, under the leadership of Deng Xiaoping, displayed a remarkable ability to renew itself, by shifting direction and embarking on a quite new economic policy, which led to a sustained period of extremely rapid economic growth and a remarkable transformation in China's situation and prospects.

Judgements about the post-1949 era have – both in China and the West, albeit in differing ways – placed overwhelming emphasis on the extent to which it represented a new departure, a rupture in the continuity and tradition of China. The reasons for this are not difficult to understand. The Chinese Communists – like the communist tradition more widely – sought to underline the extent to which they represented an utterly new kind of regime marking a complete break with the past. That, after all, is what revolutions are supposed to be about, especially socialist revolutions. The Communist Party directed its venom against many Chinese traditions, from the long-standing oppression of women to Confucian notions of hierarchy, and carried out a sweeping land reform in the name of class struggle. Meanwhile the West, with the exception of a brief period during the Second World War, has, more or less ever since the 1917 October Revolution, regarded Communist regimes as the devil incarnate. As a result, too little attempt has been made to understand them in their historical and cultural context, to appreciate the continuities with previous history and not just the discontinuities. In sum, for a variety of reasons, there has been a tendency to overlook the powerful lines of continuity between post-1949 China and the dynastic period. As Bin Wong points out, while the overt differences between Confucian and Communist ideology are clear – hierarchy versus equality, conservatism versus radicalism, harmony versus conflict – there are also important similarities between the two traditions. As in the Maoist period, for example, the Confucian tradition also emphasized the need to reduce inequality, limit the size of landholdings and redistribute land. Similarly, as we discussed earlier, the state's responsibility for moulding the outlook of the people is an old Chinese tradition, which the Communists have simply perpetuated in a distinctive form. The same can be said of the state's role in economic and social security, which the Communists continued during the Maoist period in the form of the 'iron rice bowl', with state enterprises required to provide employees with housing, education and health, as well as lifelong employment.[98]

There are political parallels, too. Both the Confucian and Communist modes of rule involved an implicit contract between the people and the state: if the state failed to meet its obligations then the peasants had, according to Mencius (372–289 BC; the foremost disciple of Confucius), a right to rebel. In the imperial era this took the form of the mandate of Heaven; in the Communist era it was expressed, in the name of class struggle, in the right of the proletariat to resist and defeat the bourgeoisie, which during the Maoist era was the pretext for the many top-down mass mobilizations that eventually culminated in Mao's own assault on the Communist state in the enormously destructive Cultural Revolution. The relationship between state and subject in both traditions was authoritarian and hierarchical, and very different from the Western tradition with its narrative of political rights and formal representative institutions. There are other examples of continuity. Confronted with the problem of the gulf between the cities and the countryside, both acknowledged the need to rule them differently. While the Confucian tradition recruited a governing elite consisting of the highly educated and literate by means of the imperial examination system, the Communists, faced with the same task, used the Party as their means of recruitment to the state, though to this day the civil service exams remain hugely important, with over 1.3 million entrants for just 12,000 jobs in 2011. Finally, in the Communist as in the Confucian tradition, elites were seen as an appendage of the state rather than as independent groups with their own forms of organization and power. The absence of a civil society and an autonomous public realm in

Communist China is not a new phenomenon: China has never had either.

There are, thus, powerful continuities between the Communist tradition and dynastic history. The PRC is an integral part of Chinese history and can only be understood in that context.[99] The historian Wang Gungwu argues that the new Communist state was 'a replacement for the old emperor-state', and that 'Mao Zedong effectively restored the idea of a charismatic founder-emperor and behaved, and he was treated very much, like an emperor with almost no limits on his power.'[100] Suisheng Zhao makes a similar point rather differently:

> A Chinese nation-state was forged under the leadership of the Communist Party and the guidance of Marxism. However, it had far more to do with Chinese nationalism, with the reassertion of China's former glory and future modernization, than with the universal principles of communism.[101]

As we shall see in Part II, the contours of Chinese modernity bear the imprint not just of the Communist present but, far more strongly, that of the Chinese past. Nonetheless, the fact remains that following more than half a century of botched, half-hearted and failed attempts to modernize the country – by the Qing dynasty, the 1911 Revolution, and under Chiang Kai-shek – China was only finally able to begin the process after the 1949 Revolution. The building blocks of modernization were numerous: the restoration of China's unity and sovereignty, the establishment of a viable and effective state, sweeping land reform, the destruction of many of the old class and elitest divisions, and the emancipation of women from their previous subjugation. Above all else, the historic significance of the 1949 Revolution was the creation of the conditions for China's long-delayed modernization and its successful implementation.

ECONOMIC TAKE-OFF

Ultimately China was undermined in the nineteenth century by its failure to industrialize at more or less the same time as the Western powers and Japan. From around 1860 there were significant examples of Chinese industrial development that were comparable with those in Japan, notably in Shanghai.[102] But, given China's vast size, they were too limited and too scattered. China, above all, lacked two crucial ingredients of Japan's modernization: a strong modernizing state and a prosperous agrarian sector that could generate the surpluses needed to fund industrialization.[103] In the second half of the nineteenth century, Chinese agriculture stagnated or even regressed as a result of the destruction wrought by growing divisions, rebellions and uprisings, the rising price of silver, floods and famines. Worse, after the defeat by the Japanese in 1894, China was almost bankrupted by the terms of its reparation payments and then found itself defenceless in the face of yet further Western and Japanese demands.[104] The Western powers exploited China's vulnerability by carving out new spheres of influence and acquiring the so-called 'leased territories'.[105] Foreign capital poured into China as the number of foreign businesses expanded rapidly, keen to exploit a situation where they could operate virtually without restraint or discrimination.[106] By 1920, Jacques Gernet writes:

> the whole Chinese economy was dependent on the big foreign banks in Shanghai, Hong Kong, Qingdao, and Wuhan, and on powerful [foreign] companies . . . The customs, the administration of the salt tax, and the postal service were run by foreigners, who kept all the profits. Western and Japanese warships and merchant shipping were everywhere – in the ports, on the coast, and on the Yangzi River network. Apart from a few Chinese firms . . . the whole modern sector of industry (cloth mills, tobacco factories, railways, shipping, cement works, soap factories, flour mills and, in the towns, the distribution of gas, water and electricity, and public transport) was under the control of foreign companies.[107]

China's plight during this period is illustrated by the fact that in 1820 its per capita GDP was $600, in 1850 it was still $600, by 1870 it had fallen to $530, in 1890 it was $540, rising very slightly to $552 in 1913 – still well below its level in 1820, almost a century earlier. By 1950 it had fallen to a mere $439, just over 73 per cent of its 1820 level.[108] These figures reveal the disastrous performance of the Chinese economy over a period of 120 years, with foreign intervention and occupation being the single most important reason. It is hardly surprising that China now refers to the period 1850–1950 as the 'century of humiliation'. Over eighty years after the Meiji Restoration – and well over a century and a half since the commencement of Britain's Industrial Revolution – China had barely begun its economic take-off.

Apart from restoring the country's unity, the central task facing the PRC was industrialization. To this end, it engaged in a huge project of land redistribution and the creation of large communes, from which it extracted considerable agricultural surpluses in the form of peasant taxes, which it then used to invest in the construction of a heavy industry sector. Its economic policy marked a major break with past practice, eschewing the use of the market and relying instead on the state and central planning in the manner of the Soviet Union, though in a less rigid and comprehensive form. Despite the wild vicissitudes of Mao's rule, China achieved an impressive annual growth rate of 4.4 per cent between 1950 and 1980,[109] more than quadrupling the country's GDP[110] and more than doubling its per capita GDP.[111] This compared favourably with India, which only managed to increase its GDP by less than three times during the same period and its per capita GDP by around 50 per cent.[112] China's social performance was even more impressive. Between 1950 and 1980, it enhanced its Human Development Index (a measure of a country's development using a range of yardsticks including per capita GDP, living standards, education and health)[113] by three and a half times (in contrast to India's increase of two and three-quarter times), as a result of placing a huge emphasis on education, tackling illiteracy, promoting equality (including gender equality) and improving healthcare.[114] This strategy also enabled China to avoid some of the problems that plagued many other Asian, African and Latin American countries, such as widespread poverty in rural areas, huge disparities of wealth between rich and poor, major discrepancies in the opportunities for men and women, large shanty towns of unemployed urban dwellers, and poor educational and health provision.[115] The price paid for these advances, in terms of the absence or loss of personal freedoms and the death and destruction which resulted from some of Mao's policies, was great, but they undoubtedly helped to sustain popular support for the government.

The first phase of Communist government marked a huge turnaround in China's fortunes. During these years, the groundwork was laid for industrialization and modernization, the failure of which had haunted the previous century of Chinese history. This period reversed a century of growing failure, restored unity and stability to the country, and secured the kind of economic take-off that had evaded previous regimes. Despite the disastrous violations and excesses of Mao, the foundations of China's extraordinary transformation were laid during the Maoist era.

5

Contested Modernity

Since we got there first, we think we have the inside track on the modern condition, and our natural tendency is to universalize from our own experience. In fact, however, our taste of the modern world has been highly distinctive, so much so that John Schrecker has seen fit to characterize the West as 'the most provincial of all great contemporary civilizations' . . . Never have Westerners had to take other peoples' views of us really seriously. Nor, like the representatives of all other great cultures, have we been compelled to take fundamental stock of our own culture, deliberately dismantle large portions of it, and put it back together again in order to survive. This circumstance has engendered what may be the ultimate paradox, namely that Westerners, who have done more than any other people to create the modern world, are in certain respects the least capable of comprehending it.

Paul A. Cohen, *Discovering History in China*

When a Western tourist first sets foot in Shanghai, Tokyo or Kuala Lumpur, peers up at the shiny high-rise buildings, casts an eye over the streets teeming with cars, walks around the shopping malls filled with the latest, and often familiar, goodies, his reaction is frequently: 'It's so modern!', and then, with barely a pause for breath, 'It's *so* Western.' And so, at one level, it is. These are countries in which living standards have been transformed and in a few cases are now on a par with those in the West. It is hardly surprising then that they share with the West much of the furniture and fittings of modernity. There is a natural tendency in all of us – an iron law perhaps – to measure the unfamiliar in terms of the familiar: we are all relativists at heart. As we see objects and modes of behaviour that we are accustomed to, so we think of them as being the same as or similar to ours. When we recognize signs of modernization and progress, we regard them as evidence that the society or culture is headed in the same direction as ours, albeit some way behind. As yet one more McDonald's opens in China, it is seen as proof positive that China is getting more Western, that it is becoming ever more like us.

Of course these impressions are accentuated by the places frequented by Westerners. Businessmen land at an international airport, travel by taxi to an international hotel, go to meetings in the financial district and then return home. This is the ultimate homogenizing experience. Modern airports are designed to look the same wherever they may be, so give or take an abundance of Chinese eateries, Hong Kong's Chek Lap Kok Airport could be Paris, Munich or Montreal. International hotels are similarly place-less, designed to meet an international formula rather than to convey any local flavour: in the lobby of an international hotel, one could be forgiven for thinking that most men on the planet wear suits, speak English and read the *International Herald Tribune*.

One might think that the experience of the expatriate who chooses to live in East Asia for a period is more illuminating. And sometimes it is. But all too often they inhabit something akin to a Western cocoon. A significant proportion of Westerners who live in East Asia are based in Singapore or Hong Kong, city-states which have gone out of their way to make themselves attractive to Western expats. Hong Kong, as a British colony for nearly a century and a half, still bears the colonial imprint, while Singapore, more than any other place in the region, has sought to make itself into the Asian home of Western multinationals, a kind of Little West in the heart of Asia. It is hardly surprising then that precious few expats in these city-states make any attempt to learn Mandarin or Cantonese: they feel there is no need. The great majority live in a handful of salubrious, Western-style residential 'colonies', enjoying a life of some privilege, such that for the most part they are thoroughly insulated from the host community: living in the Mid-Levels area on Hong Kong Island or Discovery Bay is a very different experience from Shatin in the New Territories.

The net result is that most Westerners, be they tourists, business-men or expats, spend most of their time in a familiar, sanitized, Western-style environment, making the occasional foray into the host culture rather than actually living in it: they see these countries through a Western distorting mirror. It would be wrong to suggest that we can understand nothing from observing the hardware of modernity – the buildings, malls, consumer products and entertain-ment complexes: they tell us about levels of development, priorities, and sometimes cultural difference too. However, the key to under-standing Asian modernity, like Western modernity, lies not in the hardware but in the software – the ways of relating, the values and beliefs, the customs, the institutions, the language, the rituals and festivals, the role of the family. This is far more difficult to penetrate, and even more difficult to make sense of.

THE RISE OF EAST ASIAN MODERNITY

For the first half of the twentieth century the cluster of countries that had experienced economic take-off in the nineteenth century contin-ued to dominate the elite club of industrialized nations, with virtually no additions or alterations. It was as if the pattern of the pre-1914 world had frozen, with no means of entry for those who had missed the window of economic opportunity afforded during the previous century.[1] In the 1950s the school of 'dependency theory' generalized this state of affairs into the proposition that it was now impossible for other countries to break into the ranks of the more advanced nations. But there were good reasons why the economic ground froze over. While large parts of the world had remained colonized the possibili-ties of economic growth and take-off were extremely limited. Furthermore, two world wars sapped the energies not only of the main combatants but of much of the rest of the world as well.

From the late 1950s onwards, there appeared the first stirrings of profound change in East Asia. Japan was recovering from the ravages of war at great speed – but as a fully paid-up member of the pre-1914 club of industrialized countries, its economic prowess was hardly new. Rather, what caught the eye was the rapid economic growth of the first group of Asian tigers – South Korea, Taiwan, Singapore and Hong Kong. They were small in number and even smaller in size – a medium-sized nation, a small country and two tiny city-states, all newly independent, apart from Hong Kong, which was still a colony. They had, in varying degrees, been debilitated by the war, in Korea's case also by the Korean War, and were bereft of natural resources,[2] but they began to grow at breakneck speed, with Taiwan and South Korea often recording annual growth rates of close to double-digit figures in the following three decades.[3] By the late 1970s they had been joined by Malaysia, Thailand and Indonesia. Some of the later Asian tigers – China being the outstanding example – achieved, if anything, even faster rates of growth than the early ones. The world had never before witnessed such rapid growth. (Britain's GDP expanded at a shade over 2 per cent and the United States at slightly over 4.2 per cent per annum between 1820 and 1870, their fastest periods of growth during the nineteenth century.)[4] The result has been the rapid and progressive transformation of a region with a population of around 2 billion people, with poverty levels falling to less than a quarter by 2007 (compared with 69 per cent in 1990).[5]

The myth that it was impossible for latecomers to break into the club of advanced nations has been exploded. The Asian tigers have instead demonstrated that latecomers can enjoy major advantages: they can learn from the experience of others, draw on and apply existing technologies, leapfrog old technologies, use the latest know-how and play catch-up to great effect. Their economic approach, furthermore, has largely been homespun, owing relatively little to neo-liberalism or the Washington Consensus – the dominant Western ideology from the late seventies until the financial meltdown in 2008.[6] Nor is their novelty confined to the economic sphere. The Asian tigers have given birth to a new kind of political governance, namely the

developmental state, whose popular legitimacy has rested in significant part on the ability of the state to deliver continued economic
growth.[7] The rise of the Asian tigers, however, has an altogether more
fundamental import. Hitherto, with the exception of Japan, modernity has been a Western monopoly. This monopoly has now been
decisively broken. Modernization theory, which was very influential
in American scholarship in the 1950s and 1960s, held, like Karl Marx,
that the developing countries would increasingly come to resemble
the developed world.[8] We can now test this proposition by reference
to the East Asian experience.

SPEED OF TRANSITION

A defining characteristic of all the Asian tigers (South Korea, Taiwan,
Singapore, Hong Kong, China, Malaysia, Thailand, Indonesia and
Vietnam)[9] has been the speed of their transformation. In 1950 they
were still overwhelmingly agrarian and had barely started the process
of industrialization. In 1950 79% of South Korea's population
worked in agriculture (relatively little changed from 91% in 1920);
by 1960 the figure was 61%, and today it is around 10%. In the late
1960s the farming population still comprised half of Taiwan's total
population, whereas today it accounts for a mere 8%.[10] The figure for
Indonesia in 1960 was 75% compared with 44% today, for Thailand
84% compared with 46% today, and for Malaysia 63% compared
with 18% today.[11] Eighty-five per cent of the population of China
worked in agriculture in 1950, but today that figure is hovering
around 50%. A similar story can be told in terms of the shift from the
countryside to the cities. In 1950 76% of Taiwanese lived in the countryside, whereas by 1989 – in a period of just thirty-nine years – that
figure had been almost exactly reversed, with 74% living in cities.[12]
The urban population in South Korea was 18% in 1950 and 80% in
1994; while in Malaysia, which took off later, the equivalent figures
were 27% in 1970 and 53% in 1990.[13] In China the urban population
represented 17% of the total population in 1975 and is projected to
be 46% by 2015.[14] We could also add Japan in this context, which

experienced extremely rapid growth rates following the Second World War, its GDP increasing by a factor of over fourteen between 1950 and 1990 as it recovered from the devastation of the war and completed its economic take-off with a major shift of its population from the countryside to the cities. Between 1950 and 1973, its most rapid period of growth, its GDP grew at an annual rate of 9.29%.

Compared with Europe, the speed of the shift from the countryside to the cities is exceptional. Germany's urban population grew from 15% in 1850 to 49% in 1910 (roughly coinciding with its industrial revolution), and 53% in 1950. The equivalent figures for France were 19% in 1850 and 38% in 1910 (and 68% in 1970). England's urban population was 23% in 1800, 45% in 1850, and 75% in 1910. In the United States, the urban population was 14% in 1850, 42% in 1910, and 57% in 1950.[15] If we take South Korea as our point of comparison (with a population broadly similar to that of Britain and France), the proportion of its population living in cities increased by 62% in 44 years, compared with 52% for England over a period of 110 years, 34% over 60 years for Germany (and 38% over 100 years), 19% over 60 years for France (and 49% over 120 years), and 28% over 60 years (and 43% over 100 years) for the United States. In other words, the rate of urbanization in South Korea was well over *twice* that of Germany's – the fastest of these European examples – and was achieved in approximately *two-thirds of the time*; it was *three times quicker* than France's, taking roughly *two-thirds of the time*, and *twice as quick* as that of the United States in *two-thirds of the time*.

The shift from the countryside to the cities, from working on the land to working in industry, characterizes the process of economic take-off and is the decisive moment in the emergence of modernity. From experiencing life on the land, where relatively little changes from one year to the next, or from one generation to another, industrialization marks a tumultuous transformation in people's circumstances, where uncertainty replaces predictability, the future can no longer be viewed or predicted in terms of the past, and where people are required to look forwards rather than backwards. In the nineteenth and first half of the twentieth century, the shift towards modernity as an increasingly mass phenomenon was confined to a small minority of the world, namely the West and Japan, but by the early twenty-first century it had become an increasingly mass phenomenon in much of East Asia too, with the change occurring far more rapidly in East Asia than it had earlier in Europe or North America. This relative speed of change had two important implications for the nature of East Asian modernities, which distinguishes them from their European and North American counterparts.

1. The Proximity of the Past

The fact that large-scale agrarian employment has been such a recent experience for the Asian tigers means that the past is heavily imprinted on the present and the legacy of tradition remains a living force in the era of mass modernity. Let me put this point in more human terms. In South Korea and Taiwan, the great majority of grandparents, around half of parents over fifty, and significant numbers of those over forty, will all have spent at least some of their lives working on the land. In China, where half the population still works on the land, that rural imprint is commensurately larger: not only will the great majority of grandparents have worked on the land, but so will the great majority of those over forty. As one would expect, this has a profound influence on the way in which people think and behave. Almost three-quarters of the inhabitants of Taipei, for instance, regard themselves as migrants: every Chinese New Year, the trains are booked for weeks in advance and Taiwan's north–south expressway is clogged for hours on end as the vast bulk of the capital's inhabitants make the journey south to celebrate the festival back in what they still regard as their ancestral homes. The same kind of phenomenon is repeated throughout East Asia. Shanghai is a huge metropolis of 20 million people, plus more than 3 million migrant workers who move in and out of the city every day, seeking work of one kind or another, including many farmers who occupy numerous pavements trying to sell their fruit and vegetables.[16] Shanghai, like countless Chinese cities, encapsulates a remarkable juxtaposition of the present and the past, of modernity and tradition existing cheek by jowl, as was once the case in European cities. The difference is that because East Asia is changing so quickly, the contrast between the past and the present is much more visible and far more pronounced than it was in nineteenth-century European cities.

Another expression of the imminence of the past can be found in people's attitudes and belief-systems. On the 1st and 15th of every month, it is common for the Chinese to burn incense and worship their ancestral spirits. Walk through the streets of Taipei, for example, on either of those dates and it won't be long before you see people burning fake money as an offering to their ancestors.[17] At the Qing Ming Festival at the beginning of April, people return to their villages in huge numbers and spend the day at their ancestral graves. By Western standards, Chinese societies are not very religious, but they are extremely superstitious. Every day many Taiwanese newspapers carry tips prominently displayed on their front pages about what to do and what not to do according to the old lunar calendar. Before any important event or decision – not least, a good night's gambling – many Chinese will visit the temple and pray to one of the deities. Even otherwise highly rational academics will follow deeply rooted indigenous customs. Many, for example, practise feng shui, even if they don't particularly believe in it, because it might just make a difference. In Hong Kong, no building is finalized until a feng shui expert has been consulted about its suitability and alterations duly made. In state-of-the-art computer companies in Taiwan's Hsinchu Science Park, the guy with the American doctorate hotfoot from working for years in Silicon Valley will set up a table with food and fruits, burn incense and worship the spirits for good fortune. These examples cannot be explained solely in terms of the immediate proximity of the past, since they are also clearly a function of underlying cultural difference. Whatever the reason, the persistence of pre-modern ways of thinking is a striking characteristic of many East Asian cultures.

2. The Future in the Present

As discussed earlier in the prologue to Part I, modernity is the embrace of the future as opposed to a present dominated by tradition: eyes and minds are directed forwards in time rather than backwards as previously. But the extent of the phenomenon varies. It was, and remains, more marked in the United States than in Europe, partly because the American transformation was faster than its European equivalents and partly because the United States, unencumbered by any kind of pre-capitalist tradition, is not weighed down by its past in the same way. But this orientation towards the future is even truer of East Asia than the United States, not because it is unencumbered by the past – on the contrary, the past looms very large indeed both in its proximity and the richness and longevity of the region's history – but because the speed of transformation has generated a completely different experience and expectation of change. In contrast to Europe and the United States, these countries are characterized by a form of hyper-modernity: an addiction to change, an infatuation with technology, enormous flexibility, and a huge capacity for adaptation.

Thus, if the imminence of the past is one aspect of Asian modernization, another, paradoxically, is its polar opposite, the embrace of the future and a powerful orientation towards change. This is not surprising. If an economy is growing at around 10 per cent a year – or doubling in size every seven years or so – then people's experiences and expectations are quite different from those in a Western economy expanding at 2 per cent a year. These are not just abstract macro figures: assuming that income distribution is reasonably egalitarian, which it has been in much of East Asia[18] (though no longer in China), then turbo-charged growth means a continuing revolution in the living standards of most of society, huge shifts in employment patterns, rapid urbanization, sweeping changes in the urban landscape and accelerated access to a growing range of consumer products, all within less than a generation. These are growth rates that no society (apart from post-war Japan) had previously experienced, that transform institutions like the family, that offer enormous opportunities but also place new and immense strains on the social fabric. For Britain that kind of shift took the best part of two centuries; for the early Asian tigers it has taken less than forty years. To deal with such change requires a psychology and a mindset, both on the part of the individual and society, which is quite different from the European or

North American experience. As Hung Tze Jan, a successful writer who has since become one of Taiwan's leading cyber entrepreneurs, philosophically remarked: 'We have had to change our value system so many times in such a short space of time.'[19] The result, not surprisingly, is a highly developed pragmatism and flexibility; otherwise it would be quite impossible to cope with such rapid change.

The propensity for rapid change is reflected in the distinctive character and structure of East Asian cities. Unlike European cities – or, indeed, American cities – where the height and character of buildings are carefully regulated and space arranged in zones according to use, Asian cities have no such order: they grow like Topsy, with every area having a little bit of everything and buildings coming in all shapes and sizes. While Western cities generally have a definable centre, Asian cities rarely do: the centre is in a perpetual state of motion as a city goes through one metamorphosis after another, resulting in the creation of many centres rather than one. Shanghai, for example, offers the area around the Shanghai Centre, Lujiazui, the Bund, Hongqiao and Xijiahui, as well as Pudong. Kuala Lumpur had the golden triangle, then KLCC, followed by Putrajaya. Tokyo, like Taipei and Seoul, has grown without method or concept, the product of spontaneous development. The lack of rules, regulations and order that is typical of East Asian cities produces an eclectic and intoxicating mix of benign chaos, compressed energy and inchoate excitement. People make it up as they go along. They try things out. They take risks. Seemingly the only constant is change. Scrap and build is a classic illustration, with little importance attached to conservation, in striking contrast to Europe.[20] Whereas European cities for the most part change relatively little from one decade to the next, Asian cities are constantly being turned upside down. You can rest assured that your favourite landmark in a European city – be it a cinema, a square, a building or an underground station – will still be there when you next visit; the only certainty in many Asian cities is that the furniture will once again have been rearranged so that you won't even be able to recognize the place, let alone find the landmark.[21]

Japan represents perhaps the most extreme form of this embrace of the future, or hyper-modernity.[22] Unlike Europe or the United States, you will find few old bangers on the roads, there being little demand for used cars – or anything secondhand for that matter. Instead there is a rapacious appetite for the new. Until the post-bubble crisis, Japanese car-makers thought nothing of introducing several model changes a year, rather than the Western norm of one, while the electronics firms that Japan is famous for are constantly changing their product lines. Where most of the Western fashion industry has been happy to turn out two collections a year, one in the autumn and one in the spring, Japanese designers seem to believe in continuous sartorial motion as one collection follows another at bewildering speed several times a year. Japanese youth have become the cognoscenti of fad and fashion, be it a new electronic game, a new look, the latest mobile phone or another Pokemon-style craze. Take your chair in a Japanese hair salon and, be you man or woman, you will immediately be handed a very thick catalogue offering a seemingly infinite range of possible hair-styles and colours from which to choose. Japan is the virtuoso of consumer technology. Constant improvement and innovation are a national pastime: the scooter whose lights automatically switch on as it gets dark, the business card-holder whose lid spontaneously flips open, the toilet seat with its dazzling array of dials and controls, the virtual theme park with rides beyond one's imagination, and the dance machine which renders the need for a partner redundant.

THE CONCEPT OF MODERNITY

In his book *The Consequences of Modernity*, Anthony Giddens seeks to draw a distinction between the characteristics of modernity and pre-modernity. Speaking of pre-modern society, he argues:

> The orientation to the past which is characteristic of tradition does not differ from the outlook of modernity only in being backward-looking rather than forward-looking ... Rather, neither 'the past' nor 'the future' is a discrete phenomenon, separated from the 'continuous pre-sent', as in the case of the modern outlook.[23]

In East Asian modernity, however, the present and the past are not 'discrete', in terms of perceptions, in the way Giddens suggests, nor is the future: on the contrary, the present is layered with *both* the past and the future. In other words, the past and the future are combined in East Asian modernity in a way that is quite distinct from Western modernity. It is, at one and the same time, both very young and very old. This paradox is at its most extreme in China, the oldest continuously existing polity in the world and yet now, in cities like Shanghai and Shenzhen, also one of the youngest. There is a sense of enormous ambition, a world without limits, symbolized by Pudong, one of the most futuristic cityscapes, with its extraordinary array of breathtaking high-rise buildings.[24] According to Gao Rui-qian, professor of philosophy at East China National University in Shanghai, 'China is like the adolescent who is very keen to become an adult. He can see the goal and wants to reach it as soon as possible. He is always behaving as if he is rather older than he actually is and is constantly forgetting the reality of his situation.'[25] East Asian modernity, then, is a unique combination, in terms of social and economic realities, attitudes and consciousness, of the present, the past and the future. These countries might be described as 'time-compression societies', where the past and the future are squeezed and condensed into the present. Two hundred years of experience and history elsewhere are seemingly contained within the same place and the same moment of time. Everything is rushed. There is no time to reflect. Generational differences are a gaping chasm, society like a living geological formation.

Giddens also argues that with modernity, 'Kinship relations, for the majority of the population, remain important, especially within the nuclear family, but they are no longer the carriers of intensively organized social ties across time-space.'[26] That may be true of the West but it is certainly not the case in mainland China, or Taiwan, or the Chinese diaspora: in each instance 'kinship relations', especially in the form of the extended family, are frequently 'the carriers of intensively organized social ties across time-space'. The Chinese diaspora, for example, has relied on the extended family as the means by which to organize its globally dispersed business operations, whether large or small. Taiwan, the Chinese diaspora and the more advanced parts of China are, moreover, unambiguously part of the modern world.[27] The fact is that kinship has always been far more important in Chinese than Western societies, whatever their level of development. Or take belief-systems. In his second BBC Reith Lecture in 1999, Giddens argued:

> Such views, of course, don't disappear completely with modernization. Magical notions, concepts of fate and cosmology still have a hold but mostly they continue on as superstitions, in which people only half-believe and follow in a somewhat embarrassed way.[28]

This certainly does not apply to modern Chinese societies: superstition and traditional beliefs – as we saw earlier with the worship of ancestral spirits and the prayers offered to various deities in the hope of good fortune – remain an integral part of the thinking and behaviour of most Chinese.[29]

The arrival of modernization in different parts of the world and in diverse cultures obliges us, therefore, to rethink what is meant by modernity and to recognize its diversity and plurality. We can no longer base our concept of modernity simply on the experience of North America and Europe. Our understanding of modernity is changed and expanded by the emergence of new modernities. The Chinese scholar Huang Ping argues that Chinese civilization has been so different from Western societies in so many ways that it is impossible to comprehend it, and its modernity, simply by the use of Western concepts. 'Is it not a question of whether the concepts/theories are far away from Chinese reality? China's own practice,' he concludes, 'is capable of generating alternative concepts, theories, and more convincing frameworks.'[30]

THE PRIMACY OF CULTURE

In his book *East and West*, Chris Patten, the last British governor of Hong Kong, writes: 'I find myself driven to the conclusion that what we see when we compare West and East is a consequence more of time lags than of profound cultural differences.'[31] The implication of his argument is that timing is a relatively transient question and that culture matters little. As we have seen, however, the timing and speed of industrialization and urbanization, far from being merely transient phenomena, have real and lasting effects. More fundamentally, it is a mistake to believe that cultural difference does not have a far-reaching impact on the nature of modernity. When countries are much less developed than the West – before or in the early stages of economic take-off – then it is plausible to argue that the disparities are primarily a function of their backwardness rather than any cultural difference. But the transformation of the Asian tigers, with countries like Taiwan and South Korea now at least as developed as many European nations, means that the proposition that cultural difference counts for little can now be tested in practice. The classic exemplar is post-war Japan. As we saw in Chapter 3, Japan remains, notwithstanding the fact that it is at least as advanced as the West, very different from its Western counterparts in a myriad of the most basic ways, including the nature of social relations, the modus operandi of institutions, the character of the family, the role of the state and the manner in which power is exercised. By no stretch of the imagination can Japanese modernity be described as similar to, let alone synonymous with, that of the United States or Europe.[32]

The same can be said of China. Its path towards and through modernity has been entirely different from the route followed by the West. The state is constructed in a different way and plays a different kind of role. The relationship between the present and the past is distinct, not simply because of the way in which the past bears on the process of modernization but also because, more than any other society, China is deeply aware of and influenced by its history.[33]

The long-term persistence of cultural difference is deeply rooted. In April 1998, I interviewed two Chinese-Americans in Beijing for a television programme: they had decided to go and work in China for a year, where they had never been before, to find out what it was like and to discover more about themselves. One of them, Katherine Gin, who was in her mid twenties and had spent all her life in San Francisco, made the following observation:

> I think one of the biggest differences between the Americans and the Chinese is that Americans are always trying to re-create themselves, always feel it is important to be the first person to do this or do that.

Even America as a nation is always trying to re-create itself. The Chinese rarely even ask these questions, and as a nation seem to have more of a sense of where they come from. Of course, they are changing fast, but they don't ask who they are, or constantly compare themselves with others.[34]

The irresistible conclusion is that the reason why the Chinese have a deep sense of their own identity is to be found in their long, continuous and rich history; in contrast, as products of a relatively new and young nation, Americans are in constant search of their identity.

The recognition that the Chinese exhibit certain cultural traits which can be explained by their history does not imply cultural essentialism, the idea that all nations and ethnic groups have a bundle of characteristics which remain fixed and unchanged over time. On the contrary, identities are constantly changing and being renegotiated. But that does not mean that cultural characteristics stemming from profound and very long-run influences – like climate, patterns of agriculture, language, the environment, family structure, cosmological beliefs or the longevity of history – don't persist from the past and leave their mark on the present. According to Robert Boyd and Peter J. Richerson, who have extensively researched the relationship between cultural and genetic evolution, 'an enormous amount of circumstantial evidence suggests that culturally transmitted traits are stable over time and in the face of changing environments.'[35]

THE EXTENT OF WESTERNIZATION

Walk around Taipei, the capital of Taiwan, and virtually every street name is printed in English as well as Chinese. Switch on Taiwanese television and the most popular sports are basketball and baseball. Go to a movie on Saturday night and most of them, in a country internationally renowned for its film directors, are products of Hollywood. Go window-shopping in the underground mall below People's Square in Shanghai, and many of the models used in the fashion photographs are Caucasian. Wander round the huge Ba Bai Ban department store in Pudong, and you'll probably see many banners written in English.

Many of the the top students at Shanghai's Fudan University want to do postgraduate studies at American universities or work for American multinationals in Shanghai. Middle-class Malaysians in their thirties and forties are far more likely to have visited Europe or Australia than Japan and China. Go on a shopping spree in Tokyo's fashionable Harajuka or Shibuya districts and it won't be long before you find yourself singing along to a Western pop song blaring out from a boutique or coffee shop.

I vividly recall a softly-spoken Malaysian lawyer telling me: 'I am wearing your clothes, I speak your language, I watch your films, and today is whatever date it is because you say so.'[36] Even the term 'Asia' was a European invention. Everywhere you go in the region, you feel the presence of the West. The sheer power and dynamism of Western modernity has set, and reset, the agenda for East Asia for almost two centuries. From colonialism to Hollywood, from the English language to basketball, from the solar calendar to Microsoft, from the Vietnam War to the IMF, the West has been, and is, present in the East in a way that the East has never been present in the West. Only in the form of Japan has Asian modernity, until the recent rise of China, exercised a significant impact on the West. Otherwise, the presence of the East in the West is largely confined to the mainly post-colonial migration of large numbers of Chinese, Indians, Koreans and others to North America and Europe and their consequent impact on the West in terms, first and foremost, of food, but also language, religion and culture. The constant imperative, both past and present, for Asian nations to negotiate with Western power, influence and presence – first in the era of colonialism (with every East Asian country colonized apart from Japan and Thailand) and then in the post-war era of American hegemony – constitutes a fundamental difference between East Asian and Western modernity.

This brings us to two critical questions. Firstly, to what extent have East Asian societies been influenced and shaped by Western modernity? Secondly, in the process of modernization are they becoming more Western, or less Western, or even, paradoxically, both at the same time? These questions do not lend themselves to simple answers. They vary from one society to another and from one sphere to another in any given society. History, as one would expect, affects the answers a great deal – in particular, whether or not a country was colonized, and if so when and for how long. At the one extreme lie the Philippines – first colonized by the Spanish in 1542, then by the United States in 1899, achieving independence only in 1946 – and Hong Kong, seized by the British after the First Opium War in 1842 and only returned to China in 1997; at the other lies Japan, which managed to escape colonization altogether.

In order to explore the extent of Western influence, and whether or not it is increasing, let us consider four very different examples – language, the body, food and politics.

Language

> The language that a group shares is precisely the medium in which memories of their joint history can be shared. Languages make possible both the living of a common history and the telling of it . . . Every language is learnt by the young from the old, so that every living language is the embodiment of a tradition.[37]

Languages are not simply a means of communication, but embody and articulate a culture. To lose one's language – and thousands of languages are likely to become extinct over the course of this century as they did in the last – is also to lose, in very large measure, one's culture. As Hung Tze Jan, the successful Taiwanese publisher, puts it:

> Language is essential to form an idea – as long as you keep your unique language, you keep your way of creating ideas, your way of thinking. The traditions are kept in the language. Language was an obstacle to us going out, but it also prevented others getting inside. Language was our Great Wall.[38]

East Asia is home to almost half the top twenty most widely spoken languages in the world today.[39] Unlike the European languages, which were essentially spread by overseas conquest (the reason why the number of English, Spanish or Portuguese speakers now greatly exceeds the population of the countries they originated from), East Asian languages have grown organically in their densely populated,

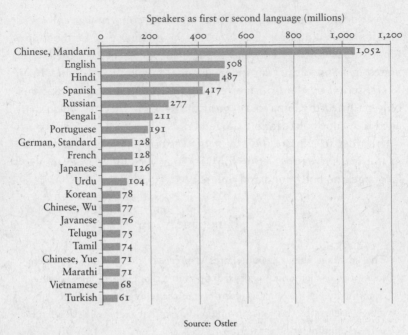

Speakers as first or second language (millions)

Language	Speakers
Chinese, Mandarin	1,052
English	508
Hindi	487
Spanish	417
Russian	277
Bengali	211
Portuguese	191
German, Standard	128
French	128
Japanese	126
Urdu	104
Korean	78
Chinese, Wu	77
Javanese	76
Telugu	75
Tamil	74
Chinese, Yue	71
Marathi	71
Vietnamese	68
Turkish	61

Source: Ostler

Figure 12. The world's top twenty languages.

rice-growing homelands, as a result of demographic trends and/or land-based territorial expansion. They are spoken overseas overwhelmingly as a result of migration and consequently only on a relatively small scale. Mandarin is the most widely spoken language in the world, far exceeding English, but the vast majority of Mandarin speakers live in China; English, by contrast, has flown the nest.

The spread of English since 1945, driven by the global pre-eminence of the United States, has not affected the popularity of the main East Asian languages in their homelands. Not only has English failed to weaken or displace the main North-East Asian languages (Mandarin, Japanese and Korean), the languages themselves have also been relatively little touched by it. Japanese, it is true, has acquired many English loanwords, mainly nouns, but this reflects the typically Japanese way of adding foreign elements to their culture while leaving the Japanese core fundamentally untouched and unaffected.[40] It is fashionable in Japan – as elsewhere in the region – to wear T-shirts bearing an English phrase, or to have shops with English names, or to see advertising with English slogans, but this has no bearing on the extent to which the Japanese speak, or even desire to speak, English. Despite an enormous cohort of English teachers and many years of compulsory English at school, the vast majority of Japanese are unable to speak English with either enthusiasm or facility.[41] Like the English, they remain linguistically insular and unembarrassed by the fact. The Chinese, on the other hand, have become hugely enthusiastic learners of English during the last decade or so and many young educated Chinese speak the language with impressive fluency. One teacher, Li Yang, who runs an operation called 'Crazy English', has taken to conducting his classes in huge stadiums with over 20,000 all chanting English phrases in unison. The number of English speakers in China has been rising rapidly ever since English was made a compulsory subject in primary schools. Indeed, it has been estimated that China may already have more English speakers than India (where in excess of 5% of the population speaks English).[42] But this Chinese enthusiasm for English in no way reflects a decline in the popularity of Chinese. On the contrary, English remains strictly a second language, acquired for the purpose of conversing with foreigners, an interlocutor language for the young, well-educated and ambitious urban elite. Chinese, unlike Japanese, possesses relatively few English loanwords – or indeed loanwords from any language – and relatively little external structural influence. It has been influenced by the rise of English, for example, in the greater use of polysyllabic words, but only in a limited way:[43] a proposal, several decades ago, to romanize Chinese by replacing characters with Pinyin transliteration came to nothing.[44]

We should not be surprised by the continuing strength and resilience of Chinese. It is a language that dates back over three thousand years. Its pictographic writing system is shared by all the various Chinese – or Sinitic – languages, including Mandarin, Cantonese, Wu and Min: over 70 per cent of Chinese, well over 800 million people, speak just one of those languages, namely Mandarin (also known as Putonghua), and the number is steadily rising as a result of the growing influence of television and the education system.[45] The fact that all Chinese languages and dialects share the same written script, even

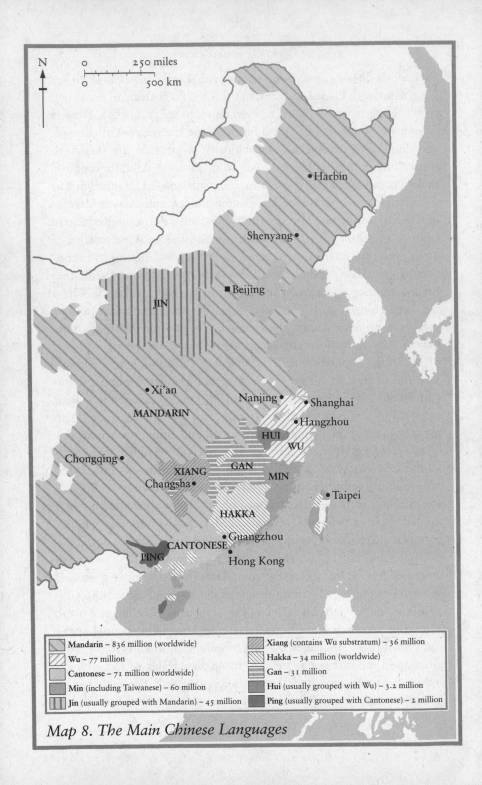

N

0 ——— 250 miles
0 ——— 500 km

• Harbin

• Shenyang

■ Beijing

JIN

• Xi'an

MANDARIN

Nanjing •   • Shanghai

• Hangzhou

HUI

WU

Chongqing •

XIANG   GAN

Changsha •   MIN

• Taipei

HAKKA

CANTONESE   • Guangzhou

PING

Hong Kong

Mandarin – 836 million (worldwide)	**Xiang** (contains Wu substratum) – 36 million
Wu – 77 million	**Hakka** – 34 million (worldwide)
Cantonese – 71 million (worldwide)	**Gan** – 31 million
Min (including Taiwanese) – 60 million	**Hui** (usually grouped with Wu) – 3.2 million
Jin (usually grouped with Mandarin) – 45 million	**Ping** (usually grouped with Cantonese) – 2 million

Map 8. The Main Chinese Languages

though they are often unintelligible to each other as spoken (being comparable in their diversity to the Romance languages), has been extremely important in maintaining a wider sense of Chinese identity. Chinese managed to survive long periods of foreign occupation by the Mongols and Manchu; although both spoke different languages, they not only failed to impose them on the Chinese, but ended up being linguistically assimilated themselves. The influence of Chinese on the neighbouring but different languages of Japanese, Korean and Vietnamese has been immense. Each originally developed writing systems for their own languages by transforming or adding Chinese characters – known as *hanja* and *kanji* in the Korean and Japanese writing systems respectively. Even though these languages are quite different in linguistic structure from Chinese, such was the prestige of ancient Chinese scholarship that, over time, they became replete with Chinese vocabulary and have remained so ever since. Those who speak Chinese often refer to it as *zhongguohuo*, or 'centre realm speech': Sino-centrism, or what I will describe later as the Middle Kingdom mentality, even extends to how the Chinese perceive their language. Chinese has even managed to survive the onslaught of the alphabetic age, though in reality, of course, it would be well-nigh impossible to create an alphabetic language which could act as the writing system of so many different Chinese languages and a fifth of the world's population.[46]

The only East Asian countries in which English has acquired a central role are Hong Kong and Singapore, where it is an official language; Malaysia, where it is very widely spoken although the official language is Bahasa Malaysia; and the Philippines, where English is still an official language alongside Tagalog. Apart from the Philippines, which was an American colony, these are all former British colonies. The popularity of English in Singapore and Malaysia owes much to the fact that – as in India – it has acted as a useful common language in a highly multiracial and multilingual environment. In the Philippines, English is used as a language of instruction in schools (from the age of twelve) in what is a complex linguistic archipelago, with Tagalog coexisting with many island dialects. The main language of Indonesia – a patchwork quilt of hundreds of languages – is Bahasa

Indonesia, with the old colonial language, Dutch, now insignificant. Similarly, in Vietnam, Cambodia and Laos, all former French colonies, French, once the official language in administration and education, has long since faded into relative obscurity.

This brings us to a further question. To what extent is English now permanently established as the global second language of choice?[47] It has been steadily strengthening its position in this respect more or less everywhere, often rapidly, with East Asia no exception. At an ASEAN (Association of South-East Asian Nations) meeting, or an international academic conference in Beijing, English is likely to be the main, or one of the main, languages of the proceedings. Throughout the region, there is a very strong desire to learn English.[48] There are several reasons why it is believed that the position English has acquired is unlikely to be reversed. Very considerable amounts of both social and personal capital have already been invested around the world in its acquisition and use, which constitute a powerful reason for its continuation and extension. English has established itself as the dominant language of a global media whose influence and penetration is likely to continue to grow.[49] The global importance of the United States ensures that English will remain the foremost language in most fields, from international business and science to the internet and diplomacy. Finally, as the vehicle for the promotion and transmission of the values and norms of a culture, the Anglo-Saxon world has a major vested interest in ensuring the perpetuation of English as the lingua franca, which provides it with considerable economic, political and cultural benefits.[50]

Although English enjoys a formidable battery of such assets, these do not render its position impregnable. The international penetration of a language is closely linked to the power and influence of its major patron. The United States may still be globally hegemonic, but, as we saw in Chapter 1, its relative global economic position is being eroded, and this is bound to impact on the fortunes of English in the longer term. English's dominant position on the internet is already under serious challenge and will certainly not be sustained even in the relatively short run, with the number of Chinese users now exceeding those in the United States.[51] Although English remains the overwhelmingly dominant language of the global media, this situation is unlikely to continue indefinitely as new non-Western players enter the global media market and the main Western providers increasingly use local languages as a means of expanding their market. This process, in fact, is already well under way. Al-Jazeera, the independent Qatar-based Arab news channel, for example, broadcasts in multiple languages, as does the Indian-owned Zee TV, while Star TV in East Asia and Phoenix TV in China (the former owned by Murdoch and the latter similarly until recently), broadcast in local languages as well as English.[52] Finally, while English has enjoyed a privileged position with new technology – especially in computing – the growing diversification of technological innovation, together with the fact that computers are now able to support a large range of languages, means that English's hitherto preponderant position in this field is by no means assured.[53]

The position of English as the global lingua franca, which is a very recent development, could therefore prove to be a relatively transient phenomenon. It is not difficult to imagine English's dominance slowly being eroded and replaced by a rather more diverse scenario. As China's influence grows in East Asia, Mandarin is becoming more widely spoken, not just by Chinese around the region, but also, as a second language, by other nationalities and ethnic groups. Mandarin is being offered as an optional or compulsory language at schools in a growing number of countries, including Thailand and South Korea, and is increasingly regarded as the language of the future. In a much weaker manner, this trend can also be seen in North America and Europe. As China becomes the economic centre of East Asia, a process already well under way (as we shall see in Chapter 9), there is a compelling reason why Japanese, Koreans, Vietnamese, Thais, Indonesians and Malaysians – to name but a few – should want to speak Mandarin. The other main languages of North-East Asia – Japanese, Korean and Vietnamese – moreover have far more in common with Chinese, from which they are partially derived, than they do with English.[54] It seems entirely possible, even likely, that in fifty years' time Chinese will have replaced, or at least joined, English as an interlocutor language in the region. If that happens, it will be the first time in China's modern history that the most widely spoken language in the world will also have acquired the status of a major second language outside its own borders.

As far as language is concerned, then, it would be quite wrong to see East Asia as subject to a one-way process of growing Westernization. The old imperial European languages, with the exception of English, are now of only marginal significance. The region's main languages remain as influential as ever in their homelands. English has, and is, greatly strengthening its position as the dominant second language, but there are reasons to doubt whether this will continue indefinitely, especially given the decline of the United States and the rise of China, with its implications for the popularity of Mandarin.[55] I will discuss the rise of Mandarin more fully in Chapter 11.

The Body

The body – by which I mean here its physical characteristics, especially skin colour, together with style of dress – tells a very different story. The influence of the West in these respects has been profound, especially in North-East Asia, and, to a lesser extent, South-East Asia. In Japan, South Korea, China, Taiwan and Hong Kong, everyday dress as worn by both men and women is highly Westernized – namely, the wearing of trousers, shirts, suits, jeans, T-shirts, skirts, blouses and dresses, for example – with traditional clothes, especially in Chinese societies, almost completely confined to relatively ceremonial occasions like weddings. The reason for the virtual disappearance of traditional attire is not obvious; after all, it has not happened in India, where the *sari* and *salwar-kameez* (Punjabi suit) for women and the *kurta-pajama* (loose top and trousers) and *bund-gala* (jacket) for men, for instance, remain ubiquitous, notwithstanding the fact that Western styles of dress are common, especially in the 'new economy' urban centres like Bangalore. Indeed, there is plenty of evidence that men and women in India are gravitating back towards traditional styles of dress.[56]

In Japan, Western dress began to spread after the Meiji Restoration. Western clothes were worn by government servants and at official ceremonies, but it was not until much later that they became popular amongst ordinary people. During wartime austerity between 1930 and 1945, simplified Japanese clothes replaced the kimono, which came to be seen as impractical. During the American occupation after the war, a period of large-scale Westernization, many people switched directly from wartime clothing to Western dress. Starting around 1960, Western dress became the preferred choice of the great majority of Japanese, with the kimono largely reserved for special occasions and, in simplified form (especially for men), for relaxing at home. The traditional kimono has far from disappeared, however. On Sundays it remains a common sight in Japanese cities and is also worn by women at weddings, rites-of-passage ceremonies and funerals. It has become a working uniform in restaurants and hotels.[57]

The Western-style dress now preferred by the Japanese retains important elements of national individuality. One example is the ubiquitous soft hat with round brim much favoured as casual wear by Japanese women. The choice of dress and footwear is also influenced by the fact that the Japanese are relatively small. Young Japanese women dress with a marked femininity, reflecting the conservative gender roles that still characterize Japanese society. For men and women alike, in dress as in so much else, there is also a strong group mentality, with less stress on individualism than is the case in the West. Thus, up to a point, there is a distinctive Japanese look, as exemplified by the *kawaii* child-woman cuteness, a girlie look which has also enjoyed some popularity outside Japan.[58] The three most famous Japanese design houses – Comme des Garçons, Yohji Yamamoto and Issey Miyake – all of which arrived on the global fashion scene in the 1970s – lie broadly within the Western tradition. However, they demonstrate a marked distinctiveness in comparison with European and American designers. Although each is very different, they are all distinguished by a strong emphasis on materials, the use of sombre and austere colours, a greater willingness to play with the boundaries, and an extremely rapid cycle of collections, although, since the introduction of 'fast fashion' by Inditex and H&M, this is no longer novel to Japan. While Western fashion is preoccupied with clothes that reveal and emphasize the female form, for these designers the shape of the body and the display of flesh are of much less concern. Indeed, Comme des Garçons' Rei Kawakubo avoids representing the body as overtly sexual. Collectively they can be seen as representing a modestly distinctive Japanese sartorial aesthetic within a global fashion world which remains Western-dominated.[59]

The Chinese story is different from the Japanese but ends up in a rather similar place. For thousands of years, Chinese dress was deeply entwined with social hierarchy, being one of its more important and visible expressions. Only the emperor, for example, was allowed to wear yellow; his sons were required to wear golden yellow, while nobles wore blue-black.[60] As Valerie Steele and John S. Major write:

> Clothing was considered a matter of great importance in ancient China. It was an instrument of the magical aura of power through which the emperor ruled the world: in addition, it served to distinguish the civilized from the barbarous, the male from the female, the high from the base, the proper from the improper – in short, it was an instrument of order in a society dedicated to hierarchy, harmony and moderation.[61]

It is not surprising, therefore, that the 1911 Revolution, which overthrew dynastic rule, was also the occasion for a sartorial revolution. The demise of the Qing court led to the dissolution of the old rules. Foot-binding for women, which had persisted for a thousand years, disappeared as did the tradition of male queues (hair worn in a long ponytail), which had been introduced by the Manchu. Chinese dress had been the subject of growing Western influence after the Opium Wars and the establishment of the treaty ports, but the rise of nationalism after 1911 made Western dress more problematic for both sexes.[62] The result was a hybrid, the most famous example being the woman's *qipao*, better known in the West as the cheongsam, which combined Chinese, Manchu and Western elements, and which became indelibly associated with Shanghai in the 1930s. Its heyday was between 1930 and 1950, though it persisted for rather longer amongst the overseas Chinese, especially in Hong Kong.[63]

The 1949 Revolution ushered in a new sartorial era. The Communist regime regarded the old styles of Chinese dress as a relic of the feudal past. In their place, the regime encouraged an egalitarian mode of dress that was loosely based around the Sun Yat-sen uniform, wrongly described in the West as the Mao suit. The Sun Yat-sen uniform, featuring a high-collared tunic, was, like the *qipao*, a hybrid style, and drew on Japanese, German and Soviet military influences. The ubiquitous Maoist style of dress, in contrast, was partly inspired by the traditional trousers, tunic and black cotton shoes of the Chinese peasant. There were no government edicts concerning dress, but the new Maoist style clearly reflected the egalitarian principles of the regime, as well as the poverty of the country.[64] Only after 1978 did this state of affairs slowly begin to change to the point where Chinese cities are now overwhelmingly dominated by Western-style dress.[65] The Maoist style of dress has almost entirely disappeared, as has the Sun Yat-sen uniform previously worn by government officials, which has largely been replaced by the Western suit. The only element of traditional Chinese dress that persists amongst ordinary people is the Chinese jacket, which still remains popular, especially amongst the old. Trousers are very widely worn by women, more so than in the West, which is in part a continuation of a much older Chinese tradition, trousers never having had the masculine connotation they once did in the West.[66] Otherwise there is little evidence of traditional Chinese dress, in either traditional or modernized form, for men or women, though it is conceivable this may change. The only exception is a relatively recent revival of the *quipao* amongst waitresses and hotel staff.

Various designers have sought to reintroduce traditional themes into modern Chinese dress. The best known example is David Tang's Shanghai Tang label, but it has experienced only limited success, the clothes in its shops mainly being bought by Westerners. Blanc de Chine, another Hong Kong firm, has similar ambitions, as does Shiatzy Chen in Taipei. Designers like Vivienne Tam, Amy Chan and Anna Sui – based mainly in the West – have also explored the use of Chinese elements in their designs. Notwithstanding these efforts, the striking feature of modern Chinese dress – certainly in contrast to India – is how Westernized it is and how little it incorporates traditional Chinese elements.[67] Over the last decade, meanwhile, various features, such as the distinctive Chinese-style collar and buttons, have become increasingly conspicuous in Western women's fashion, reflecting the growing influence of, and interest in, a Chinese aesthetic.[68] In addition, the enhanced importance of the East Asian market has also led to a small rise in the use of models from the region in Western fashion.[69]

Why have the Japanese and Chinese so comprehensively abandoned their sartorial traditions? Clearly the influence of Western modernity – in this case primarily European – has extended to what people choose to wear. If people want to be modern they feel they must dress in a Western way: Western dress is the sartorial badge of modernity. Another frequently offered explanation is practicality: traditional forms of dress are seen as largely impractical for modern living. But that does not explain why traditional elements have not found expression in a popularized and modernized form: that is what, after all, has happened with the relentlessly innovative tradition of Western dress. Long dresses and petticoats, doublets and breeches, top hats and tails, have all disappeared, along with much else, but the Western tradition of dress thrives and prospers. Interestingly, in the Japanese case, traditional (and simplified) forms of dress never came to be regarded as fundamental to the Japanese way of life, or Japanese 'realm',[70] as Kosaku Yoshino puts it, in contrast to language, food, sake and tatami mats, for example, which were. Dress was one of the elements that the Japanese were prepared to forsake and see Westernized as part of the process of post-Meiji modernization. In the Chinese case, traditional forms of dress were condemned to virtual extinction by their association with the old dynastic order. After 1978, it proved to be a relatively short sartorial journey from the ubiquitous style of dress of the Maoist era to the Western styles of today. Here, it would appear, is another, albeit perhaps surprising, example of Maoism paving the way for modernization.

A similar picture of Western influence holds throughout North-East Asia, including South Korea and Taiwan. Much the same is true of most of South-East Asia as well. The main exception is Malaysia (and to a lesser extent Indonesia), where a majority of Malay women now cover their head with the *tudung* (headscarf) and wear the *baju kurung* (a Malay style of dress consisting of sarong and upper tunic).

Given the context of rapid urbanization and a highly multiracial environment, this represents a strong statement of cultural identity. In part
the style is a return to Malay tradition, but it is also an appropriation
of various Islamic traditions, which have been given a distinctively
Malay flavour by the use of strikingly bold colours:[71] Malays have a
highly developed sense of fashion, certainly when compared with
Indian and especially Chinese Malaysians, with their somewhat drab
mimicry of Western dress codes.

If Western dress has been widely adopted in China, Japan and elsewhere for the reasons outlined, why has this not been the case in
India, or amongst Malay women, for example? It would seem that in
both instances religion has played a crucial role in sustaining traditional forms of dress. A distinctive feature of both China and Japan
– and North-East Asia generally – is the lack of any strong tradition
of organized religion. This contrasts markedly with India, where Hinduism and to a lesser extent Islam, for example, exercise an extremely
important cultural influence. In both, dress plays at least two roles:
first, it is a reflection of religious teaching, not least in the rules
governing gender dressing, and second, it may act as a means of
distinguishing followers of a religion from others. Both these considerations, for example, apply to Malay women and also to Punjabi
men, with their uncut hair and turban. Religion has proved a formidable obstacle to Western-style dress in South Asia, whereas in China
and Japan it barely constitutes a factor in dress codes.

Tokyo fashion shows use many white, as well as Japanese, models but
rarely anyone of darker skin. Comme des Garçons only ever uses
white models at its shows.[72] White models are common at Hong Kong
fashion week, along with Chinese, but there are rarely, if ever, black or
brown models. The local fashion magazines – which are often local-
ized editions of Western magazines like *Vogue* or *Elle* – carry text in
the vernacular but the models are nevertheless overwhelmingly
white.[73] A majority of fashion advertising in Hong Kong – though no
longer in Japan – uses white (rather than Chinese) models, as does
Giordano, the local equivalent of Gap; black or brown models are
never to be seen. A walk around the underground shopping mall

beneath People's Square in central Shanghai paints a not dissimilar picture: the advertising mainly features Chinese models but there are plenty of Caucasians and never anyone of darker skin. In India, on the other hand, the models on the catwalks and in the fashion magazines are overwhelmingly Indian, usually of fair complexion.[74]

In an interview with Yang Qingqing, a beauty expert and cult figure amongst Shanghai women, I sought to understand the profusion of white models and the total absence of models with darker skin.

> Chinese culture is very open. We can accept things from outside. When we look at a foreigner we will be more tolerant of their beauty. But if they are Chinese we will be more critical. Maybe distance generates an appreciation of beauty, that's why we like Western features.[75]

Despite my best efforts, she refused to be drawn on why this apparent openness did not include women of darker skin. Mei Ling, a Taiwanese beauty expert who advises Max Factor and acts as a consultant to Chinese pop singers and film stars, was altogether more forthcoming:

> In Hong Kong, Taiwan and the mainland, Chinese girls like white skin products. They think white is beautiful. People have a dream and it is about the West. We are yellow, but we don't want to be. For Max Factor, Lancôme and the rest, every season it is the same colour – white. It is very boring. We try and sell them a new colour each season, but they just want white. Asians like white skin. For seventy years – the period of make-up – the choice has always been the same – white. Because of the shape of the Chinese face – a small nose, high cheek bones, narrow eyes and absence of facial hair – skin is more important to the Chinese than to Westerners.[76]

There is a huge demand for such whitening products amongst Chinese, Japanese and Korean women and they dominate cosmetic advertising on television and in the press.[77] It is estimated that the Japanese market for whitening products was worth $5.6 billion in 2001, with China (the fastest growing market) valued at $1.3 billion. Much of the advertising aimed at Asian women by Western cosmetic companies uses images and narratives with implicit references to the aesthetic 'inferiority' of the 'dark' and 'yellow' skin tones of Asian women.[78] It is not unusual to see Chinese and Japanese women smothered in white foundation cream and looking – to Western eyes – somewhat ghostly. The racial subtext of all this is clear: black is repellent, yellow is undesirable and white is good. The desire for whiteness takes other forms. On a sunny day in China, Japan, Singapore and elsewhere, it is very common to see Chinese or Japanese women using parasols and umbrellas to shield themselves from the sun; they do not want to have tanned skin.[79]

The Japanese have long sought to distinguish themselves from other races in East Asia, especially the Chinese. In manga comics and animation films, the Japanese portray themselves in a highly Westernized manner, with big (sometimes blue) eyes, brightly coloured – even blond – hair and white skin, even though black hair, narrow brown eyes and a yellowish skin are more or less universal.[80] Generally lighter than the Chinese, they like to see themselves as white; certainly not yellow, which is how they perceive the Chinese and Koreans. For both the Japanese and the Chinese, black skin has a highly negative connotation and it is not uncommon to see black people portrayed in a derogatory way.[81] A popular advert for San Miguel beer in Hong Kong around 2000 featured a black person as little more than an imbecile. According to Mei Ling, 'They don't like to see black skin, only white skin, in the make-up catalogues that I am responsible for compiling.'[82] A senior executive for one of the top American film studios told me that there was little demand in the region for Hollywood films or TV series with black stars. The most popular look on Japanese and Chinese television and film might best be described as Eurasian – Japanese or Chinese with Western features. Jackie Chan is a case in point. For both Japanese and Chinese women, white boyfriends can enjoy a certain cachet, but the same is certainly not true of black or brown partners: they are an extremely rare sight and any such decision would require great courage.

The Western form – above all, skin colour, the defining signifier, but also other Caucasian features such as fair hair, large eyes and height – has had a profound and enduring impact on East Asian societies over the last two hundred years. It is something that is rarely commented upon and yet it is more pervasive, more psychologically far-reaching, and more fundamental in terms of identity, than most questions normally discussed in this context. For a Japanese to look in the mirror and wish to see a white person, or to emphasize those features which resemble those of a Caucasian – not easy given the profound physical differences between the two – is a powerful statement of self-image, of how a person feels about him or herself, of their sense of place in the world. It is not uncommon for the Japanese to feel physically inadequate in comparison with Westerners, complementing the sense of national inferiority and insecurity discussed in Chapter 3. Chinese can harbour similar emotions about their physical appearance, though this is much less common than amongst the Japanese.

It would be wrong to regard the predilection in East Asia for whiteness, however, as simply a product of Western influence. The desire to be white also has powerful indigenous roots. For both the Japanese and Chinese, whiteness has long carried a strong class connotation. If you are dark, it means you work on the land and are of a lower order; such a prejudice is deeply embedded in their respective national psyches and has been accentuated by modernization and urbanization, with white a symbol of urban living and prosperity and brown a metaphor for the countryside and poverty. Perceptions of different skin colours are used to define and reinforce national differences, as well as relations between races in the same country, and even between different shades within the same race. Since the Meiji Restoration, skin colour has been used by the Japanese to distinguish them from their Chinese and Korean neighbours. More widely, this hierarchy of colour is reproduced in the relationship between the fairer North-East Asia and the darker South-East Asia, and within South-East Asia between the indigenous population, the Chinese diaspora and the smaller Indian diaspora, for instance. More or less everywhere in East Asia, skin colour is a highly sensitive subject that arouses powerful feelings, perceptions and prejudices, with a near-universal desire to be fairer. The power of the Western racial model is precisely that it reinforces and interacts with very long-established indigenous views about colour. I will return to these themes in Chapter 8 in the context of China.

Food

It is fashionable to cite the spread of McDonald's in East Asia as a sign of growing Westernization. In 2008 there were 950 McDonald's stores in China (the first being opened in Shenzhen in 1990) and in 2004 there were approximately 3,500 in Japan and 300 in Malaysia. Starbucks, Kentucky Fried Chicken and Pizza Hut also have numerous outlets in the region: in 2008 KFC had more than 2,200 stores in China and in 2006 Pizza Hut had 140. A 1999 memo on fast food by McCann Erickson, which handled the advertising account in China for McDonald's, set out its appeal as follows:

> It's about modernity. The fast-food restaurant is a symbol of having made it. The new 'Western' fast-food restaurants (though predominantly the Golden Arches) become status symbol locations for the new middle class. It becomes initially their link with showing that they can live the Western (read usually 'American') lifestyle.[83]

The combined total of all US fast food stores, however, represents a very tiny fraction of the restaurants and eating places in these countries. They may attract a great deal of publicity, certainly in the West, but this gives a distorted picture of eating habits in East Asia. The overwhelming majority of people continue to consume the food indigenous to their country. Almost everyone taking lunch or dinner in Beijing or Chongqing will invariably eat Chinese food; the same can be said of the Japanese. Western fast food – including the most popular Western fast food of all, the sandwich – lives at the margins of mass eating habits. Nor do Western-style eateries enjoy a monopoly of the idea of fast food. On the contrary, Chinese and Japanese fast food restaurants – familiar to Westerners in the guise of sushi bars and noodle bars, for example – are hugely more common.

In his seminal study *Food in Chinese Culture*, K. C. Chang suggests that 'the importance of food in understanding human culture lies precisely in its infinite variability – variability that is not essential for species survival.'[84] People from different cultures eat very differently; even within the same culture there is usually considerable variation.[85] Furthermore, people display enormous attachment towards the food that they have been brought up on and with which they are intimately familiar. The instincts are tribal: in the food hall at the National University of Singapore, I was struck by how the Chinese students ate Chinese food, the Indians ate Indian, and the Malays ate Malay, with little crossover. The same can be said in the West: we might like the occasional Indian, Chinese or Mexican meal, usually heavily adapted for the local palate, but our staple diet is Western – breakfast, lunch and dinner.

At the centre of East Asia's food tradition, as with language, is China, which enjoys one of the world's most sophisticated food cultures, with an extremely long documented history, probably at least as long as that of any other food tradition.[86] Chinese cuisine, like all food cultures, has been shaped by the ingredients available and China has been particularly rich in the diversity of its plant life. Since ingredients are not the same everywhere, Chinese food acquired an indigenous character simply by virtue of those used.[87] Given the country's size and population, there are, not surprisingly, huge regional variations in the character of Chinese food; indeed, it is more appropriate to speak of Chinese cuisines rather than a single tradition, with four schools often identified, namely Shandong, Sichuan, Jiangsu and Guangdong; and sometimes eight, with the addition of Hunan, Fujian, Anhui and Zhejiang; or even ten, with the further addition of Beijing and Shanghai.[88] From very early on, Chinese cuisine incorporated foreign foodstuffs – for example, wheat, sheep and goat from Western Asia in the earliest times, Indonesian spices in the fifth century, and maize and sweet potato from North America from the early seventeenth century – all of which helped to shape the food tradition.[89] The preparation of Chinese food involves, at its heart, a fundamental division between *fan* – grains and other starch foods – and *ts'ai* – vegetable and meat dishes. A balanced meal must involve the requisite amount of *fan* and *ts'ai*.

The Chinese way of eating is characterized by flexibility and adaptability, a function of the knowledge the Chinese have acquired about their wild plant resources. When threatened by poor harvests and famine, people would explore anything edible in order to stay alive. Many strange ingredients such as wood ears and lily buds, and delicacies such as shark fins, were discovered in this way and subsequently became an integral part of the Chinese diet. Chinese cuisine is also abundantly rich in preserved foods, another consequence of the need to find a means of survival during famines and the bleak winters of northern China.[90] The Chinese attitude towards food is intimately bound up with the notion of health and the importance of eating healthily, the underlying principles of which, based on the yin–yang distinction, are specific to Chinese culture.[91] Arguably few cultures are as food-orientated as the Chinese, who, whether rich or poor, take food extremely seriously, more so even than the French.[92] For thousands of years food has occupied a pivotal position in Chinese life. The importance of the kitchen in the emperor's palace is amply demonstrated by the personnel roster recorded in *Zhou li* (the chronicle, or rites, of the Zhou dynasty, which ruled 1046–256 BC). Out of almost 4,000 people who had the responsibility of running the emperor's residential quarters, 2,271 of them handled food and wine.[93] While a standard greeting in English is 'How are you?' the Chinese equivalent is not infrequently 'Have you eaten?' K. C. Chang suggests that 'the Chinese have shown inventiveness in [food] perhaps for the simple reason that food and eating are among things central to the Chinese way of life and part of the Chinese ethos.'[94] Jacques Gernet argues, with less restraint, that 'there is no doubt that in this sphere China has shown a greater inventiveness than any other civilization.'[95]

To this picture we should add Chinese tea. No one is quite sure when tea-drinking in China began. It was already highly developed during the Tang dynasty (AD 618–907) but it certainly dates back much earlier than that. Chinese tea culture is as sophisticated, multifarious, discerning and serious as European wine culture. A traditional tea-house has no equivalent in Western culture; the diversity of teas on offer is bewildering, the ways of preparing and imbibing are intricate, the rituals elaborate, and the surroundings often fine. Although coffee is becoming more popular, tea remains overwhelmingly the national drink.[96] With the growing appetite for things Chinese, it seems likely that Chinese tea-houses will become a common sight in many Western cities before too long.

It seems faintly absurd, therefore, to suggest that Chinese food (or drink, indeed) is being Westernized by the likes of McDonald's. Of course, Chinese food has been influenced by the West, for example in terms of ingredients, but the impact has been very limited. The exceptional attachment of the Chinese to their food – in contrast to some other aspects of their culture, like clothing and architecture,[97] which they have been largely prepared to relinquish – is illustrated by the fact that overseas Chinese communities, from South-East Asia to North America, continue to eat Chinese food as their main diet.[98]

Japanese food has been subject to rather greater Western influence. Japan abounds with homespun, Western-based food, much of which was invented in the wake of the Meiji Restoration. The Japanese elite sought to imitate French cuisine in the late nineteenth century, and after the First World War Western dishes began to enter middle-class kitchens, albeit in a highly indigenized form. Essentially, foreign dishes were accommodated into the Japanese meal pattern as side dishes – thereby also mimicking the ways in which Japanese society accepted, and also cordoned off, foreign influences more generally.[99] According to Katarzyna Cwiertka:

> The basic rules concerning the blending of Japanese and Western food-stuffs, seasonings, and cooking techniques were set around the third decade of the twentieth century and have continued to be followed to this day, as Japanese cooks carry on with the adaptation of foreign elements into the Japanese context. Some combinations catch on to eventually become integral parts of the Japanese diet. Others are rejected, but they may reappear again a few decades later, advocated as new and fashionable.[100]

While the languages of East Asia are still overwhelmingly spoken within the region but not outside, this is not true of its food. Poor migrants have taken their food with them – Chinese restaurants, for example, have been the mainstay business of Chinese migrants, certainly in the early decades of settlement, as any Chinatown in the world will testify. While European food had only a limited impact on

East Asia, mainly as a result of colonialism, reverse migration, from East Asia to the West, much of it over the last forty years, has enjoyed far greater culinary influence. Chinese, Japanese, Vietnamese, Thai, Korean and Malaysian restaurants – and, of course, Indian – have become a familiar sight in the West.[101] Over the last twenty-five years, Japanese food has become very popular on the West Coast of the United States, leading to the creation of new Japanese-American hybrid dishes like the California roll.[102]

Rather than the Westernization of East Asian eating habits, it would be more appropriate to speak of the reverse, the Asianization of the Western diet. The reason has much to do with migration but is also a consequence of the sheer richness and quality of many cuisines in the region when compared with the great majority of their counterparts in Europe and North America. Take the case of Britain, the world's greatest colonizer, whose own food culture can only be described, in its contemporary state, as impoverished and threadbare (with the honourable exception of its puddings). The vacuum that was British cuisine after the Second World War has largely been filled by a myriad of foreign influences, in the first instance European, especially Italian and French, but also Asian, notably Indian and Chinese. As a consequence, its cuisine has become a hybrid: in the realm of food, Britain mirrors the characteristics of a developing country, retaining something of its own while borrowing extensively from elsewhere. The same can be said of the United States, though it started life as a European hybrid in the first place. All cuisines in the era of globalization, of course, are becoming more hybrid, but the extent of this should not be exaggerated. In East Asia food remains essentially indigenous and only hybrid at the margins, with the obvious exception of a multiracial country like Malaysia, where there has been enormous cross-fertilization in food between the Malays, Chinese and Indians, resulting in a very distinctive national cuisine.

Politics and Power

It has been widely assumed in the West that all political systems are gravitating, or at least over time will gravitate, towards a similar kind of polity, one characterized by Western-style democracy. There is also a view, based on a belief in the universal relevance of Western history, experience and practice, that power is exercised, or should be exercised, in broadly the same way everywhere. In fact, the nature of political power differs widely from one society to another.[103] Rather than speaking of a political system – with its abstract, machine-like connotations – it is more fruitful to think in terms of a political culture. The reason for this is simple: politics is rooted in, and specific to, each culture. It is, moreover, profoundly parochial. A businessman may ply his trade and skills across many different national borders, a renowned academic can lecture at universities all around the world, but a politician's gift, in terms of building a popular basis of support and the exercise of power, is rooted narrowly and specifically in the national: the skills and charisma don't travel in the same way, they are crafted and chiselled for the local audience, shaped by the intimate details of the national culture. Of course, particular leaders of major nations may be admired and appreciated across national boundaries, as Margaret Thatcher was in the 1980s, and Barack Obama has been, and Vladimir Putin was, interestingly, in China in the noughties, but that is an entirely different matter from building a domestic base and governing a particular country.

There is a profound difference between the nature of power in Western societies and East Asian societies. In the former, it is driven by the quest for individual autonomy and identity. At the centre of East Asian culture – both North-East Asian (in other words Confucian-based culture) and South-East Asian – is the individual's desire for a group, and especially family, identity: the individual finds affirmation and recognition not in their own individual identity but in being part of a group; it is through the membership of a group that an individual finds security and meaning. Further, Western governance rests, in theory at least, on the notion of utility: that government is required to deliver certain benefits to the electorate in return for their support. East Asian polities are different. Historically the function of government in East Asia has been more opaque, with, in contrast to the West, a separation between the concepts of power and responsibility: it was believed that there were limits to what a government could achieve, that other forces largely beyond human control determined outcomes, and that the relationship between cause and effect was complex and elusive. Rather than being based on utility, power was seen as an end value in itself, as intimately bound up with the collective well-being of society. Government had an essentially paternalistic role and the people saw themselves in a relationship of dependency. Although, under the pressures of modernization and economic growth, societies have been obliged to become more utilitarian – as the idea of the developmental state suggests – the traditional ways of thinking about government remain very strong.[104] This is reflected in the persistence of paternalistic one-party government in many states in the region, even where, as in Japan, Malaysia and Singapore, there are regular elections.

Although these generalizations apply to both South-East and North-East Asia, there are marked differences between the two. Here I will concentrate on the Confucian-based societies of China, Japan, Korea, Taiwan and Vietnam. The Chinese were extremely unusual in that from very early on they came to see government in primarily secular terms. Rather than presenting itself as the expression of divine authority, Confucian rule was based on the idea of an ethical order. Rulers were required to govern in accordance with the teachings of Confucius and were expected to set the highest moral standards.[105] There was an elaborate political hierarchy that presumed and required an ascending ladder of virtue on the part of office-holders. The political structure was seen as synonymous with the social order, the overall objective being a harmonious and balanced community.[106] These principles informed Chinese governance in varying degrees from the Qin through to the fall of the Qing.

The model of both society and government was based on the family, an institution intimately familiar to everyone. The individual was seen as part of society and the state in the same way as he or she belonged to his or her own family. The Confucian family was possessed of two key characteristics. The first was filial piety, the duty of the offspring to respect the authority of the father, who, in return, was required to take care of the family. As the state was modelled on the family, the father was also the role model for the state, which, in dynastic times, meant the emperor. Second, although the Chinese were not by and large religious, they shared with other Confucian societies a transcendental belief in ancestral spirits: that one's ancestors were permanently present. Deference towards one's ancestors was enacted through the ritual of ancestral worship, which served to emphasize the continuity and lineage of the family and the relatively humble nature of its present living members. The belief in ancestral spirits encouraged a similar respect for and veneration of the state as an immortal institution which represented the continuity of Chinese civilization. The importance of the family in Chinese culture can be gleaned from the special significance – far greater than in Western culture – that attaches to the family name, which always comes before the given name.[107]

Socialization via the family was and remains a highly disciplining process in Confucian societies. Children learn to appreciate that everything has its place, including them. People learn about their role and duties as citizens as an extension of their familial responsibilities. It is through the family that people learn to defer to a collectivity, that the individual is always secondary to the group. Unlike Western societies, which, historically at least, have tended to rely on guilt through Christian teaching as a means of constraining and directing individual behaviour, Confucian societies rest on shame and 'loss of face'. Discipline in Confucian societies is internal to the individual, based on the socialization process in the family, rather than externally induced through religious teaching, as in the West, though that tradition has weakened in an increasingly secular Europe.[108]

Such is the power of this sense of belonging – to one's own family, but then by extension to society and the state – that it has resulted in a strong sense of attachment to, and affinity with, one's race and nation – and, by the same token, a rejection of foreigners as 'barbarians', or 'devils', or the Other. All the Confucian countries share a biological conception of citizenship. The strong sense of patriotism that characterizes all of these societies – China, Japan, Korea, Taiwan and Vietnam – has generally been ascribed to a reaction to overbearing Western pressure, including colonialism. But this is only part of the picture, and the rather less important part: the power of identity, the rejection of outsiders and the strength of native racism is primarily a consequence of the nature of the indigenous process of socialization.[109]

The role of the family is to provide security, support and cohesion for its members. In Confucian societies, in other words, government is modelled on an institution whose focus was not on the achievement of external goals but on its own well-being, self-maintenance and self-perpetuation. It is not surprising, therefore, that a powerful feature of these societies has been the stress on unity and stability and on continuity, cohesion and solidarity. Confucian societies, thus, have a rather different conception of government to that which we are familiar with in the West, where the state is viewed as an essentially artificial construct, an external institution that people seek to hold to account, which they view with a certain suspicion, whose powers they constantly seek to define, limit and constrain. For the Chinese – and the same can broadly be said of the other Confucian societies – the state is seen as a natural and intrinsic part of society, as part of the wider common purpose and well-being. The state, like the family, is subject to neither codification nor constraint. The Chinese state has never been regarded in a narrowly political way, but more broadly as a source of meaning, moral behaviour and order. That it should be accorded such a universal role is a consequence of the fact that it is so deeply rooted in the culture that it is seen as part of the natural order of things.[110]

It is difficult for Westerners to appreciate and grasp the nature of Confucian political culture because it is so different from what they are familiar with; moreover, Westerners, accustomed to running the world for so long, are not well versed in understanding and recognizing difference. East Asian polities, as a result, are usually seen only in a very superficial light. Japan is regarded as democratic because it has elections and competing parties; yet the Japanese system works entirely differently from those in the West. Post-1949 China has been explained overwhelmingly in terms of its Communist government, with a consequent failure to understand the continuity between the Communist regime and the long thread of Chinese history. In fact, we should not be surprised either by the highly idiosyncratic nature of

Japanese politics or the umbilical cord that links Communist rule and dynastic rule. Both are examples of the way in which politics is rooted in culture.[111]

Given that East Asian polities operate by very different customs and practices to those of the West, can we draw any conclusions as to their merits and demerits? This is a tricky question, because Westerners, however broad-minded they may be, inevitably tend to apply Western criteria. They are inclined to see dependency as a negative, while East Asians veer towards the opposite view and see it as a positive. Who is right? It is impossible to make a judgement. The downside of East Asian societies might be seen as a tendency, given the strength of dependency and the paternalistic conception of government, towards authoritarianism and one-party government. On the other hand, such paternalistic leadership also has certain strengths. Because government and leaders enjoy a different kind of trust, they are given much more latitude to change direction and policies. They are not hemmed in and constrained in the same manner as Western leaders. In some ways East Asian political leaders are also more accessible and more approachable because they view their accountability to society in a more holistic way and people take a similar attitude towards them. Their greater all-round authority, rooted in the symbiotic relationship between paternalism and dependency, can also enable them to take a longer-term attitude towards society and its needs.

The highly distinctive characteristics of East Asian polities may be rooted in history, but are they declining with modernization? In some ways they are getting stronger. As the ideology of anti-colonialism has weakened, there has, if anything, been a reversion to more traditional familial and indigenous attitudes. Moreover, while the family itself is changing – in China, it is far less patriarchal than previously – it remains very different to the Western family, especially in terms of responsibilities, values and attitudes:[112] indeed, family customs have been amongst the slowest of all Asian institutions to change. Such is the profundity of the forces that have served to shape East Asian politics that it is impossible to envisage these societies somehow losing their political distinctiveness.[113]

INDIGENOUS MODERNITY

The picture that emerges from these four examples is not the scale of Westernization but, for the most part, its surprisingly restricted extent. The subjects we have considered could hardly have been more fundamental, taking us, in contrasting ways, to the very heart of societies. We can draw two general conclusions. First, if the impact of Westernization is limited, then it follows that these societies – and their modernities – remain individual and distinctive, rooted in and shaped by their own histories and cultures. It also follows that their modernization has depended not simply or even mainly upon borrowing from the West, but on their ability to transform and modernize themselves: the taproots of modernization, in other words, are native rather than foreign. Japan, the first example of Asian modernity, is a classic illustration of this. It may have borrowed extensively from the West, but the outcome was and is entirely distinctive, an ineluctably Japanese modernity. Second, if the process of modernization is simply a transplant then it cannot succeed. A people must believe that modernity is theirs in order for it to take root and flourish. The East Asian countries have all borrowed heavily from the West or Japan, usually both. Indeed, an important characteristic of all Asian modernities, including Japan's, is their hybrid nature, the combination of different elements, indigenous and foreign. But where the line of demarcation lies between the borrowed and the indigenous is crucial: if a society feels that its modernity is essentially imposed – a foreign transplant – then it will be rejected and fail.[114] This must be a further reason – in addition to the fact that colonial powers deliberately sought to prevent their colonies from competing with their own products – why, during the era of colonialism, no colonial societies succeeded in achieving economic take-off. The problem with colonial status was that by definition the colony belonged to an alien people and culture. The only exceptions were the white-settler colonies, which, sharing the race and ethnicity of the colonizing power, namely Britain, were always treated very differently; and Hong Kong, which, to Britain's belated credit, from the late fifties (a full century after its initial colonization), succeeded in becoming the first-ever industrialized colony, with the tacit cooperation of China.

Given China's long history and extraordinary distinctiveness, it is self-evident that China's modernization could only succeed if it was felt by the people to be a fundamentally Chinese phenomenon. This debate was played out over the century after 1850 in the argument over 'Chinese essence' and 'Western method' (as it was also in Japan), and it remains a controversial subject in present-day China. The conflict between Chinese tradition and Western modernity in China's modernization is well illustrated by a discussion I organized over a decade ago with four students in their early twenties from Shanghai's Fudan University, one of China's elite institutions. It is clear from the exchange that maintaining a distinct Chinese core was non-negotiable as far as these students were concerned: the two women, Gao Yi and Huang Yongyi, were shortly off to do doctorates at American universities, while the young men, Wang Jianxiong and Zhang Xiaoming, had landed plum jobs with American firms in Shanghai.[115] They were the crème de la crème, the ultimate beneficiaries of Deng Xiaoping's open-door policy, Chinese winners from globalization.

WANG: In the last century Chinese culture became marginal while Western culture became dominant. The Chinese have been much more preoccupied with the past, with their history, than the West. We have to understand why we are behind other countries, why we haven't been able to develop our country. The West has won a very great victory and this has meant a big crisis for Chinese civilization.

GAO: Our traditional values are always in conflict with modern Western values. We are always at a loss as to how to deal with this. These two value systems are always in conflict. We constantly feel the need to return to our long history to understand who we really are. The reason why we pay so much attention to our history is because the traditional way remains very powerful.

Are you more optimistic for the future? Do you think that Chinese culture will remain marginal?

WANG: Our civilization is entering a critical period. In the last century we used Western thinking to develop Chinese society and culture. That is not good. We must build up our own knowledge, our own methodology, in order to develop the country and our culture. We must build up our own things, not just bring Western thoughts to our country. That's mostly what we have done in the twentieth century. But this century I think the Chinese will develop their own knowledge.

If China does this, can it become more central and important in the world?

WANG: Not the centre of the world, but China will realize its own modernity, which will not be the same as that of the United States, nor, by the way, will it be like the Soviet Union. It will be something new.

What will be distinctive about it?

WANG: We can build our own modernity based on Chinese culture. Of course, we will use some elements of Western culture but we can't transplant that culture to China. A mistake that Western countries make, especially the United States, is to want to transplant their systems and institutions to other countries. It's wrong because it ignores the cultural core of a country. I always like to focus on the cultural core: to transform or remove the cultural core is impossible.

And the cultural core is . . . ?

WANG: Five thousand years of history.

What are the values of this cultural core?

WANG: It's composed of many elements: our attitude towards life, the family, marriage and so on. During the long history of Chinese civilization – because our country is so big – we have developed many different ideas and attitudes.

You and Zhang are both studying international finance and yet your argument is all about the distinctiveness of China.

WANG: Globalization is Westernization. But it should be a two-way process: we accept Western ideas while at the same time people in Western countries should seek to understand and maybe accept some of our ideas. Now it is not like that: we just accept Western ideas, there's no movement in the opposite direction. That's the problem. As a result, we lose something from our own culture, which worries us a lot. Now we are afraid of losing our own culture. We accept Western ideas not because they are good for us but because of their novelty. They are new to us so we accept them. But on the whole I don't think they will be good for us. Maybe in twenty years' time we will give them up.

ZHANG: Historically, there is a part of the Chinese that wants to change and a part that wants to remain the same. We are in a state of conflict, both as individuals and as a society. In the Qing dynasty we shut ourselves off from the outside world, mainly because we wanted to keep our culture and our civilization. Part of the reason for this was unacceptable: we thought we were superior to the rest of the world. When we finally opened our doors, we found that we were backward compared with Western countries. Now we have opened our doors again and with this openness we are, and will be, more and more influenced by Western countries. We are afraid we will lose our culture, our characteristics. I want to change, because the current situation in China is not so satisfactory, but at the same time I worry that when we eliminate the shortcomings in our culture maybe we will also lose the essential part of our culture, the good part of our culture.

HUANG: Even now, when Western influence is considerable and intrusive, I don't think the Chinese will lose their culture because this represents a very thick accumulation of history. It cannot change easily, even if some of the surface things change. There is a very strong core culture inside every one of us. Even if our way of life changes, that culture will not change. Our long history constantly reappears and recurs. Now we are in a period of loss. I cannot deny that. We feel a sense of loss because of the underlying conflict between modernity and tradition. But I believe that something new will come out of this: a unique China will remain.

GAO: We have been through worse periods, for example when we were colonized. I am more confident. We are in a new period when we are not being invaded but we are being influenced by the West. But for sure we will not be Westernized, the core culture will still be there.

CONTESTED MODERNITY

The balance of power in the world is changing with remarkable speed. In 1973 it was dominated by a developed world which consisted of the United States, Western Europe and Japan, together with what Angus Maddison describes as 'Western offshoots' like Australia: between them, they accounted for 58.7% of the world's GDP but only 18.4% of the world's population. By 2001, the share of global GDP accounted for by these countries had fallen to 52.0% while their share of the world's population had declined to 14.0%. The most dramatic change was the rising share of global GDP accounted for by Asia, which, excluding Japan, increased from 16.4% in 1973 to 30.9% in 2001, while its share of the world's population rose from 54.6% in 1973 to 57.4% in 2001.[116] This picture will change even more dramatically over the next few decades. It is estimated that by 2032 the share of global GDP of the so-called BRICs, namely Brazil, Russia, India and China, will exceed that of the G7, namely the US, Canada, the UK, Germany, France, Italy and Japan. And by 2027, if not rather earlier, it is projected that China will overtake the United States to become the world's largest economy.[117] To illustrate how increasingly diverse the world is likely to become, it is envisaged that the combined GDP of another eleven developing countries (Bangladesh, Egypt, Indonesia, Iran, Korea, Mexico, Nigeria, Pakistan, the Philippines, Turkey and Vietnam) could reach two-thirds of the level of the G7 by 2050.[118] Meanwhile, the developing world's share of the global population will steadily rise, though Asia's will remain relatively constant at just below 60%, with that of India and China, the two most populous countries in the world, enjoying a combined share of 37.3% in 2001,[119] projected to fall very slightly. The proportion of the world living in the developed countries, meanwhile, will continue to fall steadily.

The nineteenth and twentieth centuries marked the Age of the West. But this era is now coming to an end. By the middle of this century, when the West will be responsible for a great deal less than half the world's GDP, the Age of the West will have passed. The rise of China, India, Brazil, Korea, Taiwan and many other developing countries marks a huge shift in the balance of economic power, but it also has much wider implications. Economic prosperity serves to transform the self-confidence and self-image of societies, thereby enabling them to project their political and cultural values on a broader canvas. A striking characteristic of the Asian tigers has been the way in which, during the process of modernization, they have steadily shifted from a seemingly insatiable desire for all things Western as the symbol of the modernity they so craved – combined with a rejection of the indigenous, which was seen as synonymous with poverty and back-wardness – to a growing affirmation of the indigenous rather than the Western. In the 1970s, for example, few Taiwanese would entertain the idea of traditional Chinese furniture, but by the early nineties this attitude was starting to be superseded by a growing interest in tradi-tional artefacts. This was also true until very recently in China, but now there is a huge appetite for antique furniture, with a wealth of television programmes devoted to the subject, a consequent dearth of genuine pieces as opposed to fakes, and rapidly escalating prices.[120] Similarly in Taiwanese pop music, for example, Western influences were steadily usurped after the 1970s by local and regional mando-pop (Chinese-composed pop music sung in Mandarin).[121] In other words, tradition, rather than being rejected, has been progressively rearticulated as part of a new and native modernity.[122] The same gen-eral picture applies across the whole of East Asia, including China. In 1980 few knew or cared much about other countries in the region: all eyes were turned to the global mecca, the United States. The lines of communication were overwhelmingly east–west – in terms of infor-mation, music, politics, technology, education, film, aspiration and desire. Most East Asians knew far more about what happened in New York, Washington or London than in Tokyo, Seoul, Beijing or Kuala Lumpur. East Asians still remain remarkably intimate with what emanates from the United States – certainly compared with the over-whelming ignorance that Americans display towards East Asia – but the situation has changed markedly. Hung Tze Jan, the Taiwanese publisher quoted earlier, well describes this changed mentality: 'When I was at high school and university, we focused all our efforts on West-ern literature and ideas. My son is in his early teens and in contrast to me he has the opportunity to create something new – to read both Chinese *and* Western literature.'[123]

In the future, then, instead of there being one dominant Western modernity (itself, of course, a pluralistic phenomenon), there will be many distinct modernities. It is clear that we have already entered this era of multiple modernities: by the middle of the century we will be firmly ensconced in it. Hitherto, we have lived in a Western-made and Western-dominated world, in which the economic, political and cultural traffic has been overwhelmingly one-directional, from the West to others. That is already beginning to change, becoming a two-way, or more precisely a multi-directional process. An interesting illustration of how the old pecking order is steadily being disrupted, even inverted, can be found in the world of cricket. Formerly, cricket was largely dominated by England, together with two former white settler colonies, Australia and New Zealand. But in 2008 India, which already accounted for around 80 per cent of the game's revenues, established the Indian Premier League and its eight teams, representing various Indian cities and states, proceeded to sign up many of the world's best cricketers, much to the chagrin of the English cricket authorities, who have always thought of themselves as the centre of the game. The future of cricket now manifestly belongs on the Indian subcontinent, where the character, flavour and evolution of the game will increasingly be determined.[124] If Manchester United, Liverpool and Barcelona enjoy a global fan base in football, the likes of the Punjab and Chennai may blaze a similar trail in cricket.

The Age of the West was not only marked by economic and military dominance but by Western ascendancy in more or less every field, from culture and ideas to science and technology, and from painting and language to sport and medicine. Western hegemony meant anything associated with the West enjoyed a prestige and influence that other cultures did not. White skin colour has been preferred globally – in East Asia too, as we saw earlier in this chapter – because it was synonymous with Western power and wealth. Western-style clothes have been widely adopted for the same reason. English is the global lingua franca because of the overweening importance of the United States. The history of the West – in particular, the United States and Western Europe – is far more familiar to the rest of the world than that of any other country or region because the centrality of the West has meant that everyone else is obliged, or desires, to know about it. Western political values and ideas are the only ones that enjoy any kind of universalism for a similar reason. But now that the West is no longer the exclusive home of modernity, with the rest of the world cast in a state of pre-modernity, the global equation changes entirely. Hinduism will no more be a byword for backwardness. Nor will

Indian clothes. It will no longer be possible to dismiss Chinese political traditions as an obsolete hangover from the days of the Middle Kingdom, nor equate the Western family with modernity and dismiss those of India and China as remnants of an agrarian age. To growing numbers of people outside the West, Chinese history will become as familiar as Western history is now, if not more so. The competition, in other words, between the West and the rest will no longer be fundamentally unequal, pitting modernity against tradition, but will take place on something that will increasingly resemble a level playing field, namely between different modernities. We can already see this in the corporate world, where Korean, Japanese and Chinese companies, bearing the characteristics of the cultures from which they derive, compete with their rather different Western counterparts, often with considerable success.

The twentieth century was characterized by the ideological cleavage between socialism and capitalism, an era ushered in by the October Revolution in 1917 and which found expression in the onset of the Cold War after 1945, until finally coming to an end with the collapse of the Soviet Union in 1989–91. That world, where every conflict and division was refracted through the prism of this wider ideological schism, then proceeded to evaporate with great speed. American neo-conservatives believe that the new global divide is the war on terror – what they like to describe as the Fourth World War (the third having been the Cold War) – but this represents a basic misreading of history. The era we are now entering, in fact, can best be described as one of *contested modernity*. Unlike the Cold War, it is not defined by a great political or ideological divide but rather by an overarching cultural contest. The emergence of new modernities not only means that the West no longer enjoys a virtual monopoly on modernity, but that the histories, cultures and values of these societies will be affirmed in a new way and can no longer be equated with backwardness or, worse still, failure. On the contrary, they will experience a new sense of legitimacy and, far from being overawed by or deferential towards the West, will enjoy a growing sense of self-confidence.

Hitherto the world has been characterized by Western hubris – the Western conviction that its values, belief-systems, institutions and arrangements are superior to all others. The power and persistence of this mentality should not be underestimated. Western governments feel no compunction or restraint about lecturing other countries on the need for, and overwhelming virtue of, their versions of democracy and human rights. This frame of mind is by no means confined to governments, who, for the most part, simply reflect a popular cultural consensus. Often, Western feminists, for example, tend to assume that gender relations in the West are more advanced than elsewhere, and that they are more liberated and independent than women from other cultures. There is a deeply embedded sense of Western psychological superiority which draws on powerful economic, political, ideological, cultural and ethnic currents. The rise of a world of multiple modernity challenges that mentality, and in the era of contested modernity it will steadily be eroded and undermined. Ideas such as 'advanced', 'developed' and 'civilized' will no longer be synonymous with the West. This threatens Western societies with an existential crisis of the first order, the political consequences of which we cannot predict but will certainly be profound. The assumptions that have underpinned the attitudes of many generations of Westerners towards the rest of the world will become increasingly unsustainable and beleaguered. The West has thought itself to be universal, the unquestioned model and example for all to follow; in the future it will be only one of several, even many, possibilities. This is a scenario that, at least until very recently,[125] the West has been almost entirely unprepared for, as Paul A. Cohen, quoted at the very beginning of this chapter, suggests. In future it will be required to think of itself in relative rather than absolute terms, obliged to learn about, and to learn from, the rest of the world without the presumption of underlying superiority and the belief that ultimately it knows best as the fount of all civilizational wisdom. The bearer of this change will be China, partly because of its overwhelming size and its growing economic strength, but also because of the nature of its culture and outlook. China, unlike Japan, has always regarded itself as universal, the centre of the world, and even, for a millennium and more, believed that it actually constituted the world. The emergence of Chinese modernity will de-centre and relativize the position of the West. That is why the rise of China has such far-reaching implications.

II
The Age of China

Although parts of China are already prosperous and developed, around half of the population still lives in the countryside. China remains very much a developing country. As a consequence, Chinese modernity can only be regarded as work in progress. Some of its characteristics are already evident, others are only in embryonic form, while others still are not yet visible. It is abundantly clear, however, that Chinese modernity will differ markedly from Western modernity. The reasons for this lie not only in the present, but even more tellingly in the past. China has little in common with the West. It comes from entirely different cultural coordinates. Its politics, its state and its moral outlook have been constituted in a highly singular way, likewise its relationship with its neighbours. The fact that for many centuries the Chinese regarded themselves as constituting the world, as 'all land under Heaven', only serves to underline the country's unique character. Unlike most developing countries, furthermore, China was never colonized, even though many of its cities were. Colonization was a powerful means by which countries were Westernized, but in China its absence from vast swathes of the country meant this never happened in the same manner that it did in India or Indochina, for example. The sheer size of China, both as a continental land mass and, more importantly, in terms of population, were, of course, indispensable conditions for enabling the Chinese to think in such autarchic and universalist terms. It might be argued that all these considerations lie in the past, but it is history that shapes and leaves its indelible mark on the present. Modernity is not a free-floating product of the present, but a function of what has gone before.

The fact that China, ever since 1949, but more significantly following 1978 and the beginning of the reform period, has been single-mindedly focused on the task of modernization has served to emphasize its affinity with the West: the need to gain the US's backing for its admission to the international system, the necessity of learning and borrowing from the West's economic practice, and the opening up of the country to foreign investment and multinationals being obvious examples. But as China progresses further down the road of modernization, it will find itself less constrained by the imperatives of development, more confident about what it is and where it has come from, less anxious about being accepted and more at ease about its sense of difference.

6

China as an Economic Superpower

In August 1993, I visited Guangdong province, north of Hong Kong, for the first time. The experience is engraved on my memory. The route we took from Shenzhen to Guangzhou (the provincial capital, known as Canton in colonial times) was sometimes made up, occasionally little more than a mud track. Although we were in the middle of the countryside, the road was overflowing with pedestrians and vehicles of every conceivable kind. Played out before my eyes was the most extraordinary juxtaposition of eras: women walking with their animals and carrying their produce, farmers riding bicycles and driving pedicabs, the new urban rich speeding by in black Mercedes and Lexuses, anonymous behind darkened windows, a constant stream of vans, pick-ups, lorries and minibuses, and in the fields by the side of the road peasants working their small paddy fields with water buffalo. It was as if two hundred of years of history had been condensed into one place in this single moment of time. It was a country in motion, its people living for the present, looking for and seizing the opportunity, as if it might never be offered again. I was engulfed by an enormous torrent of energy, creativity and willpower. The British Industrial Revolution must have been a bit like this: speculative, chaotic, dynamic – and a complete bloody mess. Guangdong was certainly a mess. Everywhere you looked there was construction – seemingly everything was in the process of being changed: the half-made road along which we were travelling, the countless half-finished buildings, land being cleared as far as the eye could see. Guangdong was like a huge construction site.

Just over two years later I tried to retrace my steps with a television crew. There was not a single familiar sight I could find. The dynamic chaos had given way to order. There were brand-new expressways, bridges, factories, warehouses, and a lot more cars; and little sign of the juxtaposition of eras that had so fascinated me two years earlier. I enlisted the help of a couple of officials, but as I described the scenes I wanted to recapture on film they shrugged as if to suggest that they lay in the distant past. For me it was just two years ago; for them it could have been a different century. Guangdong, the brainchild of Deng Xiaoping, was well on the way to becoming not just the industrial centre of China, full of factories, many Hong Kong-owned, making cheap, mass-produced goods for the global market, but the workshop of the world. This is how and where China's economic transformation started.

Now Guangdong, less than two decades after that first volcanic eruption, is turning over a new page in its history. It can no longer sustain its old comparative advantage. Labour has become too expensive, too demanding, the expectations of its people transformed. The most dramatic illustration of this came in May–June 2010 when a wave of strikes broke out which resulted in huge wage increases at Foxconn, a Taiwanese-owned firm and the world's largest electronic contract manufacturer, employing 270,000 at its Shenzhen complex, at Honda and many other companies. Guangdong's factories are no longer able to compete with those in China's interior provinces, where wages are much lower. In 2007 alone, no less than 1,000 shoe factories closed in Guangdong, one-sixth of the total, while in 2008, 4,000 toy companies shut down.[1] Companies are moving production to the interior provinces and, in their place, Guangdong is seeking to move up the value ladder, develop its service industries and shift into new areas of production that rely on design and technology rather than the perspiration of its people and the migrant workers from faraway provinces. Shenzhen and Guangzhou, like many cities in Guangdong, now look well-maintained and prosperous, a far cry from former days when they resembled China's Wild West. Shenzhen may not yet enjoy Hong Kong's Western-style living standards, but it has significantly closed the gap. In little more than two decades, Guangdong has gone from the early days of the

Industrial Revolution to something not too far short of the less developed parts of Western Europe.

At the time of Mao's death in 1976, who would have predicted that China stood on the eve of a most remarkable period of economic growth that would entirely transform the face and fortunes of the country? Virtually nobody. It was as unpredictable and unpredicted as another enormously significant event – 1989 and the collapse of European Communism. China had been torn apart by the Cultural Revolution, in which the cadre that had largely steered the party through the 1950s and early 1960s had been vilified and banished by a 'popular' *coup d'état* staged at Mao's behest, involving the mobilization of tens of millions of young people in the Red Guard. The movement was opposed to privilege – whether by virtue of family history or party position – and super-egalitarian in its philosophy: a very Chinese phenomenon with echoes of the Taiping Uprising in the mid nineteenth century. By the time of Mao's death, the Cultural Revolution had subsided and stood largely discredited, but the country's future direction remained deeply uncertain. The vacuum created by Mao's death was soon filled by the return of those same old leaders who had been persecuted during the Cultural Revolution, with Deng Xiaoping at the helm. They were confronted by the economic ravages and political dislocation that were the legacy of the Cultural Revolution, but free at last to pursue their instincts and inclinations, unimpeded by the wild extremes and excesses of Mao, albeit in a situation where the party faced a severe crisis of legitimacy.

There was one favourable omen. By the end of the seventies China's relatively modest growth rate constituted something of an exception in East Asia. Many countries in the region were on the economic move: Japan was booming; South Korea, Taiwan, Singapore and Hong Kong had already experienced take-off; Malaysia, Thailand and others were in its early stages. The Chinese diaspora – centred on Hong Kong and Taiwan, but also in Singapore and Malaysia – were key players in this economic transformation. There were, in other words, examples around China's borders of the possibilities that now beckoned. The country's East Asian hinterland was being transformed by a region-wide economic revolution based on catch-up. Of course China faced unique problems, in particular its vastness and diversity, together with the legacy of civil war, turmoil and occupation. In addition it had been largely isolated, a condition which was partly self-imposed and partly a result of an American embargo (involving a total ban on all transactions with China until 1972 and a refusal to recognize the PRC rather than Taiwan as the legitimate China until 1979), together with the withdrawal of all Soviet aid and personnel in 1959. The challenges facing the new Chinese leadership, therefore, were far more formidable than those that had confronted Taiwan or South Korea, especially as these, as vassal states, had enjoyed considerable American patronage and munificence during the Cold War.

The process of reform began in 1978 with the creation of a handful of special economic zones along the south-eastern seaboard, including Guangdong province, in which the rural communes were dismantled and the peasants were given control of the land on long-term leases and encouraged to market their own produce. It was based on a step-by-step, piecemeal and experimental approach. If a reform worked it was extended to new areas; if it failed then it was abandoned. Such down-to-earth pragmatism stood in sharp contrast to the grand ideological flourishes that informed the Cultural Revolution era and the Maoist period more generally. As Deng put it, in the time-honoured tradition of pithy and popular quotes by Chinese leaders from Confucius onwards: 'Seek truth from the facts'; 'Truth is to be found in practice'; and 'Cross the river by feeling for the stones'. The new economic approach involved a different kind of mindset and way of thinking in the party and government, necessitating a massive change of personnel, starting at the top and working rapidly downwards. In 1978 Deng declared: 'To make revolution and build socialism we need large numbers of path-breakers who dare to think, explore new ways and generate new ideas.'[2] The *People's Daily* later commented that political reform was:

> a gigantic social systems engineering project, which involves straightening out the relationships between the Party and the government, power and judicial organs, mass organizations, enterprises and institutions,

and between central, local and grassroots organizations; it concerns hundreds of millions of people. This is an arduous and protracted task.[3]

The reform project has usually been seen in narrowly economic terms, as if it had few political implications. In fact Deng's project involved not just an economic revolution, but also a largely unrecognized political revolution, which entailed a complete overhaul of the state, both in its modus operandi and its personnel, with the universalist, ideological model of the Maoist era being replaced by something closer to the developmental model of the East Asian tigers. An essential element in this transformation was the decentralization of the state, which was seen as a precondition for the reform of the economic system and economic growth. Decision-making, including the granting of de facto property rights and fiscal power, was decentralized to different levels of local government.[4] As a consequence the central government budget, as a share of GDP, shrank considerably.[5]

Almost from the outset, economic growth rates were transformed from the respectable 4–5 per cent of the Mao period to an annual growth rate of 9.5 per cent between 1978 and 1992.[6] The momentum of reform, however, was seriously disrupted in 1989, little more than a decade after it began, by a massive student demonstration in Tiananmen Square that was brutally suppressed by the army. With the party leadership seriously divided, it seemed likely that the reform process would be derailed, perhaps indefinitely. In the event, there was only a short hiatus before, in the grand style of Chinese emperors, and to coincide with the Chinese New Year in 1992, Deng made a 'Southern Expedition' to the coastal heartland of China's economic revolution, during which he made a statement in Shenzhen – a brand-new city neighbouring Hong Kong – that not only reaffirmed the central importance of the market reforms but made a clarion call for the process to be intensified and accelerated, suggesting, in a famous passage, that there was nothing wrong in allowing the rich to get richer (and then eventually paying higher taxes to help the poor).[7] Until this point the reform process had largely been concentrated in the south, but now it began to move to the interior provinces and, most crucially of all, to Shanghai and the Yangzi Delta, China's former economic powerhouse. There was a further wave of foreign investment, largely from the Chinese diaspora based in Hong Kong and Taiwan (which to this day remains the largest single source of foreign inward investment), while Chinese exports, mainly to the United States, increased rapidly. An economic fever began to grip the country, encouraged by Deng's call to embrace the market economy and fuelled by the annual double-digit growth rate. Nothing more graphically symbolized the 'new frontier' economic spirit than the tens of millions of rural migrants, China's reserve army of labour, who left their farms and villages in search of the work and glitz of the city.[8] The Red Guards were now but a distant memory. There was barely a Mao suit in sight.

From the outset, Japan and the Asian tigers had been an important influence on China's economic reform.[9] These countries shared with Deng a pragmatic and non-doctrinal view of how to conduct economic policy. It was recognized, however, that none of them could, in themselves, provide a suitable model: the conditions, especially those flowing from China's enormous size and diversity, were simply too different. In the era of globalization that began around 1980, moreover, it was no longer possible for China, unlike Japan and the Asian tigers earlier, to grow its industries and companies behind a wall of tariffs until they were ready to compete in the international market. A further complicating factor was that China, as a Communist country, was still viewed with considerable suspicion by the United States: as a result, its entry into the WTO took fifteen years and was the subject of the most detailed agreement ever made with any country – contrasting strongly, for example, with the far less demanding terms required of India a few years earlier. China, for a variety of reasons, had to invent its own way.[10]

Although China enjoyed nothing like the intimacy of South Korea and Taiwan's relationship with the United States, it recognized the crucial importance of winning American support and cooperation in its pursuit of economic growth. Just as its approach to economic reform was informed by pragmatism, so too was its attitude towards the United States. The Mao–Nixon accord of 1972 marked a profound change in their relationship, with the establishment of formal diplomatic relations in 1979, the settlement of property claims, the unfreezing of assets and the granting to China of most-favoured nation treatment. These steps created the conditions for China subsequently to join the IMF and the World Bank in 1986 and be granted observer status to GATT in 1982. The value of the United States to China was increasingly evident during the 1980s: it became the most important destination for Chinese exports; growing numbers of Chinese students went to study there, including many sons and daughters of the party elite; while the US model of capitalism came to exercise a growing influence. The collapse of the Soviet Union only served to accentuate that influence, and the US's appeal was further enhanced by the economic dynamism associated with Silicon Valley and the internet. Increasingly during the nineties, however, there was a rising tide of nationalist sentiment directed against the US, which found expression in the bestseller *The China That Can Say No* and the demonstrations against the US bombing of the Chinese embassy in Belgrade.[11] American influence on China's modernization, nonetheless, persisted. Even China's own economic path and popular mood was to bear some of the signs of neo-liberalism: the worship of wealth, the embrace of entrepreneurs, acquiescence in growing inequality, the retreat of the state from the provision of public goods such as education and health, the rapid lowering of tariff barriers and the adoption of an extremely open trade regime[12] – all of which were closely associated with the reign of Deng's protégé and successor, Jiang Zemin.

The approach of the Chinese leadership, following Deng's emergence as the paramount leader, had been built on caution and pragmatism, notwithstanding the obvious radicalism of the reform process. They eschewed shock treatment and grand gestures. Although drawing on elements of neo-liberalism, they resisted the Washington orthodoxy and instead pursued a very home-grown approach.[13] They were painstakingly meticulous in the way that they sought to introduce reforms by a gradual process of constant testing and trial and error. The state, in the time-honoured Chinese fashion, remained at the heart of this process of reform, even though the latter was to involve a major contraction in its economic role, with the share of government revenue decreasing from around one-third of GDP in 1978 to 17 per cent in 2005.[14] For the Chinese leadership, the objective of economic reform was never Westernization, but rather a desire to restore the Party's legitimacy after Mao through economic growth,[15] and thereby to build a strong nation and state.[16] Political stability was accorded the highest priority. '[China's] modernization,' Deng stated, 'needs two prerequisites. One is international peace, and the other is domestic political stability.'[17] The disintegration of the Soviet Union after 1989 only served to reinforce Deng's belief in the vital importance of economic reform, an area in which the Soviet Union had palpably failed, and the need to avoid destabilizing political reforms, a trap which they saw Gorbachev as having fallen into.[18] The Asian financial crisis in 1997–8 similarly confirmed the Chinese leadership in its aversion to shock treatment: that China should move with great caution in its financial reform and resist any premature liberalization of the capital account that would allow the free movement of capital into and out of China, and consequent floating of the Chinese currency, the renminbi (also called the yuan), which might lead to speculative attacks on the currency and the consequent destabilization of the economy, as happened to South Korea, Thailand and Indonesia – to their great cost – during the Asian crisis.[19] (As a consequence, the renminbi remains, unlike the dollar, yen and euro, for example, a non-tradeable currency.)

In response to the challenge posed by an increasingly globalized economy, the Chinese leadership, mindful of the need to accelerate the process of reform, did, however, opt for one important element of shock treatment. During the nineties, by dismantling tariff barriers and allowing huge flows of foreign direct investment – in contrast to the economic strategy pursued by Japan, South Korea and Taiwan – they created a brutal competitive environment in which domestic companies desperately sought to survive against far richer and more advanced Western and Japanese rivals. This rapid opening up enabled the Chinese economy to take advantage of enormous flows of foreign capital and had the merit of forcing Chinese companies to learn from the outside world,[20] but the cost was high, with many struggling to survive. While their North-East Asian neighbours enjoyed a prolonged period of protection from external competition, during which their companies were given time to develop, China, in comparison, had none. Chinese companies were obliged to sink or swim, and the conditions attached to China's subsequent membership of the WTO

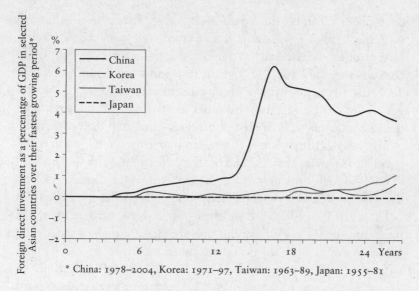

Foreign direct investment as a percentage of GDP in selected Asian countries over their fastest growing period*

* China: 1978–2004, Korea: 1971–97, Taiwan: 1963–89, Japan: 1955–81

Figure 13. The role of foreign direct investment in China compared with other Asian tigers.

meant the state faced various restrictions on the extent to which it was permitted to help state-owned enterprises, although it found various ways of circumnavigating some of them.[21]

Although the earlier phase of reform concentrated on stimulating the growth of the rural economy, by the end of the eighties the centre of gravity had decisively shifted to the cities and the industrial economy. Already, during the eighties, the Guangdong economy became a microcosm of the future shape and comparative advantage of the fast-changing Chinese economy, with Hong Kong entrepreneurs moving their manufacturing operations out of the city-state to neighbouring Guangdong province in order to take advantage of far cheaper labour; as a result, Guangdong rapidly became Hong Kong's manufacturing base. This process quickly spread north and especially eastwards during the course of the nineties, assisted by the upsurge in Western and Japanese direct investment at the end of that decade in anticipation of China's membership of the WTO in 2001. Just as China pursued an open policy on trade, it adopted a similar approach towards inward investment. Since 1978 China has received well over $500 billion in foreign direct investment, ten times the total accumulated by Japan between 1945 and 2000. In contrast to Japan – and South Korea and Taiwan – where inward foreign investment accounted for less than 1 per cent of GDP during the most rapid years of growth and never more than 2 per cent in the more recent period, China, after the 1980s, more closely resembled the South-East Asian pattern with inflows in countries like Malaysia, Thailand and Indonesia accounting for 4–6 per cent of GDP. In some provinces, it was far higher than this, notably Guangdong, where between 1993 and 2003 it was responsible for 13 per cent of GDP.[22] In 2003 China became the world's largest recipient of foreign direct investment, overtaking the United States.[23] Much of the inward investment was ploughed into the local subsidiaries of foreign multinationals with the purpose, following the example of Hong Kong, of exploiting the huge resources of cheap labour in order to make exports as globally competitive as possible. Foreign firms are presently responsible for up to 60 per cent of all Chinese exports, and dominate high-tech exports with a share of around 85 per cent.[24] China, in the process, has become the 'workshop of the world', by far the cheapest national base for low- and medium-end manufacturing on the planet.

As a result of the systematic lowering of tariffs, one of the singular features of the Chinese economy is its huge exposure to foreign trade, which accounts for around 75 per cent of GDP, far in excess of other major economies like the United States, India, Japan and Brazil, where the figure is 30 per cent or less.[25] Such exposure makes China that much more significant in the global economy; it also leaves the country more vulnerable to external shocks such as a global downturn, a US recession or growing protectionist sentiment in the West.

China is in the midst of what Marx described – writing of the British Industrial Revolution – as primitive accumulation, or what we now know as economic take-off: the process in which the majority of the working population moves from the land to industry, from the countryside to the cities. Between 1952 and 2003, agriculture's share of GDP fell from 60 per cent to 16 per cent and its share of employment from 83 per cent to 51 per cent.[26] Although it took China only 10 years to double its per capita output (1977–87) – a measure of the speed of economic take-off – compared with 58 years for the UK, 47 for the US and 11 for South Korea, after three decades of economic growth averaging 9.5 per cent,[27] around half the people still work on the land. It is estimated that even 20 years hence around 20 per cent of the population will still live in the countryside.[28] A crucial consequence of this abundant supply of rural labour is that wages for unskilled work will remain relatively depressed for several decades to come: in other words, for much longer than was the case with the earlier Asian tigers.[29] This does not mean that wages in the more developed regions like Guangdong will remain low: on the contrary, as we have seen, they have already risen considerably.[30] But in the poorer, still largely rural, interior provinces they will continue to be much lower, which is the reason why low-end manufacturing is steadily relocating there. The rapid growth of the Chinese economy since 1978 has largely been a function of the extremely high rate of investment, in the region of 40 per cent of GDP for many years, recently closer to 45 per cent, and approaching 50 per cent in 2010–11 as a result of the

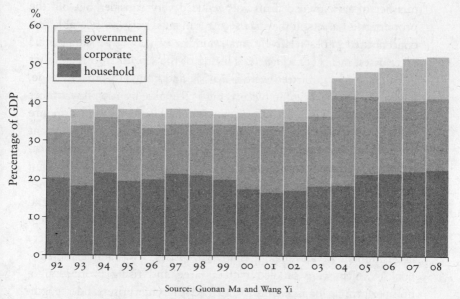

Source: Guonan Ma and Wang Yi

Figure 14. China's gross national saving.

stimulus package after the Western financial crisis.[31] Such an extremely high rate of investment has been possible because of the similarly high rate of domestic savings, running at around 40 per cent of GDP, which, together with inward investment, has provided the main funds for China's take-off. In 2001 the average Chinese household saved 25.3 per cent of its disposable income, compared with 6.4 per cent in the US in 2002. The huge savings made by Chinese families, together more recently with the high level of corporate savings, have played a key role in funding the country's rise (see Figure 14).[32]

It is instructive to compare the experiences of China and Russia because both were confronted with the problem of how to move from a command to a market economy. Russia relied on the preferred Western prescription of shock therapy, which in the nineties led to hyper-inflation, large-scale capital flight, currency collapse and default on foreign debt. In contrast China, by pursuing a more gradualist approach, avoided hyper-inflation, the government remained internationally creditworthy and there was no capital flight. In Russia, the state sector was sold off at knock-down prices to assorted cronies: in China, the total number of state-owned firms was reduced very considerably, but the proportion of assets in the state sector remained very considerable and concentrated into a relatively small number of very large state-owned enterprises. In *Forbes Magazine*'s listing of the world's 100 richest billionaires in 2007, thirteen were in Russia and none in China. In 1990, China's GDP was less than twice as big as Russia's; by 2003 it was more than six times as large. The subsequent rebound in the Russian economy, prior to the global downturn, was largely a result of the increase in the price of its oil and gas exports: unlike the Chinese economy, the Russian economy remains enormously dependent on the country's abundant natural resources. The Chinese leadership has displayed great patience and considerable competence at tackling a succession of difficult and elusive problems. At the end of the nineties, for example, the government was faced with three extremely difficult domestic issues: closing a very large number of loss-making state enterprises; overhauling the state banks, which were saddled with a large and rising proportion of non-performing loans, mainly to indebted state enterprises; and strengthening the weak fiscal position of central government. A decade later, the

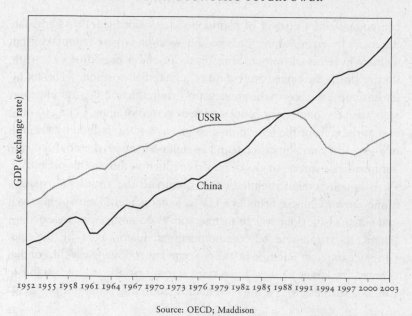

Source: OECD; Maddison

Figure 15. Economic performance of China and the USSR compared.

government had fundamentally overcome these problems, having greatly reduced the problem of indebted state enterprises, transformed the condition of the banking system and improved its own finances.[33]

Given its scale and speed, China's economic transformation is surely the most extraordinary in human history, notwithstanding the sheer novelty of Britain's as the first. The government's economic strategy, shrewd and far-sighted, has been very successful,[34] resulting in stellar economic growth and a rise in per capita income from $339 in 1990 to over $4,000 in 2010. Economic growth is no longer confined to a few 'islands' but has spread out in waves to most provinces of China, albeit in sharply varying degrees. In a remarkably short space of time, China has become the centre of global manufacturing. 'Made in China' has become synonymous with a host of mass-produced consumer products throughout the world. It produces two-thirds of the world's photocopiers, shoes, toys and microwave ovens; half its DVD players, digital cameras and textiles; one-third of its DVD-ROM drives and desktop computers; and a quarter of its mobiles, television sets, PDAs and car stereos.[35] In 2011, China became the world's largest manufacturing country in terms of output, bringing to an end a period of 110 years during which the United States had occupied that position.[36] The country has borne witness to the greatest poverty-reduction programme ever seen, with the number of people living in poverty falling from 250 million at the start of the reform process in 1978 to 80 million by the end of 1993, 29.27 million in 2001, and 26 million in 2007, thereby accounting for three-quarters of global poverty reduction during this period.[37]

Although foreign multinationals dominate the country's exports, home-grown Chinese firms like Haier, Konka, TCL, Lenovo, Huawei and Galanz have done well in such sectors as domestic appliances, computers, television and telecommunications. Encouraged by the 'Go Global' campaign initiated by the government following the turn of the century, the larger Chinese firms started to invest abroad and establish overseas subsidiaries.[38] China has made astounding economic progress,

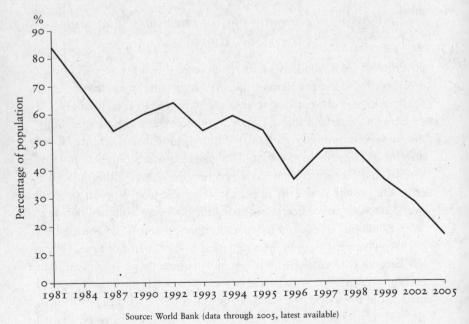

Source: World Bank (data through 2005, latest available)

Figure 16. China: poverty headcount ratio at $1.25 a day (PPP).

but its transformation is far from complete: it remains work in progress. Although it is already the world's second largest economy in terms of GDP (measured by exchange rates), having overtaken Japan in August 2010, this is far more a product of population size than economic sophistication. Can China fulfil its enormous potential and become what might be described as a comprehensive economic superpower?

HOW SUSTAINABLE IS CHINA'S ECONOMIC GROWTH?

At the centre of any discussion about China's future role in the world – let alone talk of a Chinese century – lie the country's economic prospects. A commitment to a growth rate of around 10 per cent has remained fundamental to the government's strategy. China has needed to create around 8 million jobs a year for its expanding urban population, plus another 15 million or so for the new rural migrants who seek urban employment every year.[39] Rapid economic growth will therefore remain at the heart of government strategy. It has been assumed that any serious and sustained drop in the growth rate below 8 per cent could carry the threat of serious social unrest, although the pressure to create jobs will slowly decline as the number of those aged under twenty-nine progressively falls. Can a growth rate of 7–8 per cent be sustained? What are the limits to China's present growth path? For what reasons and under what circumstances could the present strategy go awry? And what have we learned from the impact of the global contraction on China following the Western financial crisis in 2008?

China's economic success has been built upon the huge migration of rural labour into the cities which has kept labour costs remarkably low, made the country a highly attractive destination for foreign investment, and enabled Chinese manufacturing exports to be highly competitive on the global market. This has been the basic engine of China's transformation. As a model it remains far from exhausted. Around half the population still lives in the countryside, so the supply of relatively impoverished rural labour to swell the ranks of the urban labour force is set to continue for at least two decades, if not longer: it is estimated, for example, that over the next fifteen years around 326 million people will move to the cities. But the contours of the Chinese economy are, nonetheless, changing rapidly. Labour costs in the coastal regions – notably Guangdong and the Yangzi Delta – are now too high to be competitive either with countries like Vietnam and Indonesia or with China's interior provinces. Although this trend has been evident for close on a decade, the wave of strikes in Guangdong province in May–June 2010 served to dramatically accelerate this process. Foxconn, one of the biggest employers in the province and Apple's largest supplier, decided, as a result, to relocate a large part of its production to Chengdu, the capital of Sichuan province, with the consequence that by the end of 2011 it employed around 100,000 workers in the city, with an ultimate goal of 300,000, while Intel (previously in Shanghai) also moved to Chengdu, as did Dell and Lenovo; Hewlett Packard, Acer and Asustek chose nearby Chongqing (see Map 9). The differences in wage levels are stark: in Shandong and Shanxi provinces, wages are 82 per cent and 76 per cent respectively of those in Shanghai, while the figure for Chongqing, fast becoming the new frontier for the electronics industry along with Chengdu, is 61 per cent. In provinces such as Anhui, Hunan and Jiangxi, many cities are experiencing much faster economic growth as Chinese companies join the rush to invest in them, helped by China's excellent transport infrastructure.[40] As the interior provinces increasingly assume the role played by Guangdong and the Shanghai region previously, so the latter also become increasingly unattractive for migrant workers who no longer feel the need to uproot themselves in a situation where manufacturing jobs are becoming plentiful in their own home cities and provinces. Meanwhile, the likes of Shanghai and Guangdong are seeking to move up the technological ladder, upgrade their labour force, and increasingly specialize in medium and hi-tech areas of production. The government has been seeking to encourage this latter process in a variety of ways: introducing a new labour law, raising the minimum wage, encouraging highly skilled overseas Chinese who have settled in countries like the United States and Canada to return to China, hugely expanding the number of graduates and investing heavily in the universities, and greatly increasing the resources spent on research and development.

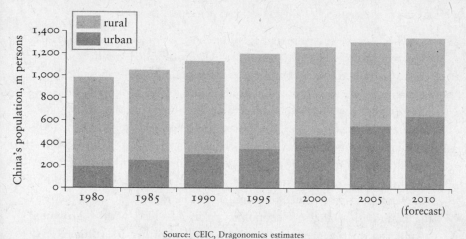

Source: CEIC, Dragonomics estimates

Figure 17. The shift from the countryside to the cities.

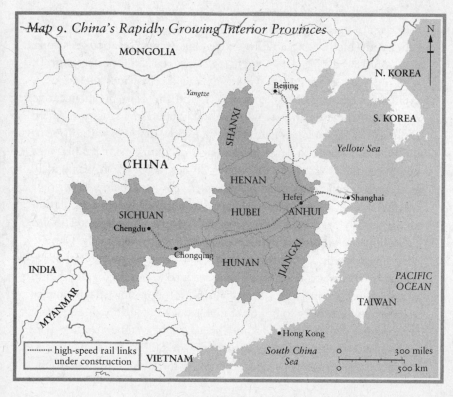

Source: National Bureau of Statistics

The Chinese economy is becoming more complex and variegated, no longer simply based on a huge supply of unskilled labour and very basic manufacturing techniques. As a consequence, priorities are shifting and the needs of more advanced regions are no longer the same as those of less developed regions. Notwithstanding this, the basic policy framework still for the most part remains relatively unchanged, resting on voluminous relatively cheap exports (over half of which foreign firms are responsible for), a very high growth rate, a huge volume of investment facilitated by massive domestic savings, and a very competitively valued renminbi. Over the next decade, this picture is bound to change as economic priorities shift, with a growing emphasis on the productivity of investment rather its volume, less reliance on exports as opposed to domestic consumption, and a slow appreciation of the renminbi, together with its gradual internationalization and modest moves towards its convertibility.

The most obvious danger facing the Chinese economy has been, and remains, its high level of dependence on trade, which makes China extremely vulnerable to exogenous events. In 2007–8, China was confronted with what might be described as a 'perfect storm', with the onset of the worst Western financial crisis since the 1930s, a rapid contraction in Western markets, and the consequent negative impact on Chinese exports. What would happen in a situation where China could no longer rely on Western export markets with, prior to the financial crisis, the European Union accounting for 22 per cent and the United States 18 per cent of Chinese exports? It was widely expected that the economic growth rate would fall below 8 per cent and even sink as low as 6 per cent.[41] There was dark speculation about rapidly rising unemployment and growing social unrest, with the serious possibility of political instability. In the event, the Chinese economy confounded most forecasts, growing at 9.6 per cent in 2008, 9.1 per cent in 2009, 10.3 per cent in 2010, and a projected figure of 9.6 per cent in 2011. The main reason for this extraordinary achievement was a $580 billion stimulus package for 2009–10, which was introduced with remarkable speed in November 2008.[42] The government thus sought to compensate for falling Western demand by encouraging domestic consumption, which accounts for around one-third of total output, but, above all, by engaging in large-scale public expenditure, on education, health and especially infrastructure. The government could do this because it enjoyed very strong finances and was therefore in a position to lavish considerable resources on stimulating the economy. The contrast between the debt-laden, low-growth Western economies and their impoverished governments, and the fast-growth, surplus-generating Chinese economy, and its cash-rich government, is stark. Furthermore, the deposit-rich Chinese banks, all state-owned or largely state-owned, were, at the government's behest, in a position to offer a huge amount of credit at generous interest rates; in contrast, the Western financial sector was effectively bankrupt.

The Chinese government is in the fortunate position of being able to afford another large stimulus package should the Western economy continue in a state of recession or near-zero growth, or face another financial meltdown. Indeed, it would probably be able to afford two or three such packages if circumstances required.[43] The Chinese economy has demonstrated its ability to survive what many thought it could not: a drastic downturn in the Western economy. The stimulus package, however, was not the only reason. Much of the East Asian economy (excluding Japan) bounced back very quickly after the initial shock in late 2008, while many developing countries, most notably India and Brazil, also continued to grow very strongly in 2009 and 2010 following a brief period of adjustment. In other words, the buoyancy of the Chinese economy was a consequence not only of the stimulus package but also of the economic strength of much of the developing world with which it enjoys growing interdependence and to which it now sends over half its exports. As a result, the Chinese economy has in some measure succeeded in decoupling itself from the Western economy. There remains, however, a longer term uncertainty. What would happen if the Western economy fails to emerge from its present impasse and remains at or near zero growth for the foreseeable future, perhaps even a decade, in rather similar fashion to what happened to Japan in the 1990s? Would the Chinese economy be able to withstand such a long-term stagnation in the Western economy? Of course, much would depend on the political consequences of such a scenario, in particular the increased likelihood of a turn towards protection in the United States and also perhaps in the European Union. It would appear that the Chinese government's strategy presently assumes that the Western economy will, at least in the medium term, resume its pre-crisis rate of growth and that its export markets will recover, although there is a growing recognition that this might not be the case.[44] The greatest external insurance against such an eventuality would be the shock absorber provided by a buoyant developing world, which is destined to become increasingly important in the global economy over the next decade, combined with the Chinese government's internal capacity, if need be, to engage in further fiscal stimulus programmes.

Let us return to the longer term issues facing the Chinese economy. As pointed out earlier, the structure of the economy has been shifting rapidly, although so far the main contours of economic strategy have, for the most part, remained largely unchanged. Indeed, in some respects the stimulus package, in relying so heavily on infrastructural investment, served to intensify the problem of over-dependence on investment rather than the productivity of that investment. The key problems which require a major shift in strategy if growth is to be sustained are: currency policy, the efficiency of investment, consumption, welfare and growing inequality, and the environment. The Chinese government is already wrestling with these problems, all of which (apart from the environment) have been made more urgent by the Western downturn.

One advantage that the government has enjoyed since 1978 is that the renminbi has remained a non-tradeable currency. This has acted as an important firewall, protecting what has become an increasingly open economy.[45] It has also enabled the authorities to control the value of the renminbi against other currencies, which has been important in ensuring that Chinese exports were competitive. The government has resisted the temptation to liberalize the capital account and allow the renminbi to float, which would have enhanced the renminbi's international role, promoted China's financial position and made it easier for Chinese firms to invest abroad. The main downside of this, apart from the loss of control over the renminbi's exchange rate, would have been that the huge volume of savings which have underpinned China's ability to invest would have fallen considerably, as savers went abroad in search of rates of return far in excess of the paltry levels they could find at home: this would have denied the country the funds for investment that it has so far enjoyed and, as a consequence, reduced the economic growth rate. In addition, a floating renminbi would have been vulnerable to the kind of speculative attack suffered by the Korean won, Thai baht and Indonesian rupiah in the Asian financial crisis.[46] Although Zhu Rongji, the then Chinese premier, intended to begin the liberalization of the capital account in 2000, the Asian financial crisis persuaded him that such a change would be imprudent. The Western financial crisis confirmed the wisdom of the Chinese leadership in continuing to regulate the capital account, despite persistent calls from the West for deregulation. As we shall see, however, the Chinese government has now taken the first steps towards liberalizing the role of the currency.

The Chinese government has come under greatly intensified pressure from the US government since the financial crisis to allow the renminbi to appreciate very significantly against the dollar as a way of reducing its huge trade deficit with China. There has been considerable domestic resistance to this from Chinese manufacturers of cheap, low-end exports who are sensitive to the fact that demand for their products would inevitably suffer; and they have been strongly supported in this by the Ministry of Commerce. The People's Bank of China, the country's central bank, on the other hand, has generally been in favour of allowing a limited appreciation of the renminbi as a way of pushing the Chinese economy in the direction of a greater emphasis on value-added production.[47] In June 2010 the currency was allowed to appreciate against the dollar and since then there has been a slow but steady process of government-controlled appreciation. The major reason for this has not been relentless American pressure, which the Chinese government is adept at ignoring, but a shifting domestic emphasis on the part of the Chinese authorities towards a more value-added economy and a reduced dependence on exports. With China's increasing economic and financial strength, furthermore, there is a growing strategic argument for encouraging the external role of the renminbi to expand. The stated aim of making Shanghai an international financial centre by 2020, the growing capital requirements of China's rapidly expanding array of international companies, and the financial rewards of the renminbi becoming a major traded currency are pushing the Chinese government in the direction of a progressive easing of the restrictions on the role of the renminbi.

Economic growth cannot depend upon a constantly rising proportion of GDP being devoted to investment, as has been the case in China, because it involves devoting an increasingly untenable proportion of the country's resources to investment, now over 50 per cent, at the expense of consumption. Too much of this investment, furthermore, has been wasteful, being ploughed into unnecessary luxurious condominiums and prestigious government buildings, for example, with local governments being particularly guilty. Future growth must depend less on investment and more on consumption. There needs to be a much greater emphasis on the efficiency of capital and improving labour productivity, rather than an overwhelming dependence on the volume of investment. China's ability to move up the technological ladder ultimately depends on this. This is already beginning to happen, with exports of cheap-end products like toys falling in the global recession and those of high-tech products rising. China also needs to reduce its present level of exposure to foreign trade, which has made it highly vulnerable to cyclical movements in the global economy, as the global recession demonstrated. There is a danger, too, especially if the Western economy fails to recover properly, that China's export drive will provoke a hostile reaction and consequent Western moves towards protectionism: indeed, there have already been clear signs of this in the US.[48] All in all, thus, China will, in future, have to shift the emphasis from exports to domestic consumption. Such a move towards higher-end production and domestic consumption would, in turn, be helped by further appreciation of the renminbi. There has been growing recognition amongst Chinese policy-makers and advisers that important changes need to be made to the model ushered in by Deng and intimately associated with his successor Jiang Zemin.[49] That process, associated with Hu Jintao, began with a shift away from the neo-liberal excesses of the nineties and towards what is termed a more harmonious society, echoing an older Confucian theme, with a new emphasis on egalitarianism, greater weight attached to social protection, a desire to lessen the importance of exports and increase that of domestic consumer spending, and also a turn away from the influence of the United States – or 'de-Americanization', as it has become known.[50] In this context, the twelfth Five Year Plan (2011–15) proposes a much bigger structural reorientation than previously envisaged (including a reduced growth rate in the region of 7 per cent), based on a growing recognition that these questions are now assuming a much greater urgency and that the longer the structural shift is postponed the more painful and difficult it will be to implement.[51]

An increasingly serious problem is that breakneck economic growth has led to China moving in a very short space of time from being a highly egalitarian society to becoming one of the more unequal in the world.[52] China's Gini coefficient – a standard measure of inequality – has risen from 0.30 in 1978 to 0.47–0.50 in 2009 (1.0 representing the most unequal possible society). The causes of inequality are threefold: the growing gulf between the coastal and interior provinces, with the richest province enjoying a per capita GDP ten times that of the poorest (compared with 8:1 in Brazil, for example);[53] that between urban and rural areas (the average urban resident earned 3.3 times as much as the average rural resident in 2009); and that between those in the formal economy and those dependent on informal economic activities.[54] It has been estimated that the richest 1 per cent of households control some 41 per cent of the country's privately held wealth. Growing inequality has led to a rising sense of anger and resentment, which has been exacerbated by the widespread belief – not mistaken – that many of the new rich have achieved their wealth as a result of corruption, often through illicit deals between government officials and the managers of newly privatized companies. A *China Daily* editorial in 2009 argued: 'This angst toward the rich is vented at those who racked up their wealth illegally. They are by no means a small group of people.'[55] On the contrary, indeed, it would appear that corruption is very widespread. Probably the most dramatic example – and there have been many high-profile cases – was in Chongqing where Bo Xilai, the new populist local Party chief, unearthed a huge network of corruption involving Wen Qiang, the former chief of police and head of the city's judicial bureau, Party officials and organized crime, leading to over 3,000 arrests and the execution of Wen Qiang.[56] The danger is that the resentment over inequality and corruption could slowly undermine the broad consensus that has hitherto sustained the reform programme.[57] At the end of 2010, the leading Chinese economist Yu Yongding argued: 'With the contrast between the opulent lifestyles of the rich and the slow improvement of basic living conditions for the poor fomenting social tension, a serious backlash is brewing.'[58] The government has begun to pay much greater attention to promoting a more egalitarian approach, including the invocation of a harmonious society, though so far with very limited effect.

A key issue, in this context, concerns the financial ability of the state to act in the ways that are needed. In the early reform period, decentralization was deliberately encouraged, with budget revenues falling from 34 per cent of GDP in 1978 to 10.8 per cent in 1995, according to the Chinese economist Hu Angang.[59] The state found itself increasingly shorn of many of its old sources of revenue and responsibility.[60] Expenditure by the state, in its turn, came to account for a rapidly declining proportion of GDP: 31 per cent in 1978, reaching a trough of around 11 per cent in 1995. By the mid 1990s there was deep concern about the loss of central state capacity that this involved, including the latter's ability to promote balanced development between the regions, and a determined attempt was made to reverse the process. There were even fears that individual provinces were beginning to operate like independent countries, with an increase in their external trade and a decline in trade flows between them.[61] As a result, the government introduced major tax reforms in 1994 including, for the first time, taxes specifically earmarked for central government; previously, central government was dependent on a share of the taxes raised in the provinces, based on a process of bargaining between the two. The central government also acquired its own tax-collecting capacity, with a large majority of revenue now being collected centrally, some of which is then redistributed to the provinces.[62] Not surprisingly, the rich provinces strongly resented losing out to central government in this way.[63] By 1999, state expenditure had recovered to 14 per cent of GDP and by 2006 to around 22 per cent, and revenues likewise.[64]

Crucially, the state needed to be able to fund its new social security programme in order to provide for the tens of millions of workers made redundant by the state-owned enterprises, which had previously been responsible for virtually all of their employees' social needs, including education, health and housing.[65] The problem is particularly severe with education and health, which have suffered from very serious public under-investment during most of the last two decades, a cause of deep popular concern and resentment.[66] In 2008 alone, education expenditure rose by 45 per cent.[67] During the Maoist period, the state was responsible for almost 100 per cent of health expenditure: the figure is now around 16 per cent, compared, for example, with about 44 per cent in the United States and over 70 per cent in Western Europe. As a result, a majority of the population can no longer afford healthcare. In April 2009 the government announced a major reform of the health system, including the short-term goal of providing basic insurance cover for 90 per cent of the population. The lack of a decent safety net and the threadbare character of key public goods fuel a sense of deep insecurity amongst many people, acting as a powerful incentive for them to save, even though the living standards of the vast majority, especially in the cities, have greatly improved.[68]

A further measure, which seems likely at some point, is the reform of the hukou household registration system, which was originally introduced in 1958. Every person is required to be registered at birth in their parents' official location and is designated as a rural or urban citizen who is eligible for social services like health, education and welfare in that area only. As a consequence, so-called migrant workers who have left their designated towns or villages and sought work in the cities are not eligible for education and health provision in those cities. This has acted as a deterrent to them bringing their families to the cities, although many do, and has led to the stigmatization of migrant workers and their families in the cities as second-class citizens, engendering a form of segregation. In effect, shorn of rights, they have been China's equivalent of Marx's reserve army of labour who have been the foot soldiers of the country's industrialization. In Beijing alone, about half of the 460,000 children born between 2007 and 2009 did not qualify for proper access to education. For almost all major cities, the hukou population is smaller than the actual population; in some cases, such as Shenzhen, the differences are huge. There is now widespread pressure for reform, including from provinces like Guangdong which, with the shift of production to the interior provinces, have found it increasingly difficult to attract migrant workers: indeed, some employers have even started to use illegal Vietnamese workers. It is estimated that Guangdong now faces a labour shortage of 2 million people. Furthermore, in the strikes of 2010, which were repeated on a much more limited scale in 2011, migrant workers have increasingly shown a willingness to stand up for themselves and fight against systemic discrimination.[69] In February 2010, in a most unusual development, a group of 13 Chinese newspapers from across the country carried an identical front-page editorial calling for the abolition of the hukou system.[70] In practice, however, little has so far been done by way of reform. According to government statistics, an estimated 153

		City districts urban areas, m persons (actual)	City districts, m persons (registered)
1	Shanghai	13.5	11.4
2	Beijing	9.9	9.7
3	Guangzhou	7.6	5.7
4	Wuhan	6.8	7.5
5	Tianjin	6.8	6.8
6	Shenzhen	6.5	1.3
7	Chongqing	6.2	9.0
8	Shenyang	4.6	4.9
9	Chengdhu	4.0	3.4
10	Dongguan	3.9	1.5

Source: 2000 Census

Table 2. Populations of China's 10 largest cities in 2000, actual and registered (hukou).

million people have left the countryside, which means that granting them full social rights in the cities where they have settled would be extremely expensive.[71]

Finally, China's growth has been extremely resource-intensive, demanding of land, forest, water, oil and more or less everything else. Herein lies one of China's deepest problems.[72] The country has to support an extremely large and, for the most part, dense population in a situation where China is, and always has been, poorly endowed with natural resources. The notable exception is rare earth minerals, with China responsible for at least 96 per cent of the world's supply of magnesium, cerium oxide, silicon, bismuth and suchlike, which are used in a range of products from mobile phones and fluorescent lights to hybrid cars and wind turbines, and the prices of which have recently soared. Otherwise, China has, for example, only 8 per cent of the world's cultivated land and yet must sustain 22 per cent of the world's population; in contrast, with less than a quarter of China's population, the United States enjoys three times as much arable land and its farmland has been under human cultivation for one-tenth of the time of China's.[73] China's development, moreover, is rapidly exhausting what limited resources it possesses. Over the last forty years almost half of China's forests have been destroyed, so that it now enjoys one of the sparsest covers in the world. In 1993 it became a net importer of oil for the first time and now depends on imports for around 60 per cent of its oil needs.

As a result, China is becoming increasingly dependent on the rest of the world for the huge quantities of raw materials that it needs for its economic growth. It is the world's largest buyer of copper, the second biggest buyer of iron ore, and the third largest buyer of alumina. It absorbs around a third of the global supply of coal, steel and cotton, and half of its cement. It is the second largest energy consumer after the US, with nearly 70 per cent produced from burning coal. In 2005 China used more coal than the US, India and Russia combined. In 2004 it accounted for nearly 40 per cent of the increase in the world demand for oil.[74] If the Chinese economy were to continue to expand at 8 per cent a year in the future, its income per head would reach the current US level in 2031, at which point it would consume

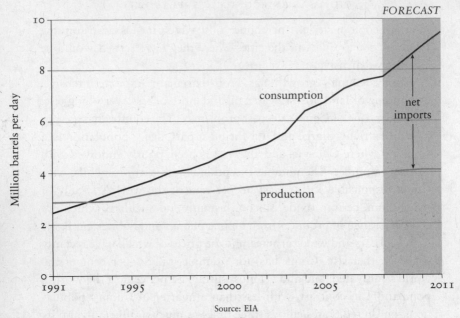

Source: EIA

Figure 18. China's oil production and consumption.

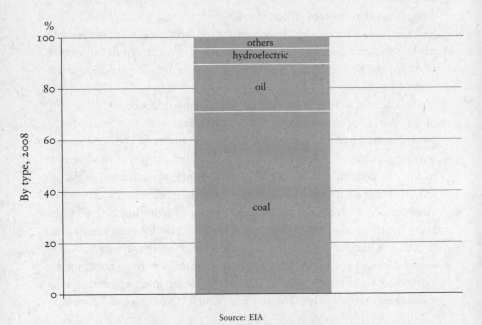

Source: EIA

Figure 19. China's energy consumption.

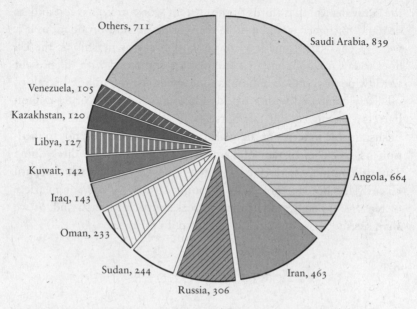

('ooo barrels per day)

Others, 711

Saudi Arabia, 839

Venezuela, 105

Kazakhstan, 120

Libya, 127

Kuwait, 142

Iraq, 143

Angola, 664

Oman, 233

Sudan, 244

Iran, 463

Russia, 306

Source: FACTS Global Energy

Figure 20. China's crude oil imports by source, 2009.

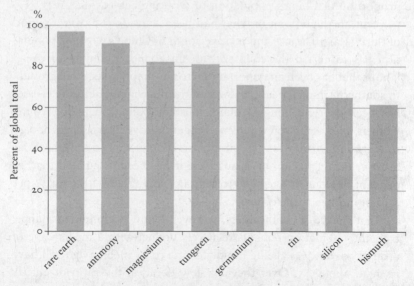

Source: 13D Research

*Figure 21. China's share of global production of
key metals and minerals.*

the equivalent of two-thirds of the current world grain harvest and its demand for paper would double the world's current production. If it were to enjoy the same level of per capita car ownership as the US does today, it would have 1.1 billion cars compared with the present worldwide total of 800 million; and it would use 99 million barrels of oil a day compared with a worldwide total production of 84 million barrels a day in 2006.[75] Of course, such a level of demand would be unsustainable in terms of the world's available resources, not to mention its global environmental impact, which would be dire. China cannot continue with the resource-intensive policy which, until recently, has been integral to its economic strategy. It has, for a variety of reasons, no choice other than to seek a new approach and, as we shall see shortly, it has already begun to do this.

GETTING OLDER

China's growth has benefited from the fact that the country has possessed a very large and also a very young population. In 2010 the proportion of China's population of working age (15–64) was 71.9 per cent, the high point of what had been a steady rise over a period of thirty years. The size and relative youth of China's working population has furnished the country with an abundant supply of cheap labour that has been an important factor in enabling its rapid growth. In southern China the labour force in the huge manufacturing centres has been overwhelmingly young; it is the young, including young women, who have been willing and eager to leave their villages and go to work in factories as migrant labour. People over 40 have been far more reluctant to uproot themselves: it has been calculated that 24 per cent of villagers aged 16–30 migrate, compared with only 11 per cent of those in their forties.

That picture of youthfulness, however, is now beginning to change: true, the population remains relatively young, with a median age of around 30, but it is ageing rapidly. By 2050 its median age will have risen to about 45. Over the next few decades, the ratio of elderly dependants to people of working age will rise from 10 per cent at present to 40 per cent by 2050. From roughly 2030, China will have more elderly dependants than children, in contrast to most developing countries where the opposite will, by and large, continue to be the case.[76] The trend towards ageing is already evident. The proportion of people aged over 60 increased from 10.4 per cent in 2000 to 13.3 per cent in 2011, while those under 16 comprised 16.6 per cent of the total compared with 23 per cent in 2000. Shanghai's ratio of residents over 60 – namely, 19 per cent – is the highest of any mainland city and by 2030 is expected to reach 32 per cent.[77] Until around 2015, the number of people of working age will continue to grow, albeit slowly, from 977 million in 2010 to about 993 million in 2015, but those aged between 15 and 24 entering the labour force will fall by almost 30 per cent over the next decade. The fact that women already comprised 44.65 per cent of the labour force in 2008 suggests that there is little room for expansion in this area.[78] China's pattern of ageing is very similar to what has happened in other East Asian countries such as Japan, South Korea, Taiwan, Hong Kong and Singapore. These, however, were already relatively rich before they started to age while China will face the problem of ageing before it manages to become rich.

The consequences of ageing – especially given the likely speed of the process – will be far-reaching. China will no longer be able to rely on a bountiful supply of labour and, as a consequence, it will become increasingly expensive. Already, migrant labour is no longer in such abundant supply in Guangdong province, which was one of the factors that helped to strengthen the hand of the workers during the wave of successful strikes in summer 2010. The rising cost of labour will make China less competitive as a centre of cheap manufacturing, although the shift towards the interior provinces will help to allay this problem in the short to medium term. Meanwhile the rise in the cost of labour will act as an increasingly powerful pressure towards a more capital- and knowledge-intensive economy. The country will also have to cope with the growing burden of a rising proportion of the population who can no longer work, combined with a contracting workforce that will be obliged to support them. The social and cultural, as well as economic, effects of this will be considerable. Chinese parents are expected to support and care for their elderly parents, in

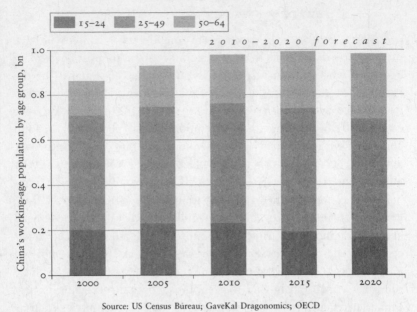

Source: US Census Bureau; GaveKal Dragonomics; OECD

Figure 22. China's ageing labour force.

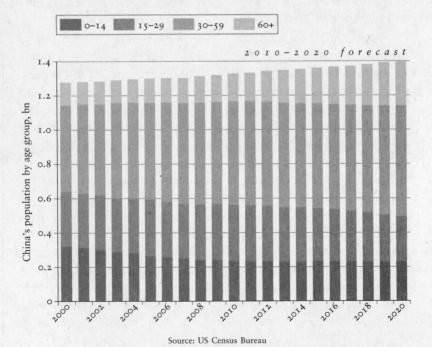

Source: US Census Bureau

Figure 23. Growing shortage of youth.

addition to bringing up their own children, assisted by their grand-parents: this is often referred to, in the context of the one-child policy, as the 4-2-1 family. As the proportion of older people rises, this will become increasingly difficult, the fear being that over time one child will be obliged to look after two parents and four grandparents. At present, there are few old people's homes while pension arrange-ments remain relatively threadbare: just 31 per cent of the workforce, mainly in the state sector, now receive public pensions and medical insurance.

There is, of course, one obvious course of action open to the Chi-nese government in order to at least alleviate the process of ageing, namely reform of the one-child policy first introduced in 1980 soon after Deng Xiaoping came to power. The one-child policy has never been quite as straightforward as the name suggests. People in the countryside have generally been allowed to have two children, while the ethnic minorities have been permitted to have more than two. Further reforms have been introduced recently: for example, if both parents have themselves been single children, then they are allowed to have two children. Considerable latitude is given to local govern-ment when it comes to family policy and a range of initiatives have

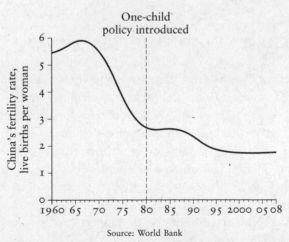

Source: World Bank

Figure 24. Falling birth rate.

recently been taken in the direction of a more liberal system, although as yet the government has refrained from announcing any comprehensive national reform to a policy which is deemed to have been a great success and which still enjoys majority popular support according to opinion polls. Nonetheless, it seems highly likely that sooner or later major changes will be forced upon the government in view of the problem of ageing. This has two fundamental causes: a low birth rate, well below the replacement level of 2.1 (it is estimated that the present fertility rate stands at 1.7), and rising life expectancy, which increased by 5.1 years to 73.1 years between 1990 and 2008 alone.[79] Clearly if China could find a way of raising the birth rate, then the problem of ageing could be postponed or at least significantly eased. But there is no certainty that even if the one-child policy was heavily modified or even abolished it would lead to a major hike in the birth rate. If the experience of other East Asian countries is a guide (and many Western nations also), as the urban population, and women in particular, become increasingly accustomed to the benefits of a career and a range of lifestyle choices, bearing and bringing up children becomes a relatively less attractive option. In the medium to long term, the ageing of China's population is going to pose a formidable challenge.

THE ENVIRONMENTAL DILEMMA

The effects of China's great paradox – namely, a huge abundance of human resources and extremely sparse natural resources – are being experienced throughout the world via the global market. China's surfeit of labour has meant that the prices of manufactured goods it produces have fallen considerably, while the prices of those commodities that China requires rose dramatically prior to the global recession. Together these constitute what might be described as the new China-era global paradigm. The great beneficiaries of China's growth, hitherto, have been the developed countries, which have enjoyed a falling real price for consumer goods, and those nations which are major producers of primary products. True, the global recession saw a sharp fall in commodity prices, but these have subsequently recovered and continued rising, driven by demand from China and India in particular and the generally buoyant economic conditions in the developing world. The International Energy Agency forecast that oil prices would rebound to more than $100 a barrel when the world economy recovered, a figure that had already been comfortably exceeded by early 2011, and would surpass $200 by 2030.[80] Rising commodity prices will make the present resource-intensive Chinese growth model increasingly, and ultimately prohibitively, expensive. Beyond a certain point, therefore, it will be impossible for China to follow the resource-intensive American model of progress; and that will happen long before China gets anywhere near the US's present living standards. Indeed, it is already clear that China has decided to pursue a less energy-intensive approach.

China, however, will find it extremely difficult to change course. For centuries it has pursued a highly extractive approach towards a natural environment which, compared with that of most nations, is extremely poorly endowed with resources, most obviously arable land and water, as measured by population density. China, for example, has only one-fifth as much water per capita as the United States. Furthermore, while southern China is relatively wet, the north, home to about half the country's population, is an immense parched region that threatens to become the world's largest desert.[81] The Chinese state, from the great canals of the Ming dynasty to the Three Gorges Dam of the present, has long viewed the environment as something that can be manipulated for, and subordinated to, human ends.[82] The level of environmental awareness, on the part of government and people alike, has been very low, though this is now changing rapidly, especially in the main cities, as exemplified by the vigorous effort to improve the quality of Beijing's air.[83] Poor societies, for obvious reasons, give greater priority to material change than virtually all other considerations, including the environment. It is much easier for a rich society to make the environment a priority than a poor society – and China remains a relatively poor society. By 2015 China will only have reached the same standard of living as most Western countries achieved in 1960 and the latter, able to draw either on their own natural resources, those of their colonies or those of newly-independent countries that were in a weak bargaining position, enjoyed the luxury of being able to grow without any concern for environmental constraints, or steeply rising commodity prices, until they were already rich.[84] In European terms, China has torn from the eighteenth century to the twenty-first century in little more than three decades, pursuing a similar resource-intensive strategy, with the environment never more than a footnote. The result is a huge ecological deficit of two centuries accumulated in just a few decades: growing water shortages, over three-quarters of river water that is unsuitable either for drinking or fishing, 300 million people lacking access to clean drinking water, rampant deforestation, sixteen of the world's twenty worst-polluted cities, acid rain affecting a third of Chinese territory, desert covering a quarter of the country, and 58 per cent of land classified as arid or semi-arid.[85]

China, still poor though it may be, will not have the option of postponing until it has achieved rich-country status in at least two of its most pressing environmental issues. Willy-nilly, it will be obliged by cost pressures to shift towards less resource-intensive technologies. With the price of oil likely to increase considerably, at least in the medium term, and already dependent on imports for 60 per cent of its oil, China has begun to seek ways of limiting its consumption by, for example, imposing heavier taxes on gas-guzzlers and encouraging the development of alternative car technologies:[86] in Shanghai, which is China's environmental leader, it now costs around £2,700 to register a new car.[87] Chinese economist Yu Yong-ding is certain the country will take action: 'A billion Chinese driving gas-hogging SUVs is just a fantasy. Believe me, the Chinese are not so stupid. China has to and will reduce its reliance on oil imports.'[88] The other irresistible environmental challenge is climate change. This has already obliged China to seek ways of limiting its production of CO_2 in the same way that it is forcing other countries to seek alternative forms of growth.[89] Like India, China has for long resisted the idea that it should be subject to the same kind of constraints as rich countries, on the grounds that the latter have been pumping greenhouse gases into the atmosphere for much longer and therefore bear a much greater responsibility for global warming. During the last forty years, China's impact on climate change has been one-sixth of that of the United States, while over the past twenty years it has been less than half of the United States and the same as that of the European Union. The major contributor to China's energy consumption, moreover, is not the domestic consumer, whose needs are minimal, but the export trade. The reality is that 40 per cent of China's energy goes into producing exports for Western markets, in other words, the source is multinationals rather than Chinese firms: the West has, in effect, exported part of its own greenhouse emissions to China.[90] The minimal historical contribution made by the developing world to global warming was recognized in the Kyoto Protocol, which excluded them from its provisions, but the refusal of the United States and Australia to participate rendered the accord largely ineffectual.

But with China having overtaken the United States as the biggest emitter of CO_2 in 2007[91] (even though its per capita CO_2 emissions remain one-seventh of those of the US),[92] the idea that countries such as China and India could be excluded from future agreements was no longer plausible, especially as the effects of global warming – already very evident in China itself, with accelerating desertification, reductions in agricultural yields, changing patterns of precipitation, the increased incidence of extreme weather like the prolonged snowfalls in central China in 2008 and the worst drought in south-west China for more than a century in 2010[93] – grow ever more serious. The environmental impact of energy use in China is particularly adverse because its dependence on coal – of a particularly dirty kind – is unusually high (60 per cent compared with 23 per cent in the US and 5 per cent in France), with carbon emissions from coal proportionately much greater than from oil and gas.[94] Although the Chinese leadership has resisted the idea that the country should be subject to internationally agreed emission targets, it has accepted the scientific argument concerning global warming and, in both speeches and the growing volume of new environmental regulations, has been

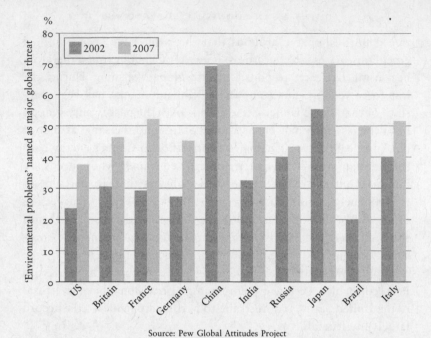

Source: Pew Global Attitudes Project

Figure 25. Growing concern over environmental problems.

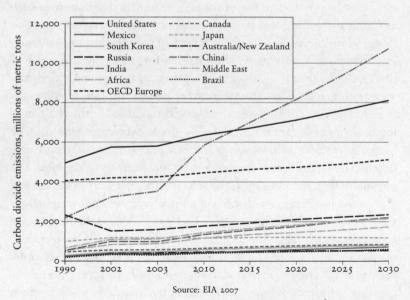

Source: EIA 2007

Figure 26. World carbon dioxide emissions by country, 1990–2030.

displaying a heightened awareness of the problem.[95] In fact, on paper China already has some of the most advanced laws in the world on renewable energy, clean production, environmental impact assessment and pollution control, though these still remain widely ignored in practice.[96] The government has so far resisted the idea that environmental considerations should detract from the priority of rapid economic growth, but there is, nonetheless, widespread recognition of their urgency at the highest levels of the Chinese leadership.[97] The need for China to embrace a green development strategy, rather than relying on the old intensive model, has been powerfully argued by the influential Chinese economist Hu Angang, who has called for a green revolution and has advocated a reduction in the economic growth rate to 8.5 per cent to this end.[98]

The Copenhagen climate conference in December 2009, which was held under the auspices of the United Nations, represented a key stage in the debate over climate change.[99] China's unilateral commitment before the conference was to reduce energy consumption per unit of GDP by 20 per cent in 2010 compared with 2005, and to reduce emissions of greenhouse gases per unit of GDP by 40–45 per cent in 2020 compared with 2005. The conference proved to be an unpredictable, conflictual and contentious affair, with China, Europe and the United States, for example, each pursuing different objectives. China forged a close alliance with India, and also Brazil and South Africa, in what became known as the Basic grouping. It also made common cause with the developing countries in the G-77, though important differences surfaced with the island nations, indicating that the unity of the developing world could no longer be taken for granted. For the first time in a major global conference in the modern era, neither the United States nor Europe was in the driving seat; indeed, Europe was not even a serious player in the final stages of the conference. The authors of the final agreement were the Basic countries led by China, with the United States playing a secondary role. No binding international targets were agreed, with China and India in particular, as developing countries committed to rapid economic growth, strongly opposed to them, citing the inviolability of the sovereignty of the nation-state. Instead, there was simply an agreement to limit global warming to no more than 2 degrees Celsius by reducing greenhouse emissions.

China, meanwhile, is making a huge commitment to renewable sources of energy. It aims to generate 15 per cent of its electricity from renewable sources by 2020 and one-third by 2050. It is already the world's largest producer of solar panels, exporting 95 per cent of its output, and in Suntech possesses the world's largest manufacturer of solar panels. In 2009 China also became the largest producer of wind turbines.[100] China is investing heavily in electric cars. It is not inconceivable that by 2015, encouraged by generous government incentives for both producers and consumers, half of all new cars could be battery-powered, though the prospects for this are looking increasingly remote. The market leader is BYD, which has ambitious plans for electric car production, including large-scale exports.[101] A hint of what the future might hold is provided by the dramatic growth in the use of electric cycles and scooters: a decade ago just a few thousand electric bikes were produced annually, whereas in 2009 22 million were sold, together with millions of kits to turn ordinary bikes into electric ones. They are rapidly becoming ubiquitous on the streets of China's cities and almost overnight China has become the global leader in the industry.[102] China is also taking bold measures to reduce vehicle emissions. In 2008 the government reduced the tax on family vehicles with engines up to 1.6 litres to 1 per cent, while at the same time increasing taxes on cars, minivans and SUVs with larger engines to as much as 40 per cent. Its fuel efficiency regulations are now far more stringent than those in the United States. It has also been investing hugely in public transport, with most of the largest cities now possessing a subway system and a high-speed rail network rapidly expanding across the country.

China has clearly set the goal of becoming the global leader in the new low carbon technologies, from solar power and wind turbines to hydrogen, hydro-power and batteries.[103] Such is the scale of the Chinese market, moreover, that whatever technologies China develops in clean and renewable energy are likely in practice to become the new global standard. With already a very considerable volume of exports, including to developed countries, it could become by far the world's leading manufacturer of renewable energy plants and at a price, furthermore, affordable to developing countries.[104]

It is still too early to draw any definite conclusions as to whether China will be able to reduce its emissions in the medium to long term. The government is certainly serious in its desire to do so, and is clear about the reasons why it matters, but it remains committed to fast economic growth which conflicts with this objective. For a long time to come, notwithstanding the enormous investment in renewable energy, China will be heavily dependent on coal for its electricity generation. Furthermore, breakneck urbanization, presently growing at 1 per cent annually, would mean that in thirty years there will be 450 million more people (or one and a half times the population of the United States) living in China's cities than is the case now, which would inevitably rachet up emissions.

LOW TECH OR HIGH TECH?

At present, China's comparative advantage lies primarily in low-end manufacturing, where it is able to exploit the huge supply of cheap unskilled labour and thereby produce at rock-bottom prices – or 'China prices', as the new global benchmark has become known – for the world market.[105] In the longer run, there are two inherent problems with this. First, in terms of the total costs of getting a product to market, the proportion represented by manufacturing is very small – around 15 per cent of the final price – with the bulk of costs being creamed off by design, marketing, branding and so forth, tasks which are still overwhelmingly carried out in the developed world.[106] It has been estimated, for example, that although the Apple iPhone is assembled in China (and therefore its whole value counts against the US trade deficit with China), the actual value added in China accounts for only 3.6 per cent of the final wholesale cost.[107] Second, most of China's exports are produced by Western and Japanese (and, in addition, Korean and Taiwanese) multinationals, with Chinese manufacturers cast predominantly in the role of subcontractors. Furthermore, the primary activity of multinationals in China hitherto has been low-cost assembly. In other words, China's role has basically been low-end manufacturing in the multifarious global operations of multinationals.[108]

There is, however, plenty of evidence that China is steadily climbing the technological ladder. Like all newcomers, it has been obliged to make it up as it goes along and find its own distinctive path. One avenue used by China to gain access to new technologies has been a combination of copying, buying, and cajoling foreign partners in joint ventures to transfer technology in return for being granted wider access to China's market. The lure of the latter has proved a powerful bargaining counter, especially with second-tier multinationals, but increasingly with first-tier as well.[109] China has already overtaken many South-East Asian countries in important areas of technology, and its ability to drive a hard bargain with foreign multinationals has been a major factor in this. While Proton, Malaysia's national car company, for example, has been unable to persuade any of its various foreign partners – most notably Mitsubishi – to transfer key technology,

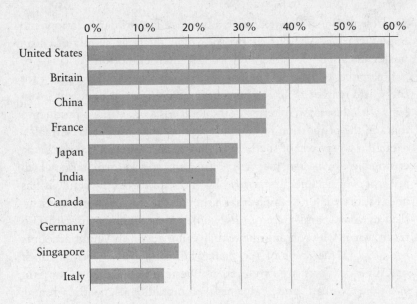

Figure 27. Percentage of multinationals with R&D centres in various countries in 2006.

the Chinese car companies have been much more successful. Indeed, technology transfer has been a general requirement in joint ventures. Moreover, as China has grown more powerful, the demand for technology transfer has become ever more insistent, with foreign companies, complain though they may, generally conceding. The Chinese market is just too big and too important for the great majority of firms to entertain the idea of exclusion.[110] There is another route by which China has been negotiating its way up the technological ladder: when foreign multinationals move their manufacturing operations to China, there is a strong tendency for other functions to follow so as to take advantage of economies of scale, for reasons of convenience, and because highly skilled Chinese labour is plentiful and cheap.[111] The textile industry in Italy, for instance, has progressively migrated to China, starting with manufacturing, followed by more value-added processes like design.[112] Microsoft, Motorola and Nokia have all established major research and development centres in Beijing, while Lucent-Alcatel has done the same in Nanjing. There are now over 1,200 foreign-invested R&D centres in China, many of which are global not just regional. As a consequence, Chinese professionals are becoming increasingly important players in the research and development (R&D) activity of multinationals.[113]

In the longer term, however, the key to China's technological potential will lie in its ability to develop its own high-level R&D capacity. Because China's growth has hitherto relied mainly on imported technologies, Chinese firms own a tiny fraction of the intellectual property rights of their core technologies. Moreover, Chinese companies have spent on average only 0.56 per cent of turnover on research and development, and even in large firms this has only risen to 0.71 per cent.[114] However, enormous efforts are being made to change this state of affairs, with the aim of increasing R&D spending from $24.6 billion (1.23 per cent of GDP) in 2004, to $45 billion (2 per cent of GDP) in 2010 (in the event it fell short at 1.75 per cent), and $113 billion (2.5 per cent of GDP) in 2020.[115] In 2006 the share of GDP accounted for by R&D in the European Union was 1.76 per cent, the US 2.62 per cent, and Japan 3.39 per cent, compared with 1.42 per cent in China. In 2011, China was poised to overtake Japan

R&D spending ($ in US billions)

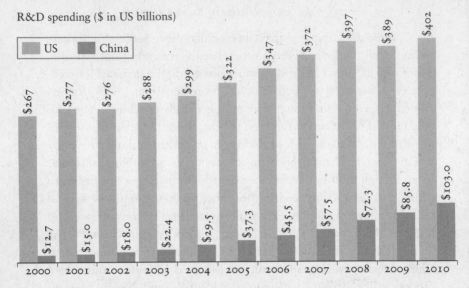

Source: National Science Foundation (US); Ministry of Science and Technology (China)

Figure 28. China's growing R&D.

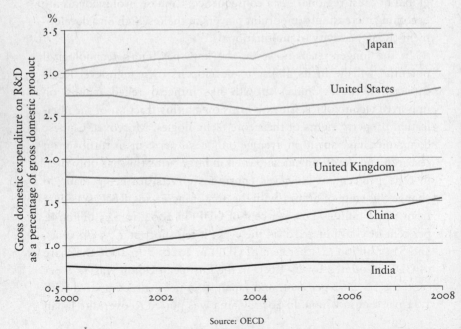

Source: OECD

Figure 29. R&D expenditure as a proportion of GDP.

and become the world's second largest spender on R&D after the United States, which continued to enjoy a very big lead.[116] China is also becoming a major player in the output of scientific papers, its contribution rising from around 2 per cent of world share in 1995 to 6.5 per cent in 2004.[117] By 2009, China had increased its share to 11 per cent, according to Thomson Reuters National Science Indicators, with the US share at 28 per cent, having fallen from 40 per cent in the early 1980s.[118] Citation rates, although very low, are also rising exponentially.[119] The overall figures hide strengths in particular areas, for example material science, analytical chemistry and rice genomics. A recent analysis of nanoscience publications shows that China ranked second behind only the US in 2004.[120] Not surprisingly, publications are concentrated amongst a handful of elite institutions such as the Chinese Academy of Science, Beijing University and Tsinghua University (also in Beijing), which China is seeking to develop as world-class centres.[121]

Among China's strengths is the fact that it possesses a large number of highly educated professionals as well as a powerful educational ethos widely shared across the population.[122] The country produced almost 4.5 million graduates in 2007 compared with 950,000 in 2000: the equivalent figures for the United States are 2.7 million in 2007 and a little over 2.1 million in 2000. In addition, a significant number of Chinese students are educated at the top American universities, with a sizeable proportion choosing to stay on and work in the US afterwards: Chinese, for example, account for around one-third of all professional and technical staff in Silicon Valley.[123] The Chinese government has been intensifying its efforts to persuade overseas Chinese to return home: 81 per cent of the members of the Chinese Academy of Sciences and 54 per cent of the Chinese Academy of Engineering are now returned overseas scholars.[124] Overall, it is estimated that around 20 per cent of Chinese professionals working overseas have now returned, thus repeating a similar pattern that occurred with earlier Korean migration.[125] The overseas Chinese represent an extremely valuable potential asset in China's efforts to raise the scientific and technical level of the economy, hence the considerable effort being expended to persuade them to return home.

The technological picture, as in virtually every other aspect of

China's development, is extremely uneven, combining the primitive, the low-tech, the medium-tech, and pockets of advanced, even very advanced, technology.[126] There is, however, little reason to doubt that China will scale the technological ladder.[127] This, after all, is exactly what happened with other Asian tigers, most obviously Japan, South Korea and Taiwan, all of which started on the lowest, imitative rungs, but which now possess impressive technological competence, with Japan and South Korea well in advance of the great majority of European countries. The evidence is already palpable that China is engaged in a similar process and with the same kind of remarkable speed.[128] It is an illusion to think that China will be trapped indefinitely in the foothills of technology. In time it will become a formidable technological power.

Unlike the early Asian tigers, Chinese firms were unable to postpone their move into foreign markets and production until they had acquired a solid financial foundation, technical competence, a well-established brand and high profitability based on domination of their home market; the major motive for many Chinese companies going abroad, in contrast, has been their desire to escape the cut-throat competition – much of it foreign – and sparse profits of the domestic market following China's accession to the WTO.[129] Peter Nolan, an expert on Chinese business, has argued that it will be extremely difficult for Chinese companies to make the A-list of multinationals precisely because they have not had the chance to build themselves up domestically behind a protectionist wall. He also suggests that over the last twenty years there has been a global business revolution, as a result of which Chinese companies, far from catching up, have fallen even further behind the top international firms, making their task even more difficult.[130]

If China fails to produce a cluster of major international firms it will stand in sharp contrast to Japan, South Korea and Taiwan.[131] But this view already seems unduly pessimistic. However difficult and different the circumstances China faces, it is busy inventing its own path of development, as Britain did as the pioneer country, the United States as the inventor of mass production, and Japan as the innovator of a new kind of just-in-time production. What might this be? Take the example of the car industry. The more expensive sectors of the market are overwhelmingly the preserve of European, American, Japanese and Korean firms, but emergent Chinese firms like BYD, Chery and Geely dominate the lowest segment.[132] Chinese firms are able to produce cars much more cheaply than foreign producers because they use a modular, or mix and match, approach rather than the integrated method of production for which Japanese firms are renowned. Firms such as Geely and Chery utilize a range of parts which are borrowed, copied or bought from foreign companies. The end product is of relatively low quality but extremely cheap. The Chevrolet Spark, which was very similar to the Chery QQ, sold for twice the price. A similar kind of approach can be seen with the Tata Nano in India, which sells for less than $2,500, half the price of the next cheapest car on the market.[133] Modular – or open architecture – production is extremely well suited to a developing country, being relatively labour-intensive and very difficult, if not impossible, for Western and Japanese firms to imitate. In the Chinese case, it was first developed by the motorcycle, truck and consumer appliance industries and then adapted by domestic car firms.[134] As in other developing countries, the low end of the market will remain by far the largest sector for some time to come. Despite fearsome competition from much better-resourced foreign producers, Chinese car manufacturers have slowly been increasing their share of the Chinese market, which

---

*1 *BYD F3 – 285,913*
 2 Buick Excelle – 241,109
 3 Hyundai Elantra (New) – 239,449
 4 Volkswagon Jetta – 224,857
 5 Honda Accord – 175,357
 6 Hyundai Elantra – 171,605
*7 *Chery QQ – 168,554*
 8 Toyota (FAW) Corolla – 157,457
 9 Toyota (Guangzhou Automobile) Camry – 154,977
*10 *Xiali Xiali – 147,547*

---

*These three models are Chinese brands

Source: www.chooseauto.com.cn

Table 3. Chinese car sales top ten, 2009.

is now the world's largest: in 2006 their combined market share was 25.6 per cent, just behind the total Japanese share of 25.7 per cent and ahead of the aggregate European share of 24.3 per cent, with Chery and Geely, the two largest, enjoying a combined share of around 10 per cent. By 2009 the share of domestic producers had risen to 32 per cent. Although analysts and industry insiders used to suggest that it would take Chinese car-makers a generation to reach

Rear-mounted engine
A $700 dollar engine is less than half the size of most, with a horsepower of 30 to 35. The Honda Fit (also known as the Jazz), one of the smallest cars sold in the United States, has 109 horsepower.

Modern comforts
Has no radio, power steering, power windows or air-conditioning.

Instrument panel
Minimal, with only a speedometer, mileometer and fuel gauge.

Windscreen wiper
One rather than the customary two.

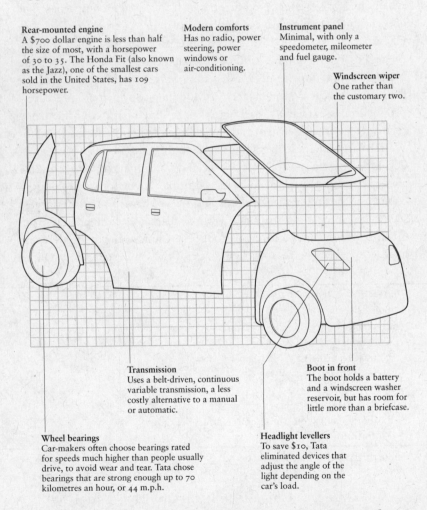

Transmission
Uses a belt-driven, continuous variable transmission, a less costly alternative to a manual or automatic.

Boot in front
The boot holds a battery and a windscreen washer reservoir, but has room for little more than a briefcase.

Wheel bearings
Car-makers often choose bearings rated for speeds much higher than people usually drive, to avoid wear and tear. Tata chose bearings that are strong enough up to 70 kilometres an hour, or 44 m.p.h.

Headlight levellers
To save $10, Tata eliminated devices that adjust the angle of the light depending on the car's load.

Figure 30. How to make a cheap car, Indian-style: the Tata Nano.

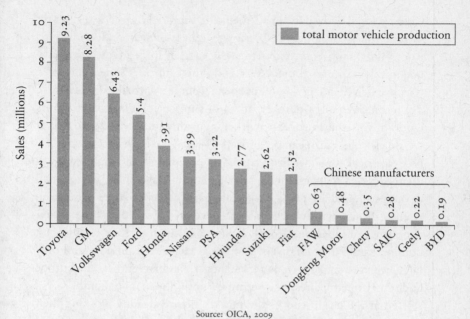

Source: OICA, 2009

Figure 31. World ranking of motor vehicle manufacturers, 2008.

globally competitive status, they now think in terms of ten or even five years. The growing competitiveness of domestic producers is being assisted by foreign takeovers, the outstanding example so far being Geely's acquisition of Volvo from Ford in 2010.[135] It seems only a matter of time before China has a couple of car firms competing on equal terms with the world's giants, especially if BYD succeeds in becoming a global leader in electric cars and hybrids.[136]

Based on the experience of the Chinese automobile industry, we should expect Chinese firms to enter at the bottom end of the global market for mass consumer goods, initially mainly in the developing world – of which there is already much evidence[137] – but later moving into the developed world. It will take time for firms like Haier, Konka, Galanz and Chery to establish themselves in Western markets, where design requirements, safety standards, tastes and expectations are very different from the 'cheap-end' advantage presently enjoyed by Chinese firms. In fact, BYD, Geely (before its acquisition of Volvo) and

Chery have already postponed their entry into the American market several times, although MG (now Chinese-owned and known as Roewe in China) launched in the UK market in 2011. A cautionary tale in this respect is provided by TCL, the Chinese TV manufacturer, which entered into a joint European venture with the French firm Thomson. It made a number of serious miscalculations based on its ignorance of the European market and announced in 2006 that it would close its European operations.[138] But TCL is an exception: Chinese electrical appliance firms have overwhelmingly chosen to establish their overseas manufacturing subsidiaries in developing rather than developed countries. There is a certain parallel, in this context, between Chinese firms initially targeting the developing world and the earlier experience of Japan and Korea. Japanese companies, for example, first dominated the then relatively poor local East Asian markets and only later began to make serious inroads into Western markets. In Europe and the United States, furthermore, both Japan and South Korea started at the cheap end of the market before steadily working their way up, Toyota being a case in point. The same will be broadly true of China, except it will probably prioritize the developing world even more strongly. Chinese exports to Africa, the Middle East, Asia and South America have been growing far more rapidly than those to the United States; indeed, Chinese exports to the developing world now account for over half its total exports. China sent more than 31 per cent of its exports to the US in 2000 but that figure had dropped to just over 22 per cent by early 2007 and is now 18 per cent.[139]

We can already identify a number of broad trends which indicate the contours of the future development of Chinese companies.[140] We will continue to see the slow but steady emergence of Chinese multinationals in areas which play to their domestic comparative advantage, in particular the sheer size of the domestic market, such as white and electrical appliances, motorcycles, trucks and cars. Examples of such companies are Haier, Galanz, Konka and BYD.[141] Another obvious area, given the country's concentration on industrialization and urbanization, is construction, infrastructure and heavy industry. Firms like Sany Heavy Industry (construction machinery), Shanghai Zhenhua Heavy Industry (construction machinery), Guangxi Liugong (wheel loaders), Sany Heavy Equipment (tunnel borers for coal-mining), Hollysys (distributed control systems in industrial automation) are not only domestic leaders but also increasingly major players in developing countries and in some cases developed countries. Shanghai Zhenhua, for example, is responsible for a critical section of the rebuilding of the earthquake-prone San Francisco Bay Bridge. Meanwhile, with China having constructed the world's largest high-speed rail network by 2009 – the size of which will exceed those of the rest of the world combined by 2012 – it is not surprising that rail manufacturers like China South Locomotive are set to become formidable global competitors, notwithstanding the fatal accident at Wenzhou in July 2011.[142] It will also be interesting to see what happens to Baidu, the internet search engine giant, which in 2011 enjoyed a 75.8 per cent share of the Chinese market and which has provided formidable opposition to Google, with the latter's market share down to a lowly 19.2 per cent. Will Baidu continue to be the overwhelmingly dominant player in the domestic market or will it also find a way of combining this with a major international presence?[143]

Chinese brands are also beginning to leave their mark in fields such as sports equipment (for example Li-Ning)[144] – linked to China's growing strength as a sporting nation – and pharmaceuticals. Li-Ning is second only to Nike in the Chinese market, with a very significant R&D spend, while in pharmaceuticals, where China's huge population offers an enormous advantage in terms of clinical trials, Simcere, a very large producer of generic drugs, is an example of a fast-rising Chinese firm. As we saw earlier, China is making a major push in renewable energy, notably solar panels, in which Suntech Power Holdings is already the global leader, and wind turbines, with firms like China High Speed Transmission, Goldwind, Sinovel and Dongfang. Renewable energy is an example of a high-tech industry in which Chinese firms are displaying a formidable competitive edge and in which they have already established a major global presence, but it is by no means alone. The most outstanding example is probably Huawei, which is China's largest telecom equipment and network technologies provider. By 2009 it had about 15 per cent of the global market in telecoms infrastructure. In late 2009 it overtook

Nokia-Siemens to become the second largest supplier of mobile network equipment in the world after Ericsson. Initially its major impact was at home and in developing markets, but it now also competes effectively in developed markets, no longer primarily on cost but on specification and quality. In 2009 it came second only to Panasonic in terms of the number of patents registered in the US, Europe and Japan. Another giant in telecommunications, of course, is China Mobile, while Lenovo became a worldwide player in computers following its purchase of IBM's computer subsidiary.[145]

The Commercial Aircraft Corporation of China (Comac), the main Chinese aerospace group, will shortly begin production of its own regional passenger jet,[146] which made its maiden flight in 2008. It is also developing a narrow-body plane which will compete directly with the Airbus 320 and the Boeing 737, with first deliveries scheduled for 2016. Meanwhile, Airbus has announced its intention of shifting some of its manufacturing capacity to China.[147] Possibly as a way of leapfrogging the development process, Comac was reported in 2007 to be considering investing in, or bidding for, six of Airbus's European plants that had been deemed surplus to requirements, although in the event no offer materialized.[148] Given time, it is inconceivable that China – already the second largest aircraft market in the world[149] – will not become a major aircraft producer in its own right. The Chinese government is in the process of introducing new rules that in time will help domestic aircraft manufacturers provide a large proportion of the 4,000 aircraft that China is expected to buy over the next twenty years. Aerospace was one of seven industries chosen in 2010 as 'new strategic industries' and earmarked for more state aid and broader policy support. The fact that China is steadily developing its space programme – it conducted a successful manned space flight in 2003, launched a lunar orbiter in 2007, had launched six satellites by late 2010 as part of its global positioning services strategy, plans to launch its own space station in 2020 and also put a man on the moon – is a further indication that China is intent on acquiring highly sophisticated technical competence in the aerospace field.[150] China is pursuing ambitious plans in other frontier areas of scientific endeavour: a Chinese supercomputer has recently been ranked as the world's second-fastest machine, thereby overtaking European and Japanese systems,[151] while it has developed the world's leading submersible, able to explore the ocean floor to greater depths than anyone else, a position previously held by the United States.[152]

The most familiar examples of the global strength of Chinese firms are its banks and oil companies. In 2007 the boom on the Shanghai Stock Exchange saw PetroChina briefly overtake Exxon as the world's largest company. By the end of 2007 China possessed three of the world's five largest companies, by value though not by sales, namely PetroChina, the Industrial and Commercial Bank of China (ICBC) and China Mobile.[153] In the 2010 Fortune Global 500, based on company revenues, three Chinese companies were listed in the top ten (Sinopec, State Grid and China National Petroleum), while in the 2010 FT Top 500, based on market value, there were also three Chinese firms, with China National Petroleum topping the list. As a broader measure of the progress being made by Chinese firms, there were 54 in the Fortune Top 500 in 2010 compared with 43 in 2008 and 9 in 2000. Some of the bigger Chinese firms are seeking to expand overseas by taking over foreign firms. Early examples were Lenovo's acquisition of IBM Computers and the Chinese oil giant CNPC unsuccessfully seeking to buy the US oil firm Unilocal; awash with cash and eager to shortcut their expansion, it is not difficult to imagine this happening on a much wider scale. All the biggest deals in 2009 were in natural resources, of which the most ambitious was Chinalco's attempt to purchase a stake in Rio Tinto, the Anglo-Australian mining group.[154] In the event it was rejected, a poignant reminder, following Unilocal, of the difficulties that Chinese companies face in concluding major deals in areas that are regarded as even vaguely sensitive.[155] Nonetheless, with many Western companies suffering from a serious shortage of cash as a result of the recession, the takeover opportunities for cash-rich Chinese companies, the oil companies in particular, remain considerable.[156] Furthermore, the establishment of the China Investment Corporation, armed with funds of $200 billion, of which some $80 billion is for external investment, will give China growing potential leverage over those foreign companies in which it decides to invest.[157]

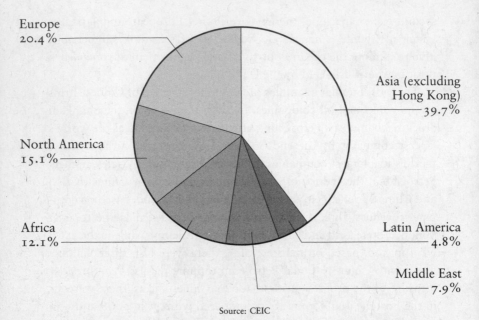

Europe
20.4%

Asia (excluding
Hong Kong)
39.7%

North America
15.1%

Africa
12.1%

Latin America
4.8%

Middle East
7.9%

Source: CEIC

*Figure 32. China's outward investment by region,
2010 (percentage of total).*

Finally, we should not forget the increasing importance of Chinese subcontractors as 'systems integrator' firms in the global supply chain of many foreign multinationals, a development which might, in the long term at least, prove to have a wider strategic significance for these multinationals in terms of their management, research capability and even ownership.[158]

Crucial to the creation of international firms is overseas direct investment. In 2010, foreign investment by Chinese companies in non-financial sectors totalled almost $70 billion (compared with $100 billion inward foreign direct investment into China). In 2008, the figure was in excess of $50 billion, a huge increase compared with 2002; official figures indicate that in 2006 60% went to Asia, 16% to Latin America, 7% each to North America and Africa, 6% to Europe and roughly 4% to Australasia (see Figures 32 and 33).[159] These figures graphically illustrate that the main area of expansion

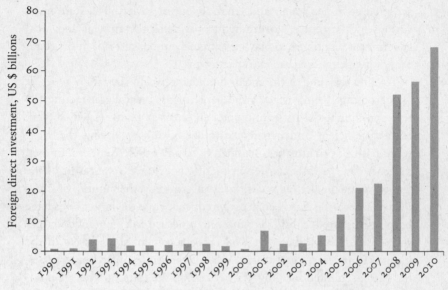

Source: United Nations Conference on Trade and Development (data as of 29 July 2011)

Figure 33. China's rapidly rising overseas direct investment.

for Chinese firms is the developing world and especially commodities. We will return to the question of Chinese foreign direct investment in a later chapter.

THE CHINESE MODEL

The transition from a command economy to a market economy, involving a major diminution in the role of the state, has understandably focused attention on the similarities between the Chinese economy and Western capitalist economies. It is becoming evident, however, that just as the Japanese and Korean economies have retained distinctive characteristics in comparison with the West, the same also applies to China, though even more so. The key difference in China's case concerns the role of the state. This should be seen as part of a much older Chinese tradition, as discussed in Chapter 4 and Chapter 7, where the state has always enjoyed a pivotal role in the economy and been universally accepted as the guardian and embodiment of society. The state in its various forms (central government, provincial government and local government) continues to play an extremely important role in the economy, notwithstanding the market reforms.

Around the time of the Asian financial crisis in the late nineties, it appeared that China was on the verge of drastically contracting the role and number of its state-owned enterprises (many of which were highly inefficient and heavily subsidized), and following the well-worn path of privatization trodden by many other countries. In fact, a decade later, a rather different picture is evident. As a result of the 'grasping the big, letting go of the small' strategy, the number of state-owned enterprises has been greatly reduced while the larger ones have been restructured, subsidized and often merged to create much larger state-owned companies. In 2008, 30 per cent of total assets in the industrial and service sectors were held by state-owned enterprises, but they accounted for only 3.1 per cent of the total number of enterprises. In other words, state-owned enterprises control a substantial part of total enterprise assets even though in terms of numbers they are marginal. Since 1999, the share of state-owned enterprises has declined from 37 per cent to less than 5 per cent in terms of numbers, and from 68 per cent to 44 per cent in terms of assets.[160] Rather than root-and-branch privatization, the government has thus sought to make the numerous state-owned enterprises that remain as efficient and competitive as possible. As a result, the top 150 state-owned firms, far from being lame ducks, have instead become enormously profitable, their aggregate profits reaching $150 billion in 2007. This has been part of a broader government strategy designed to create a cluster of internationally competitive Chinese companies, most of which are state-owned.

Unlike the approach most countries have followed with regard to state-owned firms, which has seen them enjoying various degrees of protection, and often quasi-monopoly status, the Chinese government has instead exposed them to the fiercest competition, both amongst themselves and with foreign firms. They are also, unlike in many Western countries, allowed to raise large amounts of private capital. Of the twelve biggest initial public offerings on the Shanghai Stock

Exchange in 2007, all were by state enterprises and together they accounted for 85 per cent of the total capital raised. Some of the largest have foreign stakeholders and this, despite tensions, has usually helped to improve their performance. Private investors own up to a quarter of China's largest banks. China's state-owned firms can best be described as hybrids in that they combine the characteristics of both private and state enterprises.[161] The leading state enterprises get help and assistance from their state benefactors but also have sufficient independence to be managed like private companies and can raise capital in the same way as the latter. This hybrid approach also works in reverse: some of the largest privately owned companies, like the computer firm Lenovo and the telecommunications equipment maker Huawei, have been crucially helped by their close ties with the government, a relationship which to some extent mirrors the Japanese and Korean experience. Unlike in Japan or Korea, however, where privately owned firms overwhelmingly predominate, most of China's best-performing companies are to be found in the state sector.[162] The steel industry has been awash with private investment, but the industry leader and technologically most advanced producer is the state-owned Baosteel. Chinalco, also state-owned, has become one of the world's largest producers of aluminium, and has designs on becoming a diversified metals multinational. Shanghai Electric is increasingly competing with Japan's Mitsubishi and Marubeni in bidding to build new coal-fired plants in Asia. China's two state-owned shipbuilding firms, China Shipbuilding Industry Corporation and China State Shipbuilding Corporation, are growing rapidly and starting to close the technological gap with their Korean and Japanese competitors. Chery, the state-owned car producer, with the fifth largest market share, has proved an extremely agile competitor and, given its limited resources, technologically ambitious and innovative. For the most part, it is these state-owned enterprises which are increasingly competing on the global stage with Western and Japanese companies.

The emergent Chinese model bears witness to a new kind of capitalism where the state is hyperactive and omnipresent in a range of different ways and forms: in providing assistance to private firms, in a galaxy of state-owned enterprises, in managing the process by which the renminbi slowly evolves towards fully convertible status and, above all, in being the architect of an economic strategy which has driven China's economic transformation. China's success suggests that the Chinese model of the state is destined to exercise a powerful global influence, especially in the developing world, and thereby transform the terms of future economic debate. The collapse of the Anglo-American model in the wake of the Western financial crisis will make the Chinese model even more pertinent and attractive to many countries, especially in the developing world.

A MATTER OF SIZE

The combination of a huge population and an extremely high economic growth rate is providing the world with a completely new kind of experience: China is, quite literally, changing the world before our very eyes, taking it into completely uncharted territory. Such is the enormity of this shift and its impact on the world that one might talk of modern economic history being divided into BC and AC – Before China and After China – with 1978 being the great watershed. In this section I will concentrate on the economic implications of China's size.

When the United States began its take-off in 1870, its population was 40 million. By 1913 it had reached 98 million. Japan's population numbered 84 million at the start of its post-war growth in 1950 and 109 million by the end in 1973. In contrast, China's population was 963 million in 1978 when its take-off started in earnest: that is, twenty-four times that of the United States in 1870 and 11.5 times that of Japan in 1950. It is estimated that by the projected end of its take-off period in 2020, China's population will be at least 1.4 billion: that is, fourteen times that of the United States in 1913 and thirteen times that of Japan in 1973. If we broaden this picture, India had a population of 839 million in 1990 when it started its major take-off, nearly twenty-one times that of the United States in 1870 and ten times that of Japan in 1950.[163]

Total population is only one aspect of the effect of China's scale. The second is the size of its labour force. Although China's population presently accounts for 21 per cent of the world's total, the proportion of the global labour force that it represents is, at 25 per cent, slightly higher. In 1978, when the great majority of its people worked on the land, China only had 118 million non-agricultural labourers. In 2002 that figure had already increased to 369 million, compared with a total of 455 million in the developed world. By 2020 it is estimated that there will be 533 million non-agricultural labourers in China, by which time it will exceed the equivalent figure for the whole of the developed world by no less than 100 million. In other words, China's growth is leading to a huge increase in the number of people engaged in non-agricultural labour and, as a consequence, is providing a massive – and very rapid – addition to the world's total non-agricultural labour force.

The third effect of China's rise concerns the impact of its economic scale on the rest of the world. China's average annual rate of growth of GDP since 1978 has been 9.4 per cent, over twice the US's growth rate of 3.94 per cent between 1870 and 1913. It is projected that the duration of their respective take-offs may be roughly similar: 43 years in the case of the US, 42 years for China, because, although the latter's growth rate is much faster, its population is also far larger. When the US commenced its take-off in 1870, its GDP accounted for 8.8 per cent of the world's total, rising to 18.9 per cent by 1913. In contrast, China's GDP represented 4.9 per cent of the world's total in 1978, but is likely to rise to 18–20 per cent by 2020. In both instances, their GDP growth has had a major impact on the expansion of global GDP. In the 1980s, for example, the United States made the biggest single contribution of any country, accounting for 21 per cent of the world's total increase; in the 1990s, however, China, even at its present limited level of development, surpassed the US, which remained at 21 per cent, while China contributed 27.1 per cent to the growth of global GDP.

The fourth effect is the impact China will have on world trade. Before the open-door policy, China was one of the world's most closed economies. In 1970 its export trade made up only 0.7 per cent of the world's total: at the end of the seventies, China's imports and exports together represented 12 per cent of its GDP, the lowest in the world. China's economic impact on the rest of the world was minimal for two reasons: firstly, the country was very poor, and secondly, it was very closed. But since 1978 China has rapidly become one of the world's most open economies. Its average import tariff rate will decline from 23.7 per cent in 2001 to 5.7 per cent in 2011, with most of that fall having already taken place.[164] Although its trade dependency (the proportion of GDP accounted for by exports and imports) was less than 10 per cent in 1978, by 2004 it had risen to 70 per cent, much higher than that of other large countries. China is now the world's largest exporter, the second largest importer and the second largest trading nation.

Each of these scale effects – population, labour, economy and trade – clearly has a mainly positive impact on the rest of the world, stimulating overall global growth and the expansion of national economies. But the fifth effect, China's consumption of resources, has a largely negative global impact: because the country is so poorly endowed with natural resources, its population so enormous and its economic development so intensive, its demand for natural resources has the double effect of raising the price of raw materials and depleting the world's stock of them, a process that, on the basis of recent trends, is likely to accelerate in the future.

CHINA'S GLOBAL ECONOMIC IMPACT

For what is still a poor country, with a per capita GDP of only $4,282 (at market exchange rates) in 2011, China is already having a profound impact on the world. Along with the United States, it was the main engine of global economic growth in the first decade of this century, contributing, for example, no less than one-third of the world's growth in real output between 2002 and 2005. It was widely credited with having pulled Japan out of its long-running post-bubble recession, having been responsible for two-thirds of the growth in Japan's exports and one-quarter of its real GDP growth in 2003 alone.[165] Even more dramatically, following the Western financial crisis, the continued rapid growth of the Chinese economy played a pivotal role in ensuring that the subsequent global recession was relatively mild and largely confined to the Western world.

The emergence of China as the world's cheapest producer of manufactured goods over the last two decades resulted in a sharp drop in their global price. The price of clothing and shoes in the US, for example, fell by 30 per cent in the first decade of this century. Major gainers from this have been consumers in the developed world, while the rise in commodity prices consequent upon Chinese demand has had a highly beneficial effect on primary producers, most of which are in the developing world. Anxious to secure sufficient supplies of raw materials to fuel its booming economy, China has been highly active in Africa, Latin America and the Middle East, concluding major agreements with Iran, Venezuela and the Sudan amongst many others. Two other notable net gainers have been Russia, which is a major producer of many commodities, especially oil and gas, and Australia. It is China's shortage of raw materials that has driven a major diplomatic offensive with many African and Latin American countries, including the ambitious China–Africa summit in Beijing in November 2006.[166] The main losers hitherto have been those developing countries, like Mexico, whose comparative advantage lies in similar labour-intensive production and who find themselves in direct competition with China.[167] They have also lost out to China in terms of foreign direct investment, with many international firms relocating their operations from these countries to China. The other obvious losers are blue-collar workers in the developed world who have found their jobs being outsourced to China by multinationals. In addition, of course, those countries that are not major commodity producers have suffered from the rapid increase in commodity prices resulting from China's growing demand.

The greatest impact of China's rise has been felt in East Asia. The main gainers have been the developed Asian tigers of North-East Asia – Hong Kong, South Korea and Taiwan, together with Japan. They have been the beneficiaries of cheap manufactured goods produced in China while at the same time enjoying growing demand from China for their knowledge and capital-intensive products.[168] Their own companies, meanwhile, have relocated many of their operations to China to take advantage of much cheaper labour, as in the case of the Taiwanese computer industry.[169] The losers have been the same as those in the West, namely those workers displaced by operations outsourced to China. Unlike the United States, which has a huge trade deficit with China, all of these countries enjoy either surpluses or relatively small deficits with China. The nearest example in the region to a grey area is South-East Asia, whose economies are not so dissimilar to that of China, though Singapore and Malaysia, in particular, are rather more developed. Over the last decade, the ASEAN countries have seen a large slice of the foreign direct investment they previously received going to China. They have also lost out to China in the mass assembly of electronic and computer equipment – Singapore and Malaysia being notable examples – and have, as a consequence, been forced to move up the value chain in order to escape Chinese competition.[170] The country that has suffered the greatest is Indonesia, whose economy had hitherto most closely resembled that of China. Indonesia has lost out to China through competition in areas like textiles and in terms of direct investment by those foreign multinationals which have opted for China rather than Indonesia as their preferred production base. When the China–ASEAN free trade agreement came into force on 1 January 2010, Indonesia decided unilaterally to defer implementation because of opposition from local manufacturers of cheap-end products, especially textiles, who feared they would be unable to compete with Chinese imports. On the other hand, Chinese demand for Indonesian natural resources has had a beneficial effect on its economy. On balance, China's growth has greatly benefited the ASEAN countries, with China now comfortably ensconced as their largest trading partner, their largest market, and in many cases their main provider of inward investment.[171]

A measure of China's growing impact on the world is the leverage that it enjoys in its relationship with the United States (notwithstanding the fact that the United States still has a much larger GDP than China and an immensely higher GDP per head) as a result of the economic imbalances which lie at the heart of their relationship. China is the largest exporter to the US, with Americans displaying an enormous appetite for Made in China consumer products. As the United States exports relatively little to China, the latter has enjoyed a large and rising trade surplus which has grown very rapidly since 1999.[172] China has invested this surplus in various forms of US debt, including Treasury bonds, agency bonds and corporate bonds – in effect, a Chinese loan to the US – thereby enabling American interest rates to be kept artificially low to the benefit of American consumers and especially holders of mortgages. Although the US was deeply in debt, China's continuing large-scale purchase of Treasury bonds (which I will use as shorthand for various forms of US assets held by China) allowed Americans to continue with their spending spree, and then partially helped to cushion the impact of the credit crunch. By mid 2011, China's foreign currency reserves totalled $3,197 billion – a sum greater than the annual economic output of all but nine countries.[173] The rapid growth of its foreign exchange reserves has made China a colossus in the financial world. The importance of this has become even more apparent with the Western financial meltdown. While many Western financial institutions, companies and governments have found themselves starved of liquidity, China, in contrast, is blessed with an abundance of it. Strategically, this puts China in a potentially powerful position to enhance its international financial and economic influence over the next decade, enabling it, for example, to make generous loans to developing countries and buy up suitable assets around the world. China's new-found strength was vividly illustrated in October 2011 when the European Union sought large-scale Chinese financial assistance to support its bail-out proposal for the euro.

How China deploys its reserves remains a matter of great concern, especially to the United States, since most are invested in US dollar-denominated debt. If China transferred significant amounts into other currencies – it has been suggested that it holds around 65 per cent of its reserves in dollars, 26 per cent in euros, 5 per cent in sterling and 3 per cent in yen, though this remains a closely guarded secret[174] – it would have the immediate effect of depressing the value of the dollar and forcing US interest rates to rise: the larger the sum transferred, the bigger the fall in the dollar and the larger the rise in interest rates. But the Chinese government is also faced with something of a dilemma. It would certainly make good economic sense for China to transfer a large slice of its reserves out of US Treasury bonds: the dollar depreciated steadily in 2010–11 and, given the size of the American budget deficit, it is very likely that this process will be resumed, perhaps precipitously so, which would greatly reduce the value of China's dollar holdings. China's vast dollar investments in US Treasury bonds furthermore earn miserable rates of return, which makes precious little sense for what is still a poor country.[175] However, if it tries to transfer significant sums of its reserves into other currencies, thereby provoking a further fall in the value of the dollar, then the value of its own dollar reserves will also decline. China is in a Catch-22 situation. The two great, but utterly unlike, economic powers of our time find themselves – at least for the time being – in a position of bizarre mutual dependence.[176] This was graphically illustrated in the darkest days of the financial meltdown in September 2008, when it is believed that the Chinese were pressing the US government to rescue Fannie Mae, Freddie Mac and subsequently AIG out of concern for its holdings in them, and the Americans were understandably afraid that China might otherwise sell off some of its dollar reserves, with dire consequences for the value of the dollar and its role as a reserve currency.[177]

Before these tumultuous events, China had already been exploring alternative ways of using its vast reserves other than as the United States' de facto banker. In early 2007 the government announced the formation of the China Investment Corporation, a new state agency to oversee investment of $200 billion of China's foreign currency reserves – similar to Temasek Holdings, the Singapore government's successful investment agency, which manages a $108 billion global portfolio of investments.[178] To test the water, the new agency placed $3 billion of its holdings with Blackstone, the US-based private equity group, thereby signalling Beijing's intention to switch some of its investments from US Treasury bonds into more risky equity holdings.[179] In fact it has since emerged that the State Administration of Foreign Exchange, which oversees China's reserves, had itself been investing rather more widely than was previously believed.[180] These moves heralded the beginning of China's rise as a major global financial player.[181] In the second half of 2007, as the credit crunch began to bite, the China Development Bank took a significant stake in the UK-based Barclays Bank[182] and Citic Securities formed a strategic alliance with the US investment bank Bear Stearns before the latter went bust.[183] Three Chinese banks were also in talks about acquiring a stake in Standard Chartered, the UK-based emerging markets lender.[184] But this process was halted by the Chinese government as it increasingly came to recognize the likely severity of the credit crunch and the potential threat it represented to any stakes in Western financial institutions that might be purchased. The Chinese sustained significant losses as a result of this diversification strategy: it has been estimated that the State Administration of Foreign Exchange itself lost in excess of $80 billion.[185] On the whole, however, when the financial meltdown came in September 2008, the Chinese found themselves relatively little exposed.

The relationship between the United States and China needs to be seen in a broader global and historical context. The belated acceptance of China as a member of the WTO in 2001 marked the biggest extension of the world trading system since the beginning of the contemporary phase of globalization in the late 1970s. As the largest recipient of foreign direct investment, with a non-convertible currency and soon to be the biggest trading nation, China's admission immediately transformed the nature and dynamics of the trading system. By acquiring a low-cost manufacturing base and extremely cheap imports, the developed world has been a major beneficiary of China's accession. But China itself has also been a big gainer, achieving wider access to overseas markets for its exports and receiving huge flows of inward investment, thereby helping it to sustain its double-digit growth rate.[186] At least until the Western financial crisis, China's integration into the global economy has been overwhelmingly perceived as a win-win situation. Is that likely to continue?

China's impact on the global trading system is so huge, and also in the longer term so uncertain, that this is a difficult question to answer. There are already tensions over China's relationship with the WTO: on the one hand, there are accusations from the developed countries that China is failing to implement WTO rules as it ought to, while on the other hand, both the US and the European Union are using anti-dumping clauses (designed to prevent countries selling at unfair prices) as a pretext for deploying protectionist measures against Chinese goods.[187] There has been constant controversy around Chinese exports to the US. During 2007 and subsequently these were largely concentrated on the safety of Chinese products, notably food and toys, as well as China's failure to observe intellectual property rights.[188] So far these skirmishes have been at the relative margins of their trading relationships but they could be a harbinger of growing tensions in the future. Although the present era of globalization was designed by and is the creature of the West, above all the United States, arguably the greatest beneficiary has been East Asia, especially China.[189] If the West should decide at some point that China has, indeed, been the chief beneficiary – and, what is more, *to the West's growing detriment* – then the latter is likely to become increasingly protectionist and the present global system could be undermined.

The Western financial crisis has profoundly changed the situation in terms of the outlook for the global economy. While economic prospects were relatively benign, the underlying conflicts of interest between the United States and China remained muted, but as American living standards and jobs have come under growing threat, they have become increasingly evident. The focus of the tension has been the value of the renminbi, with growing sections of American opinion, reflected in a powerful lobby within the US Congress, arguing that the Chinese currency is seriously undervalued, thereby making Chinese exports artificially cheap, and that the United States should take retaliatory action by introducing protectionist measures unless the renminbi is significantly revalued. If the United States did act in this way, then China is almost bound to retaliate. A trade war between the two countries is now more likely than at any time since the beginning of China's reform period, but it is by no means inevitable. We shall return to this issue in Chapter 10.

The Western financial crisis aside, we also need to consider China's rise from a longer-term perspective. Hitherto, the main losers in the Western world have been those unskilled and semi-skilled workers who have been displaced by Chinese competition. But their grievances have been dwarfed by the winners – the multinationals which have used China as a cheap manufacturing base and the many consumers who have benefited from China prices. What will decisively change this political arithmetic is when China, as it rapidly moves up the value chain, starts to enter spheres of production which threaten the jobs of skilled manual workers and growing numbers of white-collar workers and professionals. The process of upgrading is already underway, as the example of textiles in Prato and Como in Italy illustrates, with some of the design following manufacturing to China.[190] How quickly China upgrades its technological capacity thus lies at the heart of the likely Western response: the quicker that process proceeds, the more likely it is that the political arithmetic will change and that protectionist barriers might be erected; the slower it happens then the more likely it is that trade tensions can be managed and in some degree defused. As we saw earlier, China's rise up the technological ladder is taking place much faster than had previously been forecast. In areas like solar panels, wind energy, telecommunication networks, power transmission and high-speed trains, Chinese companies are already on a par with their Western counterparts, often by developing technology acquired in joint ventures. In other areas, such as construction machinery, machine tools, cars and electrical engineering, the major companies like Shanghai Electric are not far behind and will very soon be in a position to compete. A range of Chinese companies are already in the process of thinking about establishing plants and R&D centres in Europe, buying up key European brands and companies and poaching engineers, with Germany the most obvious target. The number of investments by China in Germany increased from seven in 2007 to 45 in 2009. In the six months to the end of March 2011, Chinese businesses invested $64.3 billion in Europe in acquisitions, trade deals and loan agreements, more than double the comparable figure for the previous period of nearly three years.[191] The economic rise of China has already led to a multiple redistribution of global economic power, including from South-East Asia to China, from Japan to China, and from Europe and the United States to China. Given that China is only a little over halfway through its take-off phase, with over 50 per cent of the population still living in the countryside, it is clear that we are only in the early stages of this process.[192] It is inconceivable that one-fifth of the world's population, embracing all the various scale effects that we have considered, can join the global economy with – by historical standards – enormous speed without ramifications which are bound to engender tension and conflict. So far China's incorporation has been relatively conflict-free. But the aura of win-win that has surrounded this process seems unlikely to continue. The political arithmetic will shift in the West as the number of losers rises, with the entirely plausible consequence that the West – the traditional proselytizer for free trade – will lead the charge towards protection and the end of the era of globalization that began in the late 1970s.[193] The present travails of the Western economy could yet be the trigger for this process.

7

A Civilization-State

Hong Kong used to be a byword for cheap labour and cheap goods. It lost that reputation when its employers started to shift their operations north of the border into the similarly Cantonese-speaking Guangdong province. Hong Kong had moved too far up the value chain: the expectations of its workers had become too great to tolerate miserable working conditions, indecently long hours and poverty wages. The old textile factories decamped north along with everything else that required the kind of unskilled labour which Hong Kong once possessed in abundance and which China, as it finally opened its borders, now enjoyed in seemingly limitless numbers. The checkpoints and fences that were thrown up around the new towns in Guangdong were eloquent testimony to the countless rural labourers who were willing to leave their villages, whether they were nearby or in a distant interior province, for the bright lights of the city and what seemed to them, though no longer those over the border in Hong Kong, like untold riches.

Guangzhou railway station was crammed with such bounty-hunters, a human tide of migrants, from morning to night, 24/7. This was the Wild East. No matter the pitiful wages and terrible conditions, welcome to the province of opportunity. Young migrant girls barely out of school, often hundreds, even thousands, of miles from home, would work crazy hours performing the simplest of repetitive tasks, making clothes, toys or fireworks for Western markets that they could not even imagine, and then retire for a few hours' sleep in their floor-to-ceiling bunk beds in cubby-hole-sized rooms in drab factory dormitories before resuming the drudgery on the morrow. But for them it was far better than eking out a much smaller pittance working the land from which they came.

Just as Hong Kong had earlier climbed the value escalator and seen living standards transformed in just a few decades, the same now began to happen in Guangdong. The expectations of locals grew and their opportunities expanded. From the most humble of beginnings, people began to make their way up their version of the career ladder. Meanwhile, as China's own standards and expectations changed, there was growing unease about the merciless exploitation of unskilled workers and migrant labour. They enjoyed no legal protection and the official trade unions were shackled and ineffectual. After years of discussion and debate, a labour law was finally introduced in 2008. It was bitterly resisted by many employers, who claimed that it would make their firms uncompetitive and drive them out of business.

Hong Kong employers were particularly prominent amongst them. Astute businessmen, enormously hard-working and pitiless to boot, they did not cross the border to escape the rising labour costs in Hong Kong in order to find themselves hamstrung by an armful of new regulations and a clutch of new expectations in southern China. Of an estimated 90,000 factories in the Pearl Delta region, nearly 60,000 are Hong Kong-owned. Many mainland Chinese employers supported them. Dubbed the country's richest woman entrepreneur, Zhang Yin, chairwoman of Nine Dragons Paper Holdings, one of the world's biggest paper-making and recycling firms, complained that workers were being given an 'iron rice bowl', a reference to the workers' contract under Mao. The powerful All-China Federation of Industry and Commerce joined the opposition, warning of more labour disputes and companies going out of business. American firms with factories in China expressed their concern; the reason why they had gone there in the first place, after all, was the dirt-cheap labour. The tame All-China Federation of Trade Unions finally found a voice and rejected any concessions to the employers.

The new law is a sign of changing times. China, just like Hong Kong, will not always be a byword for cheap goods, even cheaper labour and miserable working conditions. The universal desire to improve one's lot spells the eventual demise of an economic regime based on the cheapest labour in the world, wholly unprotected either by trade unions or the law, and exposed to the most brutal market forces. The change received its most dramatic expression so far in a wave of strikes across Guangdong province in June 2010, involving many tens of thousands of workers, most notably at Foxconn, a Taiwanese supplier of electronic products to Apple amongst others and one of the province's biggest employers, and Honda. The strikes at Foxconn followed a series of suicides, with more than a dozen workers jumping off buildings to their death. The strikers were spurred on not only by what had come to be regarded as intolerable wages and working conditions but also the new expectations aroused by the labour law. With tacit government support and passive endorsement from the official unions, the strikes resulted in huge wage increases, improved working conditions and a profound shift in attitudes. Guangdong had been changed for ever. China is in the process of moving to a new stage in its development and its political world is beginning to reflect this. Laissez-faire attitudes are being replaced by the recognition that workers' rights need to be protected and conditions improved.

There is still a widespread view in the West that China will eventually conform, by a process of natural and inevitable development, to the Western paradigm.[1] This is wishful thinking. And herein lies the nub of the Chinese challenge. Apart from Japan, for the first time in two centuries – since the advent of industrialization – one of the great powers will be from a totally non-Western history and tradition. It will not be more of the same – which is what the emergence of the United States largely represented in the late nineteenth century. To appreciate what the rise of China means, we have to understand not only China's economic growth, but also its history, politics, culture and traditions. Otherwise we will be floundering in the dark, unable to explain or predict, constantly disconcerted and surprised. The purpose of this chapter is to explore the nature of China's political difference. It is a task that is going to occupy, and tax, the Western mind for the next century.

A CIVILIZATION-STATE

China is not just a nation-state; it is also a civilization. In fact, China became a nation-state only relatively recently. One can argue over exactly when: the late nineteenth century perhaps, or following the 1911 Revolution. In that sense – in the same manner as one might refer to Indonesia being little more than half a century old, or Germany and Italy being rather more than a century old – China is a very recent creation. But, of course, that is nonsense. China has existed for several millennia, certainly for over two, arguably even three thousand years, though the average Chinese likes to round this up to more like 5,000 years. In other words, China's existence as a recognizable and continuing entity long predates its status as a nation-state. Indeed, it is far and away the oldest continuously existing polity in the world, certainly dating back to 221 BC, in some respects rather longer. This is not an arcane historical detail, but the way the Chinese – not just the elite, but taxi drivers too – actually think about their country. As often as not, it will crop up in a driver's conversation, along with references to Confucius or Mencius, perhaps with a little classical poetry thrown in.[2] When the Chinese use the term 'China' they are not usually referring to the country or nation so much as Chinese civilization – its history, the dynasties, Confucius, the ways of thinking, the role of government, the relationships and customs, the *guanxi* (the network of personal connections),[3] the family, filial piety, ancestral worship, the values, and distinctive philosophy, all of which long predate China's history as a nation-state. Unlike in Western countries, where national identity has in great part been shaped by their history as nation-states, Chinese identity is overwhelmingly a product of its civilizational history. The Chinese think of themselves not as a nation-state but as a civilization-state; or, to put it another way, Chinese civilization is like a very old geological formation, its multitudinous layers comprising the civilization-state, with the nation-state merely the top soil. Western societies are constituted on the basis of nation; China is constituted on the basis of civilization. The consequences of this difference, as we shall see, are profound and far-reaching.

Of course, there have been many civilizations. There is nothing unique in that sense about Chinese civilization. What is remarkable in the Chinese case, however, is that 'civilization' and 'state' largely coincide (the major exception being western China), not just over a relatively brief period, but over an extraordinarily long one. It is difficult to think of another similar example. This is why we can refer to China not just as a civilization, but as a civilization-state. Other countries may possess elements of a civilization-state, but none in the way that China does. A case might be made for the United States; with the destruction of the Amerindians and European settlement, a new nation and arguably a new civilization were created. But that civilization was no more than a European inheritance and, furthermore, in historical terms remains only about four hundred years old by the most generous of measures. India too can be considered a candidate but, unlike China, India, as we know it today, was a relatively recent creation of the British Raj, its previous history being far more diverse than China's.

China was to become a nation-state at the end of the nineteenth century, obliged by its own weakness to join the international system on the terms of the dominant European powers. For a century it has described itself as a nation-state rather than a civilization-state, even though its primary identity and basic character is that of a civilization-state. Today it enjoys what might be described as a double identity: as a nation-state and as a civilization-state. By history and construction it is a civilization-state; as a result of its international weakness, it was forced to become a nation-state. Or, as Lucian Pye observed with acute perception, 'China is a civilization pretending to be a nation-state.'[4] How in the future these primary and secondary identities might evolve and interact – contradictory as they are – remains an open question.

The Chinese sense of civilization helps to explain their intimacy with their own history. There are no other people in the world who are so connected to their past and for whom the past – not so much the recent past but the long-ago past – is so relevant and meaningful as the Chinese. Every other country is a spring chicken by comparison, its people separated from their long past by the sharp discontinuities of their history. Not the Chinese. China has experienced huge turmoil, invasion and rupture, but somehow the lines of continuity have remained resilient, persistent and ultimately predominant, superimposing themselves for the most part in the Chinese mind over the interruptions and breaks. The Chinese live in and through their history, however distant it might be, to a degree which is quite different from other societies. 'Of what other country in the world,' writes the historian Wang Gungwu, 'can it be said that writings on its foreign relations of two thousand, or even one thousand, years ago seem so compellingly alive today?'5 The Chinese scholar Jin Guantao argues that: '[China's] only mode of existence is to relive the past. There is no accepted mechanism within the culture for the Chinese to confront the present without falling back on the inspiration and strength of tradition.'6 The Chinese scholar Huang Ping writes:

> China is . . . a living history. Here almost every event and process happening today is closely related to history, and cannot be explained without taking history into consideration. Not only scholars, but civil servants and entrepreneurs as well as ordinary people all have a strong sense of history . . . no matter how little formal education people receive, they all live in history and serve as the heirs and spokesmen of history.7

The author Tu Wei-ming remarks:

> The collective memory of the educated Chinese is such that when they talk about Tu Fu's (712–70) poetry, Sima Qian's (died c. 85 BC) *Historical Records* [the first systematic Chinese historical text, written between 109 and 91 BC, recounting Chinese history from the time of the Yellow Emperor until the author's own time], or Confucius's *Analects*, they refer to a cumulative tradition preserved in Chinese characters . . . An encounter with Tu Fu, Sima Qian, or Confucius through ideographic symbols evokes a sensation of reality as if their presence was forever inscribed in the text.8

The earliest awareness of China as we know it today came with the Zhou dynasty, which grew up along the Yellow River Valley at the end of the second millennium BC. Already, under the previous Shang dynasty, the foundations of modern China had begun to take shape with an ideographic language, ancestor worship and the idea of a single ruler. Chinese civilization, however, still did not have a strong sense of itself. That was to happen a few centuries later through the writings of Master Kong, or Confucius (to use his Latinized name).[9] As discussed in Chapter 4, by this time the Chinese language was used for government and education, and the idea of the mandate of Heaven as a principle of dynastic governance had been firmly established. Confucius's life (551–479 BC) preceded the Warring States period (403–221 BC), when numerous states were constantly at war with each other. The triumph of the Qin dynasty (221–206 BC) brought that period to an end and achieved a major unification of Chinese territories, with the emergence of modern China typically being dated from this time.[10] Although Confucius enjoyed little status or recognition during his lifetime, after his death he was to become the single most influential writer in Chinese history (though his ideas were not always dominant; between AD 500 and AD 850, for example, they were largely eclipsed by Buddhism). For the next two thousand years China was largely shaped by his arguments and moral precepts, its government informed by his principles, and the *Analects* became established as the most important book in Chinese history. Confucianism was a syncretic mode of thinking which drew on other beliefs, most notably Taoism and Buddhism, but Confucius's own ideas remained by far the most important. His emphasis on moral virtue, on the supreme importance of government in human affairs, and on the overriding priority of stability and unity, which was shaped by his experience of the turbulence and instability of a divided country, have informed the fundamental values of Chinese civilization ever since.[11] Only towards the end of the nineteenth century did his influence begin to wane, though even during the convulsions of the twentieth century – including the Communist period – the influence of his thinking remained persistent and tangible. Ironically it was Mao Zedong, the Chinese leader most hostile to Confucius, who was to pen the *Little Red Book*, which in both form and content clearly drew on the Confucian tradition.[12]

Two of the most obvious continuities in Chinese civilization, both of which can be traced back to Confucius, concern the state and education. The state has, ever since Confucius if not earlier, been perceived as the embodiment and guardian of Chinese civilization, which is why, in both the dynastic and Communist eras, it has enjoyed such huge authority and legitimacy. Amongst its constellation of responsibilities, the state, most importantly of all, has the sacred task of maintaining the unity of Chinese civilization. Unlike in the Western tradition, the role of government has no boundaries; rather like a parent, with which it is often compared, there are no limits to its authority. Paternalism is regarded as a desirable and necessary characteristic of government. Although in practice the state has always been rather less omnipotent than this might suggest, there is no doubting the reverence and deference which the Chinese display towards it.[13] Similarly, the roots of China's distinctive concept of education and parenting lie deep in its civilizational past. Ever since Mencius (372–289 BC), a disciple of Confucius, the Chinese have always been optimistic about human nature, believing that people were essentially good and that, by bringing children up in the right manner through the appropriate parenting and education, they would acquire the correct attitudes, values and self-discipline. In the classroom, children are expected to look respectfully upwards towards the teacher and, given the towering importance of history, reverentially backwards to the past in terms of the content of their learning. Education is vested with the authority and reverence of Chinese civilization, with teachers the bearers and transmitters of that wisdom. A high priority has traditionally been placed on training and technique, as compared with the openness and creativity valued in the West, with the result that Chinese children often achieve a much higher level of technical competence at a much younger age in music and art, for example, than their Western counterparts. Perhaps this stems partly from the use of an ideographic language, which requires the rote learning of thousands of characters, and the ability to reproduce those characters with technical perfection.[14]

In stressing the continuity of Chinese civilization, it can reasonably be objected that over a period of more than two millennia, it has been through such huge and often violent disruptions and discontinuities that there can be little resemblance between China now and two millennia ago. At one level, of course, this is patently the case.

China has changed beyond recognition. But at another level the lines of continuity are stubborn and visible. This is reflected most importantly in the self-awareness of the Chinese themselves: the way in which Chinese civilization – as expressed in history, ways of thinking, customs and etiquette, traditional medicine and food, calligraphy, the role of government and the family – remains their primary point of reference.[15] Wang Gungwu argues that 'what is quintessentially Chinese is the remarkable sense of continuity that seems to have made the civilization increasingly distinctive over the centuries'.[16] Given that since 221 BC China has been unified for only 1,074 years, partially unified for 673 years, and disunited for 470 years, while experiencing several major invasions and occupations over the last millennium, this is, to put it mildly, remarkable.[17] The story of those occupations, however, also points to the strength of Chinese culture and its underlying resilience and continuity. They were, in chronological order: the proto-Mongol Liao dynasty (AD 907–1125), the first non-Chinese dynasty in north China (during the period of the Northern Song, which lay to its south); the Jin dynasty (1115–1234), which was Mongol; the Yuan dynasty (1271–1368), which was also Mongol; and the Qing dynasty (1644–1912), which was Manchu. But in each case, the foreign rulers, sooner or later, went native and were Sinicized. Chinese culture, in each instance, enjoyed a very considerable superiority over its invaders. Even the earlier Buddhist 'invasion' from India in the first century AD was to culminate in the Sinification of Buddhist teachings over a period of hundreds of years.[18]

The challenge of the West from around 1850 was an entirely different proposition: key aspects of Western culture, notably its scientific orientation and knowledge, were clearly superior to traditional Confucianism and plunged it into a deepening crisis as the Chinese largely resisted any serious reconciliation between traditional and Western values. Unlike Japan with the Meiji Restoration, China proved incapable of responding to the challenge of the West; the consequence was invasion, civil war, implosion and chronic instability. Between 1911 and 1949 virtually no institution of significance (constitution, university, press, Church, etc.) lasted in its existing form for more than a generation, such was the gravity and enduring nature of

China's impasse. The Western challenge decentred Chinese assumptions. Eventually, when all else had failed, the Chinese turned to Communism, or more specifically Maoism, which explicitly rejected Confucianism. And it was Maoism that finally and belatedly enabled modernity to take root in China. However, although officially disavowed, Confucian values and ways of thinking continued to be very influential, albeit in a subterranean form, remaining in some measure the common sense of the people. Even now, having succeeded in reversing its decline and in the midst of modernization, China is still troubled by the relationship between Chinese and Western cultures and the degree to which it might find itself Westernized, as we saw in the discussion amongst the students in Chapter 5. Somehow, through the turbulence, carnage, chaos and rebirth, China remains recognizably and assuredly Chinese, with a powerful and exceptional sense of self.

An interesting example in this context is Chinese culture, by which is meant the ensemble of social relationships, customs, values, norms and institutions which constitute and inform society. This is often perceived, especially by the Chinese themselves, to be in a state of crisis. Given China's history since 1850, this sense of dislocation is hardly surprising, with the collapse of the imperial regime, the failure of Confucianism to modernize the country, the Maoist revolution, the post-1978 period of modernization, the rapid spread of capitalism, and the arrival of many Western ideas. In such circumstances, the traditional culture has been subject to enormous upheaval and change. Not surprisingly, much of the change has been experienced as a sense of loss, especially given the deep historical roots, longevity and tenacity of traditional culture. Indeed, the latter's depth and durability is precisely why China found it so difficult to change: the forces of resistance and inertia were so immense. The disruption of the culture is therefore profound. But this does not mean that it is hobbled or enfeebled. It may be going through a process of reconstruction and renewal but in many ways it remains robust and vibrant. The fact that China has experienced such huge change and been able to sustain a double-digit growth rate with relatively little instability speaks not of a weak culture but, on the contrary, a strong and resilient one that has been able to withstand the rigours of modernization. Of course, the renewal of the culture will be a long process – it took Europe perhaps two centuries to develop a culture consonant with modernity, although China, as in everything, will take much less time. That culture will draw very heavily on the Confucian tradition – indeed, much of it remains intact – but also from what was best in Maoism as well as from the West. Contrary to what Confucian fundamentalists suggest, however, there will be no simplistic 'return to Confucianism': the latter may still persist to a remarkable extent but the fact remains that it failed to embrace and enable the modernization of China. Notwithstanding this, the lines of continuity with China's long history will be clear and indelible.

For many developing countries, the process of modernization has been characterized by a crisis of identity, often exacerbated by the colonial experience, a feeling of being torn between their own culture and that of the West, linked to an inferiority complex about their own relative backwardness. The Chinese certainly felt a sense of humiliation, but never the same kind of overwhelming and demeaning inferiority: they have always had a strong sense of what it means to be Chinese and are very proud of the fact. Such is the strength of Chineseness, indeed, that it has tended to blur and overshadow – in contrast to India, for example – other powerful identities such as region, class and language. This sense of belonging is rooted in China's civilizational past,[19] which serves to cohere an enormous population otherwise fragmented by dialect, custom, ethnic difference, geography, climate, level of economic development and disparate living standards. 'What binds the Chinese together,' Lucian Pye argues, 'is their sense of culture, race, and civilization, not an identification with the nation as a state.'[20]

The concept of the civilization-state is fundamental to China. It is the basic building block for an understanding of the country and has served to shape the country in many profound and diverse ways.[21] First, Chinese identity is derived overwhelmingly from civilizational elements such as language, familial norms, the structure of social relationships and so forth, rather than the much more recent phase of the nation-state. Second, the unity of the civilization is the defining priority of Chinese politics. Third, the maintenance and preservation of that unity is regarded as the sacred responsibility and duty of the state, thereby lending the latter an authority and legitimacy far exceeding that in a conventional nation-state. Fourth, civilizational history has shaped and defined the nature of Chinese ethnicity in a highly distinctive way, as we shall see in the next chapter, with the Han, notwithstanding China's huge population, the overwhelmingly dominant race. Fifth, although little-recognized, China, as a civilization-state of continental proportions, embraces and demands a plurality based on and necessitated by the diversity of its provinces. This found further expression recently in the constitutional settlement for Hong Kong that underpinned the 1997 handover. Such a solution, based on the principle of 'one country, two systems', is entirely alien to a nation-state, which rests on the principle of 'one country, one system', as illustrated by German reunification in 1990. Sixth, the civilization-state embodies a far more intimate relationship not simply with China's relatively recent history, as in the case of the average nation-state, but, most strikingly, with at least two millennia of history, such that the latter is constantly intervening in and acting as a guide and yardstick in the present. The term 'civilization' normally suggests a rather distant and indirect influence and an inert and passive presence. In China's case, however, it is not only history that lives but civilization itself: the notion of Chinese civilization as a living and dynamic organism rather than a static and inanimate object provides the primary identity and context by which the Chinese think of their country and define themselves. Seventh, the civilization-state serves as a continuous reminder that China is the Middle Kingdom, thereby occupying, as the centre of the world, a quite different position to all other states. The belief in Chinese superiority derives directly from this sense of civilizational greatness.

CHINA AS A CONTINENT

As a civilization-state, China has three distinctive characteristics. We have discussed two: its historical longevity and the coincidence of civilization and state. The third concerns its scale. China is of continental size, consisting of what are, in many respects, semi-autonomous

	Population	National share (%)	Comparable-sized country
Guangdong*†	104,303,132	7.8	Mexico
Shandong*†	95,793,065	7.2	Philippines
Henan*†	94,023,567	7.0	Philippines
Sichuan*	80,418,200	6.0	Germany
Jiangsu*	78,659,903	5.9	Iran
Hebei*	71,854,202	5.4	Thailand
Hunan*	65,683,722	4.9	France
Anhui*	59,500,510	4.5	UK
Hubei*	57,237,740	4.3	Italy
Zhejiang	54,426,891	4.1	Myanmar
Guangxi	46,026,629	3.5	Spain
Yunnan	44,966,239	3.4	Ukraine
Jiangxi	44,567,475	3.3	Colombia
Liaoning	43,746,323	3.3	Tanzania
Heilongjiang	38,312,224	2.9	Poland
Shaanxi	37,327,378	2.8	Canada
Fujian	36,894,216	2.8	Poland
Shanxi	35,712,111	2.7	Algeria
Guizhou	34,746,468	2.6	Canada
Chongqing	28,846,170	2.2	Malaysia
Jilin	27,462,297	2.1	Venezuela
Gansu	25,575,254	1.9	Saudi Arabia
Inner Mongolia	24,706,321	1.9	North Korea
Shanghai	23,019,148	1.7	Mozambique
Xinjiang	21,813,334	1.6	Australia
Beijing	19,612,368	1.5	Cameroon
Tianjin	12,938,224	1.0	Senegal
Hainan	8,671,518	0.7	Sweden
Hong Kong	7,003,700		Bulgaria
Qinghai	6,301,350	0.5	Paraguay
Ningxia	6,176,900	0.5	Papua New Guinea
Tibet	3,002,166	0.2	Mongolia
Macau	542,400		Solomon Islands
China	*1,316,493,591*	*100*	

* The population of each of these nine provinces is around the same size as, or larger than, the UK, France and Italy. Four of the provinces, namely Shandong, Henan, Guangdong and Sichuan, are larger than any European country including Germany.
† Just the first three provinces above – Guangdong, Shandong, Henan – have a combined population almost as large as that of the United States.

Source: Based on 2010 national census

Table 4. Population of China's provinces.

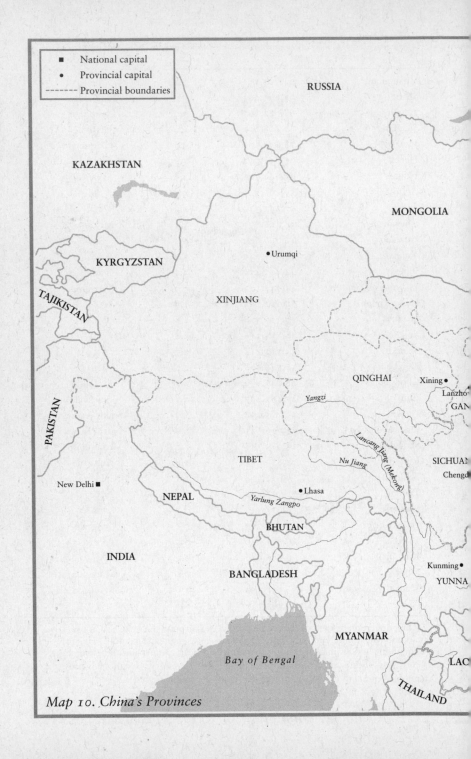

Map 10. China's Provinces

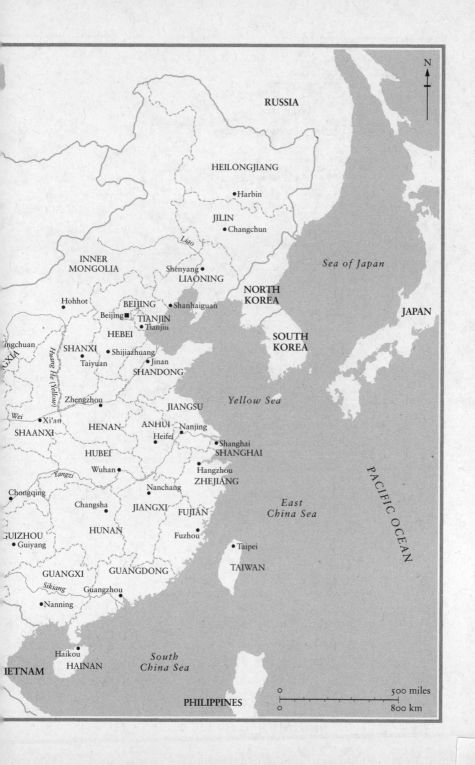

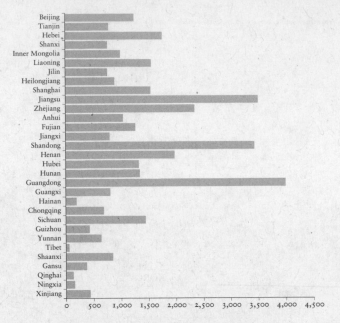

Source: China official statistics

Figure 34. GDP by province (in RMB billion), 2009.

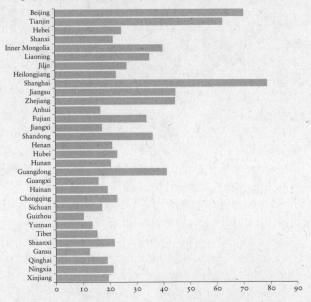

Source: China official statistics

Figure 35. GDP per capita by province
(in RMB thousand), 2009.

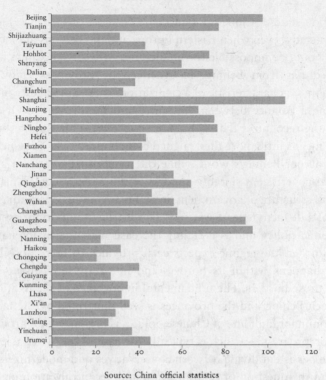

Source: China official statistics

*Figure 36. GDP per capita by cities
(in RMB thousand), 2009.*

provinces of nation-state proportions. The four provinces of Shandong, Henan, Jiangsu and Anhui, for example, have a combined population larger than that of the United States; while nine provinces have a population as large as, or larger than, that of France or the UK. It is estimated that six of China's provinces will each have an annual GDP greater than that of countries like Russia, Canada and Spain by 2020. Not surprisingly, the numerous provinces are extremely diverse in character. The disparity between their per capita incomes is vast, the structure of their economies varies greatly – for example, in their openness to the outside world and the importance of industry – their cultures are distinct, and the nature of their governance is more varied than one might expect.[22] In many respects, indeed, the provinces should be seen as akin to nation-states.[23] China's provinces are far more diverse than Europe's nation-states, even when Eastern Europe and the Balkans are included.

It would be impossible to run a country the size of China by centralized fiat from Beijing. In practice, the provinces enjoy great autonomy, a characteristic of a civilization-state. Governance involves striking a balance between the centre and the provinces. Of course everyone recognizes that ultimate power rests with Beijing: but this often means little more than feigned compliance.[24] The provinces and cities accept Beijing's word, while often choosing to ignore it, with central government suitably mindful of this.[25] Although China has a unitary structure of government, in reality its modus operandi is more that of a de facto federal system.[26] This is true of important aspects of economic policy and is certainly the case with the maintenance of social order: the regime expects each province to be responsible for what happens within its borders and not allow any disruption to cross those borders. The fundamental importance of the relationship between Beijing and the provinces is well illustrated by the fact that the dominant fault line of Chinese politics is organized not around the idea of 'progress' – which is typically the case in the West, as evinced by the persistent divide between conservatives and modernizers – but around the question of centralization and decentralization or, to put it another way, between centrifugal and centripetal forces.[27] Whether or not to allow greater freedom to the media, or to expand or restrict the autonomy of the provinces, is the dominant pulse to which Beijing beats. One of the key reforms introduced by Deng Xiaoping, as discussed in the last chapter, was to grant more freedom to provincial and local governments as a means of encouraging greater economic initiative. The result was a major shift in power from Beijing to the provinces which, by the nineties, had become of such concern to central government that it was largely reversed.[28]

There is a recognizable coherence to the life of the great majority of nation-states that is not true of China. Something major can happen in one part of the country and yet it will have little or no effect elsewhere, or on China as a whole. The traumatic events in Tiananmen Square in 1989, for example, although finding expression in many cities, had surprisingly little impact, beyond a point, on the country as a whole.

Of course, there are always effects, but the country is so huge and complex that the feedback loops work, by the norms of a nation-state, in strange and unpredictable ways. That is why it is so difficult to anticipate what is likely to happen politically.[29] It also perhaps helps to explain a particularly distinctive feature of modern Chinese leaders like Mao and Deng. Whereas in the West consistency is regarded as a desirable characteristic of a leader, the opposite is the case in China: flexibility is seen as a positive virtue and the ability to respond to the logic of a particular situation as a sign of wisdom and an indication of power. Such seeming inconsistency is a reflection of the sheer size of the country and the countless contradictions that abound within its borders. It also has practical benefits, enabling leaders to experiment by pursuing an ambitious set of reforms in a handful of provinces but not elsewhere, as Deng did with his reform programme. Such an approach would be impossible in most nation-states.

THE NATURE OF CHINESE POLITICS

The most impoverished area of debate on China, certainly in the West, concerns its politics. Any discussion is almost invariably coloured by a value judgement that, because China has a Communist government, we already know the answers to all the important questions. It is a mindset formed in the Cold War that leaves us ill-equipped to understand the nature of Chinese politics or the current regime. In the post-Cold War era, China presents us with an intriguing and unforeseeable paradox: the most extraordinary economic transformation in human history is being presided over by a Communist government during a period which has witnessed the demise of European Communism. More generally, it is a mistake to see the Communist era as some kind of aberration, involving a total departure from the continuities of Chinese politics. On the contrary, although the 1949 Revolution ushered in profound changes, many of the underlying features of Chinese politics have remained relatively unaffected, with the period since 1978, if anything, seeing them reinforced. Many of the fundamental truths of Chinese politics apply as much to the Communist period as to the earlier dynasties. What are these underlying characteristics?

Politics has always been seen as coterminous with government, with little involvement from other elites or the people. This was true during the dynastic Confucian era and has remained the case during the Communist period. Although Mao regularly mobilized the people in mass campaigns, the nature of their participation was instrumentalist rather than interactive: top-down rather than bottom-up. In the Confucian view, the exclusion of the people from government was regarded as a positive virtue, allowing government officials to be responsive to the ethics and ideals with which they had been inculcated. We should not dismiss these ideas, inimical as they are to Western sensibilities and traditions: the Confucian system constituted the longest-lasting political order in human history and the principles of its government were used as a template by the Japanese, Koreans and Vietnamese, and were closely studied by the British, French and, to a lesser extent, the Americans in the first half of the nineteenth century. Elitist as the Confucian system clearly was, it did contain an important get-out clause. While the mandate of Heaven granted the emperor the right to rule, in the event of widespread popular discontent it could be deemed that the emperor had forfeited that mandate and should be overthrown.[30]

The state has consistently been seen as the apogee of society, enjoying sovereignty over all else. In European societies, in contrast, the power of government has historically been subject to competing sources of authority, such as the Church, the nobility and rising commercial interests. In effect government was obliged to share its power with other groups and institutions. In China, at least for the last millennium, these either did not exist (there was no organized and powerful Church) or were regarded, and saw themselves, as subordinate (for example, the merchant class); the idea that different sources of authority could and should coexist was seen as ethically wrong.[31] The nearest to an exception were the great teachers and intellectuals who, though always marginal to the centre of power, could, under certain circumstances, be more influential than ministers, acting as the cultural transmitters and guardians of the civilizational tradition and the representatives of the people's well-being and conscience – even, in tumultuous times, as the emissaries and arbiters of the mandate of Heaven. Only two institutions were formally acknowledged and really mattered: one was the government and the other the family. The only accepted interest was the universal interest, represented by a government informed by the highest ethical values, be it Confucian teaching or later Marxism-Leninism-Maoism. In reality, of course, different interests did exist but they were not politically recognized and did not press to be so recognized: rather they operated out of the limelight and on an individualistic basis, lobbying government and seeking personal (rather than corporate or collective) favours which might give them exemption or advantage. Not even the merchant class were an exception to this. In the Confucian order they ranked last in the hierarchy and in practice never sought to break ranks and organize collectively. That apolitical tradition remains true to this day. They have seen themselves as a bulwark of government rather than as an autonomous interest seeking separate representation. This was the case during the Nationalist period, following the Tiananmen Square tragedy, and is exemplified by the manner in which they have been indistinguishable from government – indeed, an integral part of it – in post-handover Hong Kong. Given this lack of any kind of independent tradition of organization either in the Confucian period or more recently in the Communist period, it is hardly surprising that China has failed to develop a civil society, certainly in any recognizable Western form.[32] That may slowly be changing but the burden of history weighs heavily on the present, whatever political changes we may see.

Throughout the debate and struggles over modernization, from the late nineteenth century until today, the Chinese have sought to retain the fundamental attributes of their political system above all else; indeed, the political system has proved more impervious than any other sphere of society to Westernizing influence, both in the imperial and Communist periods. This is in contrast to most developing societies, where government has often been strongly linked to modernizing impulses and leaders were frequently drawn from the Westernized elite – as in India, for example, with the Nehru family. That was never the case in China: leaders like Mao and Deng, even if they had some familiarity with the West, could never be described as Westernized, apart from the influence of (a heavily nativized) Marxism. To this day, even over the last three decades, the ability of China's political world, unlike other institutions, to survive relatively unchanged is remarkable, a testament to its own resilience and the place it occupies in the Chinese psyche.

Chinese politics has traditionally placed a very high premium on the importance of moral persuasion and ethical example. Public officials were required to pass exams in Confucian teaching. They were expected to conform to the highest moral standards and it was to these, rather than different interest groups or the people, that they were seen as accountable. In the Communist period, Confucian precepts were replaced by Marxist (or, more accurately, Maoist) canons, together with the iconic heroes of the Long March and socialist labour. This commitment to ethical standards as the principle of government has combined with a powerful belief in the role of both family and education in the shaping and moulding of children. By the standards of any culture, the highly distinctive Chinese family plays an enormously important socializing role. It is where Chinese children learn about the nature of authority. The word of the parents (traditionally, the father's) is final and never to be challenged. In the family, children come to understand the importance of social hierarchy and their place within it. Through a combination of filial piety, on which the Chinese place greater stress than any other culture, a sense of shame, and the fear of a loss of face, children learn about self-discipline.[33] In a shame (rather than a Christian guilt) culture, Chinese children fear, above all, such a loss of face. The Chinese family and Chinese state are complementary, the one manifestly a support for the other. It is not insignificant that the Chinese term for nation-state is 'nation-family'. As Huang Ping suggests, in China 'many would take for granted that the nation-state is an extended family'.[34]

Whereas in the West the idea of popular sovereignty lies at the heart of politics, it remains largely absent in China. The concept of the nation-state was imported from Europe in the mid to late nineteenth century, with a section of the Chinese elite subsequently becoming heavily influenced by European nationalism. There was, though, a fundamental difference in how national sovereignty was interpreted. In the case of European nationalism, national sovereignty was closely linked to the idea of popular sovereignty; in China the two were estranged. While national sovereignty was accorded the highest importance, popular sovereignty was replaced by state sovereignty.[35] This was not surprising. First, as we have seen, there was a very powerful tradition of state sovereignty in China but no tradition of popular sovereignty. Second, nation-statehood was acquired at a time when China was under threat from the Western powers and Japan. In such circumstances, the overwhelming priority was national sovereignty rather than popular sovereignty. The birth of the Chinese nation-state took place in entirely different conditions from those of Europe. The European nation-states were never obliged to contend with a threat to their national sovereignty from outside their continent, as China, in common with more or less every country outside Europe, faced during the nineteenth and early twentieth century. Predictably, the colonial threat served to reinforce and accentuate China's enduring strong-state complex.[36] The imperialist threat and the domestic political tradition thus combined to infuse China's emergence into nationhood with the twin concepts of national sovereignty and state sovereignty.

One of the most fundamental features of Chinese politics concerns the overriding emphasis placed on the country's unity. This remains by far the most important question in China's political life. Its origins lie not in the short period since China became a nation-state, but in the experience and idea of Chinese civilization.[37] The fact that China has spent so much of its history in varying degrees of disunity, and at such great cost, has taught the Chinese that unity is sacrosanct. The Chinese have an essentially civilizational conception of what constitutes the Chinese homeland and the nature of its unity. The Chinese government has attached the highest priority to the return of Hong Kong, Macao and Taiwan, even though they passed out of Chinese hands (in the case of Macao and Hong Kong) a very long time ago. Furthermore, little or no weight has been given to the preferences of the people who live there.[38] Their belonging to China is seen exclusively in terms of an enduring and overriding notion of Chineseness that goes back at least two millennia if not longer: all Chinese are part of Chinese civilization, and therefore China.[39] Choice is not an issue.

Great weight is also accorded to political stability. Like Confucius, Deng Xiaoping, as cited in the last chapter, was in no doubt about its importance: '[China's] modernization needs two prerequisites. One is international peace, and the other is domestic political stability . . . A crucial condition of China's progress is political stability.'[40] The priority attached to political stability is reflected in popular attitudes.[41] In a recent survey, stability was ranked as the second most important consideration, far higher than in any other country.[42] In the Chinese mind, stability and social order rank far higher than civil and political freedoms.[43] The priority given to stability is understandable in the light of China's history, which has regularly been punctuated by periods of chaos and division, usually resulting in a huge number of deaths, both directly through war and indirectly through resulting famines and disasters. The country lost as much as a third of its population (around 35 million people dead) in the overthrow of the Song dynasty by the Mongols in the thirteenth century. It has been estimated that the Manchu invasion in the seventeenth century cost China around one-sixth of its population (25 million dead). The civil unrest in the first half of and mid nineteenth century, including the Taiping Uprising, resulted in a population decline of around 50 million. Following the 1911 Revolution and the fall of the Qing dynasty, there was continuing turbulence and incessant civil war, with a brief period of relative calm from the late twenties until the Japanese invasion, and then, after the defeat of the Japanese, a further civil war culminating in the 1949 Revolution.[44] Given this history, it is not surprising that the Chinese have a pathological fear of division and instability, even though periods of chaos and disorder have been almost as characteristic of Chinese history as periods of order.[45] The nearest parallel in Europe was the desire that consumed the continent after 1945 never to wage another intra-European war. The huge price China has paid in terms of death and bloodshed is in part perhaps the cost of trying to make a continent conform to the imperatives of a country, while Europe has paid a not dissimilar price for the opposite, namely bitter national rivalry and an absence of continent-wide identity and cohesion.

CHINA AND DEMOCRACY

In Western eyes, the test of a country's politics and governance is the existence or otherwise of democracy, defined in terms of universal suffrage and a multi-party system. This is an extremely narrow and inadequate frame of analysis. Democracy is but one aspect of a much larger picture when it comes to assessing the nature and quality of a country's governance. Take the example of Italy. In terms of the frequency of elections, it has few peers: it is always voting. Yet its governance is very weak because the state lacks legitimacy in the eyes of the people. The huge array of elections since the foundation of the modern post-war republic has singularly failed to change that state of affairs. The state lacks legitimacy because the people do not see it as their representative but rather as a somewhat foreign institution whose authority can if necessary always be subverted, ignored or evaded. The reason lies in the failure of the Risorgimento – the unification of Italy in the late nineteenth century – to create a state that succeeded in overcoming and subordinating the regional differences between its various component parts; unification was only a partially successful and partially completed project. As a consequence, it has been possible for Italians, for example, over the period since 1994 until the present to regularly elect a prime minister in Silvio Berlusconi who blatantly used the state for his own narrow personal ends: around half the electorate found his conduct perfectly acceptable because in varying degrees they shared his view of the state.

This brings us to the nature of Chinese governance. By Western norms, it is certainly not democratic. Yet the Chinese state enjoys much greater legitimacy than any Western state. The Chinese treat the state with a reverence and respect that is more or less unknown in the West; and the reason clearly has nothing to do with democracy. In other words, a state's legitimacy cannot be reduced to the existence or otherwise of democracy: on the contrary, democracy is not necessarily the most important factor in a state's legitimacy and may, as in the case of China, be relatively unimportant. The underlying reason for the legitimacy of the Chinese state is that, as discussed earlier, it is seen by the people as the embodiment and guardian of Chinese civilization, enjoying, as a consequence, something akin to a spiritual significance. It follows that what would undermine the legitimacy of a government, the present one included, is a threat to the country's unity. The attitude of the Chinese towards the state, thus, is very different to that of Westerners. For the latter, the state is an outsider, a stranger, even an interloper, whose presence should, as far as possible, be limited and confined. This is most obviously the case in the United States, with those who identify with the Tea Party, for example, regarding the state as an alien body, but even in Europe it is viewed with varying degrees of suspicion. In China, in contrast, the state and society are seen as on the same side and part of the same endeavour: the state enjoys the status of an intimate and is treated like a member of the family, not just any member but the head of the family – the patriarch himself. We can only understand the immense authority of the Chinese state in these terms, an authority which has been reinforced by the fact that, unlike in the West, it has had no serious rivals for over a millennium. This brings us to the future of democracy, as we understand it in the West, in China.

The last fifty years have seen a huge increase in the number of countries that boast some kind of democracy, though important areas of the world, notably the Middle East, Africa, Central Asia and, of course, China, are still, at least in practice, exceptions. There is little doubt that some kind of democracy is a desirable system if the circumstances are ripe and if it can take serious root in a culture. If, however, democracy amounts to little more than an alien transplant, as has been the case in Iraq, where it was imposed via the barrel of an Anglo-American gun, then the cost of that imposition, for example in terms of resistance, alienation or ethnic conflict, is likely to turn out to be far higher than any benefits it may deliver. Democracy should not be regarded as some abstract ideal, applicable in all situations, whatever the conditions, irrespective of history and culture, for if the circumstances are not appropriate it will never work properly, and may even prove disastrous. Nor should it be seen as more important than all the other criteria that should be used to assess the quality of a country's governance. For developing countries in particular, the ability to deliver economic growth, maintain ethnic harmony (in the case of multi-ethnic societies), limit the amount of corruption, and sustain order and stability, are equally, if not rather more, important considerations than democracy. Democracy, in other words, should be seen in its proper historical and developmental context: different societies can have different priorities depending on their circumstances, histories and levels of development.[46]

Very few countries have combined democracy, as it is now understood in the West, with the process of economic take-off.[47] Britain's Industrial Revolution took place in the late eighteenth and early nineteenth century. Even by 1850, however, only around one-fifth of men had the right to vote. It was not until the 1880s that most men gained the right, and not until 1918, over 130 years after the beginning of the Industrial Revolution, that women (over thirty) won the same right. Broadly speaking this picture applies to other West European countries, all of which experienced take-off without democracy. In fact the most common form of governance during Europe's industrial revolutions was the monarchical state, absolutist or constitutional. The American experience was significantly different. By 1860 a majority of white men enjoyed the right to vote, but most blacks did not acquire it, in practice, until 1965, while white women only won it in 1920: during America's economic take-off, thus, only a minority enjoyed the right to vote. In Japan, universal male suffrage was not introduced until 1925, well after the economic take-off that followed the Meiji Restoration.[48] In sum, the right to vote was not established in the developed world, except for a very small and privileged minority, until well after their industrial revolutions had been concluded (with white men in the United States constituting the nearest to an exception). The European powers, furthermore, never granted the vote to their colonies: it was still seen as entirely inappropriate for the vast tracts of the world that they colonized, even when it had become an accepted fact at home. The only exceptions in the British case were the so-called dominions like Australia and Canada, where shared racial and ethnic characteristics were the underlying reason for the display of latitude. It was not until after the great majority of former colonies gained independence following the Second World War that they were finally able to choose their form of governance. Much hypocrisy, it is clear, attaches to the Western argument that democracy is universally applicable whatever the stage of development.

Some form of democratic governance is now universal in the developed world, where economic take-off was achieved a century or more ago. In contrast, the picture predictably remains uneven in the developing world, with democracy for the most part either unusual or, at best, somewhat flawed. A similar pattern concerning democracy and levels of development broadly prevails in East Asia. Japan, as we have seen, did not achieve anything like widespread suffrage until well after its economic take-off. None of the first Asian tigers – South Korea, Taiwan, Hong Kong and Singapore – achieved take-off under democratic conditions: South Korea and Taiwan were governed by far-sighted military dictatorships, Hong Kong was a British colony bereft of democracy, while Singapore enjoyed what might be described as a highly authoritarian and contrived democracy. All, though, were blessed with efficient and strategic administrations. As developmental states, the legitimacy of their governments rested in significant part on their ability to deliver rapid economic growth and rising living standards rather than a popular mandate. Each of these countries has now achieved a level of development and standard of living commensurate with parts of Western Europe. Hong Kong, under Chinese rule since 1997, now enjoys very limited elements of democracy; Singapore's governance remains a highly authoritarian democracy; while South Korea and Taiwan have both acquired universal suffrage and multi-party systems. These last examples, together with Japan, confirm that industrialization and economic prosperity generally provide more propitious conditions for the growth of democratic forms.

In this light it seems misconceived to argue that China is now ready for, and should become, more or less forthwith, a multi-party democracy based on universal suffrage. The country is only halfway through its industrial revolution, with over 50 per cent of the population still living and working in the countryside. It is true that India remains much less developed than China and yet possesses what, by historical standards, is a remarkable democracy; but in this respect India has so far been history's great exception. Another interesting example is Indonesia, which, though an extremely diverse archipelago, now enjoys a fragile democracy. The main reason why countries have tended not to be democratic during economic take-off is that there is an inherent authoritarianism involved in an industrial revolution – the need to concentrate society's resources on a single objective – which, judging by history, people are prepared to tolerate because their own lives are dominated by the exigencies of economic survival and the desire to escape from poverty. In a sense, the attitude of the people mirrors that of government: political authoritarianism complements the authoritarian and compulsive circumstances of everyday life, with its inherent lack of choice. This helps to explain why authoritarianism rather than democracy has been the normal characteristic of economic take-off. As many have observed, there is little demand for democracy from within China. Indeed, if anything, there has been a turn away from democracy since Tiananmen Square. A combination of a fear of instability following the events of 1989, the disintegration of the Soviet Union, and what are seen as the difficulties experienced by Indonesia, Thailand and Taiwan as democracies – and also the Philippines and India – have reinforced the view of most Chinese that this is not an immediate issue: that, on the contrary, it is liable to represent a distraction from the main task of sustaining the country's economic growth.[49] Implicit in this is the not misplaced view that any move towards democracy is likely to embroil the country in considerable chaos and turmoil. This is a key reason why democracy, for the great majority of Chinese, commands little support.

Those Westerners – what we might call the ultra-democrats – who believe that democracy is more important at all times than any other matter, would, of course, take issue with this. Bruce Gilley, for example, argues that Russia could end up better off, at least in the long run, than China because it has already addressed the issue of democracy. Given China's hugely more impressive economic growth and Russia's somewhat precarious democracy, this judgement seems tenuous to say the least. Gilley also suggests that: 'Debates about issues like compulsory voting, fair electoral systems, money in politics, judicial review, and the like will be the dominant "historical" issues of our time.'[50] Major issues in the West, for sure, but in a world grappling with multifarious problems such as Western economic crisis, one superpower, the rise of China, and also perhaps India, and where ethnic conflict often presents nation-states with their greatest challenge and where for many the task of economic take-off remains all-consuming, the idea that a cluster of issues revolving around democracy will be the dominant global issue of our time betrays a highly parochial Western mentality.

While there is little sign of any significant pressure in China for what might loosely be described as Western-style democracy, there is, nonetheless, a continuing and growing demand for the accountability of government at local, provincial and national levels. So how should we approach the question of democracy in China? China is roughly at the halfway point of its economic take-off, perhaps somewhat beyond. Even twenty years hence, it is estimated that over 20 per cent of its population will still work on the land. There are many imponderables, but assuming that economic growth continues at a relatively rapid rate and political stability is broadly maintained, then it seems reasonable to expect serious moves towards democratization within that kind of timescale, possibly less.[51] In developmental terms, this would still be rather sooner than was the case with the other Asian tigers or the West. It should also be borne in mind that the political traditions of China are neither favourable nor orientated towards democracy. There is a very weak tradition of popular accountability, and state sovereignty has been preferred to popular sovereignty: government is, in effect, answerable to itself via the feedback loop of ethical norms. This is reflected in the central values that govern political behaviour, which can be summarized as sincerity, loyalty, reliability and steadfastness,[52] all of which derive from the influence of Confucianism, and, to a lesser extent, Communism. In contrast, the equivalent Western values are accountability, representation and participation. There is, moreover, as we have seen, no tradition of independent organization and only a very weak notion of civil society.

Power resides overwhelmingly in the state. Interest groups, rather than aspiring to represent themselves collectively, seek to advance their claims by private lobbying and achieving some kind of accommodation with the state. Instead of making demands on or confronting government, interest groups prefer to associate with power on an individual basis.

What serves to greatly complicate the question of democracy is that China has the size and diversity of a continent, although the site of democracy, globally speaking, has always been, and remains, exclusively the nation-state. There are no multinational, regional or global institutions that could be described as democratic.[53] Their invocation to a modicum of representivity is invariably via the nation-states that comprise them. The classic example of this phenomenon is the European Union, which makes no real claim to be democratic other than by virtue of its member-states – the European Parliament being elected but largely powerless. One of the reasons that democracy has worked in India, which is also of a continental scale, might in part be because it is far looser and more decentralized than China, so that individual states can act, in some degree, like quasi nation-states. This is certainly not the case in China, which for thousands of years has prided itself on its centralized and unitary status, even though, as we have seen, this has in practice involved a high degree of negotiated decentralization. While the more developed provinces, notably those on the eastern and southern seaboard, may already be in a position to embrace a more democratic form of polity, their progress in that direction is bound to be constrained by the far less developed condition of the majority of the country. It is possible, nonetheless, that more developed cities like Shenzhen and Shanghai may be allowed to introduce democratic reforms in advance of the rest of the country. In 2008 the Shenzhen mayor Xu Zongheng claimed that direct voting would in future account for 70 per cent of the city's residential and village committees.[54] Since 2009, it has eased legal restrictions on civic organizations such as charities and business associations, allowing them to register without direct supervision by a Party or government official, to seek private funding in China and overseas, and even to hire foreigners. It now has more than 3,500 such non-governmental organizations.[55] More far-reachingly, the Standing Committee of the National People's Congress issued a ruling at the end of 2007 that it would consider allowing direct elections for Hong Kong's leader in 2017; at present half its Legislative Council is elected. Such a solution would be in the spirit of 'one country, two systems' and lies within the tradition of a civilization-state in which different systems coexist.

Finally, we should bear in mind that China is the home of Confucian thought and practice, and consequently has experienced Confucianism in a more complete and doctrinaire form than Japan and Korea, where it was a Chinese import and therefore never enjoyed quite the same degree of overweening influence as in China. As a result, it was easier for these countries to embrace democracy by, in effect, adding a new political layer to coexist along with the older Confucian traditions and practices. It will certainly be possible for China to do the same, but the weight of what might be described as Confucian orthodoxy is likely to make it more difficult.[56]

In the long run it seems rather unlikely, given the underlying pressures for democracy that exist within increasingly sophisticated, diverse and prosperous societies, that China will be able to resist the process of democratization. The interesting question is what democracy might look like in China. There is a strong tendency in the West to view democracy in terms of a 'one size fits all' approach. In fact, the form of democracy varies greatly according to the history, traditions and culture of a society. There is no reason to believe, except on grounds of Eurocentrism, that the very specific conditions that shaped European society (and European-derived nations like the United States), and therefore European democracy, will result in the same kind of democratic structures elsewhere.[57] This is abundantly clear in the case of Japan. It certainly possesses some of the trappings of democracy that we are familiar with in the West – not surprisingly, given that the US authored Japan's post-war constitution following the latter's defeat – most notably universal suffrage and a multi-party system. Yet it is immediately evident that in practice the system works very differently. The Liberal Democrats were almost continuously in power from the mid 1950s until 2009. The other parties, apart from the occasional period of coalition government, found themselves in permanent opposition and wielded rather less power and enjoyed rather less importance in the political life of the country than the various factions within the Liberal Democrats. It remains to be seen how long the Democrats, who finally defeated the Liberal Democrats at the last election, will stay in office. Moreover, as Karel van Wolferen has observed, much of the real power is vested in the civil service, especially in particular ministries, rather than in the government itself: in other words, in that part of the state that is permanently constituted rather than in that part that is elected. The cabinet, for example, rarely meets and when it does its business is largely ceremonial.[58] The Democrats vowed to end the overweening power of the bureaucracy, but they would appear – not surprisingly given the burden of history – to have singularly failed. Notwithstanding the accoutrements of a Western-style democracy, state sovereignty continues to prevail over popular sovereignty, with the significance accorded to elections – and, therefore, popular sovereignty – much less than in the Western case. Reflecting the hierarchical character of society and Confucian influence, power has a permanent and unchanging quality that is relatively unaffected by the electoral process.

Whatever democratic political system evolves in China will bear the heavy imprint of its Confucian past. It is more difficult to judge the longer-term impact of Communism because its duration will have been far more limited. There are, though, important continuities between Confucianism and Communism – for example, in the notion of a special caste of political leadership, Confucian in the one case, Leninist in the other.[59] In North-East Asia – for these purposes, Japan, South Korea, Taiwan and Vietnam – the continuing influence of the Confucian tradition is palpable in the emphasis on education, the structure of the family, the central role of the bureaucracy and the commitment to harmony.[60] Because of the presence of a Communist government, this was, until 1978, perhaps less apparent in China, but there has been a marked revival in Confucian influence since then, a process initiated by the government during the 1990s,[61] but which has increasingly acquired a momentum of its own.[62] Reflecting Confucian influence, an editorial in the *People's Daily* argued that in order to build a market economy, it was necessary to promote 'the rule of virtue while developing the rule of law'.[63] In March 2007 the prime minister Wen Jiabao remarked: 'From Confucius to Sun Yat-sen, the traditional culture of the Chinese nation has numerous precious elements, many positive aspects regarding the nature of the people and democracy. For example, it stresses love and humanity, community, harmony among different viewpoints, and sharing the world in common.'[64] Communist Party officials in Henan province are now, amongst other things, assessed on the basis of Confucian values such as filial piety and family responsibility, while secondary school children are once more being taught the Confucian classics[65] and Confucius's birthday is again being celebrated.[66] On a practical level, the Party is now placing a new kind of emphasis on the importance of the obligations and duties shown by its cadres towards the people they represent. As part of their training, they are given test cases in which they are expected not just to consult their superiors as before, but also, more importantly, to listen to the people. This new attitude was reflected in the way in which public officials apologized for their failures in the Sichuan earthquake and milk scandal – in a manner reminiscent of the behaviour of shamed Japanese government and corporate leaders – and resigned. Significantly, the government has chosen to use the name Confucius Institutes for the numerous Chinese cultural and language centres which it has been establishing round the world.

With the decline of Marxism, the turn towards Confucianism in a country so steeped in its ethical and moral discourse is predictable.[67] It can be argued, in any case, that, for the most part, those tenets of Marxism that have had most impact in China are the ones that most chimed with the Confucian tradition – for example, self-criticism (mirroring the Confucian idea that one should direct criticism at oneself before others), the idea that rulers should be morally upright and the invoking of model workers as an example to others; by the same token, those Marxist ideas that failed were those that were most inimical to Confucianism. Even the fact that Chinese political leaders dye their hair black can be traced back to the Mencian proposition that white-haired people should be cared for rather than engage in heavy work. Most importantly of all, Confucian ideas remain embedded in the fabric of the culture: filial piety is still widely practised and endorsed, including the legal requirement that adult children care for their elderly parents. A favourite theme of Chinese television soaps concerns relationships with elderly parents. An obvious and striking characteristic of Chinese restaurants, in contrast to Western ones, is the frequency with which one sees the extended family eating together, a tradition reflected in the ubiquity of the large circular table.[68]

Confucianism should not be seen as a fixed entity, having been through many mutations during its history. Like all philosophies and religions, its longevity has depended in part upon its ability to adapt to changing circumstances and times.[69] The fact that Confucianism is a syncretic tradition has served to enhance its flexibility and adaptability. One of the most outstanding examples was the manner in which the Neo-Confucians of the Song period (AD 960–1279) assimilated Buddhism and Taoism, which were then sweeping China.[70] It would be wrong, moreover, to regard Confucianism as entirely inimical to democratic ideas. For example, Sun Yat-sen, the leader of the 1911 Revolution and the founding father of the Republic of China, said: 'Our three-*min* principles [nationalism, citizen rights and the welfare of human beings] originate from Mencius ... Mencius is really the ancestor of our democratic ideas.'[71] The mandate of Heaven, in recognizing the right of the people to rebel if the emperor failed them, was certainly a more democratic idea than its European counterpart, the divine right of kings.[72] The emperor was required to rule in a virtuous and benign way according to the ethical strictures that constituted the guidelines for his conduct, while the hierarchical structure demanded a certain degree of reciprocity, suggesting implied rights as well as duties.[73] The government was expected to grant society considerable independence from the state, and in important respects this was the case – not least in the economic sphere, as the early development of a sophisticated market illustrates. Although civil society remains very weak in China, there is a powerful tradition of *min-jian* society, or folk culture, composed of age-old Chinese customs and support systems, which to this day still represents an important area of autonomy from government.[74] In sum, Confucianism certainly lends support and succour to an authoritarian system of government, but it is also imbued with democratic and popular elements.[75]

There are a number of ways in which Confucian ideas are likely to inform a democratic China:[76] the overarching role of the state and its bureaucracy; the centrality of the family, and extended networks like clans (which help, for example, to relieve the state of some of the tasks of social welfare); the importance of *guanxi* (the web of personal relationships which inform Chinese society); the Confucian preference for resolving conflicts by mediation rather than litigation, suggesting that the resort to law and the judicial process will always be far less significant in China (and Japan) than it is in the West; and the significance that is attached to values and morality as the lodestar of people's behaviour.[77] Such age-old belief systems almost invariably have a profound effect on the way a society operates. China, like Japan and Korea, has a quite different sense of public order and behaviour compared with the norms that prevail in the West, a situation reflected in the much lower levels of crime in these societies. Indeed, these deeper societal traditions have undoubtedly helped China – and other East Asian societies – to cope with the combined vicissitudes of globalization and modernization, in effect acting as shock absorbers.[78]

Chinese democracy will share certain universal characteristics with democracies elsewhere, but will also be highly distinctive, expressive of its roots in Chinese society and traditions.[79] Most significantly, Chinese democracy is always likely to give priority to state sovereignty over popular sovereignty in the manner of Japan, but to a much greater extent in the light of its history. In other words, the state is always likely to enjoy a preponderant position over the people – because the latter believe it should do so. Given the cultural context of Confucianism and Communism, together with the extraordinary demands of governing a continent, the invention and evolution of Chinese democracy will require enormous novelty and ingenuity.[80] There is no reason to believe, in a country which is home to the world's oldest and most sophisticated statecraft, that this will prove impossible. But there seems little reason to believe that this process is in any way imminent. Nor will innovation in governance be a matter of one-way traffic. Just as China can learn from the American federal system and the European Union in governing such a vast country, so China, accounting for one-fifth of the world's population – and with arguably the world's most competent state – can offer others a model for large-scale governance, which will become increasingly important in a globalized world.

COMMUNIST RULE

The coincidence of the collapse of Soviet Communism with the suppression in Tiananmen Square persuaded most Western observers that the Chinese Communist Party would meet a similar fate. They could not have been more wrong. In contrast to Soviet Communism, which suffered from a growing state of paralysis and ossification, the Chinese party, under Deng Xiaoping, displayed great creativity and flexibility, responding to the crisis it inherited from Mao by initiating a process of reform that has transformed the living standards of the great majority of the people. The rule of the Communist Party is no longer in doubt: it enjoys the prestige that one would expect given the transformation that it has presided over. The feel-good factor, and a concomitant mood of extraordinary confidence that has been engendered, is clear from Table 5 and Figures 37–8. Indeed, what is so striking about these figures is the *contrast* between the level of satisfaction of the Chinese in their economic situation and with the economic competence of their government as compared with that of the populations in all the other countries polled: the Chinese are hugely more satisfied than anyone else. The uncertainties of 1989 are now a very distant memory. The nature of the Party's support and legitimacy has changed in the process: it is no longer primarily a function of ideology but depends increasingly on its ability to deliver economic growth together with the quality of its rule. In that sense, China has come to resemble other East Asian developmental states, though in all these cases, as discussed earlier, and also in Chapter 5, the nature of governmental authority is also deeply embedded in the culture. Even though support for the Communist Party is now more contingent, there is little cause to believe that it is fragile or vulnerable. On the contrary, it is reasonable to presume that its rule is rather more secure than has been the case at any time since the death of

Mao, which is not surprising given its success as a governing party, and is reflected in the fact that over the last decade 20 million people have applied to join annually, even though only 2 million have been admitted each year. There is pressure for more radical political reform, as illustrated by the Charter 08 manifesto, but it remains relatively isolated and heavily policed by the state.

	2002	2007	2008	2009
% Good	%	%	%	%
Poland	7	36	52	29
Kenya	7	60	–	19
Germany	27	63	53	28
Russia	13	38	52	20
S Korea	20	8	7	5
Nigeria	32	37	41	23
Turkey	14	46	21	24
Britain	65	69	30	11
US	46	50	20	17
Argentina	1	45	23	20
CHINA	52	82	82	88
Indonesia	15	23	20	48
Lebanon	5	9	10	11
Japan	6	28	13	10
Spain	–	65	35	13
France	45	30	19	14
Jordan	33	44	39	33
Pakistan	49	59	41	22
Mexico	31	51	36	30
Egypt	–	53	44	27
India	39	74	62	73
Brazil	–	–	–	–

Source: Pew Research Center

Table 5. How people have perceived their nation's national economic situation.

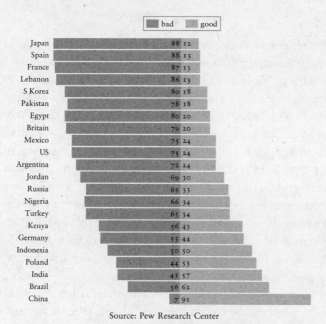

Source: Pew Research Center

Figure 37. How people view current economic situation of their country, 2010.

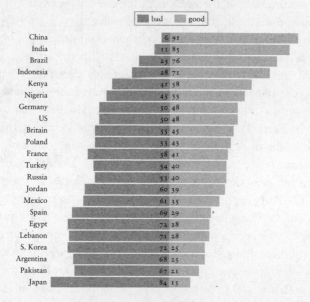

Source: Pew Research Center

Figure 38. Government rating for dealing with economy, 2010.

If the reform process has been characterized by the boldness of its economic measures, it has also been distinguished by the more limited nature of the political changes. This is not to underestimate them: on the contrary, there have extensive and far-reaching reforms of the state, notably in 1982, 1988, 1993 and 1998.[81] These have included the gradual spread of competitive elections to the great majority of villages and to some towns, for example in Guangdong and Fujian, where mayoral elections have been held.[82] There has been reform of the civil service, the decentralization of power to local government, and a limited rejuvenation of national and local parliaments. There has been a growing trend, largely as a result of economic necessity, towards rule by law (that is, the determination of issues according to a legal code) and, to a far lesser extent, towards the rule of law (that the law applies irrespective of the view of government),[83] which, according to one Chinese expert, applies in only 10–20 per cent of instances.[84] Given that the latter would require the Party's power to be constitutionally limited, thereby necessitating a fundamental change in its role, its significant extension remains both problematic and unlikely. There has been a formalization of procedures such that, for example, the president can now only serve for two terms. Relations between the military and civil power have been normalized. Compared with the pre-reform period, there is far greater political space for open discussion and serious critique,[85] with the internet now the most important arena for public debate, greatly exceeding what is possible in the conventional media, though even here censorship now operates with a rather ligher touch.[86] There have also been major reforms within the Party. Leaders are now required to retire rather than being allowed to die in office. The Sixteenth Congress in 2002 saw the first orderly transfer of power, from Jiang Zemin to Hu Jintao. Contested elections for delegates to the Party congress take place in some provinces.[87] The Party has broadened its membership, most notably, following Jiang Zemin's Three Represents reform, to include private capitalists. And the Party leadership at all levels, including the top, is more professional and better educated than it was previously, with better training for officials and the opening of MBA-style colleges for Party members.[88] Intellectuals are now involved in policy-making discussions in a more open and systematic way at the highest levels.

China's political reform has occurred gradually and incrementally. Unlike the economic reforms, the intention has never been to effect a systemic change, and certainly not to introduce Western-style democracy – rejected as incompatible with both China's traditions and present needs in the White Paper on Democracy published in 2005[89] – but rather to modernize and codify political and administrative processes, thereby seeking to promote efficiency while maintaining political stability. The purpose of village elections, for example, has been good governance and functional efficiency rather than any move towards a wider process of democratization.[90] On the other hand, there has been a major expansion in civil liberties and human rights. Hong Kong opinion, which has traditionally been very sensitive to the lack of such rights in China, has become increasingly positive about trends to the north. In a 2008 survey in Hong Kong on the anniversary of the crackdown in Tiananmen Square, 85 per cent of respondents believed that human rights in China had improved since 1989, up from 78 per cent a year earlier. And the proportion who thought that they would improve further in the following three years rose to 77 per cent from 67 per cent a year earlier. Only 2 per cent thought that China's human rights record had worsened since 1989.[91] The boundaries of what it is now possible to say and do in China have expanded greatly, unless they concern the most sensitive subjects like Taiwan, Tibet, the Falun Gong religious sect, or the role of the Communist Party. This is most clearly apparent on the internet, which, although heavily policed in a manner that contradicts the utopian idea of the internet as a censorship-free zone, still allows a wide-ranging and frank discussion on all but the most delicate topics.[92]

There is also growing pressure for accountability with regard to the conduct of officials. In 2006 there were over 90,000 'mass incidents' (demonstrations, strikes, occupations, riots, etc.) recorded by the Ministry of Public Security – a Beijing academic estimated that this figure had risen to 180,000 in 2010 – many of which concerned the appropriation of land from farmers through sweetheart deals between developers and local government, from which corrupt officials benefited financially. Although these cases usually have little or nothing to do with the national authorities, the government sought, in the face of gathering unrest, to strengthen farmers' land rights in order to prevent such seizures. A new rural reform package was announced in October 2008 that strengthened the rights of farmers by enabling them to trade in their thirty-year land-use contracts, a move which had the effect of bolstering their security of tenure.[93] Similarly, in an attempt to improve labour conditions, the government introduced a new labour law in 2008 which enhanced the role of labour unions and made it harder for employers to fire workers or rely on casual labour; the new laws have already significantly improved workers' wages and conditions. Meanwhile the government has predictably resisted the formation of independent labour associations.

The Maoist period involved the politicization of more or less the whole of society. The old Maoist slogan of 'politics in command' aptly summed up the nature of Communist rule until Mao's death in 1976, with its constant calls for mass campaigns, symbolized most dramatically by the Cultural Revolution. In contrast, during the reform era there has been a steady process of depoliticization, accompanied by a steep decline in the importance of ideology. The highly politicized and obtrusive Maoist state has given way to what now looks more like a technocratic state, in the manner of other East Asian developmental states,[94] although the powers of the Chinese state remain wide-ranging, from the one-child policy and internal migration to history books and the media.[95] As the Party has shifted from ideological to instrumental rule, from a political to a technocratic approach, its relationship with the people has become less intrusive and its visibility less apparent. There is, in effect, a new kind of social compact between the Party and the people: the task of the Party is to govern, while the people are left free to get on with the business of transforming their living standards and enjoying the rewards of rising incomes and a growing variety of consumer goods.[96] Money-making, meanwhile, has replaced politics as the most valued and respected form of social activity, including within the Party itself. The Party has actively encouraged its officials to enter business, not least as a means of galvanizing economic growth. 'Political loyalty' has in some degree been replaced by 'money' as the measure of the political worth of Party cadres, resulting in a decline in the Party's identity, a loss of its spiritual appeal and a process of internal decay.[97]

The Party has increasingly sought to transform itself from a revolutionary organization into a ruling administrative party.[98] It prioritizes technical competence, entrepreneurship and knowledge over, as previously, revolutionary credentials, military record and class background, with a technocratic class rather than revolutionaries now in charge of the Party.[99] There have been drastic changes in the social composition of the Party leadership over the last twenty years. Between 1982 and 1997 the proportion of the central committee who were college-educated rose from 55.4 per cent to 92.4 per cent. By 1997 all seven members of the standing committee of the central committee's political bureau (the top leadership) were college-educated in technical subjects like engineering, geology and physics, while eighteen of the twenty-four political bureau members were also college-educated.[100] The Party has opened its doors to the new private capitalists in an effort to widen its representation and embrace the burgeoning private sector. By 2000 20 per cent of all private entrepreneurs were members of the Party.[101] This is not surprising given that by 1995 nearly half of all private capitalists had previously been Party and government officials.[102] The large-scale shift of Party and government officials into the private sector has almost certainly been the biggest single reason for the enormous increase in corruption, as some exploited their knowledge and connections to appropriate state property, gain access to cash reserves, and line their own pockets. The problem poses a grave challenge to the Party because, if unchecked, it threatens to undermine its moral standing and legitimacy. Despite a series of major, high-profile campaigns against corruption, of which the most prominent casualty so far has been the former Communist Party chief in Shanghai, Chen Liangyu, the evidence suggests that the problem remains huge and elusive because its roots lie deep within the Party itself and the myriad of *guanxi* connections.[103]

As the country gravitates towards capitalism, changes are taking place in China's class structure that will, in the longer term, have far-reaching political implications. For the time being, however, the technocratic leadership will continue to dominate both the Party and the government, with little immediate prospect of a challenge to their position. The peasantry, though restive in response to the seizure of their land, remain weak and marginalized.[104] The working class has, until recently, seen a serious diminution in its status and influence, with protests limited to piecemeal, factory-by-factory action, but the dramatic strikes in June 2010 in Guangdong and elsewhere were on a scale not witnessed in recent years. The new class of private entrepreneurs, meanwhile, seems to be conforming to the traditional role of merchants, seeking an accommodation with, and individual favours from, the government, rather than playing an independent role of its own.[105]

In the longer run there are four possible political directions that Chinese politics might take.[106] The first is towards a multi-party system. This, for the time being, seems the least likely. The second would be the de facto recognition of factions within the Party. To some extent this process has, at least tacitly, been taking place, with former general secretary Jiang Zemin's power base resting on what came to be known as the Shanghai faction, who were associated with super-growth, privatization, pro-market policies and private entrepreneurs, in contrast to Hu Jintao's constituency, which has given greater priority to sustainable growth, social equality, environmental protection, and state support for education, health and social security.[107] Perhaps the most interesting example of this phenomenon was the thinly-veiled campaign by Bo Xilai, the Chongqing Party secretary, for a seat on the Party standing committee prior to the 2012 Party congress. In addition to pursuing highly popular policies such as more affordable housing and more polite, less corrupt police officers, he reintroduced Maoist slogans, which had more or less vanished from sight in China, with commercials on the local state television channel replaced by 'red programmes' and residents receiving 'red texts' consisting of Mao quotations on their mobile phones.[108] The third would be reforms designed to instil more life and independence into the People's Congress and the People's Consultative Conference, which are state rather than Party institutions. If all three of these directions were followed, they would result in an outcome not dissimilar from that in Japan, where there is a multi-party system in which only one party, at least until very recently, has mattered, where the various factions within the Liberal Democrats have counted for rather more than the other political parties, and where the diet enjoys a limited degree of autonomy. Another possible scenario, in this same context, is that of Singapore – in whose arrangements Deng Xiaoping showed some interest[109] – where the ruling party dominates an ostensibly multi-party system, with the opposition parties dwarfed, harassed and hobbled by the government. The fourth direction, which has been advocated by the Chinese intellectual Pan Wei, puts the emphasis on the rule of law rather than democracy, on how the government is run rather than who runs it, with state officials required to operate according to the law with legal forms of redress if they do not, and the establishment of a truly independent civil service and judiciary, a proposal which, overall, bears a certain similarity to governance in Singapore and Hong Kong.[110] Should this route be pursued then it would mark a continuing rejection of any form of democratic outcome and an affirmation of a relatively orthodox Confucian tradition of elitest government committed to the highest ethical standards.

None of these scenarios seems particularly imminent. For the foreseeable future the most likely outcome is a continuation of the process of reform already under way, notwithstanding the problems of governance consequent upon social unrest and chronic corruption.[111] The Chinese economist Yu Yongding sees corruption in particular as a very serious threat: 'What the public resents most is the collusion between government officials and business people . . . Breaking this unholy alliance will be the big test for China's leadership in 2011 and beyond. Under China's current institutional arrangements, meritocracy is a prerequisite for good governance. But meritocracy has been eroded by a political culture of sycophancy and cynicism.'[112] Meanwhile the transfer of power to a new leadership, which will begin in 2012 with Hu Jintao and Wen Jiaobao giving way to Xi Jinping and Li Keqiang, seems likely to be a well-organized and smooth transition. The Party has been displaying growing self-confidence in recent years and this is reflected, as mentioned earlier, in the optimism shown by the Chinese about their future. In an opinion poll conducted by Pew Research in March 2010 in the aftermath of the popular uprising in Egypt, 87 per cent of Chinese said they were satisfied with the way things were going in their country, compared with 28 per cent of Egyptians, while 91 per cent of Chinese characterized their country's economic situation as good, compared with only 20 per cent of Egyptians. Nearly two-thirds of Chinese judged their lives to be better than five years previously, which was a much higher proportion than in the United States and Western Europe, while nearly half of Egyptians reported a decline in their quality of life. The Chinese showed even greater confidence in the future, with 74 per cent believing that their lives would be better in five years, a far higher percentage than in the United States and Western Europe, while only 23 per cent of Egyptians anticipated a higher quality of life. In response to a question about their government's handling of the economy, the Chinese government came top with a 91 per cent approval rating, compared with 48 per cent for the US government, 45 per cent for the UK, 28 per cent for the Egyptian and 15 per cent for the Japanese. In the light of these findings, the suggestion widespread in the West at the time that the Chinese government might meet the same fate as the Egyptian government was clearly absurd. The growing confidence of the Chinese government is well captured in an interview with Wang Jisi, one of China's leading intellectuals: 'Without such an efficient, centralized and powerful government, there would not have been the China miracle . . .When other countries want to learn from China they should first of all adopt a similar form of government . . . China will remain a one-party polity for a long, long time to come. This is a reality we have to recognize. Meanwhile China will be more pluralistic and diversified politically, and will strengthen its legal system and find ways to protect human rights.'[113]

If the Chinese Communist Party spent many years on the defensive after 1989, it is now increasingly on the front foot. Notwithstanding this, there is a common view among Western commentators that the Chinese government regards itself to be weak and vulnerable, citing as evidence its recent harsh reaction to any obvious signs of dissent and its repressive treatment of oppositional voices like Liu Xiabo and Ai Weiwei. This is based, at least in part, on a misreading of how the Chinese government sees its role. In the time-honoured manner of Chinese governments, given the exceptional priority attached to the maintenance of social order, it is constantly on the alert for signs of opposition or potential threats to internal stability. Similarly it regards itself to be responsible for a vigilant and proactive policing of the boundaries of what is permissible and what is not in Chinese society. These are perceived as basic requirements of good governance, spliced no doubt with a significant dose of paranoia. As a Chinese lawyer in London reminded me, the behaviour of the Chinese state is akin to that of a Chinese parent, who always lays down clear rules regarding the behaviour of their offspring and requires them to be obeyed.

In conclusion, to return to the theme of possible future scenarios, undoubtedly the worst-case scenario for both China and the world would be the collapse and demise of the Communist Party in the manner of the Soviet Union,[114] which had a disastrous effect on Russian living standards for over a decade. The ramifications, nationally and globally, of a similar implosion in China, which has a far bigger population, a much larger economy, and is far more integrated with the outside world, would be vastly greater. A period of chaos would threaten the country's stability, usher in a phase of uncertainty and conflict, threaten a premature end to its modernization, and potentially culminate in a return to one of China's periodic phases of introspection and division. Fortunately the chances of this scenario are relatively remote. The best prospect for China, and the world, is if the present regime continues to direct the country's transformation on a similar basis of reform and mutation until such time as there can be a relatively benign transition to a different kind of era. Given China's huge success over the last thirty years, this remains by far the most likely scenario.

CHINA AS A DIFFERENT KIND OF STATE

After the Treaty of Westphalia in 1648 (which marked the end of the Thirty Years War and initiated a new order in Central Europe based on state sovereignty), the European nation-state slowly emerged as the dominant unit in the international system. The rise of China poses an implicit challenge to this idea. For the West the key operational concept is the nation-state, but for the Chinese it is the civilization-state. China's rise will present the world with formidable problems of mutual understanding. This can be illustrated by the linguistic differences: whereas in English there are different words for nation, country, state and government, the Chinese still largely use the same character for 'country' and 'state'.[115] The real difficulty, of course, lies not in the linguistic niceties but in the different cultural assumptions and meanings that are attached to those words in the two languages. The same word can have a very different meaning for an American or a French person in contrast to a Chinese, even though they might appear to be singing from the same sheet. Huang Ping believes that this cultural difference 'is going to be a huge problem'.[116] In a world hitherto dominated by Western concepts, values, institutions and propositions, to which China has been obliged to adapt, this has been a far bigger problem for China than for the West. But fast-forward to the future and it becomes clear that, as China's power and influence grow apace, it will become the West's problem much more than China's.[117] Such has been the West's dominance over the last two centuries that hitherto it has virtually never been required to address and understand the conceptual framework of a non-Western culture, certainly not as an equal.

It is a mistake to think that China will always adjust to and adopt Western cultural norms as it has over the last century. Far from China converging on the Western model and thereby conforming to the established patterns of the nation-state, there is likely to be a rather different scenario. This is not necessarily because China will want to change things: on the contrary, it has been at pains to assure the global community that it certainly does not see itself as an agent of change anxious to overthrow the established international order. But countries naturally and inevitably see the world according to their own history and experiences, an outlook that is tempered only by the constraints of geopolitics and realpolitik. The European powers, the major architects of the international system as we know it today, brought their own traditions and history to bear on the shaping and design of that system, at the core of which lay the nation-state, a European invention. The way in which the United States sees the world reflects both its European ancestry and the specific characteristics of its own formation and growth. The fact that it expanded by a continuous process of conquest and that, as a settler-nation, it had to invent itself from scratch has imbued the country with a universalizing and missionary conception of its role.[118] The rules that govern the international system may be universal in application, but that does not mean that they were universal in creation, that they emerged magically or democratically out of the international ether: on the contrary, they were the invention of those nations that were strong and dominant enough to enforce their will and to ensure that their interests were those that triumphed. As China becomes a global power, and ultimately a superpower, probably in time the dominant superpower, then it, like every other previous major power, will view the world through the prism of its own history and will seek, subject to the prevailing constraints, to reshape that world in its own image. As China's power grows, it will increasingly see the world in terms of its identity and experience as a civilization-state, with its attendant characteristics and assumptions, rather than primarily as a nation-state. It is worth noting in this context that China's claim on the Spratly and Paracel Islands in the South China Sea is based on ancient Chinese law which dates from the tributary state and civilization-state era.

There is another related sense in which China's emergence is bound to change the international system as we know it. The European nation-states that constituted the original founding core of the international system were all, roughly speaking, of a similar population: namely, in global terms, small to medium sized. Following the Second World War, the number and diversity of nation-states was dramatically transformed as a result of decolonization (and then again after 1989 with the break-up of the USSR). The second half of the twentieth century was dominated by the US and the USSR, which were both far larger than even the biggest European nation-states. Partly as a result, the West European states were encouraged to combine their power in what we now know as the European Union, a grouping of nation-states. It has become common, certainly on the part of Europeans, to see such unions of nation-states as the way forward, ASEAN and Mercosur (a regional trade agreement between four South American countries) being further examples, though neither as yet involves any pooling of sovereignty. The American perspective, for obvious reasons, has invariably placed the major emphasis on the nation-state. But the rise of China and India threatens to transform the picture again. In one sense, of course, it marks the reassertion of the nation-state. These are no ordinary nation-states, however, but states on a gargantuan scale. If this century will increasingly belong to China and India, in conjunction with the United States, then it should also be seen as the Age of the Megastate, albeit in China's case a megastate with a difference, namely a civilization-state.[119] This does not mean that unions of nation-states will go out of fashion, but their primary *raison d'être* is likely to be as a counterweight to the megastate, both the old (the United States) and especially the new (China and India).

Quite where this will leave the old Westphalian system is difficult to say. States of the scale, size and potential power of China and India will dwarf the vast majority of other countries. This will not be an entirely new phenomenon. During the Cold War, the United States and the Soviet Union both established unequal relations with their subordinate allies to an extent which frequently undermined or greatly detracted from the sovereignty of the latter. This is the case, in varying degrees, with the US's present relationship with many countries. But China and India are on a different scale even to the United States: China has more than four times the population and between them India and China comprise around 38 per cent of the world's population. As both are still only in the early stages of their transformation, it is impossible at present to be clear what this might mean in terms of their relationship with other states. The Westphalian system might survive the emergence of China and India as global powers, but it will certainly look very different than at any previous stage in its history, especially given China's status as a civilization-state.

There is one other aspect of China's emergence as a global power that is also novel. Hitherto, ever since the onset of industrialization in the late eighteenth century, the most powerful countries in the world have shared two characteristics. First, they have enjoyed one of the highest (if not the highest) GDPs of their time. Second, they have, relative to their time, also had an extremely high GDP per head: the richest nations have also had the richest populations. That was true – in rough chronological order – of Britain, France, Germany, the United States and Japan. The only exception was the USSR. That situation is about to change: China will share only one of these characteristics, not both. It already has a high GDP – the second highest in the world measured by market exchange rates. But even when it overtakes the United States in 2027, as predicted by Goldman Sachs, or even earlier, it will still have a relatively low GDP per head, and even in 2050 it will still

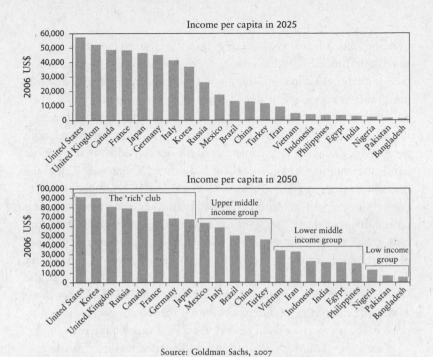

Income per capita in 2025

Income per capita in 2050

Source: Goldman Sachs, 2007

Figure 39. Future income per capita of major countries.

only belong to the 'upper middle group' rather than the 'rich club' (see Figure 39). Welcome to a new kind of global power, which is, at one and the same time, both a developed – by virtue of the size of its GDP – *and* a developing country – by virtue of its GDP per capita.

The implications of a potential superpower being both a developed and a developing country are profound and multifarious. Previously the distinction between developed and developing countries was clear and unambiguous. Indeed between 1900 and 1960 there was a fundamental cleavage between those countries that industrialized in the nineteenth century and those that did not, a situation which persisted until the rise of the Asian tigers from the late fifties. This distinction between developing and developed will in future be more shaded. The continental-sized states, namely China and India, are likely to belong to both categories for many decades: their huge populations mean that they will continue to embrace very diverse levels of development and living standards within their borders. And they are in the process of being joined by other more populous developing countries such as Brazil and Indonesia, with Russia already belonging in this category.

The fact that China and India will be both developed and developing countries suggests that they will also enjoy diverse interests, namely the motives and concerns of *both* developed and developing countries: in effect, they will have a foot in both camps. Hitherto, trade relations have been dominated by the interests of the developed world on the one hand and the developing world on the other. Where will China and India fit in this game? Will they lean towards the developed world or the developing world, or both, depending on the issue involved?[120] It is reasonable to assume that over the next twenty years or so, both will frequently make common cause with the developing world: this can already be seen in the role of and cooperation between China, India, Brazil and South Africa in the World Trade Organization. It was also very evident at the Copenhagen climate conference in December 2009, as was the emergence of differences within the bloc of developing countries, based on their levels of development and specific interests.

Assuming that both China and India continue to enjoy rapid growth for some time to come, the centre of gravity of their interests and concerns is likely to shift steadily over time from the 'developing' sectors of their economies to the 'developed', a process which will be accompanied by the growing power of those associated with the more modern parts of their economies. This is already very evident in China with the increasing power of industrial interests and the steady decline of the farmers. A by-product of these trends might be to embed fundamental divisions in these countries between the developed and developing parts, disparities that are a function of historic differences, reinforced and accentuated by their relationship to the inequalities and dynamics of the global economy.

China will also share another characteristic with India as a major power. China was partially colonized and India was completely colonized. The club of advanced countries – those that began their industrialization in the nineteenth century or, in the case of Britain, earlier – were those that did the colonizing. The United States, of course, also started life as a colony, but because its settler population consisted of migrants from Europe, especially Britain, its relationship to Britain as an imperial power was very different to those colonies whose people were of a different race and culture.[121] The US, moreover, was also later to acquire its own colonies. China and India will be the first major powers that were previously colonized and are composed of non-white races and cultures. In other words, China and India can identify with those who have been colonized in a way that the imperialist powers obviously cannot. This has greatly assisted China in its courtship of Africa, as we shall see in Chapter 10. Here is another powerful change in the texture and symbolism of global politics represented by the rise of China and, in this case, especially India.[122]

The rise of China will profoundly change the nature of the global system. This is already becoming apparent in a limited way but over the next twenty years it will become crystal-clear. For the first time in the modern era, the world's increasingly dominant player will be a civilization-state, a megastate on a completely new scale, a developing country and a former colony of the Western powers and Japan.

8

The Middle Kingdom Mentality

The journey from Fudan University on the north side of Shanghai to the Shanghai Museum in the centre must have taken the best part of an hour, perhaps longer. Over a decade ago the roads were not only congested but also in variable states of repair. Quite frequently in the course of my city travels, I found that taxi drivers had only a rather vague idea of where my destination might be and it was not entirely unusual to be left high and dry in what one hoped was the general vicinity of where one needed to be: the city was changing so quickly that road maps were out of date before they were published, giving a whole different meaning to what in London the cabbies call 'the knowledge'. On this occasion, though, there was no such problem; being a famous landmark in the central area of Shanghai assured familiarity.

My companion on the journey to interview the founder of the magnificent Shanghai Museum was a sociology student, Gao, who was in her final year at Fudan University before leaving to pursue a doctorate at one of the top American universities. She had been asked by her professor to assist me during my month's stay at Fudan and she had proved wonderfully supportive. She was one of the most intelligent and committed undergraduates I had ever met and was extraordinarily well read. More than that, she was very pleasant and agreeable company, full of suggestions, always prepared to meet my requests, as well as having plenty of ideas of her own. She helped to make my stay in Shanghai a real pleasure. On this occasion she was coming with me to assist with any translating that might be required during the interview.

In the taxi we talked about the interview, the Museum, which I had visited on a couple of previous occasions, and the interviews planned before my return home to Hong Kong in just over a week's time. Then our conversation drifted on to other subjects. Gao was naturally excited about the prospect of studying in the United States and suddenly said: 'Did you know that some Chinese students that go to America marry Americans?' I told her about the television programme I had made the previous year about the overseas Chinese, including an interview with such a mixed-race couple living in San Francisco. 'Actually, three weeks ago I saw a mixed couple at the supermarket checkout at the end of our road,' I said. 'A Chinese woman and an American guy.' Then I added after a pause: 'He was black.' Why did I say that to her? I guess there were several reasons. In Hong Kong such a couple was a rare sight – indeed, it was the only time I had ever seen one, and it had stuck in my mind. And my wife was Indian-Malaysian, possessed of the most beautiful dark brown skin, but I was painfully aware that not everyone perceived her colour in the way that I did, especially the Hong Kong Chinese.

I was totally unprepared for Gao's reaction. Her face became contorted and she reacted as if she had just heard something offensive and abhorrent. She clearly found the very thought repellent, as if it was unnatural and alien, akin to having a relationship with another species. Her reaction was a demonstration of prolonged physical repulsion the like of which I had never previously witnessed. For her, the idea was simply inconceivable. Gao was a highly educated and intelligent woman; and an extremely nice one. I was shocked. I asked her what the matter was as she writhed in disgust, but there was no answer and no possibility to reason with her. That was more or less the beginning and end of our conversation on the subject. The memory of that journey has remained with me ever since. There was, alas, no reason to think that Gao's reaction was unusual or exceptional. This was not simply the reaction of an individual but the attitude of a culture. And she was surely destined to become a member of China's elite.

What will China be like as a great power? The traditional way of answering this question is in terms of geopolitics, foreign policy and interstate relations. In other words, it is largely seen as the preserve of foreign ministries, diplomacy, bilateral talks, multinational negotiations and the military. A concentration on the formal structures of international relations, however, fails to address the cultural factors that shape the way a people think, behave and perceive others. The geopolitical approach informs how a state elite reasons and acts, while a cultural analysis, rooted in history and popular consciousness, seeks to explain the values, attitudes, prejudices and assumptions of a people. In the short run, the former may explain the conduct of relations between countries, but in the longer run people's values and prejudices are far more significant and consequential.[1] Ultimately, nations see the world in terms of their own history, values and mindset and seek to shape that world in the light of those experiences and perceptions.

Take the example of the United States. Fundamental to any understanding of American behaviour over the last three centuries is that this was a country established by European settlers[2] who, by war and disease, largely eliminated the indigenous population of Amerindians; who, having destroyed what had existed before, were able to start afresh on the basis of the European traditions that they had brought with them; who engaged in an aggressive westward expansion until they came to occupy the whole of the continent; and who were to grow rich in important measure through the efforts of their African slaves.[3] Without these building blocks, it is impossible to make any sense of subsequent American history. They help us to understand the basic contours of American behaviour, including the idea of the United States as a universal model and the belief in its manifest destiny. It is clear that race and ethnicity are fundamental to this picture. Consciously or unconsciously, they lie at the heart of the way in which people define themselves and their relationship to others.[4]

This more cultural approach is, if anything, even more important in China's case because it has only very recently come to see itself as a nation-state and engage in the protocol of a nation-state: most Chinese attitudes, perceptions and behaviour, as we saw in the last chapter, are still best understood in terms of its civilizational inheritance rather than its status as a nation-state. If we want to comprehend how China is likely to behave towards the rest of the world, then first we need to make sense of what has made China what it is today, how it has evolved, where the Chinese come from, and how they see themselves. We cannot appreciate their attitude towards the rest of the world without first understanding their view of themselves. Once again, history, culture, race and ethnicity are central to the story.

FROM DIVERSITY TO HOMOGENEITY

China, or at least the land mass we now call China, was once, like any other huge territory, occupied by a great multitude of races.[5] Today, however, China sees and projects itself as an overwhelmingly homogeneous nation, with over 91 per cent of the population defined as Han Chinese. True, the constitution defines China as a unitary, multi-ethnic state, but the other races comprise less than 9 per cent of the population, a remarkably small percentage given its vast size. A tourist who visits the three great cities of Guangzhou in the south, Shanghai in the east and Beijing in the north-east, however, ought to have no difficulty in noticing that there are very marked physical differences between their inhabitants, even though they all describe themselves as Han Chinese. While Beijingers are every bit as tall as Caucasians, those from Guangzhou tend to be rather shorter. Given that modern China is the product of a multiplicity of races, this is not surprising. The difference between China and other populous nations has not been the lack of diversity, but rather the extraordinary longevity and continuity of Chinese civilization, such that the identity of most races has, over thousands of years, been lost through a combination of conquest, absorption, assimilation, intermarriage, marginalization, extermination and government resettlement.

Like all racial categories, the Han Chinese – a product of the gradual fusion of many different races – is an imagined group. The term 'Han Chinese', indeed, only came into existence in the late nineteenth century. But such has been the power of the idea, and its roots in the long history of Chinese civilization, that it has spawned what can only be described as its own historical myth, involving the projection of the present into the distant past. That myth holds that the Chinese are and always have been of one race, that they share a common origin, and that those who occupy what is China today have always enjoyed a natural affinity with each other as one big family.[6] This has become an integral part of Chinese folklore and is shared by the Confucian, Republican and Communist traditions alike.[7] A recent official Chinese publication on patriotic education declared: 'Patriotism is a fine tradition of our Chinese nation. For thousands of years, as an enormous spiritual force, it continuously stimulated the progress of our history.'[8] There is a commonly held view amongst the Chinese that Chinese civilization commenced with the Yellow Emperor (Huang Di), who, as legend has it, was born in 2704 BC and ruled a kingdom near the Yellow River on the central plain that is regarded as the cradle of Chinese civilization. This explains why the Chinese commonly refer to their civilization as 5,000 years old. Many Chinese, both on the mainland and overseas, believe that they are genealogically descended from the Yellow Emperor.[9] Although Mao rejected the idea, it has staged something of a revival since the mid 1980s. In a speech in 1984, Deng Xiaoping suggested that the desire for the reunification of the mainland and Taiwan was innately 'rooted in the hearts of all descendants of the Yellow Emperor'.[10] A well-known intellectual, Su Xiaokang, has written: 'This Yellow River, it so happens, bred a nation identified by its yellow skin pigment. Moreover, this nation also refers to its earliest ancestor as the Yellow Emperor. Today, on the face of the earth, of every five human beings, there is one that is a descendant of the Yellow Emperor.'[11] This statement implies that the Chinese have different origins from everyone else. Like the Japanese, the Chinese have long held, albeit with significant dissenting voices, a polygenist view of the origins of *Homo sapiens*, believing that – in contrast to the generally held view that we all stem from a single ancestry in Africa – humanity has, in fact, multiple origins.[12] Peking Man, discovered in Zhoukoudian near Beijing in 1929–30,[13] has been widely interpreted in China as the 'ancestor' of the Mongoloid race.[14] In 2008 a further important discovery was made of skull fossils of a hominid – Xuchang Man – at the Xuchang site in Henan province,[15] which was believed to date back 80,000–100,000 years. An article in the *China Daily* claimed that 'the discovery at Xuchang supports the theory that modern Chinese man originated in what is present-day Chinese territory rather than Africa.' It continued, 'Extraordinary archaeological discoveries are critical to maintaining our national identity as well as the history of our ancient civilization.'[16] While internationally archaeological findings are regarded as part of a worldwide effort to understand the evolution of the human race, in China, where they are given unusual prominence, they are instead seen as an integral part of national history and are used 'to promote a unifying concept of unique origin and continuity within the Chinese nation'.[17]

Chinese historians generally describe the process of Chinese territorial expansion as one of 'unification' rather than 'conquest', with expansion being seen as a progressive evolution towards a preordained and inevitable unity. Territory, once taken, has been regarded as immutably Chinese.[18] There is a powerful underlying assumption that the numerous races and nationalities have always demonstrated undivided loyalty to the imperial regimes.[19] The truth, in fact, is rather different. Far from China's expansion to its present borders being a harmonious and natural process, the realization of a nation always waiting to be born, it was in fact, as one would expect, a complicated process of war, rivalry, ethnic conflict, hegemony, assimilation, conquest and settlement.[20] The embryo of contemporary China was born out of the military victory of the Qin kingdom (221–206 BC), following the Warring States period during which over 100 states fought for supremacy in north and central China. The Qin dynasty – which, prior to its triumph, roughly coincided with the present north-west province of Shaanxi – eventually emerged victorious over six other kingdoms and succeeded in expanding its territory sixfold.[21] During the 2,000 years that followed the Qin victory, China expanded southwards to the South China Sea, northwards to incorporate much of the steppe lands, and westwards into Central Asia. Far from this enormous geographical expansion being characterized by a natural process of fusion, peace and harmony, it predictably entailed much conflict and many wars.[22]

The growth of China is the story of the outward expansion of the

THE AGE OF CHINA

northern Chinese. The best-known area of conflict concerns the region to the north of Beijing, bordering on what we now know roughly as Mongolia and Manchuria. For thousands of years this region was contested between the northern horse-bound nomads of the steppes and the agrarian-based Chinese. The picture painted by official Chinese histories is of aggressive, rampaging nomads and peace-loving Chinese peasants.[23] While it is true that the Chinese were constantly preoccupied with the security of their northern borders – until the Qing dynasty, the steppe nomads showed themselves to be highly effective fighters – the Chinese frequently sought to conquer and hold the steppe lands to their north. Rather than seeing the Great Wall as a line of fortified defence against the nomads, in fact, it is more appropriate to regard it as the outer perimeter of an expanding Chinese empire.[24] The names of the fortifications reveal the nature of the Chinese intent: 'Tower for Suppressing the North' and 'Fort Where the Barbarians are Killed'. The Chinese saw the nomads as much their inferior, referring to them as barbarians. It was the long-running conflict between the Chinese and the steppe nomads that shaped the Chinese sense of cultural superiority, gave rise to the distinction between 'civilization' and 'barbarians', and largely conditioned Chinese thinking about 'self' and 'the other'.[25] The cleavage is not surprising: settled agricultural communities everywhere looked down on nomads as backward and primitive. Nevertheless, the Chinese and the steppe nomads, although more or less constantly at war, also experienced something of a symbiotic relationship. On several occasions, the 'barbarians' successfully conquered China and became its rulers, most famously in the case of the Mongols and later the Manchu of the Qing dynasty. Indeed, as testimony to the extent of mutual incursion and interaction over the millennia, the ruling Chinese caste was essentially a racial mix of the northern Chinese and the nomadic steppe tribes.[26] The ascendancy of the Chinese, however, is illustrated by the manner in which both the Mongols and the Manchu – and all other conquerors of China from the steppes – invariably, sooner or later, went 'Chinese' once in power. The historian Wang Gungwu has suggested that, 'in the last thousand years, the Chinese can only claim to have ruled their own country for 280 of those years', yet in every case the 'foreign' rulers adopted Confucian culture and the Confucian system of governance.[27] There is no more powerful demonstration of the advanced nature of Confucian civilization and the hegemonic influence that it exercised over the peoples around its borders.

The conquest of the lands to the south is less well known. It took place over a period of nearly three millennia and involved the movement of whole populations, the intermixing of races, and the disappearance or transformation of cultures. Some races vanished altogether, while substantial kingdoms were either destroyed or were subject to a process of absorption and assimilation. The rich foliage of these subtropical lands lent themselves to guerrilla warfare and the

Map 11. Boundaries of Ming and Qing China

Source: *Philip's Atlas of World History*

Han rulers, during the Qin and Han dynasties in particular, were kept in a more or less permanent state of insecurity.[28] By far the largest single expansion – and certainly the most rapid – took place in the early phase of the Manchu-controlled Qing dynasty, from 1644 until the late eighteenth century, when the territory under Chinese rule more than doubled. This involved the conquest of lands to the north, notably those occupied by the Mongols, and to the north-west, the homelands of the diverse Muslim populations of Turkestan.[29] Many of the peoples conquered, particularly in Central Asia and Tibet, had little or nothing in common with the Han Chinese. These lands became colonial territories of the Qing empire, huge in extent, sparsely populated and rich in some natural resources. China's expansion usually involved a combination of military force and cultural example. This was certainly true of the southern and central parts of China as well as the steppe lands. But the Qing conquest of the north-west and west was different, being achieved by the use of large-scale force and brutality.[30] Most of the Zunghars, for example, who occupied much of what we now know as Xinjiang, were exterminated.[31]

The expansion of the Chinese empire over such a long historical period involved what might be described as a steadily moving frontier or, to be more precise, many moving frontiers. One of the characteristics of Chinese expansion was the resettlement of enormous numbers of people across China, with population movement, always highly regulated, being an important instrument of government policy. The Qin, for example, deployed it on a massive scale to occupy and pacify their greatly expanded territory. One of the most remarkable examples was the huge resettlement of Sichuan province in the south-west, whose population had fallen to around half a million by 1681, but which reached 207 million in 1812 as a result of the movement of migrant-settlers, organized and orchestrated by the Qing dynasty.[32] This process is still evident today, with the steady influx of Han migrants into Inner Mongolia, where they now constitute a very large majority, and into Tibet and Xinjiang, where they represent substantial minorities, possibly even a majority in the case of the latter. Resettlement has been a key tool in the process of Chinese expansion and Hanification.

It is important, in this context, to distinguish between a land-based expansion like China's and a maritime-based expansion such as those of the European empires of Britain and France. The European colonies never acquired any degree of permanence because, except in those cases where there was overwhelming white settlement, as for example in Australia and North America, it was impossible to assimilate races and cultures which, by virtue of history, place and distance, were entirely alien. This was quite different from China, which, because of its land-based expansion, always enjoyed the advantage of proximity, thereby enabling, if need be, the process of absorption and incorporation to take thousands of years.[33] As a consequence, in terms of the consciousness of its multitudinous component groups, the Chinese empire is no longer an empire, except at its northern and especially north-western and western edges, with the population of these areas representing only 6 per cent of China's total.[34] China thus only confronts difference at – in relative terms – its demographic margins. On the other hand, in terms of land these regions are extremely important, accounting for around 64 per cent of China's land mass. Territorially speaking, China remains an empire.

FROM UNIVERSE TO NATION-STATE

Until its engagement with Europe in the nineteenth century, China saw itself in terms quite different from those of a nation-state. China believed that it was the centre of the world, the Middle Kingdom, the 'land under Heaven' (*tianxia*), on an entirely different plane from other kingdoms and countries, not even requiring a name.[35] It was the chosen land not by virtue of God, as in the case of Israel or the United States, but by the sheer brilliance of its civilization. Perhaps the best way to illustrate imperial China's mentality is by the maps of the period, dating from the sixth century BC onwards. These consisted of a series of concentric circles or rectangles, with Beijing at the epicentre, the core formed by the northern Chinese, then progressively moving outwards across China, from those fully accepted as Chinese, to the inner barbarians, the outer barbarians, the tributary states, and finally to those condemned to outer darkness, deemed incapable of being civilized, who lived in distant lands and continents (see illustration on p. 305).[36] Imperial China, in short, embraced an utterly Sinocentric view of its place in the global order. This was not a world with a common measure, as in a system of nation-states, but instead a bifurcated world, consisting of a single 'civilization' surrounded by many 'barbarians', the latter arranged according to their cultural proximity to civilization, as in a spectrum of deepening shadows. As the 'land under Heaven', imperial China was a universe in its own right, above and distinct from the rest of the world, superior in every respect, a higher form of civilization achieved by virtue of the values, morals and teachings of Confucianism and the dynastic state that embodied them. Its ideal was universalism, which was also the rationale for its expansion.[37]

Unlike a nation-state, its frontiers were neither carefully drawn nor copiously policed, but were more like zones, tapering off from civilization through the various states of barbarianism.[38] It is not surprising that the centre of the world did not require a name, for the Middle Kingdom needed no further explanation or description. Its mode of expansion was a combination of conquest and cultural example, its ideological justification that of a 'civilizing mission'.[39] The Chinese system exercised an extraordinary hegemonic influence on the entire surrounding region: on the distant island of Japan and on the Korean Peninsula, which, as we have seen, both adopted Chinese characters for their writing systems, used a form of Confucianism for their moral tenets and system of governance, and were part of China's tributary system; on the tribal nomads of the northern steppes, most of whom, when circumstances enabled or dictated, came under the Confucian spell; on what we now know as Vietnam, which was thoroughly Confucianized while fiercely defending its independence from the Chinese over many centuries; and finally, as we have seen, on the progressive Sinicization of the diverse peoples that comprise what we know as China today. Whatever the role of force, and it was fundamental, there is no brooking the huge power, influence and prestige of Chinese thinking and practice.

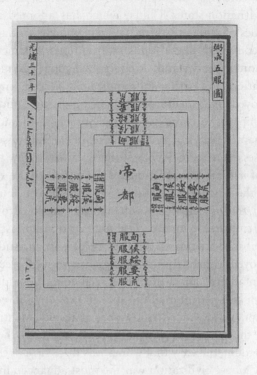

The Ancient Chinese View
of the World

The classic ancient Chinese account of the world, dating from the sixth century BC, was the Yugong, a chapter of the Shujing (Classic of History). This highly influential document describes five major concentric geographical zones emanating outwards from the capital: royal domains, princely domains, a pacification zone, the zone of allied barbarians, and the zone of savagery. These zones have conventionally been portrayed in rectangular form, in line with the cosmological notion of a square earth.

Traditional Western political theory has been at pains to draw a firm and categoric distinction between agrarian-based dynastic regimes and nation-states. China, which has adopted many of the characteristics of a nation-state while remaining essentially a civilization-state, confounds these kinds of traditional distinctions, as the lines of continuity between the Celestial Kingdom and modern China as a civilization-cum-nation-state indicate.[40] Indeed, imperial China already enjoyed, in elemental form, some of what we understand, in a broader comparative context, to be the crucial building blocks and incipient characteristics of a nation-state. In Confucianism, for example, it possessed a state ideology par excellence, by far the most advanced of its time, which imbued the outlook of the elite and also influenced the wider population.[41] The mandarin bureaucracy – schooled in the precepts of Confucianism, devoted to the idea of service and endowed with a powerful credo of administration – was by far the most sophisticated civil service of its time. And the country already enjoyed a shared written language: many dialects may have been spoken across China, most of which could be understood only by their own speakers, but all the spoken versions shared a common written script and this acted as a source of affinity, identity and cohesion across the population.[42] Finally, Sinocentrism – the idea of the Middle Kingdom, the view that China was the centre of the world, the belief that Chinese civilization was the most advanced in the world – provided what might be described as a primordial form of patriotism.[43] This was not the kind of patriotism that we associate with the nationalism of the modern nation-state, but rather a belief in their own universalism, the relevance of their culture to all peoples and societies, and its inherent superiority in relation to others. Implicit in this feeling of pre-eminence, as we shall see, was an inchoate notion of racial, as well as cultural, superiority, such that the two became intimately entwined.

Towards the end of the nineteenth century, under growing threat from the European powers and Japan, the Qing dynasty was increasingly obliged to operate according to the rules of a nation-state-based international system. The haughty view that it had previously maintained of its elevated role in relation to that of other states foundered on the rock of European superiority. The 'land under Heaven' was brought down to earth. The Middle Kingdom became just another state, now with a name, China, like any other. An elite and a people schooled in the idea of their cultural superiority entered a prolonged crisis of doubt, uncertainty and humiliation from which, a century and a half later, they are only now beginning to emerge. China, besieged by foreign powers, was forced to begin the process of defining its frontiers with the same kind of precision as other states, though such was the length of these borders and the number of its neighbours that even today those with India remain unresolved.

The belief in their cultural superiority shaken and undermined, the Chinese began a long and agonized search for a new sense of identity as circumstances grew more precarious and desperate at the end of the nineteenth century. It was during this period that the nationalist writer Zhang Taiyan introduced the term 'Han people' (*Hanren*) to describe the Chinese nation, and it rapidly acquired widespread popularity and usage.[44] 'Qin Chinese' might have been chosen, but Han was preferred, probably because the Han dynasty, which immediately followed the Qin (the first unified Chinese empire), lasted much longer: 400 years compared with a mere fifteen. The term 'Han Chinese' was an invention, nothing more than a cultural construct: there was no such race; the Han Chinese were, in reality, an amalgam of many races.[45] The purpose of the term was overtly racial, a means of inclusion and exclusion. It was used as a way of defining the Chinese against the Manchu, who formed the Qing dynasty and who, after 250 years in power, increasingly came to be seen, as their rule began to crumble, as an alien and objectionable presence. It was also directed against the Europeans, who controlled most of the treaty ports and who were seen as undermining the fabric of China and Chinese life. The deep resentment against Europeans, who were increasingly referred to in derogatory racial terms, was graphically illustrated by the xenophobic and nativist Boxer Uprising (1898–1901),[46] which marked the early beginnings of a popular Chinese nationalism, though it was not until the Japanese invasion in 1937 that this became a genuinely mass phenomenon. There are many expressions of what is frequently referred to as Chinese nationalism today, most notably directed against the Japanese – as in the demonstrations in 2005 – and also against various Western powers, especially the United States; as a result, it has become commonplace to refer to the rise of Chinese nationalism. The problem is that this suggests it is essentially the same kind of phenomenon as other nationalisms when, in fact, Chinese nationalism cannot be reduced to nation-state nationalism because its underlying roots are civilizational. Imperial Sinocentrism shapes and underpins modern Chinese nationalism. It would be more accurate to speak of a dual phenomenon, namely Chinese civilizationalism and Chinese nationalism, the one overlapping with and reinforcing the other.

THE CHINESE AND RACE

Racism is a subject that people often seek to avoid, it being deemed too politically embarrassing, any suggestion of its existence often eliciting a response of outraged indignation and immediate denial. Yet it is central to the discourse of most, if not all, societies. It is always lurking somewhere, sometimes on the surface, sometimes just below. Nor is this the least bit surprising. Human beings see themselves in terms of groups, and physical difference is an obvious and powerful signifier of them. It is but a short distance to ascribe wider cultural and mental characteristics to a group on the basis of visible physical differences: in other words, to essentialize those physical differences, to root culture in nature, to equate social groups with biological units.[47] There is a widely held view, not least in East Asia, that racism is a 'white problem': it is what white people do to others. In both China and Taiwan, the official position is that racism is a phenomenon of Western culture, with Hong Kong holding a largely similar view.[48] This is nonsense. All peoples are prone to such ways of thinking – or, to put it another way, all races harbour racial prejudices, engage in racist modes of thought and practise racism against other races. Racism, in fact, is a universal phenomenon from which no race is exempt, even those who have suffered grievously at its hands. Each racism, however, while sharing general characteristics with other racisms, is also distinct, shaped by the history and culture of a people. Just as there are many different cultures, so there are also many different racisms. White racism has had a far greater and more profound – and deleterious – effect on the modern world than any other. As white people have enjoyed far more power than any other racial group over the last two centuries, so their influence – and their prejudices – have reached much further and have had a greater impact, most dramatically as a result of colonialism. But that does not mean that other peoples do not possess similar attitudes and prejudices towards races that they believe to be inferior.[49]

This is certainly the case in East Asia. Although rarely recognized, in many parts of the region, especially in North-East Asia, the notion of identity is highly racialized. Many terms have been used in China and Japan since the late nineteenth century to represent these countries as biologically specific entities. In China these include *zu* (lineage, clan), *zhong* (seed, breed, type, race), *zulei* (type of lineage), *minzu* (lineage of people, nationality, race), *zhongzu* (breed of lineage, type of lineage, breed, race), *renzhong* (human breed, human race); while those used in Japanese include *jinshu* (human breed, human race), *shuzoku* (breed of lineage, type of lineage, breed, race) and *minzoku* (lineage of people, nationality, race).[50] Even in South-East Asia, which is racially far more heterogeneous, racial identities remain very powerful. In short, a racialized sense of belonging is often at the heart of national identity in East Asia.[51]

The importance of racial discourse in China and other Confucian societies like Japan, Singapore, Taiwan, Korea and Vietnam begs the question of why this is the case. The answer is almost certainly linked to the centrality of the family, which has been a continuing and crucial thread in the Chinese tradition (as in all Confucian societies), and which, together with the state, is the key societal institution. The family defines the primary meaning of 'we', but the family is also closely linked to the idea of lineage, which serves to define a much larger 'we'. People in China have long had the habit of thinking of people with the same name as sharing a common ancestry. Since the Ming dynasty, it has been widespread for different lineages with the same surname to link ancestors and establish fictitious kinship ties through a famous historical figure, as in the case of the Yellow Emperor. 'The entire Chinese population,' suggests Kai-wing Chow, 'could be imagined as a collection of lineages, since they all shared the same Han surnames.'[52] And the fact that there are relatively few surnames in China has served to magnify this effect: according to some estimates, 100 surnames cover 85 per cent of Chinese citizens – the three most common being Wang (92 million), Li (91 million) and Zhang (86 million) – compared with 70,000 surnames covering 90 per cent of Americans. In Chinese custom, lineage, like the family, is intimately associated with biological continuity and blood descent (an idea which enjoys core cultural significance in Confucian societies) as is, by extension, the nation itself.[53] This is reflected in the notion of citizenship, with blood the defining precondition in all these societies: indeed, it is almost impossible to acquire citizenship in any other way.[54]

Far from racism being a Western invention, it has ancient roots in both China and Japan. There is written evidence cited by Jared Diamond going back to at least 1000 BC which shows that the Chinese regarded themselves as superior to the non-Chinese and that the northern Chinese saw those in southern China as barbarians.[55] In ancient China, the ruling elite measured groups by a cultural yardstick according to which those who did not follow Chinese ways were considered to be barbarians, though the latter could subsequently be reclassified depending on the degree of their cultural assimilation.[56] Within the Middle Kingdom, the barbarians were typically divided into two categories: 'raw barbarians' (*shengfan*), who were seen as savage and resistant, and 'cooked barbarians' (*shufan*), who were regarded as tame and submissive.[57] Cooked barbarians were deemed as on the cusp of being civilized, raw barbarians as being beyond assimilation. Those living outside the borders of China were regarded as either raw barbarians or, worse, as akin to animals. The distinction between man and animal in Chinese folklore was blurred, with alien groups living outside China frequently regarded as savages hovering on the edge of bestiality and often described by the use of animal radicals (radicals are a key component of written Chinese characters), thereby identifying different non-Chinese peoples with various kinds of animals.[58] It is clear from this that the Chinese sense of superiority was based on a combination of culture and race – the two inseparably linked, the relative importance of each varying according to time and circumstance.[59] Frank Dikötter, who has written the major study in the English language on Chinese racism, argues:

> On the one hand, a claim to cultural universalism led the elite to assert that the barbarian could be 'sinicized', or transformed by the beneficial influence of culture and climate. On the other hand, when the Chinese sense of cultural superiority was threatened, the elite appealed to categorical differences in nature to expel the barbarian and seal the country off from the perverting influences of the outside world.[60]

For the most part, however, the expansive rather than the defensive view prevailed.

Skin colour assumed an early significance. From the most ancient times, the Chinese chose to call themselves white, with a light complexion highly valued and likened to white jade.[61] By the beginning of the twelfth century, the elite attached a heightened meaning to being white, with colour consciousness amongst the elite sensitized by the maritime contacts established during the Southern Song dynasty (AD 1127–1279). During this period even the newly popular image of Buddha was converted from a 'swart half-naked Indian to a more decently clad divinity with a properly light complexion', rather as Jesus was whitened in the Western Christian tradition.[62] Of course, not all Chinese had light complexions. In particular, those who laboured long and hard in the fields under a fierce sun were weather-beaten and dark-skinned. The symbolic distance, and distinction, as represented by class, and made visible in skin colour, was thus projected by the Chinese elite onto the outside world as they came into growing contact with other peoples and races. White was regarded as the centre of the civilized world, embodied by the Middle Kingdom, while black represented the negative pole of humanity, symbolized by the remotest parts of the known world. As the Chinese became familiar with more distant lands during the Ming dynasty, notably through Zheng He's voyages to Africa and South-East Asia in the fifteenth century, so their perception of skin colour and physical difference became more variegated, with Africans and aboriginals invariably placed at the bottom, and Malays and Viets just above them.[63]

During the Qing dynasty, racial categories became a central and explicit factor in the characterization of the barbarian. This represented an important shift from the cultural norms that had previously tended to prevail, even though the racial element had always been significant.[64] New racial taxonomies and classifications were elaborated, stimulated by the bloody wars of expansion that the Chinese fought in the west, which had brought them into contact with peoples very different from themselves who, throughout much of the second half of the nineteenth century, they struggled to subdue, with only partial success.[65] But it was the increasing presence and power of Europeans following the Opium Wars, and the growing crisis of the Qing dynasty that this provoked, which was to prove the rudest shock of all and produce the biggest change in Chinese attitudes, not just amongst the elite, but also at a popular level. From the 1890s, the cultural racism of ancient China was articulated into a new and popular racist philosophy by a rising class of academics and writers, who were influenced by the racial theories and social Darwinism prevalent in the West at the time. Racism now became an integral part of popular thinking, articulated in a whole range of widely circulated publications, especially amongst the urban population of the treaty ports. The new racial discourse covered every aspect of physical difference, from skin colour and hair to height, size of nose, eye colour, size of feet and body odour: no racial stone was left unturned, each physical detail explored for its alleged wider mental and cultural significance. Barbarians had routinely been described as 'devils' since earlier in the century, but now they were distinguished according to their skin colour, with Caucasians referred to as 'white devils' (*baigui*) and those of darker skin as 'black devils' (*heigui*), terms that are still in common usage. Not all devils were regarded in the same way, however: white devils were perceived as 'rulers' and black devils as 'slaves'.[66] The literature of the treaty ports was filled with contempt for those from Africa and India.

During this period, which coincided with the growing popularity of the term 'Han', the Chinese began to describe themselves as yellow rather than white, in an effort to distinguish themselves from Europeans on the one hand and those of darker skin on the other. As China sought to resist the growing European threat, the world was seen in social-Darwinist terms of the survival of the fittest, with those of darker skin perceived as having failed and thereby being condemned to inevitable oblivion, and the yellow races, headed by the Chinese, being engaged in a desperate battle for survival against the dominant white race.[67] Yellow enjoyed a strongly positive connotation in the Chinese world, given its association with the Yellow River and the Yellow Emperor. In 1925 the poet Wen Yudio, who spent some time in the United States, wrote a poem entitled 'I am Chinese', which captures the swelling sense of racially inspired Chinese nationalism, heightened in this case by his experiences in the West:

> I am Chinese, I am Chinese,
> I am the divine blood of the Yellow Emperor,
> I came from the highest place in the world,
> Pamir is my ancestral home,
> My race is like the Yellow River,
> We flow down the Kunlun mountain slope,
> We flow across the Asian continent,
> From us have flown exquisite customs,
> Mighty nation! Mighty nation![68]

The pervasiveness of racialized ways of thinking is underlined by Frank Dikötter, who chronicles countless examples, adding:

> It would be wrong to assume that these clichés have been gathered. . . simply by sieving printed material through a filter that retains racial utterances. A dredger would be needed to gather up all the racial clichés, stereotypes and images which abounded in China [as well as the West] between the wars. These clichés were the most salient feature of a racial discourse that was pervasive and highly influential; moreover it was rarely challenged. They were adopted and perpetuated by large sections of the intelligentsia.[69]

While this racism was clearly a product of imperial China's worsening predicament, an expression of a crisis of identity and a desire for affirmation and certainty as the country was drawn remorselessly into a system of nation-states on extremely unfavourable terms, it was also a function of the cultural racism that had been such a strong feature of the Celestial Kingdom over a period of almost three millennia. The rigour of the racial hierarchies that now became endemic bore a striking resemblance to the cultural hierarchy of the Confucian social order – an illustration of the complex interplay between cultural and racial forms of superiority in Chinese society.

This racialized thinking heavily influenced the nationalists, led by Sun Yat-sen, who overthrew the Qing dynasty in the 1911 Revolution. Sun saw the Chinese as a single race and believed in the inevitable confrontation of the yellow and white races:

> Mankind is divided into five races. The yellow and white races are relatively strong and intelligent. Because the other races are feeble and stupid, they are being exterminated by the white race. Only the yellow race competes with the white race. This is so-called evolution. . . among the contemporary races that could be called superior, there are only the yellow and white races. China belongs to the yellow races.[70]

Elsewhere he wrote: 'The greatest force is common blood. The Chinese belong to the yellow race because they come from the bloodstock of the yellow race. The blood of ancestors is transmitted by heredity down through the race, making blood kinship a powerful force.'[71] Initially, he dismissed the Tibetans, Mongolians, Manchu and others as numerically insignificant: he was a Han nationalist who saw the Chinese exclusively in terms of the Han, and therefore as a nation-race. But after the Revolution he was confronted with the reality of inheriting a Qing China in which, though their numbers might have been small, the ethnic minorities occupied over half the territory of China. If China was defined only in terms of the Han, then the government would be confronted with the prospect of ethnic rebellion and demands for independence – which, in the event, is what happened. In the face of this, Sun Yat-sen's nationalist government backtracked and redefined China in terms of one race and five nationalities, namely the Han, Manchu, Mongols, Tibetans and Hui: in other words, China was recognized as a multinational state, though still composed of one race, all sharing the same Chinese origins. Chiang Kai-shek continued with the general lines of this approach, but took a strongly assimilationist line, suppressing the ethnic minorities in the belief that they should be forced to adopt Han customs and practices as speedily as possible.[72]

The 1949 Revolution heralded a major shift in policy. The racist discourse which had been rife since the late nineteenth century was now officially abolished and Han nationalism firmly discouraged. China was described as a unitary multinational state, although the government, after briefly offering ethnic minorities (often referred to as nationalities) the right of self-determination, rapidly withdrew this offer.[73] Instead, they encouraged ethnic minorities to apply for official recognition of their ethnic identity status, with fifty-six eventually being accepted (including the Han). They were extremely diverse in nature: some had a very powerful sense of ethnic identity, combined with separatist aspirations (the Uighur and Tibetans), some had a strong and continuing sense of ethnic identity but no separatist ambitions (for example, the Yi),[74] some had an extremely weak sense of ethnic identity (such as the Miao, Zhuang and the Manchu),[75] while others, hangovers from a distant past before their more or less total assimilation by the Han, barely existed except as a bureaucratic entry (for example, the Bai and the Tujia).[76] This last category, in fact, encapsulates mainstream Chinese history, with the slow but remorseless process of Hanification. Those ethnic minorities with the strongest identity were granted a measure of autonomy with the establishment of five autonomous regions (known as the Inner Mongolian, Xinjiang Uighur, Guangxi Zhuang, Ningxia Hui and Tibet Autonomous Regions), enjoying limited powers of their own, including the right of the minority to appoint the chief minister; it was never intended, however, as a means by which ethnic minorities could exercise some form of autonomous rule.[77]

There are three ethnic groups that, over the last century, have sustained strong separatist movements, namely, the Mongols, Tibetans, and Uighur in Xinjiang province. The Tibetans enjoyed considerable autonomy until the Chinese occupation in 1951, while Xinjiang, which means 'new territory', saw brief independence as East Turkestan, or

Uighurstan, in 1933. Each enjoys the status of an autonomous region, though in practice that autonomy is attenuated. In the Mongolian Autonomous Region there are four times as many Han as Mongols, thereby rendering the latter relatively impotent: indeed, the homelands of China's old conquerors, the Mongols and the Manchu, are both now overwhelmingly Han. In the Tibet Autonomous Region, the Han are still outnumbered by Tibetans, while in Xinjiang, which is China's second largest producer of oil and gas, they now account for at least 40 per cent and perhaps more than half, compared with 6 per cent in a 1950s census.[78] Each of these regions thus has been subject to the classic and oft-repeated process of Han settlement, which has changed, and is continuing slowly but surely to change, their ethnic balance. Not surprisingly, relations between the Han and the Tibetans, and the Han and Uighur, who are mainly Muslims and speak a Turkic language, remain suspicious and distant.[79]

By curbing Han chauvinism, eschewing the claim that the Han represent the core of China and granting the ethnic minorities full legal equality,[80] the Communist government has avoided the worst assimilationist excesses of the Nationalist period. Under Mao, the language of race was replaced by that of class. However, the underlying attitudes of the Han have remained little changed. There is an ingrained prejudice amongst great swathes of the Han Chinese, including the highly educated, towards the ethnic minorities. According to Stevan Harrell, a writer on China's ethnic minorities, there is 'an innate, almost visceral Han sense of superiority'.[81] He quotes the example of a Han official who had worked on a government forestry project in the middle of a Yi area and who, despite living there for twenty years, had never tried Yi food, on the grounds that it was dirty and would make him sick. Far from the ethnic minorities being seen as equals, they are regarded as inferior because they are less modern. There is an underlying belief that they have to be raised up to the level of the Han, whose culture is considered as a model for the minorities to follow and emulate.[82] In other words, the Han believe that they have a civilizing mission in relation to China's ethnic minorities, with Han migrants playing a key role in this process.[83] Minority cultures are recognized at a superficial level, for example in terms of traditional dress and dance, but not treated as the equal of the Han in more substantive matters. In essence, this is not so different from the kind of Confucian ethnically infused cultural hubris that informed the imperial era. Although racialized ways of thought became less explicit after the 1949 Revolution, they never disappeared, remaining an integral, if subterranean, part of the Chinese common sense; and, since the beginning of the reform period, they have been on the rise in both popular culture and official circles.[84]

TIBET AND XINJIANG

Tibet and Xinjiang, which together account for around one-third of China's territory, provide the best insight into Chinese attitudes towards difference, with about half the population of each Tibetan or Uighur respectively, and with both groups being ethnically and racially very different from the Han. The anti-Han riots by Tibetans in Lhasa, and in neighbouring provinces to Tibet, in March 2008 were the worst seen for many decades and a powerful reminder of the simmering tensions that exist between Tibetans and Han. There were over 120 separate protests in the various Tibetan areas, the great majority non-violent.

Tibet was originally brought under loose Chinese influence by the Qing dynasty in the early decades of the eighteenth century, but its rule grew weaker until towards the end of the century the Qing intervened again and established a form of tributary rule. In the nineteenth century Chinese influence slowly waned until the Qing eventually reasserted control in 1910. Tibet enjoyed considerable autonomy in the decades after the 1911 Revolution, when China was in a state of division. Following the Chinese invasion in 1950 a new agreement was reached, but the promised autonomy never materialized and the resulting tension culminated in a major uprising in 1959 which was crushed by China, with the Dalai Lama, together with some 80,000 Tibetans, going into exile. Most countries now recognize Chinese sovereignty over Tibet, including the UK as of October 2008. The Dalai Lama, who accepts Chinese sovereignty, claims a much larger territory

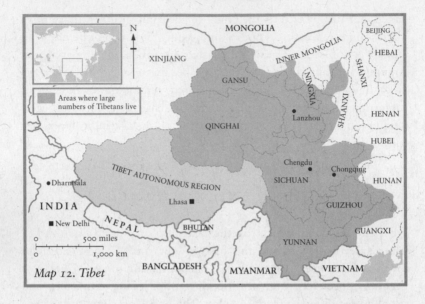

Map 12. *Tibet*

as Tibet than is presently contained within the Tibet Autonomous Region: the TAR is an administrative rather than ethnic region, with around half of Tibetans living in neighbouring provinces, as well as in India and Nepal.

The Chinese strategy towards Tibet has comprised a range of different approaches. It has pursued a policy of repression and forced assimilation, which has included refusing to recognize the Dalai Lama, restricting the role of Buddhist priests, and forbidding Tibetan students and government workers from visiting monasteries or participating in religious ceremonies. The six-year-old boy who was named Panchen Lama, the second holiest figure in Tibetan Buddhism, by the Dalai Lama in 1995 was apprehended by the Chinese authorities and has not been seen or heard of since, the Chinese instead nominating a different boy. In addition, China has encouraged large-scale Han migration to Tibet in an effort to alter the ethnic balance of the population and thereby weaken the position of the Tibetans, who for the most part live in the rural areas and in segregated urban ghettos, unlike the Han, who comprise over half the population of Lhasa and are concentrated in the urban areas. Given the rapid pace of Han migration, encouraged by the new direct rail link between Beijing and Lhasa, it is possible that the proportion of Han in the TAR could rise rapidly in the future. In what appears to have been a typical case of divide and rule, China chose to dismember the Tibetan population by putting heavily Tibetan areas under non-Tibetan jurisdiction in the neighbouring provinces of Sichuan, Qinghai and Gansu. On the other hand, China has made a major effort to generate economic growth and raise living standards in the belief that this would help win the acquiescence of Tibetans, with Tibet being heavily subsidized by Beijing. Since 1950, Tibetan living standards and life expectancy have been transformed, with annual economic growth averaging 12 per cent over the last seven years and incomes rising by more than 10 per cent annually over the last six years. The Tibetans are widely viewed by the Chinese as a backward and primitive people who should be grateful for the fact that the Chinese are seeking to bring them civilization and development.[85] This is eloquently illustrated by the Confucian-like pronouncement of Zhang Qingli, Communist Party secretary of the TAR, that: 'The Communist Party is like the parent to the Tibetan people, and it is always considerate about what the children need ... the central party committee is the real Buddha for Tibetans.'[86]

The riots of 10 March 2008, which took place on the anniversary of the failed uprising in 1959 and were by far the worst since that occasion, show that this strategy has singularly failed. Tibetan rioters attacked Han shops and businesses in the old Tibetan quarter of Lhasa, setting them alight and killing many Han Chinese. The protests continued for five days, with around 100 Tibetan and Han Chinese deaths. The government blamed the riots on a conspiracy led by the Dalai Lama, accusing him, in traditional Chinese racial terms, of being a 'wolf in monk's robes', 'a wolf with a human face and heart of a beast', 'a jackal wrapped in a habit' and the 'scum of Buddhism'.[87] The prime minister Wen Jiabao asserted that the protests were 'organized, premeditated, masterminded and incited by the Dalai clique'.[88] The two biggest Tibetan grievances concern their lack of cultural and religious freedom, and Han migration. They believe that they are systematically being turned into a minority in their own homeland and deeply resent their lack of cultural and religious freedom. The Tibetans see the Han population as having been by far the biggest beneficiaries of the economic prosperity: the Han live in the urban areas where economic change has been concentrated, run most of the businesses and shops, and dominate positions of power and privilege in the administrative apparatus. Relations between the Han and Tibetans are characterized by disdain, distrust and resentment, 'by stereotyping and prejudice and, among Tibetans, by deep feelings of subjugation, repression and fear'.[89] 'Our government has wasted our money in helping those white-eyed wolves,' commented Wang Zhongyong, a Han manager of a Lhasa handicraft shop that was destroyed in the riots. 'The relationship between Han and Tibetan is irreconcilable,' said Yuan Qinghai, a Lhasa taxi driver. 'We don't have a good impression of them, as they are lazy and they hate us, for, as they say, taking away what belongs to them. In their mind showering once or twice in their life is sacred, but to Han it is filthy and unacceptable.'[90]

The rioting, destruction and burning of Han property, and resulting Han deaths, which were shown repeatedly on Chinese television, led to a wave of anger and indignation across China. The consequence was to stoke up further Han resentment against the Tibetans and potentially lay the basis for more draconian measures, although the government, concerned about the effect the riots might have on international opinion in the build-up to the 2008 Beijing Olympics, agreed to reopen talks with representatives of the Dalai Lama. It is inconceivable that Tibet will ever be granted independence – which is not a demand of the Dalai Lama in any case – given China's attitude towards its unity and the strategic importance of Tibet. But it is not difficult to sketch out the terms of a potential settlement: the Dalai Lama would renounce his vast territorial claims to Greater Tibet, which are spurious in any event, and refrain from continuing his Western-orientated anti-Chinese campaign, while the Chinese would allow the Dalai Lama to return to Lhasa as spiritual leader, grant limited self-rule and genuine religious and cultural autonomy, while restricting Han migration. There is a precedent for such an approach: Hu Yaobang, the former secretary of the Communist Party, visited Tibet in 1980 and apologized for the behaviour of the previous thirty years, promising more autonomy and less direct Chinese rule in Tibet, although in the event nothing was to materialize.[91] In practice, the kind of settlement outlined would mark a huge change not just in the policy of the Communist government but more importantly in age-old Han attitudes towards ethnic minorities.

Following incessant military conflicts over a long period, in a drawn-out and brutal war during the 1750s, in which over a million Zunghars were slaughtered, the Qing dynasty conquered much of the territory of the Zunghar Empire, one of the last great nomadic empires. The new acquisition was named Xinjiang (New Frontier) by the Qing and was maintained as a strategic frontier zone under direct military rule with a massive military presence of 15,000–20,000 troops.[92] There were several major rebellions and it was not until 1884 that Xinjiang was finally established as a province by the Qing. In 1933 a revolt led to the establishment of the East Turkestan Republic, which was to prove short-lived. A second East Turkestan Republic came into existence with Soviet support between 1944 and 1949 but this came to an end in 1949 when the PLA entered Xinjiang.

Xinjiang is a huge desert region some 2,000 miles to the west of Beijing, fragmented by large mountain ranges. Although it accounts for one-sixth of China's surface area and is three times the size of Texas, it is sparsely populated, only 4.3 per cent of the territory being inhabitable, with the consequence that less than 2 per cent of China's population live in Xinjiang. Historically it is home to a diverse range of ethnic groups, including the Uighur, Han, Kazakh, Hui, Kyrgyz and Mongol. In 1949, more than 90 per cent of the population was Uighur, a Turkic people of Islamic faith who have more in common in terms of culture, language and religion with the peoples of what we now know as the Central Asian republics than with the Han Chinese to their east. Over the last sixty years there has been a steady migration of Han into Xinjiang which has accelerated rapidly in recent years after the government introduced a drive to open up the western regions, and especially the oil and gas industry, almost a decade ago. The oil and petrochemical sector now accounts for 60 per cent of the Xinjiang economy, Xinjiang being China's second largest oil producer, with abundant reserves of oil and gas. The Han now account for around 8.3

million of Xinjiang's population of 22 million, almost as many as the Uighur, with the Han concentrated in the urban centres, notably the capital, Urumqi, where they comprise most of the population of 2.3 million, and in the oil- and gas-producing regions in the north. As in Tibet, the socio-economic structure of the workforce reflects a very marked ethnic divide, with the Han dominating commercial activities, the bureaucracy, oil and gas, and the Uighur living in the smaller towns and the rural areas. The two communities for the most part live very separately with relations between them distant and tense.

On 5 July 2010, a serious riot broke out in Urumqi when several thousand Uighur marched in protest against the killing of two Uighur in Guangdong province on 25 June by their fellow Han workers. It is unclear how the riot in Urumqi developed but it would appear that the demonstrators were attacked by the police, which further inflamed emotions, and some of the demonstrators then went on to attack Han Chinese, resulting in over 197 deaths and at least 1,700 injured, most of whom were Han. In the following days, the Han invaded the Uighur areas, seeking revenge against the Uighur. It took more than 10,000 troops to restore order but the atmosphere remained extremely tense for several months afterwards. Just over a month after the riots, there was much panic in Urumqi over a string of syringe attacks, the nature of which has never properly been determined.[93] Such was the gravity of the situation following the riots that President Hu Jintao curtailed his visit to a G8 meeting in Rome and immediately returned to Beijing. The government blamed the riots on local separatists and subversive activities by foreign organizations, notably the World Uighur Congress, led by the exiled Rebiya Kandeer. Internet and mobile phone communications were immediately suspended and only began to be restored at the end of 2009.[94]

The underlying causes of the unrest are clearly deep and fundamental; and, as in the case of Tibet, point to the failure of central government policy. The Xinjiang economy has been growing at around 11 per cent per annum for the last six years, which is above the national average. During this period, large numbers of Han have been encouraged to settle in the region, with an inflow of 1.2 million workers in 2008 alone. The disparities between Han and Uighur are striking. Although income and unemployment figures by ethnic group are not available, according to official Xinjiang statistics, the income gap between Han-dominated urban and Uighur-dominated rural areas widened from 2.1 times in 1980 to 3.24 times in 2007. Average incomes in southern Xinjiang, where more than 90 per cent of the population is Uighur, are steadily deteriorating in comparison with the north: the income gap between the wealthiest county in the north and the poorest in the south had increased to 6.28 times by 2005.[95] The Uighur feel that the fruits of Xinjiang's energy and mineral-fuelled growth have been inequitably shared, with the Han enjoying most of the benefits. To add to this, they face widespread discrimination by the Han, who regard them to be inferior. A 15-year-old Uighur, for example, was quoted as saying: 'Everything is organized in an unfair way at school. The teachers always think the Han are better students. They look down on us'[96]

Although the initial government response to the riots blamed separatists, terrorists and foreign forces, as in the case of Tibet, it subsequently unveiled a rather more considered response which sought to provide greater financial support to the region and address the issue of how to offer specific assistance to the Uighur, especially with regard to finding employment.[97] It is clear that generalized support will not deal with the underlying problem, which is systemic discrimination against the Uighur. Indeed, as in the case of Tibet, economic growth has actually exacerbated tensions between the Han and the Uighur, who increasingly feel excluded in their own homeland. The key problems the government has to confront are those of inequality and discrimination, otherwise the situation could deteriorate even further, especially if there is a new wave of Han migration. The events in Tibet in 2008 and Xinjiang in 2010 constitute overwhelming evidence that Beijing's policy towards them has so far singularly failed.

DENIAL AND REALITY

Claims that racism is common in Chinese societies are invariably greeted with a somewhat indignant denial, as if it was a slur against the Chinese.[98] In a very interesting – and rather unusual – exchange between Chinese-Malaysians on a Malaysian website, which was initiated by a writer who attacked Chinese racism, one participant wrote: '[the claim] that racism had been an element in China's 5,000 years civilization is intellectually ignorant and by selling such unfounded statements to the non-Chinese and to Chinese friends who read no classical Chinese, it is dangerous.' Another wrote: 'The Chinese have been persecuted and been victims of racism the world over. We certainly don't need our own kind to accuse us of racism.'[99]

The standard view amongst most Chinese, indeed, is that they are not racist, that racism is essentially what happens to the Chinese in Western societies, and that Chinese societies are more or less unaffected by it.[100] To cite one example of many, in 1988 the then general secretary of the Communist Party, Zhao Ziyang, told a meeting on national unity that racial discrimination is common 'everywhere in the world except in China'.[101]

The pervasiveness of racism applies not only to China but also to Taiwan,[102] Singapore, Hong Kong and even the overseas Chinese communities. Thus it is not simply a function of isolation or insularity, of China's limited contact with the outside world. Take Hong Kong, for example, which, in contrast to China, has enjoyed a highly cosmopolitan history as a result of colonialism. Although in 2001 the then chief executive Tung Chee-hwa typically described racism as a minor problem, requiring no more than an extremely low-budget, low-profile educational campaign, in fact, it is endemic amongst the Hong Kong Chinese, who comprise around 96 per cent of the population.[103] In a survey of South-East Asians, South Asians and Africans in Hong Kong conducted by the Society of Community Organizations in 2001, around one-third said they had been turned down for a job on the basis of their ethnicity, a similar proportion had been refused rental of a flat, one-third reported that the police discriminated against them on the streets, while nearly half had experienced racial discrimination in hospital.[104] The most common targets are foreign 'helpers', usually known as 'maids', mainly Filipinas and Indonesians, who are frequently required by their Chinese domestic employers to work absurdly long hours, are treated abysmally, paid little, granted scant freedom, and, in a significant minority of cases, subjected to physical and sexual abuse. Their conditions not infrequently resemble a latter-day form of indentured labour, as is also true in Singapore and Malaysia.[105]

It might reasonably be argued that Hong Kong Chinese racism is a legacy of British rule. After they took possession of the colony following the First Opium War, the British practised systemic racism: English was the sole official language until 1974, the Chinese were prohibited from living in the exclusive Peak area from 1902, there was a miscellany of petty apartheid laws – such as the requirement, until 1897, that Chinese carry night passes – and they were excluded from high-level public employment until as late as the 1970s and, in some departments, until the mid 1990s.[106] With a truly breathtaking disregard for the truth, in 1994 the British had the gall to claim that 'racial discrimination in Hong Kong is not a problem'.[107] The fact that racism was the currency of British rule only encouraged the Chinese to behave in a similar way towards those whom they regarded to be their inferiors, namely those of darker skin. It would be naive, however, to think that British behaviour was the main cause of Chinese racism: it was clearly a contributory factor, but the fundamental reason lies in Chinese history and culture. After a major campaign in response to the death, in 2000, of Harinder Veriah, a young Malaysian lawyer of Indian descent, who complained about serious racial discrimination in a Hong Kong hospital, the government was finally forced to acknowledge that racism was a serious problem and in 2008, directly as a result of this case, belatedly introduced anti-racist legislation for the first time.[108] But Hong Kong, cosmopolitan and international as it is, remains an essentially biracial city, with whites enjoying a privileged status, along with the Chinese, and those of darker skin generally banished to the margins as second-class residents or migrant workers.[109]

So what of racism in China itself? When a people and government are in denial of their own racism, then evidence of that racism depends on the witness of those who are the object of it and, as a consequence, predominantly on anecdote rather than anything more systematic. Once there is an established culture of anti-racism – as opposed to simply a culture of racism, which is the situation in China, Taiwan and Hong Kong – it becomes possible to paint a more accurate picture of the incidence of racism, though even then the great bulk of it still remains hidden from view. In Chinese societies, and China in particular, there is no culture of anti-racism except at the very margins, because the dominant discourse of Han superiority has never been seriously and openly challenged.[110] Racist attitudes are seen as normal and acceptable rather than abnormal and objectionable. As M. Dujon Johnson, a black American scholar of China, puts it:

> In Chinese society one of the reasons that the issue of race and racism is rarely discussed openly . . . is because racism is universally accepted and justified . . . Racism is . . . an issue that is not addressed among Chinese because most Chinese see themselves as superior to darker-skinned people. Therefore, within the Chinese mindset it would be a waste of time to address an obvious fact of darker-skinned people's inferiority.[111]

In the Chinese perception there is a clear racial hierarchy. White people are respected, placed on something of a pedestal and treated with considerable deference by the Chinese; in contrast, darker skin is disapproved of and deplored, the darker the skin the more pejorative the reaction.[112] Chen Juan, a young secretary at an English language training school in Beijing, to take one of many examples, is quoted as saying: 'In my impression, black people, especially Africans, are not clean enough. To be frank, I just feel black people are too black. Definitely, I wouldn't consider having a black guy as my boyfriend, even if he were rich.'[113] People from other East Asian countries, traditionally regarded as inferior, are not immune. A Filipina friend studying at Beijing University was shocked by the level of discrimination she experienced. Unlike her white colleagues, who were treated with respect, she often found herself ignored in restaurants, with waiters refusing to serve her. Local Chinese would audibly refer to her as 'stupid' or 'ignorant'. One day she was refused entry on to a bus by the conductor in a manner that suggested that she was afflicted with a disease that the other passengers might catch; after such public humiliation she avoided travelling by bus. Dujon Johnson, who conducted a survey of the experience of black Americans and Africans in China and Taiwan based on interviews with them, describes how people frequently moved seats when a black person sat next to them on public transport, or proceeded to rub that part of their body that a black person had innocently brushed against in a crowded place as if it required cleansing. Most depressingly of all, African interviewees indicated that they tried to avoid contact with the Chinese public as much as possible and 'normally venture out only when it is necessary'.[114]

There has been a long history of discrimination against African students in China. Emmanuel Hevi, a Ghanaian who studied there in the early 1960s, wrote: 'In all their dealings with us the Chinese behaved as if they were dealing with people from whom normal intelligence could not be expected.'[115] In December 1988, after an incident between Chinese and African students at Heihai University in Nanjing, there was a march of over 3,000 Chinese students to protest against the presence of African students, with demonstrations subsequently spreading to Shanghai, Beijing and elsewhere.[116] On some of these marches, the climate was so hostile towards African students that a number of universities decided to move them out of their dormitories because of a perceived threat to their physical safety. No attempt was made by the authorities to halt or prevent the demonstrations, which went on for many days, suggesting that they perhaps enjoyed a certain measure of tacit official sympathy.[117] At Wuhan Industrial College, students marched demanding that 'all blacks be removed from China'.[118] According to Dujon Johnson, the race riots and demonstrations in 1988 were by no means unique: similar events occurred in Shanghai in 1979 and 1980, in Nanjing in 1979, 1980, 1988 and 1989, and in Beijing in 1982, 1983, 1984, 1985, 1987, 1988 and 1989.[119] In September 2007 there was a report that a group of at least twenty black men, including students, tourists and the son of a Caribbean diplomat, had been arrested by a team of police in black jumpsuits in a Beijing nightclub and severely beaten. A white American witness reported that: 'He had never seen anything so brutal. There was blood on the streets. They were basically beating up any black person they could find.'[120] It should be borne in mind that a black face remains an extremely rare sight in China. In 2006 there were reported to be 600 Africans in Beijing, 500 in Shanghai, 100 in Shenzhen and over 10,000 in Guangzhou (with a population of 12 million). These numbers have certainly grown since, mainly as a result of the expanding trade with Africa, with estimates for Guangzhou varying between 30,000 and 100,000; not surprisingly, reports of racism there have been rife.[121] No doubt this lack of familiarity with black people may partly explain the Chinese sense of suspicion and mistrust, but it cannot be the main explanation for the deep-seated racism. Dujon Johnson's account of the black experience in China avoids recounting his own experiences except at the very end when he writes, '[my experiences] demonstrated to me on a daily basis how life in Chinese society is racially segregated and in many aspects similar to a system of racial apartheid.'[122]

An incident that gained widespread national and international attention occurred in autumn 2009 just before President Obama's visit to China. Lou Jing, a twenty-year-old student at Shanghai's prestigious Theatre Academy, took part in an *American Idol*-type TV show called *Go! Oriental Angel* and was chosen as one of the final thirty contestants. Jing's mother is Chinese and her father, who she has never met, was African-American. The host, in introducing her, had said, 'her chocolate-coloured skin lights up her sunny character'. In her two months on air she was nicknamed the 'Chocolate Angel' and the 'Black Pearl' in the media. Her participation led to a wave of vitriolic online racist abuse, though there were also supportive postings. Messages criticized her skin colour as 'gross' and 'ugly'. Many refused to accept her as Chinese, preferring to describe her as African. Her mother, a teacher, was attacked for 'her disgraceful behaviour', and described as a 'slutty, thick-skinned, race traitor bitch of a mother'. Jing was shocked by the reaction and decided to try and study abroad. She felt that the lack of knowledge about racism in China meant that many people didn't even realize their comments were discriminatory or hurtful.[123]

In response to the visit of Condoleezza Rice, the then US Secretary of State, to Beijing in 2005, there was a flurry of racist postings on various websites. The Chinese writer Liu Xiaobo was moved to write in protest:

I have browsed China's three biggest portals' BBS articles [blogs] about Rice's six-nation visit . . . Just take Sina as an example. I examined over 800 BBS articles . . . excluding repetitions, there were over 600 articles. Among them, there were nearly 70 articles with racial discrimination, one-tenth of the total . . . There were only two with a gentle tone, the rest were all extremely disgusting. Many stigmatized Rice as 'really ugly' . . . 'the ugliest in the world' . . . 'I really can't understand how mankind gave birth to a woman like Rice' . . . Some directly called Rice a 'black ghost', a 'black pig' . . . 'a witch' . . . 'rubbish of Humans' . . . Some lament: Americans' IQ is low – how can they make a 'black bitch' Secretary of State . . . Some, of course, did not forget to stigmatize Rice with animal [names]: 'chimpanzee', 'bird-like', 'crocodile', 'a piece of rotten meat, mouse shit, [something] dogs will find hard to eat'.[124]

Eventually, the Chinese government felt impelled to shut down these blogs and some of the sites.[125]

The rising tide of popular nationalism in the late 1990s, as evinced by the various *The China That Can Say No* books, the student response to the US bombing of China's Belgrade embassy, and the nationalist outpourings on leading websites, also contained a significant racial dimension.[126] One of the most influential nationalist writers has been Wang Xiaodong, who co authored *China's Path under the Shadow of Globalization*, published in 1999, which became a bestseller. Wang argued that the rise of Chinese nationalism represented a healthy return to normality after the abnormal phenomenon of what he describes as 'reverse racism' in the 1980s[127] – 'the thinking that Chinese culture is inferior and the Chinese people an inferior race'[128] – when, according to him, many Chinese intellectuals looked to the United States for inspiration and denigrated their own culture. Bizarrely, Wang argues that such reverse racism 'is not very different from Hitler's racism', a remark which suggests that his own view of what constitutes racism is highly idiosyncratic and betrays little understanding of Nazism.[129]

Wang argued, in an article published after the embassy bombing in 1999, that conflict between China and the United States was inevitable because it would be racially motivated: in the eyes of the Americans and West Europeans, 'oriental' people are inferior, and he predicted that the 'race issue will become even more sensitive as biological sciences develop'.

> [T]he United States might manufacture genetic weapons that would successfully deal with those radicals who are racially different from Americans and who commit acts of terrorism against the United States. Because it is genetically much easier to differentiate Chinese from Americans than to differentiate Serbians from Americans, genetic weapons targeting the Chinese most likely would be the first to be made.[130]

In a very different vein, Ding Xueliang, a Hong Kong-based Chinese scholar, has argued that racial and cultural differences between the United States and China, together with their different political systems and national capacities, would mean that the United States would see China as its major enemy.[131]

OVERSEAS CHINESE

The overseas Chinese have suffered from widespread racism in their adopted countries, including the United States, Australia and Europe, and are rightly very sensitive about the fact. A notable characteristic of the overseas Chinese is the extent to which they tend to keep to themselves as a community. Notwithstanding the serious racism that they have historically experienced in the United States, they did not join with black Americans in the major civil rights campaigns.[132] The most important and largest Chinese communities are in South-East Asia, where they often constitute sizeable minorities – most notably Malaysia, where they account for over a quarter of the population. Historically the overseas Chinese in South-East Asia have suffered various forms of discrimination and this has been a continuing problem since these countries acquired independence following the Second World War. It is important, however, to see the wider context. The Chinese in this region invariably control a large proportion of the non-state economy, often more than half, and enjoy on average a rather higher standard of living than the indigenous ethnic majority.

It is common for them to look down on the majority race, and even avoid mixing with them more than is necessary, although many in my experience do not share such prejudices. There are, thus, two sides to the coin: the Chinese, as a minority, experience various forms of discrimination, but at the same time regard themselves as superior to the indigenous majority, hold chauvinistic attitudes towards them, and use their economic power to favour their own and discriminate against the ethnic majority.[133] Indonesian-Chinese writer and businessman Richard Oh described the attitude of the Chinese towards Indonesians: 'The Chinese community tends to recoil from society and makes very little effort to integrate. Although frightened, they are very arrogant and haughty. Where do they get this feeling of being a superior race?'[134] He volunteered that he preferred the company of Indonesians for this reason.

Such is their sense of the Chinese being the norm, and every other race being a deviation from that norm, that the overseas Chinese frequently refer to the host population as foreigners. The British author and journalist James Kynge cites a fascinating example of a Chinese community newspaper in Prato in northern Italy, which ran a front-page story about 'three foreign thieves' responsible for various burglaries in the local Chinatown. When Kynge rang the editor he discovered that not only were the 'foreign thieves' actually Italian, but that anyone who was not Chinese was automatically regarded as a foreigner, and that the same convention was used in all Chinese-language papers around the world.[135] Lucian Pye explains such a phenomenon in the following terms: 'The Chinese see such an absolute difference between themselves and others that even when living in lonely isolation in distant countries they unconsciously find it natural and appropriate to refer to those in whose homeland they are living as "foreigners".'[136]

A particularly striking feature of overseas Chinese communities is the extent to which, wherever they are living, they seek to retain their sense of Chineseness. In many South-East Asian countries, Chinese often prefer to send their children to a Chinese rather than a local school, with the Chinese community often sponsoring a large number of such schools. In many Western countries, where their relative numbers are much smaller, the Chinese community organizes Chinese Sunday schools at which their children can become conversant in Mandarin and familiar with Chinese culture. In San Francisco, which has a large Chinese population, there is an extensive 'Roots' project, where Chinese-Americans visit their ancestral villages in China in order to find out about and hopefully meet their distant relatives.[137] One of the participants in 1997, Evan Leong, then a student at the University of California, writes fascinatingly about his experiences and feelings.

> Even though my great-great-great-grandfather came to the United States more than 125 years ago, I have not homogenized to become an 'American'. No matter what people call me, what clothes I wear, what food I eat, what my tastes are, what race my friends are, or what girls I date, I still know that I am Chinese.[138]

He writes:

> The general sentiment among both groups [US-born Chinese and those newly arrived from China] was shared – that China and Chinese people were far superior to any other race.[139]

The newly arrived, moreover, enjoyed greater kudos than those born in the US because they were seen as more authentically Chinese, the opposite to what often happens with migrants from the developing world in the developed world. He also describes his family's attachment to Chinese customs:

> Even though I am so distant and different from my blood relatives in China, my American ancestors have continued to practice many Chinese customs. Our extended families gather together often for holidays and birthdays. We clean and prepare our houses and wear new clothes for Chinese New Year rituals. We pay our respects to my grandfather's grave . . . during Ching Ming and other important dates.[140]

The cohesive ties of Chinese identity have found expression in the notion of Greater China, a cultural and civilizational idea rather than a territorial or political entity.[141] Greater China is seen as embracing all Chinese, with China at the centre, encircled by Hong Kong, Macao,

Taiwan and Singapore, together with the numerous Chinese communities around the world, and has become an increasingly popular concept amongst Chinese over the last quarter century. The strength of these bonds is rooted in a shared inheritance of Chinese civilization, thereby adding a further dimension to the notion of China as a civilization-state. Despite the legacy of political differences, the overseas Chinese, especially those in Hong Kong and Taiwan, have made a formidable contribution to Chinese economic growth through huge investments in the mainland.[142] In contrast, Russian émigrés chose to shun the Soviet Union (and since its demise, one of the big problems of Russian economic growth has been large-scale capital flight), and the Indian diaspora has historically made a much less significant contribution to Indian growth than its Chinese counterpart. Strong centripetal forces operate in Greater China, as within China itself, with the Chinese, wherever they are, feeling a powerful sense of attachment to the homeland.

This found a new form of expression during the torch relay that was staged around the world as part of the build-up to the Beijing Olympics. In London, Paris, Athens and San Francisco, the celebrations were overshadowed by counter-demonstrations in protest at Chinese policy over Tibet. But elsewhere the picture was very different. In Canberra 10,000 demonstrated in favour of the Games, hugely outnumbering the protesters. In Seoul, thousands turned out in support of the Olympics, as they did in Nagano in Japan, in both cases dwarfing the number of protesters; likewise in Kuala Lumpur, Jakarta, Bangkok, Ho Chi Minh City and Hong Kong. Everywhere those demonstrating their support for the Beijing Games were overwhelmingly Chinese, either students from the mainland or people from the local Chinese community.[143]

Not surprisingly, the overseas Chinese feel enormous pride in China's rise. After almost two centuries during which their homeland was synonymous with poverty and failure, China has risen to a position of great global prominence and allure in a remarkably short space of time. Television channels the world over are pouring out programmes about China and in many countries people are signing up in large numbers to learn Mandarin. The gravitational pull exercised by China on its overseas communities has increased markedly as a result. My son's Sunday Mandarin School decided to cancel lessons for the day in order to join the London festivities for the Olympic torch relay. For them China was coming home and being embraced by their adopted city. There was real delight in China's achievement and the global recognition that the Olympics signified.

In taking to the streets in support of the Beijing Olympics in so many cities around the world and in such large numbers, the overseas Chinese proved a powerful political force in their adopted countries, as well as for the Chinese government. This kind of phenomenon, of course, is neither new nor particularly Chinese: diasporas in many countries have long played a significant role in support of their home-land, the most potent post-war example being that provided by the Jewish diaspora for Israel. The Chinese diaspora, however, has several characteristics which together mark it out as somewhat distinct. It is numerically large and spread all around the globe, from Africa to Europe, East Asia to the Americas (see Appendix); for historical and cultural reasons, it enjoys an unusually strong identification with the Middle Kingdom; and China is already a global power, and destined to become the most powerful country in the world. As its rise contin-ues and Chinese worldwide interests grow, the Chinese diaspora is likely to greatly expand, become increasingly prosperous, buoyed by China's own economic success, enjoy enhanced prestige as a result of China's rising status, and feel an even closer affinity with China.

CHINA AND DIFFERENCE

China will, like other great powers, see the world in terms of its own history and values, and seek to shape the world in accordance with them. The world, however, contains great diversity and difference. No country, not even one as large as China, can even vaguely be regarded as a microcosm of it. The attitude of China towards difference – the diverse cultures, histories, ethnicities, races and values embodied by other peoples – is therefore of great consequence. How will the Chi-nese treat people who are different from them? To what extent will a rising China respect them and seek to understand them? Will its own history allow an outlook that enables it to appreciate the very different experiences of others? These are difficult questions to answer, firstly because China has spent virtually all of its history isolated from the rest of the world – excepting its regional neighbours – and secondly because the answers obviously still lie in the future: China's present behaviour can only be regarded as a partial indicator, simply because its power and influence remain limited compared with what they are likely to be. From the foregoing discussion, there are a number of elements that should be considered.

China's own experience of race is unique. Although once comprised of countless races, China is now dominated by what the Chinese regard to be one race, the Han Chinese, with the other races – described as 'nationalities' – accounting for less than 9 per cent of the population (though this is still 105 million people).[144] 'The Chinese may have different origins,' argues Wang Xiaodong, 'but 95 per cent of them believe they are from the same race.'[145] This melding is a function of China's extraordinarily long and continuous history, the slow and long-drawn-out process by which the Han Chinese were created and came to represent and embody the overwhelming bulk of the population. It is part of the legacy of the civilization-state, combining, broadly speaking, two processes, the slow erosion of difference in the eastern part of China where the vast majority of Chinese live to this day, and the emergence over thousands of years of a very powerful sense of cultural identity. Every country is the outcome of a distinctive process of ethnic construction. In China's case it was the process of Hanization. Its strength was that the overwhelming dominance of the Han provided the cement and cohesion which bound this vast country together; without it, China would have fragmented like other empires. Its weakness was that it engendered a weak concept of and respect for difference. The Chinese writer Huang Ping puts it like this: 'The process by which the Chinese [within China] became hegemonic was the process which also resulted in the subordination and dissolving of ethnic difference – the process of the formation of Chineseness.'[146] As a consequence, the Chinese tend to downplay or disregard ethnic difference, holding it to be largely transient in the belief that over time it will converge with and ultimately metamorphosize into a Han identity. There is, as a result, a lack of recognition of other ethnicities, which are seen as subordinate, inferior, and not deserving of equal respect. The idea of overwhelming racial homogeneity, in the context of a huge population, makes the Chinese, in global terms, unique. As Jared Diamond points out, four of the world's other most populous countries – India, the United States, Brazil and Indonesia – are not only relatively recent creations but are also 'ethnic melting pots' comprising many races and languages; in contrast, China is neither recent nor a melting pot.[147] Many Han Chinese, in fact, believe that they are not only of one race, but that they share a common and distinct origin, and that, at least figuratively speaking, they are descended from the Yellow Emperor in northern China. The perception and the ideology are quite different from anywhere else in the world and inevitably pose a question about the ability of the Chinese to understand and respect the very different formation and make-up of other countries. The world's other most populous countries, in particular India, United States, Brazil and Indonesia, recognize their diverse origins and the heterogeneity of their contemporary populations; indeed, in varying degrees, they celebrate their multiracial and multicultural character. In China's case, there is a de facto coincidence of race and nation – except, relatively speaking, at the margins – which is simply not true of the other most populous countries.[148] In practice, though not formally, the Han Chinese think of themselves overwhelmingly as a nation-race.

China's own unique experience inevitably influences its perception of others. 'Because the Han Chinese see themselves as all the same,' argues Huang Ping, 'is also the reason why they see everyone else, for example Indians and Africans, in the same terms.'[149] China, in other words, faces a profound problem in trying to comprehend the nature of ethnic difference in the outside world. As we have seen, the problem is graphically illustrated by the attitude towards the Tibetans and Uighur: the Han have pursued a policy of absorption, assimilation and settlement based on a belief in their own virtue and superiority rather than a respect for and acceptance of ethnic and cultural difference. Huang Ping argues:

China has a lot of learning to do, not least . . . learning who we are, where we came from and how it happened . . . People should not take it for granted that people are Chinese. This has been the result of a historically-constructed process. They take it as a given when it is not. We can do a bit of teaching [to the outside world], but only after we have done a lot of learning.[150]

Given how historically entrenched these attitudes are, however, any serious change is bound to take an extremely long time. In the meantime, China's ethnic mentality will inevitably exercise a powerful influence over its attitude and behaviour towards other peoples: the Chinese will tend to see the world in terms of a complex racial and cultural hierarchy, with the Chinese at the top, followed by whites, and, notwithstanding the anti-imperialist line of the Maoist era, those of darker skin somewhere at or near the bottom.

Another notable feature of the Chinese is their enormous sense of self-confidence, born of their long history and the dazzling success of their civilization for large periods of time, a self-confidence which has withstood and survived quite remarkably the vicissitudes and disasters of the century between the Opium Wars and the 1949 Revolution. These, nonetheless, have left their mark. In a book entitled *The Ugly Chinaman*, which was widely circulated in China in 1986, Bo Yang, a Taiwan-Chinese, described the Chinese as constantly wavering between two extremes – 'a chronic feeling of inferiority and extreme arrogance. In his inferiority, a Chinese person is a slave; in his arrogance, he is a tyrant. In the inferiority mode, everyone else is better than he is . . . Similarly, in the arrogant mode, no other human being on earth is worth the time of day.'[151] This captures the way in which the 'century of humiliation' has affected the Chinese psyche, and the consequent brittleness of emotion. It would be wrong, however, to suggest, as Bo Yang does, that the Chinese have ever felt inferior to everyone: towards whites at times, but never towards those of darker skin. Nonetheless, what remain most striking are not the periods of doubt but, given the problems that have beset the country for most of the modern era, the fact that the Chinese have continued to regard themselves as being at the summit of the global hierarchy of race. True, in moments of vulnerability, the Chinese sometimes acknowledge that they are second to whites, or perhaps equal with them, but this is seen as a relatively temporary situation before normality is again restored. Chen Kuan-Hsing argues:

> This universal chauvinism . . . has provided a psychic mechanism for the Han to confront imperialist intervention and to make life more bearable and more liveable – 'These (white) foreign devils can beat us by material force, but can never conquer our mind' – . . . but at the same time, exactly the same logic of racist discrimination . . . can be utilized to discriminate against anyone living at the periphery of China. A sharp-edged shield can be used for self-defence, but can also be a weapon to kill . . .[152]

Another Taiwanese writer, Lu Liang, is unambiguous about underlying Chinese attitudes: 'Deep down the Chinese believe that they are superior to Westerners and everyone else.'[153] No other people from a developing country possess anything like this sense of supreme self-confidence bordering on arrogance.

It would be wrong to regard this feeling of superiority as purely or perhaps even mainly racial in character. Rather it is a combination of both cultural and racial, and has been such for thousands of years.[154] The steady expansion of the Chinese empire rested on two processes, first of conquest and second of absorption and assimilation. As we have seen, Chinese attitudes fluctuated between regarding other races as incapable of adaptation to Chinese ways, or alternatively believing that they could be assimilated, depending on how self-confident the Chinese felt at the time and the precise balance of power. Expansion, in other words, was a hegemonic project, a desire to absorb other races, to civilize them, to teach them Chinese ways and to integrate them into the Chinese self. Given that the notion of 'Chinese' was constantly being redefined in the process of expansion and absorption – including the case of those dynasties, like the Qing, that were not Chinese – it is clear that the idea of 'race' was not – and could not be – static or frozen: it was steadily, if very slowly, mutating. Thus, while race is a particularistic and exclusionary concept in the present, this did not prevent the process of hegemonic ethnic absorption and assimilation in the long run.

The fact that the Chinese regard themselves as superior to the rest of the human race, and that this belief has a strong racial component, will confront the rest of the world with a serious problem. It is one thing to hold such attitudes when China is relatively poor and power-less, quite another for those attitudes to inform a country when it enjoys huge global power and influence. Of course, there is a clear parallel with European and Western attitudes, which have similarly been based on an abiding sense of superiority rooted in cultural and racial beliefs.[155] There are, though, two obvious differences: first, China's hubris has a much longer history and second, the Chinese represent one-fifth of the world's population, a far larger proportion than, for example, Britain or the United States at their zenith have ever constituted. Precisely how this sense of superiority will inform China's behaviour as a global superpower is a crucial question.

The Chinese believe that China's rightful place is as the world's leading power, and that the last two centuries represent a deviation from the historical norm. Every Chinese leader over the last century has regarded it as his historic task to overcome the national humilia-tion represented by the colonial era and to restore China to its lost grandeur.[156] A nation like Germany may have felt a need to right past wrongs, but these grievances were invariably of relatively recent origin; uniquely, China's have lasted well over a century. The idea of China's restoration is rather succinctly expressed by Yan Xuetong, one of China's leading international relations experts:

> The rise of China is granted by nature. The Chinese are very proud of their early achievements in the human history of civilization. In the last 2,000 years China has enjoyed superpower status several times, such as the Han dynasty, the Tang dynasty and the early Qing dynasty . . . This history of superpower status makes the Chinese people very proud of their country on the one hand, and on the other hand very sad about China's current international status. They believe China's decline is a historical mistake which they should correct.
>
> . . . The Chinese regard their rise as regaining China's lost interna-tional status rather than as obtaining something new.[157]

Or, as Lucian Pye puts it: 'The most pervasive underlying Chinese emo-tion is a profound, unquestioned, generally unshakeable identification with historical greatness. Merely to be Chinese is to be a part of the greatest phenomenon of history.'[158] The rise of China and its restoration as the number one nation in the world is widely regarded as a matter of historical inevitability.

The roots of China's sense of difference, superiority and greatness lie not in its recent past as a nation-state – indeed, its period as a nation-state largely overlaps, at least until very recently, with its historical ignominy and humiliation – but in its much longer history and existence as a civilization-state. There are two key elements to this. First, there is China's belief in its cultural superiority, which dates back at least two millennia. Second, there is the idea of China's racial superiority, which is closely linked to its cultural hubris and which anchors that hubris in nature: that to be born Chinese, rather than as a 'foreigner', 'barbarian' or 'foreign devil', carries a special status and significance. Together they constitute what might be described as the Middle Kingdom mentality. The historically arresting fact is simply how old these beliefs and convictions actually are. The obvious parallel is with Egyptian, Greek and Roman civilizations: but it is unimaginable that modern Egyptians, Greeks or Italians would believe that the efflorescence of their civilizations in ancient times would offer any guide or solace as to their present or future fortunes – yet that is precisely what the Chinese almost universally believe. This is not to suggest that the Chinese identity is fixed: on the contrary, the creation of a Chinese modernity is subjecting 'Chineseness' to a process of restless change, disorientation, reconstruction and turmoil.[159] That these belief-systems date back to antiquity, however, suggests that they not only possess extraordinary historical stamina and resilience but that they are unlikely, in important respects, to change in the near future: rather, China's rise is likely to strengthen them,

The problem with Western commentary on China has been its overwhelming preoccupation with China's polity, in particular the lack of democracy and its Communist government, and, to a lesser extent, its potential military threat. In fact, the challenge posed by the rise of China is far more likely to be cultural in nature, as expressed in the Middle Kingdom mentality. Or, to put it another way, the most difficult question posed by the rise of China is not the absence of democracy but how it will handle difference. A country's attitude towards the rest of the world is determined by its history and culture as much as its interests. The power of each new hegemonic nation or continent is invariably expressed in novel ways: for Europe, the classic form was maritime expansion and colonial empires, for the United States it was airborne superiority and global economic hegemony. Chinese power, similarly, will take new and innovative forms. Certainly the Chinese tradition is very distinct from that of the West. Even though one can identify certain common traits, notably the idea of universalism, a notion of a civilizing mission, and a sense of inherent superiority, in practice they have worked very differently. Although the Chinese steadily augmented their territory as a result of land-based expansion, there has been no equivalent of Western overseas expansion or the European colonization of large tracts of the world: the West sought to remake the world in its own image in a way that Chinese manifestly did not, apart from within their own land mass. Likewise, Confucianism was never a proselytizing religion – or philosophy – in the manner of Christianity or indeed Islam. The most likely motif of Chinese hegemony lies in the area of culture and race. The Chinese sense of cultural self-confidence and superiority, rooted in their long and rich history as a civilization-state, is utterly different from the United States, which has no such legacy to draw on, and contrasts with Europe too, if less strongly. The Chinese have a deeply hierarchical view of the world based on culture and race. As a consequence, the rise of China as a global superpower is likely to lead, over a protracted period of time, to a profound cultural and racial reordering of the world in the Chinese image. As China draws countries and continents into its web, as is happening already with Africa, for example, they will not simply be economic supplicants of a hugely powerful China but also occupy a position of cultural and ethnic inferiority, or subordination, in an increasingly influential Chinese-ordered global hierarchy.

9

China's Own Backyard

In the early 1990s books about China were relatively few and far between. The story was still, for the most part, the Asian tigers, and most Western writers seemed to park themselves in Hong Kong and Singapore and view China and the region through that prism. My first visits to the region followed a similar pattern: both island-states always seemed to be on my itinerary, partly because they provided a ready-made network of contacts and partly because English was widely spoken. Given this cultural baggage, it is not surprising that China was generally seen in derivative terms: it was all a question of when and to what extent China would become infected with the Hong Kong bug. When Hong Kong was finally returned to China in 1997, the British, self-congratulatory almost to a person, were deeply sceptical as to whether the territory would thrive in the way that it had under the British; predictably they believed that China's future hung on the extent to which it became like Hong Kong. In this view, China's prospects depended on learning from everyone else, with the recommended direction of wisdom invariably proceeding from the outside inwards rather than from within outwards. This contained a kernel of truth: the transformation of the region had, indeed, begun outside China. The role and importance of Hong Kong and Singapore in this wider process, however, is a moot point; far more significant were Japan, South Korea and Taiwan, all of which looked far less like, and owed much less to, the West than these micro-states.

In fact, this mindset was deeply patronizing towards China. It suggested that China was an empty vessel that needed filling up with Western ideas and know-how. Certainly China had much to learn from the West, but its subsequent transformation has been more home-grown than Western import. In fact, if China's growth in the 1980s had relied heavily on the resources and knowledge of Hong Kong and Taiwanese entrepreneurs, by the 1990s the direction of influence was in the process of being reversed, with the Middle Kingdom once more becoming the centre of influence, power and wealth. A map of East Asia in the 1980s might reasonably have had the lines of influence and capital running from a miscellany of Hong Kong, Taiwan and the overseas Chinese into China itself. Now it is the opposite. The hubs no longer lie around China's borders but are congregated within them.

While Hong Kong is still recognizably Hong Kong, economically it has been remade by China, the size of its stock exchange now comfortably surpassed by Shanghai's in terms of market capitalization. Who now would choose to go to Hong Kong when you can find the real thing in Beijing or Shanghai? For more than a decade Taiwan has needed China vastly more than China has needed Taiwan, with its economy suffering increasingly from its relative isolation from China. Meanwhile the reversal of the lines of causation between China on one hand and Hong Kong and Taiwan on the other are being repeated on a far grander scale across the region. Everywhere the magnet is China. Where previously the story was outside China, now all roads lead to China. China's growth and dynamism are spilling over its borders, infecting countless other countries far and wide, from Laos and Cambodia[1] to South Korea and Japan, from Indonesia and Malaysia to the Philippines and Australia. East Asia is being reconfigured by China's rise. The agenda of the region is being set in Beijing.

The rise of China is best seen not from the vantage point of the United States or Europe, or for that matter Africa or Latin America, but East Asia. It is in China's own backyard that the reverberations of its rise are already being felt most dramatically and in the most far-reaching ways. If we want to understand China's rise, and what it might mean for the world, then this must be our starting point. The way in which China handles its rise and exercises its growing power in the East Asian region will be a very important indicator of how it is likely to behave as a global power.[2]

It is difficult to achieve the status of a global power without first becoming the dominant power in one's own region. Britain is unusual in this respect: it acquired global hegemony in the nineteenth century even though it didn't succeed in achieving a decisive pre-eminence in Europe. In contrast, the United States, confronted with no serious rivals, achieved overwhelming dominance in the Americas prior to becoming a global superpower in the second half of the twentieth century. China faces a far more formidable task in seeking to become the premier power in East Asia. The region accounts for one-third of the world's population and China has to contend with two rivals in particular, namely Japan and the United States, which stand in the way of its ambitions. Japan still possesses by far the most advanced economy in the region, though no longer the largest (as measured by GDP according to exchange rates), while the United States, by virtue of its military alliances, bases and especially naval presence, remains the most powerful military force in East Asia. Furthermore, China shares borders with Russia to its north and India to its south-west, both of which are powerful players. China's path to regional pre-eminence is and will continue to be a difficult and complicated process.

History, however, offers considerable encouragement for China's ambitions. Until the latter decades of the nineteenth century, China had enjoyed overwhelming regional dominance for much of the previous two millennia: it was to the Middle Kingdom that all others, in varying degrees – depending on their distance from Beijing – paid homage, acknowledging their status as the Celestial Kingdom's inferior. A hierarchical system of relations, which initially began to take shape during the Han dynasty, evolved over time to embrace, in varying degrees, much of East Asia, with China at its centre. According to this system, non-Chinese rulers were required to observe the appropriate forms and ceremonies, including the giving of tribute, in their contact with the Chinese emperor as the symbolic expression of their recognition of the superiority of the Middle Kingdom. Taken together, this pattern of relations constituted what has become known as the tribute system. During the Qing period this included receiving a noble rank in the Qing hierarchy, dating communications by the Qing calendar, presenting tribute memorials on statutory occasions together with a symbolic gift of local products, performing the kow-tow at the Qing court, receiving imperial gifts in return and being granted certain trading privileges and protection.[3] If a ruler recognized the superiority of Chinese civilization and paid tribute to the emperor, then the emperor generally pursued a policy of non-interference, leaving domestic matters to the local ruler. The system, at least in conception, was cultural and moral rather than administrative or economic, though it certainly had a very important trading dimension. The underlying basis of Chinese hegemony rested on the overwhelming strength of its economy together with the superiority of its cultural and political systems. The emperor exercised few coercive powers but maintained control for the most part symbolically. The fact that Chinese hegemony was exercised in such a light and relatively superficial way enabled it to be maintained over a huge and very diverse population for long periods of time. The tributary system embraced the Sinic core – namely Korea, Vietnam, Japan and the the small island kingdom of Liuqiu (the Ryukyu islands, now part of Japan), which were the territories most influenced by Chinese civilization, notably by the ideographic writing system, Confucian teaching and Chinese modes of governance and bureaucracy. It also extended to Central Asia, embracing the Manchu, Mongols, Uighur, Turks, Tibetans and others whose societies, cultures and languages were very different from those of China. In addition, it also included a number of South-East Asian states like Thailand, Myanmar and Malacca, which paid tribute to China or at least acknowledged Chinese suzerainty. Those countries that were closer to China in terms of geography and culture were generally considered to be more equal than those that were not. So, for example, China was considered the big brother, Korea a middle brother and Japan a younger brother.

In light of the extent of the system, the diversity of the countries and cultures embraced, and the vast time-period involved, it would be wrong to conceive of the tributary system in singular rather than plural terms, with big variations taking place from the Han, Tang, Song and Ming to the Qing. Indeed, there could be striking changes even during the course of one dynasty, with the system in the early Ming differing considerably from that in the late Ming, and likewise in the early and late Qing periods. It would also be wrong to equate the tributary system with the entirety of China's approach to international relations. In practice the latter were motivated and shaped by a range of different considerations including security, war and the balance of power, with Chinese rulers generally displaying considerable flexibility and pragmatism.[4] The most consistent overarching theme in China's international relations was the insistence on and belief in Chinese superiority. This went to the heart of the legitimacy of the imperial regime, the belief in the universal pre-eminence of the emperor as the Son of Heaven and the consequent subordinate status of all other territories and rulers, with the payment of tribute serving as the symbol of this. But the way in which in practice this sense of superiority informed and influenced China's international attitudes and actions varied according to circumstances. When China was weak, as during the Song, its rulers were in no position to demand adherence to the tributary system and were forced to treat China's neighbours as its equals.[5] Whether China was strong or weak, however, to quote the historian Wang Gungwu: 'What was exceptional was that the Chinese ruling groups were able to move back and forth between the assertion of myth and the acceptance of reality so frequently and for so long a time without abandoning this superior view of themselves.'[6] The nature of the tributary relationship varied from country to country as well as over time.[7] The classic tributary state was Korea with Japan, for example, enjoying in contrast much greater autonomy from China: indeed, for long periods Japan did not pay tribute to China, which was the case even during the early Ming when the tribute system was arguably at its zenith. No doubt this partly explains why later Japan was able to display such remarkable independence of action in the aftermath of the Meiji Restoration, with its rejection of the Sinocentric world and its turn to the West.[8] It also helps to explain South Korea's closer relationship with China today.

Notwithstanding these variations, the common thread running through the tributary system, as we have seen, was an acceptance of China's cultural superiority. This, together with China's overweening position in the region, was the reason why the acceding states acquiesced in an arrangement which they tended to regard as in their interests as well as the Middle Kingdom's.[9] The relative stability of the tributary system over such a long historical period was partly a function of its flexibility but, above all, because China was overwhelmingly dominant within it: inequality, in other words, served to promote order.[10] From the second half of the nineteenth century, with the growing power of the European nations and later Japan, together with the decline of China, the European-conceived Westphalian system, together with its colonial subsystem, steadily replaced the tributary system as the organizing principle of interstate relations in the region, or, arguably, was superimposed upon the existing system.[11]

Given that it constituted the regional system in East Asia for perhaps as long as 2,500 years, the tributary system remains deeply embedded in the historical memory of the region. Most countries in East Asia had some experience of it, often as recently as a century ago, and certainly not more than a century and a half ago. Even as it began to break down towards the end of the century, elements of the tributary system continued to survive until well into the twentieth century. While it seems inconceivable that any future Chinese hegemony in East Asia could take the form of the old tributary system, it is certainly reasonable to entertain the idea that it could bear at least some of its traces. There is still an overwhelming assumption on the part of the Chinese that their natural position lies at the epicentre of East Asia, that their civilization has no equals in the region, and that their rightful position, as bestowed by history, will at some point be restored in the future. China still frequently refers to its Asian neighbours as 'periphery countries', suggesting that old ways of thinking have not changed as much as one might think.[12] Former habits and attitudes have a strange way of reasserting themselves in new contexts. It would not be entirely surprising, therefore, if elements of the old tribute system were to find renewed expression as China once again emerges as the dominant centre of the East Asian economy.[13] Writing over forty years ago, John K. Fairbank, the author of until now the most important book on the tributary system, certainly in the English language, argued: 'Nationalist and Communist China have inherited a set of institutionalized attitudes and historical precedents not easily conformable to the European tradition of international relations among equally sovereign nation states. Modern China's difficulty of adjustment to the international order of nation-states in the nineteenth and twentieth centuries has come partly from the great tradition of the Chinese world order. This tradition is of more than historical interest and bears upon Chinese political thinking today.'[14] It is important to underline the sheer novelty – in a modern world that hitherto has been dominated by European traditions and concepts of international relations – of the Chinese tributary system. Alas, until now the latter has been overwhelmingly ignored by Western scholars, including international relations experts. Yet as a tradition it stands in stark contrast to that of the West: to lend emphasis to this point, while the colonial system was for several centuries fundamental to Europe's relationship with the world, it was never part of the Chinese world order.

We are thus confronted with a number of intriguing questions. Will China regain its regional pre-eminence? How long is that process likely to take? How might it be achieved? What might that regional pre-eminence look like, what forms will it take, and to what extent might it bear strong echoes of the tributary system?

CHINA'S NEW TURN

At the beginning of the 1990s China, with the reform era already a decade old, still existed for the most part in a state of splendid isolation, a condition that it had inherited from the Maoist era. The suppression of the Tiananmen Square demonstration exacerbated this state of affairs, leading to China's estrangement by the West and its condemnation by Japan.[15] Throughout the 1990s, China steadfastly refused to countenance being a party to any regional multilateral arrangements,[16] fearing that it would be obliged to play second fiddle to Japan, mindful that the United States was strongly opposed to regional organizations from which it might be excluded[17] and, not least, still imbued with that traditional regional aloofness born of its enduring sense of historical superiority. It was only in the early 1990s that China established diplomatic relations with South Korea, Singapore, Indonesia, Vietnam and Brunei.[18] By the end of the decade, however, China had determined on a very different strategy, one that it was to implement with breathtaking speed.

Already in 1994, it had established the Shanghai Five with Russia, Kazakhstan, Kyrgyzstan and Tajikistan, in response to the collapse of the Soviet Union in Central Asia and a desire to engage with Russia and foster cooperation on its traditionally troublesome north-western border. It was not until 2001, however, with the formal establishment of the Shanghai Cooperation Organization (SCO), that this was to be translated into something more thorough-going, with a permanent office in Shanghai, the addition of Uzbekistan and the acquisition of new and more extensive functions.[19] The purpose of the SCO appears to be three-fold: to promote cooperation in Central Asia, to counter Islamic extremism and to resist American influence in the region. Over the subsequent years, India, Iran, Pakistan and Mongolia have acquired observer status, while representatives are also invited from ASEAN and the CIS (composed of the former Soviet Republics). SCO's future is difficult to assess but it certainly represents a powerful bloc of Central Asian countries and, significantly, remains outside the aegis of American influence. The heart of China's new strategy, though, lay not so much to its north-west but to its south-east, namely South-East Asia, a region towards which, in comparison, China had for centuries displayed for the most part benign neglect and traditional indifference. It is no exaggeration to suggest that the fulcrum of China's strategy in East Asia – certainly as it has evolved over the last decade or so – came to hinge on a volte-face in its attitude towards ASEAN, the organization of the ten nations of South-East Asia that was formed in 1967.[20]

How do we explain China's belated embrace of multilateralism? First and foremost, its dramatic economic growth after 1978 generated a growing sense of self-confidence and enabled the country to entertain new and more ambitious perspectives. Second, by the turn of the century China was on the verge of membership of the World Trade Organization, thereby marking its entry into the global international system and signalling its global acceptance of multilateralism. Third, China felt increasingly comfortable about its position in the region and confident that it would not be required to play the role of subordinate to Japan. Finally, as a consequence of the Asian financial crisis in

1997–8, which ravaged the economies of South-East Asia (and South Korea), China found itself thrown into an increasingly close relationship with them. As they struggled to emerge from the effects of the crisis, now rudely aware – after a long period of spectacular economic growth – of their vulnerability to global volatility and bruised by the damaging effects of the US and IMF-imposed solutions to the crisis, the ASEAN countries began to see China in a new light.[21] From being a rival to be feared, its motives always the subject of suspicion, China increasingly came to be seen as a friend and partner, primarily because it refrained from devaluing the renminbi, a move which would have inflicted even further pain on their economies, together with its willingness to extend aid and interest-free loans during the crisis.[22] The Malaysian prime minister Mahathir Mohamad remarked in 1999: 'China's performance in the Asian financial crisis has been laudable, and the countries in this region . . . greatly appreciated China's decision not to devalue the yuan [renminbi]. China's cooperation and high sense of responsibility has spared the region a much worse consequence.'[23]

A decade earlier, a rapprochement between ASEAN and China would have been inconceivable; now it had a certain air of inevitability. But it required, on the part of the Chinese, a leap of imagination, a new kind of mindset, a willingness to abandon old ways of thinking, and a boldness that had previously characterized their domestic economic reform programme, though not their conduct of regional relations.

What was surprising was not simply that China was suddenly prepared to embrace multilateralism in the region but also the manner in which it did so. This, after all, was the country that down the ages, from Tang to Mao, had regarded its neighbours with a sense of superiority and indifference: China did not need its neighbours, but they needed it. Yet China was prepared to engage with ASEAN, an organization composed – broadly speaking – of the weakest nations in East Asia, and to do so on its terms rather than China's. China's approach, in other words, was informed by a new and unfamiliar humility. Historically, North-East Asia, home to old and powerful civilizations like Japan and Korea as well as China, has been overwhelmingly predominant over the much less developed South-East Asia, where a lower level of economic development, ethnic diversity and a weak sense of nationhood have long been manifest.[24] There was now a remarkable inversion, at least in terms of diplomacy, of this traditional state of affairs.

From the ASEAN perspective, the origins of the new rapprochement lay in two initiatives. The first was the decision taken in 1992 to establish AFTA – the ASEAN Free Trade Area – which required the ten member states to remove all barriers to free trade by 2010.[25] The second was a call made by the Malaysian prime minister Mahathir Mohamad in 1990 that East Asia should establish an East Asian Economic Group, later termed the East Asian Economic Caucus, as a means of offsetting the negative effects of the Western-dominated international economic order.[26] The proposal was supported by ASEAN but opposed by Japan, and it was only after the Asian financial crisis that it gained serious momentum. Mahathir's initiative stemmed from his conviction that membership of East Asian bodies should be confined to countries within the region and his antipathy to APEC (Asia–Pacific Economic Cooperation), which included non-Asian members like the US and Australia. In fact Mahathir's position prefigured what was to become an increasingly important fault line within the region – the exclusion or inclusion of the United States – with Japan always favouring inclusion and China, *sotto voce*, tending to favour – though not always – exclusion.

The shift in China's approach took place between 1997 and 2001.[27] At a China–ASEAN summit in 2001 – known as ASEAN+1 (i.e. China) – China proposed the creation of a China–ASEAN free trade area to be established by 2010 (with initial discussions beginning in 1999).[28] The ASEAN–China Free Trade Area, or ACFTA as it became known, was an extraordinarily bold proposal to create a market of almost 2 billion people, thereby making it by far the largest free trade area in the world. As the Chinese had originally proposed, it finally came into operation on 1 January 2010.[29] The ASEAN countries had become increasingly nervous about the effect China's growing economic power might have on their own exports and also their inward foreign investment: the Chinese proposal for a free trade area helped reassure them that China would not pursue economic growth regardless of the consequences for others. At the ASEAN–China summit in 2003, furthermore, China formally acceded to ASEAN's Treaty of Amity and Cooperation – which committed China to the core elements of ASEAN's 1967 Charter – the first non-ASEAN country to do so (India has since followed). In 2002 it also signed the Declaration on the Conduct of Parties in the South China Sea, which rejected the use of force in resolving the disputes over the Spratly and Paracel islands.[30] These had been a serious and continuing source of tension between China on the one hand and Vietnam, Taiwan, the Philippines, Malaysia and Brunei on the other, culminating in military conflict with Vietnam[31] and the Philippines.[32] The agreements between ASEAN and China were to have a major impact on the political dynamics of East Asia. Prior to them Japan, which had long been the major external player in the South-East Asian economies, had resisted entering into regional trade agreements, preferring instead to operate by means of bilateral agreements. Japan now suddenly found itself on the back foot, outmanoeuvred by China's bold diplomacy, and ever since it has been running to catch up.[33]

Already, in 1997, during the Asian financial crisis, there had been the first ASEAN+3 summit (China, Japan and South Korea) and this was later formalized into a regular event. At the ASEAN+3 summit in 2003, the Chinese premier Wen Jiabao proposed that a study be made into the feasibility of an East Asian Free Trade Area and this was agreed.[34] Following China's earlier lead, in 2005 Japan started to negotiate its own Free Trade Agreement with ASEAN, which was concluded in outline form in 2007. In 2009 Australia and New Zealand did likewise. There is now a complex web of Free Trade Agreements in the process of negotiation in East Asia intended to act ultimately as the basic infrastructure of a wider East Asian Free Trade Agreement (EAFTA), which was designed to be in place around 2007 and implemented before 2020.[35] Indeed, there is now an ASEAN+6 (which includes India, Australia and New Zealand). Whether the EAFTA ever materializes, of course, only time will tell, but the progress towards a lowering of tariffs in the region – with China in the driving seat – stands in marked contrast to the effective demise of the WTO Doha round, a point lost on neither ASEAN nor the rest of East Asia.[36]

ASEAN lies at the core of the new East Asian arrangements and has provided them with their template. Although South-East Asia has always been the poor relation in the region (in 1999, for example, the GDP of the North-East Asian economy was more than nine times that of ASEAN),[37] it would have been impossible for North-East Asia to have played the same role because the latter remains too divided, riven by the animosity between Japan and China, and to a lesser extent that between South Korea and Japan, as well as distracted by the disputes over Taiwan and the Korean Peninsula. As a result there is nothing like ASEAN in North-East Asia: such formal multilateral arrangements have been almost completely absent, although belatedly more than a decade ago China, Japan and South Korea started to hold regular meetings at the ASEAN+3 gatherings and in December 2008 decided that in future these should be free-standing tripartite meetings held independently of ASEAN. An important consequence of these various developments has been the effective exclusion of the United States from economic diplomacy in the region. This has never been China's stated aim,[38] but, intended or otherwise, it is what has happened in practice. The centrality that APEC enjoyed in the mid 1990s, and in which the US was a key player,[39] began to seem like a distant memory. In late 2011, however, the United States made a determined attempt to reassert itself into regional economic arrangements by seeking to widen the number of East Asian countries involved in its Trans-Pacific Partnership, which was first launched in 2005. Singapore and Brunei were parties to the original agreement and Malaysia, Japan and presently Vietnam are involved in negotiations to join. The marginalization of the US has also been manifest in the Chiang Mai Initiative, first agreed in 2000 on the proposal of the Chinese,[40] which involves bilateral currency swap arrangements between the ASEAN countries, China, Japan and South Korea, thereby enabling East Asian countries to support a regional currency that finds itself under attack. The scheme, which allows a member to draw on funding to address balance of payment problems and short-term lending difficulties, was increased to $120 billion after the Western financial crisis in 2008. The Chiang Mai agreement was a direct product of the Japanese proposal for an Asian Monetary Fund during the Asian financial crisis,[41] which was strongly opposed at the time by both the United States (on the grounds that it would undermine the IMF) and China (because it came from Japan). China has since swallowed its opposition – no doubt in large part due to the strengthening position of the renminbi – while the United States, weakened by the IMF debacle in the Asian financial crisis, has not resisted.[42]

If ASEAN has provided the canvas, it is the diplomatic drive and initiative of China that has actually redrawn the East Asian landscape. In effect, China has been searching out ways in which it might emerge as the regional leader.[43] Underpinning its growing influence has been the transformation in its economic power. This has been the real engine of change in East Asia, the force that is reconfiguring the region. Unlike the European Union, where economic integration followed politics, in East Asia economics has been the dynamo of change, with political change following in its wake.[44] In North-East Asia, intra-regional trade – even in the absence of formally binding agreements – accounts for in excess of 52 per cent of the total trade of the five economies (China, Japan, Taiwan and the two Koreas), a situation that was achieved in little more than a decade; the equivalent figure for the European Union is roughly 60 per cent, which it took half a century to reach.[45] Between 1991 and 2001, world trade increased by 177 per cent, whereas intra-regional trade in East Asia, despite the Asian financial crisis, increased by a staggering 304 per cent. By far the most important cause of this has been the growth of China, whose share in intra-regional trade almost doubled between 1990 and 2002 and this trend has continued unabated since.[46] With the emergence of the first Asian tigers in the early 1960s, followed by the later examples, including China itself, the East Asian economy used to be seen in terms of 'flying geese', with Japan in the lead and the others flying in formation behind.[47] But with China's rapid economic rise, Japan's role as the most important economy in the region has been eclipsed by China. Between 1980 and 2002, while China's share of East Asian exports increased from 6 per cent to 25 per cent, Japan's fell from 50 per cent to below 30 per cent; similarly, while China's share of East Asian imports over the same period increased from 8 per cent to 21 per cent, Japan's fell from 48 per cent to 27 per cent.[48] Even at the peak of its economic power, Japan's role was always limited by the fact that it steadfastly refused to open up its economy to exports from its neighbours (other than those from its own foreign subsidiaries) – or, indeed, to the rest of the world – so its influence was largely exercised by a combination of its own foreign direct investment in Japanese overseas subsidiaries, imports from those Japanese subsidiaries and Japanese exports to the region. In contrast China's influence, because it has chosen to have an extremely open economy, is far more multifarious – as a market for the products of the region, as an exporter and as a multifaceted investor.

Zhang Yunling, one of the architects of China's new strategy, and Tang Shiping have described the aim as: 'to make China a locomotive for regional growth by serving as a market for regional states and a provider of investment and technology'.[49] The most obvious expression of this has been the way in which, in less than a decade, China has become the most important market for many countries in the region; and it seems likely that it will soon be the single largest market for every country in the region (see Figures 40–42). For the ASEAN countries, the Chinese market is now three times the size of Japan's.[50] No country – not even Japan, with China becoming its largest export market in 2009, overtaking the United States – can afford to ignore

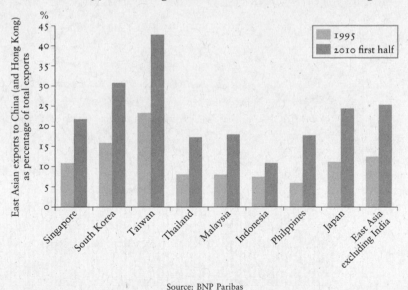

Source: BNP Paribas

Figure 40. Rapidly growing importance of Chinese market for East Asian countries.

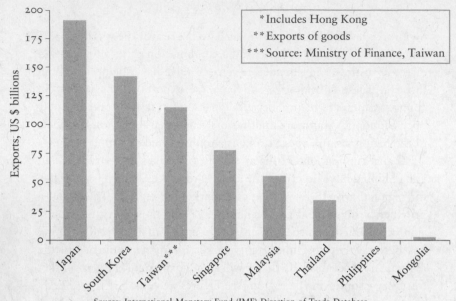

Source: International Monetary Fund (IMF) Direction of Trade Database

Figure 41. East Asian countries for which China* is their largest export** market, 2010.

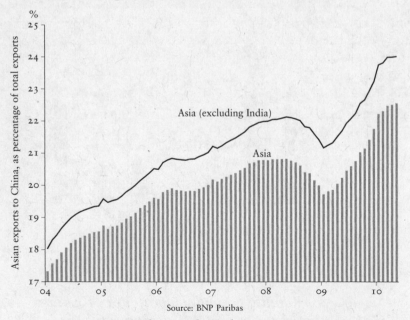

Source: BNP Paribas

Figure 42. China takes almost one-quarter of Asian exports.

the Chinese market, or China.[51] In 2010 China (including Hong Kong) accounted for over 23 per cent of Japanese exports. Since 2000, China's imports from ASEAN have increased at an annual rate of 30–40 per cent:[52] it accounted for over 17 per cent of Malaysia's exports in 2009, compared with 2 per cent in 1990; 31 per cent of South Korea's exports in 2010, compared with virtually zero in 1990; and 21.8 per cent of Australia's exports in 2010, compared with 3.7 per cent in 1992.[53] It was widely feared in South-East Asia that Chinese imports from the ASEAN countries would be overwhelmingly comprised of raw materials. Certainly these are very significant, a case in point being the huge Chinese demand for timber, which is rapidly stripping the Indonesian forests.[54] Indeed, there is considerable concern in Indonesia that, although the country has hugely benefited from Chinese demand for its natural resources, it will be unable to diversify its economy beyond resource-extraction to value-added industries.[55] In fact, however, the most important single category of ASEAN exports to China is composed of intermediate goods: components account for around half of China's imports from East Asia, though this figure also includes North-East Asia. China is where the final assembly of many products of foreign-owned multinationals (American, European, Japanese, Taiwanese and South Korean) takes place prior to their export to their final destination. Countries like Malaysia and Thailand thus occupy a crucial niche in a complex division of labour centred on China.[56] In addition, China is assuming the role of an increasingly important investor in the region, with a large quantity of investment aimed at the extractive industries and infrastructure like railways, toll roads and refineries, in order to speed the flow of natural resources to the Chinese market. In 2006, 60 per cent of China's total foreign direct investment was directed towards Asia,[57] making it by far the most important destination. As a consequence, Chinese investment in South-East Asia has helped to compensate for the decline in Western investment over the last few years.

Zhang Yunling and Tang Shiping have described China's regional strategy in the following terms: 'participate actively, demonstrate restraint, offer re-assurance, open markets, foster interdependence, create common interests, and reduce conflict'.[58] With one bold and unexpected stroke, China has succeeded, in the manner of Deng Xiaoping, in redefining the dynamics of the region, enhancing regional economic growth, as well as its own, and making itself increasingly pivotal to the economic future of the region. For sheer courage and unpredictability, China's East Asian initiative belongs to the genre of Chinese diplomacy initiated by Mao in the rapprochement with the United States that began in 1971. Even the intractable problems of North-East Asia are to some extent being redrawn by the ASEAN-based Chinese initiative, with both Japan and South Korea now involved in the creation of the East Asian Free Trade Area first proposed by the Chinese premier Wen Jiabao at the 2003 ASEAN+3 summit. It is impossible to predict the outcome of the process – or, more accurately, processes – now under way. They are open-ended and multi-layered, and could yet acquire another dimension, with the involvement of India and perhaps other South Asian countries in the future.[59] It has been suggested that one day there might be a fully-fledged East Asia Economic Union, perhaps even with a common currency, though the latter seems rather unlikely given the huge economic disparities across the region.[60] What is certain is that the renminbi will play a growing role in the region as China progressively eases the restrictions on its use and allows it to become an international currency. It is already being used in a limited way in the settlement of trade and this will grow very rapidly over the next five years, especially given the importance of China in regional trade and the continuing decline of the dollar. Rather than a new regional currency, over the next decade the renminbi will come to perform this role. Likewise, China's role in regional trade will in due course encourage a growing number of countries to in effect peg their currencies to the renminbi. Finally, albeit in the somewhat longer term, the renminbi is likely to increasingly assume the role of a reserve currency in the region; indeed, the Bank of Negara, Malaysia's central bank, is already holding the renminbi as part of its reserves.[61] It is worth noting that in the zones around China's borders – Myanmar, Mongolia, Laos, Cambodia and Vietnam – the renminbi, though not yet convertible, is already traded freely and used as a de facto reserve currency, sometimes instead of the US dollar.[62]

Not surprisingly, China's rapidly developing economic influence in the region is having wider political and cultural repercussions.[63] Everywhere, in varying degrees, the impact of China can be felt. The willingness of China to foster interdependence, to seek new arrangements, and to take into account the needs and interests of other nations has had an extremely favourable effect on how it is seen in most countries.[64] David Shambaugh, a leading US writer on China, has argued: 'Bilaterally and multilaterally, Beijing's diplomacy has been remarkably adept and nuanced, earning praise around the region. As a result, most nations in the region now see China as a good neighbour, a constructive partner, a careful listener, and a non-threatening regional power.'[65] This process was enhanced by the stark contrast over the period between 2000 and 2008 – prior to Barack Obama's election as president – between China's whole-hearted embrace of multilateralism and the United States' preoccupation with the Middle East, combined with its shift towards unilateralism during the Bush administration. China's overseas aid rose from around $260 million in 1993 to more than $1.5 billion in 2004 at a time when the US was reducing its own; as a result, China's aid to the Philippines is now four times that of the US, double what the US gives to Indonesia, and far outstrips American aid to Laos, Cambodia and Myanmar.[66] China has funded many high-profile projects, including a new presidential palace and foreign ministry building in East Timor and a parliament building in Cambodia.[67] It finances the training of Cambodian and Laotian officials in China as well as receiving a growing number of politicians and dignitaries from the region in China on visitor programmes.[68] It has opened its doors to foreign students, with over 150,000 from East Asia studying in Chinese universities in 2009. There is a growing thirst across the region to learn Mandarin – it is now a compulsory school subject in a number of countries including South Korea and Thailand – while Chinese tourists are becoming an increasingly common sight in South-East Asia, greatly outnumbering those from Japan.

As we shall see, however, China's rise is a complicated process which provokes varying reactions from countries in the region. While China made enormous progress in terms of its regional standing and acceptance between 2000 and 2009, there were growing signs of disquiet from some of its neighbours in 2010 and 2011.

SHIFTING SANDS

One of the consequences of China's growing economic importance has been that the great majority of countries in the region have tended to become more closely aligned with it. There is only one clear exception to this and that is Japan. The most dramatic and recent example of this shift has been the growing rapprochement between China and Taiwan: given the bitter enmity that has long characterized their relationship, and its historic roots, nothing more graphically serves to illustrate the change that has been taking place in the region. Even Singapore and the Philippines, two traditionally close allies of the United States, have moved much closer to China over the last decade. Rather than countries fearing the rise of China and, as a result, choosing to move closer to the United States, in general the opposite has tended to be the case, certainly prior to 2010. A senior Singaporean diplomat confidentially offered the view in 2004 that:

> The balance of influence is shifting against the United States. In the last decade the Chinese have not done anything wrong in South-East Asia. The Japanese have not done anything right, and the US has been indifferent. So already Thailand, Laos, Cambodia, and other states are defining their national interest as 'Finlandization' with respect to China. The US will never be shut out of South-East Asia completely, but there is less room for it now than in the past fifty years.[69]

As the accompanying figures suggest (Figures 43–6), attitudes in the region have grown more favourable towards China, compared with those towards the US, while China is generally seen as emerging as the new power centre in the region and as likely to become the most important economic partner of most countries. To illustrate the

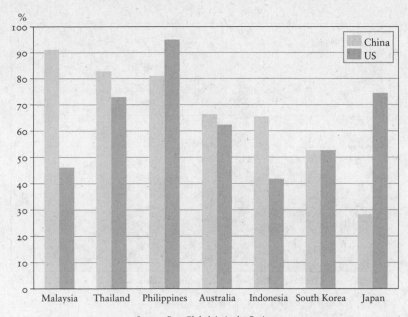

Source: Pew Global Attitudes Project

Figure 43. East Asian attitudes towards China and the United States (% 'favourable'), November 2005.

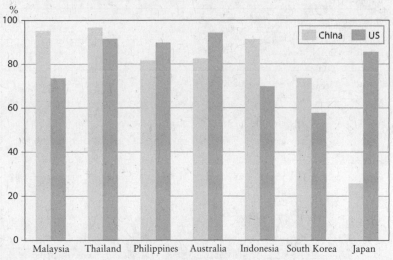

Source: Pew Global Attitudes Project

Figure 44. East Asian perceptions of bilateral relationship with China and the United States (% 'good'), November 2005.

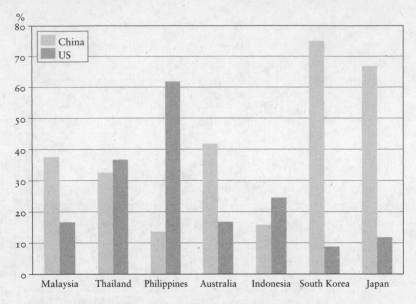

Source: Pew Global Attitudes Project

Figure 45. East Asian perceptions of Asia's future power centre (%), November 2005.

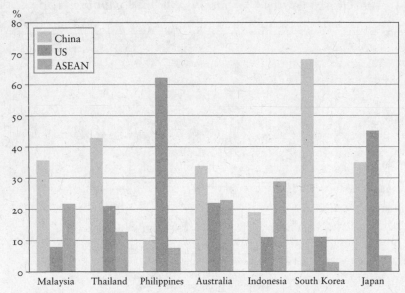

Source: Pew Global Attitudes Project

Figure 46. East Asian perceptions of their closest economic partner in 5–10 years (%), November 2005.

reconfiguration of power in East Asia towards China, I will look at three very different examples, namely Myanmar, Malaysia and South Korea; and then at the remarkable way in which Australia is being drawn into China's orbit, though strictly, of course, it belongs to the Asia–Pacific region rather than East Asia.

As a former tributary state of the Middle Kingdom, Myanmar has long enjoyed a close relationship with China, but since the late 1980s this has become more marked. The growing isolation of Myanmar – especially from and by the West – has served to increase its dependence on China for both trade and security, with the latter now by far its biggest trading partner as well as its largest source of inward investment, much to the chagrin of India, which views Myanmar as part of its own sphere of influence. A gas pipeline is presently under construction to supply China with natural gas from Myanmar, while an oil pipeline will take oil from the Middle East via Myanmar to China, thereby avoiding the Malacca Straits. The country's Chinese minority, which has grown considerably in recent years – some estimates suggest that one-third of the population of Mandalay is now Chinese – has played a very important role in this growing economic alignment with China. There is also close military collaboration between the two countries, the only such instance of this in the region (with the partial exception of North Korea). With their long shared border, Myanmar is an important ally for China because it gives its landlocked south-west provinces vital access to the Indian Ocean for their exports while also providing facilities for the Chinese navy to operate in the Indian Ocean. For a combination of historical and economic reasons – and because otherwise Myanmar would find itself even more isolated – China's relationship with Myanmar is, in fact, more intimate than that with any other country in the region.[70] Although the Myanmar government suspended work on a Chinese-backed dam in the north of the country in 2011, this is unlikely to affect what is a deep economic relationship between the two countries; nor is any possible rapprochement between Myanmar and the United States.

For geographical reasons, the archipelagic countries of South-East Asia have traditionally enjoyed a more distant relationship with

China than those like Myanmar and Vietnam that share the same land mass.[71] Furthermore, the ethnic, cultural and religious differences between China and countries like Malaysia and Indonesia are much more pronounced. Malaysia, following its independence in 1957, viewed China with considerable suspicion because of its own large Chinese minority and the fact that the Maoist regime encouraged a guerrilla war, mainly based amongst the local Chinese, against the British and, after independence, against the newly installed Malay-dominated government. With China's rapid economic growth during the reform period, together with its turn away from promoting revolutionary change elsewhere, relations steadily improved. Although the two countries have been in dispute over the Spratly Islands, the then Malaysian premier Mahathir Mohamad chose to pursue a policy of engagement with China, aware that his country could not win any naval clash.[72] He also played a critical role for more than a decade in encouraging China to become more involved in the region and with ASEAN in particular. This approach has continued subsequently, including under the new premier Najib Abdul Razak. Following his election, his first foreign trip in June 2009, after an initial visit to immediate neighbour Singapore, was significantly to Beijing, where he declared: 'Because China is a country that has moved forward so fast, I need to bring the relationship to an even greater height.'[73]

In the longer run, any deepening relationship with China is likely to have an effect on the delicate racial balance in Malaysia between the Malay majority and the Chinese minority, who presently account for more than a quarter of the population. Not surprisingly, it is the Chinese minority who are primarily involved in trade with China, who fill the planes that fly between the two countries, and who benefit the most economically from the bilateral relationship.[74] As a result, Malaysia, while seeking a closer relationship with China – which also obviously appeals to its Chinese minority – is bound to remain at the same time somewhat ambivalent about it. (The problem of an economically powerful indigenous Chinese minority is by no means confined to Malaysia: a Chinese minority, though relatively smaller than that in Malaysia, also plays the dominant role in the private sectors of Thailand, Indonesia, Myanmar, Laos, Cambodia, Vietnam and the Philippines.[75]) Notwithstanding this, the relationship between Malaysia and China has grown markedly closer over the last decade.

The most dramatic example of the way in which China's rise has transformed relations in the region has been South Korea.[76] After the Second World War it became an intimate ally of the United States, a relationship which was cemented in the Korean War, with no small part of its subsequent economic success being due to its position as an American vassal state during the Cold War. Yet over the last decade or so, until very recently, it has moved closer to China both at a governmental and a popular level.[77] China is now easily the country's largest trading partner and South Korean firms have invested heavily in the mainland, with China the largest destination for Korean foreign investment.[78] In fact, more than 30,000 South Korean firms now have operations in China. Over half the students from East Asia studying for advanced degrees in China come from South Korea, while over 60,000 Chinese students are studying in South Korea.[79] More than 2.4 million South Koreans visited China in 2009, compared with one million in 2003, while 1.5 million Chinese visited South Korea in 2010, more than double the figure in 2005. Each week, there are over 840 flights between the two countries.[80] The long-running crisis over North Korea and its nuclear weapons served to bring China and South Korea closer together during the presidencies of Kim Dae-jung and Roh Moo-hyun, as South Korea found that it had more in common with the cautious Chinese position of restraint than the more aggressive American approach under Bush. Indeed, China's handling of the crisis and its emergence as the key mediator with North Korea enhanced its standing both with South Korea and in the region more widely.[81] The fact that the United States in the meantime strengthened its defence ties with Japan further alienated South Korea, which views Japan with considerable enmity as a result of the latter's conduct during its colonial occupation of the country.[82]

South Korea's attitude towards North Korea and China on the one hand and the United States on the other, however, is volatile. After the liberal administrations of Kim Dae-jung and Roh Moo-hyun, both of which emphasized reconciliation with North Korea and sought closer relations with China, the election of conservative president Lee Myung-bak in 2008 marked a shift towards a tougher stance on North Korea and the reassertion of a much closer relationship with the United States. In early 2010 the South Korean government accused North Korea of sinking one of its naval corvettes with the loss of 46 sailors. A subsequent international investigation also blamed North Korea. For their part, the North Koreans denied any responsibility, while the Chinese declined to express an opinion. The incident drew South Korea and the United States closer together, the two staging joint naval exercises in the Yellow Sea in the aftermath of the incident, notwithstanding fierce Chinese objections. In November 2010, North Korea's artillery fired at South Korea's Yeonpyeong Island in the Yellow Sea, which is claimed by the North, with the South Koreans returning fire; two South Korean marines and two civilians were killed. Subsequently, the South Koreans staged live-fire artillery drills on the island. These incidents were amongst the most serious since the end of the Korean War. There was much speculation about the muted and defensive Chinese reaction. Clearly, in the long run, China's relationship with South Korea is far more important to it than that with North Korea: China's trade with the South, for example, is 70 times greater than that with the North. On the other hand, the Chinese would probably prefer to see the Korean Peninsula remain divided for the foreseeable future because it does not want to share a border with South Korea given its military alliance with the United States and the continuing presence of the latter's troops. The Chinese, as a consequence, are anxious to maintain a reasonably close relationship with North Korea while also seeking to ensure that the country does not implode, which would have highly unpredictable and destabilizing consequences, including a huge influx of refugees into China. They also clearly feel, given the long-standing nature of their bilateral relationship, a certain loyalty to the regime, however capricious and reckless it may be. There is no question, however, that China's relationship with Pyongyang constantly puts Beijing in a difficult and defensive position both regionally and globally: once again, these events served to strengthen the bonds between the US, South Korea and Japan, while also alienating South Korean public opinion.[83] On a rather different note, it is also important to bear in mind that a significant historical source of tension between China and South Korea concerns the precise ancestry of the ancient kingdom of Koguryo, which occupied territory in North Korea, South Korea and also over the Chinese border, and is claimed by both Korea and China as part of their history.

Notwithstanding the recent deterioration in relations between China and South Korea – a state of affairs that could be reversed depending on the result of the presidential election in 2012 – it seems likely that in the longer run South Korea will continue to move closer to China and further away from the United States. The key drivers in this process are their deep historic ties, their geographical proximity, China's growing economic might, their increasing economic interdependence, combined with the steady weakening of the US's presence and influence in the region, which will be hastened by the latter's economic decline. This could lead ultimately to the end of the US–Korean alliance, but that is very unlikely to happen within less than a decade, probably rather longer.[84] In the meantime, it is possible that the United States will eventually withdraw its troops, presently numbering 28,000, from the Korean Peninsula if and when a solution is found to the present crisis.[85] Of course, a key factor in all this is what will happen to North Korea: will it engage in a Chinese-style reform, implode, or will the present impasse continue for the foreseeable future? At some point we might eventually see the reunification of Korea, although this still seems a rather distant prospect. The rapprochement between China and South Korea is a powerful echo of earlier times when Korea was the tributary state closest to China, a situation that lasted for many centuries until China's defeat in the Sino-Japanese War.[86]

One of the most interesting and intriguing relationships concerns that between China and Australia. Australia belongs more properly to Asia–Pacific, which embraces East Asia together with those countries in or that border on the Pacific. One of the great geo-cultural anomalies is that a country that lies just to the south of Indonesia has an overwhelmingly white majority and has long been considered a Western country. Though historically part of the British Empire, ever since 1942 it has enjoyed an extremely close relationship with the United States, for most of that period being its closest and most loyal ally in the Asia–Pacific region. Over the last decade, however, China's growing economic power has exercised a mesmerizing effect on the island continent. By far the most important reason for this is China's voracious appetite for Australia's huge deposits of raw materials, especially iron ore and coal, but also alumina, diamonds, lead, zinc, gold, copper and nickel. China has now overtaken Japan as Australia's largest export market, accounting, as mentioned earlier, for 21.8 per cent of Australia's exports in 2010, compared with only 3.7 per cent in 1992: in contrast, the US's share was only 5 per cent in 2009. More generally, Australia's exports to Asia as a whole now account for 72 per cent of its total exports, with China easily taking the largest share, compared with a mere 40 per cent a decade ago.[87] Largely as a result of Chinese demand, the Australian economy has enjoyed uninterrupted growth for almost two decades, even, unlike the Western world, during the aftermath of the financial crisis. All this indicates that Australia is in the process of decoupling its fortunes from the Western economy, especially the United States. Australia is one of the relatively few countries in the world that has experienced a double benefit from China's rise, namely the falling price of manufactured goods and, most importantly in its case, the rising price of commodities. Increasingly, Australian financial markets follow signals from China rather than the US, while the correlation between the value of equities in Shanghai and Sydney has strengthened every year since 2004.[88] China's interest in Australia's vast natural deposits, furthermore, is not confined to that of a customer; its role as an investor has become increasingly important since 2007, with the purchase of stakes in Australian mining firms, including, most dramatically so far, the unsuccessful proposal by the Chinese state-owned aluminium producer Chinalco to buy a large chunk of the debt-laden Anglo-Australian mining group Rio Tinto. Meanwhile, Australia's leading service sectors, led by higher education and tourism, are increasingly dependent on the Chinese. In 2010, Australian schools enrolled an estimated 130,000 Chinese students, more than from any other foreign country. In short, Australia is being drawn remorselessly into China's sphere of economic influence, as indeed, unsurprisingly, is New Zealand.

China's growing role in Australia's prosperity has manifold and far-reaching implications. If twentieth-century Australia was dominated by New South Wales and Victoria, and the rivalry between Sydney and Melbourne, this century will be characterized by the rise of the mining states, Western Australia and Queensland, as a result of China's growing demand for their commodities. Not surprisingly, the political relationship with China has become a highly charged and contentious issue. Australia is a country that prides itself on its Anglo-Saxon identity – notwithstanding its geographical location – and its Western orientation, a significant expression of which has been its long tradition of hostility to non-white immigration. The growing importance of the Chinese connection has become increasingly controversial as manifest in the rejection of Chinalco's bid for Rio Tinto, the Australian government's decision to block a bid by China's Minmetals for Oz Minerals, and the domestic repercussions of the arrest in China of four Rio Tinto employees and their imprisonment on charges of bribery and stealing trade secrets from Chinese steel makers.[89] There has been a powerful backlash against China's desire to purchase stakes and companies in the resources sector, fuelled by the fact that China is seen as alien and non-Western but also because the Chinese companies involved are state-owned.[90] Hitherto probably the clearest political expression of China's growing importance was the election of Labour prime minister Kevin Rudd in 2007, although he was subsequently unseated in an internal party coup in 2010 and is now the country's foreign minister. A fluent Mandarin-speaker, well versed in Chinese culture and tradition, and possessed of excellent contacts in Beijing (having worked there for many years), he can be described as the first Chinese-orientated political leader to be elected in the West. Historically, the Labour Party has been much more sympathetic to the idea that Australia should orientate itself towards Asia than the Liberal Party; Rudd's predecessor as Labour prime minister, Paul Keating, was the first Australian premier to advocate a turn towards Asia; in contrast, his successor, the long-serving Liberal prime minister John Howard, could hardly have been more pro-American.

Given Australia's extraordinarily close relationship with the United States, it is difficult to predict the course of Australian politics. In introducing a new White Paper, 'Australia in the Asian Century' in 2011, the prime minister Julia Gillard clearly acknowledged the new Asian context in which Australia must prosper; however, shortly afterwards she announced that US troops would in future be stationed at a military base in northern Australia.[91] It is highly premature, therefore, to speculate that Australia will at some point distance itself from the United States and in effect bandwagon with China in the manner, for example, of South Korea or Thailand. More realistically, Australia might become increasingly sensitive about its relations with China and make these sensitivities known to the Americans. In that way Australia might become the Western voice of China. In the very much longer term, it is conceivable that Australia might move more decisively into China's orbit and become increasingly distant from the United States as the latter's power and utility wane.

The rapid rise of China, together with the decline of American power in East Asia, accentuated by the Bush administration's overwhelming preoccupation with the Middle East, means that there is a quite new fluidity and uncertainty in the region. The last decade has been dominated by China's rise and the astute diplomacy that accompanied it. From late 2009 onwards, however, the mood perceptibly changed. The reassurance that China's new strategy offered was joined by increasing anxiety about exactly how China might exercise its growing power. The critical issue in this context concerned the Spratly and Paracel Islands in the South China Sea. China began to be a little more assertive with regard to its claim of sovereignty over the islands. It continued to insist that any negotiations should be conducted on a bilateral rather than multilateral basis and an American official claimed that a Chinese official had described the islands as a 'core interest' – the term used in relation to Taiwan and the other 'lost territories', as well as Xinjiang and Tibet – though this description has never been used officially by the Chinese government. The

Chinese have also significantly increased their naval presence in the South China Sea, with a growing number of nuclear submarines operating from a new underground naval base in Hainan Island off the south coast of China.[92] These developments made some ASEAN members, especially those with a claim over the islands, more sensitive about Chinese intentions. The US Secretary of State, Hillary Clinton, was invited to attend an ASEAN regional security forum in July 2010, at which, to China's annoyance, she declared, somewhat provocatively in the circumstances, that the US would be prepared to act as mediator in the dispute over the islands. As chair of ASEAN during this period as well as a claimant to both the Paracels and the Spratlys, Vietnam played a key role in this process. Tensions between China and Vietnam have run high over the Paracels, exacerbated by the fact that the two countries have a very long history of animosity. During these months, China had captured various Vietnamese fishing boats in the vicinity of the Paracels and detained their crews.[93]

The invitation to Hillary Clinton, which was followed up by others, suggested that at least some ASEAN countries were prepared to entertain the idea that the United States could play a balancing role in the region in relation to China. Lee Kuan Yew, Singapore's elder statesman, has argued that: 'The size of China makes it impossible for the rest of Asia, including Japan and India, to match it in weight and capacity in about 20 or 30 years. So we need America to strike a balance.' The Vietnamese have been the most hawkish of ASEAN members towards China. In contrast, Alberto Romulo, the foreign secretary of the Philippines, an old American ally, flatly rejected Clinton's offer and made clear that the dispute was a matter for China and ASEAN alone. Juwono Sudarsono, a former defence minister of Indonesia, which has traditionally leaned towards the Americans, said: 'We can navigate between that rivalry, from time to time giving out signals that both the United States and China are important to us, because if we align ourselves too closely, it would be detrimental to the core values of Indonesia's foreign policy.'[94] The Lee Kuan Yew remark takes us to the nub of the concern within ASEAN: while there has been some criticism of China's present behaviour, there is much more anxiety as to how China might behave in future decades when it is far more powerful.[95] The islands are clearly regarded by the ASEAN countries as something of a litmus paper test as far as China is concerned. In this light, it is a little surprising that the Chinese allowed the situation to escalate in this manner. They have earned great respect for their conduct and approach over the last decade, but this could be squandered in a fraction of that time if the Chinese misplay their hand and arouse suspicions amongst their South-East Asian neighbours. Time is on China's side, so there is no need for them to act in an impatient or inflexible manner. In this context, it is a little puzzling that China has not yet acceded to the ASEAN request that the Code of Conduct regarding the peaceful settlement of disputes in the South China Sea be made legally binding.

More or less coinciding with this friction over the South China Sea, China found its relations with South Korea and Japan also deteriorating, the former as a result of the sinking of the naval corvette and the latter over the detention of a Chinese trawler by the Japanese. Neither of these, however, should be seen in the same light as the South China Sea dispute. The sinking of the corvette had nothing to do with China, which found itself in a no-win situation, while the capture of the Chinese trawler had more to do with hawkish, anti-Chinese elements within the Japanese government, in particular the then foreign minister, than any Chinese action. Nonetheless, the combined effect of the South China Sea dispute, together with the conflicts with South Korea and Japan, served to put China on the defensive in the region. It is also clear that the United States has consciously sought to rebuild its presence in the region, as shown by its skilful diplomacy with ASEAN, in particular Vietnam, and its use of the sinking of the corvette to draw closer to South Korea. An eloquent example of US intentions was the choice of countries in President Obama's tour of East Asia in late 2010, namely India, South Korea, Japan and Indonesia: the sub-text was manifestly China's rise and how it might be contained by what is termed 'strategic hedging'. These developments were taken a stage further in November 2011 when the Obama administration made a big push with the Trans-Pacific Partnership at the APEC summit, announced that US troops would be stationed in northern Australia, and then participated in the East Asian Summit, which it had previously ignored and now attended for the first time. (The East Asian Summit now consists of ASEAN+6, together with the US and Russia.) It is clear that the US is following China's lead and seeking to participate in ASEAN-led institutions as part of a wider offensive to counter China's growing influence and assert its own.

It would be wrong to draw too dramatic a conclusion from these recent events. The fact remains that US power in the region has been steadily receding and that of China remorselessly rising: there will be no return to the status quo ante when the US dominated the region. Indeed, post-financial crisis, the United States is significantly weaker and China considerably stronger. It is interesting to note that just before Obama's visit to Indonesia in 2010, it was announced that China would invest $6.6 billion in urgently needed infrastructure developments: this is the power of the Chinese purse, it will continue to grow apace, and the US will be increasingly unable to match it. When the Chinese premier Wen Jiabao visited Jakarta in April 2011, a further loan of $4 billion for infrastructural projects was agreed. Meanwhile, China is rapidly outdistancing the US as a trading partner: in 2009 Indonesia's trade with China totalled $23.5bn in contrast to $18.8bn with the US, with the Indonesians complaining about American protectionism.[96] Although the ASEAN countries are in varying degrees concerned about the rise of China, and several might be prepared to encourage the US to play a balancing role, none see a declining America as an alternative to the most dynamic economy in the world: they are very aware that China is the future of their region and that their relationship with it must take increasing priority over that with the United States. As revealed in Wikileaks, in a cable sent to US Democratic Senator Jim Webb after his visit to Bangkok in January 2009, King Bhumibol's deputy private secretary apologized for 'having to play the China card' but pointing out that 'as US focus on South East Asia has diminished over the last decade, China has increasingly become a more important partner for Thailand': this notwithstanding the fact that Thailand is a traditional American ally.[97] When asked whether the Philippines, a long-standing American ally, might turn to the United States for protection in the South China Sea dispute, President Benigno Aquino III replied, 'If they are around.' The

Philippines, like all the other countries in the region, recognize that it is and will be essential for them to reach an accommodation with China: as Aquino put it, 'If we were to engage in a boxing match, there's 15 of them for every one of us.'[98] Furthermore, the plans for a high-speed rail network connecting China with Thailand, Malaysia, Singapore, Laos and Cambodia, with China playing a key role in both construction and financing, will serve to greatly strengthen and accelerate China's relationship with South-East Asia, to a far greater extent than air travel could possibly achieve.[99] Nonetheless, recent events are a reminder that China's rise in the region, irresistible as it undoubtedly is, will be a complex process involving many twists and turns of fortune. Not least, China has clearly made foreign policy errors since 2009 which it will need to learn from. In particular, notwithstanding its remarkably open and concessive attitude towards ASEAN in the matter of trade negotiations, its (admittedly very limited) military build-up appears to have been conducted in a very different unilateral manner.

ECHOES OF THE PAST

In the light of the region's realignment towards China, we can now return to the question of how East Asia's relationship with China is likely to evolve and, in particular, to what extent it might bear some of the hallmarks of the tributary system. The tributary system and Westphalian system are often regarded as polar opposites and mutually exclusive, the former involving a hierarchical relationship, the latter based on relations of equality between sovereign nation-states. In fact, as mentioned in Chapter 7, the Westphalian system in practice has never been quite that simple. For most of its history it was largely confined to a group of European states, since until the second half of the twentieth century the great majority of countries in the world did not enjoy independence, let alone equality.[100] Even after these countries became sovereign nation-states, in the great majority of cases they were to enjoy nothing like equality with the United States or the West European nations, or indeed the Soviet Union. Indeed, during the Cold War nation-states experienced what was, in practice, limited sovereignty in their relationship with the superpower to which they owed their allegiance. Life has not been that dissimilar in the era of the single superpower, with most countries enjoying varying degrees of limited sovereignty in their relationship with the United States. Given the profound inequalities in interstate relations, the concept of equality in the Westphalian system is thus legalistic rather than real. In practice, as with the tributary system, it has strong hierarchical features.[101] Like the tributary system, the Westphalian system also has an influential cultural component, namely the role of hegemony and soft power. In other words, the distinction between the tributary and Westphalian systems is not quite as clear-cut as one might think. Seen in these terms, the restoration of elements of the tributary system in a modernized form does not seem so far-fetched. Some of the old building blocks, moreover, remain firmly in place. Chinese culture not only continues to enjoy great prestige throughout East Asia, but its influence is once again on the rise, aided by the presence of a much larger Chinese minority than existed in earlier times, especially in South-East Asia. Furthermore, in North-East Asia, and also Vietnam, Confucianism is a shared heritage in a not dissimilar way to the role of the Graeco-Roman tradition in Europe.

Historically, the tributary system was the international concomitant of China's identity and existence as a civilization-state. And just as the influence of the civilization-state remains deep and profound in the domestic sphere, so the persistence of the tributary state mentality is apparent in the realm of international relations. In important respects, indeed, Chinese attitudes towards concepts of sovereignty and interstate relations continue to owe at least as much to the tributary legacy as they do to the contemporary Westphalian system.[102]

A classic example is China's attitude towards maritime sovereignty, which differs fundamentally from that in Western-inspired international law. Take the dispute over the sovereignty of the Spratly and Paracel islands, which, though partially shelved for now – following the agreement with ASEAN discussed earlier – remains, in the long term, unresolved.[103] The Spratly and Paracel islands are barely islands at all, but a collection of uninhabited rocks, many of

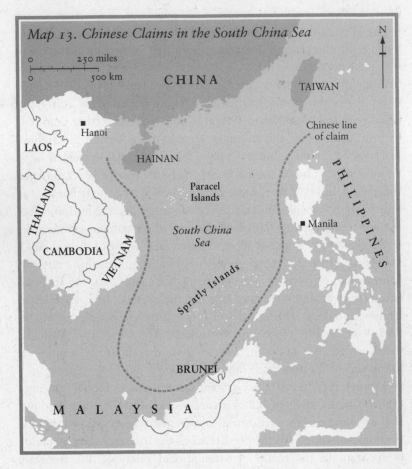

Map 13. Chinese Claims in the South China Sea

which are usually under water, situated in the South China Sea, the Spratlys to the north of East Malaysia and to the west of the Philippines, and the Paracels to the east of Vietnam. The idea of maritime sovereignty is a relatively recent innovation, dating from 1945 when the United States declared that it intended to exercise sovereignty over its territorial waters,[104] and it is this body of law that essentially forms the basis of the claim by the various South-East Asian states to the Spratlys and Paracels. China, in contrast, rests its argument on 'historic claims', namely that the islands have for thousands of years formed an integral part of the south-east frontier of the

Middle Kingdom in the same manner, for example, as the land border to the north of Beijing. Expeditions to the islands have discovered various Chinese artefacts, such as chinaware and copper cash from the Tang and Song dynasties, that have been used to buttress these 'historic claims' and demonstrate that the islands have long been a part of China. The islands are part of the folklore of Chinese culture, kept alive, in various invocations of the Chinese frontier spirit, by articles written by Chinese journalists who regularly visit the islands. They are shown on many Chinese maps as clearly within the 'historic claim line' (see map on p. 376) and therefore as part of China.[105] (It is worth noting, in this context, that Taiwan, which also claims both the Paracels and Spratlys, does so on a similar basis to China.) Hainan Island, off the southern coast of China, may be China's smallest land province, but it is also regarded – because of the extent of its maritime territory which, as claimed, reaches far into the South China Sea – as its largest 'ocean province'.[106] In 2007 Beijing established the new Sansha municipality in Hainan Province, which has jurisdiction over three islets that Vietnam claims in the Spratly and Paracel archipelagos. This led to large-scale protest demonstrations outside the Chinese embassy in Hanoi.[107] The idea of 'historic claims' finds expression in the Chinese use of intertemporal law, which concerns rights or wrongs in the historical past. Chinese legal scholars argue that: 'a judicial fact must be appreciated in the light of the laws contemporary with it, rather than the laws in force at the time when a dispute arises.'[108] This gives force and legitimacy to history rather than the present, to the laws that prevailed during the era of the tributary system rather than the present international legal system.

In 1984 Deng Xiaoping suggested 'the possibility of resolving certain territorial disputes by having the countries concerned jointly develop the disputed areas before discussing the question of sovereignty'.[109] In other words, the question of sovereignty should not necessarily delay moving forward on other issues. Deng's remark has frequently been cited by Chinese sources in the context of the islands in the South China Sea, where his approach has in practice been followed, and in relation to the Diaoyu/Senkaku islands in the East

China Sea that are disputed with Japan; it has also been suggested in connection with Taiwan.[110] While insisting on their ultimate sovereignty over the latter, the Chinese have in effect offered to shelve the matter more or less indefinitely, providing Taiwan does not seek to declare independence, illustrating the flexibility with which the Chinese are prepared to approach the issue. Alternatively, they have suggested that, providing their sovereignty over the island is accepted by the Taiwanese, Taiwan can continue to have its own government, political system and even armed forces.[111]

This highlights another fundamental difference between the Chinese conception of sovereignty and that held in the West – most clearly demonstrated in the attitude displayed by China towards the handover of sovereignty in Hong Kong. The transfer of sovereignty was regarded by the Chinese as non-negotiable, as in the case of all the so-called lost territories – namely, Taiwan, Hong Kong and Macao – which China regards, on the basis of history, culture and ethnicity, as rightly its own. But by Western standards its sovereignty has been exercised in an unusually pliant manner. The British – and Western – narrative concerning Hong Kong was that, following the handover in 1997, the Chinese would transform the territory into something that very closely resembled the mainland. This expectation has not been borne out. For the most part, Hong Kong has changed very little, its political and legal system remaining relatively unchanged since British colonial rule. The key to understanding the Chinese approach lies in 'one country, two systems', the principle which informed the territory's post-handover constitution, otherwise known as the Basic Law. As far as China was concerned, the key issue was the recognition of its sovereignty over Hong Kong rather than whether or not the territory shared the same system of government.[112] The Western approach, based on the nation-state, is quite different: sovereignty and a singular system are seen as synonymous. In fact, 'one country, two systems' lies in a millennia-old Chinese tradition that acknowledges and accepts the existence of differences between its many provinces, or, to put it another way, that such differences are an inherent and necessary part of a civilization-state. In other words, the civilization-state is based on the principle of 'one civilization, many systems'. In contrast, the

Western notion of sovereignty rests on the principle of 'one nation-state, one system', and the Westphalian system on 'one system, many nation-states'.[113] An eloquent demonstration of the difference of approach is provided by German unification in 1990 when East Germany was absorbed into West Germany exclusively on the latter's terms, with barely a trace of the former remaining.

The Chinese attitude towards sovereignty is closely related to the old Confucian concept of 'harmony with difference', which has been revived under the present Chinese leader, Hu Jintao. Some Chinese scholars, in fact, have interpreted 'one country, two systems' as an example of 'harmony with difference'. Whereas in Western discourse, harmony implies identity and a close affinity, this is not the case in Chinese tradition, which regards difference as an essential characteristic of harmony. According to Confucius, 'the exemplary person harmonizes with others, but does not necessarily agree with them; the small person agrees with others but is not harmonious with them.'[114] Agreeing with people means that you are uncritically the same as them: the opposite of harmony is not chaos but rather uniformity and homogeneity. Interestingly, in China the latter are often associated with the term 'hegemony', which is used pejoratively to describe big power behaviour – once the Soviet Union, now the United States – in contrast to 'harmony' which is seen as enabling and embracing difference.

In considering the future relationship between China and its East Asian neighbours, it is pertinent to take into account not only the historical legacy of the tributary system but also what might be described as the realpolitik of size. This was clearly a fundamental aspect of the tributary system, but arguably it is an even more powerful factor in the era of globalization and the modern nation-state. China is anxious to emphasize its desire to exercise self-restraint and respect for the interests of other states, but in the longer run, on the assumption that China continues its economic rise, the disparity between China and the other nations in the region is likely to become ever more pronounced over time. It is not difficult to imagine a scenario in which the inequality between the power of China and that of neighbouring states will be rather greater than that to be found in any other region of the world. Such overweening power will be expressed in a gamut of ways, from economic and cultural to political and military. This is the major factor that lies behind the suspicions latent in the region towards China: the fear not so much of what China is now – especially as it has gone out of its way to reassure its neighbours – but what it might be like in the future.[115] The chief of the Malaysian navy put it like this in 1996: 'as the years progress, there exist[s] . . . uncertainty in the form of China's behaviour once she attained her great power status. Will she conform to international or regional rules or will she be a new military power which acts in whatever way she sees fit?'[116] Imagine the relationship, fifty years hence, between a hugely powerful and advanced China, with a population well in excess of 1.5 billion, and Laos and Cambodia, with populations by then of perhaps around 10 million and 20 million respectively and far less developed; or, for that matter, Malaysia, with perhaps rather more than 35 million people. On grounds of size – let alone the tributary legacy – the relationship between China and its region is bound to be fundamentally different from that between the dominant country and its neighbours in any other region.

What will China be like? How will it act? It is clear that China's behaviour towards, and conception of, the region is bound to be heavily influenced by the legacy of the tributary system and its character as a civilization-state. After all, Britain's attitude towards Africa and the Middle East to this day remains strongly influenced by its colonial history, not least in its willingness to use force. In China's case, the impact of traditional ways of thinking is apparent in its attitude towards the Spratly and Paracel islands, Hong Kong and Taiwan. In its own region at least, it is clear that in many respects China does not behave in the manner of a Westphalian nation-state. China and ASEAN approach the question of the disputed islands from very different legal and theoretical standpoints. The same can be said, as we shall see shortly, of China's approach to the Taiwan question. Accepting these historically rooted conceptual differences, how assertive is China likely to be in pursuing its objectives? Is one to judge China's future behaviour by the restraint and relative magnanimity that is characteristic of the present regime, or will that be superseded by something altogether more Sinocentric? Could China slowly abandon its present extreme caution and become more forceful in its relations with other countries; for example those, such as India, Japan and the South-East Asian countries, with whom it has territorial disputes which for the time being it has agreed to shelve?[117] As China grows more powerful, it would hardly be surprising if it did become more Sinocentric: in fact, at least in the longer run, that is what one might expect. After all, with the present overwhelming emphasis on economic development and the desire to ensure that there are no distractions, restraint is at least partly a function of priorities: in the reform era, China's self-discipline has been huge and impressive. Casting our minds into the future to a time when Chinese living standards are much higher and China has established itself as the dominant power in East Asia, how might a more Sinocentric outlook express itself?

Perhaps the best way of answering this question is to look for pointers in the present, however isolated and scattered they might be. There are three examples. The first concerns the Chinese invasion of Vietnam in February 1979, which China described as a 'punitive war to teach Vietnam a lesson' about the proximity of Chinese power and its belief that the Vietnamese had not been sufficiently grateful for the assistance they had received from China during the Vietnam War.[118] The language of this war, the tone of imperial condescension, the desire to assert a hierarchical relationship, the need for big brother to teach younger brother a lesson, were a throwback to the days of the pre-modern Chinese world order and the tributary system.[119] In not dissimilar vein, China has used military force in the disputes over the islands in the South China Sea, against the Philippines in 1995 and most notably against Vietnam in 1956, 1974, and again in 1988, when China took six islands in the Spratly area, three Vietnamese ships were sunk and seventy-two Vietnamese seamen killed.[120] All these various actions clearly bear the imprint of the tributary system, the need to assert the natural hierarchical order of things, and, if necessary, punish those who dared step out of line. As we have seen, the animosity between China and Vietnam dates back many centuries and, given this, is likely to continue in the future.[121]

The second example concerns the relationship between China and Chinese citizens abroad. In autumn 2005 it was alleged that a Chinese female tourist in Malaysia had been strip-searched and subjected to violent assault by Malaysian officials. The issue was first reported by the *China Press*, a Malaysian Chinese-language newspaper, and was subsequently taken up with such vehemence by the Chinese media that the Malaysian prime minister ordered an independent investigation, as well as instructing his home affairs minister to make a special trip to Beijing in order to explain and apologize.[122] An editorial in the *China Daily*, an official government newspaper, exclaimed: 'All sensible minds cannot but be shocked by the images showing a female compatriot of ours being forced to perform "ear-squats" naked by a Malaysian policewoman in uniform. No excuse can justify brutality of such magnitude.'[123] The editorial exercised little restraint or circumspection. Yet soon afterwards it was discovered that the woman in question was not a Chinese citizen, or even Chinese for that matter, but a Malay.[124] The Chinese response to the incident was, from the outset, both disproportionate and belligerent, and based on false information culled from the Chinese-Malaysian press. It would be wrong to draw too many conclusions from one isolated incident, but the Chinese reaction, under the circumstances, was overbearing and intemperate. The Chinese treated the Malaysian government with scant respect. They didn't even have the courtesy to check the facts first. They behaved in an imperial fashion towards what they seemed to regard, in tone at least, as a lesser state. Meanwhile, the Malaysian government, for its part, acted in the manner of a suitably humble and deferential tributary state. As Chinese tourism in the region grows apace, the incident suggests that the protection afforded to Chinese citizens abroad will be attentive and proactive at best, invasive and aggressive at worst.

The final example concerns the response of the Chinese to the riots against the local Chinese in Indonesia in 1997. In the event, the Chinese government displayed considerable restraint, seeking to discourage the kind of demonstrations staged by the overseas Chinese in Hong Kong, Taiwan, New York, South-East Asia and Australia.[125] Nonetheless, to judge by postings on the internet, the reaction of many Chinese was one of considerable anger. The following post is one such example:

> My mother country, do you hear the crying? Your children abroad are crying out. Help them. I do not understand politics and do not dare talk about politics. I do not know what it means to say 'we have no long-term friends or enemies, only long-term interests', and I do not know what these interests are . . . I only know that my own compatriots are being barbarously slaughtered, they need help, and not just moral expressions of understanding and concern. My motherland, they are your children. The blood that flows from their bodies is the blood of the Han race. Their sincerity and goodwill also come from your nourishment. Help them . . .[126]

Notwithstanding these sentiments, the Chinese government acted with caution and moderation; but as Chinese power in the region grows, the relationship between China and the overseas Chinese – who wield exceptional economic power in virtually every ASEAN country,[127] and whose self-confidence, status and position will be greatly enhanced by China's rise – will become a growing factor in these countries.[128] Emboldened by the rise of China, the local Chinese may seek to take advantage of their improved bargaining position in order to enhance their power, while governments in these countries are likely to be increasingly cautious about the way they handle their Chinese minorities for fear of upsetting Beijing. The historian Wang Gungwu argues that the overseas Chinese share many characteristics with other ethnic minorities: 'But where the "Chinese" are totally different is [that] their "mother country" is near Southeast Asia, very large and populous, potentially powerful and traditionally contemptuous of the peoples and cultures of the region.'[129] On the other hand, it should be borne in mind that, historically, the imperial regimes believed that they had no responsibility towards those Chinese who, over the centuries, left the mainland to live in South-East Asia; on the contrary, they believed that they had stepped out of civilization and were therefore not deserving of protection or assistance.

TAIWAN – THE GREAT
NON-NEGOTIABLE

There have been two great exceptions to the new turn in China's regional policy. One was China's most important 'lost territory', namely Taiwan, and the other her regional colonizer and greatest adversary, Japan. While China has pursued a strategy of engagement, accommodation and compromise with virtually every other country in the region since the turn of the century, that cannot be said of its attitude towards Japan or, until very recently, Taiwan.[130]

China's attitude towards Taiwan is fraught not only because it regards the island as one of its lost territories, and therefore as historically part of China; there is an extra charge because Taiwan became a bone of contention after the civil war between the Chinese Communist Party and the nationalist Kuomintang, with the flight of Chiang Kai-shek and his forces to the island and the declaration that it was now the Republic of China, claiming sovereignty over the whole of China. As a consequence, Taiwan represents unfinished business, the only incomplete item on the Party's civil war agenda. This is a further reason why the return of Taiwan to Chinese sovereignty is the ultimate non-negotiable for the present regime and, given the strength of Chinese public opinion on the issue, probably for any other regime one could imagine as well.[131] The road since 1949 has been tortuous, from the pariah status bestowed upon China by the United States and its recognition of Taiwan rather than the People's Republic of China as the true China, to the American volte-face after the Nixon–Mao rapprochement, and then the steady international isolation of Taiwan over the last four decades. But China's ultimate objective, namely reunification, has proved beyond reach because the Taiwanese themselves have remained firmly opposed to it, with the tacit support of the Americans.

Indeed, China's hopes have been thwarted over the last two decades by a most unexpected development: a growing sense of Taiwanese identity culminating in the electoral defeat of the Kuomintang (KMT), which, in principle at least, had always supported a one-China policy, and the victory of the pro-independence Democratic Progressive Party

(DPP). After the election of the DPP's Chen Shui-bian as president in 2000, Taiwan pursued a policy of de-Sinicization and increasingly assertive nationalism. This happened to coincide with growing economic interdependence between China and Taiwan, which, though resisted for a period by Chen and his predecessor as president, Lee Teng-hui,[132] has accelerated to the point where, by 2003, half of the top 1,000 Taiwanese firms, including all the major computer companies, had invested in the mainland, usually in manufacturing subsidiaries. Around three-quarters of Taiwanese foreign direct investment presently goes to China, and there are hundreds of thousands of Taiwanese living and working in the Shanghai region and Guangdong province. The Chinese market accounted for 43 per cent of Taiwanese exports in 2010, compared with around 1 per cent in 1992, making China easily Taiwan's largest export market, far bigger than the US and Japan.[133] Will growing economic interdependence mean that the two countries are drawn irresistibly closer together, resulting in some kind of political arrangement between them? Or will the sense of difference that clearly informs Taiwanese consciousness close off that option and lead to a growing desire for de jure, and not just de facto, independence?

A key question here concerns the nature of Taiwanese identity. To what extent is it constituted as different from and in opposition to Chinese identity? And is a sense of Taiwanese identity positively correlated with support for Taiwanese nationalism and ultimately independence? As can be seen from Figure 47, between 1992 and 2006 the proportion of Taiwanese who thought of themselves simply as Chinese has been steadily declining, while those who felt themselves to be Taiwanese has been commensurately rising. However, those that consider themselves to be both Taiwanese and Chinese have consistently been the largest group – by a narrow margin, in fact, the biggest of all – accounting for almost half the electorate. The picture is, therefore, rather complex. The fact that the largest group consider themselves to be both Taiwanese and Chinese suggests that the two identities, far from being mutually exclusive, are seen by almost half the population as complementary. Many, in fact, recognize that their Taiwanese identity, based on a shared sense of history,

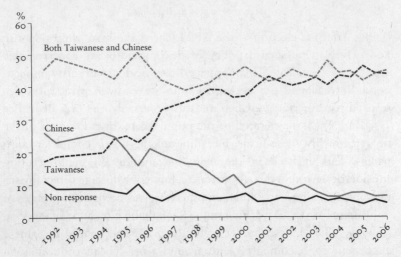

Source: Election Study Center, National Chengchi University

Figure 47. Changing Taiwanese attitudes towards Taiwanese/Chinese identity.

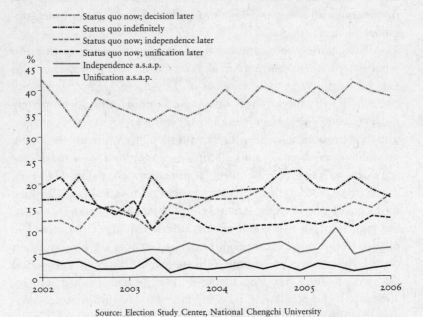

Source: Election Study Center, National Chengchi University

Figure 48. Taiwanese support for unification and for independence.

culture, place and customs, exists within and alongside their sense of being Chinese.[134] This would suggest that there is not necessarily a strong correlation between a sense of Taiwanese identity and support for independence. This is rather borne out in Figure 48. The largest group supports the status quo, with any decision on the island's status to be postponed until later, or what might be described as a 'wait and see' position. The second largest group (which enjoys half the support of the former) favours the status quo now and independence later, but this is more or less matched by those who prefer the status quo indefinitely. And not far behind this group in terms of support are those who favour the status quo and unification with China later; there is minimal backing, however, for immediate unification. Only a small minority support immediate independence, and this group combined with those who favour the status quo and independence later comprise less than a quarter of the population. Furthermore, the combined support for these two positions peaked in 1999 and has subsequently levelled off or declined slightly.

This suggests that Taiwanese identity is a diverse and malleable concept which means different things to different people. It does not appear to have a strong political content, otherwise there would be a closer correlation between Taiwanese identity and support for independence.[135] Rather than seeing the direction of Taiwan as predetermined, the situation is, in fact, fluid and open-ended. Taiwanese opinion is open to influence according to the way in which China behaves and the exigencies of Taiwanese politics, together with deeper underlying trends, including how China evolves economically and politically in the longer run, what happens to the Taiwanese economy, and the impact of economic integration between China and Taiwan.

While there is nothing inevitable about the political effects of growing economic integration, the sheer speed and extent of the process over the last few years has had a major impact on Taiwanese politics. Fear of its consequences persuaded former president Lee Teng-hui to impose restrictions on investment in China by Taiwanese companies and to hasten the process of Taiwanization in order to take advantage of what Lee saw as a window of opportunity before the dynamic of economic integration began to close down options.[136]

Chen followed suit, though he was forced to bow to pressure from Taiwanese companies and ease some of the restrictions. The growing dependence of Taiwanese companies both on the Chinese market and on their manufacturing operations in China has become an influential consideration in the minds of both Taiwanese business and the Taiwanese electorate. Whereas once the country was largely dependent on the American market, this has been supplanted in importance by the Chinese market in a manner similar to China's other neighbours. In Taiwan's case, though, this process has happened even more quickly and gone a lot further – primarily, no doubt, because of shared Chinese customs, culture and language, though other factors like geographical proximity are obviously important. Any calculation concerning Taiwan's economic future, or the prospects for living standards, must inevitably place China at the centre of the equation. It is hardly surprising that in a 2005 survey almost twice as many Taiwanese were in favour of strengthening economic ties between China and Taiwan as compared with those in favour of downgrading them.[137] And China has recently sought to use these growing connections to build links with different sections of the Taiwanese population in order to influence the political climate and put political pressure on the Taiwanese government.[138]

The manifest volatility of Taiwanese public opinion has underlined the need for China to court and influence it, yet this is a matter to which the Chinese government has historically attached relatively little importance. There are three reasons for this. First, the Chinese concept of the 'lost territories' means that Taiwan, as in the case of Hong Kong, is seen in terms of an historic claim rather than popular sovereignty: in other words, legitimacy is regarded as a matter of history rather than the present. As a consequence of this attitude, the Hong Kong people were not represented in the talks about the handover, which were conducted exclusively between the Chinese and the British.[139] This differed from what has normally happened in negotiations over decolonization, with those seeking independence from the colonial power generally represented at the conference table. Second, the Chinese attitude towards both Hong Kong and Taiwan demonstrates the overriding importance attached to state sovereignty and the absence of any tradition of popular sovereignty, a subject I discussed in Chapter 7. Third, the Chinese view of Taiwan involves a particular concept of Chineseness, which conceives of it in essentialist terms, as immutable, timeless and fixed in history, something that is inherited at birth, whether one likes it or not. This is directly related to the discussion in the last chapter about the nature of the Han Chinese, who are seen by the Chinese government as homogeneous, even though in reality the Han are a very diverse group. It follows, therefore, that the notion of a Taiwanese identity that serves to supersede or elide one's Chinese belonging is given little or no credence.[140]

As a consequence the Chinese government, at least until recently, has made little attempt to woo Taiwanese opinion. Indeed, it has often acted in a manner that served to inflame, alienate, intimidate and antagonize the Taiwanese – issuing thinly veiled threats, refusing to countenance their views, and resorting to coercive action, most notably the firing of missiles into the Taiwan Strait during the 1996 presidential election campaign.[141] Recently, however, China has been more prepared to engage with the situation in Taiwan as it actually is and thereby take Taiwanese opinion more seriously.[142] This was illustrated by its wooing of the KMT leadership in the period prior to the 2008 parliamentary and presidential elections, including the visit of the former KMT leader Lien Chan to Beijing in 2005. There is now growing optimism in Beijing based on the fact that support for Taiwanese independence seems to have peaked and a view that the majority of Taiwanese are basically pragmatic – supporting, in one form or another, the status quo. The rising economic interdependence between China and Taiwan also points in the direction of the status quo or closer political ties.

China is prepared to be patient and settle for the status quo for the indefinite future, provided Taiwan does not declare independence. This has the virtue of enabling Beijing to concentrate on China's economic development and sidelining an issue which, in the event of a military conflagration, would do untold damage to the country's global and regional standing. There is a quiet belief on the part of the Chinese that time is now on their side. Taiwan's growing economic dependence on China is one obvious reason for this, while China's own spectacular progress is clearly making the country steadily less unattractive in the eyes of the much richer Taiwanese. At the same time Taiwan, throttled by its lack of diplomatic recognition, has found itself excluded from the new regional trade arrangements centred on ASEAN.[143] Indeed, until now Taiwan and North Korea have been the only two countries in the region that did not have any free trade agreements with other Asian nations. Another factor is the improvement in China's military competence and strength across the Taiwan Strait, consequent upon the country's growing economic and technological capacity, which serves as an increasingly powerful deterrent to any adventurist action by Taipei. Furthermore, the fact that the Bush administration consistently sought to restrain President Chen Shui-bian's more outlandish schemes also served to reassure Beijing.[144] Most important of all, the sweeping victories achieved by the KMT in the parliamentary and presidential elections in early 2008 confirmed Beijing in its new sense of optimism. Weary of Chen's preoccupation with independence and concerned about the weak state of the economy, the electorate voted decisively for improved relations with the mainland, especially economic, with the new president Ma Ying-jeou promising to maintain the status quo and seek a closer relationship with China. During the eight years of Chen's presidency, annual economic growth averaged only 4 per cent while the country became an increasingly unattractive destination for foreign investment. Taiwan was finding itself bypassed as a result of its isolation.[145]

In April 2009 there was dramatic progress when China and Taiwan concluded new agreements on financial services, direct flights and fighting crime. This marked a major turning point, paving the way for a much closer relationship between the two countries. In June 2010 a landmark trade deal was agreed between China and Taiwan, known as the Economic Cooperation Framework Agreement (ECFA) and intended to be the first phase in a process of trade liberalization. China agreed to do the lion's share of opening up in the initial round, cutting its import tariffs across 539 products and services worth $13.84 billion in trade terms, with cuts on the Taiwanese side amounting to only $3 billion. It is now possible to fly directly to twenty-three Chinese cities from Taiwan, whereas prior to these recent agreements China could only be accessed via Hong Kong. In 2011 Taiwan agreed to allow Chinese investors to take stakes in its technology companies. The new rules give Chinese investors access to some of Taiwan's most globally competitive companies, such as Taiwan Semiconductor Manufacturing Company and Acer. While Taiwanese have long invested in China, Chinese investment has hitherto been forbidden in Taiwan.[146] Soon after the ECFA was signed, Taiwan announced that, with Beijing's approval, it had commenced negotiations with Singapore on a bilateral trade agreement, which could be the prelude to its eventual entry into ASEAN, thereby ending its regional isolation. Any such development, of course, would require China's blessing, which only goes to underline the pivotal importance for Taipei of continuing to move closer to Beijing: Taiwan's integration with the region depends on the extent of its intimacy with China. Together these various developments mark a sea change in Taiwan's position.[147] It seems likely that the independence movement, which with hindsight was a blind alley, is now in long-term decline, certainly in its old form, with the former president Chen Shui-bian serving a 20-year prison sentence for corruption and now a deeply discredited figure. The ECFA marks the beginning of a process which will see a huge intensification of Taiwan's economic integration with China. We have, it would seem, entered a new era which will see the relationship between the two countries growing ever closer, with the prospect of an agreement by the Chinese at some point to withdraw their missiles pointed at Taiwan.[148] It is not difficult to imagine that the end result – in time – will be some form of agreement by the Taiwanese to accept Chinese sovereignty in return for very considerable autonomy.

In light of this, Washington might contemplate at some point the idea that Taiwan is no longer a fundamental interest that must be defended at all costs.[149] Certainly, in the context of China's rise, Taiwan has enjoyed a declining priority in Washington over recent decades. The Chinese have already begun to entertain the possibility of rather looser political solutions that might one day be acceptable to the Taiwanese. For some time the Chinese have essentially offered Taiwan an enhanced variant of 'one country, two systems',[150] but this has recently been given less prominence. Perhaps the Chinese will contemplate the idea of a Chinese commonwealth or a federal commonwealth under which Taiwan would enjoy not only a high degree of autonomy, as it would under the Hong Kong formula, but also, while recognizing the symbolic sovereignty of Beijing, in effect be granted a measure of independence and even limited autonomy to act in the international sphere.[151] For now, China's growing optimism is not misplaced: the most likely scenario is a developing rapprochement and perhaps even an ultimate settlement. Of course, it is impossible to rule out a further reversal, including the return of another DPP government. If that government should at some point go for broke and declare independence, then China would almost certainly seek to reverse that action by military means, thereby embroiling the whole region and the United States in a crisis which would have far-reaching consequences.[152] Such an outcome, however, now seems more far-fetched than at any time since Chiang Kai-shek occupied the island after his defeat in the civil war. But this is all highly speculative: for now, at least, the rapprochement between China and Taiwan, further reinforced by Ma Ying-jeou's victory in the presidential election in January 2012, is the most startling and significant example of the way in which China's position in, and relationship with, East Asia is changing and steadily strengthening.

BIG BROTHER AND LITTLE BROTHER

Since 1949 Taiwan has been China's most acute regional problem. In the light of these latest developments, however, Japan has replaced Taiwan as the most difficult issue facing China in East Asia.[153] Until the Sino-Japanese War of 1894–5, which was a direct consequence of the Meiji Restoration in 1868 – with Japan's turn to the West, rejection of its own continent, especially China, and its expansionist ambitions – relations between China and Japan had been relatively harmonious. Japan had been a long-term though somewhat intermittent tributary state, honouring and acknowledging its debt to Chinese civilization and the Confucian tradition, even if at times it proved a distant and somewhat recalcitrant one – which, given its island status and advanced civilization, was hardly surprising.[154]

For well over a century, however, following the 1894 war, China's relationship with Japan has been far worse than that with any other major power. Many Chinese still see that war and the subsequent Treaty of Shimonoseki as the darkest hour in China's 'century of humiliation'. China's ignominious defeat and the extremely onerous terms inflicted on China in the peace left a particularly bitter taste. Moreover, defeat by what was seen as an inferior nation within the Chinese world order was considered to be a far greater humiliation than losing to the Western barbarians, and served to undermine the prevailing Chinese world-view. This was a case – in the Confucian discourse – of the student beating up the teacher or the younger brother beating up the older brother.[155]

The ignominy visited upon China in the 1894–5 war was compounded and accentuated by Japan's occupation of north-east China in 1931 and then its full-scale invasion of north-east, east and parts of central China in 1937; the scars these hostilities left have never been healed. To this day, the Nanjing Massacre defines the nature and identity of the Japanese as far as the Chinese are concerned and therefore in large measure their attitude towards Japan. It may have taken place over 70 years ago, but it remains an open wound, as present in the relationship between the two countries as if it had happened yesterday. Even the numbers killed – 300,000 in the Chinese interpretation – is still a highly charged issue.[156] Of course, the reason why these questions remain so alive is because the Japanese have failed to apologize properly, or demonstrate any serious sign of confronting their own past, unlike the contrition that the Germans have shown for their behaviour in the Second World War.[157] The Japanese paid dearly for their defeat at the hands of the United States – with huge casualties, the Tokyo trials, the confiscation of its overseas assets and the American occupation – but they have shown little remorse towards their Asian neighbours for their country's often barbaric behaviour, which was far worse than anything Japan meted out to the Western powers. The Nanjing Massacre was the worst example, with the mass killing and rape of civilians, but this was repeated on a smaller scale elsewhere in China, while the Japanese occupation of Korea was also marked by considerable cruelty.[158] The numerous apologies that Japan has given have been little more than formulaic, while the courts have refused to compensate the individual victims of crimes committed in Japan's name. The grudging attitude towards its various Asian neighbours is symptomatic of post-Meiji Japan – respect for the West and contempt for Asia. Nor, for most of the post-war period, has Japan needed to rethink its attitudes.[159] It rapidly re-established itself as the dominant power in the region, in a different league to its poorer neighbours, while the United States, its sponsor and protector, neither required nor desired Japan to apologize to Communist China during the Cold War, given that a new and very different set of priorities now applied.

Fast-forward fifty years and East Asia presents a different picture. Japan no longer constitutes the great exception, a Western level of development surrounded by a sea of backwardness. On the contrary, the initial group of four Asian tigers enjoy a GDP per head not far short of Japan's,[160] living standards in the region have risen enormously, and Japan's old nemesis, China, has been the subject of a remarkable economic transformation. In short, history has finally caught up with Japan.[161] As a society and culture, Japan has always been at its best when its goals – and the path towards those goals – were set in concrete. But when both the goals and the path need to be adapted to changed circumstances, and even subject to wholesale revision, Japan seems to find the shift inordinately difficult.[162] Rather like France, it tends to fiddle and delay until nothing short of a revolution – or, in Japan's case, a restoration – is required. In the face of the transformation of East Asia, and above all China, Japan has been effectively paralysed, unable to change direction, offering little other than more of the same. The ruling Liberal Democrats, who from 1955 until 2009 dominated Japanese politics, found such lateral thinking virtually impossible.[163] As Chinese East Asian expert Zhu Feng argues: 'Japan has been less prepared for the rise of China than any other country. They can't believe it. They don't want to believe it. Yet it affects them more than anyone else.'[164] For the most part, Japan has gone into denial about the rise of China, wishing that somehow it might go away or that it was perhaps a figment of everyone else's imagination.

From the early 1990s, Japanese politics began to shift to the right and become more nationalistic, a process hastened by the collapse of the Social Democratic Party, which had always been a staunch opponent of Japanese rearmament.[165] Japanese ruling politicians grew more aggressive towards China, displaying impatience with traditional deferential tendencies towards their neighbour, increased concern about China's rise, and frustration with what they saw as China's exploitation of Japan's colonial past.[166] In 1996 for the first time the proportion of those saying in an annual poll that they did not have friendly feelings towards the Chinese exceeded those that did. The crisis over North Korea and its threatened development of nuclear weapons, together with its abduction of Japanese citizens between 1977 and 1983, served to harden nationalist sentiment: indeed, the North Korean threat was seen as a proxy for the Chinese threat, thereby helping to ratchet up hostility towards China as well.[167] In 1999 an extreme nationalist, Ishihara Shintaro, was elected governor of Tokyo: previously anti-American, he quickly became rabidly hostile towards China. Meanwhile, Japan entered into a new defence agreement with the United States which was clearly directed against China and which implicitly involved Japan in the defence of Taiwan.[168] The growing enmity towards China found its fullest expression to date during Junichiro Koizumi's premiership between 2001 and 2006, with his annual visits in his official capacity as prime minister to the Yasukuni Shrine – a politically inspired memorial to Japan's fallen soldiers, including Class A war criminals – which were intended to encourage nationalism at home while also irritating and provoking China. After Koizumi, however, the short premierships of Shinzo Abe, previously regarded as hawkish towards China, Yasuo Fukuda in particular, and also Taro Aso revealed a desire in ruling circles to temper the hostility of the Koizumi era and seek a more accommodating relationship with China.[169]

The election of a Democratic government under Yukio Hatoyama in September 2009 seemed to herald a major change of direction. Hatoyama, in a fundamental break with the previous LDP administrations, emphasized the need for Japan to enjoy a different and much closer relationship with East Asia – unveiling a vision for an East Asian Community and describing Asia as Japan's 'basic sphere of being' – while at the same time seeking to establish Japan's relationship with the United States on a more equal and transparent basis.[170] It appeared as if the long overdue historic shift in Japan's approach might finally be at hand: a dramatic change in Japan's perception of its international role and position. In a singular gesture to Beijing, Hatoyama hastily arranged for Xi Jinping, Hu Jintao's heir apparent who was visiting Japan, to meet Emperor Akihito. Alas, these hopes were not to be borne out. The government ran into numerous difficulties, most notably powerful American opposition to its attempt to relocate the US base at Okinawa to somewhere else. In June 2010 Hatoyama resigned, to be replaced as prime minister by Naoto Kan, a much more conventional figure whose election signalled, to all intents and purposes, a resumption of the status quo ante: then Kan resigned in August 2011 and was replaced by Yoshihiko Noda, but there was no sign that he would return to Hatoyama's agenda, with the country consumed by the aftermath of the tsunami and the nuclear crisis.

Japan remains relatively isolated in East Asia. Although it has been generous in bestowing aid on many countries in the region, it has failed to address its wartime legacy, which is a continuing source of resentment for many of its neighbours, especially South Korea and China. It has continued to be relatively aloof from its neighbours, having refused to open up its market and resisted entering into multi-lateral, rather than bilateral, arrangements with them until its hand was finally forced by China's initiatives with ASEAN.[171] There have been two recent illustrations of Japan's continued isolation. The first concerned its failed bid to become a permanent member of the United Nations Security Council in 2005, when China succeeded in mobilizing most of the region in opposition to Japan's proposed membership, thereby effectively torpedoing it.[172] The second example was the anti-Japanese demonstrations in China in 2005, provoked partly by Japan's UN bid but mainly by the publication of a new school history textbook in Japan that sought to downplay Japanese crimes against

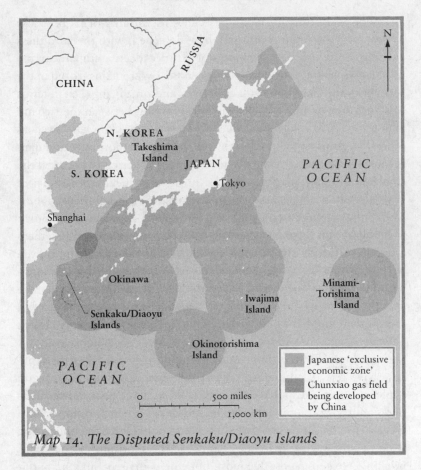

Map 14. The Disputed Senkaku/Diaoyu Islands

China during the last war;[173] in this case, as in that of the United Nations, the sympathies of the region were overwhelmingly on the side of the Chinese rather than the Japanese government.[174] In both instances, the underlying cause of Japan's isolation was the same: its failure to address not only China's grievances about the last war but nearly everyone else's as well.[175]

China's rise requires a fundamental shift in Japanese thinking – indeed, Japan's interests would have been best served if it had been willing to address the wartime treatment of its neighbours several decades ago[176] – but, notwithstanding Hatoyama's efforts, there remains little sign of it. Instead, Japan has clung to variants of its post-war stance, with the result that China has succeeded, with the adroitness of its diplomacy in the region over the last decade, in outmanoeuvring it. Meanwhile, the relationship between the two remains frozen in the manner of the Cold War, with each twist and turn being seen in terms of a zero-sum game.[177] The issues of contention between the two are many, though the historical questions clearly predominate over all others. In terms of the present, by far the most important – and dangerous – issue concerns the disputed Senkaku/Diaoyu islands and the similarly disputed maritime border in the East China Sea.[178] There have already been clashes over the islands, most notably in 1990.[179] Unlike the disputed islands in the South China Sea, there are known to be significant oil and gas deposits in the area, thereby lending them an added strategic significance. Beijing claims the islands have been part of China since the Ming dynasty, as indicated by the international maps of the period. The islands were taken by the Japanese when it colonized Taiwan after the Sino-Japanese War in 1894, and should therefore have been given up by Japan after 1945 when it lost Taiwan. China has offered to shelve the issue of sovereignty, as it has done with the Spratlys, in favour of joint development, but the Japanese have rejected the idea.[180] The Chinese, meanwhile, have begun exploration in a disputed area of sea.[181] An agreement between the two countries on joint exploration and development would serve to greatly ease tension, even though it would not resolve the underlying issue of sovereignty over the islands or the maritime border.[182] In principle, this remains the most hopeful course of action, but it requires the Japanese to drop their opposition to it. Until some kind of agreement is reached, this dispute is the one most likely to result in a serious incident and derail relations between the two countries.[183] This proved to be the case in autumn 2010 when four Japanese coast-guard patrol ships impounded a Chinese trawler in the vicinity of the islands and arrested the captain and crew under domestic Japanese law, which, given the disputed nature of the islands, was provocative. The Chinese reacted angrily and demanded their immediate release. The situation rapidly escalated into the worst diplomatic incident between the two powers since 2005, resulting, as then, in a wave of anti-Japanese demonstrations in various Chinese cities, although this time on a smaller scale. Eventually the Japanese released the crew, followed later by the captain, and withdrew the legal action, but the affair was a poignant reminder that relations between the two powers remain fragile and subject to potentially rapid deterioration.

At times of crisis, the Chinese government has generally tried to restrain popular attitudes of resentment towards Japan for fear that they might get out of control; sometimes, however, they have spilt over, as was the case with the large and angry demonstrations that took place in several Chinese cities in 2005 and again in 2010. While Taiwan and the United States have been important factors in Chinese nationalism, especially in the 1990s, its growth has been driven, above all, by feelings of resentment and hostility towards Japan. These remain much stronger than the enmity displayed towards the United States.[184] Apart from the Korean War, there is no history of conflict between China and the US. Moreover, the two countries succeeded, starting in 1971, in remaking their relationship and putting it on an entirely new footing that has survived to the present day. They are also, of course, geographically separated by the expanse of the Pacific Ocean. In contrast, the bitter enmity between the Japanese and Chinese has existed for over a century without interruption. There is simply no modern tradition of compromise or coexistence between them and yet they are by far the two most powerful countries in East Asia.[185] The Chinese may not particularly like the Americans, but they generally respect them; in contrast, as I have frequently found, the Chinese – including the highly educated – will often volunteer that they hate the Japanese.[186] The rise of China, moreover, has if anything served to harden attitudes towards Japan. As Shi Yinhong has observed, the view is now widely expressed that, 'If China concedes to Japan it means that China cannot rise. What is the point of rising if we have to concede to Japan?'[187] It is, nonetheless, strongly in China's interests to play for time. In August 2010 China replaced Japan as the largest economy in East Asia. Assuming that China continues to grow at a brisk pace, and with Japan seemingly unable to escape from the relative economic stagnation that has characterized its last two decades, and now struggling to cope with the triple effects of the 2011 earthquake, tsunami and nuclear crisis, the balance of power between the two will continue to move rapidly in China's favour,[188] with the latter steadily emerging as the fulcrum of the East Asian economy.[189] Even for Japan, China is now of great economic significance: it became Japan's largest export market in 2009, overtaking the United States, with the value of Japanese exports to China doubling between 2000 and 2003,[190] and it has also become an important manufacturing base for many Japanese multinationals. In this context, it is worth noting that while the US accounted for 30 per cent of Japan's trade in 1990, this figure had fallen to 17.7 per cent by 2010. Japan, in short, is being drawn into a relationship of growing economic interdependence with China. But this does not mean that relations between the two countries will inevitably grow more harmonious: the underlying antagonism between them is far too deeply rooted for that.

So how is the relationship between China and Japan likely to evolve? There are several possible scenarios.[191] Hitherto, Japan has essentially regarded itself as different, and apart, from the region. As we have seen, that has been the case ever since the Meiji Restoration, with Japan looking up to the West and down on Asia. The fact that this mindset has been a fundamental characteristic of Japan ever since 1868 makes the task of changing it even more difficult and daunting.[192] Since its defeat in the Second World War, Japan's detachment from Asia has been reinforced by its military dependence on the United States, with the American defence guarantee obliging Japan to look east across the Pacific Ocean rather than west to its own continent, thereby encouraging it to think of itself as an Asia–Pacific rather than East Asian power. This is illustrated by the fact that in 2007 it concluded a security pact – its only other being with the United States – with Australia, the US's closest ally in the Asia–Pacific region. Though both unstated and denied, the obvious target of the agreement is China.[193] Furthermore, as mentioned earlier, the terms of its security and defence arrangement with the United States have been significantly strengthened over the last decade.[194] The most likely scenario is that Japan continues along this same path. For the Japanese it has the great advantage of enabling them to carry on with the status quo and postponing the day when they are required to engage in a fundamental rethink – by far the biggest since 1868 – of their relationship with China in particular and East Asia in general. In China's eyes, however, the US–Japan alliance is only the second worst solution, the worst – such are China's fears of Japanese history – being a Japan that increasingly aspires to become a military force in its own right.[195] The latter process is also under way, but it is taking place slowly and within the context of Japan's alliance with the United States, rather than separately from it. In the long run, however, dependence on the United States may be unsustainable. The growing economic, political and military strength of China could at some point oblige the Japanese to rethink their attitude towards China in a more positive way, as happened briefly under Hatoyama.[196] The United States may also be persuaded at some stage that its relationship with China is rather more important than that with Japan and that its alliance with Japan should effectively be downgraded, shelved or abandoned. But any such outcome, should it ever happen, still lies far in the future.[197] The scenario that seems inconceivable, despite Chinese fears, is that Japan emerges as a stand-alone superpower to rival China: Japan is simply too small, too particularistic, too isolated and too weakly endowed with natural resources to be able to achieve this.[198]

. . . AND THE ELEPHANT

The elephant in the room or, more precisely the region, is the United States. The latter is not even vaguely part of East Asia, being situated thousands of miles to its east, but with its military alliance with Japan, its military bases in South Korea, its long-term support for Taiwan, and various other bilateral alliances and arrangements, not to mention the Korean and Vietnamese wars, it has been the dominant military power in the region ever since it replaced Europe in the 1950s. Although it still enjoys an overwhelmingly pre-eminent military presence, its political and diplomatic influence has declined rapidly over the last decade or so. A combination of the new orientation of US foreign policy after 9/11 and the new turn in Chinese foreign policy in

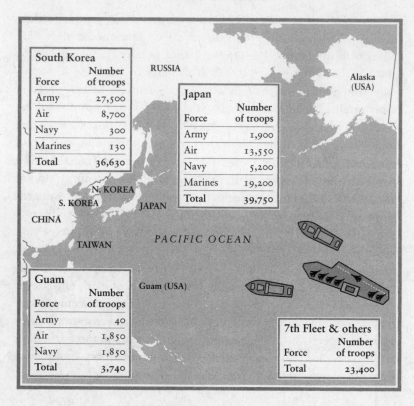

Figure 49. American troops in East Asia, 2007.

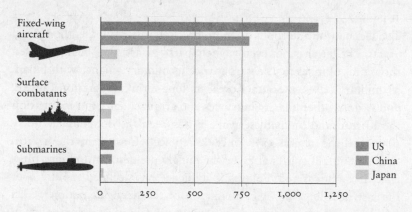

Figure 50. Naval capability, 2007.

East Asia, together with China's emergence as the fulcrum of the regional economy – one of those accidental juxtapositions of history – has transformed Chinese influence in the region, while that of the United States, hugely preoccupied with the Middle East to the virtual exclusion of all else, it would seem, declined sharply during the Bush presidency.[199] Given that the period involved was only a decade, the shift in the balance of power in the region was dramatic. In a few short years, every single country was obliged to rethink its attitude towards China and in every case – excepting Japan (but including Taiwan) – moved appreciably closer to it, including Singapore, the Philippines, Thailand and South Korea, all of which have formal bilateral alliances with the United States.[200] China's star in the region has patently been on the rise and that of the United States on the wane.[201]

It would be wrong to assume that the future will simply be a continuation of these recent trends. On the contrary, in 2010–11 the United States succeeded in making a significant comeback in the region, while China found itself on the defensive. Far from ceding the region to China, it became clear that the US was determined to try and win back lost ground. By the end of 2011, three key components of American strategy had emerged. First, the US successfully sought to consolidate and extend its two main military alliances in the region, namely those with Japan and South Korea. After the trawler incident, moreover, Japan decided to reorganize its armed forces around what it perceived to be the growing threat posed by China.[202] In addition, the US announced that it would station troops for the first time in Australia. All this represented a reassertion of the US's traditional strength in the region, namely military power.[203] Second, it managed, again with significant success, to become part of the ASEAN process, following in China's footsteps over a decade earlier. Previously the US had remained aloof, now it became diplomatically involved and proactive, as exemplified by its participation for the first time in the East Asian Summit in November 2011. This was something new for the Americans: they had clearly learnt from China's successes and their own past failings. A key plank in this approach has been a skilful attempt to give expression to the concerns felt by some ASEAN countries, notably Vietnam, the Philippines and Singapore, about China's hitherto modest naval build-up in the South China Sea (and also in the East China Sea) and, related to this, China's somewhat ham-fisted and inconsistent diplomacy around the Spratly and Paracel issue. This is the diplomatic component of the new American strategy.

Finally, the Americans are intensifying their efforts to extend the Trans-Pacific Partnership, a multilateral free trade agreement presently involving four countries but with another six in the process of negotiation. The American motivation would appear to be two-fold: a desire to extend US involvement in the most dynamic economic region in the world in the hope that this might give a boost to the American economy; and the strategic aim of wrestling the initiative from China in the field of trade agreements. The ambition, it would seem, is to shift the centre of gravity of the latter away from East Asia and towards Asia-Pacific. There is nothing new in this: it was the consistent American position throughout the 1990s, for example. On the face of it, a key aspect of the American strategy appears to be the desire to exclude China from the Trans-Pacific Partnership by setting the bar for membership impossibly high in terms of labour, intellectual property and environmental standards, and the introduction of regulatory discipline for state-owned enterprises. Trade negotiations are both complex and invariably protracted: it is impossible, at this stage, to predict the outcome. However, given China's rising economic importance in the region and America's declining position, it is difficult to imagine how the US will wrestle the initiative from China in the area of trade.

One thing can be said for certain. For a long time to come, the US will enjoy an overwhelming military predominance, at least in terms of naval and airpower, in the region. Its position is strongest in North-East Asia, where the old Cold War lines of demarcation persist to this day – to a much greater extent than anywhere else in the world. Japan's support for the US dates back to the last war; South Korea's stems from the Korean War (1950–53); and Taiwan's relationship with the US similarly dates all the way back to the 1949 revolution. It is much weaker, however, in South East Asia. So far, relations between China and the United States have remained relatively positive despite

America's attempt to reassert itself. If, however, the United States decides to go further and seeks to contain China – for example, by means of a major military build-up – then it could have very serious ramifications for their relationship, both regionally and globally.[204] A major issue that will arise in the future is the response of the United States to a growing Chinese naval presence in the West Pacific: at present the US treats these waters as effectively part of its own territory. If it persists in that view, then the West Pacific will become a growing source of tension between the two powers. Alternatively, the United States might seek to engage and cooperate with China's navy by integrating it into its own operations in the West Pacific. If that approach is followed, which at present seems unlikely, it would be a strong indication that their relationship is unlikely to be seriously derailed by China's growing power. It is possible that the US will in time – given China's growing economic and military power and the sheer expense of maintaining its existing commitments in the context of its economic decline – become increasingly reconciled to its declining influence in East Asia. The stark fact is that China's economic power and leverage in the region is increasing very rapidly, while America's is diminishing with more or less equal speed.[205] In the long term, therefore, this seems plausible. As things presently stand, China is already established as the dominant land power in the region, while the United States remains, at least for the medium term, the dominant regional maritime power.[206] While this naval strength clearly serves to restrict China's power in the region, it is also a sign of the US's growing weakness, with land power an expression of China's growing economic and political clout and maritime power almost solely a function of the US's hard power.

10

China as a Rising Global Power

Not far from Renmin University in the north-west of Beijing, there is a gargantuan Carrefour hypermarket which sells everything from clothes and refrigerators to sports equipment and food, and which takes a lifetime just to walk through let alone shop in. It is the largest supermarket I have ever used and throngs with many thousands of Beijingers every day of the week. Carrefour, French-owned and the world's second largest retailer, has 112 such hypermarkets in China, though they vary considerably in size. In April 2008 Carrefour found itself the target of a protest which spread like wildfire across China, with demonstrations taking place outside stores in Beijing, Wuhan, Heifei, Kunming, Qingdao and many other cities. The origin of the anti-Carrefour campaign was a few brief postings on China's internet bulletin boards which claimed that the retailer and one of its shareholders, LVMH, the French luxury group, had financed the Dalai Lama's government-in-exile in India. Coming hard on the heels of the riots in Tibet, it was an incendiary campaign, which was given added charge by the anger felt towards the protests in Paris against the Olympic torch relay and suggestions that President Sarkozy might boycott the Games. The large crowds that gathered outside many Carrefour hypermarkets urged shoppers to boycott the stores. Demonstrators carried pictures of Jin Jang, a wheelchair-bound Chinese athlete, who had been accosted by a French protester during the torch relay in Paris and whose treatment had incensed the Chinese public. Shoppers who bravely ventured into Carrefour stores did so under the protection of scores of riot police. The eruption of Chinese protests against Carrefour, which threatened to engulf other French companies as well, was reminiscent of those staged against Japanese companies in 2005 when relations between China and Japan reached a new nadir.

Alarmed by the threat to their Chinese operations, Carrefour vehemently denied the rumours about it funding the Tibetan government-in-exile and declared its opposition to the splitting of China. To contain the protests, China's internet gatekeepers began restricting searches using the French company's name. Meanwhile, President Sarkozy sought to defuse anger over the protests in Paris by offering a tacit apology for 'wounded' Chinese feelings. With French companies growing increasingly concerned about a boycott of their goods by Chinese consumers, Nicolas Sarkozy wrote a letter to Jin Jang, the Chinese athlete, offering his 'sympathy'. He acknowledged the 'bitterness' felt in China about the French protests and the attack on Jin Jang, referring to it as a 'painful moment' which he condemned 'in the strongest possible terms'. 'I must assure you,' he continued, 'that the incidents on that sad day, provoked by certain people, do not reflect the feelings of my fellow citizens for the Chinese people.' The letter was handed to Jin Jang in person by the head of the French Senate during an official visit to Shanghai. Mr Sarkozy also sent his chief diplomatic adviser to Beijing in an effort to calm feelings.

Earlier that year another French company, Peugeot Citroën, found itself on the wrong end of Chinese public opinion when it carried an advert in the Spanish newspaper *El Pais* featuring a computer-modified Mao Zedong scowling down from an advertising hoarding at a Citroën car. At the bottom of the ad was the slogan: 'It's true, we are leaders, but at Citroën the revolution never stops.' The ad was attacked on Chinese internet bulletin boards for 'hurting our national pride' and 'damaging the whole Chinese people'. It was hastily withdrawn by the company, which described the ad as 'inappropriate' and expressed regret for any 'displeasure' caused. Its statement read: 'We repeat our good feelings towards the Chinese people, and confirm that we respect the representatives and symbols of the country.' Then in May, Christian Dior, the French fashion brand, became the latest global company to learn the hard way about the danger of offending Chinese sensibilities. Facing the prospect of a boycott of its products, the company dropped the American actress Sharon Stone from its advertising in China after she suggested that the recent earthquake in Sichuan province was karmic retribution for how Beijing had treated Tibet. In the same month the Dalai Lama collected an honorary doctorate from the London Metropolitan University, which attracted considerable criticism in the Chinese media. In June the university's vice-chancellor met with officials at the Chinese embassy and 'expressed regret at any unhappiness that had been caused to Chinese people by the recent award'. It was widely believed that the apology was not unconnected with the fact that 434 students from China were currently studying at the university and that Chinese students have become an extremely lucrative source of revenue for British universities. In their different ways these examples testify to the importance of the Chinese market for many foreign companies and universities, and the extent to which they and their governments are prepared to bow to Chinese sensitivities. They underline the growing influence on the global stage of Chinese public opinion, concerns and attitudes.

A new world order, the future shape of which remains unclear, is being driven by China's emergence as a global power. As we saw in the last chapter, the most advanced expression of this process is in East Asia, where, in little more than a couple of decades, China has become the de facto centre of the region, an increasingly important market for every country, the key driver of the new economic arrangements presently taking shape, and the country that all others are increasingly obliged to take account of and accommodate, even if the manner of China's diplomacy has remained, at least until very recently, determinedly and self-consciously *sotto voce*. So far the changes wrought by China's rise have done little to disturb the calm of global waters, yet their speed and enormity suggest that we have entered an era of profound instability that contrasts strongly with the Cold War, for example, which was characterized by relative predictability combined with exceptional stability.

How will the impact of China's economic rise be felt and perceived in ten years' time? How will China behave twenty years hence when it will possess by far the world's largest economy and is likely to dominate East Asia? Will China continue to operate within the terms of the established international system, as it has done for the last decade or so, or become the key architect and protagonist of a new one? Will the rise of China – together with other developing countries like India – plunge the world into a catastrophic environmental and climatic crisis as a fifth of humanity rapidly acquires the living standards previously associated with the West? China certainly does not know the answers, nor does the rest of the world, whose behaviour towards China will be a powerful determinant of how China itself responds. International relations experts are fond of citing the rise of Germany and Japan in the early twentieth century as examples of nations whose new-found power could not be contained within the existing international system and whose ambitions eventually culminated in war. The rise of China will not necessarily result in military conflict – and, for the sake of humanity, we must fervently hope that it does not – but it is a sobering thought that the ramifications of China's rise for the world will be incomparably greater than those of Germany and Japan, even accounting for the difference in historical times.

The beginning of the twenty-first century marked the moment when China arrived in the global mind.[1] Until then, for most of humanity, it had largely been a story of a faraway country about which people knew little. Now, within little more than a decade, its influence has become real and tangible, no longer a set of statistics or the preserve of policy-makers, but dramatically impacting on popular consciousness around the world. Television programmes and newspaper articles on China have become commonplace. There were two main drivers of this global moment of China-awareness. First, as China established itself as the workshop of the world, 'made in China' goods began to flood global markets, from Wal-Mart in the United States to Jusco in Japan, almost overnight reducing the prices of a growing range of consumer goods, creating the phenomenon known as 'China prices'. Not surprisingly this engendered a feel-good factor about China's rise, albeit tempered by the realization that many companies and jobs were migrating to China to take advantage of the much cheaper costs of manufacturing. Second, China's double-digit growth rate fuelled a growing appetite for the world's commodities, which had the opposite effect – inflationary rather than deflationary

– of big and persistent hikes in the prices of most commodities, of which oil was the most visible and dramatic. Unless you were a major commodity-producing nation, this induced a feel-concerned factor, a growing realization that there was a downside to China's rise. The impact was, thus, felt in different ways around the world: for commodity producers in Africa, Latin America and elsewhere, it primarily meant higher prices for their exports, thereby stimulating economic growth, combined with cheaper manufactured goods; for the West and Japan it meant a large fall in the prices of consumer products and clothing, then spiralling commodity prices; for East Asia it meant a vast new market for their products and low-priced 'China goods' at home. Whatever the precise effect, and for most of the world it has so far been beneficial, China's arrival on the world market ushered in a new kind of global awareness of China: it marked the foothills of China's emergence as a global power.

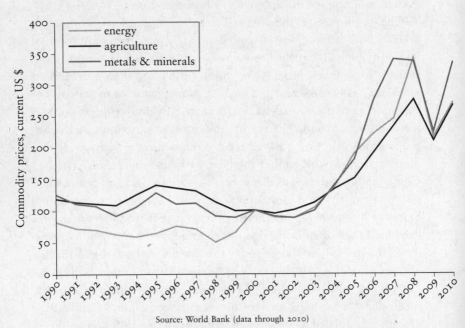

Source: World Bank (data through 2010)

Figure 51. The rising global price of commodities.

In 2001 China officially launched its 'Going Global' strategy, which was primarily intended to foster a closer relationship with commodity-producing countries and thereby secure the raw materials the country urgently required for its economic growth and huge programme of urbanization. The effects of this policy have been dramatic. In the space of less than a decade, China forged ever closer ties with many countries in Africa and Latin America, and to a lesser extent the Middle East and also Central Asia and South Asia. The West, understandably, is most interested in and concerned about how China directly impinges upon it, but China's changing relationship with the developing world is of rather greater import in China's emergence as a nascent global power. In this context, it is essential to understand the remorseless shift in economic power from the developed to the developing world, from the United States, Japan, Germany and others to the likes of Brazil, India and Indonesia, a process which has been accelerated by and become abundantly apparent as a result of the Western financial crisis. China's emphasis on the developing world should therefore be seen as part of a fundamental reconfiguration of global economic power. China's overseas direct investment increased by more than five times between 2000 and 2005, reaching $11.3 billion, and has continued to rise sharply, increasing to $56.53 billion in 2009, a 55 per cent annual growth since 2003, with East Asia the biggest single destination, followed by Latin America, the Middle East and Africa.[2]

LATIN AMERICA

In 2000 President Hu Jintao toured Brazil, Argentina, Chile and Cuba, paving the way for a series of deals which have resulted in much closer economic links. China's trade with Latin America has grown at an average annual rate of around 40 per cent since 2003. By far the most important, and dramatic, example of its expanding ties with the region is its burgeoning relationship with Brazil. Between 2000 and 2009, Brazil's exports to China rose eighteenfold, driven by the latter's demand for commodities. By 2009, China had become Brazil's most important export market, accounting for 12.5 per cent of its total exports. Soyabeans and iron ore account for two-thirds of these, and crude oil for a further 10 per cent. In contrast, although the United States took 26 per cent of Brazil's exports in 2002, the US market share had fallen to 10 per cent by 2010. While Brazil's exports to China are composed overwhelmingly of commodities, China's exports to Brazil are primarily manufactured goods. In 2010, China was comfortably the largest foreign investor in Brazil, accounting for about $17 billion of Brazil's total foreign investment inflows of $48.46 billion.[3] In late 2010 Sinopec announced that it was investing $7.1 billion to buy 40 per cent of Repsol Brasil, the Brazilian subsidiary of Repsol YPF, representing one of the company's largest investments in Latin America so far.[4] A year earlier, an agreement was signed under which Sinopec and the China Development Bank will lend Brazil's state-owned oil company Petrobas $10 billion in return for up to 200,000 barrels a day of crude oil for ten years.[5] With the discovery of one of the world's biggest-ever offshore oilfields, which is just beginning to come onstream, Brazil is set to become a major oil supplier to China. Given the size of their trading relationship, it seems very likely that within the next five years or so much of it will be paid for in renminbi rather than dollars, as at present; in effect, Brazil is likely to become an extremely important member of what might be described as the renminbi trading bloc. The fact that China and Brazil enjoy a close diplomatic and political relationship, as expressed, for example, in their membership of the BRIC grouping, will surely serve to encourage such a development.[6]

Although China's relations with Brazil, Latin America's largest economy, are comfortably the most important, its tentacles stretch right across the continent. Chinese companies have bought stakes in oilfields in Ecuador and Venezuela and have made three major investments in copper projects in Peru. In 2011, the Peruvian government estimated that Chinese investments accounted for more than $11 billion of $41 billion in existing and committed investments in the country's energy and mining sector.[7] China has agreed a currency-swap arrangement with Argentina involving the use of renminbi worth $10 billion and has concluded free-trade agreements with both

Chile and Peru. According to the World Bank, the region has experienced clear net gains from its growing links with China, largely as a result of rising commodity prices, but also because Latin American exporters have benefited from other countries growing richer as a result of their trade with China.

China is rapidly emerging as either the most important, or one of the most important, trading partners of a growing number of countries in the region. In 2010, trade with China accounted for 14 per cent of Brazil's total trade compared with 2.8 per cent in 2001; the equivalent figures for Chile were 19.2 per cent and 5.6 per cent; and for Argentina, 9.7 per cent and 4.7 per cent respectively. By 2014, China is expected to overtake the European Union as Latin America's second largest trading partner after the United States: China, in short, is already having a profound economic impact in the US's own backyard.[8] By far the most dramatic example of China's Going Global strategy, however, is Africa.

AFRICA

The attraction of Africa for China is obvious: it needs a vast range of raw materials to fuel its economic growth. In 2010 China accounted for 10 per cent of the world's consumption of crude oil, 43 per cent of zinc, 42 per cent of steel, 44 per cent of iron ore, and 39 per cent of copper.[9] As we saw in Chapter 6, China is poor in natural resources, the notable exception being rare minerals, and as a consequence has no choice but to look abroad. Africa, on the other hand, is extremely richly endowed with raw materials, and recent discoveries of oil and natural gas have only added to this. Unlike the Middle East, moreover, which continues to receive enormous American attention, Africa has been relatively neglected, having remained of relatively marginal concern to the US.[10] In 2006 the new relationship between Africa and China was publicly consummated, with Hu Jintao's tour of African capitals, followed in November by heads of state and dignitaries from forty-eight African countries attending the largest summit ever held in Beijing.[11] The Chinese premier Wen Jiabao proposed that trade between China and Africa should double between 2005 and 2010. The Chinese made a range of other undertakings, including doubling its 2006 assistance by 2009; establishing a China–Africa development fund of $5 billion to encourage Chinese companies to invest in Africa and provide support for them; increasing from 190 to over 440 the number of export items to China in receipt of zero-tariff treatment from the least developed countries in Africa; providing $3 billion of preferential loans and $2 billion of preferential buyer's credits to Africa over the next three years; cancelling debt in the form of all the interest-free government loans that matured at the end of 2005 owed by the most heavily indebted and least developed African countries; and over the next three years training 15,000 African professionals, sending 100 agricultural experts to Africa, building 30 hospitals and 100 rural schools, and increasing the number of Chinese government scholarships to African students from 2,000 per year to 4,000 per annum by 2009. At the conference major deals were signed, including for the development of an aluminium plant in Egypt, a new copper project in Zambia and a mining contract with South Africa.[12] These commitments have since been fulfilled; trade between Africa and China increased around tenfold between 2000 and 2008, from $10.6 billion to $106.84 billion, and in late 2009 Chinese premier Wen Jiabao pledged a further $10 billion in low-cost loans over the following three years, or double the commitment made in 2006.[13] Since then numerous other deals have been concluded.

Oil now accounts for over half of African exports to China,[14] with Angola its second largest provider after Saudi Arabia and well ahead of its third largest, Iran, supplying 16 per cent of all China's crude oil imports in 2009.[15] China has oil interests in Algeria, Angola, Chad, Sudan, Equatorial Guinea, Congo and Nigeria, including substantial exploration rights, notably in Angola, Sudan and Nigeria. Sudan exports half of its oil to China, representing 6 per cent of the latter's total oil needs.[16] Already around 30 per cent of all China's oil imports come from Africa and that is set to rise with the purchase of significant stakes in Nigeria's delta region.[17] Over the past decade, China's imports in all the major primary commodity categories, except ores and metals, grew much more rapidly from Africa than from the rest

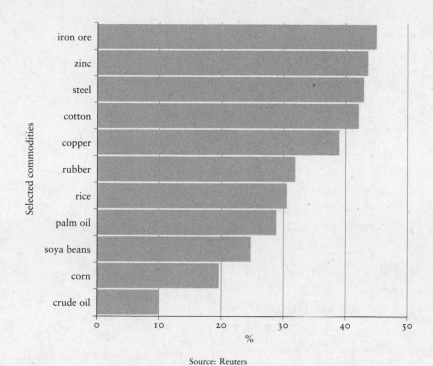

Source: Reuters

Figure 52. China's share of global consumption of commodities, 2010.

Commodity	Africa (reserves)	World (reserves)	Africa relative to world (%)
Platinum group metals (t)	63,000	71,000	89
Diamonds (million carats)	350	580	60
Cobalt (t)	3,690,000	7,000,000	53
Zirconium (t)	14	38	37
Gold (t)	10,059	35,941	28
Vanadium (t)	3,000,000	13,000,000	23
Uranium (t)	656	4,416	15
Manganese (kt)	52,000	380,000	14
Chromium (1,000t)	100,000	810,000	12
Titanium (kt)	63,000	660,000	10
Nickel (kt)	4,205	62,000	7
Coal (mt)	55,367	984,453	6

Table 6. Africa's mineral reserves versus world reserves.

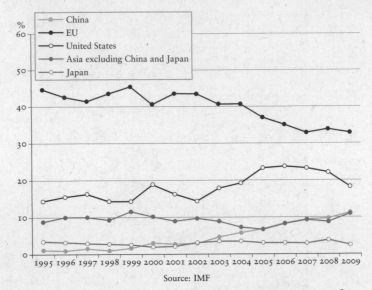

Source: IMF

Figure 53. Distribution of African exports to the major blocs, 1994–2009.

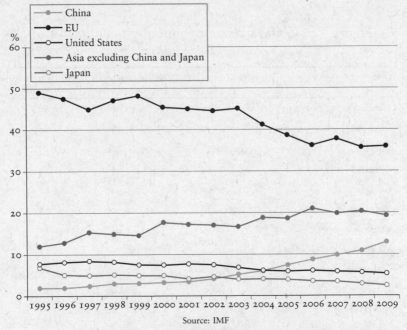

Source: IMF

Figure 54. Distribution of African imports from the major blocs, 1994–2009.

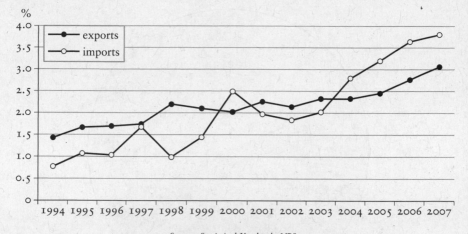

Source: Statistical Yearbook, NBS

Figure 55. Africa's share in total Chinese exports and imports.

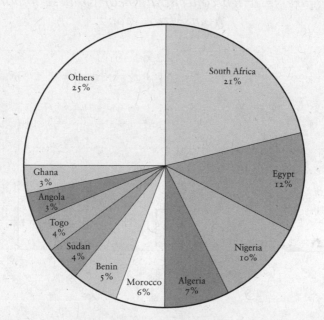

Source: UN COMTRADE, 2008

Figure 56. High concentration of Chinese exports to Africa, 2007.

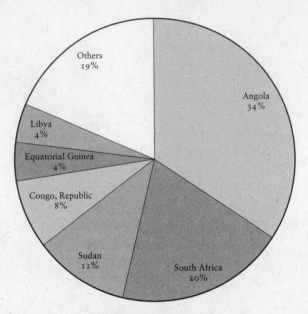

Source: UN COMTRADE, 2008

Figure 57. High concentration of Chinese imports from Africa, 2007.

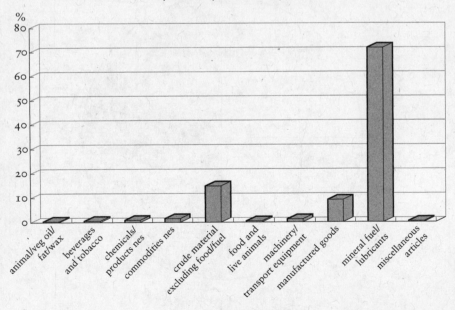

Source: UN COMTRADE, 2008

Figure 58. Africa's exports to China by product, 2007.

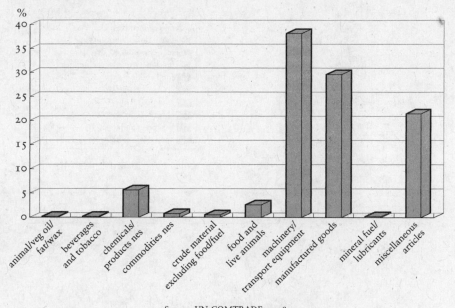

Source: UN COMTRADE, 2008

Figure 59. Africa's imports from China by product, 2007.

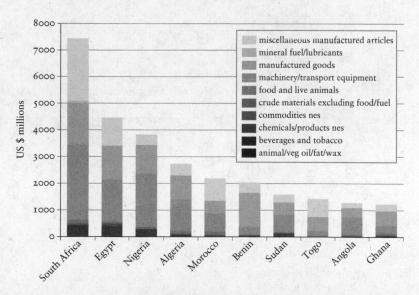

Source: UN COMTRADE, 2008

Figure 60. Key African imports from China, by country and by product, 2007.

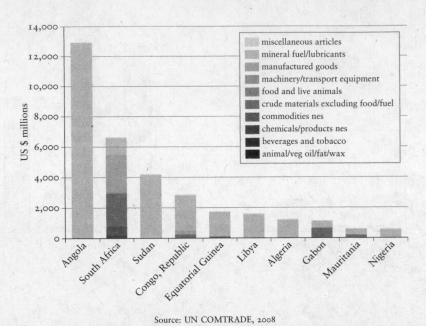

Source: UN COMTRADE, 2008

Figure 61. Key African exports to China, by country and by product, 2007.

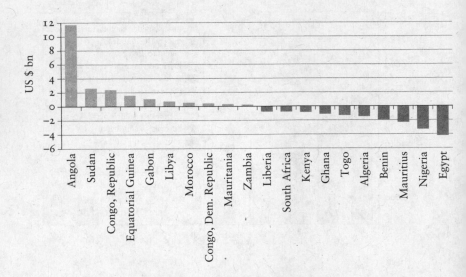

Source: Chinese Commerce Ministry, 2008

Figure 62. Africa–China balance of trade (10 leading surpluses and 10 leading deficits), 2008.

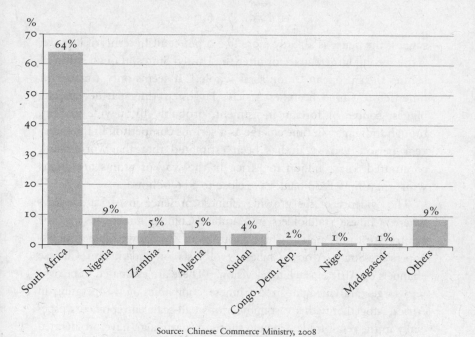

Source: Chinese Commerce Ministry, 2008

Figure 63. Destinations of China's foreign direct investment flows into Africa (2003–2008).

of the world, with, for example, Africa now accounting for a massive 20 per cent of China's total timber imports.[18] In 2008, China's major African trading partners were Angola, South Africa (the continent's largest economy), Sudan, Nigeria and Egypt (in that order). In 2009 China became South Africa's largest trading partner and also its largest export market. China's trade with Africa in 2010 totalled $126.9 billion, roughly on a par with the United States, having closed what was until even very recently a very large gap, though it still lags behind the European Union: notwithstanding this rapid rise, Africa still accounts for less than 3 per cent of total Chinese trade.[19] In the period 2005–10, sub-Saharan Africa accounted for 13.8 per cent of total Chinese outward investment, greater than the United States, Europe and Australia, but less than Asia, Latin and Central America, and the Middle East (including North Africa). It has been estimated that Chinese investment in Africa is responsible for only around 3 per cent of the total stock of foreign investments in Africa, but other estimates suggest the figure is already more like 9 per cent. In terms of flows, it is the second largest investor after the United States, though still well behind the European Union as as whole.[20] It seems only a matter of time before China becomes Africa's largest trading partner and its biggest source of foreign investment, probably by a wide margin, though India may in time emerge as a serious competitor. In the three-year period 2005–7, it has been estimated that the World Bank committed $17.4 billion to Africa in the way of grants and loans while the China Eximbank gave close to $16 billion.[21]

The evidence of the growing Chinese presence in Africa is every-where: Chinese stallholders in Zambia, Chinese lumberjacks in the Central African Republic, Chinese tourists in Zimbabwe, Chinese news-papers in South Africa, Chinese geologists in Sudan, and Chinese channels on African satellite television.[22] There are estimated to be over 900 large- and medium-sized Chinese companies now operating in Africa,[23] together with a vast number of small-scale entrepreneurs, espe-cially in the retail trade. Chinese shops, in particular, have proliferated with great speed, at times causing considerable alarm in the local African population: in Oshikango, Namibia, for example, the first shop was opened in 1999, by 2004 there were twenty-two shops, and by 2006 no less than seventy-five. In the Senegalese capital Dakar an entire city boulevard, a stretch of about a kilometre, is lined with Chinese shops selling imported women's shoes, consumer durables such as glassware, and electronic goods at rock-bottom prices.[24] The rapidly growing num-ber of direct flights between China and Africa are packed with Chinese businessmen, experts and construction workers; in contrast, there are few direct flights between Africa and the US, and the passengers are pri-marily aid workers with a smattering of tourists and businesspeople.[25]

The Chinese population in Africa has increased rapidly. It is esti-mated that it numbered 137,000 in 2001 but by 2007 had grown to over 400,000, compared with around 100,000 Western expatriates, and even this could be a serious underestimate.[26] A more generous estimate, based on Table 7, suggests a Chinese population of over 500,000, but this is excluding Angola, where the figure is estimated at 40,000, and various other countries as well.[27] The Chinese revealed that there were 35,000 nationals in Libya at the time of

Countries	Latest estimates (years in parentheses)	
Algeria	8,000+	(2006)
Benin	4,000	(2007)
Botswana	3,000–10,000	(2006–7)
Burkina Faso	1,000	(2007)
Cameroon	1,000–3,000	(2005)
Cape Verde	600–1,000	(2007)
Congo (Democratic Republic)	500	(2007)
Cote d'Ivoire	10,000	(2007)
Egypt	6,000–10,000	(2007)
Ethiopia	3,000–4,000	(2006)
Ghana	6,000	(2005)
Kenya	5,000	(2007)
Lesotho	5,000	(2005)
Liberia	600	(2006)
Madagascar	60,000	(2003)
Malawi	2,000	(2007)
Mali	2,000	(2007)
Mozambique	1,500	(2006)
Namibia	5,000–40,000	(2006)
Nigeria	100,000	(2007)
Senegal	2,000	(2007)
South Africa	200,000–300,000	(2007)
Sudan	5,000–10,000	(2004–5)
Tanzania	3,000–20,000	(2006)
Togo	3,000	(2007)
Uganda	5,000–10,000	(2007)
Zambia	4,000–6,000	(2007)
Zimbabwe	5,300–10,000	(2005–7)

Table 7. Number of Chinese in selected African countries, 2003–7.

the evacuation in early 2011. The present wave of Chinese migration is very different from earlier phases in the late nineteenth century and in the 1950s and 1960s. Apart from being on a much greater scale, the migrants now originate from all over China, rather than mainly from the south and east, and comprise a multitude of backgrounds, with many seemingly intent on permanent residence; the process, furthermore, is receiving the active encouragement of the Chinese government.[28] The burgeoning Chinese population is matched by a growing number of prosperous middle-class Chinese tourists. Tourism accounts for a substantial part of foreign exchange receipts in some African countries like Kenya and the Gambia, and it is anticipated that there will be 100 million Chinese tourists annually visiting Africa in the near future.[29] An ambitious tourism complex, for example, on Lumley Beach in Freetown, Sierra Leone – not one of the countries where Chinese influence is most pronounced – is in the pipeline, with an artist's impression in the Ministry of Tourism showing pagoda-style apartments and Chinese tourists strolling around a central fountain.[30] A further significant illustration of the expanding Chinese presence in Africa is the growing contingent of Chinese troops involved in UN peacekeeping operations. In April 2002 there were only 110 Chinese personnel worldwide but by April 2006 this had grown to 1,271 (with China rising from 46th to 14th in the international country ranking): revealingly, around 80 per cent of these troops are in Africa, placing it well above countries such as the UK, US, France and Germany.[31] In total, over 3,000 Chinese peace-keeping troops have participated in seven UN missions in Africa.[32] In addition, since 2009 China has played an increasingly important role in the international effort to prevent piracy off the Somali coast in the Gulf of Aden, the first such engagement by the Chinese navy at such a distance from its own shores.

China's impact on Africa has so far been overwhelmingly positive.[33] Indeed, it is worth asking the question as to where Africa would be without Chinese involvement: the continent had attracted little interest from the West since the mid-1970s and what aid it did receive was subject to the highly politicized conditions of the

Washington Consensus. With the West having little to offer and the Soviet Union having disappeared, China stepped into what was in many respects a vacuum. Its positive impact has been felt in various ways. First, it has driven up both demand and prices for those many African countries that are commodity exporters: this was briefly interrupted during the global downturn but has subsequently been resumed. Sub-Saharan Africa's GDP increased by an average of 4.4 per cent in 2001–4, 5–6 per cent in 2005–6, 7 per cent in 2007, falling back to 1.7 per cent in 2009 and then recovering to 4.7 per cent in 2010, compared with 2.6 per cent in 1999–2001,[34] with China clearly the major factor since it has accounted for most of the increase in the global consumption of commodities since 1998.[35] In addition, the growing availability of cheap Chinese manufactured goods has had a beneficial effect for consumers.[36] The losers have been those countries that are not commodity exporters or those producers – as in South Africa, Kenya and Mauritius, for instance – which compete with Chinese manufacturing exports.[37] Chinese textile exports have led to many redundancies in various African nations, notably South Africa, Lesotho, Nigeria and Kenya.[38] Overall, however, there have been a lot more winners than losers. Second, China's arrival as an alternative source of trade, aid and investment has created a competitive environment for African states where they are no longer mainly dependent on Western nations, the IMF and the World Bank. The most dramatic illustration of this has been Angola, which was able to break off negotiations with the IMF in 2007 when China offered it a loan on more favourable terms.[39] China's involvement has thus had the effect of boosting the strategic importance of Africa in the world economy.[40] Third, Chinese assistance tends to come in the form of a package, including important infrastructural projects like roads, railways and major public buildings, as well as the provision of technical expertise.[41] (In contrast, most Western investment in Africa is concentrated in oil and other commodities and lacks the infrastructural dimension.) There is a Chinese saying: 'to end poverty, build a road'. Infrastructure was fundamental to China's economic reform from the late 1970s onwards and its use in the African context should be seen as drawing from the Chinese experience.[42] Fourth, Chinese aid has far fewer strings attached than that of Western nations and institutions. While the IMF and the World Bank have insisted, in accord with their Western-inspired ideological agenda, on the liberalization of foreign trade, privatization and a reduced role for the state, the Chinese stance is far less restrictive and doctrinaire.[43] In addition, the West frequently attaches political conditions concerning democracy and human rights, while the Chinese argue, for their part, that it is wrong to impose political and economic conditionality in exchange for aid and that countries should be free to choose their own direction. This is consonant with the Chinese emphasis on respect for sovereignty, a principle they regard to be inviolable and which is directly related to their own historical experience during the 'century of humiliation'. In April 2006, in an address to the Nigerian National Assembly, Hu Jintao declared: 'China steadfastly supports the wish of the African countries to safeguard their independence and sovereignty and choose their roads of development according to their national conditions.'[44]

The contrasting approach of China and Western nations towards Africa, and developing countries in general, has led to a discussion amongst Africans about a distinctive Chinese model of development, characterized, amongst other things, by large-scale, state-led investments in infrastructure and support services, and aid which is less tied to the donor's economic interests and less overwhelmingly focused on the extraction of minerals as in the case of the West.[45] China's phenomenal growth, together with the huge reduction in poverty there, has also provoked enormous interest in what lessons it might offer for other developing nations.[46] An important characteristic of the Chinese model has been the idea of strong government and the eschewing of the notion of democracy, an approach which has an obvious appeal amongst the more authoritarian African governments. The Chinese academic Zhang Wei-Wei has argued that the Chinese model combines a number of different features. In contrast to the now discredited Washington Consensus, it rejects shock therapy and the big bang in favour of a process of gradual reform based on working through existing institutions. It is predicated upon a strong developmental state capable of steering and leading the process of reform. It involves a process of selective learning and cultural borrowing: China has drawn on foreign ideas, including the neo-liberal American model, as well as many that have been home-grown. And it embraces sequencing and priorities, as evidenced, for example, by a commitment to economic reforms first and political ones later, or the priority given to reforms in the coastal provinces before those in the inland provinces.[47] The idea of an alternative Chinese model of development has sometimes been described as the Beijing Consensus. There are certainly fundamental differences between the Chinese approach and the Washington Consensus, with the Chinese model both markedly less ideological and also highly experimental and pragmatic in approach, in a manner not dissimilar from that of the Asian tigers, with a willingness to adopt that which has worked and abandon that which has not. But the relevance of China's own experience as far as other developing countries are concerned is limited because of its unique characteristics, in particular its sheer size (which only India can replicate) and the highly specific nature of the Chinese state (which no country can replicate). It is interesting, in this context, that the Chinese have refrained from endorsing the idea of a Chinese model, nor have they shown much interest in the debate about the subject.[48]

It is still far too early to make any considered judgement about the likely long-term merits and demerits of China's relationship with Africa.[49] The experience has been brief and the literature remains thin. The most obvious danger for Africa lies in the fundamental inequality that exists at the heart of their relationship: China's economy is far bigger and more advanced, the largest African economy being that of South Africa, which is diminutive in comparison, while the population of Africa as a whole is less than that of China. The economic disparity between Africa and China, furthermore, seems destined to grow apace. Whatever the differences in approach between the Western powers and China, it seems likely that many of the problems in the relationship between the West and Africa, emanating from the fundamental structural inequality between them, could be reproduced, in some degree, in China's relationship with Africa.[50] The danger facing African countries is that they get locked into becoming mainly suppliers of primary commodities, unable for a variety of reasons – including unfavourable terms of trade and Chinese competition, together with domestic corruption and a lack of strategic will – to move beyond this and broaden their economic development through industrialization.

At a conference in Beijing in 2005, Moeletsi Mbeki, deputy chairman of the South African Institute of International Affairs, spelt out these fears:

> Africa sells raw materials to China and China sells manufactured products to Africa. This is a dangerous equation that reproduces Africa's old relationship with colonial powers.[51] The equation is not sustainable for a number of reasons. First, Africa needs to preserve its natural resources to use in the future for its own industrialization. Secondly, China's export strategy is contributing to the deindustrialization of some middle-income countries . . . it is in the interests of both Africa and China to find solutions to these strategies.[52]

Perhaps the country that most exemplifies this inequality is Zimbabwe, where the Chinese enjoy a significant presence in the economy, controlling areas like the railways, electricity supply, Air Zimbabwe and the Zimbabwe Broadcasting Corporation.[53] The fact that China has a carefully worked-out and comprehensive strategic approach to its relationship with Africa that is still unfolding, while the African response, in contrast, is fragmented between the many different nations, poorly informed about China, and based on an essentially pragmatic rather than strategic view, serves only to exacerbate this inequality.[54] The danger is that African nations enter into agreements with China over the exploitation of their natural resources which are too favourable to China, or use the revenues gained in a short-term fashion, perhaps corruptly, to benefit various interest groups, or possibly both. On the other side of the argument, rather than allowing China to acquire ownership of natural resources, the norm has been for African governments to grant concessions and service contracts. Moreover, Angola, to quote one example, has proved a very smart and effective negotiator with the Chinese.[55]

China's presence has been hugely welcomed across the continent, generating much enthusiasm, with favourable voices far
outnumbering critical ones.[56] Yoweri Museveni, the Ugandan president, complains that 'The Western ruling groups are conceited, full
of themselves, ignorant of our conditions'; the Chinese, he believes,
are much more 'business-like'. Senegal's president, Abdoulaye
Wade, has said that 'China's approach to our needs is simply better
adapted than the slow and sometimes patronising post-colonial
approach of European investors.'[57] Nonetheless, there has also been
unease and concern. This was most manifest in the 2006 presidential election in Zambia when the opposition candidate Michael Sata
propounded a strongly anti-Chinese line, declaring that 'Zambia is
becoming a province – no, a district – of China', and gained 29 per
cent of the vote, prompting the Chinese ambassador to hint that
China might withdraw its investments in the event of his winning
(though it should also be noted that Sata had promised to recognize
Taiwan if he won).[58] In the subsequent 2009 election, which he lost
by a margin of only 2 per cent, Sata adopted a more emollient attitude towards China, though still very critical of the treatment of
local workers by Chinese mining firms. When Sata finally won the
2011 election, he adopted a very statesmanlike attitude, specifically
welcoming foreign investment: and his first official guest was no
less than the Chinese ambassador. There have been many such accusations of labour abuses by Chinese employers, not only in Zambia
but in numerous other countries. One of the difficulties is that while
the initial Chinese investors were large state-owned companies,
subsequent Chinese migrants have tended to be small-scale or solo
operators, bringing with them the expectations and norms of their
own country, including poor levels of regulation. One of the strongest and most persistent criticisms is that Chinese companies prefer
to employ Chinese rather than local workers, with the proportion
of Chinese workers sometimes reaching as high as 70 per cent.[59] In
a World Bank survey in 2005, albeit based on a rather small sample,
Chinese companies employed around 20 per cent Chinese and 80
per cent African employees.[60] There is some evidence to suggest that

Chinese companies, mindful of these criticisms, have sought to increase the proportion of African workers. There are also frequent complaints that Chinese managers display negative attitudes towards local people.[61] Both of these points, of course, touch directly upon the question of Chinese attitudes towards those of darker skin, and especially Africans, which I discussed in Chapter 8. The evidence is still too sparse to draw any proper conclusions as yet, though the problem is unsurprising. A survey of Chinese attitudes based on a range of online sources revealed many stereotypical views about Africans, including the perception that they were 'lazy and inefficient at their workplaces', in contrast to the industry of Chinese workers, and that African men were highly sexually charged and behaved in a sexually rampant and aggressive manner.[62]

There is a widely held view, especially in the West, that China's refusal to require any conditionality in terms of governance means that it is prone to turn a blind eye to human rights abuses, such as those in Darfur.[63] That has certainly been the case, but the Chinese have recently shown growing sensitivity towards Western criticism, as well as that from within the continent itself, and as a result helped to pressure the Sudanese government into accepting the presence of a joint United Nations/African Union peacekeeping force in Darfur.[64] With the division of Sudan following the referendum, the Chinese are now faced with the challenge of establishing a good relationship with the government in the south of the country, where 80 per cent of the oil is located.[65] Notwithstanding these various criticisms, there is no evidence to suggest that China's record in Africa is any worse than the West's: on the contrary, the latter's miserable catalogue of support for corrupt and dictatorial regimes on the continent, from President Mobutu in Zaire to Idi Amin in Uganda, not to mention Europe's colonial record, which left the continent grossly ill-equipped to deal with the challenges of the post-colonial era, deprives it of much legitimacy when it comes to its criticisms of China.[66] Finally, in a rather different vein, the Chinese have become the target of terrorist groups, for example in the Niger Delta and Ethiopia, a phenomenon which is surely set to grow as the Chinese presence and influence expands and they assume the role, visibility and responsibilities of a global power not only in Africa but elsewhere too.[67]

The significance of China's African mission is enormous. Its rapidly growing influence suggests that in due course it will probably become the dominant player on the continent, and serves as a bold statement of China's wider global intentions. The speed of China's involvement in Africa, and its success in wooing the African elites, has put the West on the defensive in a continent where it has a poor historical record.[68] Unlike the 'scramble for Africa' in the late nineteenth century, which generated bitter intra-European rivalry, China's involvement has not as yet produced significant tensions with the US, Britain or France, though that could change. The establishment of the United States Africa Command (Africom) in late 2008 to coordinate its military relations and activities on the continent suggests that it is concerned about China's growing influence; it has failed, however, to find, amongst a total of 54 African states, a single one, with the exception of civil war-torn Liberia, that was willing to host its headquarters, with the rather bizarre consequence that the US's African Command is presently based in Stuttgart, Germany.[69] Apart from the rather more attractive terms that China offers African countries, one of the reasons for its remarkable progress on the continent is that it does not carry the same kind of historical baggage as the West, a fact which it regularly stresses. So, for example, China, understandably, emphasizes the fact that Zheng He's voyages to East Africa in the early fifteenth century sought no territory and took no slaves, in contrast to the Europeans. More importantly, during the Maoist period China was, in contrast to the West, a staunch supporter of the African independence movements. Thus China, with its own experience of colonization, its anti-colonial record and its status as a developing country, has more legitimacy and enjoys a greater affinity with the African nations than does the West.[70] This is reflected in the fact that in the 2007 Pew Global Attitudes Survey, for example, respondents in ten African countries expressed far more favourable attitudes towards China than they did towards the United States.

It is premature to draw any sweeping or categoric conclusions about China's involvement in Africa. Although it repeats elements of the West's relationship with the continent, it is offering a much broader package of opportunity the nature of which is still unfolding. The economic zones that Chinese firms are building in Nigeria and elsewhere – which are based on China's experience in the early stages of their reform period and were first announced in 2006 – are designed to encourage Chinese investment in African manufacturing while also seeking to persuade China's older industries to move to Africa. A recent Chinese government survey of 1,600 companies shows the growing use of Africa as an industrial base: in fact, manufacturing's share of total Chinese investment is now 22 per cent, which is not far behind mining's share of 29 per cent. Some African countries, furthermore, have made Chinese industrial investments a precondition for resource deals: in Ethiopia, two out of three Chinese firms are now in manufacturing.[71] There has also been talk of a Chinese Marshall Plan, with a fund of $500 billion drawn from the country's vast currency reserves, that would lend money to Africa and other developing countries. Whether such a scheme will materialize remains unclear, but it illustrates the kind of open-ended and dynamic thinking that characterizes the Chinese approach, the objective being the fostering of a new cycle of trade and development between China and Africa, including the expansion of low-end manufacturing in Africa.[72] One of the problems of much Western commentary on China's relationship with Africa has been the temptation to describe it in terms of a new colonialism. Given that China has no history of colonialism (the only arguable exception being the Qing dynasty's western expansion from the seventeenth century), this deserves the label of a lazy, Western-centric stereotype. Far more relevant would be to ask whether the experience of the tributary system – the approach pursued by China in East Asia – might offer us some insight into its evolving relationship with Africa.

THE MIDDLE EAST AND IRAN

Nearly two-thirds of the world's proven oil reserves are concentrated in the Arabian Gulf, with Saudi Arabia controlling over a quarter, and

Iraq and Kuwait sharing a little under a quarter. These three countries possess about half of the world's known oil reserves. Another potentially large producer in the region, Iran, accounts for a little under a tenth of world oil reserves. The Gulf States are responsible for nearly 40 per cent of world crude oil exports, with Saudi Arabia's share around 12 per cent and Iran's 7 per cent. China became a net importer of oil products in 1993 and of crude oil in 1996.[73] It now imports around half of its crude oil and it is estimated that by 2035 China will have to import over 70 per cent; it is already the second largest importer of crude oil after the United States.[74] China first became seriously concerned about its future oil supplies during the 1990s and as a result began to take steps to extend the number of supplying countries, while seeking to ensure the reliability of those supplies. In 2009, its largest supplier of crude oil was Saudi Arabia (0.839 million barrels a day), followed by Angola (0.644), Iran (0.463) and the Sudan (0.244), with around half its supply coming from the Middle East and one-third from Africa. It is therefore natural for China to seek a much closer relationship with the Middle East. Unlike Africa, however, the region is regarded by the Americans as very much their sphere of influence. The US has become increasingly embroiled there over the last thirty years, building extremely close relations with Israel and Saudi Arabia in particular, and becoming involved in two Gulf Wars with Iraq, the second largest oil producer, the invasion in 2003 culminating in the country's occupation. The Chinese, as a consequence, have trodden very warily in the region for fear of antagonizing the United States, whose relationship, ever since the reform period began, it has prioritized over all others. In contrast to Africa, which has clearly now assumed a central importance in its foreign policy, China regards the Middle East, as a result, as of only second-tier significance.[75] Nonetheless, it is interesting to note that in late 2009 China became a larger importer of Saudi oil than the United States while over ninety Chinese companies were active in the kingdom, employing around 20,000 Chinese workers, with the China Railway Construction Corporation, as part of a China–Saudi consortium, winning a contract to build a high-speed rail line between Mecca and Medina.

Over the last few years China has employed various strategies to try to secure its oil supplies from the region. It has sought to negotiate long-term energy supply arrangements, most notably a 'strategic oil partnership' with the Saudis in 1999;[76] Chinese oil companies have tried to gain rights to invest and develop oilfields in the region, including Iraq; and, finally, China has encouraged companies in the Gulf to invest in Chinese refineries in order to try to promote closer links, with the Saudis in particular being major such investors.[77]

At the heart of China's strategy in the Middle East lies Iran, with which it has long enjoyed a close relationship. The two countries have much in common. They are both very old civilizations with rich histories of achievement and a strong sense of superiority towards other states in their respective regions. They have also both suffered at the hands of the West, which they deeply resent, believing they would prosper rather more in a world no longer dominated by it. Although interests rather than attitudes have primarily driven their relationship, there is a certain sense of affinity between the two countries.[78] As an emergent global power, China has frequently sought to develop friendly relations with the more powerful states in their respective regions – Brazil and South Africa being notable examples – as this in turn is likely to enhance its own influence,[79] with Iran very much falling into this same category. China nevertheless has acted cautiously in its relationship with Iran, concerned to preserve its international reputation in the face of the militant Islamic ideology of the Iranian regime post-1979. The single most important constraining factor in China's stance towards Iran has been the attitude of the United States. China has walked a skilful diplomatic tightrope, at times cooperating with Iran in ways contrary to US policy and at other times cooperating with the United States in ways contrary to Iranian policy. Until 2010 it managed to thwart American attempts to impose economic sanctions on Iran and it successfully resisted efforts to excommunicate Iran after it had been branded as a member of 'an axis of evil' by the Bush administration.[80] China's economic relationship with Iran began to grow after the departure of the US and UK following the 1979 Revolution. The key to their blossoming partnership has been China's export of large quantities of high-tech capital goods, engineering services and arms to Iran in exchange for oil and raw materials, with trade between the two countries growing extremely rapidly during the 1990s and tenfold over the last decade.[81] In 2003 two Chinese motor vehicle manufacturers established production plants in Iran. China negotiated a major package of oil deals in 2004, as a result of which it became a key stakeholder and one of the largest foreign investors in the Iranian oil industry, in addition to Iran being one of its biggest suppliers of oil.[82] And it signed a major agreement in 2007 to develop part of the giant Yadavaran oilfield and, more recently, to develop the North Azadegan field.[83]

The future of China's relationship with Iran is open-ended. China remains constrained by the need to maintain good relations with the United States, and nowhere are American sensitivities greater than in the Middle East. The US regards Iran as an alternative power broker in the region and a major potential threat to its interests – hence its long-running hostility towards Iran. In the long run, China would probably be content to see Iran playing a major, perhaps even dominant, role in the Gulf region, given that it will be a long time, if ever, before China itself could perform such a role; every global power needs allies and Iran is China's natural ally in the Middle East. As the international relations expert John Garver argues, a dominant China in East Asia combined with a dominant Iran in West Asia could ultimately become 'a central element of a post-unipolar, China-centred Asia in the middle of the twenty-first century'.[84] It is conceivable that China is thinking in these terms with regard to a future possible multipolar system.[85] Meanwhile, in order to keep its options open, China is likely to continue to help build up Iran while seeking not to antagonize the United States. As the US seeks to ratchet up economic sanctions against Iran over the nuclear issue, it will be interesting to see whether or not China will go along with the attempted oil boycott.

There are other possible long-term scenarios. China's highest priority is Taiwan, and the biggest obstacle in the way of reunification is American military support for the island. The most likely cause of military conflict between China and the US remains Taiwan, though this is far less likely than at any time since 1949; in the event of war, China would be extremely anxious about the security of its maritime oil supply routes, especially in the Malacca Strait and the South China Sea, which could easily be severed by the US's superior air and naval power. In such an eventuality, Iran could at some point offer the possibility of a land-based supply route from West to East Asia. But there is another possible future scenario, namely that China and the US could arrive at some kind of trade-off involving Taiwan and Iran in which the US agrees to stop sending weapons to Taiwan and China volunteers to do the same with Iran. In effect, China would agree to sacrifice Iran in return for Taiwan, its greater foreign policy priority. Such a deal would represent a tacit recognition that East Asia was China's sphere of influence and the Middle East, America's.[86]

RUSSIA

During the 1980s, after two decades of bitter antagonism, China's relations with the Soviet Union began to improve. It was the collapse of the Soviet Union in the early nineties, however, that was to provide the conditions for a complete transformation in the relationship between the two countries. Russia became a pale shadow of its former Soviet self, with only half of its former GDP and less than half of its previous population, though still with around 80 per cent of its old territory.[87] Meanwhile, China embarked on its reform programme and enjoyed non-stop double-digit growth. Together, these two developments represented a huge shift in the balance of power between the two countries, with China now in a far more powerful position than its erstwhile rival. During the nineties the two countries finally agreed, after centuries of dispute, on a common border, which, at 2,700 miles, is the longest in the world. From being a highly militarized region, the border became a centre of trade and exchange. The resolution of the frontier issue enabled Russia and China to withdraw large numbers of troops from either side of the border, Russia to Chechnya and (in response to NATO's expansion) its Europe-facing territory, and China to the Taiwan Strait.[88] In the steadily improving atmosphere between the two, they established, along with several newly independent Central Asian nations, the Shanghai Cooperation Organization, for the purpose of promoting collaboration and improving security in the region. A shared, over-arching Sino-Russian concern about the overweening power of the United States in the post-Cold War world, with Russia feeling par-ticularly vulnerable following the collapse of the Soviet Union and China relatively isolated after Tiananmen Square, was a major factor in the signing of a strategic partnership agreement between the two countries in 1998.[89] China and Russia are also now part of the BRIC grouping, along with India, Brazil and latterly South Africa, which, from being no more than an economic category in a Goldman Sachs report, has since acquired a life and institutional form of its own, with annual summits of the leaders being held every year since 2009. It should also be noted that trade between China and Russia has been increasing rapidly, with a fivefold rise between 2000 and 2007.

There must, nonetheless, be serious doubts as to the strategic potential of their relationship. The underlying problem is Russia's sense of weakness, on the one hand, and China's growing strength, on the other. Although the rapprochement had much to do with Russia's sense of vulnerability following the collapse of the Soviet Union and its desire to make peace with its neighbours, that frailty also left it feeling insecure and suspicious of China. The most obvi-ous expression of this anxiety is to be found in the Russian Far East, where a population of a mere 7.5 million confronts a popula-tion of 112 million in the three provinces of China's north-east. Now that the border has been made porous, numerous Chinese have crossed into Russia to seek work and ply their trade. In 1994 Russian estimates put the number of Chinese residents in Russia's Far East at 1 million, compared with a Chinese estimate of less than 2,000. According to some demographic projections, Chinese could be the second largest minority ethnic group in the Russian Federa-tion by 2051. Exacerbating these fears is the demographic crisis facing Russia since the collapse of the Soviet Union, with its popu-lation falling from a peak of almost 149 million in 1991 to 142 million in 2010: one estimate has suggested that its population will fall to 111 million by 2050, though such projections are often wide of the mark.[90] The Russian fear of being overrun by Chinese immigration speaks both of old prejudices and new fears. The size of the Chinese population tends to arouse these anxieties elsewhere, but they are compounded in Russia's case by a long history of prejudice and conflict, the huge demographic imbalance between the two countries, and their long border.

The fact that Russia is rich in oil, gas and many other commodities – as well as being its major supplier of weapons – clearly makes it a very attractive partner for China. But Russia has proved a difficult collaborator, loath to meet its needs, certainly on the terms desired by China. In a long-running saga over the route of a new Russian east–west oil pipeline, with Russia reluctant to concede that it should go to China, as proposed by the Chinese, an agreement was finally reached in February 2009 that there would be a branch to China, in return for Chinese loans to Russian firms.[91] The Russians are wary of becoming trapped in a relationship with China where they are reduced to being the provider of raw materials for their economic powerhouse neighbour.[92] Since the turn of the century, indeed, the Russians have become increasingly protective of their oil and natural gas interests, aware that, in its weakened state, these are hugely their country's most valuable assets, especially in a global market where prices are moving steadily in their favour. Having rolled back American, European and Japanese stakes in its oil industry, Russia is hardly likely to grant Chinese oil companies a similar interest in the future. Moreover, having embraced resource nationalism under Vladimir Putin, Russia is now driving very hard bargains over its oil and gas with both Europe and its former territories. The Russian suspicion of Chinese intentions extends to the Central Asian nations that previously formed part of the Soviet Union. Russian sources, it has been reported, revealed in August 2005 that one reason for Moscow's haste in seeking to enter the former American base at Karshi Khanabad in Uzbekistan was that the Chinese had made discreet expressions of interest in acquiring it themselves.[93] China has found itself confronted with many obstacles in its desire to acquire oil and gas interests in Central Asia, with Russian resistance one of the most important. The exception hitherto has been Kazakhstan, where China has its only major oil stake in the region and from where the third leg of a major pipeline to China will finally be completed in 2011.[94] Recently, however, China has shown growing interest in Central Asia, with Turkmenistan agreeing to commit half of its vast newly discovered gas reserves to China through a new 4,350-mile pipeline that crosses Uzbekistan and Kazakhstan. It seems that Chinese influence in Central Asia is destined to grow rapidly.[95]

None of this is to suggest that the relationship between China and Russia is likely to deteriorate, though that is not inconceivable should Russian fears about the rise of China become acute, perhaps even persuading Russia, *in extremis*, to turn westwards and seek some kind of solace with the European Union or NATO. It does, however, indicate that serious tensions arising from the major imbalance of power between them are likely to constrain the potential for the relationship becoming much more than an arrangement for maintaining their bilateral relations in good order, which, given their troubled history, would in itself be no mean achievement.[96] In addition, for the time being at least, a strong mutual concern about US power is likely to bind the two countries together, as it has already, in a limited but significant way, on issues like Iraq and Iran. Russia's intervention in Georgia and subsequent recognition of South Ossetia and Abkhazia as independent states in 2008, however, were not well received in Beijing: it was another reminder that relations between the two powers are far from simple.[97]

INDIA AND SOUTH ASIA

China and India have much in common. Both are hugely populous countries, demographic superpowers, which are in the process of dramatic economic transformation. Between them they account for almost 40 per cent of the world's population. Both are continental giants, China a dominating presence in East Asia and India, at least in terms of land mass and population, in South Asia. By the mid twenty-first century, they will both be major global powers, certainly China and, in all likelihood, India too. They are in the process of redrawing the shape of the world, tilting it massively towards Asia while at the same time projecting a new kind of nation-state of continental proportions in terms of both territory and population, a very different kind of global order from when the world was dominated by a handful of small- and medium-sized European nation-states. They also share a long history of colonization by Western powers: Britain in the case of India, a miscellany (plus Japan) in the case of China. And as developing countries, they have many interests in common, as illustrated by their close collaboration in the Doha round of trade talks, climate change negotiations, most notably at Copenhagen, and in the BRIC grouping. Furthermore, China's economic growth clearly offers India a rich treasure trove of lessons and experiences. It is hardly surprising, then, that China and India are frequently bracketed together. Despite these similarities, however, in many respects the differences between them could hardly be greater, as symbolized by their long border running through the Himalayas, the greatest natural land barrier in the world, which serves to mark out what can only be described as a political and cultural chasm between the two countries. China has the longest continuous history of any country while India is a much more recent creation, only acquiring something like its present territory, or at least two-thirds of it, during the latter period of the British Raj.[98] Chinese civilization is defined by its relationship to the state whereas India's is inseparable from its caste society. India is the world's largest democracy while in China democracy remains a largely alien concept. China has a powerful sense of unity and a relatively singular identity, in contrast to India, which is blessed with a remarkable pluralism embracing many different races, languages and religions. These historical and cultural differences have served to create a sense of otherness and distance and an underlying lack of understanding. It is true that India gave China Buddhism, and that there were many other intellectual exchanges between the two countries during the first millennium and beyond, but these are now largely forgotten.[99]

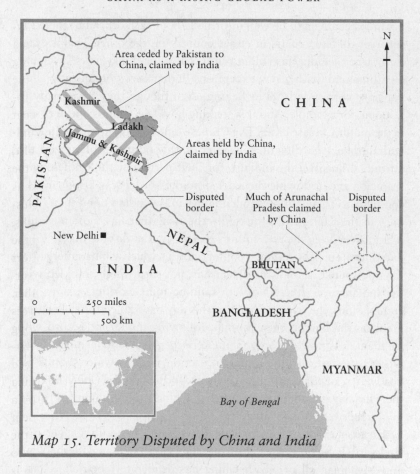

Map 15. *Territory Disputed by China and India*

For over fifty years relations between the two countries have been at best distant and suspicious, at worst antagonistic, even conflictual. After 1988 they took a turn somewhat for the better, following Rajiv Gandhi's visit to Beijing, the first by an Indian prime minister since Nehru's in 1954, but nonetheless there has still remained an underlying antipathy. The reason is partly this troubled history over the last half-century, but more fundamentally the underlying differences between the two societies and cultures, which finds reflection in the extraordinarily little contact or dialogue between them at any level. Given their geographical proximity and the sheer size of the two countries, one might expect them to be well informed about each other, but there are surprisingly few experts in either country on the other. This is especially true of India: few Indian universities or think-tanks specialize on China and, with a few exceptions, Indian news organizations do not have correspondents in Beijing, even though they have many in London, for example. And it is striking how few Indians one ever sees in the major Chinese cities. The Chinese tend to look upon the Indians with disdain, regarding them as inferior, chaotic and disorganized, the attitude dismissive; the Indians, for their part, view the Chinese with suspicion and, following their defeat in the border war, also fear. As a consequence, China looms much larger in the Indian mind than India does in the Chinese. Undoubtedly the issue that has most poisoned relations between the two countries is the border dispute that in 1962 flared into outright military conflict and in which China emerged as the undisputed victor. This defeat has, not surprisingly, rankled with the Indians ever since. Notwithstanding joint working groups and commissions, the two countries to this day have failed to reach agreement on the border, even though, following the recent accord with Vietnam, it is now the only Chinese border that remains unresolved. Other issues are also the source of friction, notably water supply: the headwaters of various Indian rivers are located on the Chinese side of the Himalayas and India fears that China's dam-building projects might deprive it of its water.[100]

Far from exercising unchallenged hegemony in South Asia, its own backyard, India finds itself confronted by Pakistan, Bangladesh, Nepal and Myanmar, all of which China has deliberately befriended as a means of balancing against India, with these countries embracing China as a way of offsetting India's overwhelmingly dominant position, and its frequently high-handed attitude, in South Asia. China has good relations with the Maoist government in Nepal; it has fostered a close relationship with Myanmar and also with Bangladesh, with economic assistance being a major factor in both cases. It has even invested $700 million in a special economic zone in Mauritius in the Indian Ocean. In the recent past, China has also made serious headway in its relationship with Sri Lanka, with China's military ordnance playing a key role in the final stages of the civil war; in contrast, India, sympathizing with the plight of the Tamils, found itself in a much more ambivalent position. Beijing has recently increased its aid to Sri Lanka fivefold and is supplying sophisticated weapons.[101] In fact, the only country in South Asia that has remained out of China's reach hitherto is the tiny Himalayan kingdom of Bhutan, an Indian protectorate. Of all China's various relationships in South Asia, however, by far the most important is that with India's bitter foe, Pakistan, which, thanks largely to China, enjoys a nuclear capability. The close political, economic and military relationship between Pakistan and China is now long established, dating back to the mid 1960s, and seems likely to endure for many years to come. Indeed, with rising tensions between the United States and Pakistan, it is possible that the latter's relationship with China could grow even closer. In December 2010, just after his visit to India, Chinese premier Wen Jiabao went to Pakistan and unveiled $35 billion in economic deals designed to deepen their alliance and tie Pakistan more closely to China's economic transformation. The various agreements were worth over twice those signed during Wen's visit to India, which amounted to $16 billion.[102] China, meanwhile, has been asked by Pakistan to build a naval base at its south-western port of Gwadar, near the Strait of Hormuz, which it expects the Chinese navy could use for the repair and maintenance of its fleet. This would give China access to the Arabian Sea and enable it to protect the growing number of Chinese tankers in the Gulf region.[103] The Chinese, however, have not so far reacted positively to this proposal. There is also speculation that the Chinese are seeking to transform the small fishing harbour of Sittwe in Myanmar into a major port, and they are presently doing the same with Hambantota in Sri Lanka. In theory at least, these ports could give China major access to various trade routes on which it is heavily dependent, provide significant listening posts and offer facilities for its shipping fleet and possibly navy.[104]

China's shrewd diplomacy has meant that India has constantly been on the back foot in South Asia, unable to assert itself in the manner which its size would suggest. Much of this has been down to the failure of India to find a modus vivendi with its neighbours that succeeds in reassuring them rather than arousing deep-seated fears about

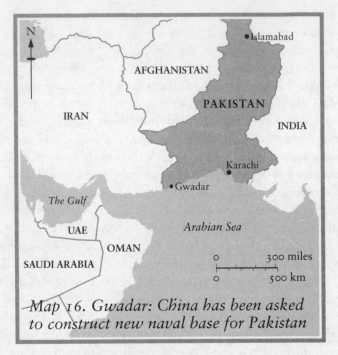

Map 16. Gwadar: China has been asked to construct new naval base for Pakistan

Sources: National Bureau of Statistics

its behaviour and intentions. In this context, it is instructive that the South Asian regional grouping established in 1985 – the South Asian Association for Regional Cooperation (SAARC), consisting of India, Pakistan, Bangladesh, Bhutan, the Maldives, Nepal, Sri Lanka and latterly Afghanistan and Myanmar – remains little more than a nominal entity, in stark contrast to ASEAN in East Asia. Furthermore, not only has India singularly failed to establish its hegemony over South Asia, it has not even tried to develop any serious influence in East Asia, notwithstanding the large Indian diaspora in South-East Asia, with which it has not succeeded in establishing any meaningful kind of relationship.[105]

In geo-political terms, there are two possible scenarios. First, China could accept that South Asia is, in effect, India's rightful sphere of influence. In practice, this seems very unlikely. Chinese influence in the region is too extensive and too well established for it to be rolled back or for China to concede that this should happen. It is an outcome which both China and its formal and informal allies in the region would resist. Indeed, as we have seen, China is continuing to extend and consolidate its bilateral relationships in South Asia. Furthermore, given that China's growth rate still exceeds that of India, albeit only narrowly, it is probably less likely than at any time in the last half-century. The second possible scenario is one in which India accepts that China's presence in South Asia is permanent and resolves to accommodate itself to this reality by, for example, conceding that an Indian–Chinese partnership is necessary for handling security problems in the region. This could even mean, at its extreme, that India acquiesces in China's pre-eminence in South Asia as well as in East Asia.[106] In this context, a major Chinese objective is to prevent the creation of any barriers which might impede the long-term growth of its presence, role and influence in Asia; other examples of this are its resistance to the widening of the US–Japan alliance and its refusal to accept any multilateral approaches or solutions to the sovereignty of the disputed islands in the South China Sea.[107] The latter scenario – Indian acceptance of China's role in South Asia – would be consonant with this objective. In reality, of course, India has been obliged over many years to adapt – de facto at least – to the growing power of China in South Asia, so large elements of this scenario already exist, at least in tacit form.[108]

China's rapid economic growth has underpinned its growing strength in South Asia. In 1950 the per capita income of India was around 40 per cent greater than that of China; by 1978 they were roughly on a par. By 1999, China's was not far short of twice that of India's and by 2009 it was over three and a half times as great.[109] Furthermore, although India's growth rate has steadily risen in recent years, it still remains slightly below that of China: in other words, China is continuing to extend its economic lead over India. Although India enjoys some economic advantages over China, notably its prowess in software, the software industry only accounts for a very small proportion of its labour force. With the two giants growing so rapidly, it is not surprising that their economic relationship has become increasingly important and a source of some hope for the future. When

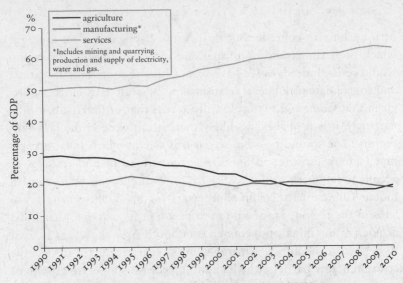

Sources: Central Statistical Organization, India, and CEIC.
Annual data fiscal year beginning in April (data through 2010)

Figure 64. Changing composition of India's GDP.

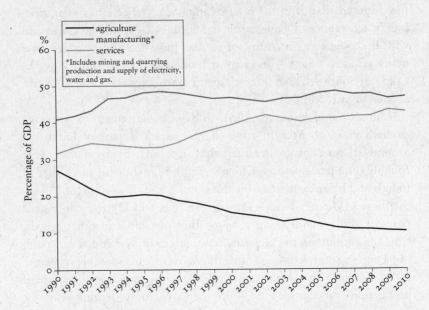

Sources: China National Bureau of Statistics and CEIC

Figure 65. Changing composition of China's GDP.

446

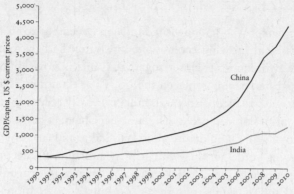

Source: International Monetary Fund (data through 2010)

Figure 66. GDP per capita for China and India.

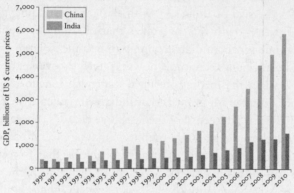

Source: International Monetary Fund (data through 2010)

Figure 67. GDP for China and India.

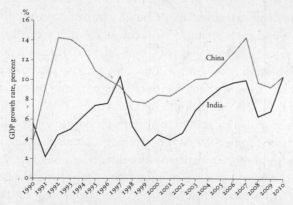

Source: International Monetary Fund (data through 2010)

Figure 68. GDP growth rate for China and India.

Chinese premier Wen Jiabao visited India in December 2010, the mood music was that growing economic cooperation had the potential to bring the two countries closer together. China is now India's largest trading partner, having replaced the US. Their economic relationship, however, remains highly unequal: India is heavily reliant on exporting large quantities of iron ore to China, while China, in contrast, exports a huge volume of manufactured goods to India, and enjoys a very large and growing trade surplus with it.[110] Manufacturing accounted for only 16 per cent of India's GDP in 2009 compared with around 43 per cent of China's, while two-thirds of India's population was still employed in agriculture in 2009 compared with less than half in China.[111] By 2009, according to IMF figures, China's economy was four times the size of India's,[112] with the gap continuing to extend. Even if India's growth rate overtakes that of China, it would take a very long time for the Indian economy to become as large as the Chinese. In short, China's economic power is likely to overshadow that of India at least in the medium term, if not much longer. Moreover, it should not be taken for granted that India will replicate the extraordinary Chinese growth record of the last three decades. There has been a tendency, in the understandable euphoria that has accompanied India's recent growth, to downplay the huge problems that it confronts: a guerrilla war in twenty states covering 40 per cent of the country's land mass, huge inequality (it has been estimated that about fifty billionaires accounted for 20 per cent of India's GDP and 80 per cent of its market capitalization in 2009, which is why it is increasingly compared with Russia rather than China), rampant corruption, and an ineffective and corrupt state.[113] All this makes the second scenario – India being obliged to live with and adapt to China's power and presence in South Asia – rather more likely. It also increases the probability that China will emerge over time not only as the dominant power in East Asia but in South Asia as well.

India naturally resents China's dominant position in its own region and is anxious to find ways of containing China's growing influence. Although the Indian premier Manmohan Singh has always emphasized that India enjoys good relations with China, over the last decade it has moved steadily closer to the United States. During the second term of the Clinton administration, the United States established a strategic partnership with India which was extended in 2006 by the Bush administration to include nuclear cooperation, an agreement which was eventually approved by the Indian parliament in 2008.[114] The agreement violated previous American policy by accepting India's status as a nuclear power, even though it was not a signatory to the Non-Proliferation Treaty. This was a pointed reminder that US policy on nuclear proliferation is a matter of interest and convenience rather than principle, as the contrasting cases of Iran and Israel in the Middle East also illustrate. The reason for the American volte-face was geo-political, the desire to promote India as a global power and establish a new US–India axis in South Asia as a counter to the rise of China.[115] During the Cold War relations between India and the US were distant and distrustful, and even after 1989 they improved little, with the US pursuing an even-handed approach to India and Pakistan and imposing sanctions on India after its nuclear tests in 1998. It is testimony to the growing American concern about China that the US was persuaded to engage in such a U-turn. For its part, India's position had previously been characterized by its relative isolation: although it had close ties with the former Soviet Union, its determinedly non-aligned status had led it to resist forming strategic partnerships with the major powers or even second-tier ones.[116] But there has been growing unease amongst sections of the Indian establishment, especially the military, about China's growing power.[117] The relationship with the United States offers India the possibility of acquiring enhanced global stature as well as a potential means of containing China's growing influence in South Asia. As if to confirm the former, in November 2010, President Obama finally lent American support to India's desire for a permanent seat on the UN Security Council, which China has hitherto refused to do. In recent years India has also drawn closer to Japan and Australia, both close American allies, as well as, to a lesser extent, Vietnam. Nor should it be forgotten that India and the US conduct joint annual naval exercises. Depending on how the US–India partnership evolves, it could very significantly change the balance of power between China and India in South Asia, persuading China to act more cautiously while at the same time emboldening India.[118] The US–India partnership raises many questions and introduces numerous uncertainties. If it proves effective and durable, then it could act as a significant regional and global counter to China. How China will respond remains to be seen: the most obvious move might be a closer relationship with Pakistan, but it is not inconceivable that China might decide to seek a strategic rapprochement with India as a means of fending off the United States and denying it a major presence in South Asia. Given India's long tradition of an independent foreign policy, together with its global ambitions, it would not easily embrace the idea of playing permanent second fiddle to the United States; a complex triangular relationship, as a result, is a quite plausible scenario.[119]

EUROPE

While the American and European economies are of a similar size, their global influence differs vastly; the United States remains the world's sole superpower, while Europe's weight in the world is far less than the sum of its parts. The reason, of course, is that Europe is divided into many nation-states and the European Union, which was created to try and transcend these differences and divisions, enjoys very limited powers and spends an inordinate amount of time and resources seeking to satisfy and reconcile the diverse interests and ambitions of its member states. As a consequence, the European Union is overwhelmingly inward- rather than outward-looking, constantly engaged in a process of institutional reform, one treaty following another, the latest example being Lisbon. This introversion has not prevented the EU from seeing itself as an embryonic model for the rest of the world and a template for how the international system should be organized: a widely held view in Europe has been that a union of nation-states pooling their sovereignty in the manner of the European Union, rather than a conventional nation-state system, is the way of the future. In other words, the EU's inward-looking mentality is combined with a much older and deeply rooted Eurocentrism – the idea of Europe as an example, leader and model for the rest of the world. Thus the EU's foreign policy has been informed by the belief that its influence will steadily spread outwards in a series of concentric circles: from Eastern Europe, to the Middle East and North Africa, and so forth.

While Europe has been obsessing over its own institutional arrangements, and in the process averting its gaze from the rest of the world, its global power and influence has been in rapid decline. In the mid 1990s, the EU's share of global trade was over 25 per cent, now it is around 20 per cent, and by 2030 it will be roughly 10 per cent; only nine European multinationals feature in the world's top fifty companies. The shift in the centre of economic gravity from the developed to the developing world has been progressively under-mining Europe's position. Europe has been vaguely aware of the process but until now has been far too preoccupied with itself and its arrangements to pay the question much attention.[120] This has been as true at a nation-state and popular level as of the European Union. A continent which was once intimate with most of the world has retreated into an intellectual and psychological bunker in which it has become increasingly unaware of and out of touch with the way in which that world is changing. In consequence, the European mentality has become steadily more defensive. China, of course, is the quintessential bearer and representative of these changes, but the European elites, in contrast to those in the United States, remain remarkably ignorant about it, with very few experts, relatively ill-informed leaders and periodic debates about China in the media which cover more or less the same ground and rehearse the same kind of issues as the previous one, and indeed the one before that; in other words, there is little in the way of a learning process. It is dif-ficult not to draw the conclusion that the blissful ignorance about China is based on an anachronistic arrogance that Europe knows – and does – best.

What has shaken Europe out of its stupor is not so much China but the Western financial crisis and its repercussions. The European banking system was hobbled, its economies contracted and subse-quent growth (with the partial exception of Germany) derisory. Governments found themselves facing huge fiscal deficits and in varying degrees set about slashing them. Worst of all, in some countries – notably Greece, Ireland and Portugal, with Spain and Italy also on the edge – the banking crisis metamorphosized into a sovereign debt crisis, which eventually led to a reluctant bail-out by the European Union, together with the IMF, a process riven by serious divisions between member countries and recurrent speculation as to whether the euro would survive. As a consequence of the financial crisis, Europe faces the prospect of an immediate and permanent diminution in its economic and political position; there will be no return to the status quo ante, the changes are too fundamental. Meanwhile, with most of Europe mired in debt and barely able to register positive growth, much of the developing world recovered quickly from the financial crisis and resumed rapid economic growth. If Europe had previously been in denial of the extent and speed with which the world was changing, now it was finally obliged to face reality: that it was in long-term decline and that its global influence was on the wane. The Western financial crisis was a spectacular wake-up call. Alas, this does not necessarily mean that Europe will adjust to the new world with which it is confronted: on the contrary, it may find it too difficult to make what would, given its history and mindset, be a huge paradigm shift in the way that it sees itself and its place in the world, and how it perceives the developing world.

The only country that appears to have weathered the storm relatively well is Germany. There are two reasons for this. First, Germany, alone of the major European nations, has succeeded in increasing the proportion of GDP accounted for by manufacturing output from 20 per cent in 1995 to 21 per cent in 2008. France and the UK, in contrast, have seen drastic reductions, the share of manufacturing in the UK falling from 18 per cent to 12 per cent and that in France from 15 per cent to 11 per cent over the same period. It is Germany's manufacturing industry that has largely been responsible for the country's success as an exporter; indeed, it has only recently been overtaken by China as the world's largest exporter. Second, by the end of 2010 China had become Germany's largest non-European export market, overtaking the United States, and it is predicted that China could become Germany's largest single export market by 2015. And it is

German manufacturing exports to China, especially capital goods, consumer products and luxury cars, that were largely responsible for the country's rapid recovery in 2009–2011. Volkswagen, the country's largest carmaker, for example, describes China as its second home market; in fact, this is an understatement, as it sells more cars in China than it does in Germany. Germany's economic resilience, it is clear, owes much to the fact that it has maintained a highly competitive manufacturing sector that has increasingly orientated itself towards the developing world and, above all, China. This contrasts sharply with the experience of the other main European economies, namely France, UK and Italy, which have singularly failed to achieve this. China is only the UK's eleventh biggest export market, smaller even than Ireland, and for Italy it is the tenth largest export market. Thus the failure of the European Union to recognize the fundamental reconfiguration of the global economy, and realign itself accordingly, has been replicated by the failure of the major national economies, bar Germany, to reorientate themselves towards the developing world, above all China. This suggests that most European economies will find it extremely difficult to resume a robust growth path, given that their trading relationships are dominated by the stagnant economies of the developed world rather than the developing economies which are driving global economic growth and likely to continue to do so in the future.

Not surprisingly, China regards the European Union in very different terms from the United States. While the latter, for all its problems is fit for purpose, a nation-state with an effective centralized state, this is palpably not the case with the European Union, which, far from being a unitary state with the capacity to think and act strategically and coherently, is an awkward amalgam and representative of different interests.[121] The United States, furthermore, is a global power in contrast to the European Union, which increasingly behaves more like a regional power and is perceived as such by China. Indeed, in East Asia, China's own region, Europe has not been a serious player since the collapse of the European empires, its role having effectively been usurped by the United States. That Europe is largely invisible in such an important region of the world bears testimony to its post-1945 global decline and its retreat into an increasingly regional role.[122] With the exception of the euro, discussion of Europe's wider global role is largely confined to what is known as 'normative power', namely the promotion of standards that are negotiated and potentially legitimized within international institutions.[123]

For the most part, Europe's response to the rise of China has been fragmented and incoherent. This is because the European Union lacks the power and authority to act as an overarching centre in Europe's relations with nations such as China. As a result, Europe generally speaks with a weak voice and more often than not with many voices, a situation which China has frequently been able to take advantage of. Europe's economic relationship with China grew considerably over the decade prior to the Western financial crisis, with a massive increase in imports of cheap Chinese manufactured goods and a significant rise in European exports to China, resulting in a growing European trade deficit with China and a loss of jobs in those industries competing with Chinese imports. Concern in Europe about the economic repercussions of China's rise was relatively muted, despite worries about the value of the renminbi and the growing trade deficit.[124] The predominant view in most countries was that China's rise had on balance been beneficial because of its negative effect on consumer prices, though in the less developed European countries like Portugal and Greece, together with the new entrants – all of which compete in varying degrees with China – the attitude was more mixed.[125]

At first, the financial crisis and its aftermath kindled a mood of heightened anxiety in many European countries, especially France and Italy, about the impact of China's rise and the effects of globalization.[126] This led to increased economic tension with China and the possibility of limited forms of action, such as anti-dumping duties and anti-subsidy tariffs, against Chinese imports.[127] While previously China's economic rise had been seen as largely benign, and for the most part beneficial, the mood became less sanguine amid growing concern about its possible consequences for Europe. A further factor fuelling this was the fear of investments by Chinese multinationals and by the Chinese Investment Corporation in key European industries.[128]

Europe has hitherto adopted a consistently haughty attitude

towards China, choosing to lecture it on what Europe saw as its many shortcomings, from its record on intellectual property rights, for example, to that on human rights and its lack of democracy. Not only has this irritated the Chinese, but it has also become harder for Europe to sustain as its position has weakened. The EU's stance on the issue of human rights has been getting progressively less support in international fora as China has grown stronger. Likewise, China's bargaining position on trade matters with the European Union has also been strengthening as its economy has become more competitive in a growing range of areas. The increasingly assertive position taken by China on the transfer of intellectual property has been an illustration of its rising confidence. Europe has hitherto tended to reassure itself that Chinese competition was restricted to cheap-end products and that this situation was likely to persist for some time into the future. This was always based on a serious underestimation of the dynamism of the Chinese economy and its ability to move much more rapidly than anticipated into more high-end products, such as high-speed rail, telecommunications, power technology, wind power and solar panels. This is precisely what is now happening, with the Chinese already able to compete, or on the verge of being able to compete, in a sophisticated range of industries like these and, in the very near future, also construction machinery, machine tools, cars and electrical engineering.[129]

What has served to fundamentally redraw the relationship between China and Europe is Europe's ongoing sovereign debt crisis and continuing economic stagnation. With the countries of southern and eastern Europe facing a severe debt crisis, many have turned to China for financial assistance. The most dramatic early example of this was a deal for Chinese banks to buy €20 billion of long-term Greek bonds; in the event it came to nought when Athens refused to sell a stake in the National Bank of Greece as part of the agreement. China's state shipping company, Cosco, it should be noted, already controls a container terminal at Piraeus under a €3.4 billion long-term concession deal and various other agreements involving shipbuilding, airports and container terminals were concluded during 2010.[130] Several Chinese companies have also signed up to a special economic zone in Sofia, while the Bulgarian government has been actively seeking to attract more Chinese investment, as has the Romanian government.[131] The deals are still limited but may well prove a sign of the future. It has not been difficult to imagine a restrictionist policy towards Chinese inward investment on the part of countries like Germany, France and the UK, but even in these cases there are growing indications that they would welcome Chinese investment: in November 2011, Lou Jiwei, the chairman of the China Investment Corporation, announced that the sovereign wealth fund was keen to invest in the UK infrastructure sector as an equity investor, and in January 2012 the fund bought 8.68 per cent of Thames Water's controlling company, a move supported by the British government. The numerous weaker European economies view Chinese investment in extremely positive terms. Italy, Spain, Portugal and Greece in particular have all strongly welcomed the fact that the Chinese have been willing to buy their sovereign debt and thereby demonstrate confidence in their financial future. As these purchases are treated as state secrets, it is impossible to know the precise sums involved, but European estimates suggested $7.5 billion in Spanish bonds and $5 billion in Portuguese debt. Not surprisingly, the weak south European economies have come to see China as something of a saviour in this situation. But even Berlin, Paris and Brussels have reason to be grateful to the Chinese for their expression of support for the euro in its hour of need.[132] When Li Keqiang, who is expected to succeed Chinese premier Wen Jiabao, toured European capitals in January 2011 he was received with an air of expectancy and not a little hope in anticipation of possible much-needed Chinese largesse for the debt-ridden and cash-starved European nations.[133] Whereas prior to the financial crisis China's need of Europe was greater than Europe's need of China, that situation has now been reversed in a very dramatic fashion. The most stark illustration of this came in October 2011 when, at the conclusion of what seemed like an interminable series of EU summits over how the euro might be saved, the French president Nicolas Sarkozy phoned Hu Jintao seeking a huge bailout loan from the Chinese government.

The Western financial crisis marked a precipitous and irreversible decline in Europe's position. Its place in the world will never be the same again. A combination of the financial crisis and the sovereign debt crisis has divided and fragmented the Union. Most countries face an era of austerity, low growth and reduced public provision. The future of the eurozone remains in doubt. The EU – and its member countries – will experience a diminished role in the world: other countries are already less keen on becoming trading partners, with alternative and more attractive suitors on offer; European influence and representation in international bodies is steadily declining, as the recent reforms in the IMF illustrate; and their aid and assistance will be less sought after by developing countries as wealthier and more generous donors, notably China, take their place. A dramatic example of the rapid decline in Europe's authority came earlier at the climate change conference in Copenhagen in 2009 when it found itself excluded from the small compact of nations – China, India, South Africa and Brazil, with the United States grudgingly admitted on sufferance at the last minute – that drew up the final agreement: it must have been the first time for two centuries or more that Europe has found itself excluded from the top table at a major international conference in which it had a powerful interest. Finally, it is worth bearing in mind that Europe will account for less than 5 per cent of the world's population by 2050, compared with 12 per cent in 1950.

The lack of any serious European diplomatic or military presence in East Asia means that, unlike the United States, which remains the key arbiter of security in the region, Europe has no major geopolitical conflicts of interest with China. When it comes to Taiwan, the Korean Peninsula or the US–Japanese alliance, all critical issues of US concern, Europe is no more than a spectator. It has no involvement in the United States' bilateral alliance system in the region. As a result, Chinese–European relations are unencumbered by such considerations.[134] The nearest such issue has been the European embargo on the supply of arms to China, which was introduced after Tiananmen Square and which China has lobbied hard to get lifted. Although the European Union eventually obliged in 2005, it rapidly reversed the decision in response to huge pressure from the United States, which turned the issue into something akin to a vote of confidence in the Atlantic Alliance. Only by making it an article of faith in the West did the US manage to hold the line, suggesting that Europe may, up to a point, be prepared to think for itself when it comes to its relations with China.[135] This is not to suggest that in the long run Europe is likely to detach itself from the United States in favour of China but the reaction of key European nations like Germany and France to the American invasion of Iraq showed that much of Europe was no longer prepared slavishly to follow the US. Relations between the US and Europe have improved significantly during the Obama presidency, though the intimacy of the Cold War period has not been restored nor is it likely to be. With the rise of China and the continuing importance of the Middle East, the transatlantic relationship is no longer pivotal for the US in the way that it once was: rather than being a universal relationship in the mould of the Cold War, the nature of cooperation is likely to vary according to the issue and region involved.[136] It seems inevitable that, as the global centre of gravity moves from the Atlantic to the Pacific, and from the West to Asia, then the United States will become increasingly interested in and preoccupied by Asia rather than Europe, which will find itself increasingly marginalized as a consequence. In such a scenario, it is likely that the United States and Europe will slowly drift apart. Furthermore, the growing power of China's huge markets, its deep pockets and its potential largesse mean, as we have seen with the sovereign debt crisis, that China has much it might offer Europe. It has shown, moreover, that it can play its cards with a very skilful diplomatic hand. But it is important not to exaggerate any such scenario; Europe is far more likely to take the side of the United States than China's in geopolitical arguments. For a variety of reasons, historical, cultural, ethnic and economic, Europe is likely to remain wedded to the US in the world that is unfolding. But in a position of American decline and growing Chinese hegemony, the relationship between Europe and the United States is likely to grow weaker and ultimately much weaker.

THE RISING SUPERPOWER AND THE DECLINING SUPERPOWER

While the domestic debate in the United States might often suggest the contrary, ever since the Mao–Nixon rapprochement of 1972 and the subsequent establishment of full diplomatic relations in 1979, the relationship between China and US has been characterized for almost four decades by stability and continuity.[137] Although it has been through many phases – the axis against the Soviet Union, the reform period and modernization, Tiananmen Square and its aftermath, China's rapid growth and its turn outwards in the late 1990s, China's emergence as a global power, and of course a succession of US presidents from Nixon, Reagan and Bush snr, to Carter, Clinton, Bush jnr and Obama – the relationship has remained on an even keel, with the United States gradually granting China access both to its domestic market and the institutions of the international system, and China in return tempering and dovetailing its actions and behaviour in deference to American attitudes. The rationale that has been used to justify the US position has been through various iterations during the course of these different phases, but there has been no shrinking from the underlying approach. It may not be immediately obvious why the US ruling elite has been so consistently supportive of this position, but the key reason surely lies in its origins. The Mao–Nixon rapprochement was reached in the dark days of the Cold War and represented a huge geo-political coup for the United States in its contest with the Soviet Union. That created a sense of ongoing loyalty and commitment to the relationship with China that helped to ensure its endurance.

China's relationship with the United States has remained the fundamental tenet of its foreign policy for some thirty years, from the outset lying at the heart of Deng Xiaoping's strategy for ensuring that China would have a peaceful and relatively trouble-free external environment that would allow it to concentrate its efforts and resources on its economic development.[138] After Tiananmen Square, Deng spoke of the need to 'adhere to the basic line for one hundred years, with no vacillation',[139] testimony to the overriding importance he attached to economic development and, in that context, also to the relationship with the United States.[140] It was, furthermore, a demonstration of the extraordinarily long-term perspective which, though alien to other cultures, is strongly characteristic of Chinese strategic thinking. The relationship with the United States has continued to be an article of faith for the Chinese leadership throughout the reform period, largely consensual and uncontested, engendering over time a highly informed and intimate knowledge of America.[141]

The contrast between China's approach towards the United States and that of the Soviet Union's prior to 1989 could hardly be greater. The USSR saw the West as the enemy; China chose, after 1972, to befriend it. The Soviet Union opted for autarchy and isolation; China, after 1978, sought integration and interdependence. The USSR shunned, and was excluded from, membership of such post-war Western institutions as the IMF, the World Bank and GATT; in contrast, China waited patiently for fifteen years until it was finally admitted as a member of the WTO in 2001. The Soviet Union embarked on military confrontation and a zero-sum relationship with the United States; China pursued rapprochement and cooperation in an effort to create the most favourable conditions for its economic growth. The Soviet Union was obliged to engage in prohibitive levels of military expenditure; China steadily reduced the proportion of GDP spent on its military during the 1980s and 1990s, falling from an average of 6.35 per cent between 1950 and 1980 to 2.3 per cent in the 1980s and 1.4 per cent in the 1990s.[142] The strategies of the two countries were, in short, based on diametrically opposed logics.[143] The Chinese approach is well illustrated by Deng's comment: 'Observe developments soberly, maintain our position, meet challenges calmly, hide our capacities and bide our time, remain free of ambition, never claim leadership.'[144] It goes without saying that the relationship between China and the United States during the reform period has, until very recently, been profoundly unequal.[145] China needed the US to a far greater extent than the US needed China. The United States possessed the world's largest market and was the gatekeeper to an international system the design and operation of which it was overwhelmingly responsible for. China was cast in the role of supplicant, or, as China expert Steven I. Levine puts it, the United States acted towards China 'like a self-appointed Credentials Committee that had the power to accept, reject, or grant probationary membership in the international club to an applicant of uncertain respectability'.[146] In the longer term, when China is far stronger, this rather demeaning experience might find expression – and payback – in the Chinese attitude towards the United States; it might be seen by them to have been another, albeit milder, expression of their long-running humiliation.

Compared with China's huge investment in its relationship with the United States, the American attitude towards China stands in striking contrast. Its relationship with China has been seen, until the financial crisis, as one of only many international relationships, and usually far from the most important. As a result, American attention towards China has been episodic, occasionally rising to near the top of the agenda, but for the most part confined to the middle tier.[147] During the first Clinton administration, for example, China barely figured.[148] Although George W. Bush made strong noises against China during his first presidential election campaign, describing it as a 'strategic competitor', China sank down the Washington pecking order after 9/11 and relations between the two rapidly returned to the status quo ante.[149] It was only after the financial crisis that the relationship between the two began to change, with talk of a G2 and a rapidly dawning realization on the part of the United States that China was indeed its most important protagonist. In line with the differential investment by the two powers in their relationship, China's impressive knowledge of the United States has not been reciprocated in Washington beyond a relatively small coterie.[150]

Following the collapse of the Soviet Union and the passing of the Cold War, the US had been obliged to rethink the rationale for its relationship with China.[151] It was not difficult. With its embrace of the market and growing privatization, China was seen, not wrongly, as moving towards capitalism. Furthermore, given China's double-digit economic growth and its huge population, it was regarded as offering boundless opportunities for US business.[152] In the 1990s China became a key element in the American hubris about globalization, which was seen as a process of Westernization that would culminate in the inevitable worldwide victory of Western capitalism, with the rest of the world, including China, increasingly coming to resemble the United States. Many assumptions were wrapped up in this hubris, from the triumph of Western lifestyles and cultural habits to the belief that Western-style democracy was of universal and inevitable applicability or, to put it another way, modernity was ineluctably Western.[153] George W. Bush declared in November 1999: 'Economic freedom creates habits of liberty. And habits of liberty create expectations of democracy . . . Trade freely with China, and time is on our side.'[154] Or, as Thomas Friedman wrote: 'China's going to have a free press. Globalization will drive it.'[155] It was regarded as axiomatic, American author James Mann suggests, that, 'the Chinese are inevitably becoming like us'.[156] This view, which is still widely held, burdens American policy towards China with exaggerated expectations that cannot possibly be fulfilled.[157] The idea of globalization which lay at its heart was profoundly flawed.

During the course of the 1990s, US policy towards China was assailed by a growing range of different interest groups, from the labour unions which, concerned about the huge increase in Chinese imports, criticized China's labour and trade practices, to human rights groups that protested about the treatment of dissidents and the subjugation of Tibet.[158] While China policy remained a presidential rather than a congressional matter, it was relatively invulnerable to the critics' complaints. However, it should not be assumed that the present American position towards China will inevitably be maintained into the indefinite future. Until the turn of the century, China impinged little on the conduct of American foreign policy, apart from in East Asia, and that was largely confined to the question of Taiwan. True, China's exports to the United States – together with the lack of competitiveness of the US's own exports – had combined to produce a huge trade deficit between the two countries, but this was mitigated by China's purchase of US Treasury bonds, which fuelled the American credit boom, and the benefit that American consumers enjoyed from the availability of ultra-cheap manufactured goods from China. But as China began to spread its wings at the beginning of the new century – its economy still growing at undiminished pace, the trade gap between the two countries constantly widening, the quantity of Treasury bonds held by China forever on the increase, Chinese companies being urged to invest abroad, the state-sponsored quest for a sufficient and reliable supply of natural resources drawing the country into Africa, Central Asia and Latin America, and its power and influence in East Asia expanding apace – it became increasingly clear that China no longer occupied the same niche as it had previously: across many continents and in many countries, the United States found itself confronted with a growing range of Chinese interests and, as a result, a steady growth in the sources of potential disagreement and conflict between the two countries.[159]

No sooner had the new century begun than two developments suggested that a major change in their relationship was possible, even though it did not appear immediately obvious at the time. First, the Bush administration abandoned the previously consensual multilateralist US foreign policy in favour of a unilateralist policy that, amongst other things, embraced the principle of pre-emptive strike. The US turned away from its previous espousal of universalism and towards a nationalism which denied or downplayed the need for alliances. The new strategy placed a priority on military strength and hard as opposed to soft power, a position made manifest in 2003 with the invasion of Iraq. The principle of national sovereignty was subordinated to the desirability of intervention for the purpose of regime-change. A new and aggressive America was born.[160] In the event, an overwhelming majority of nation-states opposed the invasion of Iraq and, according to global opinion polls, an even more decisive majority of their citizens. As the occupation faced growing opposition and was perceived to have failed, the United States became unpopular to an extent not seen in the sixty years since the Second World War.[161] Second, around 2003–5, the moment of China arrived, as global awareness of its transformation, and the meaning and effects of that transformation for the rest of the world, suddenly began to dawn. By accident, these two developments happened to coincide, thereby serving to accentuate their impact.[162] It was widely acknowledged that China was on the rise and there was a slow dawning that the US was not as omnipotent as had previously been thought. There was a growing perception that the balance of power between the two countries was starting to shift in China's favour.[163] The mood in the United States towards China grew more uncertain.[164] James Mann, in his book *The China Fantasy*, challenged what he described as the 'Soothing Scenario', namely the consensus which holds that engaging with China through trade will be to the political and economic advantage of the United States and will ultimately result in a free-market, democratic China. Mann argued that, notwithstanding China's market transformation, it by no means automatically followed that China would become democratic.[165]

The general mood of uncertainty and unease was hugely accentuated by the credit crunch which started in summer 2007 and which a year later brought the American financial sector to its knees, with illustrious names like Lehman Brothers and Bear Stearns going bankrupt and the few remaining American investment banks forced to renounce their status – Goldman Sachs, the favoured bank of recent US administrations, amongst them. In an extraordinary volte-face, the government announced a huge bail-out of the financial sector, marking a major change in the deregulated neo-liberal regime which had been the calling card of American capitalism since the late 1970s. In a few spectacular weeks the Anglo-American model had imploded, plunging the Western economies into a serious recession. The fact that the US had been living well beyond its means – and relying on Chinese credit in order to do so – underlined both the fallibility of American prosperity and a shift in the centre of economic gravity from the United States to China. The juxtaposition of China's rise and the US's financial meltdown set the scene for what will inevitably be a profound change in their relationship.

GROWING CONFLICT

Both China and the United States have sought to play down, even deny, that the financial crisis marked a turning point in their relationship. But how can it be anything other, given that it represented, and signalled to the world, a major shift in economic power from the United States to China? Nothing could ever be quite the same again. Whatever the professions to the contrary, both Chinese and American attitudes have changed as a consequence, as have those of other countries, even though there is inevitably a time lag as assumptions, perceptions, policies and strategies catch up with the new reality. In China there is now a major debate about China's future role in the world which will have a very direct bearing on its relationship with the US. Put simply, China's burgeoning economic strength and the shift in power between the US and China mean that the era of Deng Xiaoping's dictum of concentrating on growth and the elimination of poverty, while keeping a low profile and acting as very much the subordinate in its relationship with the US, is drawing to an end. The problems facing the Chinese leadership are now much more complex: to define China's role and aims in a rapidly changing world in which its power and reach are expanding remorselessly. Meanwhile the United States is for the first time – with the arguable exception of the 1980s – being obliged to face up to the reality of its own decline; although in truth the domestic discussion has barely begun, such is the scale of the problem and the novelty of the idea for the vast majority of Americans. In short, both countries have as yet taken only the first baby steps into the new world. But the change in tone is unmistakable. Where China previously sought to say nothing or wait for another country to do its bidding – for example, allowing Russia to argue the case against the American invasion of Iraq while remaining relatively silent – since the financial crisis it has been a little more willing to speak its mind. At the World Economic Forum in 2009, premier Wen Jiabao made a thinly veiled attack on the US economic model, while two months later Zhou Xiaochuan, the governor of the People's Bank of China, criticized the role of the dollar and advocated greater use of the IMF's special drawing rights (SDR).[166] This has often been characterized as a new Chinese assertiveness; it is better described as a greater willingness on the part of the Chinese to make their views public and explicit.

So where does this leave the US–China relationship? Of course, these are still very early days. We should expect nothing particularly dramatic. The Chinese are not prone to gestures or posturing, but continue to act with their trademark caution and much forethought. Even though the Deng Xiaoping era is drawing to a close, it will not be abandoned quickly or completely; on the contrary, the lines of continuity will remain very strong. With the Americans still largely in denial – and ignorance – about what their decline and the new world will bring, much will remain, at least on the surface, seemingly unchanged. The Americans will find it extremely difficult to treat the Chinese as an equal partner – as increasingly they must – because force of habit and attitude has ingrained in them a sense of superiority and ascendancy when dealing with others; and this has certainly been the case in their relations with the Chinese.

Because the US–China relationship has been relatively stable ever since the Mao–Nixon rapprochement, there has been a tendency to see it as broadly amicable, but as the Chinese international relations scholar Yan Xuetong has argued, given the major differences and conflicts of interest between them, in fact this is something of a deceit, the character of their friendship being essentially superficial.[167] This is why, in his view, the relationship constantly oscillates between friendship and enmity, optimism and pessimism. It is burdened by false expectations that are persistently disappointed, which has clearly been the case since the financial crisis. The ongoing tensions between the China and the US over currency matters are a classic illustration of this, as well as an indication of how their relationship might grow more difficult and conflictual in the future.

The immediate aftermath of the financial crisis was marked by a high degree of cooperation as governments sought to prevent the financial crisis turning into an economic depression by introducing major stimulus packages, the largest being China's. But as the success of these packages became evident, the initial wave of solidarity was replaced by growing frictions as Western economies, confronted by a growing burden of debt, tried to export their way out of recession. The United States staged a major assault on the value of the renminbi, arguing that it was as much as 25 per cent or more undervalued, thereby making Chinese exports unfairly competitive and exacerbating the American balance of trade deficit. The House of Representatives passed a bill that allowed US companies to petition for duties to be imposed on Chinese goods in retaliation for China's currency policy. In fact, though, the issue has always been more complicated than as usually presented. Over half of Chinese exports are made by foreign-owned companies and the value added in China generally accounts for only a small proportion of the total; in other words, the way in which trade figures are calculated overestimates the Chinese contribution and underestimates that of Japan, South Korea, Taiwan and other mainly East Asian countries that provide components for final assembly in China. Furthermore, as the Harvard economist Dani Rodrik has pointed out, China's reliance on an under-valued currency is partly a consequence of the fact that the industrial policies it pursued before 2001 were no longer permitted under the relatively draconian terms of its admission to the WTO.[168] Although the Chinese government allowed the renminbi to modestly appreciate once more in June 2010, it strongly resisted American pressure and counter-attacked by arguing that the two bouts of quantitative easing – in other words, printing money – introduced by the US government were deliberately aimed at reducing the value of the dollar and dollar assets. It broadened the offensive by arguing that there was a growing conflict between the domestic pressures on the dollar and its role as a reserve currency and that, as a consequence, the dollar was no longer capable of acting as the world's dominant currency. In the prelude to the Obama–Hu summit in January 2011, in an interview with the *Washington Post* and the *Wall Street Journal*, Hu Jintao said, 'the current international currency system is the product of the past'.[169] During the course of 2010 it became clear that the Chinese had rather more support than the Americans, with even Germany broadly siding with China. There had been Western suggestions that what was required was a new Plaza Accord – the agreement reached in 1985 by the main Western economies and Japan, which led to a major appreciation of the yen – but the prospects of this are slim in the extreme. The Chinese will not countenance such an agreement and, unlike the Japanese, who were a vassal state of the United States, China enjoys far greater independence of action. The Chinese will certainly allow the renminbi to appreciate, because it is increasingly in their own domestic economic interest, but they will do it in their own way and at their own speed.[170] The fact that these currency matters have become so controversial speaks to the shift in the balance of economic power between China and the US, the decline of the US and the dollar, and the rise of China as the new financial hegemon: in other words, they lie at the heart of the growing conflict between the declining power and the new rising power.

From a broader point of view, there are a number of issues which seem likely to shape the relationship between the two countries, in particular American attitudes towards China. The first concerns American views about globalization. In the 1990s globalization was seen in the US as a win-win situation, a process by which the US left its imprint on, and gained advantage in its relationship with, the rest of the world. In effect, it was something that the United States exported to the world and then reaped the benefits from at home.[171] Now, however, globalization is seen more and more like a boomerang that is returning to haunt the US.[172] Previously, the US was regarded as the overwhelming agent and beneficiary of globalization. Now the main beneficiary is perceived to be East Asia, and especially China.[173] Through globalization, China has transformed itself into a formidable competitor of the United States, with its huge trade surplus, its massive ownership of US Treasury bonds, its consequent power over the value of the dollar, and the fact that it has undermined key sectors of American manufacturing industry, with the loss of many jobs to China. The widening controversy over the value of the renminbi, the safety of Chinese exports such as food and toys, and the frequent accusations of 'unfair' competition, are a reflection of growing sensitivity towards China.[174] This is not to suggest that the balance of American opinion has shifted decisively. It was notable that in the mid-term congressional elections in November 2010 the candidates that chose to campaign vociferously on unfair Chinese competition and the migration of US jobs to China were not particularly successful. The winners, above all the US corporate giants that have moved their manufacturing operations to China and the consumers who have benefited from China prices at home, still seem to hold sway and certainly enjoy much greater influence than the losers.[175] But this could change. Rising commodity prices, especially of oil, could push American attitudes in a more negative direction. More pertinently, very slow growth and continuing high unemployment have led to growing demands for protection, which could become irresistible if these conditions persist over the next few years.[176] It is striking that, even before the credit crunch, the number of Americans who thought that trade with other countries was having a positive impact on the US fell sharply from 78 per cent in 2002 to only 59 per cent in 2007.[177]

In the longer term, as Chinese companies relentlessly climb the technology ladder, the US economy will face ever-widening competition from Chinese goods, no longer just at the low-value end, but also increasingly for high value-added products as well, just as happened earlier with Japanese and Korean firms.[178] In that process, the proportion of losers is likely to increase rapidly, as will be the case in Europe too. Such a development could further undermine the present shrinking consensus in support of free-trade globalization and strengthen support for protectionism, with the main target being Chinese imports.[179] If the United States did resort to protectionism, one of the key planks in the Sino-American relationship since the early eighties would be undermined. It would also signal a more general move towards protectionism worldwide and the conclusion of the phase of globalization that was ushered in at the end of the 1970s. The failure of the Doha round is a further indication that this kind of scenario is possible, if not yet likely.[180]

This brings us next to East Asia. There is clear evidence, as discussed in the last chapter, of a fairly dramatic shift in the balance of power in what is now the most important economic region in the world, East Asia having overtaken both North America and Europe. Nothing decisive has happened but nonetheless China has palpably strengthened its position, with even established US allies like Singapore and the Philippines hedging and seeking a closer accommodation with China. Japan, in fact, is the only country that has so far resisted being drawn closer to China. The wider significance of these developments in terms of Sino–US relations is that East Asia has, ever since the last war, been a predominantly American sphere of influence, threatened only by a weak and relatively isolated China during the Maoist period and, of course, the US's defeat in the Vietnam War. This can no longer be presumed to be the case. East Asia is becoming bipolar, with China increasingly dominant economically and the US still the main security actor. It is certainly true, as discussed in the last chapter, that the US succeeded in 2010–11 in retrieving some of the ground it had previously lost as a result of the Bush administration's preoccupation with the Middle East and neglect of East Asia. Predictably the Obama administration recognized the priority of rebuilding the US presence in the region and the determination of the Americans to do this could be a harbinger of growing tensions in the future. In the longer run, however, the strong likelihood is that America's presence in East Asia will steadily diminish as a result of its weakening economic position. The waning of American influence in East Asia would also have implications for its position globally, on the one hand serving to embolden China, and on the other acting as a marker and signal for other nations around the world.

China, meanwhile, has slowly begun to emerge as an alternative pole and example to the United States, a view which the Chinese have cautiously promoted, though in a manner very different from the kind of systemic competition that characterized the Cold War. The growing American emphasis on hard power during the Bush administration made it increasingly unpopular in the world and created a vacuum which China in a small way started to fill, not least with its embrace of multilateralism and its emphasis on its peaceful rise.[181] China's pitch is essentially to the developing rather than the developed world, with its offer of no-strings-attached aid and infrastructural assistance, its respect for sovereignty, its emphasis on a strong state, its opposition to superpower domination and its championing of a level playing field. As a package these have a powerful resonance with developing countries.[182] The main plank of American soft power is the stress placed on the importance of democracy *within* nation-states: China, by way of contrast, emphasizes democracy *between* nation-states – most notably in terms of respect for sovereignty – and democracy *in* the world system.[183] China's criticism of the Western-dominated international system and its governing institutions strikes a strong chord with the developing world at a time when these institutions are widely recognized to be unrepresentative and seriously flawed; China, in concert with other developing countries, notably India, has been in the vanguard of the movement to reform the IMF. Most powerfully of all, China can offer its own experience of growth as an example and model for other developing countries to consider and learn from, something that the United States, as the doyen of developed countries, cannot. Indeed, its own offer, the Washington Consensus, is now widely discredited. East Asia apart, there has been a significant shift of power and sentiment away from the United States and towards China in Africa and Latin America. This should not be exaggerated but it is, nonetheless, significant. Meanwhile, the spectacular failure of the neo-liberal model in the financial meltdown has seriously undermined the wider appeal of the United States. And the fact, more generally, that the American-run international economic system has been plunged into such turmoil as a result of a crisis which had its origins in the United States has served further to accentuate the loss of American power and prestige.[184] We are likely to see an intensifying rivalry between the United States and China for support in the developing world, with China increasingly being viewed as a model that might be learnt from and even, in certain respects, imitated. The fact that it has established itself as a major source of economic assistance can only serve to enhance its appeal.

This brings us finally to the question of China's military strength. This has been persistently highlighted by the United States. The Americans attach greater emphasis to military power than anything else, a position which is reflected in their continuing huge military expenditure and the importance they place on maintaining overwhelming military strength in relation to the rest of the world. In the 2002 *National Security Strategy of the United States of America*, such massive military expenditure is advocated in order to 'dissuade potential adversaries from pursuing a military build-up in hopes of surpassing, or equalling, the power of the United States'.[185] The fact is that American unipolarity has been an almost exclusively military phenomenon.[186]

The American argument that China is determined to develop a strong military capacity of its own plays on the fears of many nations, especially in East Asia. China's size and cohesiveness, together with its history of authoritarian rule, arouse doubts enough in the minds of others, so the suspicion that China is also embarked on becoming a military superpower could help to tip the balance of perception towards something closer to acute anxiety, even paranoia. This is amply borne out by the accompanying chart (Table 8) which shows that, while most publics have a relatively favourable view of China's economic rise, a large majority take a very negative view of China's

	growing economy		growing military power	
	good thing %	bad thing %	good thing %	bad thing %
US	40	47	12	79
Britain	44	42	11	74
France	32	67	12	87
Germany	37	58	16	72
Spain	36	48	11	66
Poland	39	46	17	65
Russia	49	30	14	71
Turkey	18	60	8	58
Egypt	54	42	32	55
Jordan	71	24	32	56
Lebanon	54	33	20	59
India	34	56	27	64
Indonesia	61	28	41	39
Japan	61	29	4	88
Pakistan	79	5	70	7
S Korea	45	49	7	86
Argentina	52	20	15	43
Brazil	62	21	34	40
Mexico	41	34	21	46
Kenya	90	6	66	25
Nigeria	90	5	64	20

Source: Pew Research Center, June 2010

Table 8. How China's growing power affects your country.

growing military power.[187] The political purpose behind the annual Pentagon statements on China's military spending, as well as earlier not infrequent warnings from members of the Bush administration,[188] has been to create a mood of doubt and distrust, playing in part on old Cold War fears about the Soviet Union.[189] In fact, China has opted for a different path, one that has emphasized economic growth rather than military capacity. The military budget has broadly kept pace with GDP over the last decade, after two decades during which its share of

GDP fell. As a proportion of GDP, China spends less than half the American figure.[190] Until recently, the twin objectives of China's military modernization have been to ensure that it can respond by force if necessary to any declaration of independence by Taiwan, and to pose a sufficient deterrent to any external power that might otherwise contemplate attacking China.[191] Both of these are long-established concerns, the first a product of the civil war, the second a function of China's 'century of humiliation' and its overriding concern for its national sovereignty. It should also be noted that China's ability to develop a sophisticated military capacity has been seriously constrained by the fact that its own technological level has been relatively low and that its only source of foreign arms, given the EU embargo and the US ban, has been Russia.[192] As a result, China is much weaker militarily than Japan. Only now is it in the process of constructing an aircraft carrier (based on a Soviet-designed carrier that it purchased as an unfinished hull from Ukraine in 1998) – a crucial means of power-projection – which is unlikely to be operational until 2015; and it will take China far beyond that to be able to deploy the carrier with the necessary cluster of support ships. In this context, it should be borne in mind that ten countries in the world already have at least one carrier, including the UK, which has three (though it can barely afford them), and India and Italy, which each have one.[193]

Apart from the aircraft carrier, China is now in the process of expanding its naval capability in the South China Sea, East China Sea and also the Indian Ocean. It is developing a land-based anti-ship missile which Robert Gates, the then US defense secretary, admitted would force the Pentagon to rethink the way in which its aircraft carriers were deployed;[194] and it is estimated that China now has almost as many submarines in the region as the United States. As a consequence of its growing interests in the region, and its desire to protect vital sea lanes through the South China Sea and the Strait of Malacca, China is steadily becoming a serious naval player in these waters.[195] It should be emphasized, however, that China's naval presence in the region pales into insignificance compared with that of the United States, and will do so for the indefinite future. Nonetheless, China's growing military presence will heighten the possibility of tensions between the two powers.

The danger is that at some point the United States and China will be drawn into the kind of arms race that characterized the Cold War and which produced such a climate of fear. There is no doubt that the United States feels rather more comfortable on the terrain of hard power than China, first because its military superiority is overwhelming and secondly because the language of hard power is deeply inscribed on the American psyche – partly as a result of the Cold War and partly as a consequence of the violent manner of the country's birth and expansion, as exemplified by the frontier spirit – in a way that it is not on the Chinese.[196] But there are dangers here for the United States too. The fundamental problem of China for the US is not its military strength but its economic prowess. This is what is slowly and irresistibly eroding American global pre-eminence.[197] If the US comes to see China as primarily a military issue, then it will be engaging in an act of self-deception which will divert its attention from addressing the real problems that it faces and in effect hasten the process of its own decline.[198]

These four issues – the United States' attitude towards globalization; the shift in the balance of power in East Asia; China's emergence as an alternative pole to the US; and the issue of military power – do not lie at some distant point in the future but are already in play; nor do they exhaust the likely areas of friction. As China's power and ambitions grow apace, the points of conflict and difference between the US and China will steadily accumulate. Such is the speed of China's transformation that this could happen more rapidly than we might expect or the world is prepared for: China-time passes rather more quickly than the kind of time that we are historically accustomed to. It is not difficult to imagine what some of these points of difference might be: growing competition and conflict over the sources of energy supplies – in Angola or Venezuela, or wherever; an intensifying dispute over the expanding strategic partnership between the United States and India; Chinese firms, awash with cash, threatening to take over American firms and provoking a hostile reaction (as happened in the case of the oil firm Unocal); the Chinese sovereign wealth fund, its coffers filled with the country's huge trade surplus, seeking to acquire a significant stake in US firms that are regarded as of strategic importance;[199] and a pattern of growing skirmishes over the militarization of space.[200] Moreover, China being culturally so different from the United States, in a way that was not nearly as true of the USSR, only adds to the possibility of mutual misunderstanding and resentment. Indeed, Henry Kissinger, one of the historic architects of the US–China relationship, has argued: 'The DNA of both countries could generate a growing adversarial relationship . . . unless their leadership groups take firm steps to counteract such trends.'[201] Furthermore, the fact that China is ruled by a Communist Party will always act as a powerful cause of difference as well as an easy source of popular demonization in the US, with memories of the Cold War still vivid.[202]

Potentially overshadowing all these issues in the longer run is the growing threat of climate change and the need for the world to take drastic action to reduce carbon emissions. Under the Bush administration, the United States adopted a unilateralist position, refusing to be party to the Kyoto Protocol or accept the overwhelming body of scientific opinion. As a developing country, China was not required to sign the Kyoto agreement, but now that it is the largest emitter of greenhouse gases, its exclusion from climate change agreements is insupportable from a planetary point of view; any new climate treaty will be meaningless unless it includes the United States, China and India.[203] But any agreement – involving inevitable conflict between the interests of the developed countries on the one hand and the developed on the other, with China the key protagonist for the former and the United States for the latter – will be very difficult, as was all too evident at the Copenhagen conference.[204] There, the complexity of the global debate about climate change became evident as well as the way in which China, India, Brazil and South Africa were able to command the high ground, with the United States relatively marginalized and Europe completely sidelined. The climate change issue, however, will in practice only become critical between China and the United States if and when the effects of global warming become far more serious than at present.

If relations between the US and China should seriously deteriorate, any attempt that might be entertained to exclude China from the present international economic system would simply not be an option. China has become so deeply integrated into global production systems that it would be well-nigh impossible to reverse that process. Chinese manufacturing has become a fundamental element in a complex global division of labour operated by the major Western and Japanese – and indeed Korean and Taiwanese – multinationals, which presently account for a majority of Chinese exports. The fact that the value added in China (30 per cent or much less as a rule) is only a small proportion of the total value added because of the extremely low cost of Chinese labour means that any attempt to impose sanctions on Chinese exports, for example, would inflict far greater economic harm on the many other countries involved in the production process, especially those in East Asia, than on China itself.[205] Powerful evidence of China's integration has been furnished by the global recession: from the outset China's involvement was regarded as fundamental to preventing a full-blown depression and its continuing rapid growth has been seen as vital in limiting the severity of the recession. One might add that the US's options are also limited in East Asia. If it decided to start pressurizing its East Asian allies – such as the Philippines, Singapore and Indonesia – to move away from China, it is not at all clear that it would meet with a positive response; indeed, it is conceivable that such a move might even be counter-productive because, in the event of being forced to choose, these countries might well opt for China as the rising power in the region. Finally, if the United States chooses to become more confrontational with China and engages it in an arms race, this could well harm the US's global standing rather more than China's; and China, for its part, might simply refuse to be drawn into such a military contest.[206] The problem for the United States, meanwhile, is that China's relative economic power, on which all else depends, continues to grow in comparison with that of the US.

The relationship between the United States and China is bound to change profoundly. As Chinese power grows, so will its interests and the potential areas of conflict with the United States. While the importance of cooperation will mushroom, so will the areas of rivalry. Until recently, the bilateral relationship between the US and China was one of many, as far as the US was concerned, rather than being manifestly the most important, which is clearly now the case. It is unclear how Chinese policy will evolve as the country moves beyond the Deng Xiaoping era – whether it will continue to act with such caution and circumspection or become more emphatic and assertive. Likewise, it is difficult to predict how the United States will respond to a situation where it is palpably an imperial power in decline confronted with a new and very different kind of adversary.

THE FUTURE OF THE
INTERNATIONAL SYSTEM

A key characteristic of the world's leading power is its ability to create and organize an international economic system to which other nations are willing or obliged to subscribe. Britain's version was the international gold standard system which, prior to 1914, encompassed a large part of the world in some shape or form. After Britain was finally forced to abandon the gold standard in 1931, marking the end of its global financial hegemony, the British-dominated international gold standard system gave way to an increasingly Balkanized regime based on currency areas, protected markets and spheres of interest. After 1945 the United States became the world's leading power and the new system that was agreed at Bretton Woods, and which was further elaborated in the years that followed, was essentially an American creation, made possible by the fact that the US economy was responsible for over one-third of global GDP at the end of the war. Unlike the previous British system, which was neither multilateral nor rules-based, the new US order was both. It only became truly global when China joined the WTO in 2001 and the former members of the Soviet bloc queued up to join the international system following the collapse of the Soviet Union. The relative economic decline of the US, however, has brought into question the future of the existing international economic system, including the role of the dollar.

This process of weakening has been apparent for well over a decade, though it was not until the Western financial crisis that the

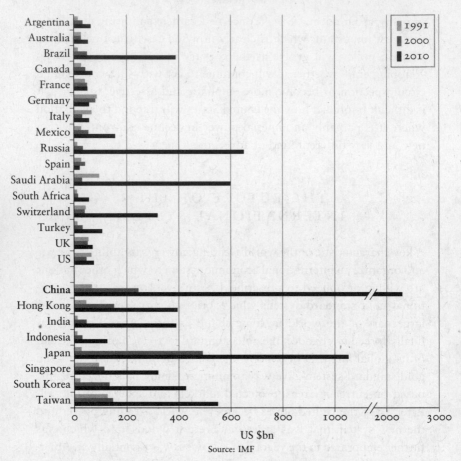

*Figure 69. The growth of East Asian foreign exchange
reserves since the Asian financial crisis.*

vulnerability of the existing system was widely recognized. To illustrate the longer-term decline of the system, let us consider the role of the International Monetary Fund and the World Bank, the two key institutions of the American system.[207] During the Asian financial crisis, Malaysia and Japan proposed that there should be an Asian Monetary Fund, such was the level of dissatisfaction within the region about the role of the IMF. This was strongly opposed by both the US and the IMF, which correctly saw the proposal as a threat to the IMF's position, and also by China, which was concerned that it had emanated from Japan. China long ago abandoned its opposition and has been actively involved with the ten ASEAN members, together with Japan and South Korea, in the Chiang Mai Initiative which started as a series of bilateral currency swap arrangements in 2000 and then in 2010 became a multilateral currency swap arrangement drawing on a foreign exchange reserves pool of US$120 billion. This has had the effect of seriously weakening to the point of marginality the role of the IMF within East Asia. In the event of another Asian financial crisis, it is highly likely that a basically regional financial solution would be found. In fact, ever since the Asian financial crisis, the IMF has become virtually redundant in the region, with countries deliberately building up huge currency reserves, as the accompanying chart (Figure 69) vividly illustrates, in order to obviate the need for IMF assistance, such was their bitter experience in 1997–9. The countries that sought IMF assistance during the crisis – Indonesia, South Korea and Thailand – have long since paid off their debts and it is difficult to imagine an East Asian country seeking IMF aid again. In a different but related way, Latin America has also moved down a similar route, seeking to avoid dependence on the IMF: Brazil, Argentina, Ecuador and Bolivia have paid off their debts and made it clear that they do not want to be dependent on the IMF in future. The underlying problem with the IMF is that while it has been run and funded by the rich developed countries, its recipients have, until the euro crisis of 2011, overwhelmingly been the developing countries; and its loan policy has been based on a highly ideological Western agenda which is now widely rejected in the developing world. As a result, an increasing number of developing countries have no longer wished to avail themselves of the IMF's assistance and the role of the IMF as a lender diminished greatly as a consequence prior to the financial crisis. Furthermore, the funds available to the IMF also declined in the period before the crisis; in comparison to the foreign exchange reserves of China and other East Asian nations, indeed, they are relatively derisory. With the Western financial crisis, the IMF experienced something of a revival: it succeeded in raising more capital and its role as a lender once more became significant, this time mainly for European countries, notably eastern and central Europe, and also, together with the European Union, in the bail-outs of Greece, Ireland and Portugal.[208] Nonetheless, its role and resources remain strictly limited and it remains a pale shadow of the body it once was.

This brings us to the World Bank. As China's financial power expands, its ability to make loans and give aid are increasing dramatically, as we saw earlier in the case of Africa, where Chinese loans have started to rival those made by the World Bank, but this is also true more generally. According to *Financial Times* research, in 2009–10 China lent more money to the entire developing world than was lent by the World Bank: specifically, the China Development Bank and China Export-Import Bank (often known as the China Exim Bank) signed loans of at least $110 billion to other developing country governments and companies during those two years, while the equivalent arms of the World Bank made loan commitments of $100.3 billion.[209] Already, in other words, the China Development Bank and the China Exim Bank are becoming more important institutions in the funding of the developing world than the World Bank. Meanwhile the WTO, with the demise of the Doha round – effectively torpedoed by China and India[210] – together with the growing popularity of the various ASEAN-related agreements, presently looks rather less important than it did a decade ago when trade liberalization was in full swing. The process of trade liberalization in East Asia since 2000, indeed, has largely bypassed the WTO, with China playing a key role through the various ASEAN-related agreements. Another institution of the present international economic system, the G7, acts as a kind of metaphor for the way in which the international system might come to look progressively less relevant, even anachronistic. Bizarrely, China, as of 2009, had still not been admitted as a member – and with the G7 being clearly unrepresentative of the global economy, it increasingly came to suffer from a chronic lack of legitimacy.[211] This was explicitly recognized in autumn 2008 when the world was faced with the prospect of the worst global recession since 1945: pride of place was taken not by a meeting of the G7, but a gathering convened by President Bush of a previously obscure entity called the G20, which included not only the rich countries but also China, India, Brazil, South Africa, Indonesia and other developing countries. It represented, at a critical moment, a belated recognition that the rich world no longer had sufficient clout on its own and that the big developing countries needed to be embraced if any action was to be effective. The G7 has since lost all credibility as a global institution: it is now effectively redundant, except perhaps as a faction for the old developed economies.[212]

The rise of China and the decline of the United States are central to the present travails of the global economy and the international financial system. Although much attention since the financial crisis has been directed towards how to narrow the gap between the surplus and deficit countries, what this fails to take proper cognizance of is that the underlying problem is not achieving short-term equilibrium but the fundamental long-term shift in economic power from the US to China.[213] The fact that China is such a huge creditor, based on its propensity to save and export, and the United States such a colossal debtor, based on its addiction to spend and import, reflects a deep change in the balance of economic power between the two countries. The American consumer boom depended on China's willingness to keep lending to the United States through the purchase of US Treasury bonds. In its present enfeebled state, the United States is still enormously dependent on China's willingness to continue buying US Treasury bonds, even though the rate of return makes little sense from a Chinese point of view: the resources of a poor country could be put to far better use, as is now openly discussed in China.[214] But the Chinese, as I discussed earlier, are in a Catch-22 situation: if they start selling US Treasury bonds, or cease buying them, the dollar will plummet and so will the value of their dollar assets. So a Faustian pact lies at the heart of the present relationship between the US and China, which is neither economically nor politically sustainable. In the first few months of 2011, there was evidence to suggest that the Chinese had begun to diversify their purchases away from the US dollar, probably by buying European government debt rather than US dollar assets, according to estimates by the Standard Chartered Bank.[215] The United States' position as the global financial centre and the dollar as the dominant reserve currency are on a Chinese life-support system. At the heart of the global financial crisis lies the inability of the United

States to continue to be the backbone of the international financial system; on the other hand, China is as yet neither able nor willing to assume that role. This is what makes the present global crisis so chronic and potentially protracted, in a manner analogous to the 1930s when Britain could no longer sustain its premier financial position and the United States was not yet in a position to take over from it. As after 1929, we are likely to lurch from one crisis to the next – beginning with the collapse of the Western (and especially US) banking system in 2008, followed by the sovereign debt crisis (so far mainly in Europe), perhaps a renewed banking crisis, growing tensions over exchange rates, the possible imposition of capital controls, moves towards protectionism, and the entirely credible prospect of an American sovereign debt crisis, followed by a collapse in the value of the dollar – until a new international financial system emerges to replace the present crisis-prone system whose viability is steadily being undermined. A World Bank report in 2011 predicted that the dollar's predominance would come to an end some time before 2025, to be replaced by a monetary system based on the dollar, euro and renminbi.[216]

In the longer run, the most likely solution to the crisis of the US-dominated system is the emergence of the renminbi as a major international currency and ultimately as a reserve currency that will replace the dollar at the heart of the global financial system. One of the most important responses of the Chinese government to the Western financial crisis has been to gingerly commence the process of internationalizing the renminbi. But this process will take a long time, at least a decade, if not more. The major obstacle to the emergence of the renminbi as a fully fledged competitor to the dollar is that it is not as yet a convertible currency, and the Chinese will move very cautiously along this path because of the negative effects it might have on the Chinese economy, which remains its overriding priority.[217]

Meanwhile, as China's power grows, together with that of other developing countries like India, the United States, along with Europe, will be obliged to adapt the international system and its institutions to accommodate their demands and aspirations, although, as demonstrated by the slowness of reform in the IMF and the G7, there has been great reluctance on the part of both the US and Europe to do so.[218] Fundamental to this has been the natural desire to retain these institutions for the promotion of Western interests and values. After China and Russia vetoed the Anglo-American bid to impose sanctions on the Zimbabwe president Robert Mugabe and some of his regime in July 2008, for example, the US ambassador to the UN, Zalmay Khalilzad, stated that Russia's veto raised 'questions about its reliability as a G8 partner'.[219] A far more dramatic illustration of this occurred in 2011 when, after the spectacular fall from grace of Dominique Strauss-Kahn and his resignation as IMF managing director, the European nations rushed to nominate a European candidate – Christine Lagarde, the French finance minister – as his replacement, despite strong European suggestions at the time of Strauss-Kahn's appointment in 2007 that the next head would not be a European and notwithstanding huge pressure from the developing world for one of its number to be chosen (including a statement from the BRIC countries attacking the convention that the managing director should be a European, as has been the case ever since 1947).[220] Significant reform of the IMF was belatedly agreed in autumn 2010, when, against European opposition, the United States accepted that Europe's voting allocation should be reduced. The Europeans were obliged to give up two of their eight seats on the 24-member board, while over 6 per cent of IMF voting power was transferred to the emerging economies, notably China and India. Brazil, Russia, India and China are now amongst the ten largest shareholders. Even with these reforms, however, the IMF remains far from representative of the global economy. The US, with a slightly increased share of 17.67 per cent of IMF quotas, retained its veto power over the Fund's key decisions, which continue to require a super-majority of 85 per cent. China, which now has a larger economy than Japan and is over a third of the size of the US economy, has a 3.65 per cent voting share, compared with Japan's 6.01 per cent and the US's 17.67 per cent.[221] Earlier, in spring 2010, the World Bank increased the voting rights of the developing countries by 3.13 per cent, giving them a total of 47.19 per cent (China's share rising by 2.77 per cent to 4.42 per cent) compared with 44 per cent previously. These are a clear sign that the Western nations are prepared to make significant concessions to the developing countries: whether they will prove sufficient remains to be seen. In an interview in 2009, the Chinese premier Wen Jiabao said that further Chinese funds for the IMF would depend upon voting reforms: they later gave $50 billion, a significant but still rather modest sum.[222]

The American international relations scholar G. John Ikenberry has argued that because the 'Western-centred system . . . is open, integrated, and rule-based, with wide and deep foundations', 'it is hard to overturn and easy to join'.[223] Elsewhere he has stated: 'Today this order is not really an American order or even a Western order. It is an international order with deep and encompassing economic and political rules and institutions that are both durable and functional.'[224] In other words, it is far more inclusive, resilient and adaptable than previous systems and therefore is likely to be reformed from within rather than replaced. There is an element of truth in this – certainly when compared with the previous British system – but it singularly fails to recognize the extent to which the system inevitably reflects and articulates the interests and objectives of the US as the hegemonic global power. The present international system is not a neutral creation based on an abstract universal interest, with the United States acting in a disinterested and altruistic fashion: on the contrary, the latter gains enormous advantage from its dominant position in the international financial system. Possessing the world's premier reserve currency, the US can run large trade deficits by virtue of the fact that those countries exporting to the US, most notably East Asia, including China, have been keen to acquire dollars for their own reserves. Such trade deficits are in reality debts whose payment can be postponed for as long as countries need dollars for their reserves. The US is thus able to act in a relatively arbitrary way – for example, by printing money (as exemplified by its resort to quantitative easing in 2010–11) and running large trade deficits (it has had a trade deficit ever since the mid sixties and increasingly large ones since the mid eighties) – in a manner that other countries cannot. As we have seen, it has dominated – and continues to dominate – the IMF by virtue of exercising a veto power that no other nation enjoys. Furthermore, US multinationals, for their part, benefit from the fact that they can avoid the transactional costs of switching from one currency to another in the financing of their trade. The US's privileged position also carries with it significant political benefits, with nations more willing to accommodate American demands, whatever they might be, in order to gain access to the dollar. The system may be international and inclusive but it clearly reflects American power and is heavily skewered in the latter's favour, both with regard to the role of the dollar and the distribution of influence within the IMF and World Bank.

In the light of such American advantage, it seems highly unlikely that, at least in the long term, the present system will survive the decline of the United States. In the short to medium term, rather than a relatively straightforward continuation of the present system, a rather more plausible scenario, extrapolating from current trends, would be what might be described as a twin-track process: first, the gradual but reluctant and inadequate reform of existing Western-centric institutions, notably the IMF and the World Bank, and perhaps also the WTO, in the face of the challenge from China and other developing countries; and second, the creation of new institutions sponsored and supported by China but also embracing other rising countries such as India and Brazil, perhaps using an institutional vehicle such as BRICS. As an illustration of reform from within, in June 2008 Justin Lin Yifu became the first Chinese chief economist at the World Bank, a position which previously had been the exclusive preserve of Americans and Europeans; the recent voting reforms in the IMF and World Bank are another example.[225] China, in other words, is likely to operate both *within* and *outside* the existing institutions, seeking to transform those institutions while at the same time, in effect, sponsoring new ones, some of which will be its own. Thus China will continue to give support to the World Bank while at the same time greatly expanding the role of the China Development Bank and the China Exim Bank in the developing world: in similar fashion, while supporting the IMF, it will back the Chiang Mai currency support initiative in East Asia (to which it contributes $38.4 billion, or one-third of the total)[226] and extend its financial assistance to countries around the world, including the indebted south European economies. The WTO is an interesting illustration of this twin-track process. With the impasse enveloping the WTO Doha round, trade agreements have continued to proceed outside the WTO framework on a regional and bilateral basis, most dramatically of all, as we saw in Chapter 9, in East Asia, with China the most important single player in this process. In time, it is possible, likely even, that these various new institutions, and others yet to be created, may effectively come to replace the existing ones: the analogy here might be the way in which the G20 has superseded the G7, notwithstanding the fact that the latter continues to exist, albeit in somewhat nominal form.

Even more dramatic than such institutional changes, however, will be impact of the decline of the dollar and its ultimate replacement by the renminbi (and before that, no doubt, various intermediate solutions). This will surely mark the demise of the US-dominated international system and the emergence of a new one in which China will be the dominant actor. The United States will strongly resist the decline of an international system from which it benefits so much: as a consequence, any transition is likely to be protracted and conflictual.[227] As during the interwar period, when British hegemony gave way to competing sterling, dollar and franc areas, it is possible to conceive of a scenario in which American hegemony is replaced, in the first instance at least, by competing regional spheres of influence. As the balance of power begins to shift decisively in China's favour, a potential division of the world into American and Chinese spheres of influence might be envisaged, with East Asia and Africa, for example, coming under Chinese tutelage, and forming part of a renminbi area, while Europe and the Middle East remain under the American umbrella. But this is purely speculative and such a process of Balkanization may not occur. Even if it does, in the longer run such arrangements are unlikely to be stable in a world which has become so integrated.[228] Rather, in time, as I have suggested, we will see the renminbi replacing the dollar as the major reserve currency as part of a new global financial system, with China the main architect and dominant player.

This brings us back to the present and the internationalization of the renminbi. Broadly speaking, there are two components to the rise of the renminbi: its use for trading purposes and as a reserve currency. The latter is likely to take at least a decade because it requires the currency to be convertible. The growing use of the renminbi for trade, however, has already started. Until very recently, the renminbi was barely used for trade purposes, despite the fact that China is the second largest economy in the world, the largest exporter of manufactured products and the biggest holder of foreign currency reserves. The reason is simple: China's capital controls and its tight restrictions on currency trade. After the financial crisis, however, the Chinese government shifted its position and decided to embark on a process of internationalizing the renminbi. The initial step was to encourage its use for trade. By June 2010 China had extended its year-old renminbi trade settlement scheme to every country in the world and to twenty Chinese provinces and cities, thereby allowing both exports and imports to be invoiced and settled in renminbi. To this end, however, countries and companies needed to be able to access renminbi offshore. This became possible shortly afterwards when China agreed to permit renminbi-denominated financial markets in Hong Kong. Then the Chinese government agreed to allow a small group of investors, including foreign central banks, limited access to China's onshore bond market. Malaysia was the first central bank to hold renminbi as part of its foreign currency reserves, but their number has steadily expanded and now includes India. South Korea's central bank has invested $370 billion of foreign exchange reserves in renminbi-denominated assets on the Chinese mainland as it seeks to diversify away from the US dollar.[229]

The result was dramatic: between June and November 2010, trade settled in renminbi amounted to Rmb340 billion compared with zero not much more than a year earlier. A growing number of Western multinationals, such as Caterpillar, Nokia, Ikea and McDonald's, are experimenting with using the renminbi in trade deals while the advantages for Chinese companies are obvious: avoiding the dollar enables them to reduce currency transaction costs and reduce foreign exchange risks. Meanwhile major banks such as HSBC, JP Morgan and Standard Chartered are rapidly building an infrastructure with which to handle worldwide renminbi transactions. The centre of this will be Hong Kong, which is the designated offshore centre for the renminbi. Most Hong Kong residents already believe that the future lies with the renminbi rather than the US dollar to which the HK dollar is currently pegged; there is a near universal expectation that the renminbi will appreciate and the US dollar depreciate and a kind of renminbi fever currently grips the former British territory. To boost the availability of the renminbi, since December 2008 the People's Bank of China, China's central bank, has also concluded currency swap arrangements with eight countries, including Argentina, Indonesia, Iceland and South Korea, totalling over Rmb800 billion, thereby enabling their trade with China to be paid for in renminbi. It seems likely that the use of the renminbi for trading purposes will take off first in East Asia – with demand already strong from Hong Kong, Malaysia, Singapore, Japan, and South Korea, for example – and then spread to other developing countries. HSBC estimated in 2010 that within three to five years at least half of China's trade flows with developing countries would be conducted in renminbi which, at about $2,000 billion, would immediately make it one of the three top global trading currencies, after the dollar and the euro, but ahead of the yen. On this basis, it is well within the bounds of possibility that in the same kind of time-frame, or a little longer, a majority of intra-East Asia trade will be conducted in the renminbi rather than, as at present, the dollar. The process by which the renminbi will be internationalized is a novel one. In the previous examples of sterling and the dollar, the process was market-driven. In China's case, it is being state-initiated rather than market-led.[230]

Within a period of five years or so, it is entirely possible that the renminbi will be highly internationalized and one of the major currencies in the settlement of trade; and within ten years it could even have supplanted the dollar in this role. Of course, only the removal of capital controls and the development of China's capital markets will allow the renminbi to become a major reserve currency, but we can now see relatively clearly how that process might develop, mindful of the fact that the Chinese authorities will not wish to allow it to jeopardize the development of the domestic economy.

11

When China Rules the World

What will the world look like in the much longer term, in twenty, or even fifty, years' time? The future, of course, is unknowable but in this chapter I will try to tease out what might be some of its more salient features. Such an approach, needless to say, is entirely speculative, resting on a range of assumptions some of which will inevitably prove to have been wrong.

Most fundamentally, I will assume that China's rise will not be derailed. China's economic growth rate, of course, is bound to decline over time, indeed the process has already started. As we discussed in Chapter 6, China is now confronted with making the difficult transition from being an export-orientated, labour-intensive economy, which is highly dependent on a very high savings ratio funding huge levels of investment, towards an increasingly innovative and capital-intensive economy, which is much less dependent on exports, much more dependent on domestic consumption and which invests a significantly reduced proportion of its GDP. In a sobering article in 2010, the leading Chinese economist Yu Yongding made a coruscating critique of the downside of the present growth model and argued that major reforms were now urgent: 'China has reached a critical juncture: without painful structural adjustments, the momentum of its economic growth could suddenly be lost.'[1] The latter scenario remains rather unlikely but without doubt the much-needed reforms will slow China's growth rate to a more manageable 7–8 per cent. It has often been suggested that China could hit the growth buffers in the same manner as Japan at the end of the 1980s: their circumstances, however, are entirely different. At that point Japan already had a very advanced economy, one of the most advanced in the world – whereas China remains overwhelmingly a developing country with a much lower GDP per head and therefore the prospect of many more years of rapid growth based on a catch-up economy and the migration of hundreds of millions from the countryside to the cities. Indeed, it would take another 25 years of rapid growth for China to achieve the same level of GDP per head that Japan enjoyed when its bubble economy burst.[2] Beyond the next decade, China's growth rate will continue to decline, perhaps to something more in the region of 5 per cent, as its economy steadily matures. Moreover, as we discussed in Chapter 6, China will increasingly face the problem of an ageing population, with a growing proportion of the population dependent on a contracting cohort that is economically active. Such a declining growth rate, however, is inevitable and in no way undermines the idea of China's continuing rise. It is also probable – certain, in fact – that within any of the longer time-frames there will be profound political changes in China, perhaps involving either the end of Communist rule or, more likely, a major metamorphosis in its character. Neither of these eventualities, however, would necessarily undermine the argument that underpins this chapter, that China, with continuing economic growth (albeit at a reduced rate), is destined to become one of the two major global powers and ultimately *the* major global power. What would demolish it is if, for some reason, China implodes in a twenty-first-century version of the intermittent bouts of introspection and instability that have punctuated Chinese history. This does not seem likely, but, given that China's unity has been under pressure – even siege – for around half of its 2,000-year life, this eventuality certainly cannot be excluded.

The scenario on which this chapter rests, then, is that China continues to grow stronger and ultimately emerges over the next half-century, or rather less in many respects, as the world's leading power. When I use the phrase 'China rules the world', I do not, of course, mean this literally: no nation ever has or ever will 'rule the world'. Rather it is a metaphor for a scenario in which China becomes the world's leading power, enjoying global hegemony in the manner of the United States, and before that Britain. Interestingly there is already a widespread global expectation that this may happen. As can be seen from Table 9, a majority of Indians, for example, believe that

	Will happen in ...			Will not replace	Don't know
	10 years	20 years	50 years		
	%	%	%	%	%
India	32	24	9	24	12
US	11	22	10	47	9
Russia	10	17	13	45	15
Japan	7	19	13	59	3
China	4	13	20	34	29

Source: Pew Global Attitudes

Table 9. Opinions on if and when China will replace the US as the dominant world power.

China will replace the United States as the dominant power within the next twenty years, while almost as many Americans and Russians believe in this scenario as think the contrary.

There is a surprisingly widely held view that the Chinese economy is already larger, as large or nearly as large as the American economy. (see Tables 10 and 11). In a Pew Global Attitudes Survey in spring 2010, more Americans, British, French, Germans, Russians and Japanese, for example, believed that the Chinese economy was larger than the American than thought the opposite, even though in the Goldman Sachs report, published in 2007, this was not projected to happen until 2027.[3] The general attitude towards China, moreover, is still relatively favourable, with a majority of countries polled having a favourable rather than unfavourable view, notably the United States, Russia, and those in the Middle East, Latin America and especially Africa (see Figure 70 and Table 12). Not surprisingly, given an economy that has been doubling in size approximately every seven years for over three decades, and the consequent transformation in living standards, the Chinese are hugely satisfied with their present economic situation, with steadily rising levels of satisfaction since 2002. In fact, the Chinese feel far better about their economic situation, invariably by a wide margin and generally by a colossal one, than the population of any other country polled (see Table 5 on p. 278 and Figures 37–8 on p. 279).

| | named as the world's leading economic power | | | | other/ |
	US %	China %	Japan %	EU %	DK %
US	38	41	8	6	7
Britain	38	44	5	8	6
France	41	47	5	7	0
Germany	18	51	8	19	4
Spain	40	34	12	8	5
Poland	44	27	9	10	11
Russia	23	27	25	9	16
Turkey	69	12	4	5	10
Egypt	42	37	12	7	1
Jordan	30	50	13	6	0
Lebanon	26	36	10	13	12
China	45	36	2	6	11
India	60	11	7	10	12
Indonesia	49	20	18	7	6
Japan	40	50	2	4	3
Pakistan	53	21	3	1	22
S Korea	77	15	1	5	3
Argentina	43	24	12	10	10
Brazil	51	18	13	5	14
Mexico	53	22	9	8	9
Kenya	61	20	7	6	6
Nigeria	55	27	7	5	7

Source: Pew Research Center, 2010

Table 10. US still seen as the leading economic power.

	2008 %	2009 %	2010 %
US	26	33	41
Germany	30	28	51
France	31	35	47
Spain	24	22	34
Britain	29	34	44
Poland	15	18	27
Russia	12	26	27
Turkey	7	9	12
Jordan	31	29	50
Egypt	27	25	37
Lebanon	22	32	36
Japan	19	21	50
Pakistan	18	26	21
S Korea	15	12	15
Indonesia	15	17	20
India	12	14	11
China	21	41	36
Mexico	17	16	22
Argentina	13	27	24
Brazil	–	–	18
Nigeria	23	18	27
Kenya	–	13	20

Source: Pew Research Centre, 2010

Table 11. But increasing numbers also see China as leading economic power.

	2002 %	2005 %	2006 %	2007 %	2008 %	2009 %	2010 %
US	–	43	52	42	39	50	49
Britain	–	65	65	49	47	52	46
France	–	58	60	47	28	41	41
Germany	–	46	56	34	26	29	30
Spain	–	57	45	39	31	40	47
Poland	–	37	–	39	33	43	46
Russia	71	60	63	60	60	58	60
Turkey	–	40	33	25	24	16	20
Egypt	–	–	63	65	59	52	52
Jordan	–	43	49	46	44	50	53
Lebanon	–	66	–	46	50	53	56
India	–	56	47	46	46	46	34
Indonesia	68	73	62	65	58	59	58
Japan	55	–	27	29	14	26	26
Pakistan	–	79	69	79	76	84	85
S Korea	66	–	–	52	48	41	38
Argentina	–	–	–	32	34	42	45
Brazil	–	–	–	–	–	–	52
Mexico	–	–	–	43	38	39	39
Kenya	–	–	–	81	–	73	86
Nigeria	–	–	59	75	79	85	76

Table 12. Proportion who regard China favourably.

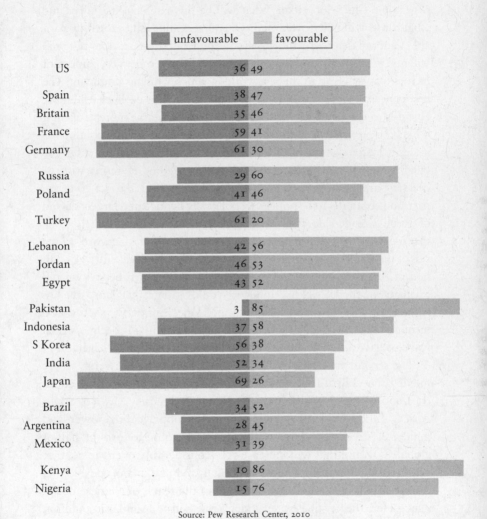

	unfavourable	favourable
US	36	49
Spain	38	47
Britain	35	46
France	59	41
Germany	61	30
Russia	29	60
Poland	41	46
Turkey	61	20
Lebanon	42	56
Jordan	46	53
Egypt	43	52
Pakistan	3	85
Indonesia	37	58
S Korea	56	38
India	52	34
Japan	69	26
Brazil	34	52
Argentina	28	45
Mexico	31	39
Kenya	10	86
Nigeria	15	76

Source: Pew Research Center, 2010

Figure 70. Views of China.

As China begins to emerge as a global power, what forms will its growing strength take? Or, to put it another way, what will a globally hegemonic China look like? What will be the extent of its power and what forms will that power take? Of course, China is not the only variable that will determine the answer to these questions: it does not, and will not, exist in isolation. Indeed, there will be two other very important factors that will help to shape a world in which China is dominant. The first concerns the United States: how quickly will it decline? The more able it is to reinvent itself in the face of China's rise, the more resilient it is likely to prove. In such a scenario, the United States would continue to act as a major constraint on the extent of Chinese hegemony. On the other hand, if the United States is unable to come to terms with its decline, paralysed by a psychosis of denial and a refusal to let go of the past, and continues to be hopelessly politically divided and largely devoid of effective leadership as a consequence, then its decline is likely to be that much faster. Furthermore, as I will discuss in the Afterword, as the rest of the world increasingly comes to recognize the degenerative condition of American power and factor this into their own behaviour and calculations, the US's global influence could wane rather more quickly. Although much less important than the United States, we should also mention the likely speed of Europe and Japan's continuing decline, which will also have a significant bearing on the extent of Chinese hegemony.

The second variable concerns the new developing powers. We are moving into a world in which the most populous developing countries, most notably India, but also Brazil, Indonesia, Mexico, South Africa, Turkey and others, will enjoy growing wealth, power and influence. Already the developing countries account for around half of global GDP and that will increase very considerably over the next 25 years. The relationship between China and the major developing countries will be a crucial determinant of the reach of Chinese dominance. Here the key question is India. Possessed of a similar population as China – albeit significantly younger – and a growth rate in recent years almost as great, India has the potential to become a serious long-term rival. But India still lags well behind China in terms of its economic development; it suffers from a grossly inefficient and corrupt state, is scarred by glaring inequality, and is confronted by guerrilla opposition across 40 per cent of the country, mainly concentrated in the south and east. For these reasons and others, it should not be taken for granted that India will follow closely in China's footsteps; if it does, however, it could act as a serious constraint on Chinese power. With the exception of India, none of the other developing countries I have mentioned can hope to rival Chinese power, but the extent to which they are able to establish themselves as regional powers will in turn oblige China to co-operate with them and serve to limit Chinese influence within their region. As a barometer of present Chinese power – and perhaps trends in the future – it is worth noting that China is becoming increasingly dominant within the BRICs grouping (Brazil, Russia, India, China – and South Africa, a recent addition, at China's behest); it presently accounts for about 12 per cent of trade in the rest of the BRICs countries – six times higher than in 2000 – while the other four countries devote only about 3 per cent of their trade to each other, a figure which has barely changed in the last decade. China, in short, is rapidly extending its lead over the other BRIC countries.[4] It is clear that we are moving towards an increasingly multipolar world compared both with the present situation and certainly the bipolar Cold War, but how multipolar, and in what ways, remains an open question.

As we peer into the future, history can in a limited way serve as some kind of guide to the nature and extent of a future Chinese hegemony. Over the last two centuries, there have been two globally dominant powers: Britain between 1850 and 1914, and the United States from 1945 to the present. Given that it is the more contemporary example, the American experience, while in no sense acting as a model, can nonetheless serve as a reference point in seeking to understand what a *Pax Sinica* might be like, including how it might be different. So what are, or have been, the characteristics of America's global hegemony?

- It has the world's largest economy.
- It has one of the world's highest GDPs per head.
- It has the world's most technologically advanced and innovative economy, as exemplified by Silicon Valley, with the highest level of expenditure on research and development.
- It is by far the world's strongest military power, which, based

on its maritime and air strength, enables it to exercise influence in every region of the world.

- Its overall global power means that it is a key factor in the calculations and attitudes of more or less every country in the world. All countries, as a consequence, enjoy, in varying degrees, limited sovereignty, from the UK and Israel to Mexico and even China.

- The international economic system was predominantly designed and shaped by the United States and its rules are still determined largely by the US.

- It is home to a large majority of the best universities in the world and has long attracted some of the most able global talent.

- English has become the global lingua franca largely because of the power and appeal of the United States.

- Hollywood dominates the global film market and, to a rather lesser extent, that of television as well.

- American corporate brand names like Google, Microsoft, Coca-Cola and Wal-Mart tend to predominate over those of other nations,[5] with many enjoying a global presence.

- The United States is not only by far the most important country in the world but New York is also, de facto, the world's capital.

- American history has become part of the global furniture, with its most important landmarks, such as the Declaration of Independence, the Civil War and the frontier spirit, familiar to the entire world. Similarly, its customs, from Thanksgiving Day to Halloween, often have a global resonance.

- American values – be it individualism, democracy, human rights, neo-liberalism, neo-Conservatism, the market, freedom or the frontier spirit – often enjoy a preponderant global influence.

- American supremacy has been associated with the global dominance of the white race and, by implication, the subordination and subjugation of other races in an informal global hierarchy of race.

Even in the case of the United States, however, whose influence is far greater than that of any other nation in history, this overweening power has never been without constraint. The concept of hegemony elaborated by the Italian Marxist Antonio Gramsci – which should be distinguished from the pejorative Chinese use of the term[6] – entails the complex interaction of coercion and consent, force and leadership, and, though it was originally advanced to explain the nature of power within societies, it is also relevant to international relations.[7] Gramsci's idea bears some resemblance to the distinction between hard and soft power employed by the American writer Joseph Nye, though Nye's approach is less conceptual and more classificatory in nature.[8] Far from hegemony being set in concrete, it is constantly contested and redefined, the balance of power never static, always in motion. Nor is it ever absolute. Even though the United States possesses almost as much military firepower as the rest of the world put together, that does not mean that it can do whatever it likes wherever it chooses, as its disastrous occupation of Iraq illustrated. Moreover, as we have observed, while it enjoys military supremacy, its economic preponderance is steadily being eroded. Although the US is the world's sole politico-military superpower, its influence varies from region to region and sphere to sphere – and in some cases it remains extremely limited. Take the unlikely example of sport. Although the US generally tops the medals tables in the Olympic Games, there are many sports in which it is not dominant and others from which it is virtually absent. The most popular American sports have remained largely confined to the US in their appeal, with the exception of basketball, while the world's most popular game is football, a European export. Similarly, apart from its domination of a key sector of the fast-food market, American cuisine enjoys little or no global influence.

So what about China? As in the case of the United States, Chinese global hegemony will reflect the country's particular characteristics, both historical and contemporary. The task here is to identify those characteristics and how they might leave their imprint on the future. It should also be borne in mind that forms of hegemony are constantly shifting and mutating in response to wider cultural, technological, military, political and economic changes. In the era of European supremacy, for example, the characteristic form of political domination was colonialism and the key expression of force-projection was the navy, but after 1945 colonialism, for a variety of reasons, became unsustainable. The American era, in contrast, is associated with air power, a global network of military bases, huge military superiority, an informal empire, dominance of the international economic system, and a global media. It is obviously impossible, beyond a point, to anticipate the new forms of modernity with which a future Chinese hegemony might be associated.

THE LONG REACH OF CHINESE HISTORY

Global history has hitherto been essentially a Western history. With the rise of China, however, that will no longer be the case. Chinese history will become familiar not just to the Chinese, or even East Asians, but to the entire world. Just as many around the globe are conversant with major events in American history (the same also being true of decisive episodes in European history – such as the French Revolution, the Enlightenment, the Industrial Revolution and the Renaissance – as a consequence of Europe's earlier supremacy), key landmarks in Chinese history will similarly become global property. This process is already under way, as the huge interest that surrounded the Terracotta Army exhibition at the British Museum in 2007–8 illustrated.[9] Of course, the grandeur and richness of Chinese history means that aspects of it, such as the Great Wall, are already well known. But this is minor compared with what lies in the future. As an indication, already in 2005 the Great Wall, one of the defining symbols of the Middle Kingdom, attracted more foreign tourists than Florence, the epicentre of Europe's Renaissance.[10]

Apart from its extraordinary longevity and bursts of efflorescent invention, the most striking feature of Chinese history is the fact that while Europe, following the fall of the Roman Empire, fragmented into many parts, and ultimately into many nations, China was already moving in exactly the opposite direction and starting to coalesce. It is this unity that has ensured the continuity of its civilization and also provided the size which remains so fundamental to China's character and impact. Unity is one of the most fundamental propositions concerning Chinese history, if not the most fundamental. If Europe provided the narrative and concepts that have informed not just Western but world history over the past two centuries, so China may do rather similarly for the next century or so, and thereby furnish the world with an entirely different story and set of concepts: namely the idea of unity rather than fragmentation, that of the civilization-state rather than the nation-state, that of the tributary system rather than the Westphalian system and colonialism, a distinctive Chinese notion of race, and an organizing political dynamic of centralization/decentralization rather than modernization/conservatism. Given the nodal importance of Chinese unity, the year 221 BC – marking the victory of the Qin, the end of the Warring States period (403–221 BC), and the beginning of modern China – will become as familiar to the world as 1776 or 1789. Qin Shihuang, the first Chinese emperor, who not only bequeathed the Terracotta Army but founded a dynastic system which was to survive until 1912, will become as widely known as Thomas Jefferson or Napoleon Bonaparte, indeed much more so.

There are many other aspects of Chinese history which will reconfigure the global discourse: the fact, for example, that China has been responsible for so many of the inventions that were subsequently adopted elsewhere, not least in the West, will help to dispel the contemporary myth that the West is history's most inventive culture. For our purposes here, the voyages of Zheng He, which predated those of Europe's great maritime explorers like Christopher Columbus, can serve as an example for this process of reconfiguration. It is widely accepted that, in ships that dwarfed those of Europe at the time, Zheng He embarked on a series of seven voyages that took him to what we now know as Indonesia, the Indian Ocean and the east coast of Africa in the early fifteenth century. The voyages of the great European explorers like Vasco da Gama and Columbus marked the beginning of Europe's long-running colonial era. For the Chinese, on the other hand, Zheng's voyages had no such consequence. There was no institution in Ming China that resembled a Navy Department and therefore, as the historian Edward Dreyer suggests, 'there was no vested interest to argue the case for sea power or for a blue water strategy, nor did China exercise what later naval theorists would call "control of the seas", even during the period of Zheng He's voyages.'[11] Zheng's voyages never had a sequel: they proved to be the final curtain in the Ming dynasty's maritime expeditions as China once again slowly turned inwards. Zheng's missions were neither colonial nor exploratory in intent: if they had been, they would surely have been repeated. They were influence-maximizing missions designed to carry out the very traditional aim of spreading China's authority and prestige in what was its known world. The Chinese had no interest in exploring unknown places, but in making peoples in its known world aware of the presence, greatness and superiority of the Chinese empire. Zheng He's expedition lay firmly within the idiom of the tributary state system, though his journeys took him much further afield than had previously been the case.[12]

History is always subject to interpretation and reinterpretation, constantly reworked in the light of a contemporary context. Given their extraordinary nature, and bearing in mind subsequent European exploits, it is not surprising that both the purpose and reach of Zheng's expeditions have been the subject of much conjecture. As China again seeks a closer relationship with South-East Asia, the fact that China has recently sponsored several commemorative exhibitions of Zheng He's expeditions in various ASEAN countries is predictable:[13] as it turns outwards once more, it remembers and reminds the world of the last such great occasion. The British historian Gavin Menzies has taken the process several steps further by arguing that the Chinese were the first to discover the Americas in 1421 and also discovered Australia.[14] While there has been much interest in, though little support for, the idea that the Chinese discovered America, when President Hu Jintao visited Australia in 2003 he gave implicit endorsement to the idea that China discovered Australia when, in an address to a joint meeting of the Australian parliament, he declared: 'Back in the 1420s, the expeditionary fleets of China's Ming dynasty reached Australian shores.'[15] These kinds of claims are likely to increase as Western-written history is contested by the growth in Chinese-written history and as China seeks to burnish its contemporary image not only by promoting its own past but also, no doubt, aggrandizing and embellishing it. The Chinese ambassador to South Africa suggested to Africans in 2007 that:

Zheng took to the places he visited [in Africa] tea, chinaware, silk and technology. He did not occupy an inch of foreign land, nor did he take a single slave. What he brought to the outside world was peace and civilization. This fully reflects the good faith of the ancient Chinese people in strengthening exchanges with relevant countries and their people. This peace-loving culture has taken deep root in the minds and hearts of Chinese people of all generations.[16]

On a light-hearted note, there is evidence to suggest that the game of golf originated in China. A Ming scroll by the artist Youqiu, entitled

Detail from The Autumn Banquet *by Youqiu, 1368.*

The Autumn Banquet and dating back to 1368, shows a member of the imperial court swinging what resembles a golf club at a small ball, with the aim of sinking it in a round hole. In Chinese the game was known as *chuiwan*, or 'hit ball'.[17]

It is reasonable to surmise that many of the sports that have previously been regarded as European inventions, and especially British, actually had their origins in other parts of the world: the British, after all, had plenty of opportunity to borrow and assimilate games from their far-flung empire and then codify the rules. As we move beyond a Western-dominated world, these kinds of discoveries and assertions will become more common, with some, perhaps many, destined to gain widespread acceptance. Not surprisingly, there is also a growing desire on the part of former colonized countries to repatriate the antiquities and artefacts that were stolen by the colonizers, claimed as their own, and which subsequently became prized exhibits at such places as the British Museum. China was no exception to this process of pillage. In 2009, for example, two bronzes were auctioned in Paris as part of the collection of the late Yves Saint Laurent, in spite of Chinese protests that they had been stolen by the British and French armies when they destroyed the Old Summer Palace in Beijing in the aftermath of the Second Opium War in 1860. In the event, the bronzes were bought by Cai Mingchao, an auctioneer and collector himself, who then refused to pay and was hailed as a hero in China. There will no doubt be countless similar disputes in the future, involving not only China but many other countries who similarly feel that their historical heritage has been looted.[18]

BEIJING AS THE NEW GLOBAL CAPITAL

At the turn of the century, New York was the de facto capital of the world. Nothing more clearly illustrated this than the global reaction to 9/11. If the same fate had befallen the far more splendid Twin Towers in Kuala Lumpur, the disaster would have been fortunate to have commanded global headlines for twelve hours, let alone months on end.

New York's prominence owes everything to the fact that it is the financial capital of the world, the home of Wall Street, as well as a great melting pot and the original centre of European immigration. New York's global status is, however, largely a post-1945 phenomenon. In 1900, during the first wave of globalization, the world's capital was London. And in 1500, arguably Florence was the most important city in the world (though in that era it could hardly have been described as the global capital). In 1000 perhaps Kaifeng in China enjoyed a similar status, albeit unknown to most of the world, while in AD 1 it was probably Rome.[19] Looking forward once again, it seems likely that in fifty years' time, if not earlier, Beijing will have assumed the status of de facto global capital. It will face competition from other Chinese cities, notably Shanghai, but as China's capital, the centre of the Middle Kingdom and the home of the Forbidden City, Beijing's candidature will be assured, assuming China becomes the world's leading power.

But this is not simply a matter of Beijing's status. We can assume that Chinese hegemony will involve at least four fundamental geopolitical shifts: first, that Beijing will emerge as the global capital; second, that China will become the world's leading power; third, that East Asia will be the world's most important region; and fourth, that Asia will assume the role of the world's most important continent, a process that will also be enhanced by the rise of India. These multiple changes will, figuratively at least, amount to a shift in the earth's axis. The world has become accustomed to looking west, towards Europe and more recently the United States: that era is now coming to an end. London might still represent zero when it comes to time zones, a legacy of its once-dominant status in the world,[20] but the global community will increasingly set its watches to Beijing time.

THE RISE OF THE CIVILIZATION-STATE

The world has become accustomed to thinking in terms of the nation-state. It is one of the great legacies of the era of European domination. Nations that are not yet nation-states aspire to become one. The nation-state enjoys universal acceptance as the primary unit and agency of the international system. After the 1911 Revolution, even China was obliged to define itself as a nation-state. But, as we have seen, China is only latterly, and still only partially, a nation-state: for the most part, it is something very different, a civilization-state. As Lucian Pye argued:

> China is not just another nation-state in the family of nations. China is a civilization pretending to be a state. The story of modern China could be described as the effort by both Chinese and foreigners to squeeze a civilization into the arbitrary and constraining framework of a modern state, an institutional invention that came out of the fragmentation of Western civilization.[21]

It is this civilizational dimension which gives China its special and unique character. Most of China's main characteristics pre-date its attempts to become a nation-state and are a product of its existence as a civilization-state: the overriding importance of unity, the power and role of the state, its centripetal quality, the notion of Greater China, the Middle Kingdom mentality, Confucian values, the idea of race, the family and familial discourse, even traditional Chinese medicine.

Hitherto, the political traffic has all been in one direction, the desire of the world, including latterly the Chinese, to conform to the established Western template of the international system, namely the nation-state. This idea has played a fundamental role in China's attempts to modernize over the last 150 years from a beleaguered position of backwardness. But what happens when China no longer feels that its relationship with the West should be uni-directional, when it begins to believe in itself and its history and culture with a new sense of confidence, not as some great treasure trove, but as of direct and operational relevance to the present? That process is well under way[22] and will only get stronger with time. This will inexorably lead to a shift in the terms of China's relationship with the international system: in effect, China will increasingly think of itself, and be treated by others, as a civilization-state rather than – or at least as well as – a nation-state. As we saw in Chapter 9, this has already begun to happen in East Asia and in due course it is likely to have wider global ramifications. Instead of the world thinking exclusively in terms of nation-states, as has been the case since the end of colonialism, the lexicon of international relations will become more diverse, demanding room be made for competing concepts, different histories and varying sizes.

THE RETURN OF THE TRIBUTARY SYSTEM

The Westphalian system has dominated international relations ever since the emergence of the modern European nation-state. It has become the universal conceptual language of the international system. As we have seen, however, the Westphalian system has itself metamorphosed over time and enjoyed several different iterations. Even so, it remains what it was, an essentially European-derived concept designed to make the world conform to its imperatives and modalities. As a consequence, different parts of the world approximate in differing degrees to the Westphalian norm. Arguably this congruence has been least true in East Asia, where the legacy of the tributary state system, and the presence of China, mean that the Westphalian system exists in combination with, and on top of, pre-existing structures and attitudes. The specificity of the East Asian reality is illustrated by the fact that most Western predictions about the likely path of interstate relations in the region since the end of the Cold War and the rise of China have not been borne out: namely, that there would be growing instability, tension and even war and that the rise of China would persuade other nations to balance and hedge against it. In the event, there have been rather fewer wars since 1989 than was the case during the Cold War, and there is little evidence of countries seeking to balance against China, with the obvious exception of Japan: on the contrary, most countries have prioritized the need for a good relationship with China, just as they did during the long history of the tributary system.[23] This suggests that the modus operandi of East Asia is rather different to elsewhere and contrasts with Western expectations formed on the basis of its own history and experience. A fundamental feature of the tributary state system was the enormous inequality between China and all other nations in its orbit, and this inequality was intrinsic to the stability that characterized the system for so long. It may well be that the new East Asian order, now being configured around an increasingly dominant China, will prove similarly stable: in other words, as with the tributary system, overweening inequality breeds underlying stability, which is the opposite to the European experience, where roughly equal nation-states were almost constantly at war with each other over many centuries until 1945, when, emerging exhausted from the war, they discovered the world was no longer Eurocentric.[24]

The idea that East Asia in future will owe as much to the tributary system as the Westphalian system will inevitably influence how China views the wider international system. Moreover if East Asia, as the most important region in the world, operates according to different criteria to other parts of the global system, then this is bound to colour behaviour and norms elsewhere. In other words, the tributary state system will not only shape China's outlook but, in the context of its global hegemony, is also likely to influence the international system more widely. As the writer David Kang suggests, the modalities of East Asia in terms of interstate relations, from being ignored or marginalized until the end of the Cold War, will increasingly assume the role of one of the world's major templates.[25]

Two key characteristics of the tributary system were the overwhelming size of China in comparison with its neighbours and a mutual acceptance of and acquiescence in Chinese superiority. In the era of globalization, these characteristics, certainly the first, might be transferred on to a wider canvas. Such will be the relative economic size and power of China that it is likely to find itself in relationships of profound inequality with many countries outside, as well as within, East Asia; as a result, they are likely to find themselves highly dependent on China. The most obvious example of this is Africa and to a lesser extent various Latin American countries like Peru and Bolivia; in other words, developing countries which are predominantly commodity-producers.[26] As China's voracious appetite for raw materials grows apace, more and more such countries are likely to enter into its orbit. In this context, it is worth noting that China, along with other countries including South Korea, India and Saudi Arabia, has been leasing and buying up farmland, especially in Africa, in order to boost its supply of food, the biggest purchase being 2.8 million hectares in Congo for a huge palm-oil plantation.[27] There is a natural but mistaken tendency to view China's emergent relationship with these countries in the same terms as those of the West, as a replay, in other words, of Western history. But China did not follow the European pattern of colonization even though it had ample opportunity to do so. Because of the huge disparity in size, and China's own history, it would be more appropriate to think of China's relationships with these countries in neo-tributary terms rather than in colonial or neo-colonial terms. To what extent the other characteristic of the tributary system – an acceptance of China's cultural superiority – might also become a factor is more difficult to judge, although given how deeply entrenched such attitudes are, and their sheer historical endurance, they will surely continue to influence Chinese perceptions and behaviour. It is important, however, to place these various points in a broader context. China's rise will be accompanied by that of other major developing countries, such as India and Brazil, and these are likely to act in some degree as a constraint on China's power and instincts.

WEIGHT OF NUMBERS

At the height of the British Empire in 1913, Britain accounted for only 2.5 per cent of the world's population, while Western Europe represented 14.6 per cent. By 2001 Western Europe's share had fallen to 6.4 per cent. In the same year, when the United States was the world's sole superpower, it comprised a mere 4.6 per cent of the world's population. The proportion accounted for by the West as a whole – including Eastern Europe and countries like Australia but excluding the former USSR – was 13.9 per cent in 2001. China, in contrast, comprised 20.7 per cent of the world's population in that year.[28] Whatever the obvious commonalities – historical, cultural and ethnic – that serve to link and cohere the Western world, this is very different from the unity and cohesion that China enjoys as a single nation. The true comparison is China's 20.7 per cent against the US's 4.6 per cent. In other words China, as the world's leading country, will enjoy a demographic weight that is qualitatively different from that of any previous hegemonic power in the modern era.

The basis of democracy is that every person counts. Hitherto this proposition has been confined within the boundaries of each individual nation-state. It has never found any form of expression at a supranational, let alone global, level, with the possible exception of the United Nations General Assembly – which, predictably, enjoys virtually no power. Institutions like the IMF and the World Bank have never sought to be democratic but instead reflect the economic and political clout of those countries that founded and control them, hence the dominance of the United States and to a lesser extent Europe, with the US alone enjoying the power of veto in the IMF. The Western world order has – in its post-1945 idiom – placed a high premium on democracy within nation-states while attaching zero importance to democracy at the global level. As a global order, it has been anti-democratic and highly authoritarian. The emergence of China as the globally dominant nation is very unlikely to usher in a new kind of democratic global governance, but the rise of developing nations like India, Brazil and Russia, along with China, will bring, in a rough and ready way, a far more democratic global economy. The huge mismatch between a relative handful of rich countries containing a very small percentage of the world's population on the one hand, and the vast majority of the world's population living in the great majority of countries enjoying very little wealth on the other, which has characterized the last two centuries, will be significantly reduced. For the developing world, including the most populous countries like China, India, Brazil and Indonesia, poverty has meant marginalization or effective exclusion from global decision-making; economic power, in contrast, is a passport to global enfranchisement. To put it another way, a global economic regime based on the BRICs (namely Brazil, Russia, India, China and South Africa), together with other developing countries, will be inherently more democratic than the

Western regime that has previously prevailed. Furthermore, the fact that China, as the top dog, is so numerous will in itself introduce a more democratic element, albeit in the crudest sense, to the global polity. One-fifth of the world, after all, is rather more representative than the US's 4.6 per cent.[29]

That China, as a global power, will be so numerous will have many consequences. China will exercise a gravitational pull and also have a centrifugal impact on the rest of the world. There will be many aspects to this push-pull phenomenon. The size of the Chinese market means that, in time, it will inevitably become by far the world's largest. As a result, it will also assume the role of de facto template for most global standards and regulations. The size of its domestic market will also have the consequence that Chinese companies will be the biggest in the world, as will the Chinese stock exchanges. In the 1950s Europeans were astounded by the scale of all things American; in the future, these will be dwarfed by the magnitude of all things Chinese. Even Las Vegas, the once unchallenged gambling capital of the world, has been overtaken by Macao: in 2010 the latter's gaming revenues were four times greater than those of Las Vegas. An example of China's centrifugal impact is offered by Chinese migration. China will be a net exporter of people, as Europe was until the mid twentieth century, but unlike the United States, which remains a net importer.[30] A small insight into what this might mean is provided by the rapid migration of hundreds of thousands of Chinese to Africa in the first decade of the twenty-first century. If the economic relationship between China and Africa continues to develop along the same lines in the future, Chinese settlers in sub-Saharan Africa could come to represent a significant minority of its population. It is not inconceivable that large numbers of Chinese might eventually migrate to Japan to compensate for its falling population, though this would require a sea-change in Japanese attitudes towards immigration. It is estimated that the Chinese minority there, legal and illegal, presently numbers up to 400,000.[31] The Chinese are already a rapidly growing minority in Russia, especially in the Russian Far East. In comparison with Americans, then, if not necessarily with the Europeans before them, the Chinese will be far more ubiquitous in the world.

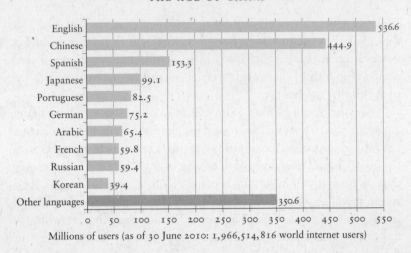

Millions of users (as of 30 June 2010: 1,966,514,816 world internet users)

Source: Miniwatts Marketing Group

Figure 71. Top ten internet languages, June 2010.

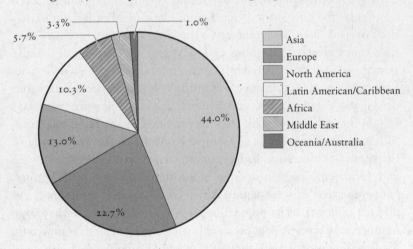

Source: Miniwatts Marketing Group

Figure 72. World internet users, March 2011.

Another example will be provided by tourism. Mainland Chinese made 54 million trips overseas in 2010 compared with 28 million in 2004, and the Chinese government expects this to rise to 100 million by 2015, though HSBC predicts 130 million.[32] The World Travel and Tourism Council estimates that by 2018 the value of Chinese tourism will almost be as great as that of the United States. The impact will be greatest in East Asia, especially South-East Asia, and Australia, where many destinations will seem as if they have been taken over by Chinese tourists, a phenomenon that hitherto has been almost exclusively Western, but which will happen on a far grander scale with the Chinese.[33] The Chinese language, similarly, will assume global importance simply because it has so many native speakers; this will contrast with recent periods of history when the USSR and later Japan were riding high but which, partly because of their relatively small populations, had little linguistic impact, apart from on Eastern Europe in the case of the Soviet Union, outside their own borders. In terms of language, it is already possible to glimpse the future through those who use the internet. Though the proportion of China's population who are internet users is far smaller than that in the United States, by 2008 the number of Chinese internet users had already overtaken the number of American users.[34]

THE CHINESE RACIAL ORDER

For the last two centuries Caucasians have enjoyed a privileged position at the top of the global racial hierarchy. During the period of European colonial empires their pre-eminent position was frequently explained in terms of racial theories designed to show the inherent superiority of the white race. Since the mid twentieth century, with the defeat of Nazism followed by colonial liberation, such explicitly racial theories have been in retreat in most regions of the world and now enjoy only minority appeal in the West. Nonetheless, if such racial theories are no longer regarded for the most part as acceptable, there remains an implicit and omnipresent global racial pecking order, with whites invariably at the top. Various factors have helped to shape this hierarchy, including levels of development, skin colour, physical characteristics, history, religion, dress, customs and centuries-old racist beliefs and prejudices. Throughout the world, white people command respect and deference, often tinged with fear and resentment, an attitude which derives from a combination of having been globally dominant for so long, huge wealth, overwhelming military power, and genuine achievement. The rise of China to surpass the West will, over time, inevitably result in a gradual reordering of the global hierarchy of race.[35]

Although possessed of an inner belief that they are superior to all others, the Chinese sense of confidence was shaken and in part undermined by the 'century of humiliation'. This found expression during the 1980s in what Wang Xiaodong has described as 'reverse racism', or a desire to ape and copy the West, and denigrate things Chinese.[36] That phase, however, is increasingly giving way to a growing sense of self-belief and a return to older attitudes. The idea that China must learn from the West is being joined by the proposition that the West needs to learn from the East.[37] The fact that the Chinese sense of superiority survived more than a century and a half of being hugely outperformed by the West is testament to its deeply ingrained nature. As China becomes a major global player, this feeling of superiority will be supported and reinforced by new rationales, arguments and evidence. Chinese racial discourse, furthermore, as we saw in Chapter 8, differs in important respects from that of Europe, primarily because its origins lie in China's existence as a civilization-state rather than as a nation-state.

In a few limited areas, such as football, athletics and popular music, the global predominance of Caucasians has come under significant challenge. But the ubiquity of the white role-model in so many spheres – business, law, accounting, academe, fashion, global political leadership – still overwhelmingly prevails. Figures like Barack Obama and Tiger Woods remain very much the exception, though the former's election as American president is highly significant in this context. Nelson Mandela came to enjoy enormous moral authority throughout the world but enjoyed little substantive power. With the rise of China, white domination will come under serious challenge for the first time in many, if not most, areas of global activity.

The pervasive importance of racial attitudes should not be underestimated. International relations scholars have persistently neglected or ignored their significance as a major determinant of national behaviour and global relations, preferring instead to concentrate on nationalism; yet, as we saw in Chapter 8, race and ethnicity are central to the way in which nations are constructed.[38] This has been well described by the Chinese international relations scholar Zi Zhongyun in the case of the United States.[39] The fact that there has been virtually no challenge to, or questioning of, widely held racial prejudices in China, that they are regarded as normative rather than abnormal and that there is no culture of anti-racism, means that they will continue to exercise a powerful influence on how China sees the world, how the Chinese at all levels of society regard others, and how China will behave as a nation. Of course, as China becomes increasingly open to the world and mixes with it on a quite new basis following centuries of being relatively closed, then some of the old prejudices are bound to wither and disappear, but the persistence of these kinds of attitudes, rooted as they are in such a long history, will remain. As the dominant global power, China is likely to have a strongly hierarchical view of the world, based on a combination of racial and cultural attitudes, and this will play a fundamental role in shaping how China views other nations and peoples and its own position at the top of the ladder.

A CHINESE COMMONWEALTH?

The concept of the West is intimately linked to European expansion and the migration of its population to far-flung parts of the world. This is a neglected issue, something that is largely taken for granted and little scrutinized. It was European emigration that led to the creation of the United States as a white-dominated society in the northern part of the American continent, and likewise in the case of Canada. The term 'Latin America' derives from the Spanish and Portuguese colonization of South America and to this day finds expression in the fact that the elite in these countries remains predominantly white and is largely descended from the original colonial families.[40] Similarly, British migration created a white Australia – which, together with New Zealand, formed in effect an Asia–Pacific outpost of the West – based on the suppression, decimation and subsequent marginalization of the indigenous Aborigine peoples. But for that, Australia and New Zealand would today be Aboriginal and Maori countries respectively, with entirely different names, languages and cultures. If European migration to South Africa had been on a much greater scale, then the large white minority population might have been in a majority, thereby making white rule permanent. The European, or white, diaspora has had a huge impact on the nature and shape of the world as we know it.

Unlike the white diaspora, which was a product of relative European power and wealth, the Chinese diaspora was largely a consequence of hunger and poverty at home, combined with the use of Chinese indentured labour in the British Empire. This notwithstanding, the Chinese diaspora in South-East Asia enjoys, relatively speaking, disproportionate economic power, while Chinese ethnic minorities more or less everywhere have experienced increasing economic success in recent decades. From being industrious but poor, the Chinese are steadily rising up the ladder of their respective adoptive homelands in both economic and cultural terms. That process is being driven in part by the growing power of China, which is serving to raise the self-confidence, prestige and status of the overseas Chinese everywhere. The multifarious links between the mainland and the Chinese diaspora, in terms of trade and Mandarin, for example, are predictably helping to enhance the economic position of the overseas Chinese. In some Western countries, notably Australia and also in Milan in Italy, where there have been clashes between the increasingly prosperous Chinese community and the local police, there has been evidence of strong resentment towards the local Chinese.[41] The recent economic success of the Chinese, who have traditionally been regarded as inferior and impoverished, has proved disconcerting for sections of the Milanese population. Similarly, in Prato in Tuscany, local feeling has recently turned against the Chinese community, where the Chinese are estimated to comprise 40,000 of a total population of 180,000, and there was a big crackdown against them by the right-wing Lega Nord mayor, backed by the Berlusconi government.[42] Yet, as China becomes steadily wealthier and more powerful, Westerners will have to get used to the idea that growing numbers of Chinese at home and abroad will be more successful and richer than they are. They will not find this easy, given how deeply rooted these preconceptions and prejudices are.

This brings us to China's attitude towards the overseas Chinese. As mentioned earlier, one of the narratives of Chinese civilization is that of Greater China, an idea which embraces the 'lost territories' of Hong Kong, Macao and Taiwan, the global Chinese diaspora and the mainland. The Middle Kingdom has always been regarded as the centre of the Chinese world, with Beijing at its heart and the disapora at its distant edges. All Chinese have held an essentially centripetal view of their world. The way that the diaspora has contributed to China's economic transformation is an indication of a continuing powerful sense of belonging. The rise of China will further enhance its appeal and prestige in the eyes of the diaspora and reinforce their sense of Chineseness. The Chinese government has sought, with considerable success, to encourage eminent overseas Chinese scholars to work and settle in China, which has been a key plank in its efforts to shift the economy towards more value-added production. Meanwhile, as discussed earlier, Chinese migration is on the increase, notably to Africa, resulting in the creation of new, as well as enlarged, overseas Chinese communities. It is estimated that there are now at least half a million Chinese living in Africa, most of whom have arrived only very recently. There are over 7 million Chinese living in each of Indonesia, Malaysia and Thailand, over 1 million each in Myanmar and Russia, 1.3 million in Peru, 3.3 million in the United States, 700,000 in Australia and 400,000 in the UK; the approximate figure for the diaspora as a whole is 45 million (excluding Taiwan), but this may well be a considerable underestimate.

Historically, imperial China regarded those who left China with disdain, regarding their departure as no less than stepping outside of civilization. Contemporary Chinese attitudes are very different, with the Chinese government encouraging some types of migration and seeking to establish a positive and supportive relationship with overseas Chinese communities. How will this relationship between China and the diaspora develop? Will the mainland at some point consider allowing dual citizenship, which at the moment it does not? Is it conceivable that in the future there might be a Chinese Commonwealth which embraces the numerous overseas Chinese communities? Or, to put it another way, what forms might a Chinese civilization-state take in a modern world in which it is predominant? A commonwealth would no doubt be unacceptable to other nations as things stand, but in the event of a globally dominant China, the balance of power would be transformed and what is politically possible redefined. The impact of any such development would, of course, be felt most strongly in South-East Asia, where the overseas Chinese are, relatively speaking, both most powerful and most numerous.

ECONOMIC POWERHOUSE

Chinese economic power will underpin its global hegemony. With the passing decades, as the Chinese economy becomes increasingly wealthy and sophisticated, so the nature of that power will no longer rest primarily on the country's demographic clout. It is impossible to predict exactly what this might eventually mean in terms of economic reach, but, given that China has a population around four times that of the United States, one might conjure with the idea that China's economy could be four times as large as that of the US at some point in the distant future. The Goldman Sachs projections in 2007, cited in Chapter 1, suggested that the Chinese economy would overtake the US economy in size in 2027 – although more recent post-financial crisis estimates indicate 2020 – and that by 2050 the Chinese economy would be almost twice the size of the American economy. China is already the world's second largest exporter and it will soon become the largest, while in 2011 it became the world's biggest producer of manufactured products. As both a huge exporter and importer (mainly of natural resources), Chinese trade already has a very large global footprint. In 1990, China was the largest trading partner of a tiny number of countries in East Asia; by 2002, this group had expanded significantly and by 2010 China had become the largest trading partner of many countries in East Asia. Even more dramatically,

Company	Country	Market value $m	Sector
1 PetroChina	China	329,259.7	oil & gas producers
2 Exxon Mobil	US	316,230.8	oil & gas producers
3 Microsoft	US	256,864.7	software & computer services
4 Industrial & Commercial Bank of China	China	246,419.8	banks
5 Apple	US	213,096.7	technology hardware & equipment
6 BHP Billiton	Australia/UK	209,935.1	mining
7 Wal-Mart Stores	US	209,000.7	general retailers
8 Berkshire Hathaway	US	200,620.5	nonlife insurance
9 General Electric	US	194,246.2	general industrials
10 China Mobile	Hong Kong	192,998.6	mobile telecommunications

Source: *Financial Times*

Table 13. Biggest global companies by market value, 2010.

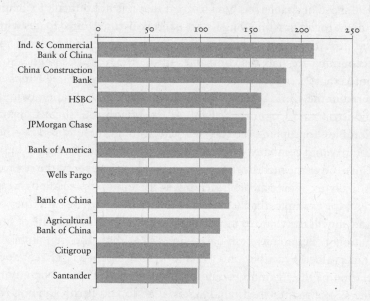

Source: Bloomberg, company prospectus

Figure 73. World's biggest banks, by market capitalization, 7 July 2010, $bn.

by 2010 China had become the largest trading partner of a growing number of countries around the world, including Brazil, Argentina, Chile, Russia, South Africa, India and Egypt. The rapid expansion of Chinese trade over the last 30 years is set to continue so that by 2030, for example, many countries in many continents are likely to count China as their biggest trading partner.

In 2010 Chinese companies accounted for two of the top five in the Forbes Global 2000 by market capitalization, and three of the top ten. According to a similar compilation by the *Financial Times*, 23 Chinese companies featured in the top 500 companies by market capitalization in 2010, which made China sixth in terms of the number of its companies that were represented (the US was first with 163 companies) and third by market value; if companies registered in Hong Kong are also included, China comes second in terms both of the number of companies represented and according to market value. In contrast, no Chinese companies featured in the top 500 in 2006 (there were seven from Hong Kong) and even in 2007 there were only eight Chinese companies in the top 500 (and eight from Hong Kong).[43] The speed of change has been so great that it is not difficult to imagine China (together with Hong Kong) overtaking the United States within the next decade in terms of companies represented and by 2030 accounting for half the companies in the top 500. It should also be noted that in 2010, according to Bloomberg, four Chinese banks featured in the world's top ten banks by market capitalization, with the Industrial and Commercial Bank of China and the China Construction Bank occupying the top two places. In all these rankings – both country and company – the renminbi exchange rate is of great importance. Over the next five years, let alone the next twenty, the renminbi is likely to appreciate considerably. If it should appreciate by 25 per cent, for example, then China's GDP will similarly rise by 25 per cent and so will the value of its companies. The Peterson Institute of International Economics estimated in 2010 that the renminbi was undervalued by 41 per cent: whether true or not, a 41 per cent appreciation of the renminbi would have made the Chinese economy half the size of that of the United States in 2010 and PetroChina one and a half times the size of ExxonMobil.[44] The potential volume of Chinese overseas investment, as China's capital account is steadily opened and the movement of capital liberalized, is huge, especially given the level of China's savings. In 2007 China had $4,800 billion in household and corporate savings, equivalent to about 160 per cent of its GDP. On the assumption that savings grow at 10 per cent per annum, China will have in the region of $17,700 billion in savings by 2020, by which time China might have an open capital account. If just 5 per cent of savings leaves the country in 2020, that would equal $885 billion in outward investments. If outflows reach 10 per cent of savings, $1,700 billion would go abroad.[45] To provide some kind of perspective, in 2001 US invisible exports totalled $451.5 billion. At the time of writing, Chinese overseas investment is still, in historical terms, in its infancy, but it is growing extremely rapidly: China's overseas investment increased from $2.85 billion in 2003 to $56.53 billion in 2009 and over $68 billion in 2010.[46] A hint of what the future might hold was provided by the investments made by Chinese banks in Western financial institutions, which, in late 2007, found themselves seriously short of capital as a result of the credit squeeze which began in August of that year. By the end of 2007 Chinese financial institutions owned 20 per cent of Standard Bank, 9.9 per cent of Morgan Stanley, 10 per cent of Blackstone, and 2.6 per cent of Barclays.[47] This, however, proved to be the high-water mark, as the Chinese government, increasingly aware of the depth of the American financial crisis, advised its banks to desist from becoming involved in rescue packages for beleaguered American and European banks.

There is plenty of evidence that China is steadily climbing the technological and scientific ladder. At present it is still a largely imitative rather than innovative economy, but the volume of serious scientific research is rising rapidly, as is expenditure on research and development, with China overtaking Japan in 2010 to become the second highest spender after the United States. China is already the fifth leading nation in terms of its share of the world's leading scientific publications and it is particularly strong in certain key areas like nanotechnology.[48] With 6.5 million undergraduates and 0.5 million postgraduates studying science, engineering and medicine, China already has the world's largest scientific workforce.[49] In 2003 and

2005 it successfully carried out two manned space missions,[50] while in 2007 it managed to destroy one of its own satellites with a ballistic missile, thereby announcing its intention of competing with the United States for military supremacy in space.[51] Over the next decade, it seems highly likely that China will emerge as a major global force in science and technology.

One of the more fundamental economic effects of the rise of China will be to transform and reshape the international financial system. The financial crisis triggered in September 2008 suggests that the US is no longer economically strong enough to underwrite the present international economic system and sustain the dollar as the world's premier reserve currency.[52] There is an immediate threat to the value of the dollar in the shape of the United States' huge budget deficit, which could lead to a crisis of confidence on the part of foreign investors and a sharp fall in the value of the dollar, thereby threatening its reserve currency status. The significance of the dollar's decline, moreover, is not confined to the financial world but has much larger ramifications for Washington's place on the international stage. Flynt Leverett, a former senior National Security Council official under President George W. Bush, has argued that: 'What has been said about the fall of the dollar is almost all couched in economic terms. But currency politics is very, very powerful and is part of what has made the US a hegemon for so long, like Britain before it.'[53] Similarly Kenneth Rogoff, former chief economist at the International Monetary Fund, wrote: 'Americans will find global hegemony a lot more expensive if the dollar falls off its perch.'[54] The consequences of a falling dollar could be manifold: nations will prefer to hold a growing proportion of their reserves in currencies other than the dollar; countries that previously pegged their currency to the dollar, including China, will choose no longer to do so; the US will find that economic sanctions against countries like Iran and North Korea no longer carry the same threat because access to dollar financing has less significance for them; countries will no longer be so willing to hold their trade surpluses in US Treasury bonds; US military bases overseas will become markedly more expensive to finance; and the American public will be less prepared to accept the costs of expensive overseas military commitments. To put it another way, the US will find it more difficult and more expensive to be the global hegemon. The same kind of processes accompanied the decline of the pound, and Britain's position as an imperial power, between 1918 and 1967.

The decline of the dollar, meanwhile, will coincide with the rise of the renminbi. As yet, the role of the renminbi is fundamentally constrained by the absence of convertibility. But over the next five to ten years that will begin to change, as discussed in the last chapter, and by 2020 the renminbi could enjoy full convertibility, enabling it to be bought and sold like the dollar. By then, if not earlier, most, if not all, of East Asia, perhaps including Japan, will be part of a renminbi currency system. Given that China is likely to be the main trading partner of most if not all East Asian nations, it will be natural for trade between them to be conducted in the renminbi, for the value of their currencies to be fixed against it rather than the dollar, which is often the case now, and for the renminbi to be used as the reserve currency of choice. As the dollar continues to weaken with the relative decline of the US economy, it will steadily, perhaps even rapidly, lose its global pre-eminence, to be replaced by a basket of currencies, with power perhaps initially being shared by the dollar, euro and yen, together with the renminbi, depending on when it acquires convertibility.[55] When the renminbi is made fully convertible, it will become one of the three major reserve currencies, along with the dollar and the euro, and is likely to rapidly replace the dollar as the world's major currency. This is a likely scenario within the next 20 years, perhaps even less.[56]

The present international financial institutions could well, in time, be superseded by new ones. Of course, it is possible that the IMF and the World Bank will be transformed into something very different with, for example, China and India eventually usurping the role of the US, but a new institutional architecture may be more likely, operating alongside a progressively marginalized IMF and World Bank. Both the IMF and the World Bank enjoy rather less power and influence than was the case even a decade ago, and this process seems likely to continue.[57]

A NEW EXEMPLAR OF CAPITALISM

In Chapter 2 I discussed how the rise of American capitalism differed from the various forms of European capitalism that had previously been predominant. The characteristics of the new and dynamic American capitalism that took shape during the century after 1850 and which served to distinguish it from its European counterparts included: a very large and relatively homogeneous consumer market, in contrast to the much smaller and highly differentiated and segmented national markets in Europe; a relative scarcity of labour that stimulated the introduction of labour-saving machinery and constant improvements in the labour process; a new form of mass assembly-line production (often referred to as Fordism), involving a much more elaborate division of labour and enjoying large economies of scale when compared to the much smaller batch-style production typical of the main west European economies; and the absence of pre-capitalist forms of social relations (as a result of the defeat and destruction of native Americans), which meant that there were few economic, political or cultural obstacles to the development of capitalist relations. Whereas in Western Europe the legacy of feudalism was evident in a multitude of ways, not least in patterns of land ownership, this was not the case in the United States where farms, for example, rapidly assumed a much larger scale. These differences, along with others, were to permeate all aspects of American life, from the economy and technology to culture and politics.

The rise of China represents at least as profound a change in the nature of capitalism as did the arrival of modern American capitalism in the nineteenth century. What are the key distinguishing characteristics of the Chinese model compared with those which we have come to associate with the United States? The Chinese market is far larger than that of the United States, thereby enabling new forms of production and marketing. The sheer scale and diversity of China, furthermore, means that it has the characteristics of a super continental-sized, even sub-global, economy. As a consequence, provinces and cities compete with each other as nation-states do in other parts of the world. HSBC projects that by 2020 China will have six provinces with an annual GDP greater than countries like Russia, Canada and Spain and a further ten with a GDP comparable to countries like Indonesia, South Africa and Switzerland. At the same time, the combination of China's dependence on the rest of the world for natural resources and its own manufacturing competitiveness means that, compared with the United States, its degree of internationalization – that is, interdependence and integration with the global economy – will be much greater. In a very different vein, China has been very significantly shaped by the effects of the 1949 Revolution, which, amongst other things, democratized land tenure and introduced far more egalitarian gender relations, thereby injecting a very powerful emancipating dynamic into Chinese society. Chinese capitalism has been shaped by the communist tradition, not only as a result of Deng Xiaoping but, even more fundamentally, by Mao Zedong. The fact that the Chinese leadership refers to Chinese capitalism as 'socialism with Chinese characteristics' is not simply a rhetorical way of emphasizing continuity with 1949, but more substantively speaks to a continuing connection with that tradition. Finally, Chinese capitalism is shaped by the fact that China is primarily a civilization-state; one of the most fundamental expressions of this is the nature of the Chinese state – ubiquitous, omnipresent, directive, strategic, and highly competent. As such, it could hardly be more different from the American model.

Unlike the American model, moreover, which became highly integrated with the other advanced economies of the time, notably those of Europe, the Chinese economy will be much more closely linked with those of the developing world. Since the latter accounts for the great majority of the world's population, the reach of the Chinese economy will be far greater than that of the American economy. Moreover, the fact that the economic transformation of other highly populous countries like India and Brazil will take place in parallel with that of China will only serve to accentuate the importance and influence of the Chinese model. The Chinese model of capitalism will come to exercise a profound influence on the nature of global development, just as the American model, now in the process of being superseded, did for well over a century before, but this time on a far greater scale.

CHINA'S BEHAVIOUR AS A GREAT POWER

In their heyday the major European nations sought to impose their designs on the rest of the world in the name of a civilizing mission. Expansion by means of colonialism was at the heart of the European project, wedded to an aggressive mentality that stemmed from Europe's own seemingly perpetual habit of intra-European wars. Not surprisingly, the United States inherited important parts of this legacy, though its very different geo-political circumstances, ensconced as it was in its own continent, also bred a powerful insularity. The United States, which was founded on the missionary zeal of the Pilgrim Fathers and their contemporaries, and later articulated in a constitution that embodied an evangelizing and universalistic credo, was possessed of a belief in its manifest destiny and that its spiritual purpose was to enlighten the rest of the world.[58] This history of manifest destiny (an expansionist ideology that dates from the original settlers), the destruction of the Amerindians, and the restless desire to expand westwards, helps us to understand the behaviour of the United States as a global superpower. What, then, of China, whose origins and history could hardly be more different?

There are two factors that have to be considered. The first, associated with the so-called realist school of international relations, lays emphasis on the importance of interests and therefore stresses how great powers tend to behave in a similar fashion in the same circumstances.[59] 'Rising powers,' as Robert Kagan argues, 'have in common an expanding sense of interests and entitlement.'[60] Accordingly China will, in this view, tend to behave like any other global superpower, notably the United States. The second factor, in contrast, emphasizes how great powers are shaped by their own histories and circumstances and therefore behave in distinct ways. As in the case of the

United States, these two different elements – the one convergent and the other divergent – will combine to shape China's behaviour as a superpower. The convergent pressure is obviously a familiar one, but the divergent tendency, a product of Chinese particularism, is less knowable and more elusive.

The historian William A. Callahan argues, in this context, that there are four different narratives present within Chinese civilization.[61] The first is what he describes as *zhongguo*, or China as a territorial state. The obvious metaphor for this is the Great Wall – the desire to keep barbarians out – linked to the nativist sentiment, a constantly recurring theme in Chinese history, as evident in the Boxer Rebellion and continuing resentment towards foreign influences, notably American and Japanese. This view appeals to a defensive and inward-looking sense of Chineseness. It might crudely be described as China's equivalent of American insularity. The second is *da zhongguo*, a metaphor of conquest. This has been intrinsic to the expansionary dynamic of the Chinese empire, as we saw in Chapter 8. In the conquest narrative, Chinese civilization is constantly enlarging and annexing new territory, seeking to conquer, subdue and civilize the barbarians on its borders. In the contemporary context, the conquest narrative aims first at restoring the 'lost territories' and then seeking to reverse the 'century of humiliation'. Yan Xuetong, a leading Chinese intellectual cited earlier, sees this in relatively benign terms: 'the Chinese regard their rise as regaining China's lost international status rather than obtaining something new . . . the Chinese consider the rise of China as a restoration of fairness rather than as gaining advantages over others.'[62] However, the conquest narrative also clearly lends itself to a much less benign and more expansionist and imperialist interpretation. The third narrative is *da zhonghua*, or conversion. This strand is as fundamental as that of conquest: the belief in the inherent superiority of Chinese civilization and the desire to convert others to its ways. To quote Mencius, the disciple of Confucius: 'I have heard of the Chinese converting barbarians but not of their being converted by barbarians.'[63] The key issue here is neither conquest nor recovery but rather defining and spreading the characteristics of Chinese civilization. As we have seen, this is implicitly, sometimes explicitly, linked to race. Cultural China, as Callahan describes it, is an open and expansive concept, resembling the notion of soft power but not reducible to it. The fourth and final narrative is that of the Chinese diaspora, of the notion of Greater China as reflected in the continuing sense of Chinese identity embodied in the diaspora. Each of these narratives is present in, and serves as a continuing influence on, contemporary Chinese attitudes. Which of the first three – which are the relevant ones here – might predominate in the future, or at any one time, is a matter of conjecture.

It is important to bear in mind the difference historically between Western and Chinese patterns of behaviour. The former have long sought to project their power overseas to far-flung parts of the world, commencing with the Portuguese, Dutch and Spanish; the Chinese, in contrast, have no tradition of expansion other than continental-based territorial incrementalism. The Europeans, perhaps conditioned by the maritime experience of the Mediterranean, were, from the late fifteenth century, seeking to expand across the oceans. China, in contrast, has always seen itself as a land-based continental power and has never regarded itself or sought to become a maritime power with overseas ambitions. The very different purposes of the voyages of Zheng He on the one hand and the great European explorers on the other are an illustration of this. To this day, the Chinese have never sought to project themselves outside their own land mass.[64] It is not insignificant that the Chinese have still not got a blue-water navy and will not acquire one for at least another decade or more. This does not mean that the Chinese will not seek in future to project their power into distant oceans and continents, but there is no tradition of this. It is reasonable to assume that China, as a superpower, will in due course acquire such a capability but, unlike the West, it has hitherto not been part of the Chinese way of thinking and behaving.

There is another factor that may reinforce this historical reserve. Although the 'century of humiliation' is often seen as a reason why China might seek to extract some kind of historical revenge – one might recall Germany and the Treaty of Versailles – it could also act as a constraining factor. The experience of invasion and partial colonization, the fact that China suffered for so long at the hands of the

Western powers and Japan, is likely to counsel caution: the German example, in other words, is entirely inappropriate – including the timescales involved, which are of an entirely different order. China will be the first great power that was a product of colonization, the colonized rather than a colonizer. As a result, China may act with considerable restraint for long into the future, even when its own power suggests to the contrary. The evidence for this lies in the present. The Chinese have gone to great lengths to act with circumspection and to reassure the world that they do not have aggressive intentions, the only exception being their attitude towards Taiwan which, as far as the Chinese are concerned, is an entirely different and separate matter. It is true that over the last half-century China has been involved in wars with the Soviet Union, India and Vietnam, but the first two were border disputes and in no instance did the Chinese display expansionist intent. This relative restraint touches on another dimension of the Chinese mentality, namely a willingness to be patient,

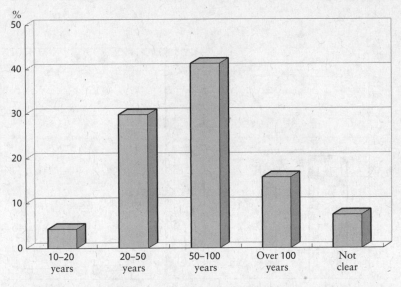

Figure 74. Response of Chinese youth to the question, 'How many years do you believe it will take for China's comprehensive national power to catch up with Western developed nations?'

to operate according to timescales which are alien to the Western political mind. This is eloquently summed up by former Chinese premier Zhou Enlai's reported response to Henry Kissinger's question in 1972 about the consequences of the French Revolution: 'It is too early to say.' Such thinking is characteristic of a civilization-state rather than a nation-state. And it is clearly reflected in Figure 74.

It has been argued that Chinese military doctrine – stemming from the ancient military strategist Sun Zi (who lived *c.* 520–400 BC, just before the Warring States period) and others – sets much greater store on seeking to weaken and isolate the enemy rather than in actually fighting him: that force, in effect, should be a last resort and that its actual use is a sign of weakness rather than strength. As Sun Zi wrote, 'Every battle is won or lost before it is ever fought.' This is certainly a very important strand in Chinese strategic culture,[65] but it would be misleading, argues the international relations expert Alastair Iain Johnston, to regard this, rather

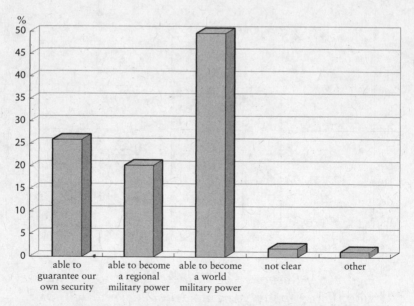

Figure 75. Response of Chinese youth to the question, 'Do you hope that China's future military power is . . . '

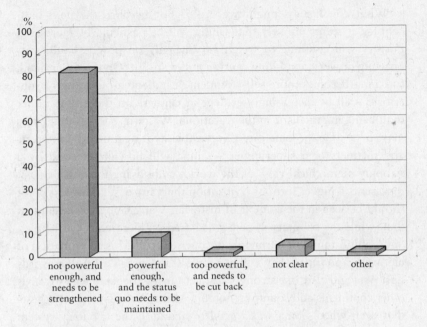

Figure 76. Response of Chinese youth to the question, 'Do you believe our military power is . . . '

than the contrary view that conflict is a constant feature of human affairs, as the dominant element in Chinese history. He writes: 'My analysis of the *Seven Military Classics* [the seven most important military texts of ancient China, including Sun Zi's *The Art of War*] . . . shows that these two paradigms cannot claim separate but equal status in traditional Chinese strategic thought. Rather the *parabellum* paradigm [that war is essential] is, for the most part, dominant.'[66] His view, however, has been strongly contested by Chinese scholars.[67] Whichever is correct, it seems likely that China will in due course acquire a very powerful military capability. In a 2003 survey of over 5,000 students drawn from China's elite universities, – a potentially significant indicator of future Chinese attitudes – 49.6 per cent believed that China in future should become a world military power, while 83 per cent felt that Chinese military power was inadequate (see Figures 75 and 76).[68]

What conclusions might we draw? For perhaps the next half-century, it seems unlikely that China will be particularly aggressive. History will continue to weigh very heavily on how it handles its growing power, counselling caution and restraint. On the other hand, as China becomes more self-confident, a millennia-old sense of superiority will be increasingly evident in Chinese attitudes. But rather than being imperialistic in the traditional Western sense – though this may, over time, become more noticeable as it acquires the interests and instincts of a superpower – China will be characterized by a strongly hierarchical view of the world, embodying the belief that it represents a higher form of civilization than any other. This last point should be seen in the context of historian Wang Gungwu's argument that, while the tributary system was based on hierarchical principles, 'more important is the principle of superiority'.[69] This combination of hierarchy and superiority will be manifest in China's attitude towards East Asia and also, one strongly suspects, in a variegated way towards other continents and countries, notably Africa. Wang Gungwu suggests that even when China was forced to abandon the tributary system and adapt to the disciplines of the Westphalian system, in which all states enjoyed formal equality, China never really believed this to be the case. 'This doubt partly explains,' argues Wang Gungwu, 'the current fear that, when given the chance, the Chinese may wish to go back to *their long-hallowed tradition of treating foreign countries as all alike but equal and inferior to China* [my italics].'[70]

The nature and longevity of its civilization, coupled with its huge population, mean that China will always have a different attitude towards its place in the world from Europe or the United States. China, similarly to the West, has always constituted itself as, and believed itself to be, universal, an example for all others. But the Chinese, rather than being expansionist like the West in the pursuit of universalism, believed the Middle Kingdom was simply superior to and above all others; thus, rather than seeking to conquer others and rule them in the manner of the West, as exemplified by the colonial system, they instead looked down upon them, preferring to remain aloof, as typified by the tributary system. Thus while Europeans regarded those of its population that settled in their colonies to be kith and kin, affording them the protection of the imperial power, the Chinese saw those who migrated as stepping outside of civilization and therefore unworthy of such protection. In an important sense, China does not aspire to run the world, because it already believes itself to be the centre of the world, this being its natural role and position. And this attitude is likely to strengthen as China becomes a major global power. As a consequence, it may prove to be rather less overtly aggressive than the West has been, but that does not mean that it will be less assertive or less determined to impose its will and leave its imprint. But it will tend to do this in a different way, through its deeply held belief in its own inherent superiority and the hierarchy of relations that necessarily and naturally flow from this.

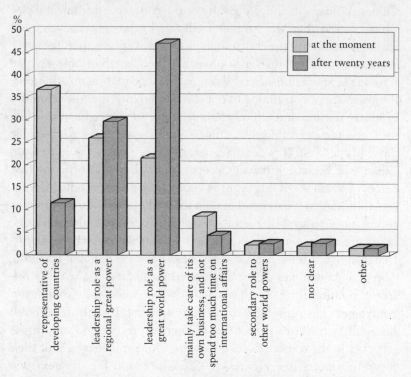

Figure 77. Response of Chinese youth to the question, 'What role do you think China should play in international affairs?'

A NEW POLITICAL POLE

Although the West finds it difficult to imagine a serious and viable alternative to its own arrangements, believing that ultimately all other countries, whatever their history or culture, are likely to converge on the Western model, China represents precisely such an alternative. To understand the nature of the Chinese polity – and how it differs from the West – one has to move beyond the present Communist regime and see China in a much longer-term context. Its underlying characteristics, as discussed in Chapter 7, can be summed up as follows: an overriding preoccupation with unity as the dominant imperative of Chinese politics; the huge diversity of the country; a continental size which means that the normal feedback loops of a conventional nation-state do not generally apply; a political sphere that has never shared power with other institutions like the Church or business; the state as the apogee of society, above and beyond all other institutions; the absence of any tradition of popular sovereignty; and the centrality of moral suasion and ethical example. Given the weight of this history, it is inconceivable that Chinese politics will come to resemble those of the West. It is possible, indeed likely, that in the longer run China will become increasingly democratic, but the forms of that democracy will inevitably bear the imprint of its deeply rooted Confucian tradition. Moreover, rather than seeing the post-1949 Communist regime as some kind of aberration from the norm of Chinese history, in many respects the Communist regime (notably the Deng and post-Deng era but also the Maoist years) lies within the national tradition.

As China emerges as a major global power, it will present a different political face to that of the West. Since the Communist government has presided over a highly successful transformation of the country, it enjoys a great deal of internal prestige and support, as reflected in the self-confidence that the Chinese display about their future prospects (see Figures 78–9). As a result, for the next two decades – perhaps rather longer – the Communist Party is likely to continue in power. Given its achievements, it would not be surprising, moreover, if it did not also enjoy a revival in, and major enhancement of, its global reputation, a process that is already under way.[71] In this context, we should think of China's Communist regime quite differently from that of the USSR: it has, after all, succeeded where the Soviet Union failed. It has also, since Deng, pursued an entirely different kind of strategy, moving away from socialism and towards capitalism. China's socialist legacy has nonetheless left a deep and continuing mark on society: the destruction of the old feudal elite in the Maoist land reform (in contrast to India); the emancipation of women from their centuries-old subjugation; an attachment to the notion of a classless society even though this is now in rapid retreat; a strong belief in egalitarianism even amongst the urban intelligentsia; and the continuing appeal of a socialist vocabulary, as in the commitment of Hu Jintao and Wen Jiabao to build a 'socialist countryside'.[72]

In this context, it is important to recognize that Mao remains a far more venerated figure in China than Deng. At the north end of Tiananmen Square, his giant portrait still hangs above the Gate of Heavenly Peace, while his body rests in an imposing mausoleum at the centre of the square and is visited by hundreds of thousands of Chinese every year. The fact that, for example, Bo Xilai, the popular Chongqing Party secretary, revived Maoist slogans as part of his campaign for a place on the Party standing committee in 2011 was eloquent testimony to Mao's continuing importance. Whatever the fortunes of the Communist regime, however, the main political impact of China on the world will be its Confucian tradition, its lack of a Western-style democracy or tradition, the centrality of the state and the relative weakness of any civil society that is likely to develop. Even a more democratic China will be profoundly different from the Western model.

In short, China will act as an alternative model to the West, embodying a very different kind of political tradition – a post-colonial society, a developing country, a Communist regime, a highly sophisticated statecraft, and an authoritarian Confucian rather than democratic polity.

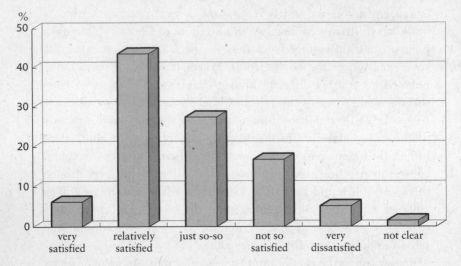

*Figure 78. Response of Chinese youth to the question,
'Are you satisfied with your current living conditions?'*

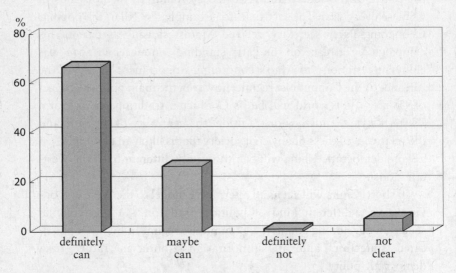

*Figure 79. Response of Chinese youth to the question,
'Do you believe you can live a better life in the future?'*

A CONTEST OF VALUES

The dominance of the West for the last two centuries has served to couch the debate about values overwhelmingly in terms of those that are civilized, a synonym for Western values, against those that are backward or reactionary, which has meant more or less all others, not least those of the Muslim world. In reality, values and cultures are far more complex and nuanced than this suggests. During the Cold War, the conflict over values was fought in highly ideological terms between capitalism and socialism. In the era of contested modernity, which will shape this century and well beyond, the debate over values will be rooted in culture rather than ideology, since the underlying values of a society are primarily the product of distinctive histories and cultures. Although on the surface these values may appear very different, in fact, there are often striking similarities. As John Gray has pointed out, there is nothing uniquely Western about tolerance, for example: 'The Ottomans practised religious toleration at a time when we did not, as did the medieval Moorish kingdom in Spain and the Buddhist kingdom of Asoka in India. Toleration could thus be described as a universal value. It's not peculiarly liberal, and it's not even peculiarly modern.'[73] Nonetheless, there is often conflict and tension between the various values that different peoples hold dear. In a world of multiple and often competing values, it will be important to find a way of enabling and allowing such conflicting values to coexist. This will be a precondition, in fact, for a globalized world of contested modernity to live in a relatively peaceful and harmonious way. It will pose the greatest challenge of all to the West because the latter has become accustomed to thinking of its own values as the norm and regarding itself as justified in imposing these on other countries and insisting that they be accepted by the international community.

There are two senses in which China will be a major protagonist in the debate about values. First, China has strongly resisted Western arguments that have sought to impugn its international reputation in terms of human rights, including its lack of democracy and the limited nature of free speech. China largely succeeded in resisting American efforts in the nineties to condemn it in these terms, mainly because it succeeded in mobilizing the support of many developing countries. In opposition, China and its supporters in the developing world argue that what should take priority are not political rights in the domestic context but economic and social rights in the international context. The argument was essentially over the differing priorities, interests and experiences of the developed countries on the one hand and the developing countries on the other. By the end of the 1990s, that argument began to fade into the background as China's growing influence began to shift the balance of power and the nature of the debate. Indeed, in the first decade of this century, it was the United States rather than China that found itself on the defensive in the debate over values because of its conduct in Iraq and its behaviour at Guantánamo. Interestingly, 127 out of 192 members of the UN General Assembly typically voted against European Union human rights positions in 2010 (compared with 117 the year before).[74]

The second sense in which China will be a protagonist is less immediately politically charged but in the longer run rather more important. As we have seen, the Chinese political order has a strong ethical component rooted in the Confucian tradition.[75] In Chinese culture a powerful distinction is made between right and wrong, as reflected, for example, in the emphasis placed in children's education at home and at school on their correct moral behaviour. Confucianism is essentially a set of precepts that prescribe appropriate forms of behaviour and in that sense, though secular rather than spiritual, is not dissimilar from major religious texts like the Bible and the Koran. These Confucian teachings underpinned the conduct of the state and the nature of Chinese statecraft during the dynastic period and are presently experiencing something of a revival. The continuing influence of Confucian culture is reflected in the highly moralistic tone that the Chinese government frequently adopts in its attitudes and pronouncements.[76] The profound differences in the values of China (and other Confucian-based societies like Japan and Korea) and those of Western societies – including a community-based collectivism rather than individualism, a far more family-orientated and family-rooted culture, and much less attachment to the rule of law and the use of law to resolve conflict – will remain pervasive and, with China's growing influence, acquire a global significance.

A MULTITUDE OF NEW CITIES AND MEGA-CITIES

In 1980 China's urban population was only 22 per cent of its total population. Today about 600 million Chinese live in cities, which is about 45 per cent of the population compared with over 80 per cent in the United States. It is projected that China's urban population will reach 926 million by 2025 and over 1 billion by 2030. Thus, between now and 2025, a period of less than 15 years, China's urban population will increase by 326 million, in other words by more than the entire population of the United States. The near doubling of the urban population over the next two decades will have huge implications for the nature and character of Chinese cities. Between 1990 and 2007, Chinese cities expanded largely by incorporating neighbouring land and their resident populations rather than longer-distance migration; in future, migration will play a much larger role, accounting for almost three-quarters of newcomers to cities. Current trends suggest that mid-sized cities, with populations between 1.5 million and 5 million, will absorb around 40 per cent of the new urban residents. Their total population will double and the number of such mid-sized cities will grow from 73 at present to 115. Meanwhile mega-cities, with populations in excess of 10 million, will also continue to grow rapidly and by 2025 will have 13 per cent of China's urban population compared with 6 per cent in 2005. Within the next two decades, there are likely to be eight mega-cities: Beijing and Shanghai will be joined by Chengdu, Chongqing, Guangzhou, Shenzhen, Tianjin and Wuhan. The population of these cities will increase almost fourfold, from 34 million to 120 million by 2025. It should be noted that the size of Chinese cities depends on how they are defined, which explains why, for example, Chongqing is frequently described as China's largest city with a population of 30 million; in fact, this covers an area the size of Austria, the

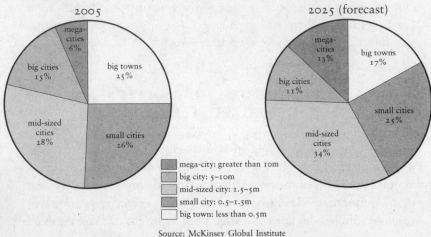

2005

mega-cities 6%

big towns 25%

big cities 15%

mid-sized cities 28%

small cities 26%

2025 (forecast)

mega-cities 13%

big towns 17%

big cities 11%

small cities 25%

mid-sized cities 34%

mega-city: greater than 10m
big city: 5–10m
mid-sized city: 1.5–5m
small city: 0.5–1.5m
big town: less than 0.5m

Source: McKinsey Global Institute

*Figure 80. Distribution of China's urban
population, by city size, %.*

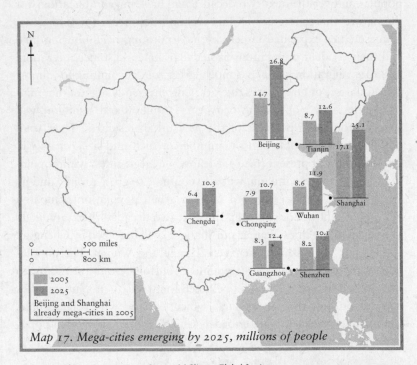

N

26.8
14.7
Beijing

8.7 12.6
Tianjin

25.1
17.1
Shanghai

6.4 10.3
Chengdu

7.9 10.7
Chongqing

8.6 11.9
Wuhan

8.3 12.4
Guangzhou

8.2 10.1
Shenzhen

0 ⎯ 500 miles
0 ⎯ 800 km

2005
2025
Beijing and Shanghai
already mega-cities in 2005

Map 17. Mega-cities emerging by 2025, millions of people

Source: McKinsey Global Institute

majority of whom are rural dwellers. The figures above are based on cities proper, in other words the concentrated urban population.[77]

The demands of such a huge process of urbanization taking place in such a short period of time will be enormous and certainly far in excess of what cities in North America and Europe experienced in the heyday of their urbanization. China will have to build 900–1,100 gigawatts of power production by 2025 to meet with the energy demand of its cities; in the same period it will also have to construct 5 billion square metres of road, 28,000 kilometres of commuter rail and erect 20,000–50,000 skyscrapers. There will be immense pressure on land, with the supply of arable land in particular constantly diminishing. Air quality, water supply, city finance, and the provision of education and health will be formidable tasks.

Not least, there is the challenge of urban transport. China's underlying problem is the density of its population. Although the United States and China have a similar surface area, China's population is four times bigger and therefore four times as dense. Whereas the United States is replete with space, in China it is at a premium. This is one reason why Americans have been able to rely on the car rather than public transport, which in the United States can best be described as either minimal or non-existent. This scenario is impossible for China. If the Chinese chose to rely mainly on the car, their cities would grind to a halt. Traffic congestion is already a major problem in cities like Beijing and Shanghai, even though by Western standards car ownership is still relatively low and many cities in recent years have built or extended their subway systems. Because of the novelty of their urbanization – namely, the scale, the speed and the density of population – the Chinese will be obliged to innovate in many areas of their urban development, not least public transport. Increasingly we will see the city of the future take shape in China and it will over time exercise a huge influence on the global imagination; in particular, Chinese cities will become an example for those in populous developing countries like India, Brazil and Mexico which face many similar problems.

The Chinese are already experimenting with a quite new kind of

Source: Shenzhen Ditege Industrial Design Co. Ltd

The Chinese megabus, a proposed new form of urban transport.

urban transport which takes up no road space and is partially solar-powered. In an effort to tackle the country's congestion and air quality problems, a Shenzhen company – Shenzhen Huashi Future Parking Equipment – has developed a vehicle which has been variously described as a jumbo-bus, megabus and straddling bus (see opposite).

The vehicle travels along fixed routes on rails that span the width of two lanes of traffic, and the passenger compartment sits high above the road surface on fence-like stilts, allowing road traffic to pass uninterrupted beneath. The hybrid vehicle – part bus, part train – can carry up to 1,200 passengers at an average speed of 40 kph (25 mph). It is powered by a combination of municipal electricity and solar power generated by panels on the long roofs of the megabus and the bus stops. The megabus, which is 6 metres (20 feet) wide, could carry as many passengers as 40 conventional buses, thereby saving an enormous amount of fuel and greatly reducing carbon emissions. The average speed would be much faster than that of a conventional bus and it would also significantly reduce traffic congestion. The cost of construction would be roughly a tenth of that for a similar length of subway. It has been estimated that by 2025 China will require 170 new mass-transit systems, so it is not surprising that considerable interest has been shown in the megabus. Beijing is constructing nine kilometres of line in its Mentougou district in order to test the system and, if successful, a further 186 kilometres will be built. Two other cities, Shijiazhuang in Hebei province and Wuhu in Anhui province, have also applied for financing for the scheme.[78]

CAN YOU SPEAK MANDARIN?

One of the consequences of the Chinese being so numerous is that there are twice as many people in the world who speak Mandarin as their first or second language as English, with the great majority of them living in China. With the rise of China, however, growing numbers of people around the world are beginning to acquire Chinese as a second language. Since 2006 this process has been actively promoted by the Chinese government with the establishment of Confucius

Institutes in many different countries, often linked to local universities. As of July 2010, there were 316 such institutes and 337 Confucius classrooms in 94 countries and regions. The Office of the Chinese Language Council International (known colloquially as Hanban) planned to establish 500 institutes by the end of 2010 and 1,000 by 2020.[79] The object of the Confucius Institutes (which are broadly modelled along the lines of the British Council, Alliance Française and the Goethe Institut) is primarily the teaching of the Chinese language, including the training of teachers in Chinese, together with the promotion of Chinese culture. It is estimated that over 40 million people worldwide were learning Chinese at the end of 2008, a figure that some predict will have risen to 100 million by 2010, and that over 2,500 universities in 100 countries run Chinese courses. The spread of Mandarin is most striking in East Asia. It is making rapid strides in Hong Kong, where Cantonese is the first language, and amongst overseas Chinese communities in South-East Asia. In South Korea there are 160,000 students studying Mandarin, an increase of 66 per cent within the past five years. In South Korea and Thailand all elementary and middle schools now offer Mandarin, and the Thai government hopes that one-third of high school students will be proficient in Mandarin by 2011.[80] It is now the second most widely taught foreign language in Japan after English. In 2009, the Malaysian Minister of Education announced that they were considering making Mandarin a compulsory language in schools. And in 2010, Kapil Sibal, the Indian Minister of Education, announced that Mandarin would be introduced into the Indian secondary schools' curriculum for the first time.[81] One of the biggest obstacles is the paucity of Mandarin teachers, so the Chinese Ministry of Education has begun dispatching groups of language teachers, partially funded by the ministry, for one- and two-year stints in Cambodia, Thailand, Indonesia, Kenya, Argentina and many other countries.[82] The attraction of Mandarin in East Asia, of course, is obvious: as China becomes the centre of the East Asian economy, the most important market for exports of countries within the region and also their major source of inward investment, the ability to speak Mandarin will be of growing importance for trade, diplomacy and cultural exchange.

In contrast, Mandarin is little taught in the West, yet even here there has been an outbreak of Mandarin-fever, albeit in a much milder form. In a survey of US high schools in 2006, 2,400 said they would consider teaching Mandarin if the resources were available. Chicago, which has set itself the aim of becoming a hub of Chinese learning, now has about 20,000 school students learning Chinese.[83] It is estimated that about 1,600 US public and private schools teach Mandarin, up from about 300 a decade ago, with the lack of trained teachers being a major constraint. Among America's approximately 27,500 middle and high schools offering at least one foreign language, the proportion offering Chinese rose to 4 per cent, from 1 per cent, between 1997 and 2008.[84] The UK reveals a not dissimilar picture, with only 2,233 entries for GCSE in 2000, and 3,726 in 2004. A small number of private schools have begun to offer Mandarin as an option, and the same has started to happen in the state system. The number of students at UK colleges and universities taking Mandarin as their main subject doubled between 2002 and 2005, while similar increases have been recorded in other European countries.[85] The relative slowness of the Western response, especially in the US and the UK, speaks to their abiding linguistic insularity – thousands of American schools have abandoned the teaching of foreign languages over the last decade – and their failure to comprehend the wide-ranging implications of China's rise.

In the era of globalization, and an increasingly globalized media, language is an important component of soft power. The emergence of English as the global lingua franca – the interlocutor language of choice – carries considerable benefits for the United States in a myriad of different ways. It is far too early yet to say what the reach of Mandarin might one day be, but it will in time probably join English as a global lingua franca and perhaps eventually surpass it. The example of the internet is interesting in this context. Bret Fausett, who runs the ICANN (Internet Corporation for Assigned Names and Numbers) blog, has argued: 'We're at the peak of the English language on the internet. As internationalized domain names are introduced over the next few years, allowing users to conduct their entire online experience in their native language, English will decline as the central language of the internet.'[86] Non-Latin domain names, in fact, started to be introduced in May 2010.

Predicting the future of a language is fraught with difficulty. As the linguistic authority David Crystal writes: 'If, in the Middle Ages, you had dared to predict the death of Latin as the language of education, people would have laughed in your face – as they would, in the eighteenth century, if you had suggested that any language other than French could be a future norm of polite society.'[87] The rise of English has coincided with, and been a product of, the global dominance of the United States. By the same token, the decline of the United States will adversely affect the position of English: the global use of a language does not exist in some kind of vacuum but is closely aligned with the power and reach of a nation-state.[88] The nascent competition between English and Mandarin for the status of global lingua franca, a contest which is likely to endure for this century and perhaps the next as well, is fascinating not least because, as languages and cultural forms, they could hardly be more different: one alphabetic, the other pictographic; one the vehicle for a single spoken language, the other (in its written form) embracing many different ones; English having grown by overseas expansion and conquest, Mandarin by a gradual process of territorial enlargement.

THE RISE OF CHINESE UNIVERSITIES

An important way in which the United States has left its mark on the world has been through its universities. It possesses what are generally regarded as the world's best universities, which attract some of the finest academics and students from around the globe. At the top US universities, researchers can enjoy facilities and resources second to none, while a degree from a university like Harvard, Berkeley or MIT carries more kudos than a degree from anywhere else, with the possible exception of Oxbridge. Great universities, of course, require huge national wealth and resources, be they public or private institutions. It is not surprising, therefore, that hitherto the West has dominated the league tables for the top universities. In the Times

Higher Education World University Rankings for 2010, US universities accounted for seven of the top ten and the UK three. In the top 30 there were three Asian universities, with Hong Kong University 21st, Tokyo University 26th, and Pohang University of Science and Technology 28th. There were six Chinese universities in the top 200, with Peking University 37th, University of Science and Technology of China 49th, Tsinghua University 58th, Nanjing University 120th, Sun Yat-sen University 171st, and Zhejiang University 197th.[89] There were five Chinese universities in the top 200 in 2004. The Shanghai Jiaotong University's Academic Ranking of World Universities[90] and a similar one published by the China Scientific Review Research Centre confirm that the top Chinese universities are making progress up the global rankings. China is also emerging as a main centre of top-flight business education, according to a *Financial Times* ranking of Executive MBAs, which shows four of the top 20 programmes are based there (including Hong Kong).[91]

Growing numbers of foreign students are taking courses at Chinese universities. During the 2003–4 academic year, 77,628 foreign students were seeking advanced degrees at Chinese universities, of

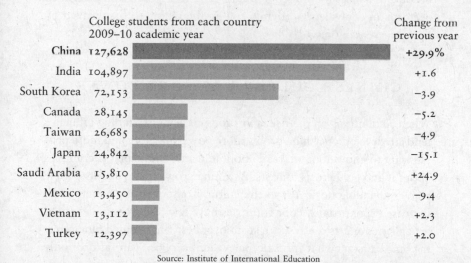

	College students from each country 2009–10 academic year	Change from previous year
China	127,628	+29.9%
India	104,897	+1.6
South Korea	72,153	−3.9
Canada	28,145	−5.2
Taiwan	26,685	−4.9
Japan	24,842	−15.1
Saudi Arabia	15,810	+24.9
Mexico	13,450	−9.4
Vietnam	13,112	+2.3
Turkey	12,397	+2.0

Source: Institute of International Education

Figure 81. College students in US, by country, 2009–10.

whom around 80 per cent were from other Asian countries. South Korea accounted for by far the largest number, almost half, but others came from Japan, Vietnam, Thailand, Indonesia, Nepal and elsewhere.[92] In addition, Chinese students study abroad in large numbers, especially in the United States and also in the UK. The number of Chinese studying in the United States was around 128,000 in the academic year 2009–10, while Chinese enrolments in the UK were around 75,000 in 2008.[93]

It seems likely that Chinese universities will, over the next two decades, rise steadily up the global rankings to eventually occupy positions within the top ten. In order to accelerate this process, the government is making determined attempts to attract leading overseas Chinese scholars to take up appointments at Chinese universities.[94] With the government spending very large sums of money in order to improve facilities and faculty, universities like Beijing, Tsinghua, Fudan and Renmin will, in time, become institutions of recognized global excellence that are increasingly able to attract some of the best scholars from around the world, Chinese or otherwise, while the trend already evident for Chinese universities to become a magnet for students in East Asia will grow as they begin to perform an equivalent academic role in the region to that played by the Chinese economy.

CHINESE CULTURE AS SOFT POWER

When a country is on the rise, a virtuous circle of expanding influence tends to develop. As China grows more powerful, more and more people want to know about it, read about it, watch television programmes about it and go there as tourists. As China grows richer and its people enjoy expanding horizons, so the cultural output of the country will increase exponentially. Poor countries have few resources to devote to art galleries or arts centres; can sustain, at best, only a small film industry and a somewhat prosaic television service; can afford only threadbare facilities for sport; while their newspapers, unable to support a cohort of foreign correspondents, rely instead on Western agencies or syndicated articles for foreign coverage. A report several years ago, for example, showed that only 15 per cent of Chinese men aged between 15 and 35 actively participated in any sporting activity, compared with 50 per cent in the US, while on average the country has less than one square metre of sports facilities per person.[95] As China grows increasingly wealthy and powerful, it can afford to raise its sights and entertain objectives that were previously unattainable, such as staging the Olympic Games, or producing multinational block-buster movies, or promoting the Shaolin Monks to tour the world with their kung fu extravaganza, or building a state-of-the-art metro system in Beijing, or commissioning the world's top architects to design mag-nificent new buildings. Wealth and economic strength are preconditions for the exercise of soft power and cultural influence.

Hollywood has dominated the global film industry for more than half a century, steadily marginalizing other national cinemas in the process. But now there are two serious rivals on the horizon. As Michael Curtin argues:

> Recent changes in trade, industry, politics and media technologies have fuelled the rapid expansion and transformation of media industries in Asia, so that Indian and Chinese centres of film and television produc-tion have increasingly emerged as significant competitors of Hollywood in the size and enthusiasm of their audiences, if not yet in gross reve-nues ... Media executives can, for the very first time, begin to contemplate the prospect of a global Chinese audience that includes more moviegoers and more television households than the United States and Europe combined.[96]

Over the last decade, mainland film directors like Zhang Yimou and Chen Kaige have joined the Taiwanese Ang Lee in becoming increas-ingly well known in the West, as have Chinese film stars like Gong Li, Jet Li, Zhang Ziyi and Hong Kong's Jackie Chan. In recent years there has been a series of big-budget, blockbuster Chinese movies, often made with money from China, Hong Kong and the United States, which have been huge box office successes, both in China and the West. Obvious examples are *Hero*, *Crouching Tiger, Hidden Dragon*, *House of Flying Daggers*, *The Forbidden Kingdom* and *Curse of the*

Golden Flower, which together mark a major shift from the low-budget, art-house films for which China was previously known. The blockbuster movies are generally historical dramas set in one of the early dynasties, drawing on China's rich history and punctuated with dramatic martial arts sequences.[97] Not surprisingly, the storylines and approaches of Hollywood and Chinese movies differ considerably, reflecting their distinctive cultures. While Hollywood emphasizes the happy ending, this is never a major concern for Chinese films; action ranks highly for Hollywood, martial arts for the Chinese; cinematic realism matters for the US, social realism for Chinese audiences. In the longer run, the Chinese film industry is likely to challenge the global hegemony of Hollywood and also to embody a distinctive set of values. It seems quite possible that, in the manner of Sony's takeover of Columbia, Chinese companies will, in time, acquire Hollywood studios, though this will probably have little effect on their output of Hollywood-style movies.[98]

It is worth noting in this context the extraordinary influence that martial arts already enjoy in the West. Fifty years ago the pugilistic imagination of Western children was overwhelmingly dominated by boxing and, to a much lesser extent, wrestling. That picture has completely changed since the 1970s. The Western pugilistic traditions have been replaced by those of East Asia, and in particular China, Japan and Korea, in the form of tae kwon do, judo and kung fu, while amongst older people t'ai chi has also grown in influence. The long-term popularity of martial arts is a striking example of how in the playground and gym certain East Asian traditions and practices have already supplanted those of the West.[99]

The economic rise of China, and of Chinese communities around the world, is changing the face of the market for Chinese art. Chinese buyers are now at least as numerous as Western ones at the growing number of New York and London auctions of Chinese art, a genre which, until a few years ago, was largely neglected by the international art market. In 2006 Sotheby's and Christie's, the world's biggest auction houses, sold $190 million worth of contemporary Asian art, most of it Chinese, in a series of record-breaking auctions in New York, London and Hong Kong. At the end of that year a painting by contemporary artist Liu Xiaodong was sold to a Chinese entrepreneur for \$2.7 million at a Beijing auction, the highest price ever paid at that time for a piece by a Chinese artist. With auction sales of \$23.6 million in 2006, Zhang Xiaogang was narrowly second to Jean-Michel Basquiat in the ArtPrice ranking of the 100 top-selling artists in the world: altogether there were twenty-four Chinese artists in the list, up from barely any five years before. In 2010, Sotheby's international head of Chinese ceramics and works of art said that in the previous five years the number of mainland clients had increased at least threefold and prices had tripled or quadrupled.[100] These changes reflect the growing global influence of Chinese art and artists.[101]

China still lags hugely behind the West, however, when it comes to the international media. Recently the Chinese government has attempted to expand their international reach, upgrading Xinhua, the state news agency, creating new overseas editions of the *People's Daily* and an English-language edition of the *Global Times*, professionalizing the international broadcasting of CCTV, and enabling satellite subscribers in Asia to receive a package of Chinese channels.[102] Compared with the international audiences achieved by Western media like CNN and the BBC, the Chinese media are still in the early stages, but the success of Al Jazeera suggests that mounting a serious challenge to the Western media is not as difficult as it once seemed. The Chinese government invested a reported \$8.7 billion in 2009–10 in its 'external publicity work', which largely meant China Central Television (CCTV), China Radio International (CRI), Xinhua News Agency and the *China Daily* newspaper. As a result, Xinhua TV is now operating a 24-hour channel along the lines of Al Jazeera. CCTV News, which competes with CNN and the BBC, uses both Chinese and non-Chinese presenters, is increasingly professional and, far from being a government mouthpiece, is acquiring a reputation for objectivity. CCTV broadcasts six international channels in five languages and claims a global audience of about 125 million. Some provincial television stations also have foreign language channels. Xinhua News Agency is highly visible in the developing world and has become the principal source of news for Africans. It has 400 correspondents posted in 117 bureaus worldwide, with plans to grow to 180 by 2020.[103] The potential of CCTV, in particular, should not be underestimated. Its broadcast of the opening ceremony of the Beijing Olympics commanded an average home audience of half a billion, rising to 842 million at its peak. Its revenues in 2008 were expected to top $2.5 billion, compared with about $1 billion in 2002. With this kind of domestic base, its international potential, as China reaches out to the world, could be enormous.[104] Meanwhile, Rupert Murdoch's News Corporation, in a tacit admission that it had failed in China, announced in 2010 that it was going to sell control of its three Chinese television channels to a Chinese state-controlled private equity fund.[105]

THE BEIJING OLYMPICS

Sport is not an activity in which China has traditionally excelled, but over the last twenty years Chinese athletes have become increasingly successful. The government has invested large sums of money in sports facilities in order to try to raise China's level of achievement, with the main emphasis being on those disciplines represented at the Olympics, where success has been seen as one of the requisite symbols of a major power. Although China has only been competing in the modern era since the Los Angeles Olympics in 1984, the investment was rewarded at the Athens Olympics in 2004 when China won 32 gold medals, behind the US but ahead of Russia. China first applied to hold the Olympics in 1993 but only in 2001 did its bid finally succeed. The 2008 Beijing Olympics was the first occasion that China had ever hosted a great global sporting event and it was clear during the build-up that the Chinese government saw them as an opportunity to demonstrate to the world what China had achieved since 1978. The preparations were enormous and lavish, with little expense spared. Magnificent new stadiums were constructed, new parks laid out, and many new roads and subway lines built – with the Games costing, including the many infrastructural projects, an estimated $43 billion. The centrepiece was the Bird's Nest, which has rapidly become one of the world's iconic landmarks – a work, notwithstanding its scale, of beauty, elegance, intricacy and intimacy. It was designed by the Swiss architects Herzog & de Meuron in collaboration with the Chinese artist Ai Weiwei, and contains many traditional Chinese motifs.[106] The Chinese authorities went to great lengths to try to deal with the pollution that envelopes Beijing on most summer days, including banning around 2 million cars a day from its streets, a measure that proved relatively effective at the time and which has been continued subsequently.[107]

The Games themselves were generally agreed to have been a tour de force. They were very well organized and ran perfectly to time, the athletes were well cared for and there were no serious mishaps. The Chinese topped the medals table for the first time, with 51 gold medals compared with 36 for the United States, although the latter's total medal haul exceeded China's by ten. Arguably the most impressive event was the opening ceremony, which was directed by the Chinese film director Zhang Yimou. The elaborate show included 15,000 performers and a three-part production focused largely on China's history; it was suffused with many typical Chinese elements, including the choreography of dancers on a giant calligraphy scroll and the serried ranks of 2,008 drummers on a traditional Chinese percussion instrument, the *fou*. It was a demonstrably confident, sure-footed and highly accessible statement to the world about Chinese history and culture.[108] After the Games, there was general agreement that China had raised the Olympic bar to a new level which it would be well-nigh impossible for others to equal, let alone surpass; as the baton passed to London, which was to hold the 2012 Games, there was some trepidation in the UK as to how it might stage an Olympics which did not pale in comparison. Notwithstanding that China is a poor country and Britain a rich one, the UK authorities made it clear from the outset that the 2012 Games would be a much more modest affair.

Apart from the Olympic events, Chinese players have recently managed to make a significant impact on the tennis circuit, with six figuring amongst the top 120 women in 2007, Zheng Jie reaching the Wimbledon women's semi-final in 2008, and Li Na reaching the Australian Open women's final and winning the French Open in 2011. The most dramatic success so far was the emergence of China's Yao Ming as one of the top basketball players in the US's NBA and a huge star in China. Like the leading European football clubs, the NBA sees China as offering a major new market for their sport.[109] The Chinese government – unlike Japan or India – sees sporting success as important to the country's status and prestige, and consequently over the coming decades China is likely to become a major player in a range of prominent sports.[110]

CHINESE FOOD AND MEDICINE

There are two ways in which China already enjoys a major global cultural influence: food and, to a rather lesser extent, traditional Chinese medicine. The global spread of Chinese cuisine has been taking place for many decades, consequent upon Chinese migration, to the point where it is now highly familiar in most parts of the world. Even if people know little about China, they are often familiar with a Chinese dish or two, and are conversant with chopsticks even if they cannot use them. Interestingly, the global influence of Chinese food stems not from China's rise but from the opposite – its previous poverty and the desire of poor Chinese to seek a better life elsewhere. Typically, migrants either sought to establish a Chinese restaurant in their adopted homeland or, more likely, get a job in one as a stepping stone to later owning a restaurant of their own. The spread of traditional Chinese medicine outside the mainland has largely been an outcome of the same process, with overseas Chinese taking the traditions of Chinese medicine with them and slowly introducing them to the host population. Both Chinese food and medicine are products of China's long and rich history and its ancestry as a civilization-state.[111] Indeed, it is interesting to reflect that what most of the world knows about China is through these two quintessentially civilizational legacies. Although their diffusion long predates China's rise, the country's growing influence can only accelerate this process. For over two centuries the Chinese cuisines familiar to foreigners have been those associated with the regions from which Chinese migrants have predominantly come, notably Guangdong and Fujian provinces; but the knowledge and availability of other cuisines is now spreading rapidly.[112] The richness and diversity of Chinese cuisine means that it is highly flexible, able to cater for many different tastes and needs, from cheap takeaways at one end to lavish, upmarket banquets at the other. Until recently it has been mainly associated with the former, but that has now changed significantly.[113] The growing popularity of Chinese food is closely linked to the post-war spread of restaurant eating in the West, a relatively new Western phenomenon, but one which dates back over a millennium in China.[114]

The global reach of traditional Chinese medicine is also likely to continue expanding. Every Chinese hospital has a department devoted to Chinese medicine, with doctors frequently qualified in both Western and Chinese medicine. When Western-style drugs are prescribed they are often combined with traditional Chinese treatments (which was my own experience in a Beijing hospital).[115] The major constraint on the development of Chinese medicine in the West has been that it is not subject to the same kind of regulation as Western medicine (though clinical trials are quite common in China).[116] Western drugs have made considerable headway in China, but traditional Chinese medicines are still favoured by most people, including the affluent middle class and the highly educated, on the grounds that they have thousands of years of experience behind them, are cheaper, and also devoid of toxic side effects. It is accepted that Western drugs are superior for diseases like cancer, but even when these are used, people will generally revert to Chinese medicines subsequently.[117] The contrast between Chinese and Western medicine eloquently sums up the difference between civilizational wisdom and scientific knowledge. Chinese medicine, rather like the world's cuisines, is a product of thousands of years of trial and error, of the everyday experience and resourcefulness of hundreds of millions of people and their interaction with their plant environment; Western medicine is a rigorous product of the scientific method and the invention and refining of chemicals. There is a widespread and growing acceptance in the West that medicinal palliatives and cures derived from civilizational experience are a valid and important part of medicine, even if we do not understand, at least as yet, how the great majority of them actually work.

THE DECLINE AND FALL OF THE WEST

The purpose of this chapter has been to explore the ways in which Chinese global hegemony is likely to grow over the next half-century. There is another side to this coin which we should consider before we conclude. The most traumatic consequences of this process will be felt by the West because it is the West that will find its historic position being usurped by China. The change that this will represent can hardly be exaggerated. For well over two centuries, in some respects much longer, the West, first in the form of Europe and later in the shape of the United States, has enjoyed overwhelming global pre-eminence. Since 1945 Europe has been obliged to adjust to the fact that it is no longer the dominant player in world politics. The sense of being less and less central to a world that it had previously dominated has been a traumatic experience for European states, especially Britain and France. One response has been the construction of the European Union as a way of mitigating the decline in the power and status of individual states. The fact that European dominance was replaced by that of the United States, however, has helped to lessen this sense of loss. Driven by the Cold War antagonism towards the Soviet Union, an enhanced and transformed concept of the West was forged which effectively enabled Western Europe, at least until 1989, to remain a major global player alongside the United States, even though it was very much the junior partner. This was no ordinary relationship between nation-states based on specific interests, however. On the contrary, the United States was a product of European migration: it had been built by Europeans (together with African slaves) and saw itself as the New World joined at the hip with the Old World whence it came. In other words, history, civilization, culture, ethnicity and race, as well as the exigencies of geo-politics, served to weld and underpin the Western alliance.

The rise of China will have no such compensations, either for a declining Europe or a dethroned United States. Europe has had some preparation for this eventuality: it has spent the last half-century trying to adjust to decline and dethronement. Even now, though, Europe still finds it extremely difficult to understand, let alone accept, its increasingly modest place in the world and to modify its sights accordingly. The case of Britain is most striking in this context. In a desperate attempt to remain a global power with a metaphorical seat at the top table, it has tenaciously hung on to the coat-tails of the United States, constantly walking in its shadow, seemingly always prepared to do its master's bidding.[118] Its foreign policy has long been a clone of that of the United States and its defence and intelligence policies are almost entirely dependent on and deeply integrated with those of the US. The UK's dependence on the US is a measure not simply of its own weakness and of its failure to find an independent place in the world following the collapse of its imperial role, but also of how traumatic it has found the idea of no longer being a great power. The relationship with the United States has been a surrogate for its lost past. Even now, though the palest shadow of the fighting machine it once was – its increasingly threadbare military resources testament to its rapid historical decline – Britain still seems to find the need to intervene militarily whenever and wherever it can, Iraq, Afghanistan and Libya being classic recent examples: the imperial mentality lives on regardless of shrunken means or changed circumstance, at times in an almost farcical manner. Europe's continuing existential crisis underlines how difficult it is for countries to adjust, not least psychologically, to a world in which their importance is greatly diminished. Europe's decline, furthermore, will certainly continue into the indefinite future. Its remarkable role over the last 400 years will never be repeated and will become an historical curiosity in the manner of the Greek and Roman Empires, whose present-day incarnations as Greece and Italy reflect the grandeur of their imperial past in little more than the survival of some of their historic buildings.

If Europe will suffer, that is nothing to the material and psychological crisis that will be faced by the United States. It is almost completely unprepared for a life in which it will no longer be globally dominant. Under the Bush administration it sought to redefine itself as the world's sole superpower, able to further its interests through unilateralism and shun the need for alliances: in other words, far from recognizing its relative decline and the prospect of a diminution in its power, it drew precisely the opposite conclusion and became intoxicated with the idea that US power could be further expanded, that America was in the ascendancy, that the world in the twenty-first century could be remade anew in the country's image. The dominant ideological force during the Bush era was neo-conservatism, which was predicated on the belief that the United States could and should assert itself in a new way. In the wake of 9/11, Washington was in thrall to a debate about empires and whether the United States was now an imperial power and what that might mean. The Bush administration represented the most extreme expression so far of an aggressive, assertive and expansionist America, but even after it was widely seen to have failed as a result of the Iraq debacle, there were not many in the United States who drew the conclusion that the country was in longer-term decline, that far from it being on the eve of a new global dominance, its power had, in fact, already peaked; on the contrary, there was a widespread perception that the United States simply needed to find a less confrontational and more consensual way of exercising its global leadership. Not even the advances made by China in East Asia were interpreted as the harbinger of a major shift in global power.

The heart-searching that accompanied the 2007–8 primary and presidential campaign around Barack Obama's candidature did not, at least until the financial meltdown just before the election, reach the conclusion that the United States would have to learn to live with decline. Even the precipitous fall in the value of the dollar in 2006–7 did not provoke fear of American decline, though a small minority of observers recognized that in the longer term the position of the dollar might come under threat. The United States thus remained largely blind to what the future might hold, still basking in the glory of its past and its present, and preferring to believe that it would continue in the future. Britain displayed a similar ignorance – and denial – about its own decline after 1918, constantly seeking to hold on to what it had gained, and only letting go when it could see no alternative. Indeed, it only began to show an underlying recognition of its own decline in the 1950s, when it became obvious that it would lose its colonies. The turning point in the United States may well prove to have been the financial meltdown in September 2008 and the near collapse of the financial system. The US National Intelligence Council report in November 2008 represented a 180-degree shift compared with its previous report just four years earlier in 2004. While the latter predicted continuing American global dominance, 'positing that most major powers have forsaken the idea of balancing the US', the new one anticipated American decline, the emergence of multipolarity, and a world in which the US would increasingly be obliged to share power with China and India. It declared: 'By 2025, the US will find itself as one of a number of important actors on the world stage, albeit still the most powerful one.'[119] Presently, only a minority – even inside the Beltway – acknowledge that the United States is in decline. But what will surely drive a growing recognition of this reality is America's huge burden of debt. This will prevent the country at every level of government, especially federal, continuing to live in the manner to which it has become accustomed. The demands of debt will be relentless and unforgiving. If America has enjoyed the intoxication of over-consumption for the best part of three decades, now it faces the prospect of a permanent hangover. The fact that Washington DC is paralysed by the political polarization that presently afflicts the country will make the task of coming to terms with the debt crisis that much more difficult and protracted. These, of course, are still early days in what will be a long process of decline, with many acts to follow over this and future decades. The biggest danger, from a global point of view, is that the United States will at some point adopt an aggressive stance that treats China as the enemy and seeks to isolate it. A relatively benign example of this was the proposal, at the time of the 2008 presidential election, by the Republican presidential candidate Senator John McCain for a 'league of democracies', designed to exclude China and Russia (which he also wanted to expel from the G8) and thereby create a new global division.[120] The longer-term fear must be that the US engages China in military competition and an arms race in something akin to a rerun of the Cold War. The United States is entering a protracted period of economic, political and military trauma. Its medium-term reaction may not be pretty: the world must hope it is not too ugly.

The fact that China derives from utterly different civilizational and historical roots to those of the West, and is possessed of quite different geographical coordinates, will greatly accentuate the Western sense of loss, disorientation and malaise. It was one thing for Britain to have been confronted with the United States – given the obvious affinities and commonalities that they enjoyed – as its rival and successor as the world's dominant power, but it is an entirely different matter for the United States to be faced with China – with whom it has nothing in common in either civilizational or political terms – as its usurper and ultimate replacement. For the United States, the shock of no longer having the world to itself – what has amounted to a proprietorial right to determine what happens on all major global questions – will be profound. With the rise of China, Western universalism will cease to be universal – and its values and outlook will become steadily less influential. The emergence of China as a global power in effect relativizes everything. The West is habituated to the idea that the world is *its* world; that the international community is *its* community; that international institutions are *its* institutions; that the world currency – namely the dollar – is *its* currency; that universal values are *its* values; that world history is *its* history; and that the world's language – namely English – is *its* language. The assumption has been that the adjective 'Western' naturally and implicitly belongs in front of each important noun. That will no longer be the case. The West will progressively discover, to its acute discomfort, that the world is no longer Western. Furthermore, it will increasingly find itself in the same position as the rest of the world was during the West's long era of supremacy, namely being obliged to learn from and live on the terms of the West. For the first time, a declining West will be required to engage with other cultures and countries on a far more equal basis and obliged to recognize and learn from their strengths. It is entirely possible – likely in fact – that in a world it no longer dominates, the West itself will begin to fray and fragment. As Australia is drawn remorselessly into the Chinese sphere of economic influence, this will surely over time weaken its links with the West. The European sovereign debt crisis has exposed new fault lines, with several of the most affected countries seeking a closer relationship with China: this could well be a harbinger of future centrifugal pressures. Meanwhile, the importance of Europe is already weakening in the American mind: in 1993, 50 per cent of Americans considered Europe to be the most important region for US interests and only 31 per cent Asia; in 2011, the balance of opinion had been reversed, with 47 per cent considering Asia to be the most important and only 37 per cent Europe.[121]

12

Concluding Remarks: The Eight Differences that Define China

Broadly speaking, there have been two kinds of Western response to the rise of China. The first sees China more or less solely in economic terms. We might call this the 'economic wow factor'. People are incredulous about the growth figures. They are in awe of what those growth figures might mean for China's position in the world. Any undue concern about their implications, moreover, is calmed by the belief that China is steadily becoming more like us, possessed of the accoutrements – from markets and stock exchanges to cars and private homes – of a modern Western society. This response is guilty of underestimating what the rise of China represents. It is a victim of tunnel vision and represents a failure of imagination. Economic change, fundamental as it may be, can only be part of the picture. This view, blind as it is to the importance of politics and culture, rests on an underlying assumption that China, by virtue of its economic transformation, will, in effect, become Western. Consciously or unconsciously, it chimes with Fukuyama's 'end of history' view: that since 1989 the world has been converging on Western liberal democracy. The other response, in contrast, is persistently sceptical about the rise of China, always expecting it to end in crisis and failure. In the light of Maoism, the collapse of the Soviet Union and the suppression of the demonstrators in Tiananmen Square, the argument runs, it is impossible for China to sustain its transformation without fundamental political change: unless it adopts the Western model, it will fail. The first view holds that China will automatically become Western, the second does not: but both share the belief that for China to succeed, it must, in effect, become Western.

This book is predicated on a very different approach. It does not accept that the 'Western way' is the only viable model. In arguing this, it should be borne in mind that the West has seen off every major challenge it has faced, culminating in the defeat after 1989 of its greatest adversary, Soviet Communism. It has a formidable track record of growth and innovation, which is why it has proved such a dynamic force over such a long period of time. Unlike the stark either/or alternatives of the great ideological era between 1917 and 1989, however, the choices are now more nuanced. The East Asian examples of modernization have all drawn from the Western experience, including China's post-1978 transformation. But to suggest that this is the key to East Asia's success or even amounts to the main story is wrong. The reason for China's transformation (like those of the other East Asian countries, commencing with Japan) has been the way it has succeeded in combining what it has learnt from the West, and also its East Asian neighbours, with its own history and culture, thereby tapping and releasing its native sources of dynamism. We have moved from the era of either/or to one characterized by hybridity.

Central to the book is the contention that, far from there being a single modernity, there will in fact be many. Until around 1970 modernity was, with the exception of Japan, an exclusively Western phenomenon. But over the last half-century we have witnessed the emergence of quite new modernities, drawing on those of the West but ultimately dependent for their success on their ability to mobilize, build upon and transform the indigenous. These new modernities are no less original for their hybridity; indeed, their originality lies partly in their possession of this characteristic. Nor will hybridity remain an exclusively Asian or non-Western condition: in the face of the growing success of East Asian societies, the West will be obliged to learn from and incorporate some of their insights and features. In a limited way this is already the case, with the West, for example, employing some of the innovations developed by the Japanese system of manufacturing – although, given that these are very much rooted in Japanese culture, often with somewhat less success. A central question concerns which elements of the Western model are indispensable and which are optional. Clearly, all successful examples of economic transformation currently on offer are based upon a capitalist model of development, although their economic institutions and policies, not to mention their politics and culture, display very wide variations. However, the proposition that the inheritance must, as a precondition for success, include Enlightenment principles such as Western-style rule of law, an independent judiciary and a certain kind of representative government is by no means proven. Japan, which is at least as advanced as its counterparts in the West, is not based on the principles of the Enlightenment, nor does it embrace Western-style democracy, even though, since the early 1950s, largely for reasons of political convenience, it has routinely been seen as doing so by the West. And even if China moves in the direction of more representative government and a more independent judiciary, as it probably will in the long term, it will surely do so in very much its own way, based on its own history and traditions, which will owe little or nothing to any Western inheritance.

The desire to measure China primarily, sometimes even exclusively, in terms of Western yardsticks, while understandable, is flawed. At best it expresses a relatively innocent narrow-mindedness; at worst it reflects an overweening Western hubris, a belief that the Western experience is universal in all matters of importance. This can easily become an excuse for not bothering to understand or respect the wisdom and specificities of other cultures, histories and traditions. The problem, as Paul A. Cohen has pointed out, is that the Western mentality – nurtured and shaped by its long-term ascendancy – far from being imbued with a cosmopolitan outlook as one might expect, is in fact highly parochial, believing in its own univeralism; or, to put it another way, its own rectitude and eternal relevance.[1] If we already have the answers, and these are universally applicable, then there is little or nothing to learn from anyone else. While the West remained relatively unchallenged, as it has been for the best part of two centuries, the price of such arrogance has overwhelmingly been paid by others, as they were obliged to take heed of Western demands; but when the West comes under serious challenge, as it increasingly will from China and others, then such a parochial mentality will only serve to increase its vulnerability, weakening its ability to learn from others and to change accordingly.

The problem with interpreting and evaluating China solely or mainly in terms of the Western lexicon of experience is that, by definition, it excludes all that is specific to China: in short, what makes China what it is. The only things that are seen to matter are those that China shares with the West. China's history and culture are dismissed as a blind alley or merely a preparation for becoming Western, the hors d'oeuvres before the Western feast. Such an approach is not only demeaning to China and other non-Western cultures; it also largely misses the point. By seeing China in terms of the West, it refuses to recognize or acknowledge China's own originality and, furthermore, how China's difference might change the nature of the world in which we live. Since the eighties and nineties, the heyday of the 'globalization as Westernization' era, when the Asian tigers, including China, were widely interpreted in these terms, there has been a dawning realization that such a huge country embodying such a rich history and civilization cannot be so summarily dismissed. We should not exaggerate – the Western consensus still sees history as a one-way ticket to Westernization – but one can detect the beginnings of a new Western consciousness, albeit still weak and fragile, which is more humble and realistic. As China grows increasingly powerful – while remaining determinedly different – the West will be forced, however reluctantly, to confront the nature and meaning of that difference. Understanding China will be one of the great challenges of the twenty-first century.

What then will be the key characteristics of Chinese modernity? They are eight in all, which for the deeply superstitious Chinese happens to be a lucky number. In exploring these characteristics, we must consider both the internal features of China's modernity and, given China's global importance, how these might impact upon and structure its global outlook and relations.

First, China is not really a nation-state in the traditional sense of the term but a civilization-state. True, it describes itself as a nation-state, but China's acquiescence in the status of nation-state was a consequence of its growing weakness in the face of the Western powers from the late nineteenth century.

The Chinese reluctantly acknowledged that China had to adapt to the world rather than insisting, in an increasingly utopian and hopeless mission, that the rest of the world should adapt to it. That cannot hide the underlying reality, however, that China is not a conventional nation-state. A century might seem a long time, but not for a society that consciously thinks of itself as several millennia old. Most of what China is today – its social relations and customs, its ways of being, its sense of superiority, its belief in the state, its commitment to unity – are products of Chinese civilization rather than its recent incarnation as a nation-state. On the surface it may seem like a nation-state, but its geological formation is that of a civilization-state.

It might be objected that China has changed so much during the period of its accommodation to the status of nation-state that these lines of continuity have been broken and largely erased. There was the inability of the imperial state (and, indeed, Confucianism) to modernize, culminating in its demise in the 1911 Revolution; the failure of the Nationalist government to modernize China, unify the country, or defeat the occupying powers (notably Japan), leading to its overthrow in the 1949 Revolution; the Maoist period, which sought to sweep away much of imperial China, from Confucius and traditional dress to the old patterns of land tenure and the established social hierarchies; followed by the reform period, the rapid decline of agriculture, the rise of industry and the growing assertion of capitalist social relations. Each of these periods represents a major disjuncture in Chinese history. Yet much of what previously characterized China remains strikingly true and evident today. The country still has almost the same borders that it acquired at the maximum extent of the Qing empire in the late eighteenth century. The state remains as pivotal in society and as sacrosanct as it was in imperial times. Confucius, its great architect, is in the process of experiencing a revival and his precepts still, in important measure, inform the way China thinks and behaves. Although there are important differences between the Confucian and Communist eras, there are also strong similarities. This is not to deny that China has changed in fundamental ways, but rather to stress that China is also marked by powerful lines of continuity – that, to use a scientific analogy, its DNA remains intact. This is a country, moreover, which lives in and with its past to a greater extent than any other: that past casts a huge shadow over its present such that, tormented by its failure to either modernize or unify, the Chinese for long lived in a state of perpetual regret and anguish. But as China now finally circumnavigates its way beyond the 'century of humiliation' and successfully concludes its 150-year project of modernization, it will increasingly search for inspiration, nourishment and parallels in that past. As it once again becomes the centre of the world, it will luxuriate in its history and feel that justice has finally been done, that it is restoring its rightful position and status in the world.[2]

When China was down, it was obliged to live according to the terms set by others. It had no alternative. That is why it reconciled itself to being a nation-state, even if it never really believed this to be the case. It was a compromise borne of expediency and necessity. But as China arrives at modernity and emerges as the most powerful country in the world, it will no longer be bound by such constraints and will increasingly be in a position to set its own terms and conditions. It will feel free to be what it thinks it is and act according to its history and instincts, which are those of a civilization-state.

Second, China, in its relationship with East Asia, is increasingly likely to be influenced by the legacy of the tributary-state, rather than nation-state, system. The tributary-state system, as we saw in Chapter 9, lasted for thousands of years and only finally came to an end at the conclusion of the nineteenth century. Even then, it was not entirely extinguished but continued – as a matter of habit and custom, the product of an enduring history – in a submerged form beneath the newly dominant Westphalian system. Up to a point, then, it never completely disappeared, even when China was a far less important actor in East Asia than it had been prior to the mid nineteenth century. The fact that the tributary-state system prevailed for so long means that it is deeply ingrained in the way that both China and East Asian states think about their relationship. As a consequence, any fundamental change in the position of China in the region, and therefore the nature of relations between China and its neighbouring states, could well see a reversion to elements of a more tributary-type relationship, albeit in a new and modernized form. The tributary system was undermined by the emergence of the European powers, together with Japan, as the dominant presence in the region, and by the remorseless decline of China. The European powers have long since exited the region; their successor power, the United States, is now a declining force; and Japan is rapidly being overshadowed by China. Meanwhile, China is swiftly resuming its position as the fulcrum of the East Asian economy. In other words, the conditions that gave rise to the dominance of the nation-state system in East Asia are crumbling, while at the same time we are witnessing the restoration of a defining feature of the tributary-state system.

The tributary-state system was characterized by the enormous inequality that existed between China on the one hand and its neighbouring states on the other, together with a mutual belief in the superiority of Chinese culture. John K. Fairbank suggests in *The Chinese World Order* that: 'If its belief in Chinese superiority persists, it seems likely that the country will seek its future role by looking closely at its own history.'[3] Given that the idea of Chinese superiority remains firmly in place, China's growing economic strength, combined with its enormous population, could return the region to a state of affairs which carries echoes of the past. China is in the process of becoming once more the most important market for virtually every single East Asian country. Nor is the huge and growing imbalance in power between China and all the other states, which historically is entirely familiar, necessarily one that other states in the region will baulk at or seek to resist, with the possible exception of Japan; indeed, all bar Japan have largely sought to move closer to China during the course of its rise rather than hedge with the United States against it. This is partly based on the habit and experience of history and partly on an accommodation with what these countries view as an inevitable and irresistible process. The rise of China and a return to something bearing some of the features of the tributary-state system will not necessarily be distinguished by instability; on the contrary, the tributary-state system was highly stable, rooted as it was in China's dominance and a mainly unchallenged hierarchical pattern of relationships. It would be quite wrong, however, to see any return to a tributary-style relationship as a simple rerun of the past – with, for example, the presidents and prime ministers of neighbouring states making ritualized trips to Beijing bearing gifts in recognition of the greatness of the Chinese president and the superiority of the latter-day Celestial Kingdom. Rather it is likely to be defined by an acceptance that East Asia is essentially a Chinese-centric order; that it embodies an implicit hierarchy in which China's position of ascendancy is duly acknowledged; and that there is an implicit recognition and acceptance of Chinese superiority.

To what extent will such tributary influences be confined to East Asia? Could it conceivably find echoes in other parts of the world? There is, of course, no tradition of a tributary-state system elsewhere: it was only present in East Asia. That, however, was when the Middle Kingdom regarded the world as more or less coterminous with East Asia. If China should approach other parts of the world with a not too dissimilar mindset, and its power is sufficiently overwhelming, could the same kind of hierarchical system be repeated elsewhere? Could there even be something akin to a global tributary system? The most obvious objection is that the tributary system in the majority of cases embraced countries like Korea, Vietnam and Japan with which China had a strong cultural affinity. This is not true of any other part of the world. The sphere to which even an extremely diluted version of the tribute system is least likely to extend is the West, by which, in this context, I mean the United States and Europe. The only possible long-term candidates, in this context, might be the weaker countries of southern and eastern Europe. But in the great majority of countries, both Europe and North America enjoy too much power. It should not be forgotten, moreover, that it was Europe which forced China, against its wishes, to forsake the tributary system in favour of the Westphalian system in the first place. It is not inconceivable, however, that in the long run Australia and New Zealand might enter into some elements of a tributary relationship with China given their relative proximity to it and their growing dependence on the Chinese economy. A tributary dimension might also re-emerge in China's relations with Central Asia. It would not be difficult to imagine echoes of the tributary system being found in China's relationship with Africa, given the enormous imbalance of power between them; perhaps, though less likely, in Latin America also, and South Asia, though not India. In each case, the key features would be China's overweening power, the dependency of countries in a multitude of ways on China, especially trade and finance, and an implicit acceptance of the virtues, if not the actual superiority, of Chinese civilization. But geographical distance in the case of Africa and Latin America, for example, will be a big barrier, while cultural and ethnic difference in all these instances will prove a major obstacle and a source of considerable resentment.

Third, there is the distinctively Chinese attitude towards race and ethnicity. The Han Chinese believe themselves to be a single race, even though this is clearly not the case. What has shaped this view is the extraordinarily long history of Chinese civilization, which has enabled a lengthy process of melding and fusing of countless different races. The sacrosanct and inviolable nature of Chinese unity is underpinned by the idea that the Han Chinese are all of one race, with even the non-Han Chinese being described in terms of separate nationalities rather than races. There is, furthermore, a powerful body of opinion in China that believes in polygenism and holds that the origins of the Chinese are discrete and unconnected with that of other branches of human-kind. In other words, the notion of China and Chinese civilization is bolstered by a widespread belief that the difference between the Chinese and other peoples is not simply cultural or historical but also biological. The non-negotiable nature of the Chinese state's attitude towards race is eloquently illustrated by its approach towards the 'lost territories' and the belief that Hong Kong and Taiwan are inseparable from China because their populations are Chinese: any idea that there might be a distinct Taiwanese identity is summarily dismissed. The Chinese attitude towards race and what constitutes being Chinese, as we noted in Chapter 8, is diametrically opposed to that of other highly populous nations such as India, Indonesia, Brazil and the United States, which explicitly recognize their multi-racial and multi-ethnic character and, in varying degrees, celebrate that fact.

It would be wrong to describe the Chinese attitude towards race as an ideological position, because it is simply too old and too deeply rooted in Chinese history for that to be the case. Certainly it went through a profound change in the late nineteenth and early twentieth centuries, but its antecedents lie deep in the long history of Chinese civilization. Nor is the attitude towards race and identity reducible to the Chinese state or government: rather, it is ingrained in the Chinese psyche. To give one contemporary illustration: support for the return of Taiwan amongst the Chinese people is, if anything, even stronger than it is at a governmental level. Given this, any democratically elected government – admittedly, a most unlikely occurrence in the next twenty years – will almost certainly be more nativist and essentialist in its attitude towards Chinese identity than the present Communist government, which, by virtue of its lack of electoral accountability, enjoys a greater independence from popular prejudices. Nor should we anticipate any significant change in Chinese attitudes on race and ethnicity. It is true that they may have been accentuated by centuries of relative isolation from the rest of the world and China's growing integration may, as a consequence, help to weaken prejudices based on the ignorance of isolation, but the fundamental roots of Chinese attitudes will remain untouched. In fact, rather than being confined to a particular period of history, China's isolation is fundamental to understanding what I have described as the Middle Kingdom mentality. China saw itself as above, beyond, separate from and superior to the rest of the world. 'Isolation', in this sense, was integral to the Chinese world-view, even during the periods, like the Song dynasty or early Ming, when China was not isolationist in policy and outlook. It helps to explain why, for example, China has had such a different attitude from the major European states towards those who settled in other lands. Europeans viewed their settlers and colonizers as an integral part of the national civilizing mission and as still belonging to the homeland; the imperial dynasty, on the other hand, viewed those who departed the Middle Kingdom with relative and continuing indifference, as if leaving China was a step down and outside civilization. This point provides us with a way of understanding the terms on which China's growing integration with the rest of the world in the twenty-first century will take place. China is fast joining the world but, true to its history, it will also remain somewhat aloof, ensconced in a hierarchical view of humanity, its sense of superiority resting on a combination of cultural and racial hubris.

Fourth, China operates, and will continue to operate, on a quite different continental-sized canvas to other nation-states. There are four other states that might be described as continental in scale. The United States has a surface area only marginally smaller than that of China, but with a population only a quarter of the size. Australia is a continent in its own right, with a surface area around 80 per cent of China's, yet its population is a meagre 21 million, less than that of Malaysia or Taiwan, with the vast majority living around its coastal perimeter. Brazil has a surface area of around 90 per cent of China's, but a much smaller population of 185 million. Perhaps the nearest parallel to China is India, with a population of equivalent size, but a surface area only a third of that of China's. Thus, although China shares certain similarities with each of these countries, its particular combination of population size and surface area is unique. Chinese modernity will come continental-sized, in terms of *both* population and physical size. This has fundamental implications not only for the way in which China has worked in the past but also for how it will work in the future. A continental-sized country is an utterly different kind of proposition to a conventional nation-state unless its population is tiny like Australia's, or it started off life as a settler-colony – as in the case of United States and Australia, which were essentially European transplants – with the homogeneity this implies. When a country is as huge as China in both physical scale and population, it is characterized by great diversity and, in certain respects, can be thought of as, in effect, a combination of several, even many, different countries. This is not to detract from the point made throughout this book about the centripetal forces that hold China together, but rather serves to make this unity an even more extraordinary phenomenon. We are dealing with a state that is at one and the same time a country and a continent – in other words, which is both national and multinational – and which therefore must be governed, at one and the same time, according to the imperatives of both a country and a multiplicity of countries.

For these reasons, amongst others, the Chinese state operates in an atypical way in comparison with conventional nation-states. The feedback loops, for example, are different. What might seem a logical consequence of a government action in an ordinary nation-state may not follow at all in China. In a country of such huge scale, furthermore, the government can conduct an experiment in one city or province without it being introduced elsewhere, which is what happened with Deng Xiaoping's reforms, even though they could hardly have been more fundamental or far-reaching in their effect. It is possible, in this context, to imagine democratic reforms being introduced in one relatively advanced province or municipality – Zhejiang or Shanghai, for example – but not others. As we saw in Chapter 7, the civilization-state embraces the concept of 'one civilization, many systems', which was introduced to the wider world in 1997 with the handover of Hong Kong to China under the formula 'one country, two systems'; but the idea of systemic differences within China's borders, in fact, has a very long history. It is conventional wisdom in the West that China should become 'democratic' in the West's own image. The democratic systems that we associate with the West, however, have never taken root on anything like such a vast scale as China, with the single exception of India: indeed, apart from India, the only vaguely comparable example is that of a multinational institution like the European Union, and this has remained determinedly undemocratic in its constitution and modus operandi. One day China may well move, in its own fashion, towards what might be described as a Chinese-style democracy, but Western calls that it should adopt a Western-style democracy, more or less forthwith, glibly ignore the huge differences that exist between a vast continental-sized civilization-state like China and the far smaller Western nation-states (not to mention the obvious truth that China is far less developed). The fact that China's true European counterpart, the European Union, is similarly without democracy only serves to reinforce the point.

Fifth, the nature of the Chinese polity is highly specific. Unlike the Western experience, in particular that of Europe, the imperial dynasty was neither obliged, nor required, nor indeed desired to share power with other competing institutions or interest groups, such as the

Church or the merchant class. China has not had organized religion in the manner of the West during the last millennium, while its merchants, for their part, instead of seeking to promote their interests by means of a collective voice, have sought favour through individual supplication. The state did not, either in its imperial or Communist form, share power with anyone else: it presided over society, supreme and unchallenged. The Confucian ethos that informed and shaped it for some two millennia did not require the state to be accountable to the people, but instead insisted on its loyalty to the moral precepts of Confucianism. The imperial bureaucracy, admission to which represented the highest possible achievement for anyone outside the dynastic circle, was schooled in Confucian morality and ethics. The efficacy of this system was evident for all to see: for many centuries Chinese statecraft had no peers in terms of efficiency, competence or its ability to undertake enormous public projects. There was just one exception to the absence of any form of popular accountability: in the event of severe popular unrest and disillusionment it was deemed that the mandate of Heaven had been withdrawn and legitimacy lay on the side of the people rather than the incumbent emperor. Apart from this *in extremis* scenario, the people have never enjoyed sovereignty: even after the fall of the imperial system, the dynastic state was replaced not by Western-style popular sovereignty but by state sovereignty.

Little has changed with Communist rule since 1949. Popular accountability in a recognizable Western form has remained absent. During the Maoist period, the legitimacy of the state was expressed in terms of a new class system in which the workers and peasants were pronounced as the new rulers; during the reform period this has partly been superseded by a de facto results-based compact between the state and the people, in which the state is required to deliver economic growth and rising living standards. As testament to the historical continuity of the Chinese state, the same key elements continue to define the nature of the Chinese polity. There is the continuing absence of any form of popular accountability, with no sign or evidence that this is likely to change – apart from the election of Hong Kong's chief executive, which may be introduced in 2017, and the present election of half its Legislative Council. Notwithstanding the convulsive changes over the last century, following the fall of the imperial state, with Nationalist government, warlordism, partial colonization, the Maoist state and the present reform period, the state remains venerated, above society, possessed of great prestige, regarded as the embodiment of what China is, and the guarantor of the country's stability and unity. It is the quintessence of China in a way that is not true of any Western society, or arguably any other society in the world. Given its remarkable historical endurance – at least two millennia, arguably much longer – this characteristic must be seen as part of China's genetic structure. The legitimacy of the Chinese state, profound and deeply rooted, does not depend on an electoral mandate; indeed, even if universal suffrage was to be introduced, the taproots of the state's legitimacy would still lie in the country's millennial foundations. And herein lies the nub of the matter: the legitimacy of the Chinese state rests on the fact that it is seen by the people as the representative and embodiment of Chinese civilization and the civilization-state. It is this which explains the exceptional legitimacy enjoyed by the state in the eyes of the Chinese.

The Chinese state remains a highly competent institution, probably superior to any other state-tradition in the world and likely to exercise a powerful influence on the rest of the world in the future. It has shown itself to be capable not only of extraordinary continuity but also remarkable reinvention. The period since 1949 has seen this happen twice, initially in the form of the Maoist state, with the Communist Party providing the embryo of the new state while acting to restore China's unity, followed by the renewal and revitalization of the state during the reform era, leading to the economic transformation of the country. In the absence of any formal mechanism of popular accountability, it is reasonable to surmise that something like the mandate of Heaven still operates: should the present experiment go seriously wrong – culminating, for example, in escalating social unrest as a result of widening inequalities, or a serious threat to the country's unity – then the hand of history might come to rest on the Communist Party's shoulder and its time be called.

Sixth, Chinese modernity, like other East Asian modernities, is distinguished by the speed of the country's transformation. It combines, in a way quite different from the Western experience of modernity, the past and the future at one and the same time in the present. In Chapter 5, I described the Asian tigers as time-compression societies. Habituated to rapid change, they are instinctively more at ease with the new and the future than is the case in the West, especially Europe. They embrace the new in the same way that a child approaches a computer or a Nintendo games console, with confidence and expectancy – in contrast to European societies, which are more wary, even fearful, of the new, in the manner of an adult presented with an unfamiliar technological gadget. The reason is that East Asian societies have not been obliged to pass through all the various sequential stages of development – and their accompanying technological phases – that have been typical of Europe and North America, so the collective mind is less filled and formatted by older ways of doing things. China's version of modernity, however, by virtue of the country's size, must also be seen as distinct from those of other East Asian societies. While countries like Taiwan and South Korea took around thirty years to move from being largely rural to becoming overwhelmingly urban, around half of China's population still live in the countryside over three decades after 1978, and the figure will still be around one-third in 2025. This makes China's passage to modernity not only more protracted than that of its neighbours but also more complex, with various stages of development continuing to coexist over many decades as a result of the persistence of a large rural sector. This is reflected in the often sharp divergence in living standards between different provinces. This juxtaposition of different levels of economic development serves to accentuate the importance and impact of the past, the countryside providing a continuous feedback loop from history. It makes China, a country already deeply engaged with its own past, even more aware of its history.

Seventh, since 1949 China has been ruled by a Communist regime. Paradoxically, perhaps the two most significant dates of the last half-century embody what are seemingly entirely contradictory events: 1989, marking the collapse of European Communism and the demise of the Soviet bloc; and 1978, signalling not only the beginning of the most remarkable economic transformation in history but also one presided over by a Communist Party. The first represents the end of a momentous era, the second the beginning of what will probably prove to be an even more remarkable one. Given the opprobrium attaching to Communism in the West, especially after 1989, it is not surprising that this has greatly coloured Western attitudes towards the Chinese Communist Party, especially as the Tiananmen Square suppression occurred in the same year as the fall of the Berlin Wall. Indeed, following the events of 1989, the Western consensus held, quite mistakenly, that the Chinese Communist Party was also doomed to fail. Western attitudes towards China continue to be highly influenced by the fact that it is ruled by a Communist Party; the stain seems likely to persist for a long time to come, if not indefinitely. In the light of recent Chinese experience, however, Communism must be viewed in a more pluralistic manner than was previously the case: the fact is that the Chinese Communist Party is very different from its Soviet counterpart. Prior to the 1917 October Revolution, support for the Soviet Communist Party was always overwhelmingly concentrated in the cities where only a tiny minority of the population lived: in contrast, it enjoyed little backing in the countryside where the vast majority lived. As a result, the Soviet Communist Party never had widespread popular backing, which is why it became so dependent on authoritarian and coercive forms of rule after 1917. The case of the Chinese Communist Party was almost exactly the opposite. Support for it was overwhelmingly concentrated in the countryside, where the great majority lived, while it enjoyed little backing in the cities, especially compared with the Nationalists. Consequently, the Chinese Communist Party enjoyed considerable popular support, unlike the Soviet Party. This was why, when Communist rule reached its nadir after the Cultural Revolution and the death of Mao, the Party had the self-confidence and intellectual resources to undertake a fundamental change of direction and pursue an entirely different strategy. It displayed a flexibility and pragmatism which was alien to the Soviet Party. Only an organization that has deep popular roots can think and act in this kind of way. In contrast, when the Soviet Party under Gorbachev finally opted for a different strategy, it was already too late and, moreover, the approach chosen was to result in the disintegration and implosion of the country.

The longer-term future of the Chinese Communist Party remains unclear: conceivably it might metamorphose into something different (which to some extent it already has), to the point of even changing its name. Whatever the longer term may hold, the Chinese Communist Party, in presiding over the transformation of the country, will leave a profound imprint on Chinese modernity and also on the wider world. It has created and re-created the modern Chinese state; it reunited China after a century of disunity; it played a critical role in the defeat of Japanese colonialism; and it invented and managed the strategy that has finally given China the promise, after a century or more of decline, of restoring its status and power in the world to something resembling the days of the Middle Kingdom. In so doing, it has also succeeded in reconnecting China to its history, to Confucianism and its dynastic heyday. Arguably all great historical transformations involve such a reconnection with the past if they are to be successful. The affinities between the Communist conception of the state and the Confucian, as outlined earlier, are particularly striking in this respect. Given that Confucian principles had reigned for two millennia, the Chinese Communist Party, in order to prevail, needed, amongst other things, to find a way, at least in part, of reinventing and re-creating those principles.

Eighth, China will, for several decades to come, combine the characteristics of both a developed and a developing country. This will be a unique condition for one of the major global powers and stems from the fact that China's modernization will be a protracted process because of the country's size: in conventional terms, China's transformation is that of a continent, with continental-style disparities, rather than that of a country. The result is a modernity tempered by and interacting with relative rural backwardness, and such a state of bifurcation will have numerous economic, political and cultural consequences. Chinese modernity cannot, and will not be able to, ignore the fact that a large segment of the country will continue to live in what is, in effect, a different historical period. We have already mentioned how this will bring China face to face with its own past for several decades to come. But it also has implications for how China will see its own interests and its relationship with other countries. Of necessity, it will regard itself as both a developing and a developed country, with the interests of both. This will find expression in many areas, including the debate over China's responsibilities concerning climate change. Over time, of course, the weight of the developing section of the economy, and the number of people that are employed in or dependent upon it, will decline, and China will increasingly behave as a developed country rather than a combination of the two. But for the next 25 years, perhaps even half a century, it will continue to display the interests and characteristics of both, an outlook which is likely to be reinforced by the sense of grievance that China feels about its 'century of humiliation' at the hands of Japan and the Western powers, especially its experience of colonization. China, in fact, will be the first great power that comes from the 'wrong' side of the great divide in the world during the nineteenth and first half of the twentieth century, a creature of the colonized rather than the colonizers, the losers rather than the winners. This experience, and the outlook it has engendered, will be an integral part of the Chinese mentality in the era of modernity, and will strongly influence its behaviour as a global power.

A broader point can be made in this context. If the twentieth-century world was shaped by the developed countries, then that of the twenty-first century is likely to be moulded by the developing countries, especially the largest ones. This has significant historical implications. There have been many suggestions as to what constituted the most important event of the twentieth century: three of the most oft-cited candidates are the 1917 October Revolution, 1989 and the fall of the Berlin Wall, and 1945 and the defeat of fascism. Such choices are always influenced by contemporary circumstances; in the last decade of the last century, 1989 seemed an obvious choice, just as 1917 did in the first half of the century. Now we have come to the end of the first decade of the new century, another, rarely mentioned, candidate presents itself in the strongest possible terms. The rise of the developing world was only made possible by the end of colonialism. For the non-industrial world, the colonial era overwhelmingly served to block the possibility of their industrialization. The imperial powers had no interest in allowing competition for their own industries from their colonies. That does not mean that the effects of colonialism were entirely negative, though in some cases, notably that of Africa, they surely were. In East Asia, Japanese colonialism in the case of Korea and Taiwan, and Western colonialism in the instance of Hong Kong and the treaty ports, did at least demonstrate the possibilities offered by industrialization, and thereby helped to plant some of the seeds of their subsequent transformation. The end of colonialism, however, was a precondition for what we are now witnessing, the growth of multiple modernities and a world in which the new modernities are likely to prove at some point decisive. With hindsight, the defeat of colonialism between 1945 and the mid 1960s, the significance of which has been greatly underestimated in the West for obvious reasons, must rate as one of the great landmarks of the last century, perhaps the greatest.

In the light of these eight characteristics, it is clear that Chinese modernity will be very different from Western modernity, and that China will transform the world far more fundamentally than any other new global power in the last two centuries. This prospect, however, has been consistently downplayed. The Chinese, for their part, have wisely chosen to play a very long game, constantly seeking to reassure the rest of the world that China's rise will change relatively little. The West, on the other hand, having been in the global driving seat for so long, finds it impossible to imagine or comprehend a world in which this is no longer the case. Moreover, it is in the nature of vested interests – which is what the West is, the United States especially – not to admit, even to themselves, that the world stands on the edge of a global upheaval the consequence of which will be to greatly reduce their position and influence in the world. China is the elephant in the room that no one is quite willing to recognize. As a result, an extraordinary shift in the balance of global power is taking place *sotto voce*, almost by stealth, except one would be hard-pressed to argue that any kind of deceit was involved either on the part of China or the United States. The contrast with previous comparable changes, for example the rise of Germany prior to 1914, the emergence of Japan in the interwar period, and the challenge of the Soviet Union, especially after 1945, is stark. Even though none carried anything like the ultimate significance of China's emergence, the threat that each offered at the time was exaggerated and magnified, rather than down-played, as in the case of China. The nearest parallel to China's ascent, in terms of material significance, was that of the United States, and this was marked by a similar sense of stealth, though this was mainly because it was the fortunate beneficiary of two world wars, which in both cases it joined rather late, that had the effect of greatly accelerating its rise in relation to an impoverished and indebted Western Europe. Even the rise of the US, however, must be regarded as a relatively mild phenomenon compared to that of China.

So far, China has appeared an outsider patiently and loyally seeking to become an insider. As a rising power, it has been obliged to converge with and adapt to the existing international norms, and in particular to defer to and mollify the present superpower, the United States, since the latter's cooperation and tacit support have been preconditions for China's wider acceptance. China has struggled long and hard since 1978 to become an accepted member of the international community with the privileges and advantages that this confers. In devoting its energies to economic growth, it came to the conclusion that it could not afford for its attention and resources to be diverted towards what, at its present stage of development, it rightly deemed to be non-essential ends. In exercising such restraint and self-discipline, the Deng and post-Deng leaderships have demonstrated remarkable perspicacity, never losing sight of the long-term objective, never allowing themselves to be distracted by short-term considerations. The economic and technological demands of globalization, meanwhile, like the political imperatives just described, have similarly obliged China to replicate and converge in order to meet established international standards and adapt to existing norms. China's passage to modernity, in other words, has also set in motion powerful convergent forces as the country has sought to learn from more advanced countries, compete successfully in global markets, attract foreign capital, assimilate the disciplines of stock exchanges and capital markets, and acquire the latest technology. The fact that an increasing number of issues, most notably climate change, require global solutions with participation from all nations, especially the very largest, is acting as a further force for convergence.

Convergence, however, is only one side of the picture. Increasingly the rise of China will be characterized by the opposite: powerful countervailing pressures that push towards divergence from the established norms. In a multitude of ways, China does not conform to the present conventions of the developed world and the global polity. As a civilization-state masquerading in the guise of a nation-state, its underlying nature and identity will increasingly assert itself. The present Westphalian system of international relations in East Asia is likely to be steadily superseded by something that carries echoes of the tributary system. A nation that comprises one-fifth of the world's population is already in the process of transforming the workings of the global economy and its structure of power. A country that regards itself, for historical, cultural and racial reasons, as the greatest civilization on earth will, as a leading global power, clearly in time require and expect a major reordering of global relationships. A people that suffered at the expense of European and Japanese imperialism will never see the world in the same way as those peoples that were its exponents and beneficiaries. A state that has never shared power with any other class, group or institution, which has never been subject to popular sovereignty, which operates on a continental scale and which, to this day, is suffused with a Confucian outlook, albeit in a distinctive and modernized Communist form, stands in sharp contrast to the credo that informs Western states and which has hitherto dominated the global community. While the West has been shaped by the Declaration of American Independence in 1776, the French Revolution in 1789, the British Industrial Revolution, the two world wars, the Russian Revolution in 1917 and the collapse of Communism in 1989, for China the great historical monuments are mostly very different: 221 BC and the beginnings of modern China; dynasties such as the Tang, Song, Ming and Qing; the Opium Wars; the 1911 Revolution; Japanese colonization between 1931 and 1945; the 1949 Revolution; and the 1978 reforms. The different historical furniture betrays a different history. China, then, if convergent, is also manifestly divergent. While the rise of China since 1978 has been characterized by the predominance of convergent tendencies, well exemplified by China's current desire to reassure the world that it is a 'responsible power', the divergent tendencies will in due course come to predominate as China grows more wealthy, self-confident and powerful. But all this lies in the future; for the next twenty years or so, as China continues its modernization, it will probably remain for the most part a status quo power.

There are two powerful forces that will serve to promote the steady reconfiguration of the world on China's terms. The fact that China is so huge means that it exercises a gravitational pull on every other nation. The nearest parallel is the United States, but the latter is on a much smaller scale. Size will enable China to set the terms of its relationships with other countries: hitherto that has been limited by China's level of development, but its gravitational power will grow exponentially in the future. China's mass will oblige the rest of the world largely to acquiesce in China's way of doing things. Moreover China's size, combined with its remorseless transformation, means that time is constantly on its side. It can afford to wait in the knowledge that the passage of time is steadily reconfiguring the world in its favour. Take its relationship with Japan: on the assumption that China's rapid growth continues, Japan will ultimately be obliged to accept China's leadership of East Asia. The same can be said, albeit less starkly, of China's relationship with the United States and Europe. With the rise of China, indeed, time itself takes on a new and different meaning: time-scales, in one sense at least, are elongated. We have become used to thinking in terms of the converse: the ever-shortening sense of time. The template for this is provided by the United States, a country with a brief history, a short memory, and a constant predilection for remaking itself. China is the opposite. It is possessed of a 5,000-year history and an extremely long memory; unsurprisingly it conceives of the future in terms of protracted time-scales. As a result, it is blessed with the virtue of patience, confident in the belief that history is on its side. If that has been the Chinese mentality since time immemorial, in the twenty-first century that belief will surely come to fruition.

So how will China act as a great power, once it is no longer confined to the straitjacket of modernization? It would be wrong to assume that it will behave like the West; that cannot be discounted, but history suggests something different. While Europe, and subsequently the United States, have been aggressive and expansionist, their tentacles reaching all over the world, China's expansion has been limited to its continent and although, in the era of globalization, that is changing and will continue to change, there is little reason to presume that it will be a West mark 2. China will become a great global hegemon, but it is likely to exercise that power in new and distinctive ways that are congruent with its history and culture. Many in the West are concerned about the absence of Western-style democracy in China, but over the last 30 years the country has become significantly more transparent and its leadership more accountable. This process is likely to continue and at some point result in a much bigger political transformation, though any democratic evolution is likely to take a markedly different form from that of the West. For the foreseeable future, however, given the success of the period since 1978, there is unlikely to be any great change. The greatest concern about China as a global power lies elsewhere, namely its deeply rooted superiority complex. How that will structure and influence Chinese behaviour and its attitudes towards the rest of the world remains to be seen, but it is clear that something so entrenched will not dissolve or disappear. If the calling card of the West has often been aggression and conquest, China's will be its overweening sense of superiority and the hierarchical mentality this has engendered.

The arrival of China as a major power marks the end of Western universalism. Western norms, values and institutions will increasingly find themselves competing with those of China. The decline of Western universalism, however, is not solely a product of China's rise, because the latter is part of a much wider phenomenon, an increasingly multipolar economic world and the proliferation of diverse modernities. The rise of competing modernities heralds a quite new world in which, perhaps, no hemisphere or country will have quite the same kind of prestige, legitimacy or overwhelming force that the West has enjoyed over the last two centuries; instead, different countries and cultures will compete for legitimacy and influence. The Western world is coming to an end; the new world, at least for the foreseeable future, will not be Chinese in the way that the previous one was Western. China, however, will enjoy a growing global hegemony and in time is likely to become, by far, the most dominant country in the world.

13

Afterword

After the Financial Crisis: The Beginning of the
Chinese World Order

The 2008 financial crisis marked a fundamental shift in the relationship between China and the United States. Nothing could or would be quite the same again. The management of the US economy was revealed to have been fatally flawed, a lightly regulated financial sector almost allowed to shipwreck the entire economy. In a few short months, the crisis served to undermine a near-universal assumption of American, and Western, economic competence; in contrast, China's economic credentials have been considerably burnished. The crisis at the same time exposed the huge levels of indebtedness that have sustained the American economy, accentuated since by the financial rescue package, while underlining the financial strength of the Chinese economy, now the world's largest net creditor with its massive foreign exchange reserves. Although hardly new, the crisis finally woke Americans up to the fact that China had become their banker, with all this meant in terms of the shifting balance of power.

But this was only the beginning. Immediately after the financial meltdown, the American economy contracted, and when it began to grow again, it was at a very slow rate. The Chinese economy, on the other hand, confounded expectations and continued to expand at a barely reduced rate, thereby emphasizing the success of the government's stimulus package and the ability of the Chinese economy to withstand the worst Western financial crisis for seven decades. To compound matters, it is now abundantly clear that the financial crisis raised the curtain on a new and protracted period of painfully low growth and greatly reduced expectations in the West, with the American

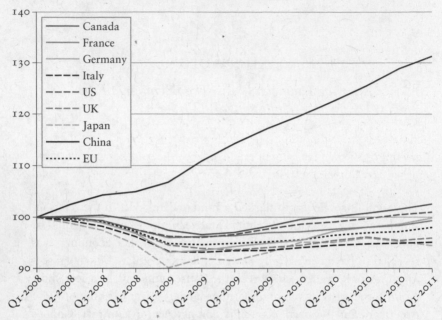

Source: OECD; China National Bureau of Statistics; Haver Analytics (data through first quarter 2011)

Figure 82. China versus the West: growth in GDP since the financial crisis.

economy – like its European counterparts – facing the prospect of years of austerity, with swingeing reductions in both government and personal expenditure, combined, for Americans at least, with the urgency of greatly reducing its trade deficit. Burdened by sovereign debt crises in Greece, Ireland, Portugal, Spain and Italy, the European integration project threatens to unravel, condemning the euro to oblivion in the process. Meanwhile the Western economies continue to teeter on the brink of another recession, with a further banking crisis and a full-scale slump not to be excluded. In contrast, the Chinese, buoyed by huge foreign exchange reserves, large trade surpluses and a high level of savings, can look forward to many more years of fast economic growth. All this adds up to an extraordinary and irreversible shift in power from the West in general, and the United States in particular, to China.

Neither the American nor the Chinese government has admitted to this shift in power; on the surface, at least, it has been business as usual. This is an illusion, but a forgivable one nonetheless. There is a strong imperative for the two countries to continue with their present modus vivendi; a shift in the tectonic plates is bound to complicate this. Signs of growing difficulty were already evident from around autumn 2009 when a whole litany of issues unsettled and ruffled their relationship: divergent and contentious positions at the Copenhagen climate change conference in December 2009; President Obama's meeting with the Dalai Lama and his decision to authorize new military aid to Taiwan, both in 2010; Google's move to pull out of China over alleged cyber-hacking; the continuing controversy over the value of the renminbi and the US's enormous trade deficit with China; continuing US naval exercises in the Yellow Sea; China's refusal to condemn publicly Pyongyang's artillery shelling of the South Korean island of Yeonpyeong in November 2010; China's seemingly more assertive position with regard to the South China Sea and Secretary of State Hillary Clinton's intervention on the issue earlier that summer; and China's strong criticism of the Federal Reserve's quantitative easing and its wider questioning of the role of the dollar. All of this happened in little more than a year and is a far from exhaustive list. Only with President Hu Jintao's state visit to Washington DC in January 2011 did relations regain a more even keel. But, no doubt, this was temporary. The underlying reason for the persistent misunderstandings and tensions is that the relationship between the two countries has changed, but neither government has yet come to terms with what that shift might mean.

This is understandable. Relations between the United States and China have been so unequal for so long that the idea of the United States being obliged to treat China as an equal is still anathema. For the Americans, the adjustment will be very painful. While the United States has grudgingly come to accept that China is, at least in certain respects, a serious adversary, one that it must, in some fields, even seek to emulate – as Obama's State of the Union Address in January 2011 acknowledged with his reference to a sputnik moment (he mentioned China only four times but it was the sub-text of the entire speech)[1] – it will be quite some time before the US can bring itself to view China as an equal. American ruling circles, after all, have only been obliged seriously to entertain the idea that their country might be in decline since the financial crisis. Although the notion of decline is now widely discussed, there is still little understanding of what it might mean or what should be done in response. As is typical of countries confronting decline, the United States is locked in old ways of thinking. Its intellectual arteries have hardened to the point where imagining a world no longer characterized by American ascendancy – let alone one in which China might be dominant – is, for the present at least, well-nigh impossible.

China is in a very different position. It is far easier for a nation whose wealth and power is growing rapidly to think in a strategic way. Unlike the Americans, who have to decide which interest or commitment has to be abandoned, the Chinese have the far more amenable task of choosing which new ones to acquire. The Western financial crisis, nonetheless, presented the Chinese leadership with a serious challenge. Like nearly everyone else, they did not anticipate either the timing or severity of the crisis and were suddenly confronted with a huge and cataclysmic event whose implications for Chinese foreign policy were clearly profound. Ever since the reform period began, Chinese foreign policy has been informed by Deng Xiaoping's dictum that the country should exercise patience and not try to assert itself or seek leadership. This approach has been pursued with remarkable discipline and great success. But the Western financial crisis has transformed China's situation and opened up quite new possibilities, thereby provoking a major debate about how the country should respond. There has already been a subtle shift in Chinese policy.

Previously the Chinese preferred, if possible, to say little, especially on such controversial subjects as the invasion of Iraq that were likely to bring China into conflict with the United States, preferring others, usually Russia, to do the talking on their behalf. Since the crisis they have become significantly more open and explicit, at least on economic matters. At the World Economic Forum in January 2009, Premier Wen Jiabao held the behaviour of the American banks responsible for the financial crisis. Two months later, Zhou Xiaochuan, the governor of the People's Bank of China – its central bank – proposed an end to the dominant role of the dollar in the international financial system and instead the use of the IMF's special drawing rights as a surrogate global currency. As the American government criticized the under-valuation of the renminbi during 2010 and subsequently, the Chinese leadership countered by reprimanding the US policy of quantitative easing, concerned that this would reduce the value of its enormous dollar holdings, and arguing that the dollar could no longer combine its domestic role with its responsibilities as the world's reserve currency. So far, then, the clearest expression of the change in the Chinese approach has been their critique of the international financial system and their obvious intention to play a far more proactive role in its reform. This new-found confidence has not been restricted to the Chinese government. In July 2010, for example, Dagong, the largest Chinese ratings agency, issued its own set of sovereign credit ratings, which pointedly differed from those issued by Moody's, Standard & Poor's and Fitch, whose credibility was severely damaged by the Western financial crisis. In particular, it not unreasonably gave a higher credit rating to China (AA+) than the United States (AA), which is technically insolvent, a fact obscured by the dollar's reserve currency status (at the time Moody's awarded the United States AAA and China a lowly A1). More generally, the Chinese have been displaying a greater confidence and even, at times, a new assertiveness, as they demonstrated when the Nobel Peace Prize was given to the dissident writer Liu Xiaobo in December 2010. The Chinese not only protested loudly, but persuaded 18 other countries, including Russia, Saudi Arabia, Egypt, Tunisia, the Philippines and Pakistan, to boycott the award ceremony. They also organized a rival Confucius Peace Prize, which was awarded to Lien Chan, the former Taiwanese vice-president, though in retrospect it appears that the prize did not enjoy official backing. [2]

CHINESE FOREIGN POLICY

Certainly for the time being, Deng's dictum will continue to inform the main contours of Chinese foreign policy.[3] Given that it has been in place for over three decades and has proved a highly successful vehicle for creating the most propitious conditions for China's rise, in particular helping to contain the anxieties and suspicions of other nations regarding what the country's transformation might mean, it will not be forsaken lightly. In truth, however, the Deng foreign policy is rapidly becoming anachronistic. Deng's approach was conceived for a country that was both poor and weak: China is still relatively poor but it is clearly no longer weak. China has a rapidly expanding range of global interests which require a foreign policy that can articulate and promote them. This need will increasingly conflict with Deng's strictures to 'hide our capabilities and bide our time; be good at maintaining a low profile; and never claim leadership'. The principles of the Deng foreign policy were simple and straightforward: ensuring the best possible external conditions for domestic economic growth and, to that end, maintaining the best possible relationship with the United States. In addition, of course, there was the importance attached to national sovereignty, which was closely linked to the protection of China's own sovereignty, a concern that can only be understood in terms of the country's history and continuing relative weakness. The Deng foreign policy was thus both highly defensive in character and overwhelmingly economic in its preoccupation. It did not have hegemonic aspirations or seek to change the world, but instead, by adopting Western norms, it had the far more modest ambition of achieving China's admission to the Western-dominated international system. Such limited horizons and truncated concerns are no longer adequate or appropriate for China's needs as a rapidly growing global power.

Its limitations have been starkly revealed by China's recent diplomatic difficulties in East Asia, especially with regard to ASEAN. As we saw in Chapter 9, after a decade of extremely successful Chinese diplomacy in East Asia, during 2010–11 the Chinese found themselves increasingly on the defensive amidst growing ASEAN concerns about Chinese policy towards the Spratly and Paracel Islands and, linked to that, China's new naval deployments in the South China Sea. A number of factors lay behind these anxieties. The sheer speed of China's economic rise constantly confounds and upsets the expectations and assumptions of other nations, especially its neighbours who are the ones most directly affected: what only recently seemed as if it belonged a long way off in the future has a habit, in China's case, of being transported with remarkable speed into the present. At the turn of the century, the Chinese proposal that the sovereignty of the islands should be shelved for the longer term, and that in the meantime they should be the subject of joint development, probably felt to the ASEAN claimants like an indefinite postponement; but China's rapidly growing power has, a decade later, sown the seeds of fresh anxiety, at least amongst some, notably Vietnam and the Philippines. This has been aggravated by the continuing lack of clarity on the part of the Chinese as to their long-term intentions with regard to the islands, a situation which was exacerbated by a relatively low-ranking Chinese official, since assigned to other duties, who suggested in 2010 that the islands were a 'core interest' (and thereby on a par, for example, with Taiwan), with the unstated implication that their sovereignty was, in effect, non-negotiable. This lack of clarity would appear to be part of a wider problem, namely that insufficient preparation and forethought has been given to the matter – and indeed, the future of East Asia more widely – by the Chinese government. The greatest fear on the part of the ASEAN claimants concerns China's naval build-up. Relatively modest though this may be, it has nevertheless served to crystallize the doubts and fears about China's long-term intentions. It would seem that the Chinese government made little or no attempt to inform, let alone consult, its ASEAN partners about the new naval deployments. This stood in sharp contrast to how China went about its economic strategy in the region, when it displayed considerable humility towards ASEAN by adopting the latter's multilateral agreements as the template for its own regional economic diplomacy. This suggests, not least, that China is far more sophisticated and sure-footed in its handling of economic diplomacy than in its unilateralist and high-handed approach to its military build-up.

The East Asian example is the clearest expression yet of how the Deng foreign policy has run its course and is no longer fit for purpose. From a more general perspective, it can be seen as a metaphor for the completely new challenges that China now faces as a global rather than an inward-looking regional power. Over the next decade it will be confronted with the daunting task of beginning to formulate a different kind of foreign policy, which is no longer overwhelmingly preoccupied with the Sino-American relationship and which does not presume that economic matters are always paramount. The broader historic significance of this shift should also be recognized. Ever since the end of the nineteenth century, and arguably since the First Opium War, Chinese foreign policy has been dominated by the country's relative impotence and the ineluctable necessity of adapting to Western norms and a Western-dominated international system. That era is now drawing to a close.

What remains unclear, at least for the most part, is what a new-style Chinese foreign policy might look like. There are, however, a number of assumptions that can be made with some confidence. Unlike present foreign policy, with its overwhelming bias towards the United States, the new one will have a comprehensive range of concerns and multiple priorities. It will give due weight towards the various continents and many countries with which China now has to deal, and China will no longer be prepared to subordinate these relationships, as a matter of course, to the exigencies of its bilateral relations with the United States. Most notably, it will give far greater emphasis to Asia, and especially East Asia, than has hitherto been the case: indeed, they are likely to become the central preoccupation of Chinese foreign policy. It is not unreasonable to characterize China's present foreign policy as mercantilist: in the great majority of cases, from Africa and East Asia to North America and Latin America, its bilateral relations are dominated by economic considerations, most notably trade and loans but increasingly also investment flows and currency issues. Chinese foreign policy, as a result, has been extremely narrowly drawn, with relatively little to offer outside the realm of economic diplomacy. The only sense in which Chinese foreign policy might be regarded as hegemonic is in its offer of a successful economic model for other developing countries: otherwise its appeal is strictly limited because, beyond a point, it has relatively little to say. A new-style foreign policy will be far more comprehensive not only in terms of the range of its relationships but also the values and narratives it seeks to embrace and promote. It will also be far more strategic in its thinking and conception. Just as Deng's domestic policy elevated the virtue and value of pragmatism, the same has been true of Chinese foreign policy. But as foreign policy becomes less adaptive and increasingly informed by Chinese interests and distinctive values, so it will become more strategic in character.

This brings us to the final contrast between the Deng approach and a new-style foreign policy. Deng, by emphasizing pragmatism and the need to adapt to existing international norms, accepted the necessity of convergence and thereby downplayed the importance of Chinese history, tradition and culture in the formulation of foreign policy. As China tries to articulate a different kind of approach, it will inevitably and irresistibly be drawn like a magnet to Chinese history in its search for inspiration and guidance.[4] There has been growing support amongst intellectuals for a distinctively Chinese view of international relations, a trend that first became evident as early as 2005. In the current debates, writers and academics are increasingly using ancient Chinese ideas such as *Wangdao* (the way of the prince) and *Badao* (the way of the hegemon), and asserting their relevance for the present-day international context. An example of such use of traditional concepts can be found in the work of the contemporary Chinese philosopher Zhao Tingyang, who suggests that 'the world' should become the highest political unit in a manner similar to the way in which the 'Middle Kingdom' was once seen as 'all land under heaven'; and that China will be a different kind of great power because, in this spirit, it will be able to embrace a new type of universalism. In a similar vein, the influential international relations scholar Yan Xuetong explores the relevance of some of the great thinkers from the Spring and Autumn Period (770–476 BC) and the Warring States period (475–221 BC) for China's foreign policy, including Confucius, Mencius, Laozi and Xunzi. Drawing from Xunzi, he distinguishes between power norms, which are about material strength, including force, and moral norms which are about winning hearts and minds. On this basis, Yan Xuetong outlines three types of rule: tyranny, which relies overwhelmingly or exclusively on power norms and which characterized the period of European domination, especially that of Britain, until 1914 and during the subsequent interwar period; hegemony, combining power norms (typically a great power's behaviour towards its enemies) and moral norms (its behaviour towards its allies) – in other words, a double-standard mentality – which characterized the behaviour of the US and USSR during the Cold War and then the US until the present; and the third type of rule is described by Xunzi as humane authority, where a nation's leadership rests exclusively on moral norms.[5] Yan Xuetong envisages China steadily developing a hegemonic capacity but in the longer run hopes that it will come to embody a new type of rule, namely one of humane authority. We are beginning to see the emergence, thus, of a more indigenous Chinese foreign policy, one rooted in and shaped by Chinese rather than Western historical and intellectual traditions – including harmony with difference, the universalism of the Middle Kingdom, sinocentrism, China's historic destiny as a great power and its moral superiority over the West. An early intimation of this was Hu Jintao's speech to the United Nations in September 2005 in which he advocated the concept of a 'harmonious world' that tolerated and included different civilizations and which embraced diversity and difference.

On this evidence, it seems highly probable that future Chinese foreign policy will differ markedly from that of the United States. Yan Xuetong argues that if China simply imitates the US it will be doomed to fail; that just as the US developed a new way of governing the world then so must China. If Chinese policy mimics that of the United States, for example in East Asia, with a huge escalation in its military expenditure to match that of the US, there will be growing tension and conflict between the two countries. China must find a different way, but it has not yet succeeded in doing so. The fact is that since Obama's election in 2008, US policy in the region has been rather more skilful than that of China. China has palpably failed to reassure its neighbours concerning its future intentions, while the United States has managed to play the security card with some effect. If China seriously wants to pursue a different kind of foreign policy from that of the United States, then East Asia will be the key test. China will need to refrain from engaging in military competition with the US in the region – in the knowledge that, with its growing economic power, time is irresistibly on its side – and instead seek to pursue its ambitions overwhelmingly by persuasion and force of example rather than force majeure. To this end, China would need to be open and public about its intentions and its objectives, including any military build-up.

Such an approach would contradict the manner of its present naval deployment in the South China Sea, which has been both unilateral and secretive. Instead, China would seek to conduct its strategic debates in public – for the benefit of both domestic and foreign audiences – and enter into a similar kind of dialogue with its neighbours over its military plans as it has over its regional economic objectives. If China should succeed in such an endeavour, it would demonstrate that, even though it may be hugely bigger and more powerful than its neighbour states, size is not synonymous with force and grunt but rather with benevolence: in such a scenario, China's ascendancy would be characterized by humane authority and would indeed represent a new kind of global leadership.

A CHINESE WORLD ECONOMIC ORDER

The driving force of China's growing influence as a global power remains its rapid economic expansion. The world has never seen its like before: a country possessed of a huge population combined with a double-digit growth rate that has been sustained for over three decades. It is this which is transforming the global order at such remarkable speed. Alas, much of the world, particularly the developed countries – the United States, certainly Japan, and perhaps above all Europe – find it almost impossible to grasp either the nature of this transformation or its speed. For the most part, they are still locked in the assumptions of the past, prisoners of the established hierarchical order and outmoded ways of thinking about China, still half-believing that its economic growth will hit the buffers and peter out. In fact, as the Chinese economy gets steadily larger, and its rapid growth rate continues, its ability to change the world is constantly accelerating: an economy growing at 10 per cent a year doubles in size roughly every seven years, but each time from a higher base. Thus, when the Chinese economy doubles in size today, its global impact is far greater than a similar doubling a decade ago, let alone 25 years ago, when it was a mere 5 per cent of its present size. Although the 12th five-year plan envisages a more modest

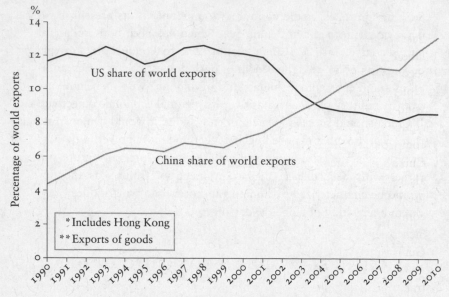

Source: International Monetary Fund (IMF) Direction of Trade Database

Figure 83. As China's* share of world exports** rises,
that of the US falls.

annual growth rate of 7 per cent, the same broad picture will still apply.

If the United States was the architect of globalization in the 1980s and 1990s – with no particular country in the ascendant in the early years of this century – since 2008 China has come to assume that role. Such is the scale of China's impact that it is now increasingly shaping the nature of globalization itself: a new Chinese-driven and Chinese-moulded globalization is emerging. What are its key characteristics? Undoubtedly the most important is trade. China is already the world's second largest trading nation and the world's largest exporter. Its share of world exports rose from below 2 per cent in 1990 to almost 11 per cent in 2010. There are two aspects to the expansion of China's trade: its highly competitive manufacturing exports and its enormous appetite for natural resources. China is now a formidable manufacturing nation. In 2011 it became the world's top manufacturing country by output, bringing to an end the

US's 110-year reign in that position.[6] Hitherto, its export prowess has been overwhelmingly based on cheap and relatively efficient labour, but with China having overtaken Japan to become the world's second highest spender on research and development in 2011, it is rapidly moving into higher-end production, such as high-speed rail, wind turbines, solar panels and sophisticated telecommunications equipment, sectors where it is more or less on a par with its Western competitors.[7] Such products account for a growing proportion of China's manufacturing exports, sourced not by foreign multinationals in China but increasingly by Chinese firms themselves. As a result, the economies of the Shanghai delta and Guangdong are steadily coming to resemble those of South Korea and Taiwan, while those of Sichuan and Hebei are beginning to look like those of Shanghai and Guangdong of the recent past.

Of equal significance in driving the huge expansion of Chinese trade (see Chapters 6 and 10) is the enormous and constantly growing demand for commodities, the scale of which has no parallel in global economic history. For many commodities, China has become the largest single source of demand and, as a consequence, has drawn a growing number of primary-producing (and mainly developing) countries into its economic orbit. By reversing the historic decline in the price of primary products, China, together with, to a much lesser extent, India, has proved an economic godsend for commodity producers. As a result of the huge and growing volume of both its exports and imports, China has, in a remarkably short period of time, become the largest trading partner (i.e. the sum of the exports and imports of both countries) for a formidable array of countries all over the world, including Brazil, Australia, Japan, India, Pakistan, Russia, Chile, Egypt, South Africa and South Korea. The phenomenon is most marked in East Asia where China is already the largest market for the exports of a majority of countries in the region. Furthermore, the share of trade (i.e. exports and imports combined) accounted for by China as a proportion of the total trade of different countries grew much more quickly between 2001 and 2010 than it did between 1992 and 2001 (see Table 14); in other words, the impact of Chinese trade is steadily accelerating. Imagine, therefore, how many more countries

Country	1992	2001	2010
Brazil	0.9%	2.8%	14.0%
Argentina	1.1%	4.7%	9.7%
Chile	2.0%	5.6%	19.2%
Colombia	0.1%	2.0%	8.1%
Venezuela	0.0%	0.8%	8.4%
Mexico	0.0%	1.4%	5.7%
United States	3.5%	6.7%	14.3%
Canada	1.5%	2.3%	7.0%
UK	0.6%	1.9%	6.2%
Italy	1.2%	2.0%	4.8%
France	1.0%	1.6%	3.8%
Spain	1.2%	1.8%	4.2%
Portugal	0.3%	0.6%	1.8%
Germany	1.3%	2.7%	6.1%
Sweden	1.1%	2.1%	3.8%
Norway	0.8%	1.8%	4.1%
Turkey	0.7%	1.5%	6.4%
Russia	NA	4.7%	8.9%
Pakistan	2.9%	4.0%	13.5%
India	0.4%	3.5%	10.5%
South Africa	NA	2.8%	13.1%
Nigeria	0.5%	2.5%	6.9%
Egypt	1.6%	3.3%	9.0%
Algeria	0.8%	0.7%	5.9%
Saudi Arabia	0.9%	3.9%	12.8%
Japan	5.0%	11.8%	20.4%
South Korea	4.0%	10.8%	22.8%
Taiwan	1.0%	32.5%	43.0%
Thailand	2.2%	5.2%	12.0%
Malaysia	2.2%	4.7%	16.3%
Indonesia	3.5%	4.6%	12.7%
Philippines	1.2%	2.7%	12.4%
Australia	3.7%	7.5%	20.6%

Source: *Financial Times*

Table 14. Share of trade with China as proportion of a country's total trade.

around the world will count China as their main trading partner in 2020. The consequence will be a further major ratcheting up of Chinese influence.

Closely linked to these changing trading patterns is the second characteristic of Chinese globalization, namely the rise of China as a major creditor and source of funds. In seeking to promote and foster its trade links, Beijing has been very active not only in signing trade agreements but also in providing long-term loans. The China Development Bank (CDB) and the China Export-Import Bank (often referred to as the China Exim Bank or CEB) – the two key institutions – made more than $110 billion available in long-term loans to developing countries in 2009–10, compared with equivalent loan commitments by the World Bank of $100.3 billion from mid-2008 to mid-2010,[8] on terms typically more generous than those of the World Bank. In the energy sector alone, the larger of the two Chinese banks, the China Development Bank, awarded loans to other developing countries – both governments and companies – of more than $65 billion in 2009–10. The total magnitude of these loans is an indicator of China's growing financial muscle and also of the World Bank's declining relative significance. The loans have played a crucial role in underpinning and cementing China's growing trading relationship with numerous developing countries all over the world, from Central Asia and Africa to the Middle East and Latin America, thereby acting as a key instrument of Chinese foreign policy. In the great majority they help to fund the extraction of raw materials and the provision of infrastructure. A classic example is the proposed high-speed rail network to South-East Asia which will bring the region closer to China by greatly reducing travel times; China will help provide much of the technology and the funding while assisting in the construction.

In some respects the CDB and the CEB can be regarded as emergent institutions of a new shadow international financial system.[9] They operate at a speed and on a scale that few other financial bodies, if indeed any, can match. In the case of the China Development Bank, different branches are given responsibility for different geographical regions with, for example, Chongqing handling the Balkans and Henan looking after southern Africa. In their reach and dynamism they carry echoes of the Rothschilds in the nineteenth century; just as the Rothschilds played a key role in financing European industrialization, the two Chinese banks are performing a not dissimilar role on the much larger canvas of the developing world in the early twenty-first century. The dramatic expansion of China's financial involvement with and growing generosity towards the developing countries stands in stark contrast with the parsimonious position of the West, where funds for the developing world are likely to go through a major contraction over the next decade, with a consequent diminution in Western status and influence.

The third characteristic of Chinese globalization is the growing internationalization of the renminbi, a process still in its relative infancy. Although China is the world's second largest trading nation and second largest economy, the renminbi has, until very recently, not enjoyed any kind of international role or presence. There has been no clearer example of the determination of the Chinese government to prioritize the country's own economic development and not allow it to be exposed to or subverted by the vagaries of international financial movements. We can expect the Chinese strategy for the renminbi to come in two stages: first, its growing use for the settlement of trade, which will come very quickly and which does not depend on the currency being made convertible; second, its utilization and deployment as a reserve currency, which will take much longer. In order for the renminbi to be used in the payment of trade, the Chinese government had to make the currency available outside China, which until very recently was not the case. This process was initiated with a currency swap arrangement with six other countries, concluded in December 2008, just after the financial crisis. Subsequently, Hong Kong was designated by the Chinese government as the offshore currency hub for the renminbi and a small but rapidly growing number of central banks have since begun to hold the currency as part their reserves, including, for example, Japan and India. The use of the renminbi in the settlement of trade will enable Chinese firms to buy their imports and sell their exports in their own currency, rather than dollars (or, to a much lesser, euros) as is the present norm, thereby avoiding the not inconsiderable transactional costs of moving between different currencies, a privilege until now largely reserved for American firms. HSBC has estimated that by 2013–15 at least half of China's trade with other developing economies will be conducted in the renminbi.[10] We can expect the use of the renminbi to follow the flows of Chinese trade, with over half of Chinese exports presently going to the developing world. The renminbi will establish its dominance initially in East Asia but will increasingly be used in the settlement of Chinese trade with Africa, Latin America, Central Asia and the Middle East. Thus, perhaps as early as 2015, a majority of trade in East Asia could be paid for in renminbi. Given that until now the dollar has been overwhelmingly the currency of choice in the settlement of East Asian trade, its future role in the region would be greatly reduced. Within the same kind of time-frame, the renminbi could become one of the world's three major trading currencies, displacing the yen, and before long overtaking the euro.

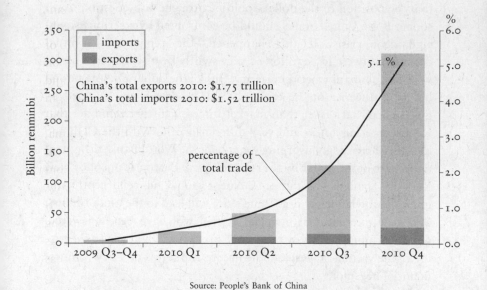

Source: People's Bank of China

Figure 84. The growing use of the renminbi in trade settlement.

The Chinese will be very cautious about making the renminbi convertible, which would be a necessary requirement for its widespread use as a reserve currency. There is no question, however, that this is its longer-term intention. Two straws in the wind, in this context, were the decision to make Shanghai a global financial centre by 2020 – which would require the convertibility of the renminbi – and the Chinese government's view that the present international financial system is no longer sustainable because of the dollar's weakness and its consequent inability to perform its present dual role as both a domestic and a reserve currency. We might expect the Chinese government to make serious moves in the direction of the renminbi's convertibility from around 2015, perhaps a little later. By that time, the renminbi could have established itself as the world's second most important trading currency, with the dollar's position as a trading currency commensurately weaker and its status as a reserve currency increasingly hobbled by Washington's continuing failure to adequately address the country's budget and trade deficits. It is possible that the position of the dollar could be brought into question much sooner if the United States should be confronted by a serious sovereign debt crisis. If this happened, the renminbi's eventual convertibility could be followed very swiftly by its emergence as the world's dominant reserve currency. Unlike the dollar and the pound before it, the rise of the renminbi will be driven and enabled by government fiat rather than market forces, a further reminder that we are entering a new and very different world. With the CDB and the CEB increasingly usurping the role of the World Bank, the potential eclipse of the dollar by the renminbi, and the replacement of New York by Shanghai as the pre-eminent global financial centre, the question of whether or not China's rise will lead to the establishment of a new international financial system will have been answered: what we cannot yet know is how the process will take place, the timing of the various stages, and the nature and forms of a new Chinese financial hegemony.

The fourth characteristic of the new era of Chinese globalization is again novel: to put it cryptically, and somewhat crudely, the locus of the new global economic system will no longer be the North, or even North–South, but rather South–South; in other words, the developing world. The evidence for this shift is already powerful. While 62 per cent of foreign exchange reserves in 1999 were held in the developed world (defined as the Western countries plus Japan),[11] compared with 38 per cent in the developing world, by 2010 the developing world held over 65 per cent, compared with less than 35 per cent in the developed world. In 1970, the developed countries accounted for 65 per cent of global manufacturing, while the share of developing countries was 35 per cent; by 2008, the share of developed countries had fallen to 52 per cent while that of developing countries had risen to 47 per cent. In 1980 the developing countries accounted for 32 per cent of global exports and 26 per cent of global imports, but by 2009 their share of global exports and imports had risen to 43 per cent and 44 per cent respectively. The accompanying

	1980–2005	2005–present
Global Economic Growth	Laggard/Dependent	Leader/Independent
Global Governance	Passive	Active
Global Commodity Prices	Price Taker	Price Setter
Global Innovation/Technology	Imitation	Innovation
Global Industry Standards	Adopt	Create/Tweak
Global Corporate Strategy	Passive/Reactive	Proactive
Global M&A	Recipient	Originator

Source: Joseph Quinlan, Fellow, Transatlantic Academy

Table 15. Global shift: the growing role of the developing nations.

table shows how, over the last three decades, the role of the developing world in global economic affairs has been transformed. With the developing world experiencing a much faster economic growth rate than the developed world – a World Bank report published in May 2011 projected a growth rate of 4.7 per cent between 2011 and 2025 for the emerging economies compared with 2.3 per cent for the advanced economies[12] – as well as accounting for the vast majority of the world's population, the global centre of economic gravity is moving remorselessly away from the developed to the developing world.

It has generally been assumed that, as China becomes more economically developed, it will increasingly orientate itself, as Japan did in an earlier period, towards the developed rather than the developing world. But this is almost certainly to misunderstand the nature of present historical trends: first, China's transformation is moving in tandem with a not dissimilar metamorphosis in the position of many other developing countries; and second, this, combined with China's huge and growing dependence on imported commodities, point to a long-term relationship between China and the developing world that is likely to grow increasingly close and intimate. China's relationship with Brazil is a classic illustration. Extraordinary as it might seem, China is already a far more important market for Brazilian exports than the United States – 15 per cent compared with 10 per cent respectively in 2010 – even though as recently as 2002 the United States still accounted for 26 per cent of Brazil's exports. The fact that the growth prospects for the developing world, including China, are so much rosier than those for the developed world will only serve to reinforce and accentuate this growing inter-relationship between China and the developing world.

This offers a rather different perspective on China's rise and America's decline. It is often thought that as China closes the gap with the United States, it will increasingly assume a similar international economic profile. But we appear to be moving towards a very different economic paradigm in which the United States, Europe and Japan, in varying degrees, will be locked into a relatively stagnant economic zone that will increasingly be dwarfed by a much larger and more dynamic developing world, in which China will be by far the most important player. China's transformation will take place cheek-by-jowl with that of the developing world and the centre of gravity of the new Chinese-shaped world economic order, with the renminbi as its premier currency, will be in the developing world rather than the developed world; at the same time, the developing countries, led by China, will increasingly shape and dominate the new global institutions – whatever they might be – which will come to characterize the Chinese economic order. Rather than a relatively straightforward process by which China displaces the United States as the premier actor in the kind of global economy that we have become familiar with, a vast global economic realignment will have the effect in the longer run of outflanking and marginalizing the United States as a global economic player – and Europe, indeed – and establishing China as the dominant economic force in a very different kind of global economy. This scenario represents a serious challenge to Western countries. Their economic future will increasingly depend on their ability to develop a large-scale trading relationship with China and the other key developing economies, which will require a major reorientation of their economic priorities and perspectives. With the notable exception of Germany, Europe has barely started along this path, with the United States and also Japan a little more advanced.

The Copenhagen climate conference in December 2009 gave an inkling of what the future might hold. Unlike any other major global conference of the last century – probably the last two, in fact – far from being dominated by the developed countries, in particular the United States and Europe, the latter found themselves largely eclipsed by what is all too frequently still referred to, in patronizing terms, as 'the rest of the world', namely the developing countries. Climate change enfranchised the world in a manner that, for example, trade-related conferences had not previously succeeded in doing. Even the smallest nations came to matter. The arbiters of the final agreement were China, India, South Africa and Brazil, who drew up the final text; the United States was only consulted at the very end, while Europe, to its chagrin, found itself excluded altogether. Copenhagen might prove to have been a template for the future.[13]

The fifth characteristic of the new Chinese order takes us to the heart of the developed world and China's growing impact upon it. Until the financial crisis, China's need of Europe was far greater than Europe's need of China: China's vulnerability was its dependence on continued access to Europe's market, whereas Europe, in contrast, required relatively little in return, unlike the United States, which relied on China continuing to purchase its public debt. As a result of the financial crisis, the relationship between China and Europe has been transformed. In varying degrees, European countries now find themselves threatened by public debt, a shortage of cash and in urgent need of an injection of resources. Previously European firms were looking for opportunities in China but increasingly the reverse has become the case. China is becoming present in Europe in three main ways: through the purchase of European government bonds, by investing in companies and by participating in European public procurement. Unsurprisingly, China has been most active, and its intervention most sought after, in southern and eastern European countries, where the economic problems have been most acute.[14]

The most visible expression of the reversal in the relationship between China and Europe has been in those countries facing a severe sovereign debt crisis, which have been anxiously seeking the support of the Chinese government in the purchase of their government bonds. In June 2010, China bought Greek bonds in return for a 35-year lease on Piraeus harbour and a deal to finance the purchase of Chinese ships. It has been estimated that China has purchased in the region of $7.5 billion of Spanish bonds and $5 billion of Portuguese debt. In June 2011 the Chinese premier Wen Jiabao said that China would buy Hungarian government bonds. It is impossible to establish from either Chinese or European sources the precise value of these purchases, but their existence is not in doubt. According to some accounts, in the first half of 2011 there was a big drop in the quantity of Chinese currency reserves invested in US assets, suggesting that they might instead have been invested in euro-denominated bonds.[15]

Meanwhile, there has been a growing, though still very limited, volume of Chinese direct investment in Europe, of which the purchase of the Volvo and MG car firms are the best-known examples. In 2006,

China's total direct investment in Europe was $1.3 billion, but in the first half of 2011 there were three separate Chinese acquisitions – of a Spanish company's Brazilian holdings, a Hungarian chemical company and a large Norwegian silicon unit – which each on their own exceeded that amount. The Chinese have also recently set the goal of acquiring stakes in high-technology small and medium-sized German companies as a means of gaining access to technology and intellectual property rights. Fosun, for example, which is China's biggest private conglomerate by sales, plans to spend $2 billion on Mittelstand technology companies.[16] Finally, the China Development Bank is increasingly active in Europe, with newly established offices in Bulgaria, Croatia, Greece, Poland, Romania, Serbia, Slovenia and elsewhere providing assistance in the financing of infrastructural projects and acquisitions. With governments in eastern Europe strapped for cash, the willingness of Chinese companies to bid at very low rates for infrastructural projects, such as road and bridge construction, is not surprisingly proving attractive.

China's financial power, combined with its largesse, is shifting European attitudes. Whereas southern European countries like Spain, Italy, Portugal and Greece had previously been far more concerned than their northern European counterparts about the threat of Chinese competition for their labour-intensive industries, they are now increasingly desperate to attract Chinese investment. Similarly, central and eastern European nations like Bulgaria and Hungary are becoming more dependent on Chinese funding as previous European sources have tended to dry up; as a result, Chinese loans are now being seen, as in the case of many developing countries, as an alternative to European or IMF loans. Predictably, these developments are affecting Europe's ability to speak with a coherent voice on China, with disparate national interests pulling in different and often contradictory directions. Germany's growing success as an exporter to China – contrasting strongly with the UK, for instance – provides a further example of this diversity of interest. The fact that China, as in other parts of the world, insists, as far as possible, on handling matters on a bilateral rather than multilateral basis, often serves to exacerbate these differences. The case of Europe shows how Chinese financial muscle has the potential to influence governments and even shift alignments not only in the developing world but also in the West. Finally, China's strong support for the euro, based on its desire to ensure that there is a strong currency other than the dollar, has boosted its reputation in the major European capitals, such as Brussels, Berlin and Paris, and has done so in a manner which de facto sidelines the United States.[17] It is a revealing instance of how China is beginning to develop a hegemonic capacity in its dealings with other nations. Indeed, all these various examples suggest how China might in the future succeed in opening up a measure of distance between Europe – or at least some European countries – and the United States.

The most dramatic illustration so far of the shift in power between Europe and China came in October 2011 at the conclusion of an EU summit designed to find a way of rescuing the euro from its potential demise. Immediately afterwards, the French president Nicolas Sarkozy telephoned the Chinese president Hu Jintao requesting a large Chinese contribution for the EU euro bail-out fund; and the following morning the head of the ESFS rescue fund flew to Beijing on a similar mission. In the event, the Chinese, concerned about the ability of the EU to honour such a loan, declined to contribute but agreed to be part of a wider IMF bail-out that included other countries. Unsurprisingly, strong views were expressed in China at the time about why a country which enjoyed a living standard of around one fifth of that of Europe should bail out a continent that was so much richer. Meanwhile, the European request for such a massive Chinese loan had the effect of bringing Europeans face to face, perhaps for the first time, with the meaning and implications of China's rise and Europe's decline. After the Second World War, a devastated and bankrupt Europe turned to the United States for financial assistance and was rewarded with the Marshall Plan. But over sixty years later the United States, now itself hugely indebted, was in no position to help: China was the only possible source of help on the scale needed.[18]

CHINESE SOFT POWER

As the outstanding example of the economic transformation of a developing country, and the largest trading partner of many nations in Africa, East Asia, Latin America and elsewhere, China already enjoys considerable respect and influence amongst developing countries. In contrast, notwithstanding its modest recent inroads in southern and eastern Europe, China still enjoys very little soft power in the West. There are two main reasons for this: first, China is still a relatively poor developing country and second, the absence of a multi-party democracy, a question we will return to in the next section. The significance of the former has been greatly underestimated: economic wealth is a fundamental determinant of a country's wider appeal. This is especially true in a globalized world in which people, wherever they live, are now far more knowledgeable than before about conditions elsewhere. There is a natural desire on the part of people in developing countries to escape poverty and improve their living standards. This creates what might be called an unwritten global hierarchy in which people aspire, at least in terms of living standards, to be like those in societies that are richer than their own while looking down upon those in societies that are poorer. The reason why the Taiwanese have not hitherto wanted to be part of China has not simply been its lack of democracy but, even more potently, the fact that the Chinese have been and still are much poorer than they are. Similarly, the reluctance of the Hong Kong population prior to 1997 to become part of China was mainly because the mainland Chinese were regarded as poorer and less civilized. In a similar vein, the Germans would not wish to exchange their living standards for those of the Greeks, let alone the Zambians, though both would aspire to enjoy those of the Germans. Clearly, China's relative poverty hugely limits its appeal as far as Western societies are concerned. There is, moreover, one further advantage that wealthy countries enjoy in terms of their appeal, namely the means to project themselves to others: Silicon Valley, great sporting events, magnificent museums and Broadway, with isolated exceptions, only lie within the capacity of a rich and developed society. It was not until 2008 that China succeeded in staging the Olympic

Games, by which time they also had the wherewithal to do so with great success.

This brings us to the nature of soft power and how it works. The main proponent of the idea of soft power has been Joseph S. Nye. In *Soft Power: The Means to Success in World Politics*, he sees hard and soft power in discrete and separate terms. He defines economic power (together with military power) as constituting hard power and asserts that 'soft power does not depend on hard power'.[19] Nye argues that 'the soft power of a country rests primarily on three resources: its culture . . . its political values . . . and its foreign policies . . .'[20] But economic power – that is, the economic wealth of a country – is a fundamental pre-condition for most soft power. This is true for two reasons: first, people aspire to be like those in wealthier societies rather than poorer ones; and second, most soft power is based on and made possible by economic wealth. Nye writes, 'Much of American soft power has been produced by Hollywood, Harvard, Microsoft, and Michael Jordan.'[21] But each of these, in varying ways, is based on or assumes huge national wealth. Which other country in the world could sustain even two of these, let alone four? It would certainly be inconceivable for Brazil, or Angola, or even China, to possess such a constellation. Only the United States, as still the richest and most advanced economy in the world, is capable of doing so. It follows that hard power and soft power cannot be treated as separate compartments as Nye argues. They may be different forms of power, but they are intimately interlinked as expressions of the overall power of a country, its ruling system and its elites. The difficulty with the concept of hard and soft power is that it treats power as fragmented and disconnected, rather than organic and integral. By chopping it up into separate parts, its dynamic nature, including the subtle interaction between different forms of power, is lost.

China's growing influence will be based on a range of different but interconnected forms of power. Of these, unquestionably the most important is its ever-expanding economic power, which is creating the conditions for it exercising much greater cultural and ideological influence – its soft power – as well as providing the wherewithal for a major increase in its military capacity. Hegemonic nations must develop an all-round capacity to lead, influence, attract, subordinate, persuade, bully and cajole other nations; and they must be able to project a view of the world which other nations are prepared to accept, whether willingly or reluctantly, including their acquiescence in the primacy of the hegemonic nation and their own subaltern relationship to it. Realizing this capacity, as we have seen with the United States, depends on a combination of economic, military, political and cultural power. These processes are already underway in China's case, albeit still at a very early stage. We are presently witnessing, for example, the extremely rapid restructuring of East Asia on the basis of China's growing regional economic dominance. As yet, however, China is still to develop a genuinely hegemonic capacity in the region, let alone something akin to a 'humane authority'.

Meanwhile, China's rising wealth will in time enable it to project itself in a variety of different ways to the world. The Beijing Olympics, the Shanghai Expo, the growing number of impressive international channels offered by CCTV, the many hundreds of Confucius Institutes established around the world, largely dedicated to the teaching and promotion of Mandarin, and the growing output of international blockbuster movies are part of what might be described as China's 'going out' cultural strategy. A poor country cannot afford such a global cultural infrastructure, but as it climbs the development ladder, China can and will.

In its heyday, America's most attractive feature for many people was that, because of its sheer wealth and dynamism, it was able to set the benchmark of modernity in so many areas. People around the world looked to the United States as a way of understanding and anticipating what the future would be like. The examples over the last 60 years have been countless: the rise of the car, suburbia, shopping malls, space exploration, the PC, skyscrapers, affordable air travel, the internet, Facebook, the iPod, fast food, Ivy League universities, jeans and Hollywood, to mention but a few. It has been able to do this because it is an extremely wealthy nation. No other country has been vaguely able to match America's performance as the exemplar of modernity. With relative economic decline, however, America's capacity to lead in the manner of old has started to wane, while China has begun to show some small but significant signs of playing such a role, albeit still in a very limited way. The most obvious example is its infrastructure, which is becoming the envy of the world: great airports, an excellent network of expressways, the Beijing–Lhasa railway (traversing the 'roof of the world'), the Pudong airport–Shanghai maglev rail link, the Three Gorges Dam, the Bird's Nest Stadium, and the world's largest high-speed rail network, which will transform China economically and socially and, ultimately, its links with the rest of East Asia. In a similar manner, China is boldly embracing a greener future with its huge investment in the manufacture of solar panels and wind turbines.

The United States, with its ageing infrastructure – antiquated railway stations, abysmal and slow rail network, indifferent airports, a ground-tracking system for air travel that dates back to the 1950s, and a stubborn addiction to the private car – already pales in comparison. Its public spending on transport and water stands at 2.4 per cent of GDP, compared with 9 per cent in China. The contrast in sheer will and foresight on such matters is sobering.[22] True, President Obama has set the aim of bringing high-speed rail to 80 per cent of Americans and broadband internet to 98 per cent of them: in his State of the Union address in 2011, he said America needs to 'out-innovate, out-educate and out-build the rest of the world'. But such projects will require the investment of enormous sums of money at a time when the United States is, in effect, broke, unlike during the so-called 'sputnik challenge' of the early 1960s when the country was still able to call upon what were, for the time, huge resources. The world will increasingly look to China in imagining the infrastructural future. Indeed, this can already be counted as part of China's emergent soft power, not only in the developing but also the developed world.

When it comes to China's soft power in a more strictly cultural sense, we need to think beyond the confines of popular culture, such as Hollywood, basketball and pop music. One of the most fundamental issues concerns parenting. Chinese values of parenting are very distinct from the values that inform parenting in the West. One of the best discussions of the two models can be found in Howard Gardner's *To Open Minds*, which, while avoiding making value-judgements, well describes the striking contrast between the two traditions.[23] There are many characteristics that differentiate them: in China, parental authority is considered sacrosanct rather than negotiable as it is in the West; Chinese parents have very high expectations of their children, much higher than in the West, and consequently demand much more of them in terms of study and achievement; likewise, Chinese parents lay down much clearer moral guidelines in terms of behaviour and responsibility, in contrast to the more laissez-faire Western mentality; and the Chinese family, both nuclear and extended, is accorded much greater importance and status within society, with parents expected to assume responsibility not only for their children but also for their own parents.

Even if it was deemed desirable, it would be impossible to transplant Chinese traditions of parenting into Western societies. Nonetheless, just as the West has exercised great influence on other cultures over the last two centuries, there is no reason in principle why China could not do the same in the future, especially in an increasingly globalized world in which distance of all kinds, including cultural, has steadily contracted. The furore in the United States in response to the publication of Amy Chua's *Battle Hymn of the Tiger Mother*[24] in early 2011 illustrates the heightened sensitivity to these issues as a result of growing misgivings about American parenting, concern about China's rise, and the superior performance of Chinese-Americans and Asian-Americans in US schools. There is a new sense of insecurity and a reluctant admission that perhaps Americans might have something to learn from Chinese culture. The mood is far from being one of moral panic, but these signals could prove early symptoms of such a condition. So far, Western interest in the relative merits of the two traditions has mainly concerned educational achievement, but the potential ramifications are much wider, including social cohesion, social inclusion, crime, delinquency and the care of the elderly.

The focus on education is not surprising. An awareness of the importance of education for national economic performance has a long history, going back to the 1870s, when Britain found itself under growing challenge from Germany. Globalization, however, has produced a much greater awareness and knowledge of relative national educational performance, not just between Western societies, where there is a long history of comparison, but between all societies, including those of East Asia. Major surveys of comparative levels of educational attainment around the world have been attracting serious media interest for several decades and for some time there has been an awareness that children in East Asia tend to out-perform their counterparts in the West. In December 2010 the latest OECD survey of the performance of 15-year-olds in mathematics, science and reading not only further confirmed this but saw the United States languishing well behind East Asian countries, and also some European ones, in what could best be described as a middling position.[25] Not only did Shanghai head the rankings in all three areas but Singapore, South Korea, Hong Kong, Taiwan and Japan – all Confucian-based societies – generally came near the top as well, notably occupying the next five places after Shanghai in maths.

On this occasion, little or no attempt was made in the United States or Britain to play down the significance of the results, as was often previously the case, with talk of rote learning and so forth; on the contrary, there was widespread recognition in the United States and Europe that East Asian countries – led by Shanghai – are out-performing the West at school, despite strenuous attempts over the last decade or so to close the gap. Of particular note in the latest survey was the extremely impressive performance of Shanghai, whose lead over everyone else was very large in all three areas and which has recently instituted a successful educational reform, based on giving much greater initiative to teachers, who are now better paid, better trained, and encouraged to participate in shaping the curriculum. The success of East Asian countries, however, cannot solely be explained in terms of their educational systems: it is also a product of the way in which those systems interact with the wider culture. As mentioned earlier, Confucian societies place much greater emphasis on education than Western societies, as exemplified by the high performance levels that parents expect and demand of their children. The explanation for their present level of educational attainment is thus to be found in part in their cultural traditions. One of the underlying strengths of the United States is the quality of its Ivy League universities, but in the

Source. OECD

Table 16. Comparative educational performance of 15-year-old students.

SCIENCE	PISA SCORE	READING	PISA SCORE	MATH	PISA SCORE
Shanghai China*	575	Shanghai China*	556	Shanghai China*	600
Finland	554	Korea	539	Singapore	562
Hong Kong, China	549	Finland	536	Hong Kong, China	555
Singapore	542	Hong Kong, China	533	Korea	546
Japan	539	Singapore	526	Taiwan	543
Korea	538	Canada	524	Finland	541
New Zealand	532	New Zealand	521	Liechtenstein	536
Canada	529	Japan	520	Switzerland	534
Estonia	528	Australia	515	Japan	529
Australia	527	Netherlands	508	Canada	527
Netherlands	522	Belgium	506	Netherlands	526
Taiwan	520	Norway	503	Macao, China	525
Germany	520	Estonia	501	New Zealand	519
Liechtenstein	520	Switzerland	501	Belgium	515
Switzerland	517	Poland	500	Australia	514
Britain	514	Iceland	500	Germany	513
Slovenia	512	United States	500	Estonia	512
Macao, China	511	Liechtenstein	499	Iceland	507
Poland	508	Sweden	497	Denmark	503
Ireland	508	Germany	497	Slovenia	501
Belgium	507	Ireland	496	Norway	498
Hungary	503	France	496	France	497
United States	502	Taiwan	495	Slovakia	497
AVERAGE SCORE	501	Denmark	495	AVERAGE SCORE	497
Czech Republic	500	Britain	494	Austria	496
Norway	500	Hungary	494	Poland	495
Denmark	499	AVERAGE SCORE	494	Sweden	494
France	498	Portugal	489	Czech Republic	493
Iceland	496	Macao, China	487	Britain	492
Sweden	495	Italy	486	Hungary	490
Austria	494	Latvia	484	Luxembourg	489
Latvia	494	Slovenia	483	United States	487
Portugal	493	Greece	483	Ireland	487

*In the study, China was represented by the city of Shanghai and by the administrative regions Hong Kong and Macao.

The OECD PISA survey of educational attainment in science, maths and reading in 65 countries, in 2009.

Source: OECD

long run the school system is far more important because it is responsible for educating the whole population rather than a tiny elite.

By taking a rather more expansive view of soft power – in this instance, infrastructure, parenting and education – it is possible to see how China could come to exercise a significant influence on Western opinion even while it is still only a relatively poor developing country. The reality of its continuing relative poverty, however, will continue to constrain its wider appeal to the much richer West far into the future.

THE CHINESE STATE

Since 2008, linked to a number of what were deemed to be 'sensitive' events, there have been a series of arrests of people associated with human rights in China. These events included the riots in Tibet in 2008, the Beijing Olympics later that year, the even more serious unrest in Xinjiang in 2009, the 20th anniversary of Tiananmen Square, the Shanghai World Expo in 2010, and the installation of a new Party and government leadership in 2012, which is probably regarded by the authorities as the most delicate of them all. In early 2011, various anonymous online calls for a 'jasmine revolution' along the lines of the Arab spring led to a further wave of arrests by the security apparatus.[26] Although the last decade has been characterized by growing openness to the outside world, increasing awareness of individual rights and a heightened concern about the need for a fair legal system, the arrest of high profile figures like Ai Weiwei and Hu Jia have seemingly contradicted this process. To add a further dimension to this picture, the Great Firewall of China, a filtering system that blocks websites hosted outside the country, began to disrupt a much larger number of sites in the early months of 2011.

Periodic clampdowns of this kind are not uncommon in China and it is often difficult to fathom the precise reasons for them, though the events listed probably provide the proximate cause. Western commentary generally interprets such behaviour as a sign that the regime feels fragile and paranoiac. While it is certainly a manifestation of the age-old preoccupation of Chinese leaders with 'stability', the two are not the same. All Chinese governments down the ages, however strong and secure, have been deeply preoccupied with stability because ruling such a vast country has always been a highly difficult act of governance requiring unusual attentiveness to the causes and sources of opposition. In other words, such a repressive response may be a sign of weakness, but not necessarily. In this instance the evidence is thin to non-existent. Although the security apparatus responded with a heavy hand to the calls for a jasmine-style rebellion, there was no sign whatsoever of any popular response: in fact, more journalists and police than would-be protesters responded to the online calls for demonstrations in February 2011.[27] The lack of support was hardly surprising: China is not Egypt. Apart from a lack of democracy, the two examples have nothing in common. According to a Pew poll in spring 2010, while 87 per cent of Chinese expressed satisfaction with their country's direction, only 28 per cent of Egyptians felt the same way. Two-thirds of Chinese believed that their lives were better than five years ago but only 18 per cent of Egyptians; almost three-quarters of Chinese expressed optimism about the future compared with 23 per cent of Egyptians.[28]

There is a very widely held Western view that the Chinese government suffers from a chronic lack of legitimacy. The reasoning is straightforward: the authority of the state is a function of democracy and, as China lacks a Western-style democracy, it follows that the Chinese state is bereft of legitimacy. Given Western assumptions and values, this is a perfectly reasonable and robust argument. It is, however, contradicted by empirical evidence. According to a survey conducted by Tony Saich of Harvard's Kennedy School, in 2009 no less than 95.9 per cent of Chinese were either relatively or extremely satisfied with the central government (although this figure fell to 61.5 per cent at the local level) (see Figure 85).[29] By any criteria, this indicates an extraordinarily high level of satisfaction and represents prima facie evidence that the legitimacy or otherwise of the Chinese state cannot be reduced to the absence of democracy; if that was the case, these figures would be drastically lower. In fact, as I argued in Chapter 7, democracy is only one determinant of a state's legitimacy; nor does it of itself ensure legitimacy, as the palpable lack of legitimacy of the Italian state since the Risorgimento serves to illustrate. Contrary to Western conventional wisdom, the Chinese state enjoys greater legitimacy than any Western state, even though Western-style democracy is entirely absent. The reason is that the authority of the Chinese state derives from an entirely different source: it is regarded by the Chinese as the protector, guardian and embodiment of Chinese civilization, its primary task being to ensure the unity of that civilization or, to put it another way, of the civilization-state. Its legitimacy has been further enhanced by the fact that, for around a millennium, the Chinese state has had, unlike Western states, no serious rivals to its authority: as a result, over this whole period there have not been any major boundaries to its powers. All this helps to explain Saich's findings. The Chinese perceive the state differently from Westerners. The latter see it as an outsider, an interloper, or even a necessary evil that must be constantly held to account and justified. The Chinese, on the other

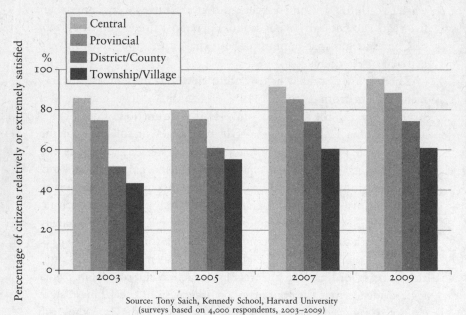

Source: Tony Saich, Kennedy School, Harvard University
(surveys based on 4,000 respondents, 2003–2009)

Figure 85. Percentage of Chinese citizens relatively satisfied or extremely satisfied with government.

hand, view the state as an intimate, as part of the family, even as the head of the family.

It is not only the nature of its legitimacy that distinguishes the Chinese state. Its historical evolution and construction have also been profoundly different from that of any Western state. It acquired a modernized form, with a centralized administration recruited by means of the imperial examination system that was capable of governing a vast country, long before this was the case in Europe; and developed a range of powers over the economy, population and the military, such as the capacity to move grain around the country and undertake huge infrastructural projects, again much earlier than Europe.[30] And these traits are still manifest in a multitude of different ways today. In fact, there is no Chinese institution that is more distinctive – or indigenous – than the Chinese state.

Its present economic role is a case in point. The nearest parallel is the East Asian developmental state, such as Japan, South Korea and Taiwan, which combine a highly activist state, a strong industrial policy, and an export-led strategy. The Chinese model, while drawing heavily on this experience, is different again. The most notable example is state ownership. In both Japan and South Korea, state ownership has been very limited: in China it is extensive. In the late 1990s, the Chinese government embarked on a major reform of state-owned enterprises (SOEs) amid widespread speculation in the West that privatization – in line with the approach pursued in many countries, including Russia – would lead to a huge diminution in their size and role. The outcome was quite different. As a result of the 'grasping the big, letting go of the small' strategy, although the number of SOEs was greatly reduced, the bigger ones were restructured, subsidized, consolidated and enlarged, such that in 2008, SOEs still held 30 per cent of total assets in the industrial and service sectors.[31] The top 150 SOEs, far from being lame ducks, have become enormously profitable. The aim was to create a cluster of internationally competitive Chinese companies, most of which were state-owned. It is difficult to think of another example like this in the world today.[32]

Unlike the approach pursued in most countries, notably in the West, where nationalized companies have enjoyed various degrees of protection and often quasi-monopoly status, the Chinese government has exposed where possible their SOEs to the fiercest market competition from other state firms, private firms and foreign companies. While SOEs get myriad help and assistance from their state benefactors, they have sufficient independence to be managed – and raise capital – in the manner of private companies. China's SOEs can best be described as hybrids that combine the characteristics of both private and state enterprises. The state's hand is also very visible in the private sector: some of the largest privately owned companies, like Lenovo and Huawei, have been crucially helped by – and depend in large measure on – their close ties with government, a relationship which to some extent mirrors Japan and South Korea. Unlike in Japan and Korea, however, where privately owned firms overwhelmingly predominate and virtually always have, most of China's best-performing companies are to be found in the state sector.

At the heart of the Chinese model, then, is a hyperactive and omnipresent state, which enjoys a close relationship with a powerful body of SOEs, a web of connections with the major firms in the private sector, and has masterminded China's economic transformation. The Chinese state is a highly dynamic institution that, since Deng Xiaoping, has been subject to a constant process of reform. Based on experimentation and trial and error, it has been continuously restructured, with institutions regularly re-purposed and incentivized.[33] This picture contrasts with the neo-liberal view that is still dominant in the West, which sees the state as inevitably prone to ossification, atrophy and anachronism.[34] We should be mindful also that the Chinese state refers to a cluster of institutions, not only the central state, but also provincial governments (nine of which are responsible for populations larger than or as large as those of France and the UK), plus mega-cities like Beijing, Shanghai and Chongqing, each with populations in the region of 20 million, as well as many lower tiers. Provincial governments have their own economic and industrial policies and their own provincial-owned enterprises, such as Chery, one of the largest Chinese car firms. Indeed, a major reason why the Chinese economy has been so dynamic is the intense competition between the various provinces and their firms.[35]

The Chinese model is unusual in another respect. It combines two characteristics which are not normally regarded as bedfellows. First, there is a ubiquitous state, operating at a national, provincial and city level, which is highly active and involved in multifarious ways in the economy and society. Second, there is, at the same time, a powerful commitment to the market and a very strong belief in competition: the Chinese government is inimical to monopolies and where they exist has sought to restructure the market in order to ensure competition.[36] The first characteristic hardly needs restating; nor should we be surprised by the commitment to the market and competition. This too is buried deep in Chinese history and the Chinese psyche, as we saw in Chapters 2 and 4. What is so peculiar – unique indeed – about the Chinese model is this combination of a hyper state and a hyper market.

Notwithstanding its highly distinctive history and circumstances, the Chinese experience has much to offer other developing countries, including, most obviously, the need for a proactive, competent and strategic state, the virtue of competition, a constant process of learning and experimentation, openness to ideas from outside, and relatively open markets. There are, however, two fundamental characteristics of China's development that no other developing country can conceivably hope to copy: first, the Chinese state itself, and second, the sheer physical and demographic size of China (with the exception of India, of course, which has a similar population).

Compared with developing countries, it is much less clear what the West can learn from the Chinese state. It seems inconceivable that Western societies would wish to imitate its model of governance. On the contrary, China's lack of democracy offends the sensibilities of most Westerners, who believe that their own experience of democracy offers a universal model for others, not least China itself. China's increasing power and influence, however, will oblige the West over time to seek a better understanding of how and why China's governance is different, including recognition of its strengths as well as its weaknesses, even though it will continue to be antipathetic to China's lack of democracy. There are, furthermore, various other aspects of the Chinese state from which the West will be required to learn. The first is 'state competence', a concern which has virtually disappeared from the Western agenda over the last 30 years in the face of the neo-liberal revolution and its overwhelming preoccupation with the market and privatization. A growing anti-state mentality has diverted and distracted attention from the need for a state that is competent and able to deliver. The second concerns the strategic capacity of the state, its ability to think and act in ways that address the long term. This is one of the great strengths of the Chinese state. In contrast, one of the great weaknesses of Western states is their fixation with the short-term. With the rise of China they will face the challenge of seeking to combine democracy with a different and much longer run notion of time, which will require a serious rethinking of the nature and forms of political governance. Finally, the distinctive Chinese paradigm of a hyper state and a hyper market could in the longer term influence the Western debate about how the relationship between the two should be seen.

All this might sound a little far-fetched, at least to many Western readers. So let us put these considerations in a wider context. The West is in the midst of its worst economic crisis since the 1930s and already, several years after the financial meltdown, it is abundantly clear that no end is in sight. Indeed, such is the gravity of the systemic crisis now afflicting Western capitalism that in all likelihood it is still only in its early stages: several years on we still have little understanding of its deeper causes and how to deal with them. Inevitably the crisis brings into question many of the underlying assumptions of the last few decades, most notably neo-liberalism, though at present there remains remarkably little recognition of this fact. In the face of the economic turmoil, the West has been intellectually paralysed, with little or no sign of any creative response and a constant recycling of old attitudes and remedies. In the longer run, the political consequences are likely to be profound. For example, the fact that the majority of Americans, as we shall see in the next section, have experienced declining real living standards for more than three decades – and that this condition also applies, albeit more recently, to an increasing number of West European countries – is likely to undermine the social contract that has underpinned the stability of Western societies for much of the post-war period.[37] Finally, the crisis, unlike that of the 1930s, coincides with a fundamental shift in global power away from the West and towards China and the developing world, which could serve to adversely affect the relative economic position of many Western countries. Over the last two centuries the West has enjoyed a highly privileged relationship with the developing world, first as colonies, then as weak post-colonial societies. As a result, the West has enjoyed privileged access to their natural resources on very favourable terms. But the growing economic power of many developing nations, combined with their own increasing demand for commodities, means that commodity prices have risen substantially, with the result that they have become increasingly expensive for the developed world. This trend is likely to continue and become more pronounced in the future.

The profundity of the crisis will, in a variety of ways, bring into question the forms of governance and political assumptions that inform Western society. Economic crises of this kind are not acts of nature but man-made events – the consequence of policies, priorities, philosophies and interests. They reflect on the competence, attitudes and ideology of the ruling groups. Like wars, such crises are a brutal and unforgiving measure of the competence, relevance, integrity and suitability of these groups. In this light, history seems likely to judge America's political system harshly. The political class (as also in the case of Britain) allowed itself to become the captive of the financial sector and its interests, thereby paving the way for the financial crisis. The American government has since found itself in a state of near paralysis, beleaguered by a polarized society, its authority constantly questioned and impugned, decision-making too often bought by powerful lobbies, of which Wall Street remains by far the most influential. It is difficult to think of a time when the American government has seemed less capable of responding to and dealing with the profound challenges that the country faces. Of course, it boasts a democratic system that has been the envy of much of the world, but that is little compensation if it is unable to deliver what is the *sine qua non* of a state, namely the ability to govern, cohere and lead society.[38] Meanwhile, the failure of European governance has, if anything, been even more spectacular, as illustrated above all by the crisis of the euro and the potential unravelling of the European project. The contrast with the competence and foresight displayed by the Chinese government in its stewardship of the country's transformation over the last three decades – surely the most remarkable performance by any state since the late 1970s, and bearing comparison with the achievement of any state over the last two centuries – is sobering. This is not to gloss over or ignore the very serious weaknesses of Chinese governance, not least large-scale corruption, but we should not allow these to distract us from recognizing its formidable achievement. The longer this contrast is sustained, the greater the likelihood that the West will find itself obliged to learn from China.

THE DECLINE OF THE UNITED STATES

The question of American decline first surfaced in the 1980s with the challenge of Japan, but was banished when the Japanese bubble economy burst, to be followed almost immediately by the euphoria that ensued after the collapse of the Soviet Union. A decade later, one of the defining assumptions of George W. Bush's presidency was that American power was now so great – with no obvious rivals on the horizon – that the world stood on the eve of a new American century. In fact, of course, as discussed in Chapter 1, the relative economic decline of the US was already underway. It was only as a result of the financial crisis, however, that the American public was forced to seriously confront the issue. It has since become widely discussed, though still only a minority accept that decline is an irreversible long-term process. Many on the right, like Charles Krauthammer, for example, believe that decline is a matter of politics: 'For America today, decline is not a condition. Decline is a choice. Two decades into the unipolar world that came about with the fall of the Soviet Union, America is in a position of deciding whether to abdicate or retain its dominance. Decline – or continued ascendancy – is in our hands.'[39] In January 2010, a poll suggested that one out of four elite Washington Democrats and Republicans recognized that the financial crisis marked the end of American international dominance.[40]

Until the financial crisis, many of the warning signs of impending difficulty, such as the country's indebtedness, the continuing budget deficit and the long-running current account deficit, had been widely ignored or seen as of only limited import. The financial crisis changed all that. There was a new awareness of American dependence on China's willingness to continue its purchase of US debt and a recognition that America's trade deficit was constantly increasing the country's indebtedness to China and others. The bail-out of the banks gave a further boost to the budget deficit so that by 2010 it was in the region of $1.6 trillion, or 10 per cent of GDP. The sum total of these annual budget deficits – the national debt – stands at around $9 trillion, much of it accumulated between 2001 and 2007: the ultimate cost of the war in Iraq alone is likely to be close to $3 trillion. By the third decade of this century, the cost of servicing the US national debt – in other words, the interest payable on the credit provided by China and others – is scheduled to be greater than the defence budget. At some point the sheer size of these deficits could culminate in a sovereign debt crisis – the belief on the part of foreign creditors that the American government might be unable to meet its financial obligations to them and, as a consequence, default. This would precipitate a withdrawal of funds from the dollar, a collapse in its value and a wholesale retreat from its use as a reserve currency.[41]

The US government is now faced with the task of drastically reducing both its budget deficit and its current account deficit. Having already suffered a serious contraction of the economy, the country is confronted with the prospect of a decade of very low economic growth, stagnant or falling real wages, and swingeing cuts in government expenditure, from education and pensions to health and defence. It is not clear how Washington is going to deal with these issues. Political debate has become deeply polarized to the point where the contending positions and narratives occupy parallel universes. The rise of the Tea Party is perhaps the best exemplar of this: it is deeply hostile to government and wants to return the country to a much earlier era of small, even very small government, as evidenced by its turn to the eighteenth century for inspiration. The causes of the growing discordance in the country are deep-rooted. It has been estimated that between 1970 and 2000, the inflation-adjusted income of 80 per cent of US earners fell by 10 per cent, while that of the top 20 per cent rose by 60 per cent.[42] Of every dollar of real income growth generated between 1976 and 2007, 58 cents went to the top 1 per cent of households.[43] In other words, the real income of the majority of the population has gradually been falling for several decades while inequality has greatly increased and social mobility – a hallowed feature of the American way of life – has also significantly declined. In response to declining incomes, the Bush administration encouraged a huge expansion in household lending, from mortgages to credit cards, which, starting with mass defaults on sub-prime mortgages, was eventually to precipitate the financial crisis. Besides the decline in living standards, there are other causes of the souring of the national mood. During the last decade, riding high on its triumph in the Cold War, America has engaged in two failed wars in Afghanistan and Iraq, which have been a huge blow to a country that takes great pride in its military prowess. Moreover, with growing talk of national decline, Americans no longer feel so confident about their previously unquestioned sense of dominance in the world. Unsurprisingly, a new mood of uncertainty has begun to infect the nation.

For most Americans, especially those who live in the inland rather than seaboard states, foreign policy, unlike defence, enjoys a relatively low priority compared with domestic issues, especially when living standards are falling significantly. In 2011, the State Department was faced with a 16 per cent cut in its budget compared with 2010. Secretary of State Hillary Clinton complained to the House of Representatives that 'we are in an information war, and we are losing that war . . . Al Jazeera is winning', while commenting that both China and Russia were increasing their international broadcasting at a time of cuts in the US networks and the BBC. In reference to China, she said: 'Let's just talk, you know, straight realpolitik. We are in competition with China. Take Papua New Guinea: huge energy find . . . ExxonMobil is producing it. China is in there every day in every way, trying to figure out how it's going to come in behind us, come under us . . . I might also mention China has about a $600 million develop-

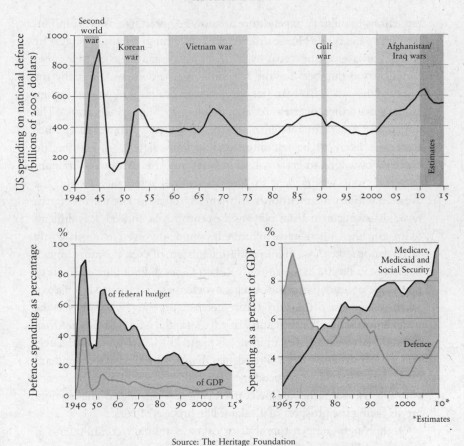

Source: The Heritage Foundation

Figure 86. America's huge defence burden.

ment programme for these Pacific island nations. And what do we have in response? Zero.'[44] As cuts grow more drastic and the consequences more profound, Clinton's comments can be regarded as the first indication of what will surely become a familiar refrain.

In comparison with the Pentagon's budget, the State Department's is tiny. Given that the defence budget accounts for around 20 per cent of the federal budget, serious cuts are inevitable sooner or later. The end of the Cold War led to large defence cuts, but the reasons then were geopolitical not economic. For the first time in seventy years, reductions in military expenditure are now required by austerity. In January 2011 the White House ordered the Pentagon to rein in its budget by $78 billion over the next five years, thereby necessitating a sizeable cut in overall troop numbers for the first time in two decades.[45] Initially the brunt of the cuts is likely to fall on purchases of new equipment, foreign military assistance, overseas bases and non-core military operations. The impact on American foreign policy of these newly straitened circumstances is likely to be felt more or less immediately, as Washington becomes unwilling to get involved in what it deems extraneous military exercises. This was evident in America's initial reluctance to join the Western military intervention in Libya in March 2011 and its subsequent rapid disengagement from playing the central role. Indeed, it is difficult to imagine the United States in future becoming involved in hugely costly interventions like those in Iraq and Afghanistan, or even the more limited operation in Bosnia in the 1990s.[46] Robert Gates did not mince his words on the eve of his departure as American defense secretary in March 2011 when he suggested that any future defense secretary who advised the president to send a big US land army to Asia, the Middle East or Africa '"should have his head examined," as General MacArthur so delicately put it'.[47] In January 2012, President Obama announced that military expenditure would be reduced by $487 billion over the next ten years, with the army and the marine corps the biggest casualties. The US military is facing the prospect of a salami-like process of cuts.

A thorough-going reappraisal of overseas military commitments is underway. There are three main areas of American involvement, apart from Iraq, which has now concluded, and Afghanistan, which is gradually being wound down: East Asia, Europe and the Middle East. For the United States, East Asia is essentially about China. The Obama administration, as discussed in Chapter 9, has made it clear that it will not reduce its military commitments in East Asia, but on the contrary will seek to intensify them. The fact that the military operations in Iraq and Afghanistan are drawing to a close will mean that more resources are available without having to increase overall defence expenditure. In the longer run, however, it is reasonable to surmise that the United States will increasingly be unable to afford the much greater military expenditure that China's growing military strength will necessitate if the United States should seek to retain its current huge military advantage over China in the region, though some on the right argue that this will be essential. Meanwhile, the US is actively extending and consolidating its alliance system in the region, based on Japan, South Korea, Australia, New Zealand, various South-East Asian countries and perhaps also, in the future, India. Where possible, moreover, it will seek to get its allies, for example Japan and South Korea, to bear a growing proportion of the costs of its military presence on their territory. Europe, for its part, will be increasingly left to the Europeans, a trend that has been evident for some time. Indeed, Robert Gates, the US defense secretary, in his final policy address in June 2011 stated: 'The blunt reality is that there will be dwindling appetite and patience in the US Congress – and in the American body politic writ large – to expend increasingly precious funds on behalf of nations that are apparently unwilling to devote the necessary resources or make the necessary changes to be serious and capable partners in their own defence.'[49] In contrast, the Middle East, given its political volatility and the importance of oil, will remain America's major overseas priority.[50]

Cutting the defence budget is bound to be a highly conflictual and traumatic process. For Americans, the armed forces are the ultimate symbol of their country's status and global power: they are deeply enshrined in American popular consciousness and inspire powerful patriotic emotions. The stars and stripes, the most visible of all national flags, flies proudly from countless buildings and, in middle America especially, outside many homes. The special place occupied by the military is illustrated by the fact that, until now, the budget presented by the Pentagon to Congress has almost never been questioned, its approval little more than a formality. Because the military, as well commanding the affection of the nation, is such a huge spender means that its budget is sustained by a vast array of interest groups: weapons manufacturers, Congress representatives in receipt of the lobbying largesse of defence contractors, the jobs and contracts on offer from the defence industry and the Pentagon, think-tanks dedicated to America's geopolitical role, and the hundreds of thousands who have served in the military.[51] It was former President Dwight D. Eisenhower who famously warned of the power of the military-industrial complex in his farewell address when he left office in 1961; and the power of that complex has grown immeasurably since, as we will no doubt discover during the coming decade.[52]

Declining imperial nations find the process of orderly retreat inordinately difficult. They are so desirous of holding on to past privileges and capabilities, there are so many vested interests committed to preserving the status quo, the idea of greatness is so addictive and beguiling, that the retreat from an imperial role and its associated commitments is almost always hugely reluctant, extremely painful, riven with conflict and, as a consequence, piecemeal and pragmatic. Britain was a classic example of this phenomenon. The most obvious exception was the Soviet Union, which simply imploded. In Britain's case, national decline was acted out in a series of tactical withdrawals obliged by growing military weakness and increasing parsimonious economic circumstance. In the long run, of course, a process of retreat informed by a strategic vision would be a far more rational approach and serve a country's interests much better. If one sought to draw up a long-term plan for how America should revitalize itself and respond to China's rise, then it would surely be very different from what is likely to transpire. The real challenge facing the United States is not military but economic. The Pentagon's huge military budget is no longer, for the most part, fit for purpose, diverting vast amounts of the country's resources into areas which have little value when it comes to the primary task of refurbishing the American economy. Not least, the country needs to spend huge sums on transforming an education system which is grossly inadequate and a sad reflection on the priorities of the world's wealthiest nation.

But over the next decade, as the pressure of austerity inexorably squeezes the federal budget, it seems entirely safe to predict that the education system will remain starved of resources, while the military-industrial complex will be far better funded than the country's true needs could possibly justify.[53] Or, to put it another way, the politics of decline, in America as in Britain before, will lead to dysfunctional outcomes because great powers, far from breaking with the imperial paradigm, tenaciously seek to hold on to it as a result of the many powerful interests that are bound up with its retention, thereby only serving to hasten the process of decline. Strategy and vision are the characteristics of rising powers; denial, a deep-seated desire to hang on to the past, and consequent disorderly retreat is the irresistible trait of declining powers.

BE PREPARED FOR A SURPRISE . . .

In 2007 Goldman Sachs suggested that the Chinese economy would surpass the size of the American economy in 2027. I vividly recall that just after the publication of the hardback edition of this book in the UK in June 2009, a very common response at the many talks I gave was that these figures were only projections and that they lay so far in the future that they were very unlikely to be borne out in practice. Not one single person, or even reviewer for that matter – and this was already nine months after the collapse of Lehman Brothers – suggested that the process might happen more quickly than these projections indicated. In the event, of course, this is exactly what is now being predicted. Instead of the Chinese economy overtaking that of the US in 2027, in 2010 that date was brought forward by BNP Paribas to 2020, and then in 2011 the *Economist* estimated that China would overtake the United States in 2018, which, at the time of writing, is just six years away. In other words, far from lying at some distant point in an unknowable future, a 'millennium-style' count-down has already commenced (see Figures 87 and 88).[54] By some indicators, of course, China has already overtaken the US. Chinese exports, for example, overtook American exports in 2007 and by 2011 exceeded them by a staggering 30 per cent. Similarly, Chinese fixed capital investment overtook that of America in 2009 and already exceeded it by more than 40 per cent in 2011. In 2010, Chinese man-ufacturing output surpassed that of the United States, as also did car sales, energy consumption and, perhaps most surprisingly, patents granted to residents. China's external financial wealth, of course, already hugely exceeds that of the United States: it enjoys total net foreign assets of $2 trillion, while America has net debts of $2.5 trillion. The one area in which United States still enjoys a huge lead is defence spending, with its expenditure five times greater than China's:

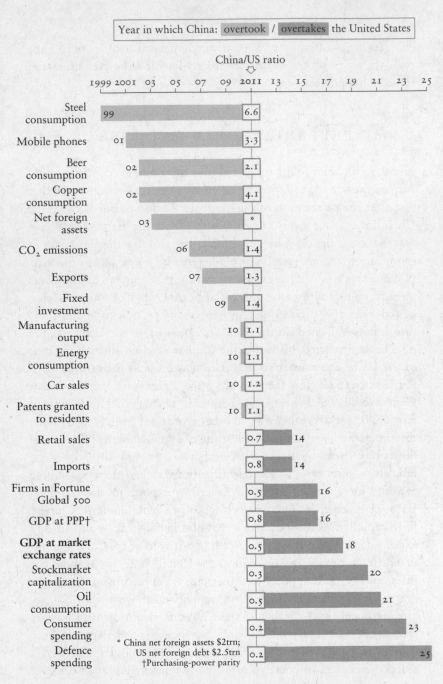

Year in which China: overtook / overtakes the United States

China/US ratio

| | 1999 | 2001 | 03 | 05 | 07 | 09 | 2011 | 13 | 15 | 17 | 19 | 21 | 23 | 25 |

Steel consumption — 99 — 6.6
Mobile phones — 01 — 3.3
Beer consumption — 02 — 2.1
Copper consumption — 02 — 4.1
Net foreign assets — 03 — *
CO_2 emissions — 06 — 1.4
Exports — 07 — 1.3
Fixed investment — 09 — 1.4
Manufacturing output — 10 — 1.1
Energy consumption — 10 — 1.1
Car sales — 10 — 1.2
Patents granted to residents — 10 — 1.1
Retail sales — 0.7 — 14
Imports — 0.8 — 14
Firms in Fortune Global 500 — 0.5 — 16
GDP at PPP† — 0.8 — 16
GDP at market exchange rates — 0.5 — 18
Stockmarket capitalization — 0.3 — 20
Oil consumption — 0.5 — 21
Consumer spending — 0.2 — 23
Defence spending — 0.2 — 25

* China net foreign assets $2trn;
US net foreign debt $2.5trn
†Purchasing-power parity

Source: *The Economist* estimates; BP; CEIC; IMF; ITU; Thomson Reuters; WIPO;
World Bank; WFE; World Steel Association

Figure 87. China is steadily overtaking the United States.

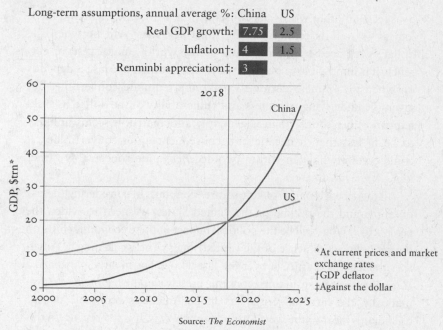

Long-term assumptions, annual average %:	China	US
Real GDP growth:	7.75	2.5
Inflation†:	4	1.5
Renminbi appreciation‡:	3	

2018

China

US

*At current prices and market exchange rates
†GDP deflator
‡Against the dollar

Source: *The Economist*

Figure 88. China becomes the World's largest economy in 2018.

and China is not projected to overtake America in this area until 2025. This brings us finally to the size of their respective economies. In 2011 America's GDP was roughly twice as big as China's, a huge change compared with 2000, when it was eight times bigger. The speed with which China has been catching the United States is quite remarkable. In the face of such an economic juggernaut, there is little the United States can do to prevent China's rise to a position of economic dominance. We can already outline what are likely to be some of the key staging posts in China's growing ascendancy.

The first, it is now clear, was the Western financial crisis which, as already discussed, marked a major shift in the balance of power between the US and China, albeit still greatly underestimated in the West. The next will be in rather less than a decade when the Chinese economy overtakes that of the United States in size. This will obviously be of huge economic significance as well as having a very palpable effect on how the world views the two countries and their prospects: in other words, its consequences will be political and ideo-logical as well as economic. The third key stage will be when the dollar is replaced by the renminbi as the world's major reserve cur-rency. It is impossible to put a date on this, not least because it depends on when the Chinese decide to make the renminbi convertible. But given the underlying weakness and vulnerability of the dollar, it could happen rather sooner than is generally anticipated. It seems unlikely to be in less than a decade but, consequent upon convertibility, it could certainly happen within two decades, quite conceivably rather less.

All these benchmarks, of course, are economic. In considering the rise of China and the decline of the United States, we need to widen the perspective. What will be the political impact of these economic shifts on the geopolitical influence of the United States? The weakening of Amer-ica's influence in East Asia over the last decade has in large part been a consequence of its shrinking economic presence in the region. More dra-matically, the financial crisis has made America's economic decline abundantly clear to the world in a quite new way. It is interesting, in this context, to reflect on the nature and causes of the Arab awakening since 2010. The Middle East has assumed a higher priority in America's for-eign policy and military commitments than any other region. Arguably one of the key factors that lay behind the Arab awakening was a per-ceived weakening in the position of the United States and the regimes that it supported. The most important expression of the Arab spring has been the Tahrir Square movement in Egypt, which overthrew Hosni Mubarak, one of America's closest allies in the region, whose govern-ment received an annual grant of $4 billion in American military aid. Furthermore, the two main Islamic parties gained 67 per cent of the vote in the subsequent Egyptian parliamentary elections held in 2011. Other indications of America's weakened position have been its unwillingness to assume the major responsibility for the bombing of Libya – which the George W. Bush presidency would surely have done in its time – and the determination of Saudi Arabia, one of America's three main allies in the region (along with Israel and Egypt, certainly under Mubarak), to ignore the strong American advice that it should not intervene militarily in Bah-rain. Most seriously of all, there are strong signs that Israel, America's most important ally in the region, is becoming increasingly isolated: Turkey, the new rising power in the region, has been adopting a more aggressive stance towards Israel; Egyptians are demonstrating growing hostility towards it; while the Palestinians, ignoring the loud objections of both the United States and Israel, have chosen to go outside the confines of the established peace process and seek the support of the wider membership of the United Nations for their right to statehood.

It would be premature to draw too strong a conclusion from these developments, but together they indicate a weakening of American influence in the Middle East. From a broader global perspective, they suggest that events could move rather more quickly than previously thought possible. When hegemons are perceived as mortal rather than omniscient, calculations change: what was previously unthinkable suddenly becomes plausible, a feeling of impotence is replaced by a sense of possibility. The classic example of this was the speed with which the Soviet empire collapsed in eastern Europe. America, of course, is a very different case, but it is entirely possible that we have overestimated its power and underestimated its vulnerability. With the financial crisis, and the downgrading of the American economy by Standard & Poor's from its long-held AAA status in August 2011, the global perception of America has changed hugely in just three years. As it becomes increasingly clear that American power is on the wane, it is reasonable to expect that its global authority will be subject to an accelerating process of erosion. This has been evident for some years in Latin America and East Asia, in both of which American hegemony has been in rapid decline. The fact, furthermore, that America's national security apparatus has tended to prioritize military aid and assistance over diplomatic and political solutions – its role in the Middle East, notably Egypt, Iraq and Yemen, being an obvious example – makes American influence that much more vulnerable to a roll-back in its military presence. Even the durability of its soft power has, as I have discussed, been exaggerated.

We should not, therefore, exclude a scenario in which American power declines far more quickly than anyone has really anticipated, with far-reaching geopolitical consequences. Hitherto, Western opinion has been overwhelmingly consumed by what it has seen as China's vulnerabilities: yet, while everyone was questioning the ability of the Chinese economy to sustain its remarkable growth, it was the American economy that foundered in dramatic style. Perhaps we have been looking in the wrong direction – and it is America's weaknesses that should and will preoccupy us. Indeed, it is conceivable that American global power will unravel far more quickly than anyone previously imagined and that within two decades its influence could be a pale shadow of what it is now. As a Chinese world order begins to take shape, the American world order is eroding with remarkable speed. Welcome to the future.

Appendix – The Overseas Chinese

For several reasons, it is difficult to estimate the number of overseas Chinese. In some instances, migration remains highly active, for example to Africa and Australia. There are also problems of definition as to precisely who the category should include, those of mixed race being an obvious example. The statistics also vary greatly in their reliability and accuracy for various reasons, including illegal immigration, the quality of censuses and definitional issues. Notwithstanding these difficulties, the table below gives a rough idea of the total size of the Chinese diaspora and the main countries in which they reside.

Chinese migration has a long history, dating back to the Ming dynasty in the case of South-East Asia. The global Chinese diaspora began in the nineteenth century, when there was a surplus of labour in the southern coastal provinces of China and Chinese workers were recruited for the European colonies, often as indentured labour. The biggest migratory movements were to South-East Asia, but the Chinese also went in large numbers during the second half of the nineteenth century to the United States, notably in search of gold and to build the railroads, and also to Australia and many other parts of the world including Europe and South Africa. Over the period 1844–88 alone over 2 million Chinese found their way to such diverse locations as the Malay Peninsula, Indochina, Sumatra, Java, the Philippines, Hawaii, the Caribbean, Mexico, Peru, California and Australia. In the second half of the twentieth century, there has been a big expansion in Chinese migration to North America, Australia and, very much more recently, Africa, as well as elsewhere.

There is a voluminous literature on the subject, including: Lynn

Pan, ed., *The Encyclopedia of the Chinese Overseas* (Cambridge, Mass.: Harvard University Press, 1999); Lynn Pan, *Sons of the Yellow Emperor: The Story of the Overseas Chinese* (London: Arrow, 1998); Robin Cohen, *Global Diasporas: An Introduction* (London: UCL Press, 1997); Susan Gall and Ireane Natividad, eds, *The Asian American Almanac: A Reference Work on Asians in the United States* (Detroit: Gale Research, 1995); Wang Gungwu, *China and the Chinese Overseas* (Singapore: Times Academic Press, 1991); Wang Lingchi and Wang Gungwu, eds, *The Chinese Diaspora: Selected Essays*, 2 vols (Singapore: Times Academic Press, 1998); Wang Gungwu, *The Chinese Overseas: From Earthbound China to the Quest for Autonomy* (London and Cambridge, Mass.: Harvard University Press, 2000).

Country	Chinese population
Indonesia	7,566,000
Thailand	7,153,000
Malaysia	7,070,000
Singapore (where Chinese are in the majority)	3,496,000
United States	3,376,000
Myanmar	1,662,000
Canada	1,612,000
Peru	1,300,000
Vietnam	1,264,000
Philippines	1,146,000
Russia	998,000
Australia	670,000
Japan	607,000
United Kingdom	347,000
Cambodia	344,000
South Africa	250,000
France	231,000
India	189,000
Laos	186,000
Brazil	152,000
New Zealand	148,000

Italy	145,000
Netherlands	145,000
Nigeria	100,000
Africa (including South Africa and Nigeria)	400,000–600,000

Notes

1 The Changing of the Guard

1. John J. Mearsheimer, *The Tragedy of Great Power Politics* (New York: Norton, 2001), p. 74.
2. Alastair Bonnett, *The Idea of the West: Culture, Politics and History* (London: Palgrave Macmillan, 2004), Chapters 1–2, 6.
3. We are already living in what is, in economic terms, a multipolar world; Pam Woodall, 'The New Titans', survey, *The Economist*, 16 September 2006. Also, Brian Beedham, 'Who Are We, Who Are They?', survey, pp. 14–16, *The Economist*, 29 July 1999.
4. Martin Wolf, 'Life in a Tough World of High Commodity Prices', *Financial Times*, 4 March 2008; Jing Ulrich, 'China Holds the Key to Food Prices', *Financial Times*, 7 November 2007.
5. 'Sharpened Focus on Sovereign Wealth Funds', *International Herald Tribune*, 21 January 2008; 'China's Stake in BP', *Financial Times*, 15 April 2008.
6. Dominic Wilson and Anna Stupnytska, 'The N-11: More Than an Acronym', *Goldman Sachs Global Economics Papers*, 153, 28 March 2007, pp. 8–9.
7. John Hawksworth and Gordon Cookson, 'The World in 2050 – Beyond the BRICs: A Broader Look at Emerging Market Growth Prospects', PricewaterhouseCoopers, March 2008, p. 3.
8. www.newamericancentury.org/statementofprinciples.htm.
9. Charles Krauthammer, 'An American Foreign Policy for a Unipolar World', Irving Kristol Lecture, American Enterprise Institute Dinner, 10 February 2004.
10. Philippe Sands, *Lawless World: America and the Making and Breaking of Global Rules* (London: Allen Lane, 2005), Chapters 3–4, 10.

11. www.globalissues.org/Geopolitics/ArmsTrade/Spending asp#InContextUS Military SpendingVersusRestoftheWorld.
12. The argument against the inviolability of national sovereignty, of course, has various rationales, notably failed states and so-called rogue states. Robert Cooper, *The Breaking of Nations: Order and Chaos in the Twenty-first Century* (London: Atlantic Books, 2003), and 'Civilise or Die', *Guardian*, 23 October 2003; Michael Ignatieff, *Empire Lite: Nation-Building in Bosnia, Kosovo and Afghanistan* (London: Vintage, 2003). Ignatieff quite wrongly suggests (p. 21) that 'we are living through the collapse into disorder of *many* [my italics] of these former colonial states' in Asia and Africa.
13. G. John Ikenberry, *Liberal Order and Imperial Ambition: Essays on American Power and World Politics* (Cambridge: Polity, 2006), p. 12.
14. Joseph S. Nye Jr, *Soft Power: The Means to Success in World Politics* (New York: Public Affairs, 2004), p. x.
15. Joshua Kurlantzick, *Charm Offensive: How China's Soft Power is Transforming the World* (New Haven and London: Yale University Press, 2007), Chapter 9.
16. Paul Kennedy, *The Rise and Fall of the Great Powers: Economic Change and Military Conflict from 1500 to 2000* (London: Fontana Press, 1988), for example pp. 472–80, 665–92.
17. Angus Maddison, *The World Economy: Historical Statistics* (Paris: OECD, 2003), p. 261.
18. Ibid., p. 258.
19. See Christopher Chase-Dunn, Rebecca Giem, Andrew Jorgenson, Thomas Reifer, John Rogers and Shoon Lio, 'The Trajectory of the United States in the World System: A Quantitative Reflection', IROWS Working Paper No. 8, University of California. A dramatic and early illustration of the effects of the UK's imperial decline was the rapid loss of British Asia between 1941 and 1945; Christopher Bayly and Tim Harper, *Forgotten Armies: The Fall of British Asia, 1941–1945* (London: Allen Lane, 2004).
20. NationalJournal.com, 'The Beltway Ponders American Global Influnece', 9 February 2010.
21. Joseph E. Stiglitz and Linda J. Bilmes, *The Three Trillion Dollar War: The True Cost of the Iraq Conflict* (London: Allen Lane, 2008), Chapter 1.
22. Adrian Wooldridge, 'After Bush: A Special Report on America and the World', *The Economist*, 29 March 2008, p. 10.
23. George W. Bush, State of the Union Address, 29 January 2002.

24. For a discussion of the US's current account deficit, see Niall Ferguson, *Colossus: The Rise and Fall of the American Empire* (London and New York: Allen Lane, 2004), Chapter 8.

25. Speech by Henry Hyde, chairman of the House International Relations Committee, 26 January, reprinted as 'The Perils of the "Golden Theory"', *Strait Times*, 21 February 2006. Paul Kennedy, 'Who's Hiding Under Our Umbrella?', *International Herald Tribune*, 31 January 2008.

26. The US has even become a net importer of investment: the difference between the overseas assets owned by Americans and the American assets owned by foreigners fell from 8 per cent of GDP in the mid 1980s to a net liability of minus 22 per cent in 2006; Niall Ferguson, 'Empire Falls', October 2006, posted on www.vanityfair.com.

27. Steven C. Johnson, 'Dollar's Decline Presents a Challenge to US Power', *International Herald Tribune*, 28–9 April, 2007.

28. 'US's Triple-A Credit Rating "Under Threat"', *Financial Times*, 11 January 2008.

29. There is no precedent for the extent of the militarization of the US economy both during the Cold War and subsequently; Eric Hobsbawm, *Globalisation, Democracy, and Terrorism* (London: Little, Brown, 2007), p. 160.

30. For an interesting discussion of the economic cost to the United States of its military expenditure, see Chalmers Johnson, 'Why the US Has Really Gone Broke', *Le Monde diplomatique*, February 2008.

31. Thomas L. Friedman, *The Lexus and the Olive Tree* (New York: Farrar, Straus and Giroux, 1999), pp. 309–22; Gerald Segal, 'Globalisation Has Always Primarily Been a Process of Westernisation', *South China Morning Post*, 17 November 1998.

32. For a discussion on the fundamental importance of cultural difference in the era of globalization, see Stuart Hall, 'A Different Light', Lecture to Prince Claus Fund Conference, Rotterdam, 12 December 2001.

33. Samuel P. Huntington, *The Clash of Civilizations and the Remaking of World Order* (New York: Simon and Schuster, 1996), Chapters 4–5.

34. Chris Patten, *East and West: China, Power, and the Future of East Asia* (London: Times Books, 1998), p. 166.

35. Francis Fukuyama, 'The End of History?', *National Interest*, summer 1989. See also for example, Edward Luttwak, *Turbo-Capitalism: Winners and Losers in the Global Economy* (London: Weidenfeld and Nicolson, 1998), p. 25.

36. John W. Dower, *Embracing Defeat: Japan in the Wake of World War II* (New York: W. W. Norton, 2000), for example Chapters 2, 6, 12, Epilogue.

37. Ezra F. Vogel, *The Four Little Dragons: The Spread of Industrialization in East Asia* (Cambridge, Mass.: and London: Harvard University Press, 1991); Jim Rohwer, *Asia Rising* (London: Nicholas Brealey, 1996), Chapters 1–3.

38. Maddison, *The World Economy: Historical Statistics*, p. 261.

39. Martin Jacques, 'No Monopoly on Modernity', *Guardian*, 5 February 2005.

40. Manuel Castells, *The Information Age: Economy, Society and Culture*, Vol. III, *End of Millennium* (Oxford: Blackwell, 1998), p. 277.

41. James Mann, *The China Fantasy: How Our Leaders Explain Away Chinese Repression* (New York: Viking, 2007), pp. 1–2, 11–12.

42. Wilson and Stupnytska, 'The N-11', p. 8.

43. G. John Ikenberry, 'The Rise of China and the Future of the West: Can the Liberal System Survive?' *Foreign Affairs*, January/February 2008, p. 2. Also Ikenberry, *Liberal Order and Imperial Ambition*, pp. 7–8.

PART I

1. Göran Therborn, *European Modernity and Beyond: The Trajectory of European Societies, 1945–2000* (London: Sage, 1995), pp. 4–5.

2. C. A. Bayly, *The Birth of the Modern World 1780–1914: Global Connections and Comparisons* (Oxford: Blackwell, 2004), p. 11.

3. Therborn, *European Modernity and Beyond*, p. 3.

4. Bayly, *The Birth of the Modern World*, p. 11.

5. Mark Elvin, 'The Historian as Haruspex', *New Left Review*, 52, July–August 2008, p. 101.

6. Ibid., p. 10.

2 The Rise of the West

1. David S. Landes, *The Wealth and Poverty of Nations* (London: Little, Brown, 1998), p. 342.

2. For a pessimistic view of China, see ibid., Chapter 21; Eric L. Jones, *The European Miracle: Environments, Economics, and Geopolitics in the History of Europe and Asia* (Cambridge: Cambridge University Press, 1981).

3. Kaoru Sugihara, 'Agriculture and Industrialization: The Japanese Experience', in Peter Mathias and John Davis, eds, *Agriculture and Industrialization* (Oxford: Blackwell, 1996), pp. 148–52.

4. Giovanni Arrighi, *Adam Smith in Beijing: Lineages of the Twenty-First Century* (London: Verso, 2007), p. 69.

5. John King Fairbank and Merle Goldman, *China: A New History* (Cambridge, Mass.: Belknap Press of Harvard University Press, 2006), p. 102.

6. Kenneth Pomeranz, *The Great Divergence: China, Europe, and the Making of the Modern World Economy* (Princeton and Oxford: Princeton University Press, 2000), pp. 34–5, 43–6, 61–2, 70, 168.

7. Mark Elvin, 'The Historian as Haruspex', *New Left Review*, 52, July–August 2008, pp. 96–7, 103.

8. Pomeranz, *The Great Divergence*, pp. 36–9, 49.

9. R. Bin Wong, *China Transformed: Historical Change and the Limits of European Experience* (Ithaca and London: Cornell University Press, 2000), pp. 27–8.

10. Paul Bairoch, 'The Main Trends in National Economic Disparities since the Industrial Revolution', in Paul Bairoch and Maurice Levy-Leboyer, eds, *Disparities in Economic Development Since the Industrial Revolution* (New York: St Martin's Press, 1975), pp. 7, 13–14.

11. Angus Maddison, *The World Economy: Historical Statistics* (Paris: OECD, 2003), pp. 249–51. In fact, the Yangzi Delta was one of Eurasia's most developed regions over a very long historical period, from 1350 to at least 1750; Bin Wong, *China Transformed*, p. 29.

12. Peter Perdue writes: 'Recent research on late imperial China has demonstrated that in most measurable aspects of demographic structure, technology, economic productivity, commercial development, property rights, and ecological pressure, there were no substantial differences between China and western Europe up to around the year 1800.' Peter C. Perdue, *China Marches West: The Qing Conquest of Central Eurasia* (Cambridge, Mass.: Belknap Press of Harvard University Press, 2005), pp. 536–7. See Arrighi, *Adam Smith in Beijing*, pp. 24–39, for an interesting discussion of these issues.

13. 'In the light of this recent research, the Industrial Revolution is not a deep, slow evolution out of centuries of particular conditions unique to early modern Europe. It is a late, rapid, unexpected outcome of a fortuitous combination of circumstances in the late eighteenth century. In view of what we now know about imperial China, Japan, and India, among other places, acceptable explanations must invoke a global

perspective and allow for a great deal of short-term change.' Perdue, *China Marches West*, p. 537.

14. Bin Wong, *China Transformed*, Chapter 5; Mark Elvin, *The Retreat of the Elephants: An Environmental History of China* (New Haven: Yale University Press, 2004), Chapters 1–4; Elvin, 'The Historian as Haruspex', p. 87.

15. Bin Wong, *China Transformed*, p. 49.

16. Pomeranz, *The Great Divergence*, pp. 63–4.

17. Robin Blackburn, 'Enslavement and Industrialisation', on www.bbc.co.uk/history; Pomeranz, *The Great Divergence*, Chapter 6, especially pp. 274–6.

18. Pomeranz, *The Great Divergence*, pp. 7, 11.

19. Ibid., p. 283; also pp. 206–7, 215, 264–5, 277, 285.

20. C. A. Bayly, *The Birth of the Modern World 1780–1914: Global Connections and Comparisons* (Oxford: Blackwell, 2004), pp. 62–71, 92.

21. Perdue, *China Marches West*, pp. 538, 542, 548.

22. 'The capabilities of the Qing to manage the economy were powerful enough that we might even call it a "developmental agrarian state"': ibid., p. 541.

23. Ibid., p. 540.

24. Bin Wong, *China Transformed*, p. 138.

25. Ibid., p. 149.

26. Ibid., pp. 147–9.

27. Elvin, 'The Historian as Haruspex', pp. 98–9; Fairbank and Goldman, *China*, pp. 180–81; William H. McNeill, *The Rise of the West: A History of the Human Community* (Chicago and London: University of Chicago Press, 1991), pp. 525–9.

28. Maddison, *The World Economy: Historical Statistics*, p. 249.

29. 'The source of Chinese weakness, complacency, and rigidity, like the Industrial Revolution itself, was late and recent, not deeply rooted in China's traditional culture.' Perdue, *China Marches West*, p. 551; also p. 541.

30. Arrighi, *Adam Smith in Beijing*, p. 27.

31. Paul A. Cohen, *Discovering History in China: American Historical Writing on the Recent Chinese Past* (New York: Columbia University Press, 1984), p. 79.

32. Perdue, *China Marches West*, p. 538.

33. Bin Wong, *China Transformed*, p. 47.

34. Charlotte Higgins, *It's All Greek to Me* (London: Short Books, 2008), pp. 77–8.

35. Ibid., p. 21. Also Deepak Lal, *Unintended Consequences* (Cambridge, Mass.: MIT Press, 1998), p. 73.

36. Lal, *Unintended Consequences*, p. 76; Bayly, *The Birth of the Modern World*, p. 82.

37. Landes, *The Wealth and Poverty of Nations*, p. 201; Elvin, 'The Historian as Haruspex', pp. 85, 97, 102.

38. Bayly, *The Birth of the Modern World*, pp. 291–3.

39. Andre Gunder Frank, *ReOrient: Global Economy in the Asian Age* (Berkeley: University of California Press, 1998), p. 343.

40. Bayly, *The Birth of the Modern World*, p. 469.

41. Ibid., p. 12; Lal, *Unintended Consequences*, p. 177.

42. Norman Davies, *Europe: A History* (Oxford: Oxford University Press, 1996), pp. 1259, 1266–7, 1282–4.

43. Christopher Bayly and Tim Harper, *Forgotten Armies: The Fall of British Asia, 1941–1945* (London: Allen Lane, 2004), p. 33.

44. Göran Therborn, *European Modernity and Beyond: The Trajectory of European Society: 1945–2000* (London: Sage, 1995), pp. 24, 68–70.

45. Ibid., p. 68.

46. Maddison, *The World Economy: Historical Statistics*, p. 260.

47. Therborn, *European Modernity and Beyond*, pp. 21–4.

48. Not fundamentalism, however, which unusually originated in the United States.

49. Ibid., pp. 21–4, 68, 356.

50. Alan Macfarlane, *The Origins of English Individualism* (Oxford: Blackwell, 1979), p. 196, quoted by Lal, *Unintended Consequences*, p. 75.

51. Göran Therborn, *Between Sex and Power: Family in the World, 1900–2000* (London: Routledge, 2004), pp. 119–23; also pp. 108–12.

52. The old white settler colonies enjoyed a very different relationship with Britain to that of the non-white colonies, and this was reflected in their far greater economic prosperity; Angus Maddison, *The World Economy: A Millennial Perspective* (Paris: OECD, 2006), pp. 184–5.

53. Samuel P. Huntington, *The Clash of Civilizations and the Remaking of World Order* (New York: Simon and Schuster, 1996), pp. 48–53; Eric Hobsbawm, *The Age of Empire 1875–1914* (London: Weidenfeld and Nicolson, 1987), Chapter 3.

54. Hobsbawm, *The Age of Empire*, pp. 57–9, 70–73.

55. Bayly, *The Birth of the Modern World*, pp. 127–8.

56. Niall Ferguson, 'Empire Falls', October 2006, posted on www.vanityfair.com, pp. 1–2.

57. Hobsbawm, *The Age of Empire*, p. 65.

58. Bayly, *The Birth of the Modern World*, p. 397.

59. Hobsbawm, *The Age of Empire*, pp. 68–9.

60. Maddison, *The World Economy: Historical Statistics*, p. 262; Maddison, *The World Economy: A Millennial Perspective* (Paris: OECD, 2006), p. 114.

61. Jonathan D. Spence, *The Search for Modern China*, 2nd edn (New York: W. W. Norton, 1999), pp. 229–34.

62. Elvin, 'The Historian as Haruspex', p. 104.

63. For a more positive view of the impact of colonialism, see Niall Ferguson, *Empire: How Britain Made the Modern World* (London: Penguin, 2004), pp. 365–81, especially pp. 368–71.

64. Therborn, *European Modernity and Beyond*, p. 40.

65. Landes, *The Wealth and Poverty of Nations*, p. 431.

66. Bayly, *The Birth of the Modern World*, pp. 182, 397–8, 409.

67. Quoted in Arrighi, *Adam Smith in Beijing*, p. 3.

68. Therborn, *European Modernity and Beyond*, pp. 5–6. Apart from the European and American passages through modernity, there are two other types. The third is that represented by East Asia, where local ruling elites, threatened by Western colonization, sought to modernize their countries in order to forestall this threat: the classic example of this is Japan. (The East Asian model will be the subject of the next chapter.) The fourth type concerns those countries that were successfully colonized and which were obliged to modernize after finally achieving national independence. History suggests that this last category has faced by far the biggest problems.

69. Samuel P. Huntington, *Who Are We?: America's Great Debate* (London: The Free Press, 2005), pp. 44–5.

70. Ibid., p. 40.

71. Ibid., pp. 53–4.

72. Landes, *The Wealth and Poverty of Nations*, p. 301.

73. Maddison, *The World Economy: Historical Statistics*, p. 261.

74. Robert Kagan, *Dangerous Nation: America and the World 1600–1898* (London: Atlantic Books, 2006), Chapter 11; Niall Ferguson, *Colossus: The Rise and Fall of the American Empire* (London: Allen Lane, 2004), Chapter 1; Hobsbawm, *The Age of Empire*, p. 58; Eric Hobsbawm, 'America's Neo-Conservative World Supremacists Will Fail', *Guardian*, 25 June 2005.

75. G. John Ikenberry, *Liberal Order and Imperial Ambition: Essays on American Power and World Politics* (Cambridge: Polity, 2006), pp. 6–8.

76. Alastair Bonnett, *The Idea of the West: Culture, Politics and History* (London: Palgrave, 2004), Chapter 1; Huntington, *The Clash of Civilizations*, pp. 69–72; John Gray, *False Dawn: The Delusions of Global Capitalism* (London: Granta Books, 1998), p. 125.

77. Bonnett, *The Idea of the West*, p. 25.

78. J. M. Roberts, *The Triumph of the West* (London: Phoenix Press, 2001), p. 291. See McNeill, *The Rise of the West*, pp. 806–7, however, for a more cautious view.

3 Japan – Modern But Hardly Western

1. Interview with Chie Nakane, Tokyo, June 1999.

2. Michio Morishima, *Why Has Japan 'Succeeded'?: Western Technology and the Japanese Ethos* (Cambridge: Cambridge University Press, 1984), p. 20.

3. The first constitution, adopted in AD 604, for example, was an overwhelmingly Confucian document; ibid., p. 26.

4. Ibid., pp. 10, 34.

5. Ibid., pp. 35–6, 7.

6. Ibid., pp. 9, 32, 34.

7. Ruth Benedict, *The Chrysanthemum and the Sword: Patterns of Japanese Culture* (London: Secker and Warburg, 1947), pp. 68–9.

8. David S. Landes, *The Wealth and Poverty of Nations* (London: Little, Brown, 1998), Chapter 22.

9. Benedict, *The Chrysanthemum and the Sword*, p. 61; Karel van Wolferen, *The Enigma of Japanese Power: People and Politics in a Stateless Nation* (New York: Vintage, 1990), p. 74.

10. Morishima, *Why Has Japan 'Succeeded'?*, pp. 14–15, 45; Benedict, *The Chrysanthemum and the Sword*, pp. 61–4.

11. Morishima, *Why Has Japan 'Succeeded'?*, pp. 53–4; Benedict, *The Chrysanthemum and the Sword*, p. 61; Landes, *The Wealth and Poverty of Nations*, pp. 355–6.

12. Endymion Wilkinson, *Japan Versus the West: Image and Reality* (London: Penguin, 1990), p. 54; G. C. Allen, *A Short Economic History of Modern Japan* (London: George Allen and Unwin, 1962), pp. 20–21.

13. Morishima, *Why Has Japan 'Succeeded'?*, pp. 68–9.

14. Ibid., pp. 41–2, 74–5, 89–93.

15. Ibid., pp. 70–71, 75, 90; Benedict, *The Chrysanthemum and the Sword*,

p. 77. For a fuller discussion of this period see, for example, Landes, *The Wealth and Poverty of Nations*, Chapter 23.

16. Robert Kagan, *Dangerous Nation: America and the World 1600–1898* (London: Atlantic Books, 2006), p. 328.

17. Wilkinson, *Japan Versus the West*, pp. 57, 61.

18. Benedict, *The Chrysanthemum and the Sword*, pp. 72–3.

19. Morishima, *Why Has Japan 'Succeeded'?*, p. 85.

20. Ibid., pp. 74, 78, 89; Benedict, *The Chrysanthemum and the Sword*, pp. 73–4.

21. 'Modernization was created by a state without a class struggle': interview with Peter Tasker, Tokyo, June 1999.

22. Kosaku Yoshino, *Cultural Nationalism in Contemporary Japan* (London: Routledge, 1992), p. 123. Also, Chie Nakane, *Japanese Society* (London: Weidenfeld and Nicolson, 1970).

23. Yoshino, *Cultural Nationalism in Contemporary Japan*, p. 128.

24. Interview with Peter Tasker, Tokyo, June 1999; interview with Tatsuro Hanada, Tokyo, June 1999.

25. Yoshino, *Cultural Nationalism in Contemporary Japan*, p. 2; Wilkinson, *Japan versus the West*, pp. 44–5.

26. Yoshino, *Cultural Nationalism in Contemporary Japan*, pp. 12–20; interviews with Kosaku Yoshino, Tokyo, June 1999 and June 2005.

27. Benedict, *The Chrysanthemum and the Sword*, p. 10.

28. Ibid., pp. 47–8, 55.

29. Van Wolferen, *The Enigma of Japanese Power*, p. 160.

30. Benedict, *The Chrysanthemum and the Sword*, pp. 98–9.

31. Deepak Lal, *Unintended Consequences* (Cambridge, Mass.: MIT Press, 1998), pp. 12–13, 91–3, 148; Benedict, *The Chrysanthemum and the Sword*, pp. 103, 113–15, 122, 166, 171, 222–4.

32. *Suicide Rates* (World Health Organization, 2007). The rates for women are 12.8 for Japan, 4.2 for the US, 3.3 for the UK and 6.6 for Germany.

33. Morishima, *Why Has Japan 'Succeeded'?*, pp. 86, 107–17; van Wolferen, *The Enigma of Japanese Power*, Chapter 6.

34. Lucian W. Pye, *Asian Power and Politics: The Cultural Dimension of Authority* (Cambridge, Mass.: Harvard University Press, 1985), p. 179; van Wolferen, *The Enigma of Japanese Power*, pp. 213, 221.

35. See Alan Macfarlane, *Japan Through the Looking Glass* (London: Profile Books, 2007), for an interesting discussion of Japan's distinctive modernity.

36. Lal, *Unintended Consequences*, p. 150.

37. Benedict, *The Chrysanthemum and the Sword*, p. 70; Yoshino, *Cultural Nationalism in Contemporary Japan*, pp. 68–95.
38. Yoshino, *Cultural Nationalism in Contemporary Japan*, p. 199.
39. Van Wolferen, *The Enigma of Japanese Power*, Chapter 5; Chalmers Johnson, *Japan: Who Governs? The Rise of the Developmental State* (New York: W. W. Norton, 1995), Chapter 6, especially pp. 124–40; Lal, *Unintended Consequences*, p. 146; interview with Tadashi Yamamoto, Tokyo, June 1999.
40. Van Wolferen, *The Enigma of Japanese Power*, Chapter 2; Martin Fackler, 'Opposition works hard to get another shot at running Japan', *International Herald Tribune*, 26 August 2009; Martin Fackler, 'Hacking away at bureaucracy', *International Herald Tribune*, 25 March 2010; Naoto Nonaka, 'The End of LDP Rule and its Meaning', *AJISS-Commentary*, No. 78. The conception of leadership is also very different from the Western model, less about strong leaders and much more concerned with consensus-building; Pye, *Asian Power and Politics*, p. 171.
41. Van Wolferen, *The Enigma of Japanese Power*, p. 29.
42. Interview with Yoshiji Fujita, Research Director, Glaxo Japan, June 1999.
43. Wilkinson, *Japan Versus the West*, pp. 4, 5, 45, 135.
44. By 1980, Japan had more or less drawn level with the European Community and the United States in terms of GDP per head, and during the 1980s pulled well ahead by this measure; ibid., p. 5.
45. Interview with Yoshiji Fujita, Research Director, Glaxo Japan, June 1999. As Takamitsu Sawa has written: 'Drunk with joy for having realised a major goal, the Japanese were at a loss to define the next goal. Suffering from a sense of despair they wasted the next decade.' 'Japan's Paradox of Wealth', *Japan Times*, 30 May 2005.
46. Interview with Peter Tasker, Tokyo, June 1999.
47. Interview with Shunya Yoshimi, Tokyo, 1999.
48. Interview with Valerie Koehn, Tokyo, June 1999; interview with Shunya Yoshimi, Tokyo, June 1999; Sawa, *Japan Times*, 30 May 2005.
49. Yoshino, *Cultural Nationalism in Contemporary Japan*, p. 11.
50. Quoted in Alastair Bonnett, *The Idea of the West: Culture, Politics and History* (London: Palgrave Macmillan, 2004), p. 69.
51. Morishima, *Why Has Japan 'Succeeded'?*, p. 96.
52. Van Wolferen, *The Enigma of Japanese Power*, p. 258.
53. Morishima, *Why Has Japan 'Succeeded'?*, p. 131.
54. Christopher Bayly and Tim Harper, *Forgotten Armies: The Fall of British Asia, 1941–1945* (London: Allen Lane, 2004), p. 3.

55. Van Wolferen, *The Enigma of Japanese Power*, p. 331; Benedict, *The Chrysanthemum and the Sword*, p. 96.
56. Wilkinson, *Japan Versus the West*, p. 67.
57. Interview with Masahiko Nishi, University of Ritsumeikan, Kyoto, November 2005.
58. Racist adverts and books are not uncommon; for example, 'Mandom Pulls the Plug on Racist TV Commercial', *Japan Times*, 15 June 2005, and '"Sambo" Resurrectionists: What's Racist?', 16 June 2005 (concerning publication of *Little Black Sambo*).
59. Van Wolferen, *The Enigma of Japanese Power*, pp. 265, 267; Frank Dikötter, ed., *The Construction of Racial Identities in China and Japan* (London: Hurst, 1997), p. 6.
60. Yoshino, *Cultural Nationalism in Contemporary Japan*, pp. 22–9.
61. Wilkinson, *Japan Versus the West*, p. 77.
62. 'Forum Mulls Ways to Make Racial Discrimination Illegal Here', *Japan Times*, 2 July 2005; 'UN Investigator Tells Japan to Draft Law Against Racism', *Japan Times*, 13 July 2005.
63. Bill Emmott, 'The Sun Also Rises', survey, *The Economist*, 8 October 2005, p. 6.
64. Macfarlane, *Japan Through the Looking Glass*, pp. 224–5.

4 China's Ignominy

1. This account is based on: Jonathan D. Spence, *The Search for Modern China*, 2nd edn (New York: W. W. Norton, 1999), pp. 121–3, 154–60; Julia Lovell, *The Great Wall: China against the World 1000 BC–AD 2000* (London: Atlantic Books, 2006), pp. 1–10; John King Fairbank and Merle Goldman, *China: A New History* (Cambridge, Mass.: Belknap Press of Harvard University Press, 2006), pp. 196–7; Alain Peyrefitte, *The Collision of Two Civilizations: The British Expedition to China in 1792–4* (London: Harvill, 1993), pp. 13, 76, 150–51, 291.
2. Paul A. Cohen, *Discovering History in China: American Historical Writing on the Recent Chinese Past* (New York: Columbia University Press, 1984), p. 79.
3. Ibid., pp. 81, 151–2; Huang Ping, '"Beijing Consensus", or "Chinese Experiences", or What?', unpublished paper, 2005, pp. 5–8; Zheng Yongnian, *Will China Become Democratic?: Elite, Class and Regime Transition* (Singapore: Eastern Universities Press, 2004), p. 85.
4. Jacques Gernet, *A History of Chinese Civilization*, 2nd edn (Cambridge:

Cambridge University Press, 1997), pp. 103–6; Jared Diamond, *Guns, Germs and Steel: A Short History of Everybody for the Last 13,000 Years* (London: Vintage, 1998), pp. 323; also pp. 413–16.

5. Fairbank and Goldman, *China*, p. 61.

6. Ibid., pp. 80, 114, 116, 120.

7. Mark Elvin, *The Pattern of the Chinese Past* (London: Eyre Methuen, 1973), pp. 21–2.

8. Fairbank and Goldman, *China*, p. 56.

9. Mark Elvin, *The Pattern of the Chinese Past*, p. 93.

10. Ibid., pp. 51, 106; Nicholas Ostler, *Empires of the Word: A Language History of the World* (London: HarperCollins, 2005), p. 171; for successive historical examples of this phenomenon, see Lovell, *The Great Wall*.

11. Ostler, *Empires of the Word*, pp. 113–73, especially pp. 116–17, 168–9.

12. Gernet, *A History of Chinese Civilization*, pp. 14–15, 265–6; Fairbank and Goldman, *China*, pp. 168–9.

13. Gernet, *A History of Chinese Civilization*, pp. 319–20.

14. Fairbank and Goldman, *China*, pp. 89, 167–9; Maddison, *The World Economy: A Millennial Perspective* (Paris: OECD, 2006), p. 42.

15. Quoted in Elvin, *The Pattern of the Chinese Past*, pp. 144–145. Also pp. 133–9.

16. Ibid., pp. 176–7.

17. Fairbank and Goldman, *China: A New History*, p. 88, also Chapter 4.

18. Ibid., Chapter 4; Gernet, *A History of Chinese Civilization*, Chapters 14, 15.

19. Elvin, *The Pattern of the Chinese Past*, pp. 198–9.

20. Ibid., Chapter 15, especially pp. 331–41, 347–8; Fairbank and Goldman, *China*, pp. 88, 93–5, 101–2.

21. Gernet, *A History of Chinese Civilization*, pp. 347–8.

22. Elvin, *The Pattern of the Chinese Past*, pp. 203–4, 214–15, 222.

23. Ibid., pp. 204–25; David S. Landes, *The Wealth and Poverty of Nations* (London: Little, Brown, 1998), pp. 93–8; Lovell, *The Great Wall*, pp. 183–4.

24. Quoted in Elvin, *The Pattern of the Chinese Past*, p. 217.

25. Gernet, *A History of Chinese Civilization*, pp. 326–9; Fairbank and Goldman, *China*, p. 93.

26. Edward L. Dreyer, *Zheng He: China and the Oceans in the Early Ming Dynasty, 1405–1433* (New York: Pearson Longman, 2007), pp. 166–71.

27. See Chapter 7.
28. Fairbank and Goldman, *China*, pp. 168–9.
29. Angus Maddison, *The World Economy: Historical Statistics* (Paris: OECD, 2003), p. 249.
30. Quoted by Andre Gunder Frank, *ReOrient: Global Economy in the Asian Age* (Berkeley: University of California Press, 1998), p. 279. See Giovanni Arrighi, *Adam Smith in Beijing: Lineages of the Twenty-First Century* (London: Verso, 2007), pp. 25–6, 58–9, 69.
31. R. Bin Wong, *China Transformed: Historical Change and the Limits of European Experience* (Ithaca and London: Cornell University Press, 2000), p. 27. 'Until about 1800', argues Andre Gunder Frank, 'the world economy was by no stretch of the imagination European-centred nor in any significant way defined by or marked by any European-born "capitalism" – it was preponderantly Asian-based.' Frank, *ReOrient*, pp. 276–7.
32. Fairbank and Goldman, *China*, p. 180.
33. Elvin, *The Pattern of the Chinese Past*, pp. 298–316; also, pp. 286–98.
34. James Kynge, *China Shakes the World: The Rise of a Hungry Nation* (London: Weidenfeld and Nicolson, 2006), pp. 131–2.
35. Elvin, *The Pattern of the Chinese Past*, pp. 314–15.
36. Ibid., pp. 281–2; Bin Wong, *China Transformed*, pp. 34, 41–4, 49; Mark Elvin, 'The Historian as Haruspex', *New Left Review*, 52, July–August 2008, p. 96.
37. Gernet, *A History of Chinese Civilization*, p. 53.
38. Bin Wong, *China Transformed*, p. 76.
39. It can also be argued that if, like Europe, China had been composed of a group of competitive nation-states, this would have made governance rather less forbidding and might also, at times, have stimulated greater innovation; Lucian W. Pye, *Asian Power and Politics: The Cultural Dimensions of Authority* (Cambridge, Mass.: Harvard University Press, 1985), p. 64.
40. Bin Wong, *China Transformed*, p. 92.
41. Lovell, *The Great Wall*, pp. 148–50.
42. Michio Morishima, *Why Has Japan 'Succeeded'?: Western Technology and the Japanese Ethos* (Cambridge: Cambridge University Press, 1984), p. 12; Lovell, *The Great Wall*, pp. 148–9.
43. Angus Maddison, *Chinese Economic Performance in the Long Run, Second Edition, Revised and Updated: 960–2030 AD* (Paris: OECD, 2007), pp. 24–6.
44. Bin Wong, *China Transformed*, p. 96.

45. Ibid., p. 97.
46. Ibid., p. 96.
47. Ibid., p. 97.
48. Ibid., p. 99; quote is p. 97.
49. Ruth Benedict, *The Chrysanthemum and the Sword: Patterns of Japanese Culture* (London: Secker and Warburg, 1947), p. 49.
50. Bin Wong, *China Transformed*, p. 100.
51. Ibid., p. 90.
52. Fairbank and Goldman, *China*, pp. 40, 48; Karel van Wolferen, *The Enigma of Japanese Power: People and Politics in a Stateless Nation* (New York: Vintage, 1990), pp. 241–2.
53. Peter Nolan, *China at the Crossroads* (Cambridge: Polity Press, 2004), pp. 134–40.
54. Ibid., pp. 130–34; Bin Wong, *China Transformed*, pp. 90–91.
55. The nature of the tributary system, and its relationships, is discussed fully in Chapter 10.
56. Bin Wong, *China Transformed*, pp. 93–5.
57. Cohen, *Discovering History in China*, p. 16.
58. Ibid., p. 18.
59. Fairbank and Goldman, *China*, pp. 206–12.
60. Gernet, *A History of Chinese Civilization*, pp. 546–65; Spence, *The Search for Modern China*, pp. 171–80; Bin Wong, *China Transformed*, p. 155.
61. Cohen, *Discovering History in China*, pp. 21, 29.
62. Zheng Yangwen, '"Peaceful Rise of China" After "Century of Unequal Treaties"? How History Might Matter in the Future', pp. 2, 7, in Anthony Reid and Zheng Yangwen, eds, *Negotiating Asymmetry: China's Place in Asia* (Singapore: NUS Press, 2009); Suisheng Zhao, *A Nation-State by Construction: Dynamics of Modern Chinese Nationalism* (Stanford: Stanford University Press, 2004), p. 48. For good reason, in both Japan and China the treaties imposed by the foreign powers were known as the unequal treaties.
63. Peter C. Perdue, *China Marches West* (Cambridge, Mass., Belknap Press of Harvard University Press, 2005), p. 554.
64. Bin Wong, *China Transformed*, pp. 89, 154; Lucian W. Pye, *The Spirit of Chinese Politics* (Cambridge, Mass.: Harvard University Press, 1992), p. 234.
65. Gernet, *A History of Chinese Civilization*, pp. 577–84.
66. Spence, *The Search for Modern China*, p. 220.
67. Ibid., p. 222; Gernet, *A History of Chinese Civilization*, p. 569.

68. The missionaries attracted a great deal of hostility from the Chinese; Cohen, *Discovering History in China*, p. 45.

69. The psychological and intellectual impact of the foreign presence on the Chinese population was profound; ibid., pp. 141–2.

70. Fairbank and Goldman, *China*, pp. 227–9.

71. Cohen, *Discovering History in China*, pp. 23–43; Gernet, *A History of Chinese Civilization*, pp. 566–74; Spence, *The Search for Modern China*, pp. 223–9; Zhao, *A Nation-State by Construction*, p. 53.

72. Cohen, *Discovering History in China*, pp. 29–30.

73. Ibid., pp. 22–4, 29–30, 32, 56–7; C. A. Bayly, *The Birth of the Modern World 1780–1914: Global Connections and Comparisons* (Oxford: Blackwell, 2004), p. 179; Gernet, *A History of Chinese Civilization*, pp. 590–98; Tong Shijun, 'Dialectics of Modernisation', Chapter 5, unpublished PhD, University of Bergen, 1994.

74. Zheng Yongnian, *Will China Become Democratic?: Elite, Class and Regime Transition* (Singapore: EAI, 2004), p. 85.

75. Cohen, *Discovering History in China*, p. 32.

76. Gernet, *A History of Chinese Civilization*, pp. 626–33; Bin Wong, *China Transformed*, p. 164.

77. Sun Shuyun, *The Long March* (London: HarperPress, 2006), for an account of this remarkable episode.

78. Iris Chang, *The Rape of Nanking* (London: Penguin, 1998), Chapter 2, and pp. 215–25.

79. Chen Jian, *Mao's China and the Cold War* (Chapel Hill and London: University of North Carolina Press, 2001), p. 20.

80. Ibid., p. 21.

81. Fairbank and Goldman, *China: A New History*, pp. 331–2.

82. Bin Wong, *China Transformed*, pp. 164, 170–73.

83. Cohen, *Discovering History in China*, p. 135.

84. Ibid., p. 132.

85. Meghnad Desai, 'India and China: An Essay in Comparative Political Economy', seminar paper, Asia Research Centre, London School of Economics, 2003, p. 5; revised version available to download from www.imf.org.

86. Cohen, *Discovering History in China*, p. 132; Bin Wong, *China Transformed*, p. 200; Lovell, *The Great Wall*, pp. 219, 242.

87. Bin Wong, *China Transformed*, p. 259.

88. Cohen, *Discovering History in China*, p. 144.

89. Zhao, *A Nation-State by Construction*, p. 107.

90. Fairbank and Goldman, *China*, Chapters 16, 17; Spence, *The Search*

for Modern China, Chapters 17, 18; Gernet, *A History of Chinese Civilization*, Chapter 30.

91. Zheng Yongnian, *Will China Become Democratic?*, pp. 84–6.

92. Zhao, *A Nation-State by Construction*, pp. 99, 108; Fairbank and Goldman, *China*, pp. 316–23.

93. Ibid., p. 117.

94. Bin Wong, *China Transformed*, p. 193.

95. Fairbank and Goldman, China, p. 329.

96. Ibid., pp. 176, 262. Zhao, *A Nation-State by Construction*, p. 97.

97. Wang Gungwu, 'Rationalising China's Place in Asia, 1800–2005: Beyond the Literati Consensus', p. 5, in Reid and Zheng, *Negotiating Asymmetry*.

98. Bin Wong, *China Transformed*, p. 194.

99. Ibid., pp. 70, 194–7, 205.

100. Wang Gungwu, 'Rationalizing China's Place in Asia', in Reid and Zheng, *Negotiating Asymmetry*, p. 5.

101. Zhao, *A Nation-State by Construction*, p. 119.

102. Elvin, 'The Historian as Haruspex', pp. 89, 104.

103. Gernet, *A History of Chinese Civilization*, p. 571.

104. Ibid., pp. 603, 610–12.

105. Ibid., pp. 578–9, 602–3.

106. Ibid., pp. 612–13.

107. Ibid., p. 613.

108. Maddison, *The World Economy: A Millennial Perspective*, pp. 558, 562; see also pp. 548, 552.

109. Maddison, *Chinese Economic Performance*, p. 70.

110. Ibid., p. 552. See also Desai, 'India and China', p. 11.

111. Maddison, *The World Economy: A Millennial Perspective*, p. 562.

112. Ibid., pp. 552, 562.

113. The Human Development Index (HDI) is an index combining measures of life expectancy, literacy, educational attainment and GDP per capita for countries worldwide. It is claimed as a standard means of measuring human development. It has been used by the United Nations Development Programme since around 1990.

114. Desai, 'India and China', pp. 9–10.

115. Bin Wong, *China Transformed*, p. 273.

5 Contested Modernity

1. Paul Krugman, *The Return of Depression Economics* (London: Allen Lane, 1999), pp. 16–17, 23.
2. Ezra F. Vogel, *The Four Little Dragons: The Spread of Industrialization in East Asia* (Cambridge, Mass.: Harvard University Press, 1991), pp. 13, 42–3.
3. Manuel Castells, *The Information Age: Economy, Society and Culture*. Vol. III, *End of Millennium* (Oxford: Blackwell, 1998), pp. 244–64.
4. Angus Maddison, *The World Economy: Historical Statistics* (Paris: OECD, 2003), p. 260. These are average annual compound growth rates.
5. World Bank, 'Will Resilience Overcome Risk? East Asia Regional Outlook', November 2007, posted on www.worldbank.org, p. 11. Poverty is defined as earning $2 per day or less.
6. Danni Rodrik, *One Economics Many Recipes: Globalization, Institutions, and Economic Growth* (Princeton: Princeton University Press, 2007), pp. 18–20.
7. Castells, *The Information Age*: III, *End of Millennium*, pp. 270–71.
8. As S. N. Eisenstadt wrote: 'Most of the studies of modernization in general and of convergence of industrial societies in particular . . . stressed that the more modern or developed different societies [became], the more similar . . . they [would] become in their basic, central, institutional aspects, and the less the importance of traditional elements within them.' Cited in Paul A. Cohen, *Discovering History in China: American Historical Writing on the Recent Chinese Past* (New York: Columbia University Press, 1984), p. 78.
9. Post-war Japan might also be included on the grounds of its growth, but has been excluded because of its earlier industrial transformation.
10. Fu-Chen Lo and Yue-Man Yeung, eds, *Emerging World Cities in Pacific Asia* (Tokyo: United Nations University Press, 1996), p. 155; *UN Human Development Report 1997* (New York: Oxford University Press, 1997), p. 182.
11. Eric Hobsbawm, *Globalization, Democracy, and Terrorism* (London: Little, Brown, 2007), p. 33; *UN Human Development Report 1997*, p. 182.
12. Lo and Yeung, *Emerging World Cities in Pacific Asia*, p. 183.
13. Ibid., pp. 155, 338; *UN Human Development Report 1997*, p. 192.
14. United Nations Development Programme, *Rapport mondial sur le développement humain 1999* (Paris: De Boeck Université, 1999), p. 198.

15. Paul Bairoch, *De Jéricho à Mexico: Villes et économie dans l'historie* (Paris: Gallimard, 1985), p. 288.

16. 'Shanghai Tops 20m', *China Daily*, 5 December 2003.

17. This practice first appeared during the Song dynasty (AD 960–1279), shortly after the spread of paper money for commercial purposes; Kenneth Dean, 'Despotic Empire/Nation-State: Local Responses to Chinese Nationalism in an Age of Global Capitalism', in Chen Kuan-Hsing, ed., *Trajectories: Inter-Asia Cultural Studies* (London: Routledge, 1998), p. 169.

18. World Bank, *The East Asian Miracle* (Washington, DC: Oxford University Press, 1993), pp. 29–32.

19. Interview with Hung Tze Jan, Taipei, March 1999.

20. Interview with Tatsuro Hanada, Tokyo, June 1999.

21. Acknowledgements to Ti-Nan Chi, Bing C. P. Chu and Chu-joe Hsia in Taipei; Tatsuro Hanada, Takashi Yamashita, Mark Dytham and Astrid Klein in Tokyo; and Wu Jiang and Lu Yongyi in Shanghai.

22. Interview with Toshiya Uedo, Tokyo, June 1999.

23. Anthony Giddens, *The Consequences of Modernity* (Cambridge: Cambridge University Press, 1997), p. 105.

24. Pudong was conceived, in 1992, as a completely new business and financial centre for Shanghai. Across the Huangpu River from the Bund, it represents an extraordinary urban and architectural leap into the new century: Cheng Youhua, et al., 'Urban Planning in Shanghai towards the 21st Century', in *Dialogue* (Taipei), February/March 1999, pp. 48–55.

25. Interview with Gao Rui-qian, Shanghai, April 1999.

26. Giddens, *The Consequences of Modernity*, p. 108.

27. The literature on the Chinese diaspora, and the role of the family and kinship, is voluminous: see, for example, Lynn Pan, *Sons of the Yellow Emperor: The Story of the Overseas Chinese* (London: Arrow, 1998); Robin Cohen, *Global Diasporas: An Introduction* (London: UCL Press, 1997), Chapters 4, 7; Joel Kotkin, *Tribes: How Race, Religion, and Identity Determine Success in the New Global Economy* (New York: Random House, 1992), Chapter 6.

28. 'Risk', available at www.bbc.co.uk/radio4/reith1999/lecture2.shtml.

29. Mark Elvin, 'Secular Karma: The Communist Revolution Understood in Traditional Chinese Terms', in Mabel Lee and A. D. Syrokomia-Stefanowski, eds, *Modernisation of the Chinese Past* (Sydney: University of Sydney, School of Asian Studies, 1993), p. 75.

30. Huang Ping, '"Beijing Consensus", or "Chinese Experiences", or What?', unpublished paper, 2005, p. 8.

31. Chris Patten, *East and West: China, Power, and the Future of East Asia* (London: Times Books, 1998), p. 166.

32. For an interesting discussion of Japan's specificity, see Alan Macfarlane, *Japan Through the Looking Glass* (London: Profile Books, 2007).

33. Howard Gardner, *To Open Minds* (New York: Basic Books, 1989), p. 280.

34. BBC2, *Proud to be Chinese* (broadcast December 1998), transcript of interview with Katherine Gin.

35. Boyd and Richerson, *Culture and Evolutionary Process* (Chicago: Chicago University Press, 1985), p. 60.

36. Interview with Shad Faruki, Kuala Lumpur, August 1994.

37. Nicholas Ostler, *Empires of the Word: A Language History of the World* (London: HarperCollins, 2005), p. 7.

38. Interview with Hung Tze Jan, Taipei, March 1999.

39. The reason why Arabic is not included in the top 20 is that, although it is spoken by in excess of 200 million people as a first language, the various dialects are mutually unintelligible, so that they can be regarded as languages rather than dialects. The largest is Egyptian Arabic with 46 million speakers.

40. James Stanlaw, 'English in Japanese Communicative Strategies', in Braj B. Kachru, ed., *The Other Tongue: English Across Cultures* (Urbana: University of Illinois Press, 1992), pp. 181–4. It has been estimated that 8 per cent of the total Japanese vocabulary is derived from English, with virtually no reverse traffic; ibid., p. 183. Also Braj B. Kachru, *Asian Englishes: Beyond the Canon* (Hong Kong: Hong Kong University Press, 2005), p. 81.

41. Kachru, *Asian Englishes*, pp. 191–2. A survey in 1998 found that 81.7 per cent of Japanese only speak Japanese even though virtually no one else speaks their language; Dentsu Institute for Human Studies, *Life in the Era of Globalisation: Uncertain Germans and Japanese Versus Confident Americans and British, the Second Comparative Analysis of Global Values* (Tokyo: July 1998). Also, Kachru, *Asian Englishes*, Chapter 4.

42. Alexandra Stevenson, 'India losing English advantage to China', *Financial Times*, 19 November 2009; David Graddol, *English Next India* (London: British Council, 2010).

43. Chin-Chuan Cheng, 'Chinese Varieties of English', in Kachru, ed., *The Other Tongue*, p. 166.

44. Ostler, *Empires of the Word*, pp. 146, 155.

45. Ibid., pp. 116–17.

46. Ibid., pp. 117, 144, 156–7, 162.

47. David Graddol, *The Future of English* (London: British Council, 1997), pp. 8–9.

48. 'Talk in English, Please, Korean Kids Told', *International Herald Tribune*, 25–6 March 2006.

49. Graddol, *The Future of English*, pp. 60–61; 'Across All Cultures, English Says It All', *International Herald Tribune*, 10 April 2007; 'At Global Business Schools, English Adds Up', *International Herald Tribune*, 11 April 2007.

50. Ostler, *Empires of the Word*, Chapter 1.

51. 'China Soon to be the World's Biggest Internet User', *Guardian*, 25 January 2007.

52. Michael Curtin, *Playing to the World's Biggest Audience: The Globalization of Chinese Film and TV* (Berkeley: University of California Press, 2007), p. 8; Bella Thomas, 'What the World's Poor Watch on TV', *Prospect*, 82, January 2003.

53. Graddol, *The Future of English*, pp. 60–61.

54. Ostler, *Empires of the Word*, pp. 162–3.

55. Graddol, *The Future of English*, pp. 58–9.

56. Amy Kazmin, 'India: designers create a world of colour with a royal touch', *Financial Times*, 31 August 2010.

57. Kayoko Aikawa, 'The Story of Kimono', in Atsushi Ueda, ed., *The Electric Geisha: Exploring Japan's Popular Culture* (Tokyo: Kodansha International, 1994), pp. 111–15.

58. Suzy Menkes, 'Hitting the High Cs: Cool, Cute and Creative', *International Herald Tribune*, 21 March 2006.

59. Lise Skov, 'Fashion Trends, Japonisme and Postmodernism, or What Is So Japanese About Comme des Garçons?', in John Whittier Treat, ed., *Contemporary Japan and Popular Culture* (Honolulu: University of Hawai'i Press, 1996), pp. 137–65. Also interview with Valerie Koehn, Tokyo, May–June 1999; Menkes, 'Hitting the High Cs'.

60. Valery M. Garrett, *Chinese Clothing: An Illustrated Guide* (Oxford: Oxford University Press, 1994), p. 35.

61. Valerie Steele and John S. Major, *China Chic: East Meets West* (New Haven: Yale University Press, 1999), p. 16; also pp. 13–35. Also, Garrett, *Chinese Clothing*; interview with Qiao Yiyi, fashion designer, Shanghai, April 1999.

62. See Karl Gerth, *China Made: Consumer Culture and the Creation of the Nation* (Cambridge, Mass.: Harvard University Asia Centre, 2003), Chapter 2.

63. Steele and Major, *China Chic*, pp. 31–5, 37–53; also Chapter 9.

64. Ibid., pp. 55–62; also Chapter 10.

65. Ibid., pp. 63–7.

66. Ibid., p. 44.

67. Ibid., Chapter 4; interview with Shiatzy Chen, Taipei, March 1999; seminar on Chinese dress, Hong Kong, September 1999 (including Blanc de Chine).

68. Steele and Major, *China Chic*, Chapter 4; 'Asian Ideas Seep into Creations on the West Coast', *International Herald Tribune*, 11 March 2002.

69. Herman Wong, 'On Global Catwalks, a New Face that's Hot – Asian', *China Daily*, 24 May 2006.

70. Kosaku Yoshino, *Cultural Nationalism in Contemporary Japan* (London: Routledge, 1992), p. 112.

71. Interview with Abdul Rahman Embong, Kuala Lumpur, March 2001.

72. Interview with Valerie Koehn, Tokyo, May–June 1999.

73. Otto Pohl, 'The West's Glossy Magazines "Go Forth and Multiply"', *International Herald Tribune*, 14–15 February 2004.

74. Suzy Menkes, 'Whose Sari Now?', *International Herald Tribune*, 17 May 2008.

75. Interview with Yang Qingqing, Shanghai, April 1999.

76. Interview with Mei Ling, Taipei, March 1999.

77. 'What Price Glamour? A Hard Lesson in Asia', *International Herald Tribune*, 2 May 2006.

78. Amina Mire, 'Giving You a Radiant White Skin "Because You Are Worth It"': The Emerging Discourse and Practice of Skin-whitening', unpublished abstract for PhD, University of Toronto, 2004, p. 16.

79. Ibid., for a fascinating account of the racial subtext of the whitening cosmetic industry, and the central role of East Asia. Also, Amina Mire, 'Pigmentation and Empire: The Emerging Skin-whitening Industry', *A CounterPunch Special Report*, 28 July 2005, pp. 6–8. Umbrellas carried by women as protection from the sun remain a peculiar and distinctive Chinese and Japanese preoccupation.

80. Felipe Fernandez-Armesto, *Millennium: A History of Our Last Thousand Years* (London: Bantam Press, 1995), pp. 683–4.

81. John G. Russell, 'Race and Reflexivity: The Black Other in Contemporary Japanese Mass Culture', in Treat, ed., *Contemporary Japan and Popular Culture*, pp. 17–19, 29–32; also Leo Ching, 'Yellow Skin, White Mask: Race, Class and Identification in Japanese Cultural Discourse', in Chen Kuan-Hsing, ed., *Trajectories: Inter-Asia Cultural Studies* (London: Routledge, 1998), pp. 65–86.

82. Interview with Mei Ling, Taipei, March 1999.
83. *Pulse Bites: Consumer Insights Around the World*, 1 April 1999, p. 4; 'In China, a Big Appetite for Americana', *International Herald Tribune*, 26 February, 2002.
84. K. C. Chang, ed., *Food in Chinese Culture: Anthropological and Historical Perspectives* (New Haven: Yale University Press, 1977), p. 3.
85. Ibid., p. 3.
86. Ibid., p. 4.
87. Ibid., pp. 6–7.
88. David Y. H. Wu and Sidney C. H. Cheung, eds, *The Globalization of Chinese Food* (London: RoutledgeCurzon, 2002), p. 4.
89. Ibid., p. 3; Chang, *Food in Chinese Culture*, pp. 5, 7; Jacques Gernet, *A History of Chinese Civilization*, 2nd edn (Cambridge: Cambridge University Press, 1996), p. 428.
90. Chang, *Food in Chinese Culture*, pp. 7–9.
91. Ibid., pp. 9–10.
92. Ibid., p. 363.
93. Ibid., p. 11.
94. Ibid., pp. 13–14.
95. Jacques Gernet, *Daily Life in China on the Eve of the Mongol Invasion, 1250–76* (Stanford: Stanford University Press, 1962), p. 135.
96. Fuchsia Dunlop, 'Enthused by China's Tea Infusions', *Financial Times*, 11–12 September 2004.
97. Dan Levin, 'Shanghai looks to glorious past', *International Herald Tribune*, 4 May 2010.
98. Chang, *Food in Chinese Culture*, p. 375; Wu and Cheung, *The Globalization of Chinese Food*, p. 5; also Chapters 3, 8–11.
99. Katarzyna Cwiertka, 'Culinary Globalization and Japan', *Japan Echo*, 26: 3, June 1999, pp. 53–8.
100. Ibid., p. 56.
101. Wu and Cheung, *The Globalization of Chinese Food*, p. xviii.
102. Cwiertka, 'Culinary Globalization and Japan', pp. 56–8.
103. As the American Sinologist Lucian W. Pye argues: 'In different times and places people have thought of power in very different ways ... theories which seek to specify general propositions about power miss the point entirely.' Lucian W. Pye, *Asian Power and Politics: The Cultural Dimensions of Authority* (Cambridge, Mass.: Harvard University Press, 1985), p. viii.
104. Ibid., pp. x, 26, 53.
105. Interview with Chih-Yu Shih, Taipei, 1999.

106. Pye, *Asian Power and Politics*, Chapter 3.
107. Interview with Tong Shijun, Shanghai, April 1999.
108. Pye, *Asian Power and Politics*, p. 327. Also Deepak Lal, *Unintended Consequences* (Cambridge Mass.: MIT Press, 1998), pp. 13, 153.
109. Pye, *Asian Power and Politics*, pp. 62, 80.
110. Interview with Chien Sechin Yung-Xiang, Taipei, March 1999.
111. There is one sphere in which profound cultural differences are accepted and acknowledged in the West, namely the way in which, for example, the nature of Japanese and Korean firms reflects the cultures of their respective countries; Charles Hampden-Turner and Fons Trompenaars, *Mastering the Infinite Game: How East Asian Values are Transforming Business Practices* (Oxford: Capstone, 1997), especially Chapters 5–7; Fons Trompenaars, *Riding the Waves of Culture: Understanding Cultural Diversity in Business* (London: Nicholas Brealey, 1993), Chapter 11; 'A Global Toyota Faces Dilution of Its Culture', *International Herald Tribune*, 15 February 2007.
112. See Göran Therborn, *Between Sex and Power: Family in the World, 1900–2000* (London: Routledge, 2004), pp. 119–26; also Gavin W. Jones, 'Not "When to Marry" but "Whether to Marry": The Changing Context of Marriage Decisions in East and Southeast Asia', in Gavin Jones and Kamalini Ramdas, eds, *Untying the Knot: Ideal and Reality in Asian Marriage* (Singapore: NUS, 2004).
113. On the contrary, as Lucian Pye suggests, the form of modernization 'will be significantly different from that produced by western individualism': Pye, *Asian Power and Politics*, p. 334.
114. In philosophical vein, the director and founder of the Shanghai Museum, Ma Chengyuan, puts it like this: 'China is now in the preliminary stage of modernization so the whole environment is very open – people have their space to do what they like. During the first stage of openness, many things come from outside. But if they can't gain their roots in Chinese society, they will fade away.' Interview with Ma Chengyuan, Shanghai, April 1999.
115. The people are real but the names are fictitious. The discussion took place in April 1999.
116. Maddison, *The World Economy: Historical Statistics*, pp. 258, 261.
117. Dominic Wilson and Anna Stupnytska, 'The N-11: More Than an Acronym', *Goldman Sachs, Global Economic Papers*, 153, 28 March 2007, p. 8.
118. Ibid., p. 4.
119. Maddison, *The World Economy: Historical Statistics*, p. 258.

120. Dan Levin, 'In China, love of old is something new', *International Herald Tribune*, 5 February 2010.

121. According to Johnny Tuan, who runs his own pop music label, Western pop music, the music of choice for many in the 1970s, now represents a very small segment of a market in which mando-pop is overwhelmingly dominant. Interview with Johnny Tuan, Chairman, Rock Records Co. Ltd, Taipei, March 1999; also interview with Wei-Chung Wang, Taipei, March 1999.

122. Another example is the revival of traditional instruments, for example, the *kayagŭm* in South Korea. Hee-sun Kim, 'Kayagŭm Shin'Gok, New Music for Antiquity: Musical Construction of Identity in Contemporary South Korea', unpublished paper, 2005.

123. Interview with Hung Tze Jan, Taipei, March 1999.

124. 'Revolution for a New Ruling Class as the Money-spinning IPL Gets Started', *Daily Mail*, 17 April 2008; Richard Williams, 'It's the End of the World as We Know It (and Cricket Will Be Fine)', *Guardian*, 22 April 2008.

125. This has begun to change as reflected in recent books such as Fareed Zakaria, *The Post-American World* (London: Allen Lane, 2008) and Bill Emmott, *Rivals: How the Power Struggle Between China, India and Japan Will Shape Our Next Decade* (London: Allen Lane, 2008). Also see Kishore Mahbubani, *The New Asian Hemisphere: The Irresistible Shift of Global Power to the East* (New York: Public Affairs, 2008).

PART II
6 China as an Economic Superpower

1. 'Guangdong Factories Drop Cheap for Chic', *South China Morning Post*, 17 March 2008.

2. John Gittings, *The Changing Face of China* (Oxford: Oxford University Press, 2005), p. 186.

3. *People's Daily*, 1 July 1987, quoted in ibid., p. 186, also pp. 165, 178, 184.

4. Zheng Yongnian, *Discovering Chinese Nationalism in China: Modernization, Identity, and International Relations* (Cambridge: Cambridge University Press, 1999), pp. 31–2.

5. Zheng Yongnian, *Will China Become Democratic?: Elite, Class and Regime Transition* (Singapore: EAI, 2004), p. 34.

6. Zheng Yongnian, *Discovering Chinese Nationalism in China*, pp. 31–2.
7. Wang Zhengyi, 'Conceptualising Economic Security and Governance: China Confronts Globalisation', *Pacific Review*, 17:4 (2004), p. 526; Gittings, *The Changing Face of China*, p. 252; Zheng Yongnian, *Will China Become Democratic?*, p. 241; Zhao Suisheng, *A Nation-State by Construction: Dynamics of Modern Chinese Nationalism* (Stanford: Stanford University Press, 2004), p. 217.
8. Gittings, *The Changing Face of China*, p. 254.
9. Deng offered his pragmatic support for the model of the East Asian developmental state; Zhao, *A Nation-State by Construction*, p. 30.
10. Peter Nolan, *Transforming China: Globalisation, Transition and Development* (London: Anthem Press, 2005), pp. 185, 187–8.
11. Zhao, *A Nation-State by Construction*, pp. 142–7, 242. Also, Shi Anbin, 'Mediating Chinese-ness: Identity Politics and Media Culture in Contemporary China', in Anthony Reid and Zheng Yangwen, eds, *Negotiating Asymmetry: China's Place in Asia* (Singapore: NUS Press, 2009,), p. 16.
12. Wang Hui, *China's New Order* (Cambridge, Mass.: Harvard University Press, 2003), pp. 96–124; interview with Wang Hui, Beijing, 23 May 2006; interview with Fang Ning, Beijing, 7 December 2005; and Wang Xiaodong, 'Chinese Nationalism under the Shadow of Globalisation', lecture at the London School of Economics and Political Science, 7 February 2005.
13. Danni Rodrik, *One Economics Many Recipes: Globalization, Institutions, and Economic Growth* (Princeton: Princeton University, 2007), pp. 238–9.
14. Angus Maddison, *Chinese Economic Performance in the Long Run, Second Edition, Revised and Updated: 960–2030 AD* (Paris: OECD, 2007), pp. 64, 89.
15. Wang Gungwu, 'Rationalizing China's Place in Asia, 1800–2005: Beyond the Literati Consensus', in Reid and Zheng, *Negotiating Asymmetry*, p. 5.
16. Gittings, *The Changing Face of China*, p. 186.
17. Zheng Yongnian, *Will China Become Democratic?*, p. 33.
18. Ibid., pp. 238–9.
19. Yu Yongding, 'Opinions on Structure Reform and Exchange Rate Regimes Against the Backdrop of the Asian Financial Crisis', unpublished paper, Japanese Ministry of Finance, 2000, pp. 1–11; Wang Yizhou, 'Political Stability and International Relations in the Process of

Economic Globalisation – Another Perspective on Asia's Financial Crisis', unpublished article, Beijing, 2000, pp. 1–13; and Wang Zhengyi, 'Conceptualising Economic Security and Governance: China Confronts Globalisation', *Pacific Review*, 17:4 (2000), p. 542.

20. Yu Yongding, 'China's Structural Adjustment', unpublished paper, Seoul Conference, 2005, p. 2.

21. Nolan, *Transforming China*, p. 61; Lex, 'China and International Law', *Financial Times*, 30 April 2008. Also, Dani Rodrik, 'Making Room for China in the World Economy', paper prepared for AEA session on 'Growth in a Partially De-Globalized World', December 2009, pp. 1–12, especially pp. 5–7,10–12.

22. Barry Naughton, *The Chinese Economy: Transitions and Growth* (Cambridge, Mass: MIT Press, 2007), pp. 404–5.

23. Clyde Prestowitz, *Three Billion New Capitalists: The Great Shift of Wealth and Power to the East* (New York: Basic Books, 2006), p. 61.

24. George J. Gilboy, 'The Myth behind China's Miracle', *Foreign Affairs*, July/August 2004, pp. 4–5.

25. 'The Dragon and the Eagle Survey', *The Economist*, 2 October 2004, p. 11.

26. Maddison, *Chinese Economic Performance in the Long Run*, p. 69.

27. Yu Yongding, 'China's Structural Adjustment', p. 1.

28. Interview with Yu Yongding, Singapore, 3 March 2006.

29. Andy Xie, *Asia/Pacific Economics*, report for Morgan Stanley, November 2002.

30. 'Guangdong Factories Drop Cheap for Chic', *South China Morning Post*, 17 March 2008; 'End of an Era for Pearl River Delta', *South China Morning Post*, 9 February 2008.

31. Yu Yongding, 'China's Rise, Twin Surplus and the Change of China's Development Strategy', unpublished paper, Namura Tokyo Club Conference, Kyoto, 21 November 2005, p. 12.

32. Ibid., p. 11.

33. Maddison, *Chinese Economic Performance in the Long Run,* pp. 94–6.

34. Interview with Yu Yongding, Beijing, 6 December 2005: Wang Gungwu, 'Rationalizing China's Place in Asia', in Reid and Zheng, *Negotiating Asymmetry*, p. 5.

35. Prestowitz, *Three Billion New Capitalists*, p. 74.

36. Peter Marsh, 'China noses ahead as top goods producer', *Financial Times*, 13 March 2011.

37. Joseph Stiglitz, 'Development in Defiance of the Washington Consensus', *Guardian*, 13 April 2006.

38. Oded Shenkar, *The Chinese Century: The Rising Chinese Economy and Its Impact on the Global Economy, the Balance of Power and Your Job* (New Jersey: Wharton School Publishing, 2006), p. 114.

39. Yu Yongding, 'China's Macroeconomic Development, Exchange Rate Policy and Global Imbalances', unpublished paper, Asahi Shimbun Symposium, October 2005, pp. 2–3.

40. Geoff Dyer, 'China: A new core rises', *Financial Times*, 3 August 2010; Kathrin Hille, 'Chinese pay rises encourage move to cheaper provinces', *Financial Times*, 26–27 June 2010; Kathrin Hille, 'China's computer makers march inland', *Financial Times*, 23 May 2011.

41. The World Bank predicted a fall of almost 2 per cent in China's growth rate in 2008 as compared with 2007; 'China "On Course for Growth Slowdown"', *Financial Times*, 4 February 2008.

42. Yu Yongding, 'China's stimulus shows the problem of success', *Financial Times*, 25 August 2009.

43. Interview with Yu Yongding, Beijing, July 2010.

44. Stephen S. Roach, 'Manchurian Paradox', Morgan Stanley, 27 April 2009.

45. Interview with Yu Yongding, Singapore, 3 March 2006; and Yu Yongding, 'Opinions on Structure Reform and Exchange Rate Regimes'.

46. Yu Yongding, 'Opinions on Structure Reform and Exchange Rate Regimes', pp. 1, 6–8.

47. Keith Bradsher, 'Currency dispute hots up in China', *International Herald Tribune*, 26 March 2010.

48. Yu Yongding, 'Opinions on Structure Reform and Exchange Rate Regimes', p. 2.

49. Yu Yongding, 'China's Structural Adjustment', pp. 1–5.

50. Interview with Zhu Wenhui, Beijing, 20 November 2006; interview with Fang Ning, Beijing, 7 December 2005; and interview with Wang Hui, Beijing, 23 May 2006.

51. Yu Yongding, 'A different road forward', *China Daily*, 23 December 2010.

52. Peter Nolan, *China at the Crossroads* (Cambridge: Polity Press, 2004), p. 15.

53. Maddison, *Chinese Economic Performance in the Long Run*, p. 98.

54. Wang Zhengyi, 'Conceptualising Economic Security and Governance', pp. 531–4; Zheng Yongnian, *Will China Become Democratic?*, pp. 296–301.

55. 'Wrath for the wealthy', *China Daily*, 22–23 August 2009.

56. Geoff Dyer, 'China: A populist rising', *Financial Times*, 9 March 2010;

Cao Li, 'Busting the Bribe Tribe', *China Daily*, 20 August 2009; Richard McGregor, 'Chinese steel executive beaten to death', *Financial Times*, 26 July 2009.

57. Gittings, *The Changing Face of China*, pp. 274–5.

58. Yu Yongding, 'A different road forward', *China Daily*, 23 December 2010.

59. Quoted in Zheng Yongnian, *Discovering Chinese Nationalism in China*, p. 32; Barry Naughton, *The Chinese Economy: Transitions and Growth* (Cambridge, Mass. and London: MIT Press, 2007), pp. 430–38.

60. Wang Zhengyi, 'Conceptualising Economic Security and Governance', pp. 534–5.

61. Zheng Yongnian, *Will China Become Democratic?*, pp. 104–5.

62. Ibid., pp. 136–7.

63. Zheng Yongnian, *Discovering Chinese Nationalism in China*, p. 32.

64. Nolan, *China at the Crossroads*, p. 30; Naughton, *The Chinese Economy*, pp. 430–38.

65. David Shambaugh, 'The Rise of China and Asia's New Dynamics', in Shambaugh, ed., *Power Shift: China and Asia's New Dynamics* (Berkeley: University of California Press, 2005), p. 18.

66. 'Year of the Three Big Headaches', *South China Morning Post*, 4 January 2007.

67. 'China's Priorities', *Financial Times*, 9 March 2008.

68. Yu Yongding, 'China's Structural Adjustment', p. 5.

69. Jamil Anderlini, 'Unrest spreads among China's migrant masses', *Financial Times*, 17 June 2011.

70. Jamil Anderlini, 'Call to end China citizen registration system', *Financial Times*, 1 March 2010.

71. Chloe Lai, 'Delta firms urge hukou reform amid labour shortage', *South China Morning Post*, 17 April 2010; He Huifeng, 'Illegal Vietnamese workers flood delta factories', *South China Morning Post*, 23 April 2010.

72. Yu Yongding, 'China's Rise, Twin Surplus and the Change of China's Development Strategy', pp. 24–5.

73. 'What Will the World Gain from China in 20 Years?' *China Business Review*, March/April 2003.

74. Zha Daojiong, 'China's Energy Security and Its International Relations', *China and Eurasia Forum Quarterly*, 3:3 (November 2005), p. 44; and Yu Yongding, 'The Interactions between China and the World Economy', unpublished paper, Nikkei Simbon Symposium, 5 April 2005, p. 2.

75. Lester R. Brown, 'A New World Order', *Guardian*, 25 January 2006.

76. 'A survey of ageing populations: China's predicament', *The Economist*, 25 June 2009.

77. Cary Huang, 'Leadership wakes to grey storm of ageing population', *South China Morning Post*, 2 November 2009.

78. 'Socialist workers', *The Economist*, 10 June 2010.

79. Kathrin Hille, 'China faces pressure to alter one-child policy', *Financial Times*, 28 April 2011.

80. Javier Blas and Carola Hoyos, 'IEA Predicts Oil Price to Rebound to $100', *Financial Times*, 5 November 2008.

81. Joseph Kahn and Jim Yardley, 'As China Roars, Pollution Reaches Deadly Extremes', *New York Times*, 26 August 2007.

82. Elizabeth C. Economy, *The River Runs Black: The Environmental Challenge to China's Future* (Ithaca: Cornell University Press, 2004), Chapter 2; Mark Elvin, *The Retreat of the Elephants: An Environmental History of China* (New Haven and London: Yale University Press, 2004), pp. 460–71.

83. Michael Wines, 'Beijing's skies begin to clear', *International Herald Tribune*, 19 October 2010.

84. John Warburton and Leo Horn, 'China's Crisis: A Development Perspective (Part One)', 25 October 2007, posted on www.chinadialogue.net.

85. Gaoming Jiang and Jixi Gao, 'The Terrible Cost of China's Growth', 12 January 2007, posted on www.chinadialogue.net; Economy, *The River Runs Black*, p. 18; Warburton and Horn, 'China's Crisis: A Development Perspective (Part One)'.

86. 'Chinese Carmakers Veer to Green', *International Herald Tribune*, 21–22 April 2007.

87. 'Can Shanghai Turn Green and Grow?', posted on www.bbc.co.uk/news; Lex, 'Chinese Cars', *Financial Times*, 6 July 2007.

88. Yu Yongding, 'The Interactions between China and the World Economy', p. 3.

89. 'China Gains on US in Emissions', *International Herald Tribune*, 9 November 2006.

90. Warburton and Horn, 'China's Crisis'.

91. 'China Gas Emissions "May Pass US"', 25 April, 2007, posted on http://newsvote.bbc.co.uk. The International Energy Agency originally estimated that China would surpass the US in 2009 as the biggest emitter of the main gas linked to global warming.

92. www.foundation.org.uk/801/311002_2pdf.

93. Jonathon Porritt, 'China Could Lead the Fight for a Cooler Climate', 13 November 2007, posted on www.chinadialogue.net (accessed 2/6/08). The Chinese National Climate Change Assessment Report has predicted that by 2020 the average temperature in China will increase by between 1.1 °C and 2.1 °C.

94. Maddison, *Chinese Economic Performance in the Long Run*, p. 97.

95. 'Climate Key Issue for Wen at Asean Talks', *South China Morning Post*, 19 November 2007.

96. Warburton and Horn, 'China's Crisis (Part One)'.

97. 'Economy is More Important, China Says', *International Herald Tribune*, 5 June 2007; Porritt, 'China Could Lead the Fight for a Cooler Climate.'

98. Hu Angang, 'Green Development: The Inevitable Choice for China, Parts One and Two', posted on www.chinadialogue.net (accessed 2/6/08).

99. European Council on Foreign Relations and Asia Centre à SciencesPo, 'Climate Policies After Copenhagen', *China Analysis*, 27, pp. 1–11.

100. Keith Bradsher, 'Coal abounds, but China veers to sun and wind, too', *International Herald Tribune*, 3 July 2009; Eric Ng, 'China catching up with Europe on solar farms', *South China Morning Post*, 19 April 2010; Dominic Ziegler, 'Reaching for Renaissance: A Special Report on China and Its Region', *The Economist*, 31 March 2007.

101. Kandy Wong, 'Subsidy doubts delay BYD's electric car', *Financial Times*, 24 February 2010.

102. 'Pedals of fire', *The Economist*, 15 May 2010.

103. Keith Bradsher, 'Chinese firms take commanding lead in production of renewable energy', *International Herald Tribune*, 2 June 2010; Keith Bradsher, 'China taking solar challenge to US turf', *International Herald Tribune*, 26 August 2009.

104. John Warburton and Leo Horn, 'China's Crisis: A Development Perspective (Part Two), 25 October 2007, posted on www.chinadialogue. net; Keith Bradsher and David Barboza, 'Pollution from Chinese Coal Casts a Global Shadow', *New York Times*, 11 June 2006.

105. Chunli Lee, 'Strategic Alliances of Chinese, Japanese and US firms in the Chinese Manufacturing Industry: The Impact of "China Prices" and Integrated Localization', paper presented for the Fairbank Center for East Asia Research, Harvard University, October 2004.

106. James Kynge, *China Shakes the World: The Rise of a Hungry Nation* (London: Weidenfeld and Nicolson, 2006), pp. 160–62.

107. Andrew Batson, 'Sum of iPhone parts: trade distortion', *Wall Street Journal*, 16 December 2010.

108. Gilboy, 'The Myth behind China's Miracle', pp. 4–5.

109. Kynge, *China Shakes the World*, pp. 108–10, 112; Shenkar, *The Chinese Century*, pp. 66–8.

110. Kynge, *China Shakes the World*, p. 109. Geoff Dyer, 'Wen calls bluff of moaning multinationals', *Financial Times*, 20 July 2010; Jamil Anderlini, 'German industrialists attack Chinese', *Financial Times*, 18 July 2010; Jamil Anderlini, 'Foreign Companies "losing out" in China', *Financial Times*, 2 September 2010; Charles Grant, 'Is China being beastly to foreign investors?', Centre for European Reform, 30 July 2010.

111. Prestowitz, *Three Billion New Capitalists*, pp. 147, 149; Kynge, *China Shakes the World*, pp. 83–4; Shenkar, *The Chinese Century*, p. 165.

112. Kynge, *China Shakes the World*, pp. 72, 78–82.

113. Prestowitz, *Three Billion New Capitalists*, p. 143.

114. James Wilsdon and James Keeley, *China: The Next Science Superpower?* (London: Demos, 2007), p. 9.

115. Ibid., p. 7.

116. Gautam Naik, 'China is poised to top Japan in R&D', *Wall Street Journal*, 16 December 2010.

117. Wilsdon and Keeley, *China*, p. 16.

118. Liz Gooch, 'Researchers in Asian countries raise their scientific profiles worldwide', *International Herald Tribune*, 13 September 2010.

119. Ping Zhou and Loet Leydesdorff, 'The Emergence of China as a Leading Nation in Science', *Research Policy*, 35 (2006), pp. 86–92, 100; Wilsdon and Keeley, *China*, pp. 16–17.

120. Zhou and Leydesdorff, 'The Emergence of China as a Leading Nation in Science', p. 100.

121. Wilsdon and Keeley, *China*, p. 32.

122. Nicholas D. Kristof, 'The Educated Giant', *International Herald Tribune*, 29 May 2007.

123. Wilsdon and Keeley, *China*, p. 29.

124. Zhou and Leydesdorff, 'The Emergence of China as a Leading Nation in Science', p. 84.

125. Wilsdon and Keeley, *China*, pp. 30–31; Geoff Dyer, 'How China is Rising Through the Innovation Ranks', *Financial Times*, 5 January 2007; Shenkar, *The Chinese Century*, p. 74; Gittings, *The Changing Face of China*, p. 263.

126. Suntech Power Holdings, for example, has grown big and successful as China's leading maker of silicon photovoltaic solar cells; Thomas L. Friedman, 'China's Sunshine Boys', *International Herald Tribune*, 7

December 2006. Also 'China Climbs Technology Value Chain', *South China Morning Post*, 30 March 2007; Victor Keegan, 'Virtual China looks for Real Benefits', *Guardian*, 1 November 2007; 'High-tech-Hopefuls: A Special Report on Technology in India and China', *The Economist*, 10 November 2007.

127. 'Chinese Patents in "Sharp Rise"', posted on www.bloc.co.uk/news.

128. 'China Makes a Move into High-value Exports', *International Herald Tribune*, 7 June 2007.

129. Nolan, *Transforming China*, p. 206.

130. Ibid., pp. 205, 233–93.

131. Nolan, *China at the Crossroads*, p. 24.

132. Chunli Lee, 'China Targets Detroit', *World Business*, April 2006, pp. 30–32. Local car-makers dominate cars priced below RMB 100,000 ($12,000); foreign car-makers all those above. Ibid., pp. 30–32; also 'Minicars Drive Geely', *South China Morning Post*, 16 September 2006.

133. 'India's Car for the Common Man', posted on www.bbc.co.uk (accessed 13/5/08). Also Anand Giridharadas, 'Spirit of Gandhi Inspires a Bargain', *International Herald Tribune*, 8 January 2008.

134. Chunli Lee, 'Trends of Open Product Architecture and Internationalisation of Private Companies in the Chinese Automobile Industry', *Aichi University Economic Review*, 169 (November 2005), pp. 3–5, 10–14, 23–5; Chunli Lee, Jin Chen and Takahiro Fujimoto, 'Chinese Automobile Industry and Product Architectures', unpublished paper; Chunli Lee, 'Product Development by Chinese Automakers: The Dilemma of Imitation and Innovation', unpublished working paper for International Vehicle Program, MIT, July 2007, pp. 1–30.

135. Norihiko Shirouzu, 'Volvo's Big China Gamble', *Wall Street Journal*, 14 September 2010; John Reed, 'Geely seals deal to buy Volvo from Ford', *Financial Times*, 28 March 2010.

136. Patti Waldmeir, 'Chinese aim to be king of the road', *Financial Times*, 22 April 2010; Matthew Symonds, 'A global love affair', a special report on cars in emerging markets, *The Economist*, 15 November 2010. Also, Neil Gough, 'US rollout of BYD's all-electric car delayed', *South China Morning Post*, 24 August 2010.

137. Geely, for example, has announced that it will assemble cars in Indonesia; 'Geely to Make Cars in Indonesia as Malaysia Refuses to Host Plant', *South China Morning Post*, 28 September 2006. 'Chery Gears Up for US Roll-out', *South China Morning Post*, 26 April 2006.

138. 'TCL to Close TV Factories in Europe', *South China Morning Post*, 1 November 2006.

139. 'US Market is Losing Its Appeal to China', *International Herald Tribune*, 18 April 2007.

140. For an interesting survey of Chinese companies with a major commitment to R&D expenditure, see Research-Works, 'R&D: China's Growing Competitive Edge', Shanghai, 27 February 2010, pp. 1–88.

141. For the steady penetration of Chinese TV sets into the US market, see Shenkar, *The Chinese Century*, pp. 152–3; and *China Goes Global* (London: *Financial Times*, 2005).

142. Robert Wright, 'China on track to join ranks of train manufacturers', *Financial Times*, 1 March 2010; Toh Han Shih, 'China high-speed rail to take global lead by 2012', *South China Morning Post*, 26 October 2009.

143. Alexandra Stevenson, 'Google's China market share: declining', *Financial Times*, 22 April 2011.

144. 'Faced with a Steep Learning Curve', *Financial Times* special report on global brands, 23 April 2007; 'China Aims for Spot among Top World Brands', *South China Morning Post*, 5 October 2006.

145. Lenovo is the world's fourth biggest PC seller; Sonia Kolesnikov-Jessop, 'Putting Lenovo's Brand on the Global Map', *International Herald Tribune*, 27–8 September 2008.

146. 'China's Plane Ambitions Take Off', posted on www.bbc.co.uk/news.

147. 'Airbus Near a Deal for Assembly Line in China', *International Herald Tribune*, 16 March 2006.

148. 'Chinese Group to Bid for All Six Airbus Plants', *Guardian*, 19 June 2007.

149. Simon Rabinovitch, 'China to take shot at aircraft duopoly', *Financial Times*, 4 August 2011; 'Air Battle on the Ground in China', *International Herald Tribune*, 28 February 2007.

150. 'China Plans Space Station in 2020' and 'China Launches First Moon Orbiter', posted on www.bbc.co.uk/news.

151. John Markoff, 'China seeks supercomputing edge', *International Herald Tribune*, 1 June 2010.

152. William J. Broad, 'China plans to lead world in getting to bottom of sea', *International Herald Tribune*, 13 September 2010.

153. 'PetroChina Overtakes Exxon After Shanghai Debut', *Financial Times*, 5 November 2007; Gideon Rachman, 'China Has Risen', international affairs blog, *Financial Times*, 9 November 2007; also Andy Xie, 'China's Bubble May Burst But the Impact Will Be Limited', *Financial Times*, 16 October 2007.

154. 'A Complex Rationale for China's Raid on Rio', *Financial Times*, 13 February 2008.

155. Shujie Yao, 'China will learn from failed Chinalco-Rio deal', *Financial Times*, 7 June 2010; Sundeep Tucker, 'Chinese déjà vu', *Financial Times*, 9 June 2010.

156. Lex, 'Chinese Oil Majors', *Financial Times*, 29 October 2008.

157. 'China Turns Risk Averse, Even as Capital Outflows Rise', *Financial Times*, 17 January 2008.

158. Nolan, *Transforming China*, pp. 222, 227–8.

159. Lawrence Brainard and Jonathan Fenby, 'Chinese Takeout', *Wall Street Journal*, 20 February 2007.

160. Naughton, *The Chinese Economy*, p. 313. Gao Xu, 'State-owned enterprises in China: How big are they?' EastAsiaPacific/Blog, World Bank, posted 19 January 2010.

161. Geoff Dyer and Richard McGregor, 'China's Champions: Why State Ownership is No Longer Proving a Dead Hand', *Financial Times*, 16 March 2008.

162. Yasheng Huang, *Capitalism with Chinese Characteristics: Entrepreneurship and the State* (Cambridge: Cambridge University Press, 2008), pp. 277–80.

163. The figures in this section are mainly based on Hu Angang, 'Five Major Scale Effects of China's Rise', unpublished seminar paper, East Asia Institute, National University of Singapore, 2005, pp. 1–14; also Angus Maddison, *The World Economy: Historical Statistics* (Paris: OECD, 2003).

164. Yu Yongding, 'The Interactions between China and the World Economy', p. 4.

165. 'The Dragon and the Eagle Survey', *The Economist*, 2 October 2004, p. 29.

166. See, for example, Roger F. Noriega, 'China's Influence in the Western Hemisphere', statement before the House Sub-committee on the Western Hemisphere, Washington, DC, 16 April 2005; Prestowitz, *Three Billion New Capitalists*, p. 241; and Leni Wild and David Mepnam, eds, *The New Sinosphere: China in Africa* (London: Institute for Public Policy Research, 2006).

167. Prestowitz, *Three Billion New Capitalists*, p. 240; Shenkar, *The Chinese Century*, p. 110; 'Latin Textile Makers Feel Chinese Pressure', *International Herald Tribune*, 2 April 2007.

168. Prestowitz, *Three Billion New Capitalists*, p. 137.

169. Ibid., p. 199.

170. Shenkar, *The Chinese Century*, p. 113.

171. Gary Clyde Hufbauer and Yee Wong, 'Prospects for Regional Free

Trade in Asia', working paper, Institute for International Economics, Washington, DC, October 2005, p. 4; Prestowitz, *Three Billion New Capitalists*, p. 226.

172. Yu Yongding, 'China's Rise, Twin Surplus and the Change of China's Development Strategy', pp. 26–30.

173. Simon Rabinovitch, 'China calls on US to "protect investors"', *Financial Times*, 20 July 2011.

174. Andrew Batson, 'China May Get More Daring With Its $1.07 Trillion Stash', *Wall Street Journal*, 15 February 2007.

175. 'China Money Trouble: Where to Park It All', *International Herald Tribune*, 6 March 2007.

176. 'China Voices Alarm at Dollar Weakness', *Financial Times*, 19 November 2007; Keith Bradsher, 'Rising Cost of Buying US Debt Puts Strain on China's Economy', *International Herald Tribune*, 4 September 2008.

177. Also, Lex, 'China and Fannie Mae', *Financial Times*, 17 July 2008.

178. 'China Acts to Become Huge Global Investor', *International Herald Tribune*, 10–11 March 2007.

179. 'Beijing to Take $3bn Gamble on Blackstone', *Financial Times*, 18 May 2007.

180. 'China's Two Trillion Dollar Question', editorial, *Financial Times*, 11 September 2008.

181. For a broader view of the rise of such funds, see Martin Wolf, 'The Brave New World of State Capitalism', *Financial Times*, 16 October 2007.

182. 'China Aids Barclays on ABN Amro', *Financial Times*, 23 July 2007; 'The Chinese Bank Plan is One to Watch', *Financial Times*, 23 July 2007.

183. 'Bear Stearns in Landmark China Deal', *Financial Times*, 22 October 2007.

184. 'Chinese Banks Seek Stake in StanChart', *Financial Times*, 18 November 2007. Earlier in 2007, the Bank of China was reported as being interested in acquiring a US bank; 'Bank of China Seeking US Acquisition Targets', *South China Morning Post*, 22 January 2007.

185. Jamil Anderlini, 'Chinese lost billions in diversity drive', *Financial Times*, 15 March 2009.

186. Wang Zhengyi, 'Conceptualising Economic Security and Governance', p. 541.

187. Elizabeth Economy, 'China, the United States and the World Trade Organization', Council on Foreign Relations, Washington, DC, 3 July

2002, pp. 1–4; Shen Boming, 'The Challenges Ahead: China's Membership in WTO', 2002, available to download from www.cap.lmu.de/transatlantic/download/Shen_ Boming.doc, p. 7; Shenkar, *The Chinese Century*, pp. 167–8; Yu Yong Ding, 'The Interactions between China and the World Economy', pp. 4–5.

188. 'China Tackles Tainted Food Crisis', 'Scandal-hit China Food Firms Shut', 'Chinese-made Toys Recalled in US' and 'Bush Tackles Scares over Imports', all posted at www.bbc.co.uk/news; 'US Trade Body Sets Stage for Action on Beijing "Subsidies"', *South China Morning Post*, 18 December 2006: 'Mattel Apologises to "the Chinese People"', *Financial Times*, 21 September 2007; 'Beijing Overhauling Food Safety Controls', *International Herald Tribune*, 7 June 2007.

189. Wang Zhengyi, 'Conceptualising Economic Security and Governance', p. 541.

190. Kynge, *China Shakes the World*, pp. 72, 78–82.

191. Daniel Schäfer, 'China and Germany: Reflected glory', *Financial Times*, 18 January 2011; Peter Marsh, 'Focus on deals high up in value chain', *Financial Times*, 25 April 2011.

192. In its projections for 2020, the World Bank suggested that the developed world would continue to be a net beneficiary of China's rise because of the latter's demands for its capital-intensive manufactured products together with services, and because of the significant terms of trade gains that would accrue from its growing demand for these products. But they would continue to lose out in labour-intensive manufactured products as China moved up the value-added chain. Countries that are close competitors of China – like India, Indonesia and the Philippines – would probably still benefit, but they would find the prices of their major exports falling; while less developed countries which were not endowed with natural resources would find China's continued growth having a relatively neutral economic effect at best. See World Bank, *China Engaged: Integration with the Global Economy* (Washington, DC: 1997), pp. 29–35.

193. Kynge, *China Shakes the World*, pp. 118–20.

7 A Civilization-State

1. James Mann, *The China Fantasy: How Our Leaders Explain Away Chinese Repression* (New York: Viking, 2007), pp. 1–7.

2. James Kynge, *China Shakes the World: The Rise of a Hungry Nation*

(London: Weidenfeld and Nicolson, 2006), p. 203; and Julia Lovell, *The Great Wall: China against the World 1000 BC–AD 2000* (London: Atlantic Books, 2006), pp. 30 and 27.

3. Lucian W. Pye, *The Spirit of Chinese Politics* (Cambridge, Mass.: Harvard University Press, 1992), pp. 207, 212–17.

4. Pye, *The Spirit of Chinese Politics*, p. 235.

5. Wang Gungwu, 'Early Ming Relations with Southeast Asia: A Background Essay', in John King Fairbank, ed., *The Chinese World Order: Traditional China's Foreign Relations* (Cambridge, Mass.: Harvard University Press, 1968), p. 61. Also, Henry Kissinger, *On China* (London: Allen Lane, 2011), p. 2.

6. Cited in Zheng Yongnian, *Will China Become Democratic?: Elite, Class and Regime Transition* (Singapore: EAI, 2004), p. 81.

7. Huang Ping, '"Beijing Consensus", or "Chinese Experiences", or What?', unpublished paper, 2005, p. 6.

8. Tu Wei-ming, *The Living Tree: The Changing Meaning of Being Chinese Today* (Stanford: Stanford University Press, 1994), pp. 3–4.

9. Daniel A. Bell and Hahm Chaibong, eds, *Confucianism for the Modern World* (Cambridge: Cambridge University Press, 2003), p. 1.

10. Wang Gungwu, *The Chineseness of China: Selected Essays* (Oxford: Oxford University Press, 1991), pp. 2–3.

11. Peter Nolan, *China at the Crossroads* (Cambridge: Polity Press, 2004), p. 154.

12. Interview with Huang Ping, Beijing, 10 December 2005.

13. Tu Wei-ming, *The Living Tree*, p. 17.

14. Howard Gardner, *To Open Minds* (New York: Basic Books, 1989), p. 269; also pp. 13–14, 150, 217. Pye, *The Spirit of Chinese Politics*, pp. 94–5. Given that calligraphy, the drawing and reproducing of characters, forms the basis of Chinese art, it is unsurprising that it is of a quite different content and style to Western art. Which, one might ask, is the better system? Howard Gardner, the American educationalist, argues that both have their strengths. The point that needs stressing here, though, is the fundamental difference between the two and their deep historical and cultural roots; in the light of this, we should not expect to witness any serious pattern of convergence. Gardner argues: 'It [is] disastrous to inject – unexamined – our notions of education, progress, technology into alien cultural contexts: it [is] far more timely to understand these alternative conceptions on their own terms, to learn from them if possible, and for the most part to respect (rather than to tamper with) their assumptions and their procedures.' Gardner, *To Open Minds*, p. 118.

15. Interview with Huang Ping, Beijing, 10 December 2005; Huang Ping, '"Beijing Consensus", or "Chinese Experiences", or What?', p. 7.
16. Wang Gungwu, *The Chineseness of China*, p. 2.
17. Diana Lary, 'Regions and Nation: The Present Situation in China in Historical Context', *Pacific Affairs*, 70:2 (Summer 1997), p. 182.
18. Tu Wei-ming, *The Living Tree*, p. 4.
19. Also, Shi Anbin, 'Mediating Chinese-ness: Identity Politics and Media Culture in Contemporary China', in Anthony Reid and Zheng Yangwen, eds, *Negotiating Asymmetry: China's Place in Asia* (Singapore: NUS Press, 2009), p. 13.
20. Lucian W. Pye, 'Chinese Democracy and Constitutional Development', in Fumio Itoh, ed., *China in the Twenty-first Century: Politics, Economy, and Society* (Tokyo: United Nations University Press, 1997), p. 209.
21. William A. Callahan, *Contingent States: Greater China and Transnational Relations* (Minneapolis: University of Minnesota Press, 2004), pp. 81, 109.
22. David S. G. Goodman and Gerald Segal, *China Rising: Nationalism and Interdependence* (London: Routledge, 1997), pp. 32, 44–5.
23. Ibid., pp. 31–2.
24. Pye, 'Chinese Democracy and Constitutional Development', pp. 209–10.
25. Minxin Pei recounts a classic example of this concerning Hubei province and former Premier Zhu Rongji. See his 'How One Political Insider is Using His Influence to Push Rural Reforms', *South China Morning Post*, 2 January 2003.
26. Zheng Yongian, *Will China Become Democratic?*, p. 329.
27. Pye, *The Spirit of Chinese Politics*, p. 209.
28. Zheng Yongnian, *Discovering Chinese Nationalism in China* (Cambridge: Cambridge University Press, 1999), pp. 30–33, 40–41.
29. Pye, 'Chinese Democracy and Constitutional Development', pp. 208–10; and Pye, *The Spirit of Chinese Politics*, pp. 209–10.
30. Pye, *The Spirit of Chinese Politics*, pp. 13–14, 17.
31. Ibid., pp. 24–5.
32. Pye, 'Chinese Democracy and Constitutional Development', pp. 210–13.
33. Ibid., pp. 28–9, 76, 80, 87–8, 91, 94–6, 100.
34. Interview with Huang Ping, Beijing, 10 December 2005.
35. Zheng Yongnian, *Discovering Chinese Nationalism in China*, p. 22.
36. Ibid., pp. 22–3.

37. Pye, *The Spirit of Chinese Politics*, p. 236.

38. Callahan, *Contingent States*, pp. 154, 158–9.

39. Ibid., p. 38.

40. Cited in Zheng Yongnian, *Will China Become Democratic?*, p. 33. Also Suisheng Zhao, *A Nation-State by Construction* (Stanford: Stanford University Press, 2004), pp. 226–7.

41. In the words of a leading government adviser, Fang Ning: 'China will have a future only if it maintains stability.' Interview with Fang Ning, Beijing, 7 December 2005.

42. The average ranking for other countries was 23; 2003 Roper Survey of Global Attitude, cited in Joshua Cooper Ramo, *The Beijing Consensus* (London: The Foreign Policy Centre, 2004), p. 23.

43. Rein Müllerson, 'Crouching tiger hidden dragon: Which will it be?', *Eurozine*, http://www.eurozine.com/articles/2010-04-29-mullerons-en. html. Accessed 30/04/2010.

44. Nolan, *China at the Crossroads*, pp. 73–5.

45. Mao himself offers an interesting angle on this question. While he delivered a new period of stability, he was always tempted to plunge the country into a new period of instability, as in the Great Leap Forward and the Cultural Revolution.

46. Martin Jacques, 'Democracy Isn't Working', *Guardian*, 22 June 2004.

47. Zheng Yongnian, *Will China Become Democratic?*, p. 36.

48. Nolan, *China at the Crossroads*, p. 67.

49. Interview with Zhu Wenhui, Beijing, 20 November 2005.

50. Bruce Gilley, *China's Democratic Future: How It Will Happen and Where It Will Lead* (New York: Columbia University Press, 2004), p. 246.

51. See, for example, Lee Kuan Yew interview, April 2004, in Ramo, *The Beijing Consensus*, pp. 62–3.

52. Pye, *The Spirit of Chinese Politics*, p. 15.

53. The nearest example is the United Nations.

54. 'Shenzhen Officials to Adopt New Mindset', *South China Morning Post*, 10 March 2008.

55. Jeremy Page, 'China Tests New Political Model in Shenzhen', *Wall Street Journal*, 18 October 2010.

56. Zheng Yongnian, *Will China Become Democratic?*, pp. 79–80.

57. The characteristics of the major Western countries that helped to shape their democracies include, amongst other things, that they were the first to industrialize, had colonial possessions and were relatively ethnically homogeneous.

58. Karel van Wolferen, *The Enigma of Japanese Power: People and Politics in a Stateless Nation* (New York: Vintage, 1990), Chapters 1–3, 5, 8, 16.

59. Pye, *The Spirit of Chinese Politics*, p. ix.

60. Bell and Chaibong, *Confucianism for the Modern World*, pp. 7, 356–9, 368.

61. Zhao, *A Nation-State by Construction*, pp. 228–9.

62. Callahan, *Contingent States*, p. 41.

63. 1 February 2001, quoted in Zheng Yongnian, *Will China Become Democratic?*, p. 95; also Callahan, *Contingent States*, pp. 31–2.

64. Quoted in Daniel A. Bell, *China's New Confucianism: Politics and Everyday Life in a Changing Society* (Princeton: Princeton University Press, 2008), p. 9.

65. Raymond Zhou, 'Let Sages Enrich Us, Not Polarize Us', *China Daily*, 10–11 December 2005.

66. Interview with Kang Xiaoguang, Beijing, 1 December 2005.

67. Zheng Yongnian, *Will China Become Democratic?*, p. 91; and interview with Kang Xiaoguang, Beijing, 1 December 2005. Kang was the first to propose the idea of the Confucius Institute to the government. He has suggested that Confucianism should replace Marxism in education.

68. Bell, *China's New Confucianism*, pp. 9–12.

69. Paul A. Cohen, *Discovering History in China: American Historical Writing on the Recent Chinese Past* (New York: Columbia University Press, 1984), p. 32

70. Bell and Chaibong, *Confucianism for the Modern World*, p. 26.

71. Ibid., p. 9.

72. Pye, *The Spirit of Chinese Politics*, p. 17.

73. Wang Gungwu, *The Chineseness of China*, p. 171.

74. Chen Kuan-Hsing, 'Civil Society and Min-jian: On Political Society and Popular Democracy', *Cultural Studies*, 17:6 (2003), pp. 876–96.

75. Zheng Yongnian, *Will China Become Democratic?*, pp. 82–3; Callahan, *Contingent States*, p. xxxiv.

76. For a discussion of Confucian ideas in practice, see ibid., pp. 210–14. Wang Gungwu argues there are three types of Confucian thinking; see *China and the Overseas Chinese* (Singapore: Times Academic Press, 1991), pp. 259–61.

77. Bell and Chaibong, *Confucianism for the Modern World*, pp. 15–19.

78. Ibid., pp. 12–13.

79. Rein Müllerson, 'Crouching tiger hidden dragon: Which will it be?', *Eurozine*, 29 April 2010, p. 3.

80. For an interesting discussion of some of these issues, see Bell, *China's New Confucianism*, pp. 14–18.

81. David Shambaugh (ed.), *The Modern Chinese State*, pp. 167, 174–81.

82. Zheng Yongnian, *Will China Become Democratic?*, p. 140; and interview with Yu Zengke, Beijing, 22 May 2006.

83. Zheng Yongnian, *Will China Become Democratic?*, pp. 48–70; Wang Zhengxu, 'Understanding Democratic Thinking in China', seminar paper, East Asia Institute, National University of Singapore, 28 April 2006.

84. Interview with Yu Zengke, Beijing, 22 May 2006.

85. Jude Howell, ed., *Governance in China* (Oxford: Roman and Littlefield, 2004), pp. 3, 8, 9.

86. In 2006 China had 132 million internet users, the second largest number after the US. See Christopher R. Hughes and Gudrun Wacker, eds, *China and the Internet: Politics of the Digital Leap Forward* (London: Routledge, 2003), Chapter 3; and Wang Xiaodong, 'Chinese Nationalism under the Shadow of Globalisation', lecture at the London School of Economics and Political Science, 7 February 2005. Also, interview with Yu Yongding, Beijing, 4 August 2011.

87. Interview with Yu Zengke, Beijing, 22 May 2006.

88. Zheng Yongnian, *Will China Become Democratic?*, pp. 198–9, 212.

89. www.china.org.cn/english/2005/Oct/145718.htm. Accessed 15 June 2008.

90. Zheng Yongnian, *Will China Become Democratic?*, pp. 126–7.

91. 'Tiananmen Recedes in Hong Kong', *International Herald Tribune*, 5 June 2008.

92. Naomi Klein, 'Police State 2.0', *Guardian,* 3 June 2008.

93. Edward Wong, 'A Bid to Help Poor Rural China Catch Up', *International Herald Tribune*, 13 October, 2008; 'On Solid Ground', *South China Morning Post*, 23 February, 2008.

94. Zheng Yongnian, *Will China Become Democratic?*, p. 256.

95. Howard W. French, 'Letter from China', *International Herald Tribune*, 15 June 2006.

96. Zheng Yongnian, *Will China Become Democratic?*, pp. 244–5.

97. Ibid., pp. 245–6.

98. Howell, *Governance in China*, p. 30; Zheng Yongnian, *Will China Become Democratic?*, p. 159.

99. Zheng Yongnian, *Will China Become Democratic?*, p. 229.

100. Ibid., pp. 256–60.

101. Ibid., p. 269.

102. Ibid., p. 266.

103. Ibid., pp. 93, 265–6. The examples are legion: 'China Oil Tycoon Placed Under Arrest', *South China Morning Post*, 27 December 2006; 'China Fund Says Almost $1 billion Misused', *International Herald Tribune*, 25–6 November 2006; and 'Shenzhen Tycoon on Trial for Theft', *South China Morning Post*, 13 November 2006.

104. Seminar paper by Song Weiquiang, Aichi University, 21 May 2005. According to the Ministry of Public Security, the number of disturbances to public order rose to 87,000 in 2005 (*South China Morning Post*, 20 January 2006). See also Song Weiquiang, 'Study on Massive Group Incidents of Chinese Peasants', Ph.D. dissertation, Nankai University, 20 April 2006, pp. 4–5.

105. Zheng Yongnian, *Will China Become Democratic?*, pp. 283–90, 302–8; Jie Chen and Bruce J. Dickson, *Allies of the State: China's Private Entrepreneurs and Democratic Change* (Harvard University Press: Cambridge, Mass., and London, 2010), pp. 156–8.

106. Zheng Yongnian, *Will China Become Democratic?*, pp. 308–17.

107. Mark Leonard, *What Does China Think?* (London: Fourth Estate, 2008), p. 48.

108. Kathrin Hille and Jamil Anderlini, 'China: Mao and the next generation', *Financial Times*, 2 June 2011; Kathrin Hille, 'Maoist revival gathers pace in Chongqing', *Financial Times*, 24 May 2011.

109. Interview with Yu Zengke, Beijing, 22 May 2006.

110. Mark Leonard, *What Does China Think?*, pp. 64–6, 74–5.

111. Howell, *Governance in China*, pp. 227–8.

112. Yu Yongding, 'A different road forward', *China Daily*, 23 December 2010.

113. Yoichi Funabashi, interview with Wang Jisi, *Asahi Shimbun*, 12 June 2010.

114. Nolan, *China at the Crossroads*, pp. 72, 77.

115. John Fitzgerald, *Awakening China: Politics, Culture, and Class in the Nationalist Revolution* (Stanford: Stanford University Press, 1996), p. 85. These terms and others such as 'sovereignty' and 'ethnicity' were often Western imports. Shi Anbin, 'Mediating Chinese-ness', p. 2, in Reid and Zheng, *Negotiating Asymmetry*.

116. Interview with Huang Ping, Beijing, 10 December 2005.

117. Callahan, *Contingent States*, p. xxi.

118. Robert Kagan, *Dangerous Nation: America and the World 1600–1898* (London: Atlantic Books, 2006), pp. 15–17, 130–33, 137, 250–51.

119. Martin Jacques, 'Strength in Numbers', *Guardian*, 23 October 2004.

120. Interview with Yu Yongding, Singapore, 3 March 2006.
121. Kagan, *Dangerous Nation*, Chapters 1–4.
122. David C. Kang, 'Getting Asia Wrong: The Need for New Analytical Frameworks', *International Security*, 27:4 (Spring 2003), p. 84.

8 The Middle Kingdom Mentality

1. William A. Callahan, *Contingent States: Greater China and Transnational Relations* (Minneapolis: University of Minnesota Press, 2004), pp. 2, 26.
2. Eric Hobsbawm, 'America's Neo-Conservative World Supremacists Will Fail', *Guardian*, 25 June 2005.
3. Bob Herbert in *International Herald Tribune*, 2 March 2007, from David Brion Davis, *Inhuman Bondage: The Rise and Fall of Slavery in the New World* (New York: Oxford University Press, 2005).
4. For a recognition of the importance of race and ethnicity in the formulation of foreign policy, see Thomas J. Christensen, Alastair Iain Johnston and Robert S. Ross, 'Conclusions and Future Directions', in Alastair Iain Johnston and Robert S. Ross, eds, *New Directions in the Study of China's Foreign Policy* (Stanford: Stanford University Press, 2006), pp. 410–11.
5. Jared Diamond, *Guns, Germs and Steel: A Short History of Everybody for the Last 13,000 Years* (London: Vintage, 1998), p. 324; Julia Lovell, *The Great Wall: China Against the World 1000 BC–AD 2000* (London: Atlantic Books, 2006), p. 48; and Jacques Gernet, *A History of Chinese Civilization*, 2nd edn (Cambridge: Cambridge University Press, 1996), Chapter 1.
6. Suisheng Zhao, *A Nation-State by Construction: Dynamics of Modern Chinese Nationalism* (Stanford: Stanford University Press, 2004), pp. 39, 40, 166–7; W. J. F. Jenner, 'Race and History in China', *New Left Review*, 11 (September/October 2001), p. 71.
7. Peter C. Perdue, *China Marches West: The Qing Conquest of Central Eurasia* (Cambridge, Mass.: Belknap Press of Harvard University Press, 2005), p. 508.
8. Quoted in Zhao, *A Nation-State by Construction*, p. 40.
9. Barry Sautman, 'Myths of Descent, Racial Nationalism and Ethnic Minorities in the People's Republic of China', in Frank Dikötter, ed., *The Construction of Racial Identities in China and Japan: Historical and Contemporary Perspectives* (London: Hurst and Company, 1997), p. 79; and Zhao, *A Nation-State by Construction*, pp. 167, 171.

10. Sautman, 'Myths of Descent', p. 81.

11. Frank Dikötter, introduction to his *The Construction of Racial Identities in China and Japan*, p. 1.

12. Jenner, 'Race and History in China', pp. 74–6.

13. www.unesco.org/ext/field/beijing/whc/pkm-site.htm.

14. Frank Dikötter, 'Racial Discourse in China: Continuities and Permutations', in his *The Construction of Racial Identities in China and Japan*, p. 20; and Sautman, 'Myths of Descent', pp. 84–9.

15. Jonathan Watts, 'Ancient Skull Offers Clues to Origins of Chinese', *Guardian*, 23 January 2008.

16. 'Stirring Find in Xuchang', *China Daily*, 28 January 2008.

17. John Reader, *Missing Links: The Hunt for Earliest Man* (London: Penguin, 1999), p. 111, quoted in Dikötter, 'Racial Discourse in China', p. 29; Zhao, *A Nation-State by Construction*, pp. 168–9; and Sautman, 'Myths of Descent', p. 87.

18. Geoff Wade, 'Some Topoi in Southern Border Historiography During the Ming (and Their Modern Relevance)', in Sabine Dabringhaus and Roderich Ptak, eds, *China and Her Neighbours: Borders, Visions of the Other, Foreign Policy 10th to 19th Century* (Wiesbaden: Harrassowitz, 1997), p. 147.

19. Perdue, *China Marches West*, pp. 510–11.

20. Zhao, *A Nation State by Construction*, p. 169; interview with Wang Xiaodong, Beijing, 29 August 2005; and Wade, 'Some Topoi', pp. 135–57.

21. Zheng Yangwen, 'Move People Buttress Frontier: Regime Orchestrate [*sic*] Migration-Settlement in the Two Millennia', workshop on 'Asian Expansions: The Historical Processes of Polity Expansion in Asia', Asia Research Institute, National University of Singapore, 12–13 May 2006, p. 1.

22. Johnston argues that Chinese military strategy, contrary to much conventional wisdom, has traditionally placed the major emphasis on what he calls a 'parabellum' approach – that conflict is a constant feature of human affairs; Alastair Iain Johnston, *Cultural Realism: Strategic Culture and Grand Strategy in Chinese History* (Princeton: Princeton University Press, 1995), pp. 249–59. Wang Xiaodong points out: 'Chinese academics say China has a peaceful history but the Qing dynasty was very violent in its imperial expansion. When people tell you that China was peaceful, it is lies.' Interview with Wang Xiaodong, Beijing, 29 August 2005.

23. Lovell, *The Great Wall*, pp. 43–4.

24. Ibid., p. 83.
25. 'The Mongol threat was defined in essentially racialist, zero-sum terms.' Johnston, *Cultural Realism*, p. 250.
26. Lovell, *The Great Wall*, p. 109.
27. Wang Gungwu, *Joining the Modern World: Inside and Outside China* (Singapore and London: Singapore University Press and World Scientific, 2000), p. 11.
28. Gernet, *A History of Chinese Civilization*, pp. 124–6; and Lovell, *The Great Wall*, p. 37.
29. Perdue, *China Marches West*, pp. 333–42.
30. Ibid., p. 544.
31. Ibid., p. 345.
32. Zheng Yangwen, 'Move People Buttress Frontier', pp. 1–4, 11–12.
33. David S. Landes, *The Wealth and Poverty of Nations* (London: Little, Brown, 1998), p. 425.
34. Zhao, *A Nation-State by Construction*, pp. 23, 176.
35. Ibid., pp. 44–6.
36. Callahan, *Contingent States*, pp. 82, 85–6.
37. Ibid., p. 34; and Zhao, *A Nation-State by Construction*, pp. 41–3.
38. R. Bin Wong, *China Transformed: Historical Change and the Limits of European Experience* (Ithaca and London: Cornell University Press, 2000), p. 103; Peter C. Perdue, 'Why Do Empires Expand?', workshop on 'Asian Expansions: The Historical Processes of Polity Expansion in Asia', Asia Research Institute, National University of Singapore, 12–13 May 2006; and Callahan, *Contingent States*, p. 87.
39. Callahan, *Contingent States*, pp. 26–7.
40. Zhao, *A Nation-State by Construction*, pp. 13–16.
41. Wang Gungwu, *China and the Chinese Overseas* (Singapore: Times Academic Press, 1991), pp. 259–61.
42. Nicholas Ostler, *Empires of the Word* (London: HarperCollins, 2005), pp. 116–73, especially pp. 116–17, 156–7.
43. Zhao, *A Nation-State by Construction*, p. 43.
44. Ibid., p. 46.
45. Chen Kuan-Hsing, *Asia as Method: Towards De-Imperialization* (Durham and London: Duke University Press, 2010), Epilogue: The Imperial Order of Things, or Notes on Han Chinese Racism, pp. 257–68. An earlier version, 2009, is available at www.inter-asia.org/khchen/online/Epilogue.pdf; and Leo K. Shin, *The Making of the Chinese State: Ethnicity and Expansion on the Ming Borderlands* (Cambridge: Cambridge University Press, 2006), pp. 4–5.

46. Zhao, *A Nation-State by Construction*, pp. 22, 62–3, 253–4.

47. Dikötter, introduction, pp. 1, 5.

48. M. Dujon Johnson, *Race and Racism in the Chinas* (Milton Keynes: AuthorHouse, 2007), p. 94.

49. Martin Jacques, 'Global Hierarchy of Race', *Guardian*, 20 September 2003.

50. Dikötter, introduction, p. 3.

51. Ibid., p. 2.

52. Kai-wing Chow, 'Imagining Boundaries of Blood: Zhang Binglin and the Invention of the Han "Race" in Modern China', in Dikötter, ed., *The Construction of Racial Identities in China and Japan*, p. 48; also p. 44.

53. Sautman, 'Myths of Descent', pp. 79–80; Lucian W. Pye, *Asian Power and Politics: The Cultural Dimensions of Authority* (Cambridge, Mass.: Harvard University Press, 1985), pp. 80–81, 196, 329.

54. Dikötter, *The Discourse of Race in Modern China* (London: Hurst and Company, 1992), p. 32; Allen Chan, 'The Grand Illusion: The Long History of Multiculturalism in an Era of Invented Indigenisation', p. 6, unpublished paper for Swedish-NUS conference, 'Asia-Europe and Global Processes', Singapore, 14–16 March 2001. It is easier for an ethnic Chinese born in Malaysia or Canada to get Hong Kong citizenship than it is for a Hong Kong-born person of Indian or Philippine background; Philip Bowring, 'China and Its Minorities', *International Herald Tribune*, 3 March 2008.

55. Diamond, *Guns, Germs and Steel*, pp. 331–2; and Lovell, *The Great Wall*, pp. 35, 108.

56. John King Fairbank, ed., *The Chinese World Order: Traditional China's Foreign Relations* (Cambridge, Mass.: Harvard University Press, 1968), pp. 278, 281.

57. Dikötter, *The Discourse of Race in Modern China*, p. 9.

58. Ibid., pp. 1, 3–4; Fairbank, *The Chinese World Order*, pp. 27–8; Lovell, *The Great Wall*, p. 35; Kuan-Hsing Chen, 'Notes on Han Chinese Racism'; and Wade, 'Some Topoi', p. 144.

59. Dikötter, *The Discourse of Race in Modern China*, p. 6.

60. Ibid., p. 29; Fairbank, *The Chinese World Order*, pp. 21, 281.

61. Dikötter, *The Discourse of Race in Modern China*, pp. 10–13.

62. Ibid., p. 11.

63. Ibid., pp. 12–13.

64. Ibid., p. 25.

65. Christian Tyler, *Wild West China: The Taming of Xinjiang* (London: John Murray, 2003), pp. 56–87, 269.

66. Dikötter, *The Discourse of Race in Modern China*, pp. 38–52, 129.

67. Ibid., pp. 55–6, 68–9.

68. Quoted in ibid., p. 158.

69. Ibid., p. 149.

70. Quoted in Johnson, *Race and Racism in the Chinas*, p. 39.

71. Quoted in Dikötter, *The Discourse of Race in Modern China*, p. 125.

72. Zhao, *A Nation-State by Construction*, pp. 22, 66–70, 172.

73. Ibid., pp. 172, 176–95.

74. Colin Mackerras, 'What is China? Who is Chinese? Han-minority Relations, Legitimacy, and the State', in Peter Hays Gries and Stanley Rosen, eds, *State and Society in 21st-Century China* (London: RoutledgeCurzon, 2004), pp. 216–17.

75. 'Voice of an Empire, All But Extinct', *International Herald Tribune*, 17–18 March 2007.

76. Stevan Harrell, ed., *Cultural Encounters on China's Ethnic Frontiers* (Seattle: University of Washington Press, 1995), pp. 29–32.

77. Zhao, *A Nation-State by Construction*, pp. 180–84.

78. John Gittings, *The Changing Face of China* (Oxford: Oxford University Press, 2005), p. 313; *International Herald Tribune*, 6–7 October 2001.

79. Zhao, *A Nation-State by Construction*, pp. 204–5; Mackerras, 'What is China?', pp. 224–7; and Christopher R. Hughes, *Chinese Nationalism in the Global Era* (London: Routledge, 2006), pp. 123–4. Also Geoff Dyer and Jamil Anderlini, 'Distant Thunder: Separatism Stirs on China's Forgotten Frontier', *Financial Times*, 17 August 2008.

80. Harrell, *Cultural Encounters on China's Ethnic Frontiers*, p. 23.

81. Ibid., p. 25.

82. Ibid., pp. 25–7; Zhao, *Nation-State by Construction*, pp. 202–8. Also, 'China: Minority Exclusion, Marginalization and Rising Tensions', *Human Rights in China*, Minority Rights Group International, 2007.

83. Pál Nyíri, 'The Yellow Man's Burden: Chinese Migrants on a Civilizing Mission', *The China Journal*, No. 56, July 2006, pp. 91–2.

84. Dikötter, 'Racial Discourse in China', pp. 25–6; Jenner, 'Race and History in China', pp. 70, 73–6.

85. For a very sensitive view of Tibetan culture, and the nature of Chinese attitudes, see Sun Shuyun, *A Year in Tibet: A Voyage of Discovery* (London: HarperPress, 2008), for example, pp. 2–3, 37–8. Also, Geoff Dyer, 'The Great Brawl of China', *Financial Times*, 11 July 2008.

86. Jim Yardley, 'After the Fury in Tibet, Firm Hand Trembles', *International Herald Tribune*, 18 March 2008.

87. Howard W. French, 'Again, Beijing Cues Up Its Propaganda Machine', *International Herald Tribune*, 4 April 2008.

88. Jim Yardley and Somini Sengupta, 'Beijing Blames the Dalai Lama', *International Herald Tribune*, 19 March 2008.

89. Howard W. French, 'Side By Side in China, While Still Worlds Apart', *International Herald Tribune*, 20 March 2008.

90. Quoted in ibid.

91. Sun Shuyun, *A Year in Tibet*, p. 66.

92. Jonathan D. Spence, *The Search for Modern China* (New York and London: W. W. Norton, 1999), p. 97.

93. Kristine Kwok, 'Thousands protest over Urumqi syringe attacks', *South China Morning Post*, 4 September 2009.

94. Choi Chi-yuk and Ng Tze-wei, 'Xinjiang to lift blackout in "gradual and orderly" way', *South China Morning Post*, 30 December 2009.

95. Kathrin Hille and Richard McGregor, 'Trouble at the margin', *Financial Times*, 10 July 2009.

96. Ibid.

97. Cui Jia and Zhu Zhe, 'Xinjiang support package unveiled', *China Daily*, 21 May 2010; Kathrin Hille, 'China acts to tackle Uighur tension', and 'Development unlikely to drown out disharmony', *Financial Times*, 3–4 July 2010.

98. Many have remarked on what they see as the racism of Chinese societies and communities. Howard Gardner, the American educationalist, writes: 'As a group, the Chinese tend to be ethnocentric, xenophobic and racist. Most people prefer to be with their own kind . . . but few have come to feel as strongly about this separatism over the millennia as the Han.' (*To Open Minds* (New York: Basic Books, 1989), p. 130.) Colin Mackerras suggests: 'Many Chinese care little for the minorities, let alone their cultures, and tend to look down on them.' ('What is China?', p. 221.) Lucian Pye writes: 'The most pervasive underlying Chinese emotion is a profound, unquestioned, generally unshakable identification with historical greatness . . . This is all so self-evident to the Chinese that they are hardly aware when they are being superior to others.' (*The Spirit of Chinese Politics* (Cambridge, Mass.: Harvard University Press, 1992), p. 50.) Chen Kuan-Hsing writes: 'Reports on the insensitive ways in which mainland Chinese businesses operate in Africa suggest that Han Chinese racism may become a global problem.' pp. 258–9; 'Han racism existed long before China's encounter with the West and is found today in mainland China's interactions with its Asian neighbours and within the Han population.' pp. 259–60;

'I think the supposedly heated debate on Chineseness is not nearly hot enough. It has not reached the heart of the matter: universal chauvinism.' p. 266 (*Asia as Method*).

99. www.malaysiakini.com/letters/33156 also 33115. Other discussions include: http://shanghai.asiaxpat.com/forums/speakerscorner/threads/ 65529.asp; http:www.chinahistoryforum.com/index.php?s=982bfbe0 8a75508b7a9de815588c6f12&showtopic=9760&st=15&p=4788117 &#entry4788117.

100. Johnson, *Race and Racism in the Chinas*, pp. 7, 94.

101. Sautman, 'Myths of Descent', p. 75.

102. Chen, *Asia as Method*, p. 266. There is little difference between racial attitudes in China and Taiwan; Johnson, *Race and Racism in the Chinas*, pp. 4, 42–3.

103. For example, Barry Sautman and Ellen Kneehans, 'The Politics of Racial Discrimination in Hong Kong', *Maryland Series in Contemporary Asian Studies*, 2 (2000); and Kelley Loper, 'Cultivating a Multicultural Society and Combating Racial Discrimination in Hong Kong', *Civic Exchange*, August 2001.

104. Sautman and Kneehans, 'The Politics of Racial Discrimination in Hong Kong', p. 17.

105. Ibid., pp. 73–6. Thirteen per cent of Hong Kong families with children of twelve or older employ a foreign domestic worker; according to a survey by the Asian Migrant Centre, almost a quarter were abused; *South China Morning Post*, 15 February 2001. 'Malaysian Jailed for Maid Attacks', 27 November 2008, posted on www.bbc.co.uk/news.

106. Sautman and Kneehans, 'The Politics of Racial Discrimination in Hong Kong', pp. 21–4.

107. Ibid., p. 12.

108. www.harinderveriah.com/articles.html; also, Martin Jacques, 'It seemed impossible . . . ,' *Observer*, 4 April 2010.

109. In fact, Indians have been living in Hong Kong since 1841.

110. Chen, *Asia as Method*, pp. 257–68.

111. Johnson, *Race and Racism in the Chinas*, p. 45.

112. Ibid., pp. 50–51.

113. 'Racial rethinking as Obama visits', *Washington Post*, 14 November 2009.

114. Ibid., pp. 76–7.

115. Dikötter, *The Discourse of Race in Modern China*, p. 194.

116. Dikötter, *The Construction of Racial Identities in China and Japan*, pp. 25–6; Erin Chung, 'Anti-Black Racism in China' (12 April 2005) and

'Nanjing Anti-African Protests of 1988–89', posted on www.amren. com/mtnews/archives/2005/04/nanjing_antiafr.php.

117. Johnson, *Race and Racism in the Chinas*, pp. 48, 50, 71.

118. *New York Times*, 19 January 1989, cited by Johnson, *Race and Racism in the Chinas*, p. 46.

119. Ibid., pp. 41, 44–50.

120. Jennifer Brea, 'Beijing Police Round Up and Beat African Expats', *Guardian*, 26 September 2007.

121. Barry Sautman and Yan Hairong, 'Friends and Interests: China's Distinctive Links with Africa', *African Studies Reviews* 50:3 (December 2007), p. 91; Tania Branigan, '"If I see them, I run. That's how I live." Africans living on the edge in China', *Guardian*, 7 October 2010.

122. Johnson, *Race and Racism in the Chinas*, pp. 147–8.

123. Louisa Lim, 'Mixed-Race TV Contestant Ignites Debate in China',11 December 2009, www.npr.org/templates/story.php?storyId=120311417; 'Lou Jing, and Fear of a Black China', 31 December 2009, www.dim sum.co.uk/china/lou-jing-and-fear-of-a-blackchina.html.

124. This was published on www.ncn.org. See also Martin Jacques, 'The Middle Kingdom Mentality', *Guardian*, 16 April 2005.

125. Johnson, *Race and Racism in the Chinas*, p. 91.

126. Zhao, *A Nation-State by Construction*, pp. 139–46, 156–7; and Hughes, *Chinese Nationalism in the Global Era*, pp. 111–12.

127. Wang Xiaodong, 'Chinese Nationalism under the Shadow of Globalisation', lecture at the London School of Economics and Political Science, 7 February 2005, p. 1.

128. Quoted in Zhao, *A Nation-State by Construction*, p. 153.

129. Wang Xiaodong, 'Chinese Nationalism under the Shadow of Globalisation', p. 1.

130. Quoted in Zhao, *A Nation-State by Construction*, pp. 154–5.

131. Ibid., p. 155.

132. Johnson, *Race and Racism in the Chinas*, pp. 123, 125, 132–3, 137.

133. Amy Chua, *World on Fire: How Exporting Free Market Democracy Breeds Ethnic Hatred and Global Instability* (London: William Heinemann, 2003), pp. 28–46.

134. Interview with Richard Oh, Jakarta, February 2004.

135. James Kynge, *China Shakes the World: The Rise of a Hungry Nation* (London: Weidenfeld and Nicolson, 2006), p. 87.

136. Pye, *The Spirit of Chinese Politics*, p. 56.

137. Chinese Cultural Center, San Francisco, conference 'In Search of Roots', 28 February 1998.

138. Evan Leong, 'Are You Chinese?', paper presented at the same conference.
139. Ibid., p. 9.
140. Ibid., p. 11.
141. Callahan, *Contingent States*, pp. 5, 22, 41.
142. Hideo Ohashi, 'China's Regional Trade and Investment Profile', in David Shambaugh, ed., *Power Shift: China and Asia's New Dynamics* (Berkeley: University of California Press, 2005), p. 83.
143. Michael Fullilove, 'Chinese Diaspora Carries Torch for Old Country', *Financial Times*, 18 May 2008; Geoff Dyer and Peter Smith, 'Chinese Rally to the Torch in Australia', *Financial Times*, 21 April 2008; 'Seoul Raps Chinese Protesters at Torch Rally', *South China Morning Post*, 29 April 2008; 'Chinese-Australians in Large Show of Support for Torch', *South China Morning Post*, 25 April 2008. Also Erik Eckholm, 'Chinese Abroad Exult in Glory of Olympics', *International Herald Tribune*, 12 August 2008.
144. According to the 1999 census; Zhao, *Nation-State by Construction*, pp. 192–3. Also, Robyn Iredale, Naran Bilik, Wang Su, Fei Guo and Caroline Hoy, *Contemporary Minority Migration, Education and Ethnicity in China* (Cheltenham: Edward Elgar, 2001).
145. Interview with Wang Xiaodong, Beijing, August 2005.
146. Interview with Huang Ping, Beijing, May 2006.
147. Diamond, *Guns, Germs and Steel*, p. 323.
148. Jenner, 'Race and History in China', p. 57.
149. Interview with Huang Ping, Beijing, May 2006.
150. Ibid.
151. Quoted in Jonathan D. Spence, *The Search for Modern China*, 2nd edn (New York: W. W. Norton, 1999), p. 679.
152. Chen, 'Notes on Han Chinese Racism'.
153. Interview with Lu Liang, Taipei, March 1999.
154. Fairbank, *The Chinese World Order*, pp. 36–8.
155. Martin Jacques, 'Global Hierarchy of Race', *Guardian*, 20 September 2003.
156. Zhao, *A Nation-State by Construction*, p. 51.
157. Yan Xuetong, 'The Rise of China in Chinese Eyes', *Journal of Contemporary China*, 10:26 (2001), pp. 33–4.
158. Pye, *The Spirit of Chinese Politics*, p. 50.
159. Shi Anbin, 'Mediating Chinese-ness: Identity Politics and Media Culture in Contemporary China', in Anthony Reid and Zheng Yangwen, eds, *Negotiating Asymmetry: China's Place in Asia* (Singapore: NUS Press, 2009), p. 19.

9 China's Own Backyard

1. Thomas Fuller, 'Asia Builds a New Road to Prosperity', *International Herald Tribune*, 31 March 2008.
2. Zhang Yunling and Tang Shiping, 'China's Regional Strategy', in David Shambaugh, ed., *Power Shift: China and Asia's New Dynamics* (Berkeley: University of California Press, 2005), pp. 51–2.
3. John King Fairbank, ed., *The Chinese World Order: Traditional China's Foreign Relations* (Cambridge, Mass.: Harvard University Press, 1968), pp. 10–11; Alexander Vuving, 'Traditional and Modern Sino-Vietnamese Relations', in Anthony Reid and Zheng Yangwen, eds, *Negotiating Asymmetry: China's Place in Asia* (Singapore: NUS Press, 2009), p. 2.
4. For an interesting discussion of new ways of thinking about traditional Chinese foreign policy, including the tributary system, see Zhang Feng, 'Rethinking the "Tribute System": Broadening the Conceptual Horizon of Historical East Asian Politics', *Chinese Journal of International Politics*, Volume 2, 2009, pp. 545–74.
5. Ibid., p. 567.
6. Wang Gungwu, 'Early Ming Relations with Southeast Asia: A Background Essay', in Fairbank, *The Chinese World Order*, p. 62.
7. Seo-Hyun Park, 'Small States and the Search for Sovereignty in Sinocentric Asia: The Case of Japan and Korea in the Late Nineteenth Century', in Reid and Zheng, *Negotiating Asymmetry*, pp. 3–10.
8. Ibid., pp. 3–11.
9. Chung-in Moon and Seung-won Suh, 'Overcoming History: The Politics of Identity and Nationalism', *Global Asia*, 2:1 (5 April 2007), pp. 35–6.
10. David C. Kang, 'Getting Asia Wrong: The Need for New Analytical Frameworks', *International Security*, 27:4 (Spring 2003), pp. 66–7.
11. Ibid., p. 11; William A. Callahan, *Contingent States* (Minneapolis: University of Minnesota Press, 2004), p. 89.
12. Suisheng Zhao, ed., *Chinese Foreign Policy* (New York: M. E. Sharpe, 2004), p. 256.
13. Wang Gungwu, 'China and Southeast Asia', in Shambaugh, *Power Shift*, p. 197; Kang, 'Getting Asia Wrong', p. 84.
14. Fairbank, *The Chinese World Order*, p. 4.
15. Though the ASEAN countries importantly did not condemn China, see David Shambaugh, 'Return to the Middle Kingdom? China and Asia in the Early Twenty-first Century', in Shambaugh, *Power Shift*, p. 26.

16. It became merely a consultative partner of the ASEAN Regional Forum in 1994.

17. Wang Jisi, 'China's Changing Role in Asia', p. 4, available at www.irchina.org.

18. Yu Bin, 'China and Russia: Normalizing Their Strategic Partnership', in Shambaugh, *Power Shift*, p. 232. China has also managed to agree all its borders with its East Asian neighbours, the outstanding exception being those with India.

19. Shambaugh, *Power Shift*, p. 30; John W. Garver, 'China's Influence in Central and South Asia: Is It Increasing?', in Shambaugh, *Power Shift*, p. 211; and Yu Bin, 'China and Russia', p. 236.

20. Zhang Yunling, *East Asian Regionalism and China* (Beijing: World Affairs Press, 2005), pp. 31-2.

21. Ibid., p. 67.

22. Shambaugh, 'Return to the Middle Kingdom? China and Asia in the Early Twenty-first Century', in Shambaugh, *Power Shift*, pp. 26-7.

23. Quoted in David C. Kang, *China Rising: Peace, Power, and Order in East Asia* (New York: Columbia University Press, 2007), p. 131.

24. Anthony Reid, 'Nationalisms in South East Asia', Asia Research Institute, National University of Singapore seminar paper, 24 January 2006.

25. Shee Poon Kim, 'East Asian New Regionalism: Toward Economic Integration?', *Ritsumeikan International Affairs*, 5 (2003), p. 70.

26. Zhang Yunling, *East Asian Regionalism and China*, p. 3; Shee Poon Kim, 'The Political Economy of Mahathir's China Policy: Economic Cooperation, Political and Strategic Ambivalence', *Annual Review of International Studies*, 3 (2004), p. 7.

27. Shambaugh, 'Return to the Middle Kingdom?', p. 27.

28. www.aseansec.org/16646.htm; and Wang Gungwu, 'China and Southeast Asia', p. 204.

29. Zhang Yunling, *East Asian Regionalism and China*, p. 18.

30. Shambaugh, *Power Shift*, p. 32; and Callahan, *Contingent States*, p. 71.

31. Rex Li, 'Security Challenge of an Ascendant China: Great Power Emergence and International Stability', in Zhao, *Chinese Foreign Policy*, p. 28.

32. Callahan, *Contingent States*, p. 66. An 8,000-strong contingent of Marines is based on Hainan Island for the purpose of defending China's claims.

33. Zhang Yunling, ed., *Designing East Asian FTA: Rationale and Feasibility* (Beijing: Social Sciences Academic Press, 2006), p. 61; Nobutoshi

Akao, 'Re-energizing Japan's Asean Policy', *AJISS-Commentary*, 2 August 2007, posted on www.jiia.or.jp/en.

34. Chu Shulong, 'US Security Strategy in Asia and the Regional Security Regime: A Chinese View', paper for IIPS International Conference, Tokyo, 30 November–1 December 2004.

35. Zhang Yunling, *East Asian Regionalism and China*, pp. 24, 29.

36. David M. Lampton, 'China's Rise in Asia Need Not Be at America's Expense', in Shambaugh, *Power Shift*, p. 312.

37. Kim, 'East Asian New Regionalism', p. 65.

38. Zhang and Tang, 'China's Regional Strategy', pp. 52–3.

39. Michael Yahuda, 'The Evolving Asian Order: The Accommodation of Rising Chinese Power', in Shambaugh, *Power Shift*, p. 349.

40. Jim O'Neill et al., 'China and Asia's Future Monetary System', *Goldman Sachs Global Economics Paper*, 129 (12 September 2005), p. 11; for details of the Chiang Mai Initiative, see www.unescap.org/pdd/publications/bulletin2002/ch8.pdf.

41. Zhang Yunling, *East Asian Regionalism and China*, p. 54.

42. Ibid., p. 29; also Martin Wolf, 'Asia Needs the Freedom of Its Own Monetary Fund', *Financial Times*, 19 May 2004.

43. Interview with Zhu Feng, Beijing, 16 November 2005.

44. Zhu Feng, 'Regionalism, Nationalism and China's Regional Activism in East Asia', unpublished paper, 2006, p. 4; and Takashi Inoguchi, 'Nationalism, Globalisation and Regional Order in North-East Asia: The Case of Japan at the Dawn of the Century', paper presented at conference on 'Nationalism and Globalisation in North-East Asia', Asia Research Centre, London School of Economics, 12 May 2007.

45. Ibid., p. 6.

46. Hideo Ohashi, 'China's Regional Trade and Investment Profile', in Shambaugh, *Power Shift*, p. 72; Guillaume Gaulier, Françoise Lemoine, Deniz Ünal-Kesenci, 'China's Integration in East Asia: Production Sharing, FDI and High-Tech Trade', *CEPII Working Paper No. 2005-09*, pp. 35–6.

47. Wang Zhengyi, 'Contending Regional Identity in East Asia: ASEAN Way and Its Implications', unpublished paper, 2001, pp. 12–15; World Bank, *The East Asian Miracle: Economic Growth and Public Policy* (New York: Oxford University Press, 1993), Chapters 1, 4.

48. Gaulier, Lemoine and Ünal-Kesenci, 'China's Integration in East Asia', p. 34.

49. Zhang and Tang, 'China's Regional Strategy', p. 51.

50. Interview with Zhang Yunling, Beijing, 17 May 2006.

51. Lampton, 'China's Rise in Asia Need Not Be at America's Expense', p. 311.

52. Zhang and Tang, 'China's Regional Strategy', p. 62.

53. Lampton, 'China's Rise in Asia Need Not Be at America's Expense', p. 310.

54. Jane Perlez, 'Forests in Southeast Asia Fall to Prosperity's Axe', *New York Times*, 29 April 2006; 'China and the East Asia Survey', *The Economist*, 5 May 2007.

55. Anthony Deutsch and Henry Sender, 'Indonesia uneasy about links with China', *Financial Times*, 30 April/1 May 2011.

56. Zhang and Tang, 'China's Regional Strategy', p. 62; and Ohashi, 'China's Regional Trade and Investment Profile', p. 76.

57. Lampton, 'China's Rise in Asia Need Not Be at America's Expense', p. 311.

58. Zhang and Tang, 'China's Regional Strategy', p. 54.

59. Interview with Zhang Yunling, Beijing, 17 May 2006.

60. Interview with Yu Yongding, Singapore, 3 March 2006; Yu Yongding, 'The Interactions between China and the World Economy', Nikkei Simbon Symposium, 5 April 2005, pp. 5, 7; Jim O'Neill et al., 'China and Asia's Future Monetary System', p. 13.

61. Ibid., p. 5; interview with Yu Yongding, Singapore, 3 March 2006.

62. Joshua Kurlantzick, *Charm Offensive: How China's Soft Power is Transforming the World* (New Haven: Yale University Press, 2007), pp. 105–6.

63. Clyde Prestowitz, *Three Billion New Capitalists: The Great Shift of Wealth and Power to the East* (New York: Basic Books, 2006), pp. 229–30.

64. Lampton, 'China's Rise in Asia Need Not Be at America's Expense', pp. 307, 317.

65. David Shambaugh, 'China Engages Asia: Reshaping the Regional Order', *International Security*, 29:3 (Winter 2004/5), p. 64.

66. Kurlantzick, *Charm Offensive*, p. 98.

67. Ibid., pp. 99–100; 'China's "Soft Power" Is Winning Allies in Asia', *International Herald Tribune*, 12 July 2007.

68. Kurlantzick, *Charm Offensive*, pp. 102–3.

69. Quoted in Kang, *China Rising*, p. 127. This was a personal communication with the author.

70. Kim, 'The Political Economy of Mahathir's China Policy', pp. 1, 3–4, 11, 15–16; Wang Gungwu, 'China and Southeast Asia', p. 191; and Garver, 'China's Influence in Central and South Asia', pp. 219–20.

71. Wang Gungwu, 'China and Southeast Asia', pp. 194, 198.
72. Kim, 'The Political Economy of Mahathir's China Policy', pp. 10–12.
73. Cary Huang, 'Najib calls for expanded yuan role', *South China Morning Post*, 5 June 2009.
74. Ibid.
75. Amy Chua, *World on Fire: How Exporting Free Market Democracy Breeds Ethnic Hatred and Global Instability* (London: William Heinemann, 2003), pp. 25–44.
76. Jae Ho Chung, 'China's Ascendancy and the Korean Peninsula: From Interest Revaluation to Strategic Realignment?', in Shambaugh, *Power Shift*, pp. 151–62; Kang, *China Rising*, Chapter 5.
77. Ibid., p. 151; Victor D. Cha, 'Engaging China: The View from Korea', in Alastair Iain Johnston and Robert S. Ross, eds, *Engaging China: The Management of an Emerging Power* (London: Routledge, 1999), pp. 32–56.
78. Shambaugh, 'Return to the Middle Kingdom?', pp. 33–4.
79. South Korea sends more than 13,000 students a year to China, a figure equal to the total number of Koreans who studied in the US at the height of US–South Korean relations between 1953 and 1975; Kurlantzick, *Charm Offensive*, p. 117.
80. Shambaugh, 'China Engages Asia', p. 79.
81. Chung, 'China's Ascendancy and the Korean Peninsula', pp. 156, 160–61.
82. Ibid., p. 160.
83. For an interesting Chinese view of these issues, see Zhu Feng, 'China Policy Toward North Korea: A New Twist', *PacNet*, Pacific Forum CSIS, No. 60, 8 December 2010. Also, Sharon Lafraniere and Martin Fackler, 'North Korea fires only words after South's drill', *International Herald Tribune*, 20 December 2010; David Pilling, 'Kim Jong-il plays his aces', *Financial Times*, 23 November 2010; Andrei Lankov, 'The Yeonpyeong Island Incident: why it happened, why nothing can be done, and what to expect: some thoughts', *North Korean Economy Watch*, http://www.nk econwatch.com/2010/11/29/lankov-on-the-shelling-of-yonpyong/, accessed 20 December 2010.
84. Ibid., pp. 161–2.
85. Jonathan D. Pollack, 'The Transformation of the Asian Security Order: Assessing China's Impact', in Shambaugh, *Power Shift*, pp. 338–9, 342.
86. South Korea, however, is fiercely protective of its independence and identity, and took considerable offence over an interpretation by Chinese historians in 2003 that the ancient kingdom of Koguryo (37 BC–

AD 668) had been part of China. Intense diplomatic activity in 2004 saw the dispute shelved; Shambaugh, 'China Engages Asia', p. 80.

87. Peter Smith and Richard McGregor, 'Good Days: Australia Prospers from China's Resource Needs', *Financial Times*, 2 April 2008. Also 'A Ravenous Dragon', a special report on China's quest for resources, *The Economist*, 15 March 2008, pp. 8–9; David Pilling, 'A rock lobster lesson for booming Australia', *Financial Times*, 8 December 2010.

88. Peter Smith, 'China drives engine of Australia's success', *Financial Times*, 2 February 2010; Lex column, 'The People's Bank of Australia', *Financial Times*, 2 February 2010.

89. Peter Smith, 'Australia bars China bid for Oz Minerals', *Financial Times*, 27 March 2009; Daniel Ren, '"Harsh jail" terms for Rio Tinto four', *South China Morning Post*, 30 March 2010. The four pleaded guilty and were dismissed by Rio Tinto.

90. Mark Thirlwell, 'Dealing with the Dragon: Australia and Chinese Inward Investment', 1 April 2010, *Clingendael Asia Studies*.

91. Gwen Robinson and Peter Smith, 'Australia in push to strengthen US defence ties', *Financial Times*, 26 July 2011; 'Australia Shifts Course, Away from US', posted on www.bbc.co.uk/news; Greg Barnes, 'Australia Finds a New Role as Sino-US Matchmaker', *South China Morning Post*, 26 February 2008; and 'Rudd Hitches Australia's Future to Rising China', *South China Morning Post*, 14 August 2008. Shiro Armstrong, 'Australia's Asian Future', *East Asia Forum*, http://www.eastasiaforum.org/2011/10/09/australia-s-asian-future/.

92. Geoff Dyer, 'Power play in the South China Sea', *Financial Times*, 9 August 2010; Geoff Dyer, 'Beijing's elevated aspirations', *Financial Times*, 10 November 2010.

93. Greg Torode and Minnie Chan, 'Vietnam buys submarines to counter China', *South China Morning Post*, 17 December 2009.

94. Norimitsu Onishi, 'US and China court Indonesia', *International Herald Tribune*, 10 November 2010.

95. David Pilling, 'A recipe for trouble in China's backyard', *Financial Times*, 29 September 2010.

96. Norimitsu Onishi, 'US and China court Indonesia', *International Herald Tribune*, 10 November 2010; Daniel Dombey and Gideon Rachman, 'US and the world: Mapped out', *Financial Times*, 2 June 2010.

97. James Kynge, Richard McGregor, Daniel Dombey, Martin Arnold, Helen Warrell and Cynthia O'Murchu, 'The China Syndrome', *Financial Times*, 3 March 2011.

98. David Pilling, 'Asia's quiet anger with "big, bad" China', *Financial Times*, 1 June 2011.

99. Toh Han Shih, 'Rail plan may boost China's regional sway', *South China Morning Post*, 22 November 2010.

100. Fairbank, *The Chinese World Order*, p. 61.

101. For an interesting discussion of these issues, see Wang Gungwu, 'Early Ming Relations with Southeast Asia: A Background Essay', in Fairbank, *The Chinese World Order*, pp. 60–62. Also Park, 'Small States and the Search for Sovereignty in Sinocentric Asia', p. 3.

102. Callahan, *Contingent States*, pp. 77, 81.

103. It should be noted that the Chinese continue to insist that negotiations over the sovereignty of the islands must be conducted on a bilateral rather than a multilateral basis, another echo of the tributary system; Callahan, *Contingent States*, pp. 97–8.

104. Ibid., p. 62.

105. Ibid., p. 94.

106. Ibid., pp. 33, 66–7, 78, 83. The Chinese claim the Senkaku/Diaoyu islands in the East China Sea on the same basis; Erica Strecker Downs and Phillip C. Sanders, 'Legitimacy and the Limits of Nationalism: China and the Diaoyu Islands', in Michael Brown et al., eds, *The Rise of China* (Cambridge, Mass.: MIT Press, 2000), p. 51; also Callahan, *Contingent States*, p. 72.

107. Willy Lam, 'China Flexes Its New Muscle', *International Herald Tribune*, 21 December 2007.

108. Chen Hurng-yu and Pan Shiying, cited in Callahan, *Contingent States*, p. 96.

109. Ibid., p. 63.

110. Reinhard Drifte, *Japan's Security Relations with China since 1989: From Balancing to Bandwagoning* (London: RoutledgeCurzon, 2003), p. 53.

111. Callahan, *Contingent States*, pp. 179–80.

112. Ibid., pp. 158–61, 166, 174.

113. Ibid., p. 141.

114. Cited in ibid., pp. 158–9; also p. 143.

115. Michael D. Swaine, 'China's Regional Military Posture', in Shambaugh, *Power Shift*, p. 277.

116. Quoted in Amitav Acharya, 'Containment, Engagement, or Counter-dominance? Malaysia's Response to the Rise of China', in Johnston and Ross, *Engaging China*, p. 131; also Kim, 'The Political Economy of Mahathir's China Policy', p. 11.

117. Christopher R. Hughes, *Chinese Nationalism in the Global Era* (London: Routledge, 2006), pp. 154–5.

118. Alexander Vuving, 'Traditional and Modern Sino-Vietnamese Relations', in Reid and Zheng, *Negotiating Asymmetry*, p. 9.

119. Zhao, *Chinese Foreign Policy*, p. 270.

120. Li, 'Security Challenge of an Ascendant China', p. 28; Callahan, *Contingent States*, p. 66.

121. Shambaugh, 'China Engages Asia', p. 81; Kang, 'Getting Asia Wrong', p. 81.

122. 'Abuse Claims Spark Uproar', *China Daily*, 28 November 2005; 'Malaysia Urged to Probe Women Abuse Cases', *China Daily*, 30 November 2005; 'Police Abuse Images Hurt Tourist Confidence', editorial, *China Daily*, 30 November 2005.

123. 'Malaysia Urged to Probe Women Abuse Cases', *China Daily*, 30 November 2005.

124. 'Oriental Daily in Danger of Getting Suspended', *Strait Times*, 20 January 2006.

125. Hughes, *Chinese Nationalism in the Global Era*, p. 81; also Callahan, *Contingent States*, p. 54.

126. Quoted in Hughes, *Chinese Nationalism in the Global Era*, p. 82.

127. The ethnic Chinese account for the following proportion of the total population: Malaysia 29%; Brunei 15%; Cambodia 5%; Indonesia 3.5%; Myanmar 20%; Philippines 2.0%; Thailand 10%; Vietnam 3%. Acharya, 'Containment, Engagement, or Counter-dominance?', p. 134; Chua, *World on Fire*, p. 34.

128. The Chinese government actively promotes its relations with the overseas Chinese; Kurlantzick, *Charm Offensive*, p. 77; also pp. 125–7.

129. Wang Gungwu, *China and the Chinese Overseas* (Singapore: Times Academic Press, 1991), p. 302.

130. Suisheng Zhao, *A Nation-State by Construction: Dynamics of Modern Chinese Nationalism* (Stanford: Stanford University Press, 2004), pp. 280–88.

131. Zhu Feng, 'Why Taiwan Really Matters to China', 30 November 2004, posted on www.irchina.org

132. Chu Yun-han, 'The Political Economy of Taiwan's Identity Crisis: Implications for Northeast Asia', paper given at conference on 'Nationalism and Globalisation in Northeast Asia', Asia Research Centre, London School of Economics, 12 May 2007.

133. Richard Bush, 'Taiwan Faces China: Attraction and Repulsion', in Shambaugh, *Power Shift*, p. 173; Chu Yun-han, 'The Political Economy of Taiwan's Identity Crisis', p. 3.

134. Chu Yun-han, 'The Political Economy of Taiwan's Identity Crisis', p. 9.

135. Chu Yun-han, 'The Political Economy of Taiwan's Identity Crisis', p. 7; Bush, 'Taiwan Faces China', pp. 179–80.

136. Chu Yun-han, 'The Political Economy of Taiwan's Identity Crisis', p. 5.

137. 2005 Taiwan Security Survey, Centre for Election Studies, National Chengchi University, cited in Chu Yun-han, 'The Political Economy of Taiwan's Identity Crisis', p. 8.

138. Ibid. pp. 12, 14.

139. Callahan, *Contingent States*, p. 158.

140. Ibid., pp. 181–2.

141. Ibid., p. 193.

142. Chu Yun-han, 'The Political Economy of Taiwan's Identity Crisis', p. 13.

143. Ibid., pp. 13–14.

144. Ibid., p. 13; Swaine, 'China's Regional Military Posture', pp. 275–6.

145. 'Taiwanese Voted for Ma to Fix the Economy Above All Else', *South China Morning Post*, 24 March 2008; 'New Leader in Taiwan Must Strike a Balance', *International Herald Tribune*, 24 March 2008.

146. Robin Kwong, 'Taiwan to open tech industry to Chinese investment', *Financial Times*, 27 February 2011.

147. Robin Kwong, 'China and Taiwan sign landmark deal', *Financial Times*, 29 June 2010; David Pilling, 'China's bear hug has benefits for wary Taiwan', *Financial Times*, 24 June 2010; Robin Kwong, 'Taiwan begins trade talks with Singapore', *Financial Times*, 5 August 2010.

148. Minnie Chan and Ng Tze-wei, 'Missiles will go one day, Taiwan told', *South China Morning Post*, 24 September 2010.

149. Callahan, *Contingent States*, p. 181; Lampton, 'China's Rise in Asia Need Not Be at America's Expense', p. 321; Robert S. Ross, 'The Geography of Peace: East Asia in the Twenty-first Century', in Brown et al., *The Rise of China*, p. 199.

150. Callahan, *Contingent States*, p. 179.

151. Chu Yun-han, 'The Political Economy of Taiwan's Identity Crisis', p. 15; Callahan, *Contingent States*, pp. 179–80.

152. Bush, 'Taiwan Faces China', p. 183.

153. For example, Shi Yinhong, workshop on Sino-Japanese relations, Renmin-Aichi University conference, Beijing, 8 December 2005.

154. Park, 'Small States and the Search for Sovereignty in Sinocentric Asia', pp. 3–11.

155. Peter Hays Gries, *China's New Nationalism: Pride, Politics, and Diplomacy* (Berkeley: University of California Press, 2004), pp. 39, 70–71.

156. Ibid., p. 79. The best-known recent book, arguing that over 300,000

were killed, is Iris Chang, *The Rape of Nanking* (London: Penguin, 1998). For a Japanese view that denies there was a massacre of any kind, see Higashinakano Shudo, *The Nanking Massacre: Facts Versus Fiction, a Historian's Quest for the Truth* (Tokyo: Sekai Shuppan, 2005), especially Chapter 17. The question remains deeply contentious, with a group of right-wing Liberal Democrat deputies suggesting in a report in June 2007 that only 20,000 died; see 'Japan MPs Play Down 1937 Killings', 19 June 2007, on www.bbc.co.uk/news.

157. The English-language *Japan Times*, for example, constantly carries stories about attempts by Chinese and Korean citizens to seek legal redress for their treatment in the last war, which the Japanese courts summarily dismiss; see for instance, *Japan Times*, 20 April 2005. Also Satoh Haruko, 'The Odd Couple: Japan and China – the Politics of History and Identity', *Commentary*, 4 (9 August 2006), Japanese Institute of International Affairs.

158. Jonathan D. Spence, *The Search for Modern China*, 2nd edn (New York: W. W. Norton, 1999), pp. 423–4, 439. Japan's occupation of Korea between 1910 and 1945 included sex slavery and the kidnapping of Korean women for the Japanese army, the burning down of Korean villages, the banning of the Korean language and religions, and the forced changing of names.

159. Interview with Kyoshi Kojima, Tokyo, June 1999.

160. In 2001 both Hong Kong and Singapore enjoyed a slightly higher GDP per head than Japan, while Taiwan's was 78 per cent and South Korea's was 71 per cent of Japan's; Angus Maddison, *The World Economy: Historical Statistics* (Paris: OECD, 2003), pp. 184–5.

161. Satoh, *The Odd Couple: Japan and China, the Politics of History and Identity* (Japan Institute of International Affairs, 7 August 2006).

162. Interview with Peter Tasker, Tokyo, 8 June 1999.

163. Satoh, *The Odd Couple*.

164. Interview with Zhu Feng, Beijing, 16 November 2005.

165. Drifte, *Japan's Security Relations with China since 1989*, pp. 78–9.

166. Ibid., p. 79; Mike M. Mochizuki, 'China–Japan Relations: Downward Spiral or a New Equilibrium?', in Shambaugh, *Power Shift*, p. 137.

167. Drifte, *Japan's Security Relations with China since 1989*, p. 77.

168. Ibid., pp. 80–81, 83, 88–9; Mochizuki, 'China–Japan Relations', p. 147.

169. David Pilling, 'Less Toxic Relations between Japan and China', *Financial Times*, 6 February 2008.

170. Banyan, 'Japan's love-bubbles for China', *The Economist*, 30 January

2010; Gavan McCormack, 'The US–Japan Security Treaty at 50: Entering Uncharted Waters', 24 June 2010, *Clingendael Asia Studies and Clingendael Asia Forum.*

171. Zhang Yunling, *Designing East Asian FTA*, p. 61.

172. *Japan Times*, 13 April 2005; Shi Yinhong, 'The General Situation of the China–Japan Relations and the Imperative for a Composite Strategy', workshop on Sino-Japanese relations, Renmin-Aichi University conference, Beijing, 2005, p. 2.

173. Ibid., pp. 2–3; *Japan Times*, 13 April 2005.

174. For example, *Japan Times*, 17 April 2005 and 19 June 2005.

175. *International Herald Tribune*, 2 April 2007.

176. Drifte, *Japan's Security Relations with China since 1989*, pp. 183–4.

177. Shi Yinhong, 'The General Situation of the China–Japan Relations and the Imperative for a Composite Strategy', pp. 1, 5.

178. Drifte, *Japan's Security Relations with China since 1989*, pp. 55–60; Shi Yinhong, 'The General Situation of the China–Japan Relations and the Imperative for a Composite Strategy', pp. 3–5.

179. Drifte, *Japan's Security Relations with China since 1989*, pp. 49–51.

180. Frank Ching, 'Diaoyu peace in our time?' *South China Morning Post*, 3 November 2010.

181. Ibid., p. 59.

182. Reinhard Drifte, 'Japanese–Chinese Territorial Disputes in the East China Sea – Between Military Confrontation and Economic Cooperation', pp. 35–6 (unpublished working paper, available to download from http://eprints.lse.ac.uk).

183. Zhao, *A Nation-State by Construction*, pp. 273–5.

184. Interview with Shi Yinhong, Beijing, 26 August 2005.

185. Satoh, *The Odd Couple*; Hirano So, 'Study of Contemporary Political History of East Asian Region – from the Chain Effect of Chinese and Japanese Nationalism Perspective', workshop on Sino-Japanese relations, Renmin-Aichi University conference, Beijing, 8 December 2005.

186. Gries, *China's New Nationalism*, pp. 38, 40; interview with Shi Yinhong, Beijing, 26 August 2005.

187. Shi Yinhong, workshop on Sino-Japanese relations, Renmin Aichi University conference, Beijing, 2005.

188. Perhaps this is the underlying reason for China's more self-confident stance in its relationship with Japan, as evinced by Hu Jintao. Kokubun Ryosei, 'Did the Ice Melt between Japan and China?', conference on 'Nationalism and Globalisation in Northeast Asia', Asia

Research Centre, London School of Economics, 12 May 2007, pp. 1, 9, 11–12.

189. Lampton, 'China's Rise in Asia Need Not Be at America's Expense', p. 320; Michiyo Nakamoto, 'Asia: Displacement activity', *Financial Times*, 22 August 2010.

190. Michiyo Nakamoto, 'China Ousts US as Top Japanese Market', *Financial Times*, 21 August 2008; www.rieti.go.jp/en/columns/a01_0109.html.

191. For a different and optimistic view of their future relationship, based on demographic trends, see Howard W. French, 'For Old Rivals, a Chance at a Grand New Bargain', *International Herald Tribune*, 9 February 2007.

192. Martin Jacques, 'Where is Japan?', seminar paper presented at the Faculty of Media and Communications, Aichi University, 27 July 2005; Martin Jacques, 'The Age of America or the Rise of the East: The Story of the 21st Century', *Aichi University Journal of International Affairs*, 127 (March 2006), pp. 7–8.

193. 'We're Just Good Friends, Honest', *The Economist*, 17 March 2007, p. 73.

194. Drifte, *Japan's Security Relations with China since 1989*, pp. 88–99; Thomas J. Christensen, 'China, the US–Japan Alliance, and the Security Dilemma in East Asia', in Brown et al., *The Rise of China*, pp. 148–9.

195. Christensen, 'China, the US–Japan Alliance, and the Security Dilemma in East Asia', p. 138.

196. For an example of a powerful Japanese voice that believes Japan must rethink its relationship with China, especially after the 2011 tsunami, see Yoichi Funabashi, 'Tokyo has no option but to cleave to China', *Financial Times*, 17 May 2011.

197. Drifte, *Japan's Security Relations with China since 1989*, pp. 180–82.

198. Ross, 'The Geography of Peace in East Asia', pp. 176–8.

199. Interview with Shi Yinhong, Beijing, 19 May 2006; *Strait Times*, 6 February 2006; Jane Perlez, 'As US Influence Wanes, a New Asian Community', *International Herald Tribune*, 4 November 2004.

200. Shambaugh, 'China Engages Asia', p. 93; Kang, 'Getting Asia Wrong', pp. 58, 79, 81–2.

201. It is quite likely that the US will, over time, reduce its land-based military presence in the region; Pollack, 'The Transformation of the Asian Security Order', pp. 338–9, 343.

202. Mure Dickie, 'Japan to shift focus of defence to China', *Financial Times*, 14 December 2010; Minnie Chan, 'Japan's submarine plan raises arms race fears', *South China Morning Post*, 22 October 2010.

203. Yuha Hayashi and Julian E. Barnes, 'Gates Leaves Beijing, Will Press Japan to Expand Its Defense Role', *Wall Street Journal*, 13 January 2011; John Pomfret, 'US raises pressure on China to rein in N. Korea', *Washington Post*, 6 December 2010.

204. Kang, 'Getting Asia Wrong', p. 65; Zhang and Tang, 'China's Regional Strategy', pp. 56–7. A form of containment is the strategy advocated in Aaron L. Friedberg, *A Contest for Supremacy: China, America, and the Struggle for Mastery in Asia* (New York and London: W. W. Norton, 2011), especially Chapter 11.

205. David Pilling, 'Hillary's charm offensive in China's backyard', *Financial Times*, 27 July 2011.

206. Ross, 'The Geography of Peace in East Asia', pp. 170, 187, 190.

10 China as a Rising Global Power

1. Interview with Shi Yinghong, Beijing, 26 August 2005.

2. 'Reaching for a Renaissance: A Special Report on China and Its Region', *The Economist*, 31 March 2007, p. 6; Bijun Wang and Yiping Huang, 'Is there a China model of overseas direct investment?', http://www.eastasiaforum.org/2011/04/12/is-there-a-china-model-of-overseas-direct-investment/, accessed 9 May 2011.

3. Joe Leahy, 'Brazil and China trade tensions set to rise', *Financial Times*, 30 January 2011.

4. Leslie Hook, 'Repsol and Sinopec join forces in Brazil', *Financial Times*, 1 October 2010.

5. 'The dragon in the backyard', Briefing: Latin American geopolitics, *The Economist*, 15 August 2009.

6. Joe Leahy, 'Drawn into an ever closer embrace', *Financial Times*, 20 May 2011; Joe Leahy, 'Financial flows: Commodities are central to defining the relationship', *Financial Times*, 20 May 2011; Martin Wolf, 'Manufacturing at risk from global shift to Asia', *Financial Times*, 20 May 2011.

7. Naomi Mapstone, 'Cash flow into Peru mine brings rights fear', *Financial Times*, 19 January 2011.

8. Joshua Kurlantzick, *Charm Offensive: How China's Soft Power is Transforming the World* (New Haven and London: Yale University Press, 2007), p. 95.

9. Based on FT research, *Financial Times*, 17 January 2011; Shell, *Shell Global Scenarios to 2025: The Future Business Environment – Trends,*

Trade-offs and Choices (Washington, DC: Institute for International Economics, 2005), p. 129.

10. Raymond W. Copson, 'US Response to China's Rise in Africa: Policy and Policy Options', in Marcel Kitissou, ed., *Africa in China's Global Strategy* (London: Adonis and Abbey, 2007), p. 71.

11. Stephen Marks, introduction in Firoze Manji and Stephen Marks, eds, *African Perspectives on China in Africa* (Oxford: Fahamu, 2007), p. 1.

12. Ibid., pp. 2–3.

13. James Lamont and Geoff Dyer, 'China eyes industrial bases in Africa', *Financial Times*, 3 December 2009.

14. Daniel Large, 'As the Beginning Ends: China's Return to Africa', in Manji and Marks, *African Perspectives on China in Africa*, p. 158.

15. Barry Sautman and Yan Hairong, 'Honour and Shame? China's Africa Ties in Comparative Context', in Leni Wild and David Mepham, eds, *The New Sinosphere* (London: Institute for Public Policy Research, 2006), p. 54; Chris Alden, *China in Africa* (London: Zed Books, 2007), p. 67.

16. Ndubisi Obiorah, 'Who's Afraid of China in Africa? Towards an African Civil Society Perspective on China–Africa Relations', in Manji and Marks, *African Perspectives on China in Africa*, pp. 47–8.

17. Alden, *China in Africa*, p. 12.

18. John Rocha, 'A New Frontier in the Exploitation of Africa's Natural Resources: The Emergence of China', in Manji and Marks, *African Perspectives on China in Africa*, p. 22.

19. Leni Wild and David Mepham, introduction in Wild and Mepham, *The New Sinosphere*, p. 2.

20. Deborah Brautigam, *The Dragon's Gift: The Real Story of China in Africa* (Oxford: Oxford University Press, 2009), pp. 183–4; Sautman and Yan, 'Honour and Shame?', p. 58.

21. Brautigam, *The Dragon's Gift*, p. 182; also, Kurlantzick, *Charm Offensive*, p. 97.

22. John Blessing Karumbidza, 'Win–Win Economic Co-operation: Can China Save Zimbabwe's Economy?', in Manji and Marks, *African Perspectives on China in Africa*, p. 89.

23. Alden, *China in Africa*, pp. 14, 39–40; Kitissou, *Africa in China's Global Strategy*, p. 171.

24. Alden, *China in Africa*, p. 49; 'A Troubled Frontier: Chinese Migrants in Senegal', *South China Morning Post*, 17 January 2008.

25. Howard W. French, 'Chinese See a Continent Rich with Possibilities', *International Herald Tribune*, 15 June 2007.

26. Sautman and Yan, 'Honour and Shame?', p. 59.

27. Alden, *China in Africa*, pp. 52–3.

28. Ibid., pp. 52–3, 55, 84–5.

29. Abah Ofon, 'South–South Co-operation: Can Africa Thrive with Chinese Investment?', in Wild and Mepham, *The New Sinosphere*, p. 27.

30. Lindsey Hilsum, 'China, Africa and the G8 – or Why Bob Geldof Needs to Wake Up', in Wild and Mepham, *The New Sinosphere*, pp. 6–7.

31. Mark Curtis and Claire Hickson, 'Arming and Alarming? Arms Exports, Peace and Security', in Wild and Mepham, *The New Sinosphere*, p. 41.

32. Alden, *China in Africa*, p. 26.

33. Interview with Jeffrey Sachs, 'Africa's Long Road Out of Poverty', *International Herald Tribune*, 11 April 2007.

34. Marks, introduction in Manji and Marks, *African Perspectives on China in Africa*, p. 5.

35. Raphael Kaplinsky, 'Winners and Losers: China's Trade Threats and Opportunities for Africa', in Wild and Mepham, *The New Sinosphere*, p. 16.

36. Ibid., p. 18.

37. Ibid.

38. Alden, *China in Africa*, pp. 79–82.

39. Ibid., pp. 44, 68.

40. Rocha, 'A New Frontier in the Exploitation of Africa's Natural Resources', p. 29.

41. Examples of public projects include the construction of an extension to the parliament building in Uganda, presidential palaces in Kinshasa and Harare, and new offices for the ministries of foreign affairs in Angola and Mozambique; Alden, *China in Africa*, p. 23.

42. Brautigam, *The Dragon's Gift*, p. 308.

43. Kaplinsky, 'Winners and Losers', pp. 12–13.

44. Text of Chinese president's speech to Nigerian General Assembly, 27 April 2006, posted on www.fmprc.gov.cn.

45. Sautman and Yan, 'Honour and Shame?', p. 58.

46. Kaplinsky, 'Winners and Losers', pp. 12–13; Marks, introduction in Manji and Marks, *African Perspectives on China in Africa*, pp. 6–7.

47. Zhang Wei-Wei, 'The Allure of the Chinese Model', *International Herald Tribune*, 1 November 2006.

48. The best discussion of this subject can be found in Barry Naughton, 'China's Distinctive System: can it be a model for others?', *Journal of Contemporary China*, 19:65 (June 2010), pp. 437–60.

49. For an interesting discussion of China's involvement in Africa in a broader historical context, see Barry Sautman and Yan Hairong, 'East Mountain Tiger, West Mountain Tiger: China, the West, and "Colonialism" in Africa', *Maryland Series in Contemporary Asian Studies*, 3 (2006).

50. Barry Sautman and Yan Hairong, 'Friends and Interests: China's Distinctive Links with Africa', *African Studies Review*, 50:3 (December 2007), p. 78.

51. See John Reed, 'China's Africa Embrace Evokes Imperialist Memories', *Financial Times*, 27 September 2006.

52. Moeletsi Mbeki, *South African Journal of International Affairs*, 13(1): 7 (2006), quoted in Marks, introduction in Manji and Marks, *African Perspectives on China in Africa*, p. 5.

53. Karumbidza, 'Win-Win Economic Co-operation', p. 95.

54. Rocha, 'A New Frontier in the Exploitation of Africa's Natural Resources', p. 31; Sautman and Yan, 'Honour and Shame?', pp. 55–6. Chris Alden argues that 'at the regional and multilateral levels African reactions to Beijing have been basically lacking in any strategic approach, as well as being fundamentally uncoordinated.' Alden, *China in Africa*, p. 77.

55. 'Briefing: The Chinese in Africa', *The Economist*, 23 April 2011.

56. Stefan Halper, *The Beijing Consensus: How China's Authoritarian Model will Dominate the Twenty-First Century* (New York: Basic Books, 2010), pp. 233–4; Howard W. French and Lydia Polgreen, 'China Brings Its Deep Pockets to Africa', *International Herald Tribune*, 13 August 2007; Alden, *China in Africa*, p. 35.

57. Gideon Rachman, 'China's increasing influence', *Financial Times*, 24 April 2010.

58. Alden, *China in Africa*, pp. 74–6; Michelle Chan-Fishel, 'Environmental Impact: More of the Same?' in Manji and Marks, *African Perspectives on China in Africa*, p. 144.

59. Rocha, 'A New Frontier in the Exploitation of Africa's Natural Resources', p. 25.

60. Brautigam, *The Dragon's Gift*, p. 229.

61. Karumbidza, 'Win-Win Economic Co-operation', p. 101.

62. Simon Shen, 'A constructed (un)reality on China's re-entry into Africa: the Chinese online community perception of Africa (2006–2008)', *Journal of Modern African Studies*, 47:3 (2009), pp. 435–7.

63. Ali Askouri, 'China's Investment in Sudan: Displacing Villages and Destroying Communities', in Manji and Marks, *African Perspectives*

on China in Africa, pp. 74, 80; Curtis and Hickson, 'Arming and Alarming?', p. 41.

64. Jim Yardley, 'China Offers Defense of Its Darfur Stance', *International Herald Tribune*, 8–9 March 2008; Alden, *China in Africa*, pp. 120, 123–4.

65. Geoff Dyer, 'Beijing and troubled nations: Signals of a shift', *Financial Times*, 20 January 2011.

66. Sautman and Yan, 'Honour and Shame?', p. 57.

67. 'Rebels Raid China-run Oil Facility in Ethiopia', *International Herald Tribune*, 25 April 2007; 'Chinese Worker Abducted in Niger', posted on www.bbc.co.uk/news, 7 July 2007; Obiorah, 'Who's Afraid of China in Africa?', pp. 51–2.

68. Alden, *China in Africa*, pp. 102, 106–7, 118, 129.

69. Chris Thompson, '"We can do the job fine from here"', *FT Magazine*, 19/20 June 2010.

70. Alden, *China in Africa*, pp. 9–10, 15, 18–20, 31.

71. 'Briefing: The Chinese in Africa', *The Economist*, 23 April 2011.

72. Geoff Dyer, 'China's policy: Anxious to shed colonial image and foster a new cycle of trade', *Financial Times*, 14 June 2010; James Lamont and Geoff Dyer, 'China eyes industrial bases in Africa', *Financial Times*, 3 December 2009.

73. Zha Daojiong, 'China's Energy Security and Its International Relations', *China and Eurasia Forum Quarterly*, 3:3 (November 2005), p. 40.

74. Ibid., p. 42; http://www.eia.doe.gov/cabs/China/Oil.html, accessed 2 December 2010.

75. John W. Garver, *China and Iran: Ancient Partners in a Post-Imperial World* (Seattle: University of Washington Press, 2006), p. 293.

76. Hassan M. Fattah, 'Avoiding Political Talk, Saudis and Chinese Build Trade', *New York Times*, 23 April 2006.

77. Phar Kim Beng and Vic Y. W. Li, 'China's Energy Dependence on the Middle East: Boon or Bane for Asian Security?', *China and Eurasia Forum Quarterly*, 3:3 (November 2005), p. 24.

78. Garver, *China and Iran*, pp. 2–17.

79. Ibid., p. 28.

80. Ibid., pp. 281, 283.

81. Ibid., pp. 237, 246.

82. Ibid., pp. 256, 265, 271, 275.

83. 'Iran Signs $2bn Oil Deal with China', *Financial Times*, 9 December 2007.

84. Garver, *China and Iran*, p. 295.
85. Ibid., p. 295.
86. Ibid., pp. 296–7.
87. Lowell Dittmer, 'Ghost of the Strategic Triangle: The Sino-Russian Partnership', in Suisheng Zhao, ed., *Chinese Foreign Policy* (New York: M. E. Sharpe, 2004), p. 217.
88. Ibid., p. 213.
89. Ibid., pp. 220–21.
90. Ibid., p. 215.
91. Yu Bin, 'China and Russia: Normalizing Their Strategic Partnership', in David Shambaugh, ed., *Power Shift: China and Asia's New Dynamics* (Berkeley: University of California Press, 2005), pp. 238–9; http://www.eia.doe.gov/cabs/China/Oil.html, accessed 2 December 2010.
92. Stephen Blank, 'China, Kazakh Energy, and Russia: An Unlikely Ménage à Trois', *China and Eurasia Forum Quarterly*, 3:3 (November 2005), p. 105.
93. Ibid., pp. 107–8.
94. Ibid., pp. 105–8.
95. Alexander Monro and Dana Denis-Smith, 'China taps into the heart of Turkmenistan's gas fields', *Financial Times*, 17 December 2009; 'Riches in the near abroad', *The Economist*, 30 January 2010.
96. Lowell Dittmer, 'Ghost of the Strategic Triangle', pp. 220–21.
97. Geoff Dyer, 'Russia Fails to Secure Regional Backing', *Financial Times*, 28 August 2008; Geoff Dyer, 'Russia Could Push China Closer to the West', *Financial Times*, 27 August 2008; Bobo Lo, 'Russia, China and the Georgia Dimension', *Centre for European Reform Bulletin*, 62 (October/November 2008).
98. Meghnad Desai, 'India and China: An Essay in Comparative Political Economy', seminar paper, Asia Research Centre, London School of Economics, 2003, p. 3; revised version available to download from www.imf.org.
99. Amartya Sen, *The Argumentative Indian: Writings on Indian History, Culture and Identity* (London: Allen Lane, 2005), pp. 161–90, especially p. 164.
100. John W. Garver, *Protracted Contest: Sino-Indian Rivalry in the Twentieth Century* (Seattle: University of Washington Press, 2001), pp. 79–80.
101. James Lamont and Amy Kazmin, 'Fear of influence', *Financial Times*, 13 July 2009.
102. James Lamont and Farhan Bokhari, 'China signs $35 bn in deals with Pakistan', *Financial Times*, 19 December 2010.

103. Farhan Bokhari and Kathrin Hille, 'Pakistan turns to China for naval base', *Financial Times*, 22 May 2011.

104. Iskander Rehman, 'Keeping the Dragon at Bay: India's Counter-Containment of China in Asia', *Asia Security*, 5:2, 2009, pp. 122–3.

105. Ibid., pp. 370–73; Prasenjit Duara, 'Visions of History, Trajectories of Power: China and India since De-colonisation', in Anthony Reid and Zheng Yangwen, eds, *Negotiating Asymmetry: China's Place in Asia* (Singapore: NUS Press, 2009), p. 6. Also, Bill Emmott, *Rivals: How the Power Struggle between China, India and Japan Will Shape Our Next Decade* (London: Allen Lane, 2008), pp. 50–51; Vikas Kumar, 'Why is SAARC Perennially Gridlocked and How can it be Revitalized?', *Clingendael Asia Forum*, 16 December 2010.

106. Garver, *Protracted Contest*, p. 368.

107. Ibid., p. 374.

108. Ibid., p. 384.

109. Desai, 'India and China', pp. 2, 8, 10, 12; Martin Wolf, 'On the Move: Asia's Giants Take Different Routes in Pursuit of Economic Greatness', *Financial Times*, 23 February 2005.

110. Tom Wright, 'Wen touts deals and trade ties on trip to India', *Wall Street Journal*, 16 December 2010.

111. Simon Long, 'India and China: The Tiger in Front', survey, *The Economist*, 5 March 2005, p. 10; Shell, *Shell Global Scenarios to 2025*, pp. 137–43; David Pilling, 'India Hits Bottleneck on Way to Prosperity', *Financial Times*, 24 September 2008.

112. Measured in terms of GDP exchange rates. It is over twice as large measured by GDP purchasing power parity; *The Economist, The World in 2007* (London: 2006), pp. 106–7.

113. The inequality figures were compiled by the Asian Development Bank; James Lamont and James Fontanella-Khan, 'India: Writing is on the wall', *Financial Times*, 21 March 2011.

114. Gideon Rachman, 'Welcome to the Nuclear Club, India', *Financial Times*, 22 September 2008.

115. Jo Johnson and Edward Luce, 'Delhi Nuclear Deal Signals US Shift', *Financial Times*, 2 August 2007.

116. Garver, *Protracted Contest*, pp. 376–7.

117. Charles Grant, 'India's Role in the New World Order', *Centre for European Reform Briefing Note* (September 2008).

118. Roger Cohen, 'Nuclear Deal With India a Sign of New US Focus', *International Herald Tribune*, 4–5 March 2006; Rajan Menon and Anatol Lieven, 'Overselling a Nuclear Deal', *International Herald*

Tribune, 7 March 2006; John W. Garver, 'China's Influence in Central and South Asia: Is It Increasing?', in Shambaugh, *Power Shift*, p. 223.

119. Rehman, 'Keeping the Dragon at Bay: India's Counter-Containment of China in Asia', pp. 125–9.

120. Richard Youngs, *Europe's Decline and Fall: The Struggle against Global Irrelevance* (London: Profile Books, 2010), Chapter 1.

121. Katinka Barysch with Charles Grant and Mark Leonard, *Embracing the Dragon: The EU's Partnership with China* (London: Centre for European Reform, 2005), p. 77.

122. Dominique Moisi, 'Europe Must Not Go the Way of Decadent Venice', *Financial Times*, 12 July 2005.

123. For example, Zaki Laïdi, 'How Europe Can Shape the Global System', *Financial Times*, 30 April 2008.

124. Patrick Messerlin and Razeen Sally, 'Why It is Dangerous for Europe to Bash China', *Financial Times*, 13 December 2007.

125. European Commission, 'The Challenge to the EU of a Rising China', in *European Competitiveness Report* (Luxembourg: 2004).

126. In the Italian general election in 2008, growing fears about globalization, amongst other things, were reflected in very big increases in the vote for the anti-globalization, anti-immigration Lega Nord in Milan, Turin, Venice, Bologna and Florence; Erik Jones, 'Italy's Bitterness Could Blight Berlusconi', *Financial Times*, 16 April 2008.

127. Charles Grant with Katinka Barysch, *Can Europe and China Shape a New World Order?* (London: Centre for European Reform, 2008), especially pp. 10–13; also Chapter 3.

128. Ibid., pp. 38–40; James Kynge, *China Shakes the World: The Rise of a Hungry Nation* (London: Weidenfeld and Nicolson, 2006), pp. 82–92, 118–9, 213.

129. Daniel Schäfer, 'China and Germany: Reflected glory', *Financial Times*, 18 January 2011.

130. Kerin Hope and Jamil Anderlini, 'Athens turns to Beijing for bond sale', *Financial Times*, 27 January 2010; Kerin Hope, 'China prepares to invest in Greek projects', *Financial Times*, 14 June 2010.

131. Jonathan Hoslag, 'China builds a bridge across the Danube', *Financial Times*, 27 June 2010. Also, 'Hu wraps up Portugal trip with offer to help fight crisis', *South China Morning Post*, 8 November, 2010.

132. Jamil Anderlini, 'China extends help to tackle euro crisis', *Financial Times*, 21 December 2010; Victor Mallet, 'China's Spanish debt buys put at €6bn', *Financial Times*, 6 January 2011. Also, Lou Jiwei, 'China

can help West build economic growth', *Financial Times*, 27 November 2011; Jamil Anderlini, George Parker and Chris Giles, 'China boost for Osborne growth plans', *Financial Times*, 28 November 2011.

133. James Kynge, Geoff Dyer and James Blitz, 'Bear gifts for friends', *Financial Times*, 15–16 January 2011.

134. Barysch, Grant and Leonard, *Embracing the Dragon*, p. 67.

135. Ibid., pp. 60–65.

136. Shell, *Shell Global Scenarios to 2025*, pp. 126, 144; François Heisbourg, 'Europe Must Be Realistic about Life After Bush', *Financial Times*, 6 February 2008; Philip Stephens, 'A Futile European Contest for Obama's Ear', *Financial Times*, 10 November 2008.

137. James Mann, *The China Fantasy: How Our Leaders Explain Away Chinese Repression* (New York: Viking, 2007), p. 40.

138. Shambaugh, 'Return to the Middle Kingdom?', in Shambaugh, *Power Shift*, p. 28; Bates Gill, 'China's Evolving Regional Security Strategy', in Shambaugh, *Power Shift*, p. 248.

139. Quoted by Joseph Y. S. Cheng and Zhang Wankun, 'Patterns and Dynamics of China's Strategic Behaviour', in Zhao, *Chinese Foreign Policy*, p. 196.

140. For example, Liu Ji, 'Making the Right Choices in Twenty-first Century Sino-American Relations', in ibid., p. 248.

141. For example, David M. Lampton, *Same Bed, Different Dreams: Managing US–China Relations, 1989–2000* (Berkeley: University of California Press, 2001), pp. 372–3.

142. David M. Lampton, 'China's Rise in Asia Need Not Be at America's Expense', in Shambaugh, *Power Shift*, p. 314.

143. Zheng Yongnian, *Discovering Chinese Nationalism in China* (Cambridge: Cambridge University Press, 1999), p. 150.

144. Quoted by Suisheng Zhao in *A Nation-State by Construction: Dynamics of Modern Chinese Nationalism* (Stanford: Stanford University Press, 2004), pp. 35–6.

145. Steven I. Levine, 'Sino-American Relations: Practicing Damage Control', in Samuel S. Kim, ed., *China and the World: Chinese Foreign Policy Faces the New Millennium*, 4th edn (Oxford: Westview Press, 1998), pp. 94–5.

146. Ibid., p. 98.

147. Ibid., p. 93.

148. Ibid., p. 97.

149. Cheng and Zhang, 'Patterns and Dynamics of China's Strategic Behaviour', p. 200; Mann, *The China Fantasy*, pp. 3, 84–8.

150. Lampton, *Same Bed, Different Dreams*, pp. 372–3.

151. Suisheng Zhao, 'Chinese Foreign Policy', in Zhao, *Chinese Foreign Policy*, p. 15.

152. Levine, 'Sino-American Relations', p. 95; Mann, *The China Fantasy*, pp. 1–2.

153. Ibid., pp. 11–12.

154. George W. Bush, 'A Distinctly American Internationalism', speech at Ronald Reagan Library, Simi Valley, California, 19 November 1999.

155. Thomas I. Friedman, *The Lexus and the Olive Tree: Understanding Globalization* (New York: Farrar, Strauss and Giroux, 1999), p. 154.

156. Mann, *The China Fantasy*, p. 12.

157. Levine, 'Sino-American Relations', p. 96.

158. Ibid., pp. 96–7.

159. Robert Ross, 'Engagement in US China Policy', in Alastair Iain Johnston and Robert S. Ross, eds, *Engaging China: The Management of an Emerging Power* (London: Routledge, 1999), p. 179.

160. Lampton, 'China's Rise in Asia Need Not Be at America's Expense', p. 318; *National Security Strategy of the United States of America* (Washington, DC: September 2002); Martin Jacques, 'The Neo-Con Revolution', *Guardian*, 31 March 2005.

161. 'Image of US Falls Again', *International Herald Tribune*, 14 June 2006; 'Unease About Big Powers "Rising"', 27 June 2007, posted on www.bbc.co.uk news; 'Distrust of US Gets Deeper But Not Wider', *International Herald Tribune*, 28 June 2007.

162. Interview with Shi Yinhong, Beijing, 26 August 2005.

163. Robert Ross, 'Engagement in US China Policy', pp. 179–80.

164. Kenneth Lieberthal, 'Why the US Malaise over China?', *YaleGlobal Online*, January 19 2006.

165. Mann, *The China Fantasy*, Chapter 1.

166. Andrew Edgecliff-Johnson et al., 'Wen and Putin lecture western leaders', *Financial Times*, 29 January 2009; 'China pushes for new global super-currency', *South China Morning Post*, 24 March 2009.

167. Yan Xuetong, 'The Instability of China–US relations', *The Chinese Journal of International Politics* (2010), pp. 1–30, especially pp. 14–23.

168. Dani Rodrik, 'Making room for China in the world economy', December 2009, http://www.hks.harvard.edu/fs/drodrik/Research%20papers/Making%20room%20for%20China.pdf; accessed 20 June 2010.

169. Interview with Hu Jintao, *Washington Post*, 17 January 2011.

170. Michael Spence, 'The west is wrong to obsess about the renminbi', *Financial Times*, 21 January 2010.

171. Friedman, *The Lexus and the Olive Tree*, pp. 372–3.

172. 'Red States and Blue Collars', *Financial Times*, 3 August 2007. Hilary Clinton has expressed doubts about whether the Doha round should be revived; 'Clinton Doubts Benefits of Doha Revival', *Financial Times*, 2 December 2007. There has been a major shift amongst mainstream economists, with growing scepticism about the virtues of globalization; Dani Rodrik, 'The Death of the Globalization Consensus', July 2008, posted on www.project-syndicate.org.

173. Clyde Prestowitz, 'The Yuan Might Shift; the Imbalances Won't', *International Herald Tribune*, 1 June 2005; Prestowitz, *Three Billion New Capitalists*, p. 193.

174. Kynge, *China Shakes the World*, pp. 220–21.

175. Mann, *The China Fantasy*, pp. 59–63.

176. David Pilling, 'The President-Elect Must Ease Asian Anxieties', *Financial Times*, 5 November 2008.

177. Pew Global Attitudes Project, *World Publics Welcome Global Trade – But Not Immigration*, 4 October 2007, posted on http://pewglobal. org, p. 14.

178. For respective figures for the number of science and engineering graduates and doctorates in China and the US, with the latter comparing unfavourably, see Prestowitz, *Three Billion New Capitalists*, pp. 132–4. Also, David M. Lampton, 'What Growing Chinese Power Means for America', hearing before the US Senate Committee on Foreign Relations, East Asian and Pacific Affairs Sub-committee, 7 June 2005, pp. 4, 6.

179. Kynge, *China Shakes the World*, pp. 108–14, 117–21, 212–13.

180. Martin Jacques, 'The Death of Doha Signals the Demise of Globalisation', *Guardian*, 13 July 2006.

181. Lampton, 'China's Rise in Asia Need Not Be at America's Expense', p. 322.

182. Ibid., p. 317.

183. Ibid., p. 317.

184. Jeffrey Sachs, 'Amid the Rubble of Global Finance, a Blueprint for Bretton Woods II', *Guardian*, 21 October 2008.

185. Quoted in Lampton, 'China's Rise in Asia Need Not Be at America's Expense', p. 318.

186. Joseph S. Nye, 'Soft Power and the War on Terror', in *Shell Global Scenarios to 2025*, p. 80.

187. Pew Research Center, Global Attitudes Survey 2010, released 17 June 2010.

188. For example, Vice-President Cheney's warnings about Chinese military

spending in February 2007, 'Cheney Warns on Chinese Build-up', 23 February 2007, posted on www.bbc.co.uk/news; 'Rice Assails China on Australia Trip', *International Herald Tribune*, 17 March 2006.

189. The Pentagon has described China as the country with the 'greatest potential to compete militarily' with the US; 'Pentagon Sees China as Rival', *Financial Times*, 5 February 2006.

190. Edward Carr, 'Brushwood and gall', A special report on China's place in the world, *The Economist*, 4 December 2010, p. 7.

191. Peter H. B. Godwin, 'Force and Diplomacy: China Prepares for the Twenty-first Century', in Kim, *China and the World*, p. 188.

192. Yu Bin, 'China and Russia: Normalizing Their Strategic Partnership', p. 240; David Lague, 'Russia-China Arms Trade Wanes', *International Herald Tribune*, 3 March 2008.

193. Kathrin Hille, 'Carriers back China's global reach', *Financial Times*, 17 December 2010; Kathrin Hille, 'China reveals aircraft carrier plans', *Financial Times*, 17 December 2010.

194. Kathrin Hille, 'China missile may cause power shift', *Financial Times*, 28 December 2010.

195. Edward Carr, 'Brushwood and gall', *The Economist*, 4 December 2010, pp. 6–7.

196. Lampton, 'China's Rise in Asia Need Not Be at America's Expense', p. 318; Niall Ferguson, *Colossus: The Rise and Fall of the American Empire* (London: Allen Lane, 2004), Chapters 1, 2; Robert Kagan, *Dangerous Nation: America and the World 1600–1898* (London: Atlantic Books, 2006).

197. For example, Ferguson, *Colossus*, Chapter 8.

198. Howard W. French, 'Is the US Plunging into "Historical Error"?', *International Herald Tribune*, 1 June 2006; Lampton, 'What Growing Chinese Power Means for America', pp. 2–12.

199. 'Chinese Fund Takes $5bn Morgan Stanley Stake', *Financial Times*, 19 December 2007. As of mid December 2007, the Chinese enjoyed stakes of 20%, 9.9%, 10%, 2.6% and 6.6% in Standard Bank, Morgan Stanley, Blackstone, Barclays and Bear Stearns respectively; 'Morgan Stanley Taps China for $5bn', *Financial Times*, 19 December 2007. This, of course, was before the credit crunch.

200. This has already happened in a limited way with China demonstrating its ability to destroy a satellite and then the US doing likewise; 'Chinese Missile Test Against Satellite Was No Surprise to US', *International Herald Tribune*, 24 April 2007; 'US Missile Hits Defunct Satellite', *Financial Times*, 21 February 2008.

201. Katrin Bennhold, 'Mutual trust called crucial to US–China relations', *International Herald Tribune*, 13 September 2010.

202. Aaron L. Friedberg, *A Contest for Supremacy: China, America, and the Struggle for Mastery in Asia* (New York and London: W. W. Norton, 2011), pp. 42–5; Martin Wolf, 'Why America and China Cannot Afford to Fall Out', *Financial Times*, 8 October 2003.

203. 'Reaching for a Renaissance: A Special Report on China and Its Region', *The Economist*, 31 March 2007, p. 13.

204. Elizabeth C. Economy, *The River Runs Black: The Environmental Challenge to China's Future* (Ithaca: Cornell University Press, 2004), Chapter 8; 'China Wants Others to Bear Climate Curbs', *International Herald Tribune*, 7 February 2007; 'Politics Shift as the Planet Heats Up', *International Herald Tribune*, 7–8 April 2007.

205. Lampton, 'What Growing Chinese Power Means for America', p. 10; Lampton, 'China's Rise in Asia Need Not Be at America's Expense', p. 321; Kynge, *China Shakes the World*, pp. 160–61.

206. Levine, 'Sino-American Relations', p. 110.

207. Editorial, 'Not yet out of the Bretton Woods', *Financial Times*, 29 September 2009.

208. Alan Beattie, 'A reach regained', *Financial Times*, 22 April 2010.

209. Geoff Dyer, Jamil Anderlini and Henry Sender, 'China's lending hits new heights', *Financial Times*, 17 January 2011.

210. Keith Bradsher, 'About-face Puts China on Side of India Over High Food Tariffs', *International Herald Tribune*, 31 July 2008.

211. 'World Economic Net Fights to Keep Role: World Bank, IMF and WTO Struggling Under Globalization and Other Pressures', *International Herald Tribune*, 23 May 2007; Timothy Garton Ash, 'One Practical Way to Improve the State of the World: Turn G8 into G14', *Guardian*, 24 January 2008.

212. Anna Fifield, 'G7 meets amid doubts over relevance', *Financial Times*, 6–7 February 2010.

213. Martin Wolf, 'Why China's exchange rate policy concerns us', *Financial Times*, 8 December 2009.

214. Geoff Dyer, 'China's Dollar Dilemma', *Financial Times*, 22 February 2009.

215. Jamil Anderlini and Tracy Alloway, 'Trades reveal China shift from dollar', *Financial Times*, 20 June 2011.

216. James Politi, 'World Bank sees end to dollar's hegemony', *Financial Times*, 17 May 2011.

217. Yu Yongding, 'Comments', IMF Reform Conference, 10 October

2005, and 'The Interactions between China and the World Economy', unpublished paper, Nikkei Simbon Symposium, 5 April 2005.

218. Bob Davis, 'IMF Gives Poor Countries Scarce New Voting Count', *Wall Street Journal*, 31 March 2008; Mark Weisbrot, 'The IMF's Dwindling Fortunes', *Los Angeles Times*, 27 April 2008; Jeffrey Sachs, 'How the Fund Can Regain Global Legitimacy', *Financial Times*, 19 April 2006; George Monbiot, 'Don't Be Fooled By This Reform: The IMF Is Still the Rich Man's Viceroy', *Guardian*, 5 September 2006; Joseph Stiglitz, 'Thanks for Nothing', *Atlantic Monthly*, October 2001.

219. 'Fury as Zimbabwe Sanctions Vetoed', 12 July 2008, posted on www.bbc.co.uk/news.

220. Alan Beattie, 'IMF succession: A contested quarry', *Financial Times*, 25 May 2011; 'Statement from Bric IMF directors', *Financial Times*, 24 May 2011; Martin Wolf, 'Europe should not control the IMF', *Financial Times*, 24 May 2011.

221. Song Jung-a, 'G20 agrees historic reform of IMF', *Financial Times*, 23 October 2010.

222. 'Interview: Message from Wen', *Financial Times*, 1 February 2009; 'China to buy $50 billion of IMF's first bonds', *International Herald Tribune*, 4 September 2010.

223. G. John Ikenberry, 'The Rise of China and the Future of the West: Can the Liberal System Survive?', *Foreign Affairs*, January/February 2008, p. 1 (available at www.foreignaffairs.org).

224. G. John Ikenberry, 'China and the Rest Are Only Joining the American-Built Order', *New Perspectives Quarterly*, Volume 25, No. 3, Summer 2008.

225. Martin Jacques, 'The Citadels of the Global Economy are Yielding to China's Battering Ram', *Guardian*, 23 April 2008.

226. Joseph P. Quinlan, *The Last Economic Superpower: The Retreat of Globalization, the End of American Dominance, and What We Can Do About It* (New York: McGraw Hill, 2011), p. 97.

227. Yu Yongding, 'The Evolving Exchange Rate Regimes in East Asia', unpublished paper, 12 March 2005, p. 9.

228. Interview with Shi Yinhong, 19 May 2006.

229. Kevin Brown, Robert Cookson and Geoff Dyer, 'Malaysian boost for Beijing's renminbi hopes', *Financial Times*, 19 September 2010; Song Jung-a and Robert Cookson, 'South Korea seeks to shift reserves to China', *Financial Times*, 4 May 2011.

230. Robert Cookson and Geoff Dyer, 'Yuan direction', *Financial Times*, 14 December 2010; Shai Oster, Dinny McMahon and Tom Lauricella,

'Offshore Trading in Yuan Takes Off', *Wall Street Journal*, 14 December 2010; Chen Xingdong, 'RMB convertibility and two-way floating', *Economics Inside China*, September 2010, BNP Paribas, pp. 16–17; Cary Huang, 'Najib calls for expanded yuan role', *South China Morning Post*, 5 June 2010; James Kynge, 'China's "locally global" financial reforms', *Financial Times*, 27 November 2009; Friedrich Wu, 'The Renminbi Challenge: the future role of the Chinese currency', *The International Economy*, Fall 2009, pp. 32–53.

11 When China Rules The World

1. Yu Yongding, *China Daily*, 23 December 2010.
2. Martin Wolf, 'Wen is right to worry about China's growth', *Financial Times*, 21 September 2010.
3. Dominic Wilson and Anna Stupnytska, 'The N-11: More Than an Acronym', *Goldman Sachs Global Economics Paper*, 153 (28 March 2007), p. 8. This followed an earlier paper in 2003 which suggested 2041; Dominic Wilson and Roopa Purushothaman, 'Dreaming with BRICs: The Path to 2050', *Goldman Sachs Global Economics Paper* 99 (2003), p. 10.
4. Jamil Anderlini, 'China cements role as top of the Brics', *Financial Times*, 14 April 2011.
5. 'Faced with a Steep Learning Curve', *Financial Times* special report on global brands, 23 April 2007.
6. William A. Callahan, *Contingent States: Greater China and Transnational Relations* (Minneapolis: University of Minnesota, 2004), pp. 158–9.
7. Antonio Gramsci, *Selections from the Prison Notebooks* (London: Lawrence and Wishart, 1971), pp. 12–13, 206–8, 333, 416–18.
8. Joseph S. Nye Jr, *Soft Power: The Means to Success in World Politics* (New York: Public Affairs, 2004), Chapter 1.
9. Maev Kennedy, 'On the March: Terracotta Army Aims for Ticket Office Triumph', *Guardian*, 8 February 2007.
10. 'Great Wall Overtakes Florence for Tourists', 20 May 2005, posted on http://news.ft.com.
11. Edward L. Dreyer, *Zheng He: China and the Oceans in the Early Ming Dynasty, 1405–1433* (New York: Pearson Longman, 2007), p. 170.
12. My thanks to Zhang Feng for these observations. See also 'Columbus

or Zheng He? Debate Rages On', *China Daily*, 19 July 2007, especially the views of Ge Jianxiong.

13. 'Chinese Maritime Hero Commemorated', *China Daily*, 30 August 2005.

14. Gavin Menzies, *1421: The Year China Discovered The World* (London: Bantam Books, 2003).

15. Geoff Wade, 'Don't Be Deceived: Our History Really is Under Serious Attack', *Canberra Times*, 27 April 2006.

16. Quoted in Chris Alden, *China in Africa* (London: Zed Books, 2007), p. 19.

17. Patrick L. Smith, 'Museum's Display Links the Birth of Golf to China', *International Herald Tribune*, 1 March 2006.

18. Tim Johnson and Julie Sell, 'Getting relics home', *South China Morning Post*, 5 March 2009; Geoff Dyer, 'Beijing bronzes expose faultline with west', *Financial Times*, 6 March 2009.

19. Nicholas D. Kristof, 'Glory is as Ephemeral as Smoke and Clouds', *International Herald Tribune*, 23 May 2005.

20. Dava Sobel, *Longitude* (London: Fourth Estate, 1998).

21. Lucian W. Pye, *The Spirit of Chinese Politics* (Cambridge, Mass.: Harvard University Press, 1992), p. 235.

22. Suisheng Zhao, *A Nation-State by Construction: Dynamics of Modern Chinese Nationalism* (Stanford: Stanford University Press, 2004), pp. 147–9.

23. David C. Kang, 'Getting Asia Wrong: The Need for New Analytical Frameworks', *International Security*, 27:4 (Spring 2003), pp. 57, 61–5.

24. Ibid., pp. 66–8, 79–82.

25. Ibid., pp. 57–85.

26. It is noteworthy that in 2006 the Chinese government committed to establish special economic enclaves in five African countries where Chinese businesses are to enjoy privileged treatment as well as preferential access to Chinese capital and African markets; Chris Alden, Daniel Large and Ricardo Soares de Oliveira, eds, *China Returns to Africa: A Rising Power and a Continent Embrace* (London: Hurst, 2008), pp. 357–8.

27. 'Buying farmland abroad: Outsourcing's third wave', *The Economist*, 21 May 2009.

28. Angus Maddison, *The World Economy: Historical Statistics* (Paris: OECD, 2003), p. 258.

29. For a very interesting article on the decline of the United States, and

the West, in this context, see Niall Ferguson, 'Empire Falls', October 2006, posted on www.vanityfair.com.

30. Angus Maddison, *The World Economy. A Millennial Perspective* (Paris: OECD, 2006), p. 128.

31. Howard W. French, 'For Old Rivals, a Chance at a Grand New Bargain', *International Herald Tribune*, 9 February 2007.

32. Alan Wheatley, 'Preparing for China's tourist boom', *International Herald Tribune*, 21 December 2010.

33. Wolfgang Georg Arlt, *China's Outbound Tourism* (London: Routledge, 2006), pp. 67, 227–8.

34. 'China Soon to be World's Biggest Internet User', *Guardian*, 25 January 2007; 'US Slips on the Web', *International Herald Tribune*, 11 May 2006.

35. Martin Jacques, 'Global Hierarchy of Race', *Guardian*, 20 September 2003.

36. Wang Xiaodong, 'Chinese Nationalism Under the Shadow of Globalisation', lecture, London School of Economics, 7 February 2005, pp. 1–2.

37. Zhao, *A Nation-State by Construction*, pp. 147–9.

38. Alastair Iain Johnston and Robert S. Ross, *New Directions in the Study of China's Foreign Policy* (Stanford: Stanford University Press, 2006), pp. 410–11.

39. Zi Zhongyun, 'The Clash of Ideas: Ideology and Sino-US Relations', in Suisheng Zhao, ed., *Chinese Foreign Policy: Pragmatism and Strategic Behaviour* (New York: M. E. Sharpe, 2004), pp. 224–42.

40. Richard Gott, 'Latin America is Preparing to Settle Accounts with Its White Settler Elite', *Guardian*, 15 November 2006; Amy Chua, *World on Fire: How Exporting Free Market Democracy Breeds Ethnic Hatred and Global Instability* (London: William Heinemann, 2003), Chapter 2.

41. 'A Battle of Cultures in Milan's Chinatown', *International Herald Tribune*, 27 April 2007; also 'Chinese Entrepreneurs Upset French Neighbors', *International Herald Tribune*, 6 June 2007.

42. Guy Dinmore, 'Tuscan town turns against Chinese migrants', *Financial Times*, 8 February 2010.

43. www.ft.com/FT500.

44. Geoff Dyer, 'Consequences of stronger RMB dawn on US', *Financial Times*, 23 February 2010.

45. Jing Ulrich, 'Insight: China Prepares for Overseas Investment', *Financial Times*, 7 August 2007.

46. United Nations Conference on Trade and Development, data as of 29 July 2011. Also 'China's Overseas Investment Rises 60% Annually', 2 February 2007, posted on www.chinadaily.com.cn/bizchina.

47. 'Morgan Stanley Taps China for $5bn', *Financial Times*, 19 December 2007; Tony Jackson, 'The Chinese Bank Plan is One to Watch', *Financial Times*, 23 July 2007; Geoff Dyer and Sundeep Tucker, 'In Search of Illumination: Chinese Companies Expand Overseas', *Financial Times*, 3 December 2007.

48. Zhou Ping and Loet Leydesdorff, 'The Emergence of China as a Leading Nation in Science', *Research Policy*, 35 (2006), pp. 83–104.

49. Geoff Dyer, 'The Dragon's Lab – How China is Rising Through the Innovation Ranks', *Financial Times*, 5 January 2007.

50. 'Chinese Spacecraft Back to Earth', 17 October 2005, posted on www.bbc.co.uk/news.

51. 'China's Missile Test Holds Signal for US', *International Herald Tribune*, 20–21 January 2007; 'China Uses Space Technology as Diplomatic Trump Card', *International Herald Tribune*, 24 May 2007.

52. 'It's a Multi-Currency World We Live In', *Financial Times*, 26 December 2007; Benn Steil, 'A Rising Euro Threatens American Dominance', *Financial Times*, 22 April 2008.

53. Daniel Dombey, 'America Faces a Diplomatic Penalty as the Dollar Dwindles', *Financial Times*, 27 December 2007.

54. Quoted in ibid.

55. Ibid.

56. Avinash D. Persaud, 'The Dollar Standard: (Only the) Beginning of the End', posted on http://opendemocracy.net; Avinash D. Persaud, 'When Currency Empires Fall', posted on www.gresham.ac.uk.

57. Mark Leonard, *What Does China Think?* (London: Fourth Estate, 2008), p. 120.

58. Eric Hobsbawm, 'America's Neo-Conservative World Supremacists Will Fail', *Guardian*, 25 June 2005.

59. Alastair Ian Johnston, *Cultural Realism: Strategic Culture and Grand Strategy in Chinese History* (Princeton: Princeton University Press, 1995), pp. 258–9.

60. Robert Kagan, *Dangerous Nation: America and the World 1600–1898* (London: Atlantic Books, 2006), p. 304.

61. Callahan, *Contingent States*, pp. 28–44.

62. Yan Xuetong, 'The Rise of China in Chinese Eyes', *Journal of Contemporary China*, 10:26 (2001), p. 34.

63. Callahan, *Contingent States*, p. 34.

64. Robert Ross, 'The Geography of Peace: East Asia in the Twenty-first Century', in Michael Brown et al., eds, *The Rise of China* (Cambridge, Mass.: MIT Press, 2000), pp. 189–90, 193.

65. Callahan, *Contingent States*, pp. 34–7.

66. Johnston, *Cultural Realism*, p. 249.

67. Callahan, *Contingent States*, pp. 34–5.

68. Wang Xiaodong, *Chinese Youth's Views on the World: A Survey Report* (Beijing: China Youth Research Centre, 2003), pp. 27–8.

69. Wang Gungwu, 'Early Ming Relations with Southeast Asia: A Background Essay', in John King Fairbank, ed., *The Chinese World Order: Traditional China's Foreign Relations* (Cambridge, Mass.: Harvard University Press, 1968), p. 61.

70. Ibid.

71. Interview with Shi Yinhong, Beijing, 19 May 2006.

72. Pankaj Mishra, 'Getting Rich', *London Review of Books*, 30 November 2006, pp. 6–7.

73. John Gray, '(Re-)Ordering the World: Dilemmas of Liberal Imperialism', *RSA Journal*, 2:6 (2002), p. 52. Also, Akash Kapur, 'Upholding a tradition of tolerance', *International Herald Tribune*, 12 February 2010.

74. Richard Gowan and Franziska Branter, *The EU and Human Rights at the UN: 2010 Review*, European Council on Foreign Relations, 2010.

75. Lucian W. Pye, 'China: Erratic State, Frustrated Society', *Foreign Affairs*, 69:4 (Fall 1990), pp. 56–74.

76. Ibid., pp. 56–74.

77. The statistics and projections are based on Janamitra Devan, Stefano Negri, and Jonathan R. Woetzel, 'Meeting the challenges of China's growing cities', *The McKinsey Quarterly*, 2008 Number 3, pp. 107–116; also, Kam Wing Chan, 'Measuring the urban millions', *China Economic Quarterly*, March 2009, pp. 21–6 and Tom Miller, 'Big cities, small cities', *China Economic Quarterly*, March 2009, pp. 27–31.

78. Bettina Wassener and Andrea Deng, 'Taking the high road, with 1,200 aboard', *International Herald Tribune*, 18 August 2010; Niall Firth, '3D Express Coach: The Chinese bus that solves traffic jams by letting you drive UNDERNEATH it', *Daily Mail*, 7 August 2010.

79. 'Foreign and Chinese Delegates Flock to First Confucius Institute Conference', 6 July 2006, posted on http://english.peopledaily.com.cn.

80. 'Chinese Language Fever Brings Opportunities and Harmony to the World', 13 July 2006, posted on http://english.people.com.cn; Michael Vatikiotis, 'The Soft Power of "Happy Chinese"', *International Herald Tribune*, 18 January 2006.

81. James Lamont, 'Turning deaf ear to Mandarin no longer wise', *Financial Times*, 3 October 2010; James Lamont and Geoff Dyer, 'Wen's trip to India stirs old squabbles', *Financial Times*, 14 December 2010.

82. Joshua Kurlantzick, *Charm Offensive: How China's Soft Power is Transforming the World* (New Haven and London: Yale University Press, 2007), pp. 68–9.

83. 'Chicago Hub of Chinese Learning in US', *China Daily*, 17 May 2006.

84. Sam Dillon, 'Foreign Languages Fade in Class – Except Chinese', *New York Times*, 20 January 2010.

85. Julian Borger, 'America in "Critical Need" of Mandarin', *Guardian Weekly*, 10–16 March 2006; 'Demand for Chinese Language Courses in US Soars', *China Daily*, 23 November 2005; 'Mandarin Lessons for All – in UK School', *Strait Times*, 21 January 2006; 'The Future is … Mandarin', *Guardian*, 6 April 2004; 'Mandarin Learning Sours Outside China', 29 July 2007, posted on www.bbc.co.uk/news.

86. 'English Today, Mandarin by 2020?', September 2006, posted on www.pbs.org; 'Beijing Sets Up Its Own Internet Domains', *International Herald Tribune*, 21 March 2006.

87. David Crystal, *English as a Global Language* (Cambridge: Cambridge University Press, 1997), p. 113.

88. Ibid., Chapter 1; p. 117.

89. http://www.timeshighereducation.co.uk/world-university-rankings/ 2010-2011/top-200.html; accessed 19 April 2011.

90. http://ed.sjtu.edu.cn/ranking.htm.

91. Della Bradshaw, 'Chinese Business Schools Move Up Rankings', *Financial Times*, 31 October 2004.

92. David Shambaugh, 'China Engages Asia: Reshaping the Regional Order', *International Security*, 29:3 (Winter 2004/5), p. 78.

93. http://www.nytimes.com/2010/11/15/us/15international.html; accessed 19 April 2011.

94. Howard W. French, 'China Luring Scholars to Make Universities Great', *New York Times*, 28 October 2008; Arian Eunjung Cha, 'Opportunities in China Lure Scientists Home', *Washington Post Foreign Service*, 20 February 2008.

95. Xan Rice, 'China's Long March', *Observer Sport Monthly*, 80 (October 2006).

96. Michael Curtin, *Playing to the World's Biggest Audience: The Globalization of Chinese Film and TV* (Berkeley: University of California Press, 2007), p. 3; also p. 10.

97. Steve Rose, 'The Great Fall of China', *Guardian*, 1 August 2002;

interview with Gong Li, 'I Don't Go to Hollywood. Hollywood Goes to China', *Guardian*, 6 April 2007; David Barboza, 'Made-in-China Blockbusters: Success that Can Sting', *International Herald Tribune*, 29 June 2007; Mark Landler, 'Paper Tigers, Hidden Knockoffs Flood Market', *International Herald Tribune*, 4 July 2001.

98. See Gary Gang Xu, *Sinascape: Contemporary Chinese Cinema* (Oxford: Rowman and Littlefield, 2007).

99. 'KungFuBustle', *China Business Weekly*, 14–20 November 2005.

100. Vivienne Chow, 'Newly rich mainlanders push antique prices through the roof', *South China Morning Post*, 15 March 2010.

101. David Barboza, 'At Christie's Auction, New Records for Chinese Art', *International Herald Tribune*, 29 November 2006; David Barboza, 'In China's New Revolution, Art Greets Capitalism', *International Herald Tribune*, 4 January 2007; Jonathan Watts, 'Once Hated, Now Fêted – Chinese Artists Come Out From Behind the Wall', *Guardian*, 11 April 2007; Souren Melikian, 'The Chinese Advance: More Bids, Many Buys', *International Herald Tribune*, 8–9 April 2006.

102. Kurlantzick, *Charm Offensive*, p. 63.

103. David Shambaugh, 'China flexes its soft power', *International Herald Tribune*, 8 June 2010.

104. David Barboza, 'The Games Are Golden for Beijing Network', *International Herald Tribune*, 23–24 August 2008.

105. Kathrin Hille and Tom Mitchell, 'News Corp sells control of its China TV channels', *Financial Times*, 9 August 2010.

106. Edwin Heathcote, 'Power Games', *Financial Times*, 19 July 2008; Nicolai Ouroussoff, 'Beijing Unveils a Landmark Olympics Stadium', *International Herald Tribune*, 7 August 2008.

107. Shi Jiangtao and Al Guo, 'Clear View for the Games?', *South China Morning Post*, 21 July 2008.

108. Christopher Clarey, 'Spectacle Has Viewers Floating on Air in Beijing', *International Herald Tribune*, 9–10 August 2008.

109. Pete Thamel, 'Future of NBA Lies in China and Millions of Fans', *International Herald Tribune*, 11 August 2008.

110. Frank Ching, 'Sport For All in China', *South China Morning Post*, 8 September 2004; Rice, 'China's Long March'; Brook Larmer, 'The Center of the World', *Foreign Policy*, September–October 2005; Ian Whittell, 'How a Small Step for Yao Can Become a Giant leap for China', *The Times*, 10 February 2007; Chih-ming Wang, 'Capitalizing the Big Man: Yao Ming, Asian America, and the China Global', *Inter-Asia Cultural Studies*, 5:2 (2004).

111. David Y. H. Wu and Sidney C. H. Cheung, eds, *The Globalization of Chinese Food* (London: RoutledgeCurzon, 2004), pp. 2–7; P. Y. Ho and F. P. Lisowski, *A Brief History of Chinese Medicine and Its Influence* (Singapore: World Scientific, 1998), p. 37.

112. Wu and Cheung, *The Globalization of Chinese Food*, pp. 5–6.

113. Ibid., pp. 10–11.

114. Ibid., pp. 9–10.

115. Ho and Lisowski, *A Brief History of Chinese Medicine*, pp. 52–3.

116. Alok Jha, 'Not Just a Bunch of Plant Extracts', *Guardian*, 25 March 2004; Mure Dickie, 'Chinese Traditional Medicine Gets a Dose of Modernisation', *Financial Times*, 7 November 2003; 'Traditional Chinese Medicine: Potions and Profits', *The Economist*, 27 July 2002.

117. 'A Tough Sell for Western Drugs', *International Herald Tribune*, 26 December 2007.

118. Tony Blair's premiership perhaps constituted the most extreme case of this.

119. US National Intelligence Council, *Global Trends 2025: A Transformed World* (November 2008), p. xi; also pp. 1–2, 97. (Posted on www.dni.gov/nic/NIC_2025_project.html.)

120. Robert Kagan, 'The Case for a League of Democracies', *Financial Times*, 13 May 2008; Gideon Rachman, 'Why McCain's Big Idea is a Bad Idea', *Financial Times*, 5 May 2008.

121. Based on Pew Research Center polls; Andrew Kohut, 'Friend or Foe? How Americans see China', *Wall Street Journal*, 13 January 2011.

12 Concluding Remarks: The Eight Differences that Define China

1. Paul A. Cohen, *Discovering History in China: American Historical Writing on the Recent Chinese Past* (New York: Columbia University Press, 1984), p. 95.

2. Yan Xuetong, 'The Rise of China in Chinese Eyes', *Journal of Contemporary China*, 10:26 (2001), pp. 33–4.

3. John King Fairbank, ed., *The Chinese World Order: Traditional China's Foreign Relations* (Cambridge, Mass.: Harvard University Press, 1968), p. 62.

13 Afterword

1. Keith B. Richburg, 'Is China a rival to the US? Many Chinese think not – or not yet', *Washington Post*, 8 February 2011.
2. Andrew Ward and Geoff Dyer, 'Nineteen countries shun Nobel Prize ceremony', *Financial Times*, 7 December 2010; Geoff Dyer and Ralph Jennings, 'China snubs Nobel with rival peace prize', *Financial Times*, 8 December 2010.
3. David Shambaugh, 'Coping with Conflicted China', *The Washington Quarterly*, Winter 2011, pp. 18–19.
4. Henry Kissinger, *On China* (London: Allen Lane, 2011), p. 2.
5. Yan Xuetong, *Ancient Chinese Thought, Modern Chinese Power* (Princeton: Princeton University Press, 2011), especially Chapters 1–3; Yan Xuetong, 'International leadership and norm evolution', *Chinese Journal of International Politics*, Vol. 4, no. 3 (autumn 2011), pp. 233–64.
6. Peter Marsh, 'China noses ahead as top goods producer', *Financial Times*, 13 March 2011.
7. Daniel Schäfer, 'China and Germany: Reflected glory', *Financial Times*, 18 January 2011.
8. Based on research by the *Financial Times*: Geoff Dyer, Jamil Anderlini and Henry Sender, 'China's lending hits new heights', *Financial Times*, 17 January 2011.
9. Geoff Dyer, David Pilling and Henry Sender, 'A strategy to straddle the planet', *Financial Times*, 17 January 2011.
10. Cited in Robert Cookson and Geoff Dyer, 'Yuan direction', *Financial Times*, 14 December 2010.
11. 'Developed nations' refers to the US, Canada, Japan, Australia, New Zealand, the UK, Ireland, Belgium, France, Germany, Spain, Portugal, Italy, the Netherlands, Sweden, Switzerland, Denmark, Norway, Finland and Austria.
12. James Politi, 'World Bank sees end to dollar's hegemony', *Financial Times*, 17 May 2011.
13. Andrew Ward, 'The old world order is melting away', *Financial Times*, 17 December 2009.
14. François Godement and Jonas Parello-Plesner with Alice Richard, 'The Scramble for Europe', Policy Brief, European Council on Foreign Relations, July 2011, pp. 1–12.
15. Simon Rabinovitch, 'China calls on US to "protect investors"', *Financial Times*, 20 July 2011.

16. Daniel Schäfer, 'China and Germany: Reflected Glory', *Financial Times*, 18 January 2011.

17. Liz Alderman, 'Beijing seen striving for influence in Europe', *International Herald Tribune*, 2 November 2010; Henry Sender, 'China has much to gain from supporting the euro', *Financial Times*, 3 February 2011; David Oakley and Anousha Sakoui, 'China offers Spain 1bn euro confidence vote', *Financial Times*, 12 July 2010.

18. Simon Rabinovitch, 'ESFS head optimistic of China's support', *Financial Times*, 28 October 2011; Jamil Anderlini and Richard Milne, 'China could play a key role in EU rescue', *Financial Times*, 27 October 2011; Yu Yongding, 'Bejing will not ride to eurozone's rescue', *Financial Times*, 31 October 2011.

19. Joseph S. Nye, *Soft Power: The Means to Success in World Politics* (New York: Public Affairs, 2004), p. 8.

20. Ibid., p. 11.

21. Ibid., p. 17.

22. 'America's transport infrastructure: Life in the slow lane', *The Economist*, 30 April 2011.

23. Howard Gardner, *To Open Minds* (New York: Basic Books, 1989), pp. 9–15, 118, 150–51, 217–18.

24. Amy Chua, *Battle Hymn of the Tiger Mother* (New York: Penguin Press, 2011)

25. OECD, *PISA 2009 Results: What Students Know and Can Do – Student Performance in Reading, Mathematics and Science, Volume 1* (Paris: OECD, 2010), pp. 54–6, 134–5, 151–2; D. D. Guttenplan and Sam Dillon, 'West picks through the rubble as Chinese shine in student test', *New York Times*, 8 December 2010; Nick Anderson, 'US students in middle of global pack', *Washington Post*, 7 December 2010; Henry Mance, 'Why are Chinese schoolkids so good?' http://blogs.ft.com/beyond-brics/2010/12/07/why-are-chinese-schoolkids-so-good/(accessed 8/12/2010).

26. Jamil Anderlini and Kathrin Hille, 'China: A sharper focus', *Financial Times*, 10 May 2011.

27. Geoff Dyer, Kathrin Hille and Patti Waldmeir, 'Chinese steer clear of "Jasmine revolution"', *Financial Times*, 20 February 2011.

28. James Bell, 'Upbeat Chinese May Not Be Primed for a Jasmine Revolution', *Pew Research Center Publications*, 31 March 2011.

29. Tony Saich, 'Chinese governance seen through the people's eyes', *East Asia Forum*, 24 July 2011.

30. R. Bin Wong, *China Transformed: Historical Change and the Limits of*

European Experience (Ithaca and London: Cornell University Press, 2000), pp. 90–91, 96–7, 99.

31. Gao Xu, 'State-owned enterprises in China: How big are they?', East AsiaPacific/Blog, World Bank, posted 19 January 2010.

32. Geoff Dyer and Richard McGregor, 'China's Champions: Why State Ownership is No Longer Proving a Dead Hand', *Financial Times*, 16 March 2008.

33. Barry Naughton, 'China's Distinctive System: can it be a model for others?', *Journal of Contemporary China* 19:65 (June 2010), pp. 452–7. There were extensive and far-reaching reforms of the Chinese state, notably in 1982, 1988, 1993 and 1998, far greater than anything attempted in the West during this period, and this remains a continuing process; David Shambaugh (ed.), *The Modern Chinese State*, pp. 167, 174–81.

34. Karen Tumulty and Ed O'Keefe, 'The government tends to resist reorganization', *Washington Post*, 28 January 2011.

35. Barry Naughton, 'China's Distinctive System: can it be a model for others?', pp. 445, 447–8.

36. Ibid., pp. 444–5.

37. Chris Giles, 'Spectre of stagnating incomes stalks globe', *Financial Times*, 27 June 2011.

38. Francis Fukuyama, 'US democracy has little to teach China', *Financial Times*, 17 January 2011.

39. Charles Krauthammer, 'Decline is a Choice: the New Liberalism and the end of American ascendancy', *The Weekly Standard*, Volume 015, Issue 05, 19 October 2009.

40. Robert Moran, 'The Beltway Ponders America's Global Influence', *NationalJournal.com*, 9 February 2010.

41. Nouriel Roubini, 'A presidency heading for a fiscal train wreck', *Financial Times*, 28 October 2010.

42. Michael Mandelbaum, *The Frugal Superpower: America's Global Leadership in a Cash-Strapped Era* (New York: Public Affairs, 2010), p. 24.

43. Raghuram G. Rajan, *Fault Lines: How Hidden Fractures Still Threaten the World Economy* (Princeton and Oxford: Princeton University Press, 2010), p. 8.

44. James Kynge, Richard McGregor, Daniel Dombey, Martin Arnold, Helen Warrell and Cynthia O'Murchu, 'The China Syndrome', *Financial Times*, 3 March 2011.

45. Nathan Hodge and Julian E. Barnes, 'Pentagon Faces the Knife', *Wall Street Journal*, 7 January 2011.

46. Michael Mandelbaum, *The Frugal Superpower*, pp. 5, 183.

47. Richard McGregor, 'US loses its appetite for job as the world's policeman', *Financial Times*, 3 March 2011.

48. Aaron L. Friedberg, *The Contest for Supremacy: China, America, and the Struggle for Mastery in Asia* (W. W. Norton: New York, 2011), Chapter 11.

49. Peter Spiegel, 'Gates warns Nato alliance at risk', *Financial Times*, 10 June 2011.

50. Mandelbaum, *The Frugal Superpower*, pp. 186–90.

51. Andrew J. Bacevich, *Washington Rules: America's Path to Permanent War* (New York: Metropolitan Books, 2010), p. 228.

52. Ibid., pp. 32–4; David Ignatius, 'Ike was right: Cut defense', *Washington Post*, 26 January 2011.

53. Four new Republican governors have made swingeing cuts in state spending, especially education, during the course of 2011 in an attempt to reign in state deficits; 'The right's brave swingers', *The Economist*, 17 September 2011.

54. Chen Xingdong, 'China in 2015: Growth Transition', in Chen Xingdong, Isaac Meng and Hiroshi Shiraishi, *China in 2015*, BNP Paribas, October 2010, pp. 3–94, especially p. 24; Economic Focus, 'How to get a date', *The Economist*, 31 December 2011.

Guide to Further Reading

It is difficult, a little invidious even, to select a relative handful of books from the vast range of sources – including books, academic and newspaper articles, lectures, talks, seminars, personal conversations, conference proceedings and countless interviews – that I have used in writing this book. Nonetheless, having spent years burrowing away, I feel it is my responsibility to offer a rather more selective list of books for the reader who might want to explore aspects of the subject matter a little further. I cannot provide any titles that offer the same kind of sweep as this book but no doubt, in due course, as China's rise continues, there will be several and eventually a multitude.

I have mainly used three general histories of China, though others have been published more recently. The best is John King Fairbank and Merle Goldman, *China: A New History* (Cambridge, Mass.: Belknap Press of Harvard University Press, 2006), but I also found Jonathan D. Spence, *The Search for Modern China*, 2nd edn (New York: W. W. Norton, 1999), and Jacques Gernet, *A History of Chinese Civilization*, 2nd edn (Cambridge: Cambridge University Press, 1996), very useful. Julia Lovell, *The Great Wall: China against the World 1000 BC–AD 2000* (London: Atlantic Books, 2006), is a highly readable account of the Wall as a metaphor for the long process of China's expansion, while Peter C. Perdue, *China Marches West: The Qing Conquest of Central Eurasia* (Cambridge, Mass.: Belknap Press of Harvard University Press, 2005), is a formidable account of the huge expansion of Chinese territory that took place under the Qing dynasty. Edward L. Dreyer, *Zheng He: China and the Oceans in the Early Ming Dynasty, 1405–1433* (New York: Pearson Longman, 2007), examines one of the most remarkable achievements in Chinese history. Although Jared Diamond, *Guns, Germs and Steel: A Short History of Everybody for the Last 13,000 Years* (London: Vintage, 1998), only has a little about China, in a few short pages he demonstrates just how untypical Chinese civilization is in the broader global story.

There are many books that deal with Europe's rise and the failure of China to industrialize from the end of the eighteenth century. Kenneth Pomeranz, *The Great Divergence: China, Europe, and the Making of the Modern World Economy* (Princeton and Oxford: Princeton University Press, 2000), and R. Bin Wong, *China Transformed: Historical Change and the Limits of European Experience* (Ithaca and London: Cornell University Press, 2000), have been amongst the most prominent recently in arguing that Europe's rise was largely a consequence of contingent factors; Pomeranz's book has become a key book in this context. Mark Elvin, *The Pattern of the Chinese Past* (London: Eyre Methuen, 1973), still remains essential reading for those seeking an explanation of why China lost out on industralization. I also found C. A. Bayly, *The Birth of the Modern World 1780–1914: Global Connections and Comparisons* (Oxford: Blackwell, 2004), by taking a global frame of reference, useful in arriving at a broader picture.

Göran Therborn, *European Modernity and Beyond: The Trajectory of European Societies, 1945–2000* (London: Sage, 1995), offers a powerful argument on the exceptionalism of European modernity. Deepak Lal, *Unintended Consequences* (Cambridge, Mass.: MIT Press, 1998), raises interesting questions concerning long-running cultural differences between diverse peoples and civilizations and what lies behind them. There is one outstanding book on the nature of Japanese culture, and that is Ruth Benedict's *The Chrysanthemum and the Sword: Patterns of Japanese Culture* (London: Secker and Warburg, 1947), which, though written over sixty years ago, remains a classic on how to analyse cultural difference. Kosaku Yoshino, *Cultural Nationalism in Contemporary Japan* (London: Routledge, 1992), offers interesting insights into Japanese identity, while Michio Morishima, *Why Has Japan 'Succeeded'?: Western Technology and the Japanese Ethos* (Cambridge: Cambridge University Press, 1984), is an excellent general history.

On the nature and extent of East Asia's Westernization, discussed in Chapter 5, I would mention K. C. Chang, *Food in Chinese Culture: Anthropological and Historical Perspectives* (New Haven: Yale University Press, 1977), and especially Nicholas Ostler, *Empires of the Word* (London: HarperCollins, 2005), which tells the story of world history through languages and makes some illuminating points about Mandarin in this context. Lucian W. Pye, *Asian Power and Politics: The Cultural Dimensions of Authority* (Cambridge, Mass.: Harvard University Press, 1985), provides a perceptive account of the distinctive characteristics of East Asian politics, though it is much stronger on North-East than South-East Asia.

Moving into Part II, many books have been published on China's rise but the great majority tend to deal with its economic aspects, with surprisingly few taking a more general approach. One of the most useful of these is James Kynge, *China Shakes the World: The Rise of a Hungry Nation* (London: Weidenfeld and Nicolson, 2006), which is highly readable and has a distinctive take. I would also mention David M. Lampton, *The Three Faces of Chinese Power: Might, Money, and Minds* (Berkeley: University of California Press, 2008). Paul A. Cohen, *Discovering History in China: American Historical Writing on the Recent Chinese Past* (New York: Columbia University Press, 1984), raises interesting questions about the nature of American writing and interpretation of contemporary China. Although arguably a little dated, Lucian W. Pye, *The Spirit of Chinese Politics* (Cambridge, Mass.: Harvard University Press, 1992), displays a remarkable ability to grasp some of the underlying characteristics of Chinese politics, in a very accessible manner, which has few if any peers. On the civilization-state and related matters, I would highly recommend William A. Callahan, *Contingent States: Greater China and Transnational Relations* (Minneapolis: University of Minnesota Press, 2004). Callahan is one of the few Western writers who does not view China through a mainly Western prism, but seeks to understand it on its own terms.

The speed of Chinese economic growth means that books inevitably tend to become a little dated rather quickly. Barry Naughton, *The*

Chinese Economy: Transitions and Growth (Cambridge Mass.: MIT Press, 2007), is a comprehensive review of Chinese economic development after 1949 and subsequently during the reform period, while Peter Nolan, *Transforming China: Globalisation, Transition and Development* (London: Anthem Press, 2005), offers an interesting assessment of the global prospects for Chinese companies. Elizabeth C. Economy, *The River Runs Black: The Environmental Challenge to China's Future* (Ithaca: Cornell University Press, 2004), discusses China's environmental challenge, which can explored in more topical fashion on www.chinadialogue.net, a website devoted to China's environment.

Zheng Yongnian, *Will China Become Democratic?: Elite, Class and Regime Transition* (Singapore: EAI, 2004), is a very useful assessment of political trends in contemporary China, while Suisheng Zhao, *A Nation-State by Construction: Dynamics of Modern Chinese Nationalism* (Stanford: Stanford University Press, 2004), provides an excellent analysis of the development of the Chinese nation-state. Christopher R. Hughes, *Chinese Nationalism in the Global Era* (London: Routledge, 2006), is one of a number of recent books exploring Chinese nationalism.

As explained in Chapter 8, all too little has been written about race and ethnicity in China, though there is more on the Chinese sense of cultural superiority. In the parched territory of the former, Frank Dikötter, *The Discourse of Race in Modern China* (London: Hurst and Company, 1992), remains, alas, something of an oasis. I would like to be able to mention books by Chinese writers but there is really only one, the important essay (written as Epilogue) by Chen Kuan-Hsing in his book *Asia as Method: Towards De-Imperialization* (Durham and London: Duke University Press, 2010). A version of this can also be found at www.interasia.org/khchen/online/Epilogue.pdf. Wang Gungwu, *The Chineseness of China: Selected Essays* (Oxford: Oxford University Press, 1991), is, as the title suggests, a perceptive and informative study of China's distinctiveness.

As for China's relationship with East Asia, there remains no better book on the tributary-state system than John King Fairbank, ed., *The Chinese World Order: Traditional China's Foreign Relations*

(Cambridge, Mass.: Harvard University Press, 1968). The best survey of China's present relations with its neighbours is David Shambaugh, ed., *Power Shift: China and Asia's New Dynamics* (Berkeley: University of California Press, 2005).

On China's relationship with the wider world, John W. Garver's two books – *China and Iran: Ancient Partners in a Post-Imperial World* (Seattle: University of Washington Press, 2006) and *Protracted Contest: Sino-Indian Rivalry in the Twentieth Century* (Seattle: University of Washington Press: 2001), are models of their kind. There are many books on the Sino-American relationship, with David M. Lampton, *Same Bed, Different Dreams: Managing US–China Relations, 1989–2000* (Berkeley: University of California Press, 2001), being the most comprehensive.

On a contemporary note, Mark Leonard, *What Does China Think?* (London: Fourth Estate, 2008), provides an interesting guide to present thinking across a range of subjects amongst Chinese intellectuals and policy-makers.

In a different vein, Henry Kissinger's *On China* (London: Allen Lane, 2011) is a fascinating account of China by one of the authors of the Mao–Nixon rapprochement. Unlike the vast majority of Western politicians, Kissinger displays a shrewd appreciation, and respect for, all that is different about China.

Finally, for those of a statistical persuasion, there are two books by that doyen of historical statistics, Angus Maddison, who sadly died in 2010, namely *Chinese Economic Performance in the Long Run, Second Edition, Revised and Updated: 960–2030 AD* (Paris: OECD, 2007) and *The World Economy* (Paris: OECD, 2007). The latter combines two volumes originally published separately: 1: *A Millennial Perspective* and 2: *Historical Statistics*. They provide essential data for anyone who wants to understand Chinese historical trends. All economic historians owe him a debt of gratitude.

Select Bibliography

Acharya, Amitav, 'Containment, Engagement, or Counter-dominance? Malaysia's Response to the Rise of China', in Alastair Iain Johnston and Robert S. Ross, eds, *Engaging China: The Management of an Emerging Power* (London: Routledge, 1999)

Aikawa, Kayoko, 'The Story of Kimono', in Atsushi Ueda, ed., *The Electric Geisha: Exploring Japan's Popular Culture* (Tokyo: Kodansha International, 1994)

Akao, Nobutoshi, 'Re-energizing Japan's Asean Policy', *AJISS-Commentary*, 2 August 2007, posted on www.jiia.or.jp/en/

Alden, Chris, *China in Africa* (London: Zed Books, 2007)

—— Daniel Large and Ricardo Soares de Oliveira, eds, *China Returns to Africa: A Rising Power and a Continent Embrace* (London: Hurst, 2008)

Alderman, Liz, 'Beijing seen striving for influence in Europe', *International Herald Tribune*, 2 November 2010

Allen, G. C., *A Short Economic History of Modern Japan* (London: George Allen and Unwin, 1962)

Anderlini, Jamil, 'Chinese lost billions in diversity drive', *Financial Times*, 15 March 2009

—— 'German industrialists attack Chinese', *Financial Times*, 18 July 2010

—— 'Foreign Companies "losing out" in China', *Financial Times*, 2 September 2010

—— 'China extends help to tackle euro crisis', *Financial Times*, 21 December 2010

—— 'China cements role as top of the Brics', *Financial Times*, 14 April 2011

—— with Alloway, Tracy, 'Trades reveal China shift from dollar', *Financial Times*, 20 June 2011

Anderson, Benedict, *Imagined Communities: Reflections on the Origin and Spread of Nationalism* (London: Verso, 1983)

—— *The Spectre of Comparisons: Nationalism, Southeast Asia, and the World* (London: Verso, 1998)

Anderson, Nick, 'US students in middle of global pack', *Washington Post*, 7 December 2010

Arlt, Wolfgang Georg, *China's Outbound Tourism* (London: Routledge, 2006)

Arrighi, Giovanni, *Adam Smith in Beijing: Lineages of the Twenty-First Century* (London: Verso, 2007)

Askouri, Ali, 'China's Investment in Sudan: Displacing Villages and Destroying Communities', in Firoze Manji and Stephen Marks, eds, *African Perspectives on China in Africa* (Oxford: Fahamu, 2007)

Bacevich, Andrew J., *Washington Rules: America's Path to Permanent War* (New York: Metropolitan Books, 2010)

Bairoch, Paul, *De Jéricho à Mexico: Villes et économie dans l'historie* (Paris: Gallimard, 1985)

—— and Maurice Levy-Leboyer, eds, *Disparities in Economic Development since the Industrial Revolution* (New York: St Martin's Press, 1975)

Barthes, Roland, *Empire of Signs* (New York: Hill and Wang, 1982)

Barysch, Katinka, with Charles Grant and Mark Leonard, *Embracing the Dragon: The EU's Partnership with China* (London: Centre for European Reform, 2005)

Batson, Andrew, 'Sum of iPhone parts: trade distortion', *Wall Street Journal*, 16 December 2010

Bayly, C. A., *The Birth of the Modern World 1780–1914: Global Connections and Comparisons* (Oxford: Blackwell, 2004)

Bayly, Christopher, and Tim Harper, *Forgotten Armies: The Fall of British Asia, 1941–1945* (London: Allen Lane, 2004)

Beattie, Alan, 'A reach regained', *Financial Times*, 22 April 2010

—— 'IMF succession: A contested quarry', *Financial Times*, 25 May 2011

Beedham, Brian, 'Who Are We, Who Are They?', survey, *The Economist*, 29 July 1999

Bell, Daniel A., *China's New Confucianism: Politics and Everyday Life in a Changing Society* (Princeton: Princeton University Press, 2008)

—— and Hahm Chaibong, eds, *Confucianism for the Modern World* (Cambridge: Cambridge University Press, 2003)

Benedict, Ruth, *The Chrysanthemum and the Sword: Patterns of Japanese Culture* (London: Secker and Warburg, 1947)

Beng, Phar Kim, and Vic Y. W. Li, 'China's Energy Dependence on the Middle East: Boon or Bane for Asian Security?' *The China and Eurasia Forum Quarterly*, 3:3 (November 2005)

Bennhold, Katrin, 'Mutual trust called crucial to US–China relations', *International Herald Tribune*, 13 September 2010

Bernstein, Richard, and Ross H. Munro, *The Coming Conflict with China* (New York: Alfred A. Knopf, 1997)

Bickers, Robert, *The Scramble for China: Foreign Devils in the Qing Empire, 1832–1914* (London: Allen Lane, 2011)

Biers, Dan, *Crash of '97* (Hong Kong: Far Eastern Economic Review, 1998)

Bin Wong, R., *China Transformed: Historical Change and the Limits of European Experience* (Ithaca and London: Cornell University Press, 2000)

Blackburn, Robin, 'Enslavement and Industrialisation', posted on www.bbc.co.uk/history

Blank, Stephen, 'China, Kazakh Energy, and Russia: An Unlikely Ménage à Trois', *The China and Eurasia Forum Quarterly*, 3:3 (November 2005)

Bokhari, Farhan, and Kathrin Hille, 'Pakistan turns to China for naval base', *Financial Times*, 22 May 2011

Bonnett, Alastair, *The Idea of the West: Culture, Politics and History* (London: Palgrave Macmillan, 2004)

Bowring, Philip, 'China and Its Minorities', *International Herald Tribune*, 3 March 2008

Bracken, Paul, *Fire in the East: The Rise of Asian Military Power and the Second Nuclear Age* (London: HarperCollins, 1999)

Bradsher, Keith, 'Currency dispute hots up in China', *International Herald Tribune*, 26 March 2010

—— 'Coal abounds, but China veers to sun and wind, too', *International Herald Tribune*, 3 July 2009

—— 'Chinese firms take commanding lead in production of renewable energy', *International Herald Tribune*, 2 June 2010

—— 'China taking solar challenge to US turf', *International Herald Tribune*, 26 August 2009

Branigan, Tania, '"If I see them, I run. That's how I live." Africans living on the edge in China', *Guardian*, 7 October 2010

Brautigam, Deborah, *The Dragon's Gift: The Real Story of China in Africa* (Oxford: Oxford University Press, 2009)

Broad, William J., 'China plans to lead world in getting to bottom of sea', *International Herald Tribune*, 13 September 2010

Brown, Kerry, *Struggling Giant: China in the 21st Century* (London: Anthem Press, 2007)

Brown, Kevin, Robert Cookson and Geoff Dyer, 'Malaysian boost for Beijing's renminbi hopes', *Financial Times*, 19 September 2010

Brown, Lester R., 'A New World Order', *Guardian*, 25 January 2006

Brown, Michael, et al., eds, *The Rise of China* (Cambridge, Mass.: MIT Press, 2000)

Bush, George W., State of the Union Address, 29 January 2002

Bush, Richard, 'Taiwan Faces China: Attraction and Repulsion', in David Shambaugh, ed., *Power Shift: China and Asia's New Dynamics* (Berkeley: University of California Press, 2005)

Callahan, William A., *Contingent States: Greater China and Transnational Relations* (Minneapolis: University of Minnesota Press, 2004)

—— *China: The Pessoptimist Nation* (Oxford: Oxford University Press, 2010)

Carr, Edward, 'Brushwood and gall', A special report on China's place in the world, *The Economist*, 4 December 2010

Castells, Manuel, *The Information Age: Economy, Society and Culture*: Vol. I, *The Rise of the Network Society*, 1996; Vol. II, *The Power of Identity*, 1997; Vol. III, *End of Millennium*, 1998 (Oxford: Blackwell)

Cha, Victor D., 'Engaging China: The View from Korea', in Alastair Iain Johnston and Robert S. Ross, eds, *Engaging China: The Management of an Emerging Power* (London: Routledge, 1999)

Chan, Allen, 'The Grand Illusion: The Long History of Multiculturalism in an Era of Invented Indigenisation', unpublished paper for Swedish-NUS conference, 'Asia-Europe and Global Processes', Singapore, 14–16 March 2001

Chan, Kam Wing, 'Measuring the urban millions', *China Economic Quarterly*, March 2009, pp. 21–6

Chan, Minnie, and Ng Tze-wei, 'Missiles will go one day, Taiwan told', *South China Morning Post*, 24 September 2010

——'Japan's submarine plan raises arms race fears', *South China Morning Post*, 22 October 2010

Chang, Gordon G., *The Coming Collapse of China* (London: Arrow Books, 2002)

Chang, Iris, *The Rape of Nanking* (London: Penguin, 1998)

Chang, Jung, and Jon Halliday, *Mao: The Unknown Story* (London: Jonathan Cape, 2005)

Chang, K. C., *Food in Chinese Culture: Anthropological and Historical Perspectives* (New Haven: Yale University Press, 1977)

Chase-Dunn, Christopher, et al., 'The Trajectory of the United States in the World System: A Quantitative Reflection', IROWS Working Paper No. 8, University of California

Chen Jian, *Mao's China and the Cold War* (Chapel Hill, NC: University of North Carolina Press, 2001)

Chen Kuan-Hsing, ed., *Trajectories: Inter-Asia Cultural Studies* (London: Routledge, 1998)

—— ed., 'Civil Society and Min-jian: On Political Society and Popular Democracy', *Cultural Studies*, 17:6 (2003)

—— 'Notes on Han Chinese Racism', unpublished paper, 2007 (revised version, 2009, available at www.inter-asia.org/khchen/online/Epilogue.pdf)

—— *Asia as Method: Towards De-Imperialization* (Durham, NC and London: Duke University Press, 2010)

Chen Jian, *Mao's China and the Cold War* (Chapel Hill and London: The University of North Carolina Press, 2001)

Chen, Jie, and Bruce J. Dickson, *Allies of the State: China's Private Entrepreneurs and Democratic Change* (Cambridge, Massachusetts and London: Harvard University Press, 2010)

Chen Xingdong, 'RMB convertibility and two-way floating', *Economics Inside China*, September 2010, BNP Paribas

Cheng Chin-Chuan, 'Chinese Varieties of English', in Braj B. Kachru, ed., *The Other Tongue: English Across Cultures* (Urbana and Chicago: University of Illinois Press, 1992)

Cheng Youhua, et al., 'Urban Planning in Shanghai towards the 21st Century', *Dialogue* (Taipei), February/March 1999

Ching, Frank, 'Diaoyu peace in our time?' *South China Morning Post*, 3 November 2010

Ching, Leo, 'Yellow Skin, White Mask: Race, Class and Identification in Japanese Cultural Discourse', in Chen Kuan-Hsing, ed., *Trajectories: Inter-Asia Cultural Studies* (London: Routledge, 1998)

Choi Chi-yuk and Ng Tze-wei, 'Xinjiang to lift blackout in "gradual and orderly" way', *South China Morning Post*, 30 December 2009

Chow, Kai-wing, 'Imagining Boundaries of Blood: Zhang Binglin and the Invention of the Han "Race" in Modern China', in Frank Dikötter, ed., *The Construction of Racial Identities in China and Japan: Historical and Contemporary Perspectives* (London: Hurst and Company, 1997)

Chow, Vivienne, 'Newly rich mainlanders push antique prices through the roof', *South China Morning Post*, 15 March 2010

Christensen, Thomas J., 'China, the US–Japan Alliance, and the Security Dilemma in East Asia', in Michael Brown et al., eds, *The Rise of China* (Cambridge, Mass.: MIT Press, 2000)

——Alastair Iain Johnston and Robert S. Ross, 'Conclusions and Future Directions', in Alastair Iain Johnston and Robert S. Ross, eds, *New Directions in the Study of China's Foreign Policy* (Stanford: Stanford University Press, 2006)

—— Robert Cookson and Geoff Dyer, 'Yuan direction', *Financial Times*, 14 December 2010

Chu Shulong, 'US Security Strategy in Asia and the Regional Security Regime: A Chinese View', paper for IIPS International Conference, Tokyo, 30 November–1 December 2004

Chu Yun-han, 'The Political Economy of Taiwan's Identity Crisis: Implications for Northeast Asia', paper given at conference on 'Nationalism and Globalisation in Northeast Asia', Asia Research Centre, London School of Economics, 2007

Chua, Amy, *World on Fire: How Exporting Free Market Democracy Breeds Ethnic Hatred and Global Instability* (London: William Heinemann, 2003)

—— *Battle Hymn of the Tiger Mother* (New York: The Penguin Press, 2011)

Chua, Beng-Huat, 'Postcolonial Sites, Global Flows and Fashion Codes: A Case-study of Power *Cheongsams* and Other Clothing Styles in Modern Singapore', *Postcolonial Studies*, 3:3 (2000)

—— 'Conceptualising an East Asian Popular Culture', *Inter-Asian Cultural Studies*, 5:2 (2004)

Chung, Erin, 'Anti-Black Racism in China', 12 April 2005, and 'Nanjing Anti-African Protests of 1988–89', posted on www.amren.com

Chung, Jae Ho, 'China's Ascendancy and the Korean Peninsula: From Interest Revaluation to Strategic Realignment?', in David Shambaugh, ed., *Power Shift: China and Asia's New Dynamics* (Berkeley: University of California Press, 2005)

Clarke, J. J., *Oriental Enlightenment: The Encounter Between Asian and Western Thought* (London: Routledge, 1997)

Cohen, Paul A., *Discovering History in China: American Historical Writing on the Recent Chinese Past* (New York: Columbia University Press, 1984)

Cohen, Robin, *Global Diasporas: An Introduction* (London: UCL Press, 1997)

Confucius, *The Analects*, trans. Arthur Waley (Beijing: Beijing Foreign Languages Teaching and Research Press, 1997)

Cooper, Robert, *The Breaking of Nations: Order and Chaos in the Twenty-first Century* (London: Atlantic Books, 2003)

—— 'Civilise or Die', *Guardian*, 23 October 2003

Copson, Raymond W., 'US response to China's Rise in Africa: Policy and Policy Options', in Marcel Kitissou, ed., *Africa in China's Global Strategy* (London: Adonis and Abbey, 2007)

Crystal, David, *English as a Global Language* (Cambridge: Cambridge University Press, 1997)

Cui Jia and Zhu Zhe, 'Xinjiang support package unveiled', *China Daily*, 21 May, 2010

Curtin, Michael, *Playing to the World's Biggest Audience: The Globalization of Chinese Film and TV* (Berkeley: University of California Press, 2007)

Curtis, Mark, and Claire Hickson, 'Arming and Alarming? Arms Exports, Peace and Security', in Leni Wild and David Mepham, eds, *The New Sinosphere* (London: Institute for Public Policy Research, 2006)

Cwiertka, Katarzyna, 'Culinary Globalization and Japan', *Japan Echo*, 26:3 (June 1999)

Dabringhaus, Sabine, and Roderich Ptak, eds, *China and Her Neighbours: Borders, Visions of the Other, Foreign Policy 10th to 19th Century* (Wiesbaden: Harrassowitz, 1999)

Davies, Norman, *Europe: A History* (Oxford: Oxford University Press, 1996)

Davis, David Brion, *Inhuman Bondage: The Rise and Fall of Slavery in the New World* (New York: Oxford University Press, 2005)

Dean, Kenneth, 'Despotic Empire/Nation-State: Local Responses to Chinese Nationalism in an Age of Global Capitalism', in Chen Kuan-Hsing, ed., *Trajectories: Inter-Asia Cultural Studies* (London: Routledge, 1998)

Dentsu Institute for Human Studies, *Life in the Era of Globalisation: Uncertain Germans and Japanese Versus Confident Americans and British, the Second Comparative Analysis of Global Values* (Tokyo: July 1998)

Desai, Meghnad, 'India and China: An Essay in Comparative Political Economy', seminar paper, Asia Research Centre, London School of Economics, 2003. Revised version available to download from www.imf.org.

Deutsch, Anthony, and Henry Sender, 'Indonesia uneasy about links with China', *Financial Times*, 30 April/1 May 2011

Devan, Janamitra, Stefano Negri, and Jonathan R. Woetzel, 'Meeting the challenges of China's growing cities', *The McKinsey Quarterly*, 2008, Number 3, pp. 107–16

Diamond, Jared, *Guns, Germs and Steel: A Short History of Everybody for the Last 13,000 Years* (London: Vintage, 1998)

Dickie, Mure, 'Japan to shift focus of defence to China', *Financial Times*, 14 December 2010

Dikötter, Frank, *The Discourse of Race in Modern China* (London: Hurst and Company, 1992)

—— ed., *The Construction of Racial Identities in China and Japan:*

Historical and Contemporary Perspectives (London: Hurst and Company, 1997)

—— Introduction to his *The Construction of Racial Identities in China and Japan*

—— 'Racial Discourse in China: Continuities and Permutations', in his *The Construction of Racial Identities in China and Japan*

—— *Mao's Great Famine: The History of China's Most Devastating Catastrophe, 1958–62* (London: Bloomsbury, 2010)

Dillon, Sam, 'Foreign Languages Fade in Class – Except Chinese', *New York Times*, 20 January 2010

Dinmore, Guy, 'Tuscan town turns against Chinese migrants', *Financial Times*, 8 February 2010

Dittmer, Lowell, 'Ghost of the Strategic Triangle: The Sino-Russian Partnership', in Zhao Suisheng, ed., *Chinese Foreign Policy: Pragmatism and Strategic Behavior* (New York: M. E. Sharpe, 2004)

Dombey, Daniel, and Gideon Rachman, 'US and the world: Mapped out', *Financial Times*, 2 June 2010

Dore, R., *The End of Jobs for Life? Corporate Employment Systems: Japan and Elsewhere* (London: Centre for Economic Performance, 1996)

Dower, John W., *Embracing Defeat: Japan in the Wake of World War II* (New York: Norton, 2000)

Downs, Erica Strecker, and Phillip C. Sanders, 'Legitimacy and the Limits of Nationalism: China and the Diaoyu Islands', in Michael Brown et al., eds, *The Rise of China* (Cambridge, Mass.: MIT Press, 2000)

Dreyer, Edward L., *Zheng He: China and the Oceans in the Early Ming Dynasty, 1405–1433* (New York: Pearson Longman, 2007)

Drifte, Reinhard, 'Japanese–Chinese Territorial Disputes in the East China Sea – Between Military Confrontation and Economic Cooperation', unpublished working paper, available to download from http://eprints.lse.ac.uk

—— *Japan's Foreign Policy for the 21st Century* (Basingstoke: Macmillan, 1998)

—— *Japan's Security Relations with China since 1989: From Balancing to Band-wagoning* (London: RoutledgeCurzon, 2003)

Duara, Prasenjit, *Rescuing History from the Nation: Questioning Narratives of Modern China* (Chicago and London: The University of Chicago Press, 1995)

—— *The Global and Regional in China's Nation-Formation* (Oxford and New York: Routledge, 2009)

—— 'Visions of History, Trajectories of Power: China and India since De-colonisation', in Anthony Reid and Zheng Yangwen, eds, *Negotiating Asymmetry: China's Place in Asia* (Singapore: NUS Press, 2009)

Dunlop, Fuchsia, 'Enthused by China's Tea Infusions', *Financial Times*, 11–12 September 2004

Dyer, Geoff, 'The Great Brawl of China', *Financial Times*, 11 July 2008

—— 'How China is Rising Through the Innovation Ranks', *Financial Times*, 5 January 2007

—— 'Russia Could Push China Closer to the West', *Financial Times*, 27 August 2008

—— 'Russia Fails to Secure Regional Backing', *Financial Times*, 28 August 2008

—— 'Beijing bronzes expose faultline with west', *Financial Times*, 6 March 2009

—— 'Consequences of stronger RMB dawn on US', *Financial Times*, 23 February 2010

—— 'China: A populist rising', *Financial Times*, 9 March 2010

—— 'China's policy: Anxious to shed colonial image and foster a new cycle of trade', *Financial Times*, 14 June 2010

—— 'Wen calls bluff of moaning multinationals', *Financial Times*, 20 July 2010

—— 'China: A new core rises', *Financial Times*, 3 August 2010

—— 'Power play in the South China Sea', *Financial Times*, 9 August 2010

—— 'Beijing's elevated aspirations', *Financial Times*, 10 November 2010

—— 'Beijing and troubled nations: Signals of a shift', *Financial Times*, 20 January 2011

—— and Jamil Anderlini, 'Distant Thunder: Separatism Stirs on China's Forgotten Frontier', *Financial Times*, 17 August 2008

—— Jamil Anderlini and Henry Sender, 'China's lending hits new heights', *Financial Times*, 17 January 2011

—— Ralph Jennings, 'China snubs Nobel with rival peace prize', *Financial Times*, 8 December 2010

—— Richard McGregor, 'China's Champions: Why State Ownership is No Longer Proving a Dead Hand', *Financial Times*, 16 March 2008

—— and David Pilling and Henry Sender, 'A strategy to straddle the planet', *Financial Times*, 17 January 2011

Economy, Elizabeth C., 'China, the United States and the World Trade Organization', Council on Foreign Relations, Washington, DC, 3 July 2002

—— *The River Runs Black: The Environmental Challenge to China's Future* (Ithaca: Cornell University Press, 2004)

Edgecliff-Johnson, Andrew, et al., 'Wen and Putin lecture western leaders', *Financial Times*, 29 January 2009

Eichengreen, Barry, *Exorbitant Privilege: The Rise and Fall of the Dollar and the Future of the International Monetary System* (New York: Oxford University Press, 2011)

Elvin, Mark, *The Pattern of the Chinese Past* (London: Eyre Methuen, 1973)

—— 'Secular Karma: The Communist Revolution Understood in Traditional Chinese Terms', in Mabel Lee and A. D. Syrokomia-Stefanowski, eds, *Modernisation of the Chinese Past* (Sydney: University of Sydney, School of Asian Studies, 1993)

—— *The Retreat of the Elephants: An Environmental History of China* (New Haven and London: Yale University Press, 2004)

—— 'The Historian as Haruspex', *New Left Review*, 52, July–August 2008

Emmott, Bill, 'The Sun Also Rises', survey, *The Economist*, 8 October 2005

—— *Rivals: How the Power Struggle Between China, India and Japan Will Shape Our Next Decade* (London: Allen Lane, 2008)

European Commission, 'The Challenge to the EU of a Rising China', in *European Competitiveness Report* (Luxembourg: 2004)

European Council on Foreign Relations and Asia Centre à SciencesPo, 'Climate Policies After Copenhagen', *China Analysis*, 27

Fairbank, John King, ed., *The Chinese World Order: Traditional China's Foreign Relations* (Cambridge, Mass.: Harvard University Press, 1968)

—— and Merle Goldman, *China: A New History* (Cambridge, Mass.: Belknap Press of Harvard University Press, 2006)

Featherstone, Mike, ed., *Global Culture: Nationalism, Globalization and Modernity* (London: Sage, 1990)

Fenby, Jonathan, *The Penguin History of Modern China: The Fall and Rise of a Great Power, 1850–2008* (London: Allen Lane, 2008)

Ferguson, Niall, *Colossus: The Rise and Fall of the American Empire* (London: Allen Lane, 2004)

—— *Empire: How Britain Made the Modern World* (London: Penguin, 2004)

—— 'Empire Falls', October 2006, posted on www.vanityfair.com

—— *Civilization: The West and the Rest* (London: Allen Lane, 2011)

Fernandez-Armesto, Felipe, *Millennium: A History of Our Last Thousand Years* (London: Bantam Press, 1995)

Fifield, Anna, 'G7 meets amid doubts over relevance', *Financial Times*, 6–7 February 2010

Firth, Niall, '3D Express Coach: The Chinese bus that solves traffic jams by letting you drive UNDERNEATH it', *Daily Mail*, 7 August 2010

Fishman, Ted C., *China, Inc.: The Relentless Rise of the Next Great Super-power* (London: Pocket Books, 2005)

Fitzgerald, John, *Awakening China: Politics, Culture, and Class in the Nationalist Revolution* (Stanford: Stanford University Press, 1996)

Frank, Andre Gunder, *ReOrient: Global Economy in the Asian Age* (Berkeley: University of California Press, 1998)

French, Howard W., 'Is the US Plunging into "Historical Error"?', *International Herald Tribune*, 1 June 2006

—— 'For Old Rivals, a Chance at a Grand New Bargain', *International Herald Tribune*, 9 February 2007

—— 'Chinese See a Continent Rich with Possibilities', *International Herald Tribune*, 15 June 2007

—— 'Side by Side in China, While Still Worlds Apart', *International Herald Tribune*, 20 March 2008

—— 'Again, Beijing Cues Up its Propaganda Machine', *International Herald Tribune*, 4 April 2008

—— 'China Luring Scholars to Make Universities Great', *New York Times*, 28 October 2008

—— and Lydia Polgreen, 'China Brings Its Deep Pockets to Africa', *International Herald Tribune*, 13 August 2007

Friedman, Thomas L., *The Lexus and the Olive Tree: Understanding Globalization* (New York: Farrar, Straus and Giroux, 1999)

—— 'Democrats and China', *International Herald Tribune*, 11–12 November 2006

—— 'China's Sunshine Boys', *International Herald Tribune*, 7 December 2006

—— *The World is Flat: A Brief History of the Globalized World in the Twenty-first Century* (London: Allen Lane, 2005)

—— and Michael Mandelbaum, *That Used to be US: What Went Wrong with America? And How it Can Come Back* (London: Little, Brown, 2011)

Fukuyama, Francis, 'The End of History?', *National Interest*, 16, Summer 1989

—— *The End of History and the Last Man* (London: Hamish Hamilton, 1992)

—— *Trust: The Social Virtues and the Creation of Prosperity* (London: Hamish Hamilton, 1995)

—— 'US democracy has little to teach China', *Financial Times*, 17 January 2011

Funabashi, Yoichi, Interview with Wang Jisi, *The Asahi Shimbun*, 12 June 2010

—— 'Tokyo has no option but to cleave to China', *Financial Times*, 17 May 2011

Gall, Susan, and Irene Natividad, eds, *The Asian American Almanac: A Reference Work on Asians in the United States* (Detroit: Gale Research, 1995)

Gardner, Howard, *To Open Minds* (New York: Basic Books, 1989)

Garrett, Valery M., *Traditional Chinese Clothing in Hong Kong and South China, 1840–1980* (Hong Kong: Oxford University Press, 1987)

—— *Chinese Clothing: An Illustrated Guide* (Oxford: Oxford University Press, 1994)

Garrison, Jim, *America as Empire: Global Leader or Rogue Power?* (San Francisco: Berrett-Koehler Publishers, 2004)

Garver, John W., *Protracted Contest: Sino-Indian Rivalry in the Twentieth Century* (Seattle: University of Washington Press, 2001)

—— 'China's Influence in Central and South Asia: Is It Increasing?', in David Shambaugh, ed., *Power Shift: China and Asia's New Dynamics* (Berkeley: University of California Press, 2005)

—— *China and Iran: Ancient Partners in a Post-Imperial World* (Seattle: University of Washington Press, 2006)

Gaulier, Guillaume, Françoise Lemoine and Deniz Ünal-Kesenci, 'China's Integration in East Asia: Production Sharing, FDI and High-Tech Trade', *CEPII Working Paper No. 2005–09*

Gernet, Jacques, *Daily Life in China on the Eve of the Mongol Invasion, 1250–76* (Stanford: Stanford University Press, 1962)

—— *A History of Chinese Civilization*, 2nd edn (Cambridge: Cambridge University Press, 1996)

Gerth, Karl, *China Made: Consumer Culture and the Creation of the Nation* (Cambridge, Mass.: Harvard University Press, 2003)

Giddens, Anthony, *The Consequences of Modernity* (Cambridge: Cambridge University Press, 1997)

Gilboy, George J., 'The Myth behind China's Miracle', *Foreign Affairs*, July–August 2004

Gill, Bates, 'China's Evolving Regional Security Strategy', in David Shambaugh, ed., *Power Shift: China and Asia's New Dynamics* (Berkeley: University of California Press, 2005)

Gilley, Bruce, *China's Democratic Future: How It Will Happen and Where It Will Lead* (New York: Columbia University Press, 2004)

Gittings, John, *The World and China, 1922–1972* (London: Eyre Methuen, 1974)

—— *The Changing Face of China* (Oxford: Oxford University Press, 2005)

Godwin, Peter H. B., 'Force and Diplomacy: China Prepares for the

Twenty-First Century', in Samuel S. Kim, ed., *China and the World: Chinese Foreign Policy Faces the New Millennium*, 4th edn (Oxford: Westview Press, 1998)

Gooch, Liz, 'Researchers in Asian countries raise their scientific profiles worldwide', *International Herald Tribune*, 13 September 2010

Goodman, David S. G., and Gerald Segal, *China Rising: Nationalism and Interdependence* (London: Routledge, 1997)

Goody, Jack, *The East in the West* (Cambridge: Cambridge University Press, 1996)

Gough, Neil, 'US rollout of BYD's all-electric car delayed', *South China Morning Post*, 24 August 2010

Gowan, Richard, and Franziska Branter, *The EU and Human Rights at the UN: 2010 Review*, European Council on Foreign Relations, 2010

Graddol, David, *The Future of English* (London: British Council, 1997)

—— *English Next India*, British Council, 2010

Gramsci, Antonio, *Selections from the Prison Notebooks* (London: Lawrence and Wishart, 1971)

Grant, Charles, 'India's Role in the New World Order', Centre for European Reform Briefing Note (September 2008)

——'Is China being beastly to foreign investors?', Centre for European Reform, 30 July 2010

—— and Katinka Barysch, *Can Europe and China Shape a New World Order?* (London: Centre for European Reform, 2008)

Gray, John, *False Dawn: The Delusions of Global Capitalism* (London: Granta Books, 1998)

—— '(Re-)ordering the World: Dilemmas of Liberal Imperialism', *RSA Journal*, 2:6 (2002)

Gries, Peter Hays, *China's New Nationalism: Pride, Politics, and Diplomacy* (Berkeley: University of California Press, 2004)

—— and Stanley Rosen, eds, *State and Society in 21st-Century China* (London: RoutledgeCurzon, 2004)

Guttenplan, D. D., and Sam Dillon, 'West picks through the rubble as Chinese shine in student test', *New York Times*, 8 December 2010

Hall, Stuart, 'A Different Light', lecture to Prince Claus Fund Conference, Rotterdam, 12 December 2001

Halper, Stefan, *The Beijing Consensus: How China's Authoritarian Model will Dominate the Twenty-First Century* (New York: Basic Books, 2010)

Hampden-Turner, Charles, and Fons Trompenaars, *Mastering the Infinite Game: How East Asian Values are Transforming Business Practices* (Oxford: Capstone, 1997)

Harootunian, Harry, *The Empire's New Clothes: Paradigm Lost, and Regained* (Chicago: Prickly Paradigm Press, 2004)

Harrell, Stevan, ed., *Cultural Encounters on China's Ethnic Frontiers* (Seattle: University of Washington Press, 1995)

Hawksworth, John, and Gordon Cookson, 'The World in 2050 – Beyond the BRICs: A Broader Look at Emerging Market Growth Prospects', March 2008, posted on www.pwc.com, p. 3

Hayashi, Yuha, and Julian E. Barnes, 'Gates Leaves Beijing, Will Press Japan to Expand Its Defense Role', *Wall Street Journal*, 13 January 2011

He Huifeng, 'Illegal Vietnamese workers flood delta factories', *South China Morning Post*, 23 April 2010

Heisbourg, François, 'Europe Must Be Realistic About Life After Bush', *Financial Times*, 6 February 2008

Held, David, *Democracy and the Global Order: From the Modern State to Cosmopolitan Governance* (Cambridge: Polity Press, 1995)

Hendry, Joy, ed., *Interpreting Japanese Society: Anthropological Approaches* (London: Routledge, 1986)

Higashinakano Shudo, *The Nanking Massacre: Facts Versus Fiction, A Historian's Quest for the Truth* (Tokyo: Sekai Shuppan, Inc., 2005)

Higgins, Charlotte, *It's All Greek to Me* (London: Short Books, 2008)

Hille, Kathrin, 'Chinese pay rises encourage move to cheaper provinces', *Financial Times*, 26–27 June 2010

—— 'China acts to tackle Uighur tension', and 'Development unlikely to drown out disharmony', *Financial Times*, 3–4 July 2010

—— 'Carriers back China's global reach', *Financial Times*, 17 December 2010

—— 'China reveals aircraft carrier plans', *Financial Times*, 17 December 2010

—— 'China missile may cause power shift', *Financial Times*, 28 December 2010

—— 'China faces pressure to alter one-child policy', *Financial Times*, 28 April 2011

—— 'Maoist revival gathers pace in Chongqing', *Financial Times*, 24 May 2011

—— and Jamil Anderlini, 'China: Mao and the next generation', *Financial Times*, 2 June 2011

—— and Richard McGregor, 'Trouble at the margin', *Financial Times*, 10 July 2009

—— and Tom Mitchell, 'News Corp sells control of its China TV channels', *Financial Times*, 9 August 2010

Hilsum, Lindsey, 'China, Africa and the G8 – or Why Bob Geldof Needs to Wake Up', in Leni Wild and David Mepham, eds, *The New Sinosphere* (London: Institute for Public Policy Research, 2006)

Ho, P. Y., and F. P. Lisowski, *A Brief History of Chinese Medicine and Its Influence* (Singapore: World Scientific, 1998)

Hobsbawn, Eric, *The Age of Empire 1875–1914* (London: Weidenfeld and Nicolson, 1987)

—— *Age of Extremes: The Short Twentieth Century 1914–1991* (London: Michael Joseph, 1994)

—— 'America's Neo-conservative World Supremacists Will Fail', *Guardian*, 25 June 2005

—— *Globalisation, Democracy, and Terrorism* (London: Little, Brown, 2007)

Hobson, John M., *The Eastern Origins of Western Civilization* (Cambridge: Cambridge University Press, 2004)

Hodge, Nathan, and Julian E. Barnes, 'Pentagon Faces the Knife', *Wall Street Journal*, 7 January 2011

Hook, Leslie, 'Repsol and Sinopec join forces in Brazil', *Financial Times*, 1 October 2010

Hope, Kerin, and Jamil Anderlini, 'Athens turns to Beijing for bond sale', *Financial Times*, 27 January 2010

—— 'China prepares to invest in Greek projects', *Financial Times*, 14 June 2010

Hoslag, Jonathan, 'China builds a bridge across the Danube', *Financial Times*, 27 June 2010

Howell, Jude, ed., *Governance in China* (Oxford: Roman and Littlefield, 2004)

Hu Angang, 'Five Major Scale Effects of China's Rise', unpublished seminar paper, East Asia Institute, National University of Singapore, 2005

—— 'Green Development: The Inevitable Choice for China, Parts One and Two', posted on www.chinadialogue.net

Hu Jintao, Interview, *Washington Post*, 17 January 2011

Huang, Cary, 'Najib calls for expanded yuan role', *South China Morning Post*, 5 June 2009

—— 'Leadership wakes to grey storm of ageing population', *South China Morning Post*, 2 November 2009

—— 'Najib calls for expanded yuan role', *South China Morning Post*, 5 June 2010

Huang Ping, '"Beijing Consensus", or "Chinese Experiences", or What?', English-language unpublished paper, 2005

—— and Cui Zhiyuan, eds, *China and Globalization: 'Washington Consensus', 'Beijing Consensus', or What?* (Chinese-language edition) (Beijing: Social Sciences Academic Press, 2006)

Huang, Yasheng, *Capitalism with Chinese Characteristics: Entrepreneurship and the State* (Cambridge: Cambridge University Press, 2008)

Hufbauer, Gary Clyde, and Yee Wong, 'Prospects for Regional Free Trade in Asia', working paper, Institute for International Economics, Washington, DC, October 2005

Hughes, Christopher R., *Chinese Nationalism in the Global Era* (London: Routledge, 2006)

—— and Gudrun Wacker, eds, *China and the Internet: Politics of the Digital Leap Forward* (London: Routledge, 2003)

Huntington, Samuel P., *The Clash of Civilizations and the Remaking of World Order* (New York: Simon and Schuster, 1996)

——*Who Are We? America's Great Debate* (London: The Free Press, 2005)

Hutton, Will, *The Writing on the Wall: China and the West in the 21st Century* (London: Little, Brown, 2007)

Hyde, Henry, 'The Perils of the "Golden Theory"', *Strait Times*, 21 February 2006

Ignatieff, Michael, *Empire Lite: Nation-Building in Bosnia, Kosovo and Afghanistan* (London: Vintage, 2003)

Ignatius, David, 'Ike was right: Cut defense', *Washington Post*, 26 January 2011

Ikenberry, G. John, *Liberal Order and Imperial Ambition: Essays on American Power and World Politics* (Cambridge: Polity, 2006)

—— 'The Rise of China and the Future of the West: Can the Liberal System Survive?', *Foreign Affairs*, January–February 2008

—— 'China and the Rest Are Only Joining the American-Built Order', *New Perspectives Quarterly*, Volume 25, No 3, Summer 2008

Inoguchi, Takashi, 'Nationalism, Globalisation and Regional Order in North-East Asia: The Case of Japan at the Dawn of the Century', paper presented at conference on 'Nationalism and Globalisation in North-East Asia', Asia Research Centre, London School of Economics, 12 May 2007

Itoh, Fumio, ed., *China in the Twenty-first Century: Politics, Economy, and Society* (Tokyo: United Nations University Press, 1997)

Jacques, Martin, 'Global Hierarchy of Race', *Guardian*, 20 September 2003

—— 'Democracy Isn't Working', *Guardian*, 22 June 2004

—— 'Strength in Numbers', *Guardian*, 23 October 2004

—— 'No Monopoly on Modernity', *Guardian*, 5 February 2005

—— 'The Neo-con Revolution', *Guardian*, 31 March 2005

—— 'The Middle Kingdom Mentality', *Guardian*, 16 April 2005

—— 'Where Is Japan?', seminar paper presented at Faculty of Media and Communications, Aichi University, 27 July 2005

—— 'Imperial Overreach is Accelerating the Global Decline of America', *Guardian*, 28 March 2006

—— 'The Age of America or the Rise of the East: The Story of the 21st Century', *Aichi University Journal of International Affairs*, 127 (March 2006)

—— 'The Death of Doha Signals the Demise of Globalisation', *Guardian*, 13 July 2006

—— 'America Faces a Future of Managing Imperial Decline', *Guardian*, 16 November 2006

—— 'The Citadels of the Global Economy are Yielding to China's Battering Ram', *Guardian*, 23 April 2008

—— 'It seemed impossible . . .', *Observer*, 4 April 2011

Jenner, W. J. F., 'Race and History in China', *New Left Review*, 11 (September–October 2001)

Jin, Yi Kai, 'Big and Beautiful, the New Shanghai City', *Dialogue* (Taipei), February–March 1999

Johnson, Chalmers, *Japan: Who Governs? The Rise of the Developmental State* (New York: W. W. Norton, 1995)

—— *Blowback: The Costs and Consequences of American Empire* (London: Time Warner, 2000)

—— *The Sorrows of Empire: Militarism, Secrecy and the End of the Republic* (London: Verso, 2004)

—— 'Why the US Has Really Gone Broke', *Le Monde diplomatique*, February 2008

Johnson, M. Dujon, *Race and Racism in the Chinas* (Milton Keynes: Author House, 2007)

Johnson, Steven C., 'Dollar's Decline Presents a Challenge to US Power', *International Herald Tribune*, 28–29 April 2007

Johnson, Tim, and Julie Sell, 'Getting relics home', *South China Morning Post*, 5 March 2009

Johnston, Alastair Iain, *Cultural Realism: Strategic Culture and Grand Strategy in Chinese History* (Princeton: Princeton University Press, 1995)

—— and Robert S. Ross, eds, *Engaging China: The Management of an Emerging Power* (London: Routledge, 1999)

—— eds, *New Directions in the Study of China's Foreign Policy* (Stanford: Stanford University Press, 2006)

Jomo K. S., ed., *Tigers in Trouble: Financial Governance, Liberalisation and Crises in East Asia* (London: Zed Books, 1998)

Jones, Eric L., *The European Miracle: Environments, Economics, and Geopolitics in the History of Europe and Asia* (Cambridge: Cambridge University Press, 1981)

Jones, Gavin W., 'Not "When to Marry" but "Whether to Marry": The Changing Context of Marriage Decisions in East and Southeast Asia', in Gavin Jones and Kamalini Ramdas, eds, *Untying the Knot: Ideal and Reality in Asian Marriage* (Singapore: NUS Press, 2004)

Kachru, Braj B., ed., *The Other Tongue: English Across Cultures* (Urbana and Chicago: University of Illinois Press, 1992)

—— *Asian Englishes: Beyond the Canon* (Hong Kong: Hong Kong University Press, 2005)

Kagan, Robert, *Paradise and Power: America and Europe in the New World Order* (London: Atlantic Books, 2003)

—— *Dangerous Nation: America and the World 1600–1898* (London: Atlantic Books, 2006)

—— 'The Case for a League of Democracies', *Financial Times*, 13 May 2008

Kahn, Joseph, and Jim Yardley, 'As China Roars, Pollution Reaches Deadly Extremes', *New York Times*, 26 August 2007

Kang, David C., 'Getting Asia Wrong: The Need for New Analytical Frameworks', *International Security*, 27:4 (Spring 2003)

—— *China Rising: Peace, Power, and Order in East Asia* (New York: Columbia University Press, 2007)

Kaplan, Robert D., *Monsoon* (New York: Random House, 2010)

Kaplinsky, Raphael, *Globalization, Poverty and Inequality* (Cambridge: Polity, 2005)

—— 'Winners and Losers: China's Trade Threats and Opportunities for Africa', in Leni Wild and David Mepham, eds, *The New Sinosphere* (London: Institute for Public Policy Research, 2006)

Kapur, Akash, 'Upholding a tradition of tolerance', *International Herald Tribune*, 12 February 2010

Karumbidza, John Blessing, 'Win-Win Economic Co-operation: Can China Save Zimbabwe's Economy?', in Firoze Manji and Stephen Marks, eds, *African Perspectives on China in Africa* (Oxford: Fahamu, 2007)

Katz, Richard, *Japan, the System that Soured: The Rise and Fall of the Japanese Economic Miracle* (New York: M. E. Sharpe, 1998)

Katzenstein, Peter J., and Takashi Shiraishi, *Network Power: Japan and Asia* (Ithaca: Cornell University Press, 1997)

Kazmin, Amy, 'India: designers create a world of colour with a royal touch', *Financial Times*, 31 August 2010

Kennedy, Paul, *The Rise and Fall of the Great Powers: Economic Change and Military Conflict from 1500 to 2000* (London: Fontana Press, 1988)

—— *Preparing for the Twenty-first Century* (London: HarperCollins, 1993)

—— 'Who's Hiding Under Our Umbrella?', *International Herald Tribune*, 31 January 2008

Khanna, Parag, *The Second World: Empires and Influence in the New Global Order* (London: Allen Lane, 2008)

Kim, Hee-sun, 'Kayagŭm Shin'Gok, New Music for Antiquity: Musical Construction of Identity in Contemporary South Korea', unpublished paper, 2005

Kim, Samuel S., ed., *China and the World: Chinese Foreign Policy Faces the New Millennium*, 4th edn (Oxford: Westview Press, 1998)

Kim, Shee Poon, 'East Asian New Regionalism: Toward Economic Integration?', *Ritsumeikan International Affairs*, 5 (2003)

—— 'The Political Economy of Mahathir's China Policy: Economic Cooperation, Political and Strategic Ambivalence', *Annual Review of International Studies*, 3 (2004)

Kissinger, Henry, *On China* (London: Allen Lane, 2011)

Kitissou, Marcel, ed., *Africa in China's Global Strategy* (London: Adonis and Abbey, 2007)

Klein, Naomi, 'Police State 2.0', *Guardian*, 3 June 2008

Kohut, Andrew, 'Friend or Foe? How Americans see China', *Wall Street Journal*, 13 January 2011

Kotkin, Joel, *Tribes: How Race, Religion, and Identity Determine Success in the New Global Economy* (New York: Random House, 1992)

Krauthammer, Charles, 'An American Foreign Policy for a Unipolar World', Irving Kristol Lecture, American Enterprise Institute Dinner, 10 February 2004

—— 'Decline is a Choice: the New Liberalism and the end of American ascendancy', *The Weekly Standard*, Volume 015, Issue 05, 19 October 2009

Kristof, Nicholas D., 'Glory is as Ephemeral as Smoke and Clouds', *International Herald Tribune*, 23 May 2005

—— 'The Educated Giant', *International Herald Tribune*, 29 May 2007

Krugman, Paul, *The Return of Depression Economics* (London: Allen Lane, 1999)

Kuhn, Philip A., *Origins of the Modern Chinese State* (Stanford: Stanford University Press, 2002)

Kumar, Vikas, 'Why is SAARC Perennially Gridlocked and How can it be Revitalized?', *Clingendael Asia Forum*, 16 December 2010

Kurlantzick, Joshua, *Charm Offensive: How China's Soft Power is Transforming the World* (New Haven and London: Yale University Press, 2007)

Kwok, Kristine, 'Thousands protest over Urumqi syringe attacks', *South China Morning Post*, 4 September 2009

Kwong, Peter, *The New Chinatown* (New York: Hill and Wang, 1987)

Kwong, Robin, 'China and Taiwan sign landmark deal', *Financial Times*, 29 June 2010

—— 'Taiwan begins trade talks with Singapore', *Financial Times*, 5 August 2010

—— 'Taiwan to open tech industry to Chinese investment', *Financial Times*, 27 February 2011

Kynge, James, *China Shakes the World: The Rise of a Hungry Nation* (London: Weidenfeld and Nicolson, 2006)

—— 'China's "locally global" financial reforms', *Financial Times*, 27 November 2009

—— Geoff Dyer and James Blitz, 'Bear gifts for friends', *Financial Times*, 15–16 January 2011

—— Richard McGregor, Daniel Dombey, Martin Arnold, Helen Warrell, and Cynthia O'Murchu, 'The China Syndrome', *Financial Times*, 3 March 2011

Lafraniere, Sharon, and Martin Fackler, 'North Korea fires only words after South's drill', *International Herald Tribune*, 20 December 2010

Lal, Deepak, *Unintended Consequences* (Cambridge, Mass.: MIT Press, 1998)

Lam, Willy, 'China Flexes Its New Muscle', *International Herald Tribune*, 21 December 2007

Lamont, James, and Farhan Bokhari, 'China signs $35bn in deals with Pakistan', *Financial Times*, 19 December 2010

—— and Geoff Dyer, 'China eyes industrial bases in Africa', *Financial Times*, 3 December 2009

—— and Geoff Dyer, 'Wen's trip to India stirs old squabbles', *Financial Times*, 14 December 2010

—— and James Fontanella-Khan, 'India: Writing is on the wall', *Financial Times*, 21 March 2011

—— 'Turning deaf ear to Mandarin no longer wise', *Financial Times*, 3 October 2010

—— and Amy Kazmin, 'Fear of influence', *Financial Times*, 13 July 2009

Lampton, David M., *Same Bed, Different Dreams: Managing US–China Relations, 1989–2000* (Berkeley: University of California Press, 2001)

—— 'China's Rise in Asia Need Not Be at America's Expense', in David Shambaugh, ed., *Power Shift: China and Asia's New Dynamics* (Berkeley: University of California Press, 2005)

—— 'What Growing Chinese Power Means for America', hearing before the US Senate Committee on Foreign Relations, East Asian and Pacific Affairs Subcommittee, 7 June 2005

—— *The Three Faces of Chinese Power: Might, Money, and Minds* (Berkeley: University of California Press, 2008)

Lan, Yuk-yuen, *The Practice of Chineseness* (Hong Kong: CyDot, 1999)

Landes, David, *The Wealth and Poverty of Nations* (London: Little, Brown, 1998)

Lankov, Andrei, 'The Yeonpyeong Island Incident: why it happened, why nothing can be done, and what to expect: some thoughts', North Korean Economy Watch, http://www.nkeconwatch.com/2010/11/29/lankov-on-the-shelling-of-yonpyong/

Large, Daniel, 'As the Beginning Ends: China's Return to Africa', in Firoze Manji and Stephen Marks, eds, *African Perspectives on China in Africa* (Oxford: Fahamu, 2007)

Larmer, Brook 'The Center of the World', *Foreign Policy* (September–October 2005)

Lau, D. C., trans., *Mencius* (London: Penguin, 1970)

Leahy, Joe, 'Brazil and China trade tensions set to rise', *Financial Times*, 30 January 2011

——'Drawn into an ever closer embrace', *Financial Times*, 20 May 2011

——'Financial flows: Commodities are central to defining the relationship', *Financial Times*, 20 May 2011

Lee, Chunli, 'Strategic Alliances of Chinese, Japanese and US firms in the Chinese Manufacturing Industry: The Impact of "China Prices" and Integrated Localisation', unpublished paper presented to the Fairbank Center for East Asia Research, Harvard University, October 2004

—— 'Trends of Open Product Architecture and Internationalisation of Private Companies in the Chinese Automobile Industry', *Aichi University Economic Review*, 169 (2005)

—— 'China Targets Detroit', *World Business*, April 2006

—— 'Product Development by Chinese Automakers: The Dilemma of

Imitation and Innovation', unpublished working paper for International Vehicle Program, MIT, July 2007

—— Jin Chen and Takahiro Fujimoto, 'Chinese Automobile Industry and Product Architectures', unpublished paper

Lee, Mabel, and A. D. Syrokomia-Stefanowski, eds, *Modernisation of the Chinese Past* (Sydney: University of Sydney, School of Asian Studies, 1993)

Leonard, Mark, *Why Europe Will Run the Twenty-first Century* (London: Fourth Estate, 2005)

—— *What Does China Think?* (London: Fourth Estate, 2008)

Leong, Evan, 'Are You Chinese?', paper for Chinese American Youth Program, Roots Conference, San Francisco, 1998

Levin, Dan, 'In China, love of old is something new', *International Herald Tribune*, 5 February 2010

—— 'Shanghai looks to glorious past', *International Herald Tribune*, 4 May 2010

Levine, Steven I., 'Sino-American Relations: Practicing Damage Control', in Samuel S. Kim, ed., *China and the World: Chinese Foreign Policy Faces the New Millennium*, 4th edn (Oxford: Westview Press, 1998)

Li, Cao, 'Busting the Bribe Tribe', *China Daily*, 20 August 2009

Li, Rex, 'Security Challenge of an Ascendant China: Great Power Emergence and International Stability', in Zhao Suisheng, ed., *Chinese Foreign Policy: Pragmatism and Strategic Behavior* (New York: M. E. Sharpe, 2004)

Lieberthal, Kenneth, 'Why the US Malaise Over China?', YaleGlobal Online, 19 January 2006

Lieven, Anatol, *America Right or Wrong: An Anatomy of American Nationalism* (Oxford: Oxford University Press, 2004)

Lim, Louisa, 'Mixed-Race TV Contestant Ignites Debate in China', 11 December 2009, www.npr.org/templates/story.php?storyId=120311417

Little, Ian, *Picking Winners: The East Asian Experience* (London: Social Market Foundation, 1996)

Lo, Bobo, 'Russia, China and the Georgia Dimension', *Centre for European Reform Bulletin* 62 (October–November 2008)

Lo, Chih-cheng, 'An Inconvenient Truth: The Rise of Taiwanese Identity and Its Impacts', paper given at conference on 'Nationalism and Globalisation in North-East Asia', Asia Research Centre, London School of Economics, 12 May 2007

Lo, Fu-chen, and Yue-man Yeung, eds, *Emerging World Cities in Pacific Asia* (Tokyo: United Nations University, 1996)

Long, Simon, 'India and China: The Tiger in Front', survey, *The Economist*, 5 March 2005

Loper, Kelley, 'Cultivating a Multicultural Society and Combating Racial Discrimination in Hong Kong', *Civic Exchange*, August 2001

Lovell, Julia, *The Great Wall: China Against the World 1000 BC–AD 2000* (London: Atlantic Books, 2006)

—— *The Opium War: Drugs, Dreams and the Making of China* (London: Picador, 2011)

Lu Xun, *The True Story of Ah Q*, trans. Yang Xianyi and Gladys Yang (Hong Kong: Chinese University Press, 2002)

Luttwak, Edward, *Turbo-Capitalism: Winners and Losers in the Global Economy* (London: Weidenfeld and Nicolson, 1998)

McCann Erickson, *Pulse(r) Bites: Consumer Insights Around the World*, 2 (Beijing: 1 April 1999)

McCormack, Gavin, 'The US–Japan Security Treaty at 50: Entering Uncharted Waters', 24 June 2010, Clingendael Asia Studies and Clingendael Asia Forum

Macfarlane, Alan, *The Origins of English Individualism* (Oxford: Blackwell, 1979)

—— *Japan Through the Looking Glass* (London: Profile Books, 2007)

McGreal, Ian P., *Great Thinkers of the Eastern World* (London: HarperCollins, 1995)

McGregor, Richard, 'Chinese steel executive beaten to death', *Financial Times*, 26 July 2009

—— *The Party: The Secret World of China's Communist Rulers* (London: Allen Lane, 2010)

Mackenzie, Michael, and Gillian Tett, 'Moody's warns US over credit rating fears', *Financial Times*, 3 February 2010

Mackerras, Colin, 'What is China? Who is Chinese? Han–Minority Relations, Legitimacy, and the State', in Peter Hays Gries and Stanley Rosen, eds, *State and Society in 21st-Century China* (London: Routledge Curzon, 2004)

McNeill, William H., *The Rise of the West: A History of the Human Community* (Chicago and London: University of Chicago Press, 1991)

McRae, Hamish, *The World in 2020: Power, Culture and Prosperity: A Vision of the Future* (London: HarperCollins, 1994)

Maddison, Angus, *The World Economy: Historical Statistics* (Paris: OECD, 2003)

—— *The World Economy: A Millennial Perspective* (Paris: OECD, 2006)

—— *Chinese Economic Performance in the Long Run, Second Edition, Revised and Updated: 960–2030 AD* (Paris: OECD, 2007)

Mahbubani, Kishore, *The New Asian Hemisphere: The Irresistible Shift of Global Power to the East* (New York: Public Affairs, 2008)

Mallet, Victor, 'China's Spanish debt buys put at €6bn', *Financial Times*, 6 January 2011

Mance, Henry, 'Why are Chinese schoolkids so good?' http://blogs.ft.com/ beyond-brics/2010/12/07/why-are-chinese-schoolkids-so-good/

Mandelbaum, Michael, *The Frugal Power: America's Global Leadership in a Cash-Strapped Era* (New York: Public Affairs, 2010)

Manji, Firoze, and Stephen Marks, eds, *African Perspectives on China in Africa* (Oxford: Fahamu, 2007)

Mann, James, *The China Fantasy: How Our Leaders Explain Away Chinese Repression* (New York: Viking, 2007)

Mapstone, Naomi, 'Cash flow into Peru mine brings rights fear', *Financial Times*, 19 January 2011

Markoff, John, 'China seeks supercomputing edge', *International Herald Tribune*, 1 June 2010

Marsh, Peter, 'China noses ahead as top goods producer', *Financial Times*, 13 March 2011

——— 'Focus on deals high up value chain', *Financial Times*, 25 April 2011

Martinez, D. P., *The Worlds of Japanese Popular Culture* (Cambridge: Cambridge University Press, 1998)

Mearsheimer, John J., *The Tragedy of Great Power Politics* (New York: W. W. Norton, 2001)

Menkes, Suzy, 'Hitting the High Cs: Cool, Cute and Creative', *International Herald Tribune*, 21 March 2006

——— 'Whose Sari Now?', *International Herald Tribune*, 17 May 2008

Menzies, Gavin, *1421: The Year China Discovered the World* (London: Bantam Books, 2003)

Miller, Tom, 'Big cities, small cities', *China Economic Quarterly*, March 2009, pp. 27–31

Minxin Pei, 'How One Political Insider is Using His Influence to Push Rural Reforms', *South China Morning Post*, 2 January 2003

Mire, Amina, 'Giving You a Radiant White Skin "Because You Are Worth It": The Emerging Discourse and Practice of Skin-whitening', unpublished abstract for Ph.D., University of Toronto, 2004

——— 'Pigmentation and Empire: The Emerging Skin-Whitening Industry', *A CounterPunch Special Report* (2005), posted on www.counterpunch.org

Mishra, Pankaj, *An End of Suffering: The Buddha in the World* (London: Picador, 2004)

——— 'Getting Rich', *London Review of Books*, 30 November 2006

Mitchell, Tom, and Geoff Dyer, 'Heat in the Workshop', *Financial Times*, 14 October 2007

Mochizuki, Mike M., 'China–Japan Relations: Downward Spiral or a New Equilibrium?', in David Shambaugh, ed., *Power Shift: China and Asia's New Dynamics* (Berkeley: University of California Press, 2005)

Monro, Alexander, and Dana Denis-Smith, 'China taps into the heart of Turkmenistan's gas fields', *Financial Times*, 17 December 2009

Montes, Manuel F., and Vladimir V. Popov, *The Asian Crisis Turns Global* (Singapore: Institute of Southeast Asian Studies, 1999)

Moon, Chung-in, and Seung-won Suh, 'Overcoming History: The Politics of Identity and Nationalism', *Global Asia*, 2:1 (2007)

Moran, Robert, 'The Beltway Ponders America's Global Influence', *National Journal.com*, 9 February 2010

Morishima, Michio, *Why Has Japan 'Succeeded'?: Western Technology and the Japanese Ethos* (Cambridge: Cambridge University Press, 1984)

Morris, Ian, *Why the West Rules For Now: The Patterns of History and What They Reveal About the Future* (London: Profile Books, 2010)

Müllerson, Rein, 'Crouching tiger hidden dragon: Which will it be?', *Eurozine*, http://www.eurozine.com/articles/2010-04-29-mullerons-en.html

Naik, Gautam, 'China is poised to top Japan in R&D', *Wall Street Journal*, 16 December 2010

Naisbitt, John, *Megatrends Asia: The Eight Asian Megatrends That Are Changing the World* (London: Nicholas Brealey, 1996)

Nakamae International Economic Research, *Scenarios for the Future of Japan: Research Material* (Nihon Keizai Shimbun, Inc. (Nikkei) and Global Business Network, 1999)

Nakamoto, Michiyo, 'Asia: Displacement activity', *Financial Times*, 22 August 2010

Nakane, Chie, *Japanese Society* (London: Weidenfeld and Nicolson, 1970)

Nathan, Andrew J., and Robert S. Ross, *The Great Wall and the Empty Fortress: China's Search for Security* (New York: W. W. Norton, 1997)

Naughton, Barry, *The Chinese Economy: Transitions and Growth* (Cambridge, Mass.: MIT Press, 2007)

—— 'China's Distinctive System: can it be a model for others?', *Journal of Contemporary China*, 19:65 (June 2010)

New American Century Project, *Statement of Principles*, http://www.newamericancentury.org/statementofprinciples.htm

Ng, Eric, 'China catching up with Europe on solar farms', *South China Morning Post*, 19 April 2010

Nodskov, Kim, *The Long March to Power: The New Historic Mission of the People's Liberation Army* (Copenhagen: Royal Danish Defence College Publishing House, 2009)

Nolan, Peter, *China at the Crossroads* (Cambridge: Polity Press, 2004)

—— *Transforming China: Globalisation, Transition and Development* (London: Anthem Press, 2005)

Noriega, Roger F., 'China's Influence in the Western Hemisphere', statement before the House Sub-committee on the Western Hemisphere, Washington, DC, 6 April 2005

Norins, Martin R., *Gateway to Asia: Sinkiang: Frontier of the Chinese Far West* (New York: The John Day Company, 1944)

Nye, Joseph S., Jr, *The Paradox of American Power: Why the World's Only Superpower Can't Go It Alone* (Oxford: Oxford University Press, 2002)

—— *Soft Power: The Means to Success in World Politics* (New York: Public Affairs, 2004)

Nyíri, Pál, 'The Yellow Man's Burden: Chinese Migrants on a Civilizing Mission', *The China Journal*, No. 56, July 2006

Oakley, David, and Anousha Sakoui, 'China offers Spain 1bn euro confidence vote', *Financial Times*, 12 July 2010

Obiorah, Ndubisi, 'Who's afraid of China in Africa? Towards An African Civil Society Perspective on China–Africa Relations', in Firoze Manji and Stephen Marks, eds, *African Perspectives on China in Africa* (Oxford: Fahamu, 2007)

OECD, *PISA 2009 Results: What Students Know and Can Do – Student Performance in Reading, Mathematics and Science*, Volume 1 (Paris: OECD, 2010)

Ofon, Abah, 'South–South Co-operation: Can Africa Thrive with Chinese Investment?', in Leni Wild and David Mepham, eds, *The New Sinosphere* (London: Institute for Public Policy Research, 2006)

Ohashi, Hideo, 'China's Regional Trade and Investment Profile', in David Shambaugh, ed., *Power Shift: China and Asia's New Dynamics* (Berkeley: University of California Press, 2005)

Ohnuki-Tierney, Emiko, *Kamikaze, Cherry Blossoms, and Nationalisms: The Militarization of Aesthetics in Japanese History* (Chicago: The University of Chicago Press, 2002)

O'Neill, Jim, et al., 'China and Asia's Future Monetary System', *Goldman Sachs Global Economics Paper*, 129 (12 September 2005)

Onishi, Norimitsu, 'US and China court Indonesia', *International Herald Tribune*, 10 November 2010

—— 'US and China court Indonesia', *International Herald Tribune*, 10 November 2010

Oster, Shai, Dinny McMahon, and Tom Lauricella, 'Offshore Trading in Yuan Takes Off', *Wall Street Journal*, 14 December 2010

Ostler, Nicholas, *Empires of the World: A Language History of the World* (London: HarperCollins, 2005)

Overholt, William H., *China: The Next Economic Superpower* (London: Weidenfeld and Nicolson, 1993)

Page, Jeremy, 'China Tests New Political Model in Shenzhen', *Wall Street Journal*, 18 October 2010

Pan, Lynn, *Sons of the Yellow Emperor: The Story of the Overseas Chinese* (London: Arrow, 1998)

—— *The Encyclopedia of the Chinese Overseas* (Cambridge, Mass.: Harvard University Press, 1999)

Park, Seo-Hyun, 'Small States and the Search for Sovereignty in Sinocentric Asia: The Case of Japan and Korea in the Late Nineteenth Century', in Anthony Reid and Zheng Yangwen, eds, *Negotiating Asymmetry: China's Place in Asia* (Singapore: NUS Press, 2009)

Patten, Chris, *East and West: China, Power, and the Future of East Asia* (London: Macmillan, 1998)

Perdue, Peter C., *China Marches West: The Qing Conquest of Central Eurasia* (Cambridge, Mass.: Belknap Press of Harvard University Press, 2005)

—— 'Why Do Empires Expand?', workshop on 'Asian Expansions: The Historical Processes of Polity Expansion in Asia', Asia Research Institute, National University of Singapore, 12–13 May 2006

Perkins, Dwight H., 'History, Politics, and the Sources of Economic Growth: China and the East Asian Way of Growth', in Fumio Itoh, ed., *China in the Twenty-first Century: Politics, Economy, and Society* (Tokyo: United Nations University Press, 1997)

Persaud, Avinash D., 'The Dollar Standard: (Only the) Beginning of the End', posted on www.opendemocracy.net

—— 'When Currency Empires Fall', posted on www.gresham.ac.uk

Pew Global Attitudes Project, *World Publics Welcome Global Trade – But Not Immigration*, 4 October 2007, posted on http://pewglobal.org

Pew Research Center, *Global Attitudes Survey 2010*, released 17 June 2010

Peyrefitte, Alain, *The Collision of Two Civilizations: The British Expedition to China in 1792–4* (London: Harvill, 1993)

Pilling, David, 'Asia's quiet anger with "big, bad" China', *Financial Times*, 1 June 2011

—— 'China's bear hug has benefits for wary Taiwan', *Financial Times*, 24 June 2010

—— 'A recipe for trouble in China's backyard', *Financial Times*, 29 September 2010

—— 'Kim Jong-il plays his aces', *Financial Times*, 23 November 2010

—— 'A rock lobster lesson for booming Australia', *Financial Times*, 8 December 2010

Pohl, Otto, 'The West's Glossy Magazines "Go Forth and Multiply"', *International Herald Tribune*, 14–15 February 2004

Politi, James, 'World Bank sees end to dollar's hegemony', *Financial Times*, 17 May 2011

Pollack, Jonathan D., 'The Transformation of the Asian Security Order: Assessing China's Impact', in David Shambaugh, ed., *Power Shift: China and Asia's New Dynamics* (Berkeley: University of California Press, 2005)

Pomeranz, Kenneth, *The Great Divergence: China, Europe, and the Making of the Modern World Economy* (Princeton and Oxford: Princeton University Press, 2000)

Pomfret, John, 'US raises pressure on China to rein in N. Korea', *Washington Post*, 6 December 2010

Porritt, Jonathon, 'China Could Lead the Fight for a Cooler Climate', 13 November 2007, posted on www.chinadialogue.net

Portal, Jane, ed., *The First Emperor: China's Terracotta Army* (London: British Museum Press, 2007)

Prestowitz, Clyde, 'The Yuan Might Shift; the Imbalances Won't', *International Herald Tribune*, 1 June 2005

—— *Three Billion New Capitalists: The Great Shift of Wealth and Power to the East* (New York: Basic Books, 2006)

Pye, Lucian W., *Asian Power and Politics: The Cultural Dimensions of Authority* (Cambridge, Mass.: Harvard University Press, 1985)

—— *The Spirit of Chinese Politics* (Cambridge, Mass.: Harvard University Press, 1992)

—— 'Chinese Democracy and Constitutional Development', in Fumio Itoh, ed., *China in the Twenty-first Century: Politics, Economy, and Society* (Tokyo: United Nations University Press, 1997)

Quinlan, Joseph P., *The Last Economic Superpower: The Retreat of Globalization, The End of American Dominance, and What We Can Do About It* (New York: McGraw Hill, 2011)

Rajan, Raghuram G., *Fault Lines: How Hidden Fractures Still Threaten the World Economy* (Princeton and Oxford: Princeton University Press, 2010)

Rachman, Gideon, 'Why McCain's Big Idea is a Bad Idea', *Financial Times*, 5 May 2008

—— 'Welcome to the Nuclear Club, India', *Financial Times*, 22 September 2008

—— 'China's increasing influence', *Financial Times*, 24 April 2010

Ramo, Joshua Cooper, *The Beijing Consensus* (London: Foreign Policy Centre, 2004)

Reader, John, *Missing Links: The Hunt for Earliest Man* (London: Penguin, 1999)

Reed, John, 'Geely seals deal to buy Volvo from Ford', *Financial Times*, 28 March 2010

Rehman, Iskander, 'Keeping the Dragon at Bay: India's Counter-Containment of China in Asia', *Asia Security*, 5:2, 2009

Reid, Anthony, 'Nationalisms in South East Asia', seminar paper, Asia Research Institute, National University of Singapore, 24 January 2006

—— and Zheng Yangwen, eds, *Negotiating Asymmetry: China's Place in Asia* (Singapore: NUS Press, 2009). The book is based on papers given at an international conference on 'Rationalizing China's Place in Asia, 1800 to 2005', organized by the Asia Research Institute, National University of Singapore, 3–4 August 2006; it is these original drafts that were my sources, so my page references may not match the published book.

Ren, Daniel, '"Harsh jail" terms for Rio Tinto four', *South China Morning Post*, 30 March 2010

Research-Works, *R&D: China's Growing Competitive Edge*, Shanghai, 27 February 2010.

Rice, Xan, 'China's Long March', *Observer Sport Monthly*, October 2006

Richburg, Keith B., 'Is China a rival to the US? Many Chinese think not – or not yet', *Washington Post*, 8 February 2011

Roach, Stephen S., 'Manchurian Paradox', Morgan Stanley, 27 April 2009

Roberts, J. M., *The Triumph of the West* (London: Phoenix Press, 2001)

Rocha, John, 'A New Frontier in the Exploitation of Africa's Natural Resources: The Emergence of China', in Firoze Manji and Stephen Marks, eds, *African Perspectives on China in Africa* (Oxford: Fahamu, 2007)

Rodrik, Dani, *One Economics, Many Recipes: Globalization, Institutions, and Economic Growth* (Princeton: Princeton University Press, 2007)

—— 'Making room for China in the world economy', December 2009, http://www.hks.harvard.edu/fs/drodrik/Research%20papers/Making%20room%20for%20China.pdf

Rohwer, Jim, *Asia Rising: How History's Biggest Middle Class Will Change the World* (London: Nicholas Brealey, 1996)

Ross, Robert S., 'Engagement in US China Policy', in Alastair Iain Johnston and Robert S. Ross, eds, *Engaging China: The Management of an Emerging Power* (London: Routledge, 1999)

—— 'The Geography of Peace: East Asia in the Twenty-first Century', in Michael Brown et al., eds, *The Rise of China* (Cambridge, Mass.: MIT Press, 2000)

—— and Zhu Feng, eds, *China's Ascent: Power, Security, and the Future of International Politics* (Ithaca and London: Cornell University Press, 2008)

Roubini, Nouriel, 'A presidency heading for a fiscal train wreck', *Financial Times*, 28 October 2010

Russell, John G., 'Race and Reflexivity: The Black Other in Contemporary Japanese Mass Culture', in John Whittier Treat, ed., *Contemporary Japan and Popular Culture* (Honolulu: University of Hawai'i Press, 1996)

Ryosci, Kokubun, 'Did the Ice Melt between Japan and China?', conference on 'Nationalism and Globalisation in North-East Asia', Asia Research Centre, London School of Economics, 12 May 2007

Sachs, Jeffrey, 'Amid the Rubble of Global Finance, a Blueprint for Bretton Woods II', *Guardian*, 21 October 2008

Sands, Philippe, *Lawless World: America and the Making and Breaking of Global Rules* (London: Allen Lane, 2005)

Satoh, Haruko, *The Odd Couple: Japan and China, the Politics of History and Identity* (Japan Institute of International Affairs, 7 August 2006), available on http://yaleglobal.yale.edu

Saul, John Ralston, *The Collapse of Globalism and the Reinvention of the World* (London: Atlantic Books, 2005)

Sautman, Barry, 'Myths of Descent, Racial Nationalism and Ethnic Minorities in the People's Republic of China', in Frank Dikötter, ed., *The Construction of Racial Identities in China and Japan: Historical and Contemporary Perspectives* (London: Hurst and Company, 1997)

—— 'Honour and Shame? China's Africa Ties in Comparative Context', in Leni Wild and David Mepham, eds, *The New Sinosphere* (London: Institute for Public Policy Research, 2006)

—— 'Friends and Interests: China's Distinctive Links with Africa', *African Studies Review*, 50:3 (December 2007)

—— and Ellen Kneehans, 'The Politics of Racial Discrimination in Hong Kong', *Maryland Series in Contemporary Asian Studies*, 2 (2000)

—— and Yan Hairong, 'East Mountain Tiger, West Mountain Tiger: China, the West, and "Colonialism" in Africa', *Maryland Series in Contemporary Asian Studies*, 3 (2006)

Schäfer, Daniel, 'China and Germany: Reflected glory', *Financial Times*, 18 January 2011

Schell, Jonathan, *The Unconquerable World: Power, Nonviolence, and the Will of the People* (London: Allen Lane, 2003)

Schiller, Ben, 'The Axis of Oil: China and Venezuela', 2 March 2006, posted on www.opendemocracy.net

Schilling, Mark, *The Encyclopedia of Japanese Pop Culture* (New York: Weatherhill, 1997)

Sen, Amartya, *Development as Freedom* (Oxford: Oxford University Press, 1999)

—— *The Argumentative Indian: Writings on Indian History, Culture and Identity* (London: Allen Lane, 2005)

Sender, Henry, 'China has much to gain from supporting the euro', *Financial Times*, 3 February 2011

Shambaugh, David, ed., *The Modern Chinese State* (Cambridge: Cambridge University Press, 2000)

—— *Modernizing China's Military: Progress, Problems, and Prospects* (Berkeley: University of California Press, 2004)

—— 'China Engages Asia: Reshaping the Regional Order', *International Security*, 29:3 (Winter 2004/5)

—— ed., *Power Shift: China and Asia's New Dynamics* (Berkeley: University of California Press, 2005)

—— 'Return to the Middle Kingdom? China and Asia in the Early Twenty-first Century', in David Shambaugh, ed., *Power Shift: China and Asia's New Dynamics* (Berkeley: University of California Press, 2005)

—— *China's Communist Party: Atrophy and Adaptation* (Berkeley: University of California Press, 2008)

—— 'China flexes its soft power', *International Herald Tribune*, 8 June 2010

—— 'Coping with Conflicted China', *The Washington Quarterly*, Winter 2011

—— Eberhard Sandschneider and Zhou Hong, *China–Europe Relations: Perceptions, Policies and Prospects* (London and New York: Routledge, 2008)

Shell International Ltd, *Shell Global Scenarios to 2025: The Future Business Environment – Trends, Trade-offs and Choices* (London: 2005)

Shen, Boming, 'The Challenges Ahead: China's Membership in the WTO', 2002, posted on www.cap.Imu.de/transatlantic/download/Shen_Boming.doc

Shen, Simon, 'A constructed (un)reality on China's re-entry into Africa: the Chinese online community perception of Africa (2006–2008)', *Journal of Modern African Studies*, 47: 3 (2009)

Shenkar, Oded, *The Chinese Century: The Rising Chinese Economy and Its Impact on the Global Economy, the Balance of Power and Your Job* (New Jersey: Wharton School Publishing, 2006)

Shi Anbin, 'Mediating Chinese-ness: Identity Politics and Media Culture in Contemporary China', in Anthony Reid and Zheng Yangwen, eds, *Negotiating Asymmetry: China's Place in Asia* (Singapore: NUS Press, 2009)

Shi Yinhong, 'China and the North Korea Nuclear Problem: Diplomatic Initiative, Strategic Complexities, and Relevance of Security Multilateralism', unpublished paper, Beijing, 2004

—— 'China's "Capitalist Transition" and China's Foreign Policy', unpublished paper, Beijing, 2005

—— 'The General Situation of the China–Japan Relations and the Imperative for a Composite Strategy', workshop on Sino-Japanese relations, Renmin-Aichi University conference, Beijing, 2005

—— 'China and the North Korea Nuclear Problem: Diplomatic Initiative, Strategic Complexities, and Relevance of Security Multilateralism', in Guoguang Wu and Helen Lansdowne, eds, *China's Turn to Multilateralism: Foreign Policy and Regional Security* (London and New York: Routledge, 2008)

—— 'The Impact of China's Capitalist Transition on Foreign Policy', in Christopher A. McNally, ed., *China's Emergent Political Economy: Capitalism in the Dragon's Lair* (London and New York: Routledge, 2008)

'China–Japan Political Relations and the Imperative Strategic Management', in Niklas Swanström and Ryosei Kokubun, eds, *Sino-Japanese Relations: The Need for Conflict Prevention and Management* (Newcastle upon Tyne, UK: Cambridge Scholars Publishing, 2008)

Shibusawa, Masahide, Zakaria Haji Ahmad and Brian Bridges, *Pacific Asia in the 1990s* (London: Routledge, 1992)

Shih, Toh Han, 'China high-speed rail to take global lead by 2012', *South China Morning Post*, 26 October 2009

—— 'Rail plan may boost China's regional sway', *South China Morning Post*, 22 November 2010

Shin, Leo K., *The Making of the Chinese State: Ethnicity and Expansion on the Ming Borderlands* (Cambridge: Cambridge University Press, 2006)

Shirk, Susan L., *China: Fragile Superpower* (Oxford: Oxford University Press, 2007)

Shirouzu, Norihiko, 'Volvo's Big China Gamble', *Wall Street Journal*, 14 September 2010

Smith, Peter, 'Australia bars China bid for Oz Minerals', *Financial Times*, 27 March 2009

—— 'China drives engine of Australia's success', *Financial Times*, 2 February 2010

So, Hirano, 'Study of Contemporary Political History of East Asian Region – from the Chain Effect of Chinese and Japanese Nationalism Perspective', workshop on Sino-Japanese relations, Renmin-Aichi University conference, Beijing, 2005

Song, Weiquiang, seminar paper, Aichi University, 21 May, 2005

—— 'Study on Massive Group Incidents of Chinese Peasants', Ph.D. dissertation, Nankai University, 20 April 2006

Song Jung-a, 'G20 agrees historic reform of IMF', *Financial Times*, 23 October 2010

—— with Robert Cookson, 'South Korea seeks to shift reserves to China', *Financial Times*, 4 May 2011

Soros, George, *The Crisis of Global Capitalism* (New York: Public Affairs, 1998)

Spence, Jonathan D., *The Chan's Great Continent: China in Western Minds* (New York: W. W. Norton, 1998)

—— *The Search for Modern China*, 2nd edn (New York: W. W. Norton, 1999)

Spence, Michael, 'The west is wrong to obsess about the renminbi', *Financial Times*, 21 January 2010

Stanlaw, James, 'English in Japanese Communicative Strategies', in Braj B. Kachru, ed., *The Other Tongue: English Across Cultures* (Urbana and Chicago: University of Illinois Press, 1992)

'Statement from Bric IMF directors', *Financial Times*, 24 May 2011

Steele, Valerie, and John S. Major, *China Chic: East Meets West* (New Haven: Yale University Press, 1999)

Stephens, Philip, 'A Futile European Contest for Obama's Ear', *Financial Times*, 10 November 2008

Stevenson, Alexandra, 'India losing English advantage to China', *Financial Times*, 19 November 2009

—— 'Google's China market share declining', *Financial Times*, 22 April 2011

Stiglitz, Joseph E., 'Thanks for Nothing', *Atlantic Monthly*, October 2001

—— *Globalization and Its Discontents* (London: Allen Lane, 2002)

—— 'Development in Defiance of the Washington Consensus', *Guardian*, 13 April 2006

—— *Making Globalization Work* (London: Allen Lane, 2006)

—— and Linda J. Bilmes, *The Three Trillion Dollar War: The True Cost of the Iraq Conflict* (London: Allen Lane, 2008)

Suettinger, Robert L., *Beyond Tiananmen: The Politics of US–China Relations 1989–2000* (Washington, DC: The Brookings Institution, 2003)

Sugihara, Kaoru, 'Agriculture and Industrialization: The European Experience', in Peter Mathias and John Davis, eds, *Agriculture and Industrialization* (Oxford: Blackwell, 1996)

Sun Shuyun, *The Long March* (London: HarperPress, 2006)

—— *A Year in Tibet: A Voyage of Discovery* (London: HarperPress, 2008)

Suryadinata, Leo, *Southeast Asian Chinese: The Socio-Cultural Dimension* (Singapore: Times Academic Press, 1995)

Swaine, Michael D., 'China's Regional Military Posture', in David Shambaugh, ed., *Power Shift: China and Asia's New Dynamics* (Berkeley: University of California Press, 2005)

Symonds, Matthew, 'A global love affair', A special report on cars in emerging markets', *The Economist*, 15 November 2010

Tadashi, Yamamoto, ed., *Deciding the Public Good: Governance and Civil Society in Japan* (Tokyo: Japan Center for International Exchange, 1999)

Terrill, Ross, *The New Chinese Empire: And What It Means for the United States* (New York: Basic Books, 2003)

Therborn, Göran, *European Modernity and Beyond: The Trajectory of European Societies, 1945–2000* (London: Sage, 1995)

—— *Between Sex and Power: Family in the World, 1900–2000* (London: Routledge, 2004)

Thirlwell, Mark, 'Dealing with the Dragon: Australia and Chinese Inward Investment', 1 April 2010, *Clingendael Asia Studies*

Thomas, Bella, 'What the World's Poor Watch on TV', *Prospect*, 82 (January 2003)

Thompson, Chris, '"We can do the job fine from here"', *FT Magazine*, 19/20 June 2010

Tong, Shijun, *Dialectics of Modernisation* (Bergen: University of Bergen, 1994)

Torode, Greg, and Minnie Chan, 'Vietnam buys submarines to counter China', *South China Morning Post*, 17 December 2009

Touraine, A., *Critique de la modernité* (Paris: Fayard, 1992)

Treat, John Whittier, ed., *Contemporary Japan and Popular Culture* (Honolulu: University of Hawai'i Press, 1996)

Trompenaars, Fons, *Riding the Waves of Culture: Understanding Cultural Diversity in Business* (London: Nicholas Brealey, 1993)

Tu Wei-ming, *The Living Tree: The Changing Meaning of Being Chinese Today* (Stanford: Stanford University Press, 1994)

Tucker, Sundeep, 'Chinese déjà vu', *Financial Times*, 9 June 2010

Tumulty, Karen, and Ed O'Keefe, 'The government tends to resist reorganisation', *Washington Post*, 28 January 2011

Tyler, Christian, *Wild West China: The Taming of Xinjiang* (London: John Murray, 2003)

Ueda, Atsushi, ed., *The Electric Geisha: Exploring Japan's Popular Culture* (Tokyo: Kodansha International, 1994)

Ulrich, Jing, 'China Holds the Key to Food Prices', *Financial Times*, 7 November 2007

United Nations, *UN Human Development Report* (New York: Oxford University Press, 1997)

United Nations Development Programme, *Rapport mondial sur le développement humain 1999* (Paris: De Boeck Université, 1999)

United States National Intelligence Council, *Global Trends 2025: A Transformed World* (November 2008)

Van Hear, Nicholas, *New Diasporas: The Mass Exodus, Dispersal and Regrouping of Migrant Communities* (London: UCL Press, 1998)

Veriah, Harinder: see the website in her memory at www.harinderveriah. com

Vermander, Benoit, 'The Law and the Wheel', *China Perspectives*, 24 (July–August 1999), Hong Kong

Vogel, Ezra F., *The Four Little Dragons: The Spread of Industrialization in East Asia* (Cambridge, Mass.: Harvard University Press, 1991)

—— *Is Japan Still Number One?* (Selangor Darul Ehsan, Malaysia: Pelanduk Publications, 2000)

Vuving, Alexander, 'Traditional and Modern Sino-Vietnamese Relations', in Anthony Reid and Zheng Yangwen, eds, *Negotiating Asymmetry: China's Place in Asia* (Singapore: NUS Press, 2009)

Wade, Geoff, 'Some Topoi in Southern Border Historiography during the Ming (and Their Modern Relevance)', in Sabine Dabringhaus and Roderich Ptak, eds, *China and Her Neighbours: Borders, Visions of the Other, Foreign Policy 10th to 19th Century* (Wiesbaden: Harrassowitz, 1997)

—— 'Don't Be Deceived: Our History Really is Under Serious Attack', *Canberra Times*, 27 April 2006

Wade, Robert, *Governing the Market: Economic Theory and the Role of*

Government in East Asian Industrialization (Princeton: Princeton University Press, 1990)

Waldmeir, Patti, 'Chinese aim to be king of the road', *Financial Times*, 22 April 2010

Waley-Cohen, Joanna, *The Sextants of Beijing: Global Currents in Chinese History* (New York: W. W. Norton, 1999)

Wallerstein, Immanuel, *Geopolitics and Geoculture: Essays on the Changing World-system* (Cambridge: Cambridge University Press, 1991)

Wang, Bijun, and Yiping Huang, 'Is there a China model of overseas direct investment?', http://www.eastasiaforum.org/2011/04/12/is-there-a-china-model-of-overseas-direct-investment/

Wang Chaohua, ed., *One China: Many Paths* (London: Verso, 2003)

Wang Chih-ming, 'Capitalizing the Big Man: Yao Ming, Asian America, and the China Global', *Inter-Asia Cultural Studies*, 5:2 (2004)

Wang Gungwu, 'Early Ming Relations with Southeast Asia: A Background Essay', in John King Fairbank, ed., *The Chinese World Order: Traditional China's Foreign Relations* (Cambridge Mass.: Harvard University Press, 1968)

—— *China and the Chinese Overseas* (Singapore: Times Academic Press, 1991)

—— *The Chineseness of China: Selected Essays* (Oxford: Oxford University Press, 1991)

—— *Joining the Modern World: Inside and Outside China* (Singapore and London: Singapore University Press and World Scientific, 2000)

—— *The Chinese Overseas: From Earthbound China to the Quest for Autonomy* (London and Cambridge, Mass.: Harvard University Press, 2000)

—— 'China and Southeast Asia: The Context of a New Beginning', in David Shambaugh, ed., *Power Shift: China and Asia's New Dynamics* (Berkeley: University of California Press, 2005)

Wang Hui, *China's New Order* (Cambridge, Mass.: Harvard University Press, 2003)

—— *The End of the Revolution: China and the Limits of Modernity* (London: Verso, 2009)

Wang Jisi, 'China's Changing Role in Asia', available at www.irchina.org

—— Interview with Yoichi Funabashi, *The Asahi Shimbun*, 12 June 2010

Wang Ling-chi and Wang Gungwu, eds, *The Chinese Diaspora: Selected Essays*, 2 vols (Singapore: Times Academic Press, 1998)

Wang Xiaodong, *Chinese Youth's Views on the World: A Survey Report* (Beijing: China Youth Research Centre, 2003)

—— 'Chinese Nationalism under the Shadow of Globalisation', Lecture, London School of Economics, 7 February 2005

Wang Yizhou, 'Political Stability and International Relations in the Process of Economic Globalisation – Another Perspective on Asia's Financial Crisis', unpublished article, Beijing, 2000

—— ed., *Construction within Contradiction: Multiple Perspectives on the Relationship Between China and International Organizations* (Beijing: China Development Publishing House, 2003)

Wang Zhengyi, 'Conceptualising Economic Security and Governance: China Confronts Globalisation', *Pacific Review*, 17:4 (2004)

—— 'Contending Regional Identity in East Asia: ASEAN Way and Its Implications', unpublished paper, 2001

Warburton, John, and Leo Horn, 'China's Crisis: A Development Perspective (Part One)', 25 October 2007, posted on www.chinadialogue.net

Ward, Andrew, 'The old world order is melting away', *Financial Times*, 17 December 2009

—— and Geoff Dyer, 'Nineteen countries shun Nobel Prize ceremony', *Financial Times*, 7 December 2010

Wassener, Bettina, and Andrea Deng, 'Taking the high road, with 1200 aboard', *International Herald Tribune*, 18 August 2010

Watts, Jonathan, *When A Billion Chinese Jump: How China Will Save Mankind – or Destroy It* (London: Faber and Faber, 2010)

Weidenbaum, Murray, and Samuel Hughes, *The Bamboo Network: How Expatriate Chinese Entrepreneurs are Creating a New Economic Superpower in Asia* (New York: The Free Press, 1996)

Wheatley, Alan, 'Preparing for China's tourist boom', *International Herald Tribune*, 21 December 2010

Wild, Leni, and David Mepham, eds, *The New Sinosphere: China in Africa* (London: Institute for Public Policy Research, 2006)

Wilkinson, Endymion, *Japan Versus the West: Image and Reality* (London: Penguin, 1990)

Williams, Richard, 'It's the End of the World As We Know It (and Cricket Will Be Fine)', *Guardian*, 22 April 2008

Wilsdon, James, and James Keeley, *China: The Next Science Superpower?* (London: Demos, 2007)

Wilson, Dominic, and Anna Stupnytska, 'The N-11: More Than an Acronym', *Goldman Sachs Global Economics Papers*, 153 (28 March 2007)

—— and Roopa Purushothaman, 'Dreaming with BRICs: The Path to 2050', *Goldman Sachs Global Economics Papers*, 99 (2003)

Wolf, Martin, 'Why America and China Cannot Afford to Fall Out', *Financial Times*, 8 October 2003

—— *Why Globalization Works* (New Haven: Yale University Press, 2005)

—— 'The Brave New World of State Capitalism', *Financial Times*, 16 October 2007

—— 'Life in a Tough World of High Commodity Prices', *Financial Times*, 4 March 2008

—— 'Why Agreeing a New Bretton Woods is Vital', *Financial Times*, 4 November 2008

—— 'Why China's exchange rate policy concerns us', *Financial Times*, 8 December 2009

—— 'Wen is right to worry about China's growth', *Financial Times*, 21 September 2010

—— 'Faltering in a stormy sea of debt', *Financial Times*, 19 April 2011

—— 'Manufacturing at risk from global shift to Asia', *Financial Times*, 20 May 2011

—— 'Europe should not control the IMF', *Financial Times*, 24 May 2011

Wolferen, Karel van, *The Enigma of Japanese Power: People and Politics in a Stateless Nation* (New York: Vintage, 1990)

Wong, Herman, 'On Global Catwalks, a New Face That's Hot – Asian', *China Daily*, 24 May 2006

Wong, Kandy, 'Subsidy doubts delay BYD's electric car', *Financial Times*, 24 February 2010

Wood, Frances, *No Dogs and Not Many Chinese* (London: John Murray, 1998)

Woodall, Pam, 'The New Titans', survey, *The Economist*, 16 September 2006

Wooldridge, Adrian, 'After Bush: A Special Report on America and the World', *The Economist*, 29 March 2008, p. 10

World Bank, *The East Asian Miracle: Economic Growth and Public Policy* (Washington, DC: Oxford University Press, 1993)

—— *At China's Table: Food Security Options* (Washington, DC: 1997)

—— *China Engaged: Integration with the Global Economy* (Washington, DC: 1997)

—— *Clear Water, Blue Skies: China's Environment in the New Century* (Washington, DC: 1997)

—— *Financing Health Care: Issues and Options for China* (Washington, DC: 1997)

—— *Old Age Security: Pension Reform in China* (Washington, DC: 1997)

—— *Sharing Rising Incomes: Disparities in China* (Washington, DC: 1997)

—— 'Will Resilience Overcome Risk? East Asia Regional Outlook', November 2007, posted on www.worldbank.org

Wright, Robert, 'China on track to join ranks of train manufacturers', *Financial Times*, 1 March 2010

—— Wright, Tom, 'Wen touts deals and trade ties on trip to India', *Wall Street Journal*, 16 December 2010

Wu, David Y. H., and Sidney C. H. Cheung, eds, *The Globalization of Chinese Food* (London: RoutledgeCurzon, 2002)

Wu, Friedrich, 'The Renminbi Challenge: the future role of the Chinese currency', *The International Economy*, Fall 2009

www.ft.com/FT500

www.timeshighereducation.co.uk/world-university-rankings/2010-2011 top-200.html

Xie, Andy, *Asia/Pacific Economics*, report for Morgan Stanley, November 2002

Xinran, *What the Chinese Don't Eat* (London: Vintage Books, 2006)

Xu, Gao, 'State-owned enterprises in China: How big are they?' EastAsia Pacific/Blog, World Bank, posted 19 January 2010

Xu, Gary Gang, *Sinascape: Contemporary Chinese Cinema* (Oxford: Rowman and Littlefield, 2007)

Yahuda, Michael, *Hong Kong: China's Challenge* (London: Routledge, 1996)

—— 'The Evolving Asian Order: The Accommodation of Rising Chinese Power', in David Shambaugh, ed., *Power Shift: China and Asia's New Dynamics* (Berkeley: University of California Press, 2005)

Yan Xuetong, 'The Rise of China in Chinese Eyes', *Journal of Contemporary China*, 10:26 (2001)

—— 'The Instability of China–US relations', *The Chinese Journal of International Politics*, 2010

—— *Ancient Chinese Thought, Modern Chinese Power* (Princeton: Princeton University Press, 2011)

Yao, Shujie, 'China will learn from failed Chinalco-Rio deal', *Financial Times*, 7 June 2010

Yardley, Jim, 'China Offers Defense of Its Darfur Stance', *International Herald Tribune*, 8–9 March 2008

—— 'After the Fury in Tibet, Firm Hand Trembles', *International Herald Tribune*, 18 March 2008

—— and Somini Sengupta, 'Beijing Blames the Dalai Lama', *International Herald Tribune*, 19 March 2008

Yoshino, Kosaku, *Cultural Nationalism in Contemporary Japan* (London: Routledge, 1992)

Youngs, Richard, *Europe's Decline and Fall: The Struggle against Global Irrelevance* (London: Profile Books, 2010

Yu Bin, 'China and Russia: Normalizing Their Strategic Partnership', in David Shambaugh, ed., *Power Shift: China and Asia's New Dynamics* (Berkeley: University of California Press, 2005)

Yu Yongding, 'Opinions on Structure Reform and Exchange Rate Regimes Against the Backdrop of the Asian Financial Crisis', unpublished paper, Japanese Ministry of Finance, 2000

—— 'The Interactions Between China and the World Economy', unpublished paper, Nikkei Simbon Symposium, 5 April 2005

—— 'China's Macroeconomic Development, Exchange Rate Policy and Global Imbalances', unpublished paper, Asahi Shimbun Symposium, October 2005

—— 'China's Rise, Twin Surplus and the Change of China's Development Strategy', unpublished paper, Namura Tokyo Club Conference, Kyoto, 21 November 2005

—— 'China's Structural Adjustment', unpublished paper, Seoul Conference, 2005

—— 'China's stimulus shows the problem of success', *Financial Times*, 25 August 2009

—— 'A different road forward', *China Daily*, 23 December 2010

Zakaria, Fareed, *The Post-American World* (London: Allen Lane, 2008)

Zha Daojiong, 'China's Energy Security and Its International Relations', *China and Eurasia Forum Quarterly*, 3:3 (2005)

Zhang Feng, 'Rethinking the "Tribute System": Broadening the Conceptual Horizon of Historical East Asian Politics', *Chinese Journal of International Politics*, Volume 2, 2009

Zhang, Peter G., *IMF and the Asian Financial Crisis* (Singapore: World Scientific, 1998)

Zhang Wei-Wei, 'The Allure of the Chinese Model', *International Herald Tribune*, 1 November 2006

Zhang Yunling, *East Asian Regionalism and China* (Beijing: World Affairs Press, 2005)

—— ed., *Designing East Asian FTA: Rationale and Feasibility* (Beijing: Social Sciences Academic Press, 2006)

—— and Tang Shiping, 'China's Regional Strategy', in David Shambaugh, ed., *Power Shift: China and Asia's New Dynamics* (Berkeley: University of California Press, 2005)

Zhao Suisheng, ed., *Chinese Foreign Policy: Pragmatism and Strategic Behavior* (New York: M. E. Sharpe, 2004)

—— *A Nation-State by Construction: Dynamics of Modern Chinese Nationalism* (Stanford: Stanford University Press, 2004)

Zheng Yangwen, 'Move People Buttress Frontier: Regime Orchestrate [*sic*] Migration-Settlement in the Two Millennia', workshop on 'Asian Expansions: The Historical Processes of Polity Expansion in Asia', Asia Research Institute, National University of Singapore, 12–13 May 2006

Zheng Yongnian, *Discovering Chinese Nationalism in China* (Cambridge: Cambridge University Press, 1999)

—— *Will China Become Democratic?: Elite, Class and Regime Transition* (Singapore: EAI, 2004)

Zhou Ping and Loet Leydesdorff, 'The Emergence of China as a Leading Nation in Science', *Research Policy*, 35 (2006)

Zhu Feng, 'Why Taiwan Really Matters to China', 2004, available at www. irchina.org

—— 'Regionalism, Nationalism and China's Regional Activism in East Asia', unpublished paper, 2006

—— 'China Policy Toward North Korea: A New Twist', *PacNet*, Pacific Forum CSIS, No. 60, 8 December 2010

Ziegler, Dominic, 'Reaching for a Renaissance: A Special Report on China and Its Region', *The Economist*, 31 March 2007

Permissions

Permissions

The author and the publishers are grateful to the following for permission to reproduce graphically represented statistical material:

13D Research (Fig. 21); Bloomberg (Fig. 73); CEIC (Fig. 32); Central Statistical Organization, India and CEIC (Fig. 64); Centre for Arms Control and Non-Proliferation (Fig. 5); China Official Statistics (Figs. 34–6); China Youth Research Centre (Figs. 74–9); Chinese Commerce Ministry (Figs. 63–4); Dentsu Institute for Human Studies (Figs. 7–11; Table 1); *The Economist* (Figs. 87–8); Election Study Centre, National Chengchi University (Figs. 47–8); Energy Information Administration (Figs. 18, 19, 26); FACTS Global Energy (Fig. 20); GEIC and GaveKal Dragonomics (Fig. 17); *Financial Times* (Tables 13, 14); Goldman Sachs (Figs. 4, 40, derived from Dominic Wilson and Anna Stupnytska, 'The N-11: More than an Acronym', *GS Global Economic Papers* 153, 2007, p. 11); Guonan Ma and Wang Yi (Fig. 14, derived from 'China's High Saving Rate: Myth and Reality', *BIS Working Papers* 312, 2010, p. 7); HarperCollins (Fig. 12, derived from Nicholas Ostler, *Empires of the Word*, 2005, p. 526); Heritage Foundation (Fig. 86); Institute of International Education (Fig. 81, derived from *Open Doors*, 2007); International Monetary Fund (Figs. 1, 2, 41, 53, 54, 66–9, 83); McKinsey Global Institute (Fig. 80); Miniwatts Marketing Group (Figs. 71, 72); National Bureau of

Statistics (China) (Fig. 55); National Bureau of Statistics (China) and CEIC (Fig. 65); National Science Foundation (US), Ministry of Science and Technology (China) (Fig. 28); Organization for Economic Co-operation and Development (Fig. 6, derived from Angus Maddison, *The World Economy*, 2003, p. 179; Fig. 15, derived from Angus Maddison, *Chinese Economic Performance in the Long Run*, revised edition, 2007, p. 61; Fig. 29; Table 16); OECD, National Bureau of Statistics (China), and Haver Analytics (Fig. 82); OICA (Fig. 31); People's Bank of China (Fig. 85); Pew Research Centre/Pew Global Attitudes Project (Figs. 25, 37, 38, 43–6, 70; Tables 5, 8–12); BNP Paribas (Figs. 40, 42); Joseph Quinlan, Transatlantic Academy (Table 15); Reuters (Fig. 52); Tony Saich, Kennedy School, Harvard University (Fig. 85); United Nations (Fig. 3); United Nations Conference on Trade and Development (Fig. 33); UN COMTRADE (Figs. 56–61); US Census Bureau (Fig. 23); US Census Bureau, GaveKal Dragonomics, and OECD (Fig. 22); World Bank (Figs. 16, 24, 51); www.chooseauto.com.cn (Table 3).

Every effort has been made to contact copyright holders. The author and publishers would be happy to make good in future editions any errors or omissions brought to their attention.

Index

Maps and figures are given in *italics*

impact on the world, 20–21
increasingly sidelined by China,
608–9
and India, 449–50
industrial employment peak, 41
and the international financial
system, 482–8
inventor of mass production, 218
and Iran, 434
and Iraq, 439, 463, 465, 499, 538,
558, 625–6, 628
and Japan, 14, 61–2, 67, 70, 73
late-twentieth-century dominance,
289–90
Latin American trade fall, 412
living standards and China, 207
military spending cuts, 628
and modernity, 125, 579–80
multiracial/multi-ethnic recognition, 569
as a nation-state, 18
new world order, 585–90
no industrial phase, 42
no tribute system, 568
Olympic Games, 552
opposed to regional organizations,
348
and Pakistan, 443
population comparisons with
China, 257, 509–11, 511, 541,
571
population/economic take off, 44,
230–32
in the post-Cold War world, 437
preoccupation with the Middle
East, 359, 370, 413, 433–6,
469
and protectionism, 192
quality of life, 285–6
racism towards Chinese, 330
rise of, 49, 50–54, 243
shift in economic power, 3

and soft power, 470, 610–16,
631–6
and South Africa, 425
and South Korea, 365–7
spectacular period of growth, 9
spread of Mandarin, 544
and Taiwan, 384–5, 392, 435–6
and Tea Party thinking, 266
and the UK, 2, 52, 84, 108, 557,
560–61, 726n.118
universities, 546–7, 547
urban population of, 122, 539
and US–Japan alliance, 365,
400–401
voting rights, 267
War of Independence, 40
world's dominant power, 1–2, 6–7
United States Africa Command
(Africom), 431
universalism, 14, 39, 165, 304, 306,
341, 463, 532, 560, 583,
593–4
urban transport, 541–3, 542
Urumqi, 322
US–India Civil Nuclear Agreement
2008, 449
US–Japan security pact (1951), 14
US–Japan security pact (2007), 400
US–Korean alliance, 367
USSR see Russia; Soviet Union
US Treasury bonds, 235–6, 462, 468,
481, 522
Uzbekistan, 349, 438–9

Venezuela, 235, 412, 474
Vietnam
and China, 375, 381, 404, 442
and Confucianism, 260, 273, 304
diplomatic relations with China,
348
and disputed territories, 371
French victory in, 102